BIOLOGICAL
BOUNDARIES
OF LEARNING

THE CENTURY PSYCHOLOGY SERIES

Kenneth MacCorquodale
Gardner Lindzey
Kenneth E. Clark

EDITORS

BIOLOGICAL BOUNDARIES OF LEARNING

Martin E. P. Seligman

University of Pennsylvania

Joanne L. Hager

Cornell University

PRENTICE-HALL, INC.
Englewood Cliffs, N.J.

We dedicate this volume to those men and women whose work we include, and above all to those who may use it to go beyond it.

Credits

1. From John Garcia and Robert Koelling, "Relation of Cue to Consequence in Avoidance Learning," *Psychonomic Science*, 4 (1966), 123–124. Reproduced by permission of the authors and *Psychonomic Science*.
2. From John Garcia, Frank Ervin, and Robert Koelling, "Learning with Prolonged Delay of Reinforcement," *Psychonomic Science*, 5 (1966), 121–122. Reproduced by permission of the authors and *Psychonomic Science*.
3. From John Garcia, Brenda McGowan, and Kenneth Green, "Biological Constraints on Conditioning," in A. H. Black and W. F. Prokasy, eds., *Classical Conditioning II: Current Research and Theory*. Copyright ©1972. Reproduced by permission of Appleton-Century-Crofts.
4. From Samuel Revusky and Erwin Bedarf, "Association of Illness with Prior Ingestion of Novel Foods," *Science*, 155 (Jan. 13, 1967), 219–220. Copyright 1967 by the American Association for the Advancement of Science.
5. From Paul Rozin, "Specific Aversions as a Component of Specific Hungers," *Journal of Comparative and Physiological Psychology*, 64 (1967), 237–242. Reproduced by permission of the author and the American Psychological Association.
6. From Donna Zahorik and Steven Maier, "Appetitive Conditioning with Recovery from Thiamine Deficiency as the Unconditioned Stimulus," *Psychonomic Science*, 17(5) (1969), 309–310. Reproduced by permission of the authors and *Psychonomic Science*.
9. From Marvin Nachman, "Limited Effects of Electroconvulsive Shock on Memory of Taste Stimulation," *Journal of Comparative and Physiological Psychology*, 73 (1) (1970), 31–37. Reproduced by permission of the author and the American Psychological Association.
11. From Edward L. Thorndike, from *Animal Intelligence*, 1898, pp. 6–28. Reproduced by permission of Columbia University Press.
12. From Czeslawa Dobrezecka, Genowefa Szwejkowska, and Jerzy Konorski, "Qualitative versus Directional Cues in Two Forms of Differentiation," *Science*, 153 (July 1, 1966), 87–89. Copyright 1966 by the American Association for the Advancement of Science.
13. From Robert Bolles and Sally Seelbach, "Punishing and Reinforcing Effects of Noise Onset and Termination for Different Responses," *Journal of Comparative and Physiological Psychology*, 58 (1964), 127–131. Reproduced by permission of the authors and the American Psychological Association.
14. From Paul Brown and Herbert Jenkins, "Auto-Shaping of the Pigeon's Key-Peck," *Journal of the Experimental Analysis of Behavior*, 11 (1968), 1–8. Reproduced by permission of the authors and the Society for the Experimental Analysis of Behavior. Copyright 1968 by the Society for the Experimental Analysis of Behavior.
15. From David Williams and Harriet Williams, "Auto-Maintenance in the Pigeon: Sustained Pecking Despite Contingent Non-reinforcement," *Journal of the Experimental Analysis of Behavior*, 12 (1969), 511–520. Reproduced by permission of the authors and the Society for the Experimental Analysis of Behavior. Copyright 1969 by the Society for the Experimental Analysis of Behavior.
16. From Vaughn Stimbert, "A Comparison of Learning Based on Social or Nonsocial Discriminative Stimuli," *Psychonomic Science*, 20 (3) (1970), 185–186. Reproduced by permission of the author and *Psychonomic Science*.
17. From Keller Breland and Marian Breland, "The Misbehavior of Organisms," *American Psychologist*, 16 (1961), 681–684. Reprinted by permission of the authors and the American Psychological Association.
18. From Robert Bolles, "Species-Specific Defense Reactions and Avoidance Learning," *Psychological Review*, 77 (1970), 32–48. Reproduced by permission of the author and the American Psychological Association.

19. From Philip Hineline and Howard Rachlin, "Escape and Avoidance of Shock by Pigeons Pecking a Key," *Journal of the Experimental Analysis of Behavior*, 12 (1969), 533–538. Reproduced by permission of the authors and the Society for the Experimental Analysis of Behavior. Copyright 1969 by the Society for the Experimental Analysis of Behavior.

20. From James Allison, Daniel Larson, and Donald Jensen, "Acquired Fear, Brightness Preference, and One-Way Shuttlebox Performance," *Psychonomic Science*, 8 (7) (1967), 269–270. Reproduced by permission of the authors and *Psychonomic Science*.

22. From John Garcia, Richard Kovner, and Kenneth Green, "Cue Properties versus Palatibility of Flavors in Avoidance Learning," *Psychonomic Science*, 20 (1970), 313–314 Reproduced by permission of the authors and *Psychonomic Science*.

23. From Niko Tinbergen, from *The Study of Instinct*, 1951. Reproduced by permission of the author and The Clarendon Press, Oxford.

24. From Hardy Wilcoxon, William Dragoin, and Paul Kral: "Illness–Induced Aversions in Rat and Quail: Relative Salience of Visual and Gustatory Cues," *Science*, 171 (Feb. 26, 1971), 826–828. Reproduced by permission of the authors and *Science*. Copyright 1971 by the American Association for the Advancement of Science.

25. From Aubrey Manning, *An Introduction to Animal Behavior (Contemporary Biology Series)*. Edward Arnold (Publishers) Ltd., London.

26. From Gilbert Gottlieb, "Imprinting in Relation to Parental and Species Identification by Avian Neonates," *Journal of Comparative and Physiological Psychology*, 59 (1965) 345–356. Reproduced by permission of the author and the American Psychological Association.

27. From Stephen Emlen, "Celestial Rotation: Its Importance in the Development of Migratory Orientation," *Science*, 170 (Dec. 11, 1970), 1198–1201. Copyright 1970 by the American Association for the Advancement of Science.

28. From M. E. Bitterman, "Phyletic Differences in Learning," *American Psychologist*, 1965, 396–410. Reproduced by permission of the author and the American Psychological Association.

29. From Peter Marler, "A Comparative Approach to Vocal Learning: Song Development in White-Crowned Sparrows," *Journal of Comparative and Physiological Psychology*, Monograph (May, 1970), 1–25. Reproduced by permission of the author and the American Psychological Association.

30. From Eric H. Lenneberg, "On Explaining Language," *Science*, 164 (May 9, 1969), 635–643. Reproduced by permission of the author and the American Association for the Advancement of Science. Copyright 1969 by the American Association for the Advancement of Science.

31. From R. Allen Gardner and Beatrice T. Gardner, "Teaching Sign Language to a Chimpanzee," *Science*, 165 (Aug. 15, 1969), 664–672. Reproduced by permission of the authors and the American Association for the Advancement of Science. Copyright 1969 by the American Association for the Advancement of Science.

32. From Arnold Sameroff, "Can Conditioned Responses Be Established in the Newborn Infant?", *Developmental Psychology*, 5 (1971), 411–442. Reproduced by permission of the author and the American Psychological Association.

33. From Hans G. Furth, *Piaget and Knowledge: Theoretical Foundations.* Copyright 1969. Reprinted by permission of the author and Prentice-Hall, Inc., Englewood Cliffs, New Jersey.

34. From G. Terence Wilson and Gerald C. Davison, "Aversion Techniques in Behavior Therapy; Some Theoretical and Metatheoretical Considerations," *Journal of Consulting and Clinical Psychology*, 33 (3) (1968), 327–329. Reproduced by permission of the authors and the American Psychological Association.

35. From Martin E. P. Seligman, " Phobias and Preparedness," *Behavior Therapy,* 2 (1971), 307–320. By permission of Academic Press, Inc.

CONTENTS

ACKNOWLEDGMENTS

So many conversations. So many memos and papers passed back and forth. So many ideas generously given and eagerly received. So much other help. With gratitude we mention: Norman Adler, Phil Best, Jeff Bitterman, Abe Black, Bob Bolles, Jerry Bruner, Jack Burton, Bill Dilger, Tom Eisner, Steve Emlen, W. K. Estes, Jeff Galef, John Garcia, Trixie Gardner, Rochel Gelman, D. O. Hebb, Apollo and Xanthippe, Jim Kalat, Eric Lenneberg, Steve Maier, Marwood Roto-Rooter, Neal Miller, Sue Mineka, Debby Mueller, Jack Nachmias, National Institutes of Mental Health Grants 19604 and 16546 to M. Seligman, Howie Rachlin, Sam Revusky, Chris Risley, Paul Rozin, Barry Schwartz, Kerry and Amy Seligman, Dick Solomon, J. D. R. Staddon, Phil Teitelbaum, Dave Williams, and many others.

BIOLOGICAL
BOUNDARIES
OF LEARNING

They forget that even the capacity to learn, to learn at all, to learn only at a definite stage of development, to learn one thing rather than another, to learn more or less quickly, must have some genetic basis.

Sir Julian Huxley, Essays of a Humanist

INTRODUCTION

This book is about a reunion of thought among students of behavior and about an attempted resolution of the instinct-learning controversy. The past decade has seen an accelerating convergence of thought between the psychology of learning and behavioral biology after almost a half-century of separate development. Since Pavlov and Thorndike, psychologists of learning have searched for general laws, laws which hold across species and across experimental conditions. Behavioral biologists, particularly the ethologists led by Lorenz and Tinbergen, focused on instinctive behaviors of individual species in their natural habitat. Preoccupied with its own subject matter, each tradition minimized the significance of the other's findings; even the initial theoretical encounters between ethologists and comparative psychologists did not have wide impact. For the "general-process" learning theorist, instinctive factors affecting what experimental subjects could learn in the laboratory were annoyances, technical problems to be circumvented. Thus, for example, learning experiments typically use a small, homogeneous acoustic chamber intended to isolate the animal from the wealth of extraneous stimuli available in his natural environment and to ensure undivided attention to the artificial contingencies imposed upon him. For the behavioral biologist, on the other hand, learning can inconveniently mask the effects of releasing stimuli, genetic endowment, and motivation on behavior. One ideal ethological observation is of the animal's first exposure to the releasing stimuli, before experience can act. But we believe that far from being antagonistic, these two traditions are proving to be complementary.

This book was put together by two students of psychology who with many learning theorists have come to recognize that learning has important biological and evolutionary constraints. In it are compiled the reasons that have impelled many investigators to accept this conclusion, and in sum they are the reason we have come to it. Our book is more than an anthology, however; it is also the statement of a theory in a somewhat unconventional format. The headnotes present the theory, and the readings appear as they support, exemplify, and elaborate its development. There is one view which virtually all the researchers represented here hold in common: What an organism learns in the laboratory or in his natural habitat is the result not only of the contingencies which he faces and has faced in his past but also of the contingencies which his species faced before him—its evolutionary history and the genetic outcome.

Our path to this conclusion begins with a reexamination of why psychologists ever trained white rats to press bars for little pellets of flour or sounded metronomes followed by meat powder for domestic dogs. After all, when in the real world do rats encounter levers which they must learn to press in order to eat, and when do our pet dogs ever come across clicking metronomes which signal meat powder? There is a premise which underlies these endeavors, and it is often overlooked: It is the fundamental premise of the general process view of learning.

THE EQUIPOTENTIALITY PREMISE

Psychologists had hoped that in the simple, controlled world of levers and mechanical feeders, of metronomes and meat powder, something quite general would emerge. If we took an arbitrary action such as pressing a lever and an arbitrary organism such as an albino rat, and set it to work pressing the lever for an arbitrary foodstuff, *by virtue of* the very arbitrariness of this contingency, we would find features of the rat's behavior general to real-life instrumental learning. Similarly, if we took a dog, filtered out extraneous noises and sights, and paired a metronome's clicking with meat powder squirted into his mouth, what we discovered about the salivation of the dog might tell us about the learning of associations in general. For instance, when Pavlov found that salivation stopped occurring to a click which formerly signaled meat powder but no longer did, he hoped that this was an instance of a *law*, "experimental extinction," which would apply beyond the stimuli and responses he happened to choose. What captured the interest of the psychological world was the possibility that such laws described the general characteristics of behavior acquired when one event is paired with another. When Thorndike found that cats learned only gradually to pull strings to escape from puzzle boxes, the intriguing hypothesis was that voluntary learning in general was by trial and error. In both these situations, the very arbitrariness and unnaturalness of the experiment was assumed to guarantee generality, since the situation would be uncontaminated by past experience the organism might have had and by special biological propensities that he might bring to it.

General-process learning theorists believe that what an organism learns about is a matter of relative indifference. In classical conditioning, the choice of conditioned stimulus (CS), unconditioned stimulus (US), and response matters little; that is, all CS's and US's can be associated more or less equally well, and general laws exist which describe the acquisition, extinction, inhibition, delay of reinforcement, and spontaneous recovery for all CS's and US's. In instrumental learning, the choice of response and reinforcer matters little; that is, all emitted responses and reinforcers can be associated about equally well, and general laws exist which describe acquisition, extinction, discriminative control, shaping, and generalization gradients for all responses and reinforcers. We call this assumption the equipotentiality premise, and we suggest that it lies at the heart of general-process learning theory.

Equipotentiality is hardly a straw man. Quotations from major learning theorists document its pervasiveness.

> It is obvious that the reflex activity of any effector organ can be chosen for the purpose of investigation, since signalling stimuli can get linked up with any of the inborn reflexes (Pavlov, 1927, p. 17).

any natural phenomenon chosen at will may be converted into a conditional stimulus . . . any visual stimulus, any desired sound, any odor, and the stimulation of any part of the skin (Pavlov, 1928, p. 86).

All stimulus elements are equally likely to be sampled and the probability of a response at any time is equal to the proportion of elements in S′ [the stimulus array] that are connected to it. . . . On any acquisition trial all stimulus elements sampled by the organism become connected to the response reinforced on that trial (Estes, 1959, p. 399).

The general topography of operant behavior is not important, because most if not all specific operants are conditioned. I suggest that the dynamic properties of operant behavior may be studied with a single reflex (Skinner, 1938, pp. 45—46).

THE EQUIPOTENTIALITY PREMISE REEXAMINED

The equipotentiality premise places a special premium on the investigations of arbitrary, as opposed to naturally occurring, contingencies. Such events, since they are supposedly uncontaminated by the experience or biology of the organism, provide paradigms for the discovery of general laws of learning. More than sixty years of research in both the instrumental and classical conditioning traditions have yielded considerable data showing that similar laws hold over a wide range of more or less arbitrarily chosen events: The shape of generalization gradients is pretty much the same for galvanic skin responses classically conditioned to tones with shock as the US (Hovland, 1937) and for salivating to pressure at different points on the back with food as the US (Pavlov, 1927). Partial reinforcement causes greater resistance to extinction than continuous reinforcement regardless of whether rats are bar pressing for pellets or pigeons are key pecking for grain. Examples of similarly general laws could be multiplied at great length.

Inherent in the emphasis on arbitrary events, however, is a danger: *The laws may not be general, but peculiar to abitrary events.*

PREPAREDNESS: AN ALTERNATIVE TO EQUIPOTENTIALITY

It is a truism that an organism brings to any experiment certain equipment and predispositions either more or less appropriate to the situation. It brings specialized sensory and response apparatus with a long evolutionary history which has modified it into its present appropriateness or inappropriateness. Often forgotten is the fact that in addition to sensory-motor apparatus, the organism brings associative apparatus which also has a long and specialized evolutionary history. This specialization may make certain contingencies easier to learn about than others, more difficult to forget, more readily generalizable, and so on.

Our presentation will focus on ease of learning. For example, when an organism is placed in a classical conditioning experiment, not only may the CS be more or less perceptible to the animal and the US more or less evocative of a response, *but also the CS and US may be more or less associable.* The animal may be more or less prepared by the evolution of its species to associate a given CS and US or a given response and reinforcer. If evolution has affected the associability of specific events, then it is possible, even likely, that the very *laws* of learning might vary from one class of situations to another with the preparedness of the animal. If this is so, general-process learning theorists may have discovered only a subset of the laws of learning: the laws of learning about arbitrarily concatenated events, those associations which are selected to be equipotential.

We can define the dimension of preparedness operationally. Confront an animal with a CS paired with a US or with a response which produces a reinforcer. Depending on what these are, the animal will be either prepared, unprepared, or contraprepared to learn about the contingency. *The relative preparedness of an animal for learning about a contingency is defined by how degraded the input can be before that output reliably occurs which means that learning has taken place.* It does not matter how input or output are specified, as long as that specification is used consistently for all points on the continuum. Input can be specified by number of trials, length of delay of reinforcement, number of bits of information, etc., and output by frequency, latency or probability of response, correctness of the subject's hypothesis, appropriateness of a cognitive strategy, enlargement of a repertoire, etc. Thus, using the preparedness dimension is independent of whether one is an S-R theorist, an information processing theorist, an ethologist, an eclectic, or what have you.

What does it mean to say that contingency$_1$ (C_1) was learned with more "degraded input" than contingency$_2$ (C_2)? There are several ways input can be degraded. If the animal learned C_1 after 2 trials and C_2 only after 25 trials, we would say that C_1 was learned with more "degradation of input" than C_2, and was therefore more prepared. If both are learned in two trials, but C_1 is learned with a 60-minute delay of reinforcement and C_2 with only a 5-second delay, C_1 is more "degraded" than C_2, and therefore more prepared. If C_1 and C_2 were both learned in two trials and with the same delay of reinforcement, but learning occurs for C_1 if every other 100 milliseconds of the events are filtered out, but C_2 can be learned only without any filtering, C_1 is more prepared than C_2. (Such filtering is "degradation of input" in its most literal sense.) Probability is yet another dimension of degradation of input: If learning occurs in 10 trials with the same delay and the same filtering, but only if one element of the contingency predicts the other with a probability of 1.0 for C_2, and learning can occur with probability of 0.5 in C_1, C_1 is more prepared. Degradedness of input is a multidetermined and open-ended concept: Any of several criteria satisfy it. Such concepts are common in psychological theory: Hunger, for example, can be specified by hours of deprivation, *or* weight loss, *or* amount of quinine which an animal will tolerate and still eat, *or* amount of shock he will tolerate to get to food. Preparedness, like hunger, has the advantage of openendedness, but also a disadvantage: To the extent that the correlation among the different criteria is low, the usefulness of the concept is weakened, and this, of course, is an empirical question.

The reader should notice that we have focused on acquisition as our defining operation for preparedness. We might have selected resistance to extinction; maximum delay of reinforcement, flatness of generalization gradient or any of a host of others as our criterion. We do not know that all these will covary with ease of acquisition, and remain open to the possibility that they will not. It may turn out that one preparedness dimension is an oversimplification. If significant laws of learning do not covary with preparedness defined by the acquisition criterion, we may need several independent preparedness dimensions. We suggest acquisition preparedness, however, as a first approximation of the way the pie should be sliced.

Let us illustrate how to place a given case on the continuum for classical conditioning. If the organism makes the relevant response consistently from the very first presentation of the CS on, such behavior is a clear case of instinctive responding, the extreme of the prepared end of the dimension. An example would be using as a CS the sound of a cap gun, which elicits a startle reflex to produce a startle CR. If the animal makes the conditioned response consistently after only a few pairings, it is somewhat prepared. If the response emerges after many pairings, the organism is unprepared. If acquisition occurs only after very many pairings or does not occur at all, the organism is said to be contra-prepared[1] for the association. Number of pairings is a measure that makes the dimension continuous, and *implicit in the preparedness dimension is the premise that "learning" is continuous with "instinct."* Typically ethologists have explored situations from the prepared side of the dimension, while general-process learning theorists have largely restricted themselves to the unprepared region. The contraprepared part of the dimension has been largely uninvestigated.

Strictly speaking, the labels "prepared," "unprepared," and "contraprepared" can be used only relatively. Except for the very extremes of the dimension in which the required behavior occurs at once or never, nothing can be said to be absolutely prepared, unprepared, or contraprepared, but only more or less than something else. So, for example, if it takes a rat three pairings of the taste of licorice and apomorphine poisoning to show a full-blown aversion to licorice, and 129 pairings of licorice and foot shock for an aversion to develop, it would be inexact to say that the licorice-illness association was prepared and the licorice-shock association unprepared. Rather, the licorice-illness association was more prepared, or less unprepared, than the licorice-shock association.

PREPAREDNESS AS AN EMPIRICAL HYPOTHESIS

Preparedness is more than an alternative to the equipotentiality premise, and it is more than just a name for an ease of learning continuum. We propose four general hypotheses which transform it into an effective theoretical tool with explanatory and predictive power: (1) Different laws of learning vary with the dimension of ease of conditionability. (2) Different physiological substrata vary with the dimension. (3) Different cognitive mechanisms vary with the dimen-sion. (4) As the word "preparedness" implies, the selective pressures exerted on a species determine where a contingency falls on the dimension. These hypotheses will be elaborated and supported in our headnotes and in the readings.

Most of the articles which follow provide evidence which challenges equipotentiality, and can be viewed within a preparedness framework. For many years, ethologists and others (for an excellent example, see Breland and Breland, p. 181, this volume) have been gathering a wealth of evidence to challenge the premise. Curiously, however, these data had little impact on the general-process camp, and while not totally ignored, they were not theoretically incorporated; in view of differences in methodology, this is perhaps understandable. More persuasive to the general-process theorist should be the findings which have recently sprung up within his own tradition. Conditioning and training paradigms have generated a considerable body of evidence to challenge the premise. As we look over both this evidence and that from behavioral biology, we shall find the dimension of preparedness a useful integrative device. The experimental and theoretical papers we now present support the view that events are not all equipotential. Taken together, they clearly demonstrate that learning has its biological boundaries.

[1] The term "contraprepared" carries more baggage than the operational definition we have given it; it tends to imply an explanation as well as a description of the difficulty or impossibility of learning. "Contraprepared" literally means "prepared against," and connotes more than the absence of preparation or the presence of a *tabula rasa*. It implies that there has been selective evolutionary pressure against the association and preparation for an antagonistic mechanism such as a competing response.

We choose to rely primarily upon our operational definition, although we recognize that the continuum as defined connotes an evolutionary mechanism. The basic problem in defining "contrapreparedness" in terms of a competing association would be that the notion of competition is often used carelessly in psychology. So, for example, it is said that rats have trouble learning to press bars to avoid shock because they "freeze," and freezing competes with bar pressing. We know of no theory, however, which specifies in advance what competes with what; rather, response competition and facilitation are invoked *post hoc*. It seems possible to us that a theory of topographic incompatibility may arise to provide an explanation of the mechanism of contrapreparedness, but in our present ignorance, the strictly operational definition—that acquisition is very difficult or impossible —is more appropriate. So while it may well be that all contraprepared associations result from competition with more prepared associations (see Bolles, p. 189, and Breland and Breland, p. 181, this volume), we regard this as an empirical question, not a matter to be decided by a definition.

I

CLASSICAL CONDITIONING

Sauce Béarnaise is an egg-thickened, tarragon-flavored concoction, and it used to be my (MEPS) favorite sauce. It now tastes awful to me. This happened several years ago, when I felt the effects of the stomach flu about six hours after eating filet mignon with sauce Béarnaise. I became violently ill and spent most of the night vomiting. The next time I had sauce Béarnaise, I couldn't bear the taste of it. At the time, I had no ready way to account for the change, although it seemed to fit a classical conditioning paradigm: CS (sauce) paired with US (illness) and UR (vomiting) yields CR (nauseating taste). But if this was classical conditioning, it violated at least two Pavlovian laws: *The delay between tasting the sauce and vomiting was about 6 hours, and classical conditioning isn't supposed to bridge time gaps like that. In addition, neither the filet mignon, nor the white plates off which I ate the sauce, nor Tristan und Isolde, the opera that I listened to in the interpolated time, nor my wife, Kerry, became aversive. Only the sauce Béarnaise did. Moreover, unlike much of classical conditioning, it could not be seen as a "cognitive" phenomenon, involving expectations. For I soon found out that the sauce had not caused the vomiting and that a stomach flu had: Steve Maier and I had been working together at the lab for the previous week, and 3 days after the sauce Béarnaise I picked up the phone to ask him what had happened in the interim. A groan answered: "How should I know, I've been sick with the stomach flu for 3 days and was about to call you and ask." This information, combined with the fact that Kerry (who also ate the sauce Béarnaise) did not get sick, convinced* me that it was not the sauce but the flu that was the culprit. *Yet in spite of this knowledge, I could not later inhibit my aversion.*

That same week, the first of a series of articles by John Garcia and his collaborators appeared, and illuminated the sauce Béarnaise phenomenon for me. We now see this as an epoch-making article and do not hesitate to call it a classic. Strangely enough, these early Garcia articles came out in what were then relatively out-of-the-way journals, Psychonomic Science *and* Communications in Behavioral Biology. *They had been rejected by the blue-ribbon journals of experimental psychology,* The Journal of Comparative and Physiological Psychology, Science, *and* The Psychological Review. *Our readers might be interested to know that when he retired as editor of* The Journal of Comparative and Physiological Psychology, *William K. Estes, the distinguished learning theorist, sent a letter to John Garcia. In it he said that he had one regret about his term of office, rejecting the Garcia and Koelling article. This is recorded not as gossip but because such rejections are common in the history of scientific revolution (Kuhn, 1962), and apologies are not. It is this important article which we present first.*

In Garcia and Koelling's paradigm experiment rats are exposed to a taste and an audiovisual stimulus paired with radiation sickness. Only the taste and not the audiovisual stimulus becomes aversive. In the complementary experiment, rats are given the same two CS's paired now with foot shock. Only the audiovisual stimulus and not the taste becomes aversive.

In this one experiment, we have both ends as well as the middle of the preparedness continuum. Rats are prepared to associate tastes with illness. For in spite of a long CS-US interval (it takes about 1 hour for the x-rays to produce illness), and the presence of other perceptible CS's, only taste was associated with nausea, and light and noise were not. Further, rats are relatively unprepared, perhaps contraprepared, to associate external events with nausea and to associate taste with foot shock. Finally, the association of foot shock with light and sound seems less prepared than taste-nausea but more prepared than taste-shock. The evolutionary edge which this preparedness would give seems obvious: Animals who are poisoned by a distinctively flavored food and survive do well not to eat it again. Selective advantage should accrue, moreover, to those rats whose associative apparatus bridges a very long CS-US interval and ignores continguous and interpolated external CS's when they are poisoned.

I

RELATION OF CUE TO
CONSEQUENCE IN
AVOIDANCE LEARNING

John Garcia and Robert A. Koelling

A great deal of evidence stemming from diverse sources suggests an inadequacy in the usual formulations concerning reinforcement. Barnett (1963) has described the "bait-shy" behavior of wild rats which have survived a poisoning attempt. These animals utilizing olfactory and gustatory cues, avoid the poison bait which previously made them ill. However, there is no evidence that they avoid the "place" of the poisoning.

In a recent volume (Haley & Snyder, 1964) several authors have discussed studies in which ionizing radiations were employed as a noxious stimulus to produce avoidance reactions in animals. Ionizing radiation like .many poisons produces gastrointestinal disturbances and nausea. Strong aversions are readily established in animals when distinctively flavored fluids are conditionally paired with x-rays. Subsequently, the gustatory stimulus will depress fluid intake without radiation. In contrast, a distinctive environmental complex of auditory, visual, and tactual stimuli does not inhibit drinking even when the compound stimulus is associated with the identical radiation schedule. This differential effect has also been observed following ingestion of a toxin and the injection of a drug (Garcia & Koelling, 1965).

Apparently this differential effectiveness of cues is due either to the nature of the reinforcer, i.e., radiation or toxic effects, or to the peculiar relation which a gustatory stimulus has to the drinking response, i.e., gustatory stimulation occurs if and only if the animal licks the fluid. The environmental cues associated with a distinctive place are not as dependent upon a single response of the organism. Therefore, we made an auditory and visual stimulus dependent upon the animal's licking the water spout. Thus, in four experiments reported here "bright-noisy" water, as well as "tasty" water was conditionally paired with

From *Psychonomic Science*, 4(1966), 123–124.

This research stems from doctoral research carried out at Long Beach V. A. Hospital and supported by NIH No. RH00068. Thanks are extended to Professors B. F. Ritchie, D. Krech and E. R. Dempster, U. C. Berkely, California.

radiation, a toxin, immediate shock, and delayed shock, respectively, as reinforcers. Later the capacity of these response-controlled stimuli to inhibit drinking in the absence of reinforcement was tested.

METHOD

The apparatus was a light and sound shielded box (7 in. x 7 in. x 7 in.) with a drinking spout connected to an electronic drinkometer which counted each touch of the rat's tongue to the spout. "Bright-noisy" water was provided by connecting an incandescent lamp (5 watts) and a clicking relay into this circuit. "Tasty" water was provided by adding flavors to the drinking supply.

Each experimental group consisted of 10 rats (90 day old Sprague-Dawley males) maintained in individual cages without water, but with Purina Laboratory Chow ad libidum.

The procedure was: A. One week of habituation to drinking in the apparatus without stimulation. B. Pretests to measure intake of bright-noisy water and tasty water prior to training. C. Acquisition training with: (1) reinforced trials where these stimuli were paired with reinforcement during drinking, (2) nonreinforced trials where rats drank water without stimuli or reinforcement. Training terminated when there was a reliable difference between water intake scores on reinforced and nonreinforced trials. D. Post-tests to measure intake of bright-noisy water and tasty water after training.

In the x-ray study an audiovisual group and a gustatory group were exposed to an identical radiation schedule. In the other studies reinforcement was contingent upon the rat's response. To insure that both the audiovisual and the gustatory stimuli received equivalent reinforcement, they were combined and simultaneously paired with the reinforcer during acquisition training. Therefore, one group serving as its own control and divided into equal subgroups, was tested in balanced order with an audiovisual and a gustatory test before and after training with these stimuli combined.

One 20-min. reinforced trial was administered every three days in the x-ray and lithium chloride studies. This prolonged intertrial interval was designed to allow sufficient time for the rats to recover from acute effects of treatment. On each interpolated day the animals received a 20-min. nonreinforced trial. They were post-tested two days after their last reinforced trial. The x-ray groups received a total of three reinforced trials, each with 54 r of filtered 250 kv x-rays delivered in 20 min. Sweet water (1 gm saccharin per liter) was the gustatory stimulus. The lithium chloride group had a total of five reinforced trials with toxic salty water (.12 M lithium chloride). Non-toxic salty water (.12 M sodium chloride) which rats cannot readily distinguish from the toxic solution was used in the gustatory tests (Nachman, 1963).

The immediate shock study was conducted on a more orthodox avoidance schedule. Tests and trials were 2 min. long. Each day for four consecutive acquisition days, animals were given two nonreinforced and two reinforced trials in an NRRN,RNNR pattern. A shock, the minimal current required to interrupt drinking (0.5 sec. at 0.08-0.20 ma), was delivered through a floor grid 2 sec. after the first lick at the spout.

The delayed shock study was conducted simultaneously with the lithium chloride on the same schedule. Non-toxic salty water was the gustatory stimulus. Shock reinforcement was delayed during first trials and gradually increased in intensity (.05 to .30 ma) in a schedule designed to produce a drinking pattern during the 20-min. period which resembled that of the corresponding animal drinking toxic salty water.

RESULTS AND DISCUSSION

The results indicate that all reinforcers were effective in producing discrimination learning during the acquisition phase (see Fig. 1), but obvious differences occurred in the post-tests. The avoidance reactions produced by x-rays and lithium chloride are readily transferred to the gustatory stimulus but not to the audiovisual stimulus. The effect is more pronounced in the x-ray study, perhaps due to differences in dose. The x-ray animals received a constant dose while the lithium chloride rats drank a decreasing amount of the toxic solution during training. Nevertheless, the difference between post-test scores is statistically significant in both experiments (p. < 0.01 by ranks test.)

Apparently when gustatory stimuli are paired with agents which produce nausea and gastric upset, they acquire secondary reinforcing properties which might be described as "conditioned nausea." Auditory and visual stimulation do not readily acquire similar properties even when they are contingent upon the licking response.

In contrast, the effect of both immediate and delayed shock to the paws is in the opposite direction. The avoidance reactions produced by electric shock to the paws transferred to the audiovisual stimulus but not to the gustatory stimulus. As one might expect, the effect of delayed shocks was not as effective as shocks where the reinforcer immediately and consistently followed licking. Again, the difference between post-test intake scores is statistically significant in both studies (p. < 0.01 by ranks test). Thus, when shock which produces peripheral pain is the reinforcer, "conditioned fear" properties are more readily acquired by auditory and visual stimuli than by gustatory stimuli.

It seems that given reinforcers are not equally effective for all classes of discriminable stimuli. The cues, which the animal selects from the welter of stimuli in the learning situation, appear to be related to the consequences of the subsequent reinforcer. Two speculations are offered: (1) Common elements in the time-intensity patterns of stimulation may facilitate a cross modal generalization from reinforcer to cue in one case and not in another. (2) More likely, natural selection may have favored mechanisms which associate gustatory and olfactory cues with internal discomfort since the chemical receptors sample the materials soon to be incorporated into the internal environment. Krechevsky (1933) postulated such a genetically coded hypothesis to account for the predispositions of rats to respond systematically to specific cues in an insoluble maze. The hypothesis of the sick rat, as for many of us under similar circumstances, would be, "It must have been something I ate."

References

Barnett, S. A. *The rat: a study in behavior.* Chicago: Aldine Press, 1963.

Garcia, J., & Koelling, R. A. A comparison of aversions induced by x-rays, toxins, and drugs in the rat. *Radiat. Res.*, 1967, sup. 7, 439–450.

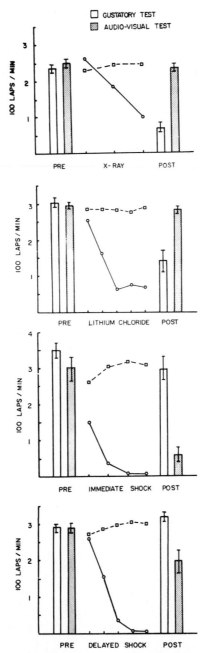

FIG. 1 The bars indicate water intake (± St. Error) during a gustatory test (a distinctive taste) and an audiovisual test (light and sound contingent upon licking) before and after conditional pairing with the reinforcers indicated. The curves illustrate mean intake during acquisition.

Haley, T. J., & Snyder, R. S. (Eds.) *The response of the nervous system to ionizing radiation.* Little, Brown & Co., 1964.

Krechevsky, I. The hereditary nature of 'hypothesis.' *J. comp. Psychol.*, 1932, 16, 99–116.

Nachman, M. Learned aversion to the taste of lithium chloride and generalization to other salts. *J. comp. physiol. Psychol.*, 1963, 56, 343–349.

A few months after the preceding article, Garcia, Ervin, and Koelling dropped the second shoe. They systematically varied the interval between taste CS and poisoning and found that the taste became aversive even with delays of up to 75 minutes. Their finding that much longer delays can be tolerated with illness than with conventional US's removes a second mystery from the sauce Béarnaise phenomenon. Just as the Garcia and Koelling findings illuminate why only the taste of the sauce and not Tristan und Isolde, *the white plates, or my wife became aversive, so this article illuminates how conditioning might have occurred with a 6-hour delay between the taste and illness.*

Like the first, this article did not receive a congenial reception in some quarters. One investigator, who had worked for years on delay of reinforcement, remarked publicly, "Those findings are no more likely than birdshit in a cuckoo clock." Nevertheless, they have been replicated many times.

2

LEARNING WITH PROLONGED

DELAY OF REINFORCEMENT

John Garcia, Frank R. Ervin,

and Robert A. Koelling

It is considered axiomatic in theory and practice that no learning will occur without immediate reinforcement. For example, a hungry rat will not learn to press a lever for food unless the response is immediately followed by food (primary reinforcement) or by a signal which has been associated with food in the past (secondary reinforcement). Food can be described as rewarding, but the same general rule has been applied to punishing agents also. Delays of the order of 3 to 45 sec. have a deleterious effect upon learning in a wide variety of experimental situations. The significance of these findings for reinforcement theory was discussed by Spence (1947) and a recent review (Renner, 1964) reveals there has been no major modification of the temporal contiguity aspect. However, our data indicates that immediate reinforcement is not a general requirement for all learning.

METHOD

Young adult male rats (Sprague-Dawley, 300 to 400 gm) were maintained in individual cages with Purina Laboratory Chow ad lib. Drinking was restricted to a 10-min. period each day. After one week of habituation to this schedule, treatment began.

In Experiment A, five groups (N = 8 each) were treated. One experimental group (Sac-Apo:inj) was given a gustatory cue in its drinking water (1 gm saccharine per liter) and after a delay was injected with a drug which produced gastric disturbances (7 mg/kg apormorphine hydrochloride I.P.). The animals were injected in serial order at 1-min. intervals with the first animal injected at 5 min. and the last one at 12 min. after the saccharine water bottle was removed

From *Psychonomic Science*, 5(1966), 121–122.

This research was supported by Grant No. CA-07368 and NASA Contract No. NsG262-63 and, NIH Career Award No. K3-MH-19,434 to Frank R. Ervin.

from the home cage. One control group (Sac-Sal:inj) drank saccharin-water and was injected with saline, while another control (Wat-Apo:inj) drank water and was injected with apomorphine. An additional experimental group (Sac-Apo:inj) received delayed injections in serial order from 15 to 22 min. post-drinking. Other rats (Sac-Shock), immediately after drinking saccharin-water, were taken from their cages and placed in a box with an electric grid floor and three shocks (0.5 sec. pulses at 3 ma) were delivered within 1 min. to the paws.

All groups received four treatments, one every third day and then three extinction tests (i.e. no injections or shock) on the same schedule. Between treatment days, the animals were given water for 10 min.

In Experiment B, five experimental groups (N = 6 each) drank saccharin-water and received apomorphine injections (15 mg/kg I.P.) with delays of 30, 45, 75, 120 and 180 min. Five treatments were administered, one every third day. One control group drank saccharin-water but received no injection.

RESULTS AND DISCUSSION

The apomorphine injected animals (Sac-Apo:inj) displayed a progressive decrease in intake of saccharin-water indicating that the pairing of this distinctly flavored fluid with the drug effects produced a gustatory aversion (Fig. 1). The difference in saccharin-water intake between the apomorphine injected group and their saline injected controls (Sac-Sal:inj) was statistically significant after two injections (p < .01 by ranks test). The decrement increased following each drug administration and then was reversed during the extinction trials. Apomorphine injections had no effect on those animals (Wat-Apo:inj) which drank water every day, demonstrating that differential reinforcement of the gustatory cue is necessary to produce the fluid intake decrement (Fig. 1).

The magnitude of the decrement in saccharin intake produced by four doses of apomorphine (Sac-Apo:inj) was independent of the delay of the reinforcing injection (r = 0) from 5 to 22 min. Furthermore, Experiment B indicated that five apomorphine injections could produce a significant effect at delays up to 75 min. (Fig. 2).

Apomorphine causes nausea and emesis in humans, but in rats emesis is blocked by the cardiac sphincter. Our doses caused the animals to stop eating for 30 min. and caused visible signs of illness within several minutes in most animals.

The rats receiving electrocutaneous shock (Sac-Shock) displayed a significant increase in saccharin-water intake after the first shock (Fig. 1). This increase may be due to the activating effects of shock rather than to associative learning. However, the contrast between shock rats and drug rats in their responses to handling and treatment was also marked. The drug and control animals progressively habituated to handling and injection, but the shock animals made strong attempts to escape after the first shock trial. This observation supports a previous study indicating that the avoidance reactions induced by electrocutaneous shock were readily transferred to auditory and visual signals but not to gustatory ones. Conversely, the avoidance reactions induced by X-ray or toxin were readily transferred to gustatory cues but not to auditory and visual ones (Garcia & Koelling, 1966).

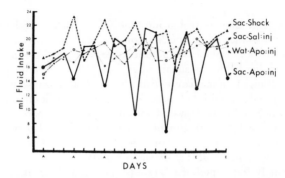

FIG. 1 Experiment A: Daily mean fluid intake during a ten-minute period on acquisition days (A) extinction days (E) and water intake on days between treatments. Only the group receiving saccharin followed by an apomorphine injection (Sac:Apo:inj) learned to reduce saccharin-water intake. Neither apomorphine (Wat-Apo:inj) nor saccharin alone (Sac-Sal:inj) had an appreciable .effect, while saccharin followed by shock (Sac-Shock) had a converse effect.

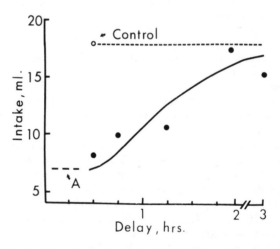

FIG. 2 Experiment B: Mean fluid intake of saccharin-flavored water on the first extinction day, following five conditional pairings of saccharin and apomorphine for groups differing in delay of injection. Results of Experiment A are also indicated.

Two sources, outside of the traditional laboratory studies of learning, indicate similar learning with prolonged delays of reinforcement. Aversions have been produced with a discrimination learning paradigm where one gustatory cue is paired with ionizing radiation and an alternative cue is not so paired (Garcia et al., 1961). Yet, this effect of radiation is not manifested until over an hour post-exposure (Smith et al., 1965). Aversions have been established for unflavored water and for merely sniffing a distinctive odor during exposure, indicating that the phenomenon is not dependent upon lingering traces of a strongly flavored solution (Garcia & Koelling, 1965). Furthermore, animals on water-deprivation invariably consume a large meal of dry food so that the gustatory and olfactory cues are immediately followed by intervening stimulation via these modalities which is not differentially reinforced.

Rats utilizing olfaction and gustation also learn to avoid poisons with slow cumulative effects, such as dicoumarin which gradually reduces the clotting power of the blood and eventually causes internal bleeding. These bait-shy responses in many cases do not develop until hours after the ingestion of the bait (Barnett, 1963).

These data indicate anew that the mammalian learning mechanisms do not operate randomly, associating stimuli and reinforcers only as a function of recency, frequency and intensity. The omnivorous rat displays a bias, probably established by natural selection, to associate gustatory and olfactory cues with internal malaise even when these stimuli are separated by long time periods. Auditory, visual and tactual stimuli are not so readily associated with malaise, though they also are discriminable and informative, i.e., suprathreshold and differentially reinforced. On the other hand, the latter cues are more readily associated with peripheral pain. In this case, both cue and reinforcer are localized in external space by the rat and under "natural" conditions, escape movements are particularly adaptive. This bias has a practical diagnostic value for drug research. Since the gustatory aversion is sensitive to toxicity yet insensitive to peripheral pain, it can be conveniently used in conjunction with injection and surgical procedures.

References

Barnett, S. A. *The rat: A study in behavior.* Chicago: Aldine Press, 1963.

Garcia, J., Kimeldorf, D. J., & Hunt, E. L. The use of ionizing radiation as a motivating stimulus. *Psychol. Rev.*, 1961, 68, 383–395.

Garcia, J., & Koelling, R. A. A comparison of aversions induced by X-rays, toxins and drugs in the rat. *Radiat. Res.*, 1965, 1967, sup. 7, 439–450.

Garcia, J., & Koelling, R. A. Relation of cue to consequence in avoidance learning. *Psychon. Sci.*, 1966, 4, 123–124.

Renner, K. E. Delay of reinforcement: A historical review. *Psychol. Bull.*, 1964, 5, 341–361.

Spence, K. W. The role of secondary reinforcement in delayed reward learning. *Psychol. Rev.*, 1947, 54, 1–8.

Smith, J. C., Taylor, H. L., Morris, D. D., & N. Hendricks, J. Further studies of x-ray conditioned aversion during the post exposure period. *Radiat. Res.* 1965, 24, 423-431.

Garcia, McGowan, and Green's overview of the five years of research following the original findings includes summaries of numerous replications and variations on the original phenomena, and a theoretical integration of neurological, evolutionary, and behavioral evidence.

3

BIOLOGICAL CONSTRAINTS
ON CONDITIONING

John Garcia, Brenda K. McGowan,
and Kenneth F. Green

During the last fifty years a theoretical trend has occurred in American Psychology which has virtually take the organism out of learning. Curiously enough, this process can be traced back to the physiologist, I. P. Pavlov (1928), who stressed the equivalence of stimuli in his *Lectures on Conditioned Reflexes*:

> if our hypothesis as to the origin of the conditioned reflex is correct, it follows that any natural phenomenon chosen at will may be converted into a conditioned stimulus. . . . Any visual stimulus, any desired sound, any odour, and the stimulation of any part of the skin, whether by mechanical means or by the application of heat or cold. . . .

Since all perceptible stimuli were assumed to be equivalent, it was assumed further that the specific nature of the afferent tracts involved and their central integrations were idle neurological speculations which obscured the true task of the learning theorist, K. W. Spence (1947) formulated this position in his paper entitled "The role of secondary reinforcement in delayed reward learning."

> psychologists have come to realize that explanation of behavioral events does not *necessarily* involve reduction to its physiological determinants. Accepting the task of the psychologist as being that of establishing interrelationships (laws) within the realm of those observable events (responses and environmental situations) that are his particular concern, these theorists have introduced a variety of new types of constructs to aid them in their purpose. In the case of learning phenomena, a number of theoretical interpretations have recently been offered which make little or no use of neurophysiological concepts.

From A. H. Black and W. F. Prokasy (Eds.). *Classical Conditioning II: Current Research and Theory* (New York: Appleton-Century-Crofts, 1972).

This research was supported by NIH Grants (RH 00589, MH 14380 and AEC (30-1)-3698.

Opposing trends such as achievements of Lashley in the neural basis of learning and Tryon's beginnings in genetic determinants of maze behavior had little impact upon learning theory. Spence's doctrine remained dominant until the present day among students of learning whether their predilections favored rigorous mathematical theorizing or no theorizing at all. W. K. Estes (1959) relegated all physiological variables to a seemingly minor role in statistical learning theory assuming

> that all empirical independent variables (causal variables, antecedent conditions, or determinants of behavior) which enter into behavioral laws influence behavior by way of stimulation. This does not mean that hormones, genetic determiners, surgical interventions, and the like are considered unimportant, but simply that they are considered in a formal behavioral theory only as determiners of parameter values. . . .

B. F. Skinner, on the one hand, cogently criticized theoretical conceptions and statistical devices which "lumped" individual behavioral patterns into meaningless means; and on the other hand, advocated experimental procedures which had precisely the same "lumping" effect upon individual and species differences. He demonstrated that, given a lever box and a fixed interval schedule, all animals produced scalloped cumulative curves (Skinner, 1959):

> Pigeon, rat, monkey, which is which? It doesn't matter. Of course, these species have behavioral repertoires which are as different as their anatomies. But once you have allowed for differences in the ways in which they make contact with the environment, and in the ways in which they act upon the environment, what remains of their behavior shows astonishingly similar properties.

For many psychologists, determination of differential organismic parameter values or specification of the ways different organisms made contact with and acted upon the environment was the meaty part of behavior. A number of critics protested vigorously, for example Beach (1950) and Hebb (1960) and, across the Atlantic, the antithetical movement, Ethology, exemplified by Tinbergen (1951) and Lorenz (1965), stressed evolution and species-specific behavior.

Perhaps the most dramatic reaction was the defection of the Brelands, who, armed with the "impeccable empiricism" of the American learning labs, had established a business venture engineering a wide range of conditioned behaviors in a variety of animals for department store displays, television commercials, zoos, and amusement parks. Their behavioral engineering successes became financially rewarding but their failures to establish stable conditioning in many cases proved theoretically more interesting. Well-trained animals drifted away from their conditioned repertoires toward instinctual patterns of responding which paradoxically required greater physical output and delayed or decreased the likelihood of reinforcement. Moreover, increasing the drive (deprivation time) actually intensified the drift. Breland and Breland (1961) concluded:

these assumptions (that the animal comes to the laboratory as a virtual *tabula rasa*, that species differences are insignificant, and that all responses are about equally conditionable to all stimuli) are no longer tenable. After 14 years of continuous conditioning and observation of thousands of animals, it is our reluctant conclusion that the behavior of any species cannot be adequately understood, predicted, or controlled without knowledge of its instinctive patterns, evolutionary history, and ecological niche.

In spite of our early successes with the application of behavioristically oriented conditioning theory, we readily admit now that ethological facts and attitudes in recent years have done more to advance our practical control of animal behavior than recent reports from American "learning labs."

Like the Brelands, many of us concerned with other "applied problems" such as assessing the "side-effects" of nutrients, toxins, drugs, and X rays also encountered theoretical contradictions. We were not concerned with upsetting learning theory; quite the contrary, we were eager to display to the physician, the pathologist, and physical scientist, the elegance of modern behavioral techniques and the predictive power of our learning principles. The practical problem of describing the behavioral effects of therapeutic treatments and weighing their beneficial and detrimental consequences for the organism was challenge enough.

Unlike the Brelands, we confined ourselves to laboratory animals treated in the traditional laboratory conditions with the usual instrumentation. The behavioral techniques served us well and the often maligned white rat proved to be an excellent subject. Behavioral effects proved to be the most sensitive biological tests for the effects of X rays and new insights were gained on the effects of toxins. Only the "empty-organism" theories proved to be totally inadequate.

Let us review some of these earlier findings and present some new data which raise some questions regarding traditional conceptualizations in conditioning and learning.

ARE TEMPORAL CONDITIONING PARAMETERS LIMITED TO SECONDS OR LESS?

In some early experiments rats were exposed to low radiant flux from a small cobalt 60 source for eight hours once a week. The total dose per day was relatively small by radiobiological standards (75 rads) and the most notable effect was a depression in food and water consumption during the exposure period (Garcia, Kimeldorf, Hunt, & Davies, 1956). The water measures in particular exhibited a progressive decrease as if the animals were learning to limit water intake during exposure. In contrast, consumption in the home cages during the remainder of the week appeared to be normal. Surprisingly, the animals displayed the same depressed consumption when, on the following week, they were returned to the radiation chambers and tested under sham conditions, i.e., without actually exposing the animals to the gamma rays.

This depressed food and water consumption was apparently a conditioned response, but could such gross temporal intervals be considered a conditioning schedule? One needs only to refer to a standard text such as Kimble (1967) to see that traditional conditioning experiments deal in seconds and fractions thereof.

Later we suspected that the critical stimulus was a subtle taste factor in the water and that the depressed food intake was a result of the decreased water intake. In the radiation chamber, the rats drank water from a drinking spout attached to plastic test tubes; in the home cage they drank from the tubes attached to glass bottles. Informal tests by Robert A. Koelling, conducted by hand in the animal room, indicated that the previously irradiated animals would refuse water which had been allowed to stand overnight in plastic test tubes, but they would drink water which had been allowed to stand in water bottles. Apparently the rats could discriminate the water in plastic bottles which they received during radiation on the basis of taste, and learned to reject it because it was conditionally associated with exposure.

The radiation-induced aversion resembled the "bait-shy behavior" displayed by wild rats surviving the effect of a poisoned bait (Barnett, 1963; Garcia & Koelling, 1967). Bait-shy animals subsequently avoided baits which tasted like the one that contained the poison for long periods after the original toxicosis.

This hypothesis was supported by more rigorous tests in which the flavor of saccharin was conditionally associated with the noxious effects of radiation exposures (Garcia, Kimeldorf, & Koelling, 1955). Except for the fact that the stimulus presentations lasted for hours rather than seconds, these aversive effects appeared to resemble the traditional avoidance conditioning results when temporal relations of the CS (saccharin drinking) and the US (radiation exposure) were varied. Simultaneous presentation was most effective, backward presentation was least effective, and forward trace presentation was intermediately effective (Garcia & Kimeldorf, 1957).

Figure 1 illustrates the phenomena in laboratory rats long after a single conditional pairing of flavor and illness. These animals were first deprived of water for 24 hours. The X-ray group was allowed to drink a saline solution (.12 M sodium chloride) and then exposed to 100 r of 280 KV filtered X rays. The lithium group drank approximately 10 ml of a toxic salt solution (.12 M lithium chloride). The control group drank water and was subsequently exposed to 100 r of X rays. All the animals were then returned to their home cages without further treatment or testing.

Thirty-two days later they were again deprived of water for 24 hours and then all three groups were presented with saline (.12 M sodium chloride) for 10 minutes. Figure 1 indicates that seven of the ten X-ray animals displayed a depressed intake, drinking less than the lowest control value. The lithium group displayed an even more marked effect, indicating that the lithium chloride-induced aversion readily generalizes to sodium chloride solutions as Nachman (1963) has already shown. Aversions, whether induced by radiation or toxins, appear to be reliable even under these adverse conditions where the initial test was delayed for 32 days.

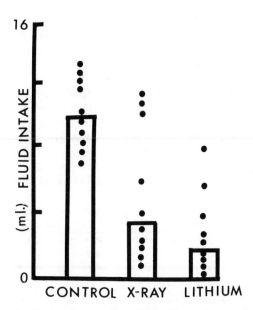

FIG. 1 Amount of saline (.12 M sodium chloride) consumed on the first test conducted 32 days after a single conditional pairing of taste and illness. The X-ray group was exposed to 100 r while drinking the saline, the lithium group drank a toxic solution (.12 M lithium chloride), and the control group drank water during an exposure to 100 r X-ray.

Other experiments have indicated that radiation effects parallel toxin effects very closely. Aversions have been induced in recipient rats by transfusions of blood from irradiated donors (Hunt, Carroll, & Kimeldorf, 1948), by intraperitoneal injections of serum from irradiated donors (Garcia, Ervin, & Koelling, 1967), and by injections by emetic drugs or toxic agents (Garcia & Koelling, 1967).

DO ALL STIMULUS ELEMENTS IN THE ACQUISITION SITUATION BECOME CONDITIONED STIMULI?

While bait-shy animals readily avoid the poison baits after suffering the effects of poison, they do not avoid the place where they ate the poison. Apparently they do not acquire strong avoidance tendencies for those stimulus elements (visual, tactual, etc.) which define the spatial location of the poison even though they have a profound aversion for the stimulus elements which define the food (taste and smell). In a similar way, it proved to be much more difficult to train an animal to avoid a distinctive compartment in which it suffered radiation exposure than it was to teach it to avoid a distinctive substance consumed before exposure (Garcia, Kimeldorf, & Hunt, 1961).

Figure 2A summarizes the results of an experiment in which a number of different stimuli were conditionally paired with an identical series of X-ray exposures (Garcia & Koelling, 1967). The bars in Figure 2A indicate the relative capacity of various conditional stimuli to suppress drinking in an extinction test. The visual, auditory, and tactual stimuli of the distinctive compartment (place group) were completely ineffective, while a distinctive flavor (taste group) was most effective.

A distinctive perfume in the radiation chamber (smell group) proved to have an intermediate effect, which is interesting since the olfactory system has two important functional roles for these animals. It can be used like vision to identify a place or used like taste to identify a food. In our experiment described above, the odor of the perfume permeated the compartment, that is, it did not emanate from the food itself. If the odor had been attached to the food, and increased in strength as the animal approached the food, it would probably have been a more effective CS.

Figure 2B summarizes the results of another experiment in which the same compound stimulus was conditionally paired with a toxin or a shock to the paws (Garcia & Koelling, 1966). By means of an electronic circuit, an audiovisual

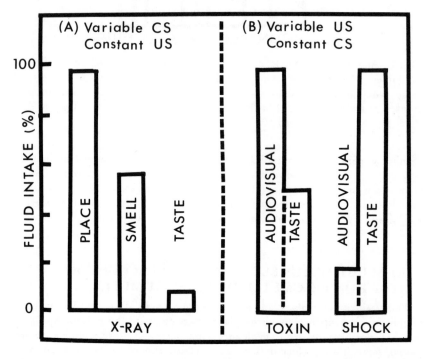

FIG. 2 Summary of several experiments in which (A) various CS_s were conditionally paired with identical X-ray exposures and (B) the same compound stimulus was paired with a toxin injection or shock to the paws. The capacity of each component CS to depress drinking was measured under extinction conditions (replotted from Garcia & Koelling, 1967; Garcia, McGowan, Ervin, & Koelling, 1968).

signal, as well as a flavor, was made contingent upon the animal's licking the water spout. The toxin group was then punished with toxicosis for drinking in the presence of the compound stimulus, while the shock group was punished by electrocutaneous shock to the paws for drinking under the same circumstances.

The double bars in Figure 2B indicate the results of two extinction tests for each group; one in which the capacity of the audiovisual component to depress drinking was tested alone under extinction conditions, and the other in which the taste component was tested alone under similar circumstances. The audiovisual elements proved ineffective as conditional stimuli when paired with toxin but very effective when paired with shock. Conversely, the taste (and possibly smell) elements were ineffective when paired with shock but very effective when paired with toxin.

Similar results were obtained in other experiments (Garcia, McGowan, Ervin, & Koelling, 1968). The noxious effects of X-ray exposure does not cause the animal to reject food on the basis of visual cues (size of pellet) as measured by latency to pick up the pellet. But radiation does change the animal preference as measured by the amount eaten, when a taste cue is provided. The painful effects of electric shock cause the animal to hesitate on the basis of visual cues but it does not decrease the animal's preference for a taste cue.

DO SIGNALS AND CUES (CS) ACQUIRE FEAR (DRIVE) PROPERTIES?

The use of electrocutaneous shock as a US has proved more curious to us than X rays or toxins. When a rat is shocked immediately after drinking a highly preferred flavor, it is likely to increase its intake on the next trial (Garcia, Ervin, & Koelling, 1966), even when the shock has been delivered to the mouth while drinking (Dietz & Capretta, 1966). This behavior does not seem to fit well with Neal Miller's definition of a learned fear quoted below (Miller, 1951).

> A learnable drive or reward is one that can be acquired by a previously ineffective cue as a result of learning. Thus, if a child has not previously feared dogs learns to fear them after having been bitten, it shows that fear is learnable. Similarly, if appropriate training causes a previously ineffective token or coin to serve as reward, we may call it a learned reward.

Unpublished data from our laboratory indicate that rats can be taught to avoid drinking a distinctive fluid if electric shock is promptly delivered after a few licks at the spout, but this treatment will not change the animal's preference for the fluid in its home cage where it has never been shocked. Thus, the animal in the context of the electric grid is able to use the taste cue to avoid shock with skeletal motor responses, but this taste can scarcely be said to acquire "fear properties" since it maintains its "reward properties" in the home cage. If one attempts to salvage Miller's conceptualization by specifying that the cue acquires fear only in its original contextual setting, then its transituational generality is lost, limiting its usefulness as an explanatory concept. On the other hand, when illness is used to change the rat's preference for a taste cue, the animal will avoid it as well in situations where it has never been ill, fulfilling the transituational requirement.

Even when the visual aspects of food (pellet size) were followed by electric shock, rats did not learn to fear this "previously ineffective cue." Hungry rats prefer large pellets and apparently continue to prefer them even after learning to avoid them. Some rats solved their dilemma by seizing large pellets and carrying them to where they could eat them while sitting among the small pellets. Clearly it seems more reasonable to say that the size of the pellet acquired the property to signal the advent of shock than to say that it acquired fear properties.

DOES CONDITIONING REQUIRE AN UNCONDITIONED RESPONSE?

In most of our radiation-induced aversion studies, saccharin-flavored water (CS) was followed by radiation (US) regardless of the animal's response, hence it can be described as a Pavlovian or classical conditioning procedure. But while it is reasonable in a strictly operational sense to designate X ray as the US it is difficult to point to an unconditioned response (UR). Bitterman (1962) points out quite clearly the importance of a clear-cut UR for the classical conditioning paradigm:

> In a Pavlovian experiment, the choice of reinforcement restricts the choice of a behavioral indicator; while the conditioned and uncondi- tioned responses are not always (as Pavlov thought) identical, the investigator must be guided in his search for evidence of learning by the functional properties of the reinforcing stimulus.

Now let us examine some data on the effect of X rays on drinking in the rat illustrated in Figure 3. The upper curve illustrates cumulative drinking measured by a lick counter for one group (N = 8) of rats drinking water on three test days. The pre-X curve indicates baseline water consumption after the animals had been habituated to drinking in the radiation chamber. The X-ray curve indicates the same group drinking on the exposure day, when the UR (200 r of 280 KV filtered X ray) was applied during the first three minutes of the drinking period. The post-X curve illustrates drinking three days later. Radiation does not depress drinking either on the exposure day nor on the post-X day, i.e., there is no apparent UR effect upon water consumption.

The lower curve depicts cumulative drinking of saccharin-flavored water (one gram per liter) for two groups (N = 8 each) on two test days. Both groups had been habituated with water to the same extent as the water group in the upper curves. The sham curve depicts drinking in one group during sham exposure (i.e., when shielded by lead from the X rays), and post-S curve indicates that their saccharin drinking rate was slightly increased when they were tested a second time three days later. The X-ray curve depicts saccharin drinking under the same exposure conditions as the water group above. Note that X rays do not depress drinking of flavored water either during the three-minute exposure nor during

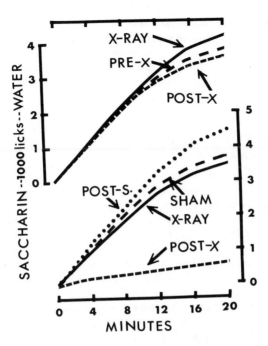

FIG. 3 Mean cumulative drinking curves for the three groups of rats. The upper curves depict drinking unflavored water by one group on three occasions; before, during, and after X-ray exposure. The lower curves depict two groups drinking saccharin-flavored water on two occasions; during X-ray or sham exposure, and after X-ray or sham exposure.

the 17-minute period which followed the exposure. Again no aversive response (CR or UR) is obvious during the conditional pairing of the saccharin flavor (CS) and the X-ray (US). However, when these animals were tested a second time (post-X) they displayed a marked depression in saccharin drinking as if a latent aversive response (CR) had developed in the interim. While the radiation procedures resemble classical conditioning procedures, the conditioned response in no way resembles the functional properties of the reinforcing stimulus.

Recently we discussed the complexities of the X-ray stimulus (Garcia, Green, & McGowan, 1969) pointing out that this pervasive form of energy produces a host of chemical changes, some operating via the olfactory epithelium cause immediate orienting responses. Thus, if the onset of X ray is followed immediately by shock to the rat's paws it is an adequate signal (Garcia, Buchwald, & Feder, 1964), but if the onset of X ray is not followed immediately by a reinforcer, the animal habituates, that is, it no longer orients or arouses to X-ray onset (Garcia, Buchwald, Bach-SC-Rita, Feder, & Koelling, 1963). This particular aspect of the X-ray stimulus cannot be the "reinforcer" (US) which establishes the profound aversive responses. Other responses follow. High sublethal exposures to X rays are followed by a symptom-free period which may last from thirty minutes to several hours after which an illness develops. Human patients report nausea, monkeys vomit, and rats become inactive. The onset, intensity and duration of these symptoms are a function of the total dose received by the organism. This "radiation sickness syndrome" is the most likely reinforcing stimulus (US) yet this formulation leads to still other theoretical difficulties.

IS IMMEDIATE REINFORCEMENT NECESSARY FOR ALL LEARNING?

The results of the study shown in Figure 3 make more sense if we assume that the X rays did not have an immediate noxious effect; thus the animals continued to drink saccharin-water during three-minute exposure and the seventeen minutes which followed. Later the animals became ill and thus developed an aversion for the substance most recently consumed. But Spence (1947) laid down the axiom in 1947 that reinforcement must occur within seconds to be effective. More recently, Perkins (1968) has succinctly restated this proposition: "All reinforcement is assumed to be immediate; delayed rewards are effective if and only if the delay is mediated by secondary reinforcement or a change in the effective attractiveness of stimuli present during the delay."

Early experiments with X rays employed "trace conditioning" procedures (the onset of radiation beginning many minutes after the drinking period) and low doses (10r-30r) which were probably followed by the prolonged symptom-free period, thus the noxious reinforcement may have been delayed a half hour or more.

Since the onset and action of the noxious X-ray effect is difficult to specify, we turned to the use of a fast acting emetic injection (16 mg/kg apomorphine sulphate) as the noxious reinforcer. Starting with a group of 16 rats we varied the delay of the injection from five to twenty-two minutes (Garcia, Ervin, & Koelling, 1966). Figure 4, a scatter diagram with delay of injection plotted against degree of aversion, indicates that delaying the injection within this interval had no effect.

Subsequent exploration indicated that the emetic injections had to be delayed more than an hour before the strength of the aversion was attenuated to an appreciable degree. Other laboratories have reported significant aversions when X-ray exposure has been delayed for many hours. Revusky (1968), employing sucrose, found aversions with seven-hour delays while Smith and Roll (1967) found similar effects for saccharin and radiation with a 12-hour interval.

ARE CHAINS OF MEDIATORS REQUIRED IN DELAYED REINFORCEMENT?

In order to support the notion of immediate reinforcement, mediating chains of S-R events (often more easily postulated than operationally specified) are invoked to account for apparent delays in reinforcement. When X-ray exposures or injections are delayed hours, it could be argued that the ingestion of flavored fluid institutes a chain of postingestional factors which bridge the interval from

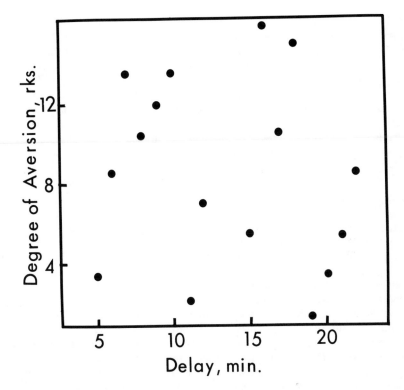

FIG. 4 Scatter diagram where degree of gustatory aversion is plotted against delay of the reinforcement. Sixteen rats were given four conditional pairings of saccharin-flavored water followed by apomorphine injections with the inter-stimulus interval varied prior to this test (Garcia, Ervin, & Koelling, 1966).

ingestion to the final reinforcing illness. Recently we presented evidence on this problem (Garcia, Green, & McGowan, 1969) and here we will only summarize.

First let us consider the CS. Temperature as well as visual aspects of food are ineffective cues—a chemical attribute of the ingested material is required. It might be argued that chemicals lingering in the mouth and other parts of the system provide a series of stimulus events to bridge the long interval between consumption and delayed internal reinforcement. This does not seem likely. Minute amounts of transient ephemeral chemicals, a subtle odor or taste, are sufficient to insure conditioning.

Consider the following sequence of events in which one-half ml. hydrochloric acid per liter of water served as the taste CS. After the sour water is swallowed, it is mixed with the higher concentration of stomach acids. Then the hungry rat is allowed to eat dry laboratory chow for one hour before it is exposed to X rays which take effect even later. Under these conditions the sour water is as effective as lingering tastes such as quinine or saccharin.

Rozin (1969) also addressed himself to the problem of peripheral mediation in a series of feeding experiments. He also found that rats could be trained to avoid a particular solution with delayed injections of apomorphine and that aversive reactions with long CS-US intervals could be much more easily established with taste as a CS than with any other cue. Significantly, he showed that rats could learn to avoid one of two concentrations of the same substance (either higher or lower) when ingestion of that concentration was followed, after 30 minutes, by an apomorphine injection. Since both concentrations have similar aftertastes, Rozin concluded that long-delay learning is probably centrally mediated, reflecting specialization of learning and memory in feeding control systems.

Smell and taste, the first stimuli in the complex chain of consumption, play the primary role in generating preferences and aversions in feeding. Borer (1968) has shown that rats, fitted with intragastric self-injection tubes which bypass the oral receptors, display the normal preference for sweet or dilute salt solutions. They neither prefer nutrients nor refuse hypertonic salt solutions. Postingestional stimuli do not exert much influence despite the fact that they are temporally closer to that ultimate reinforcement of metabolic need reduction.

Aversions do not develop for the last thing eaten, but for the substance made contingent upon illness. Revusky and Bedarf (1967) have demonstrated that when two substances are eaten in sequence prior to illness, novelty is a much more potent factor than recency in determination of the aversion.

Let us now consider the adequate reinforcer (US) for long CS-US interval learning. An internally referred (visceral) state appears to be required. Delayed beneficial injections, such as thiamine injection for thiamine deficient animals, are as effective for elevating gustatory preferences as noxious injections are for depressing preferences (Garcia, Ervin, Yorke, & Koelling, 1967). But, peripheral pain, an externally referred (cutaneous) stimulus, is not an adequate reinforcer. It will not change the animal's taste preference even when applied immediately.

Admittedly, the notion that ingestion produces a chain of stimulus events which bridge the long CS-US interval is one that is difficult to exclude with complete conviction. But even if this were the case, gustatory-visceral conditioning would still be difficult to understand in S-R terms. No one would expect to establish avoidance responses in a few trials if a tone was turned on (and left on) and electric shock was delivered hours later; not even if a symphony of tones were used to bridge the CS-US interval.

CONDITIONING: CLASSICAL, INSTRUMENTAL, OR PSEUDO?

The exclusion of organismic structure and process from consideration has led the learning theorist to place undue emphasis upon the external experimental laboratory procedures. Distinctions between Pavlovian as opposed to Thorndikian conditioning, elicited as opposed to emitted responses, associative as opposed to nonassociatve procedures, are virtually raised to the level of behavioral laws. Behavior is a continuous process and at times we seem to forget that stimuli and responses are not discrete entities but two aspects of the same behavioral event, necessarily isolated from the stream of behavior for the purpose of analysis and discussion.

It is difficult enough to distinguish between classical and instrumental conditioning on procedural grounds; it is impossible to maintain the distinction on a functional oganismic basis. Pavlov's broad class includes "any natural phenomena," the emitted operant with its response-produced stimuli, as well as stimuli emanating from externally controlled energy sources. This particular CS (i.e., the operant response) is followed by a US (i.e., the reinforcer) in the classical temporal sequence. Unconditioned responses follow the reinforcer in the same functional sequence. The rat salivates instrumentally as it presses the lever for food as surely as the dog salivates classically when it hears the bell signaling food.

The principle difference between the two methods lies in the particular segment of the behavioral sequence the investigator selects as his criterion of learning. In classical conditioning he attends to changes in topography and timing of behavioral events which follow reinforcement, and when sufficient modification and stability has occurred he labels these events conditioned response. In instrumental conditioning, on the other hand, the investigator attends to the timing and topography of behavioral events which precede reinforcement; when sufficient modification and stabilization occurs, he labels these events conditioned responses. Confusion occurs when, as learning proceeds, the classical responses begin to anticipate the reinforcer and thus instrumentally modify its effects upon the animal.

When the reinforcer is programmed at regular intervals, as in the classical temporal conditioning or in the instrumental fixed interval schedule, it is impossible to tell which procedure is in use, or for that matter, whether the procedure is a nonassociative one as habituation is generally thought to be. Only when we examine the behavioral indices employed by the investigator can we decide which of these methods have been employed. Obviously, this is of little import to the animal or to us. It is of much more interest to know the nature of the reinforcing stimulus and how the afferent input is handled in the central nervous system.

Nonassociative procedures have traditionally been looked upon with suspicion by learning theorists. When some investigators demonstrated changes in saccharin preference following noncoincidental radiation and in backward paradigms (McLaurin, Farley, Scarborough, & Rawlings, 1964; McLaurin, 1964), there was much concern as to whether radiation-induced aversions were genuine or pseudoconditioned responses. This issue for learning in general has been concisely stated by Rescorla (1967):

> The operations performed to establish Pavlovian conditioned reflexes require that the presentation of an unconditioned stimulus be contingent upon the occurrence of a conditioned stimulus. Students of conditioning have regarded this contingency between CS and US as vital to the definition of conditioning and have rejected changes in the organism not dependent upon this contingency (such as sensitization or pseudoconditioning) as not being "true" conditioning (i.e., associative).

When we are attempting to divine the internal workings of the animal, pseudoconditioning may in some situations be the method of choice. Depressions in intake of saccharin-flavored water can be obtained with backward and pseudoconditioned conditioning paradigms as well as with forward and genuine conditioning paradigms. The results complement rather than contradict each other.

Figure 5 depicts cumulative drinking curves for three groups of animals on two occasions immediately after having received injections of a nitrogen mustard, which produces illness, i.e., inactivity, loss of appetite, and diarrhea (Green, McGowan, Garcia, & Ervin, 1968). The upper curves indicate there is no consistent effect of these doses upon drinking water. The medium-dose group drank more than the zero-dose group while the high-dose group seemed to decrease its rate after about 12 minutes. As with radiation, there is no obvious unconditioned effect upon water intake.

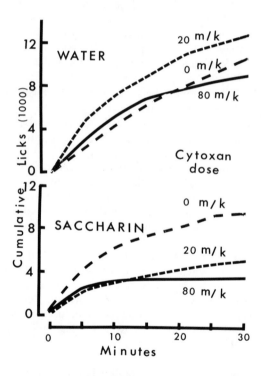

FIG. 5 Mean cumulative drinking curves for six groups of rats in a backward or pseudoconditioning paradigm. The upper curves depict three control groups drinking water after varying injections of a nitrogen mustard. The lower curve depicts three groups drinking saccharin-flavored water after similar treatment. Note these animals had no previous conditional pairing of saccharin and injection. (From K. R. Green, B. K. McGowan, J. Garcia, & F. R. Ervin. Onset of baitshyness. *American Psychological Convention*, 1968, Fig. 1. Copyright 1968 by the American Psychological Association and reproduced by permission.)

The lower curve depicts drinking saccharin-water immediately after injection of nitrogen mustard. Note that there is a consistent dose-dependent decrement in drinking although these animals have never been subjected to a contingency between saccharin and the noxious injection. This nonassociative procedure in which the noxious agent is applied prior to drinking reveals the same adaptive behavior on the part of the organism as associative procedures where the noxious agent is delayed long after drinking.

When animals are subjected to a regular series of emetic injections, even an innocuous injection of saline produces adaptive behavior which resembles illness. Figure 6 illustrates this phenomena (Green, McGowan, & Garcia, unpublished data). The conditioned illness group (N = 4) had previously received four prior injections of apomorphine but on the test day were given a saline injection. Immediately afterwards they were placed in their drinking box and presented

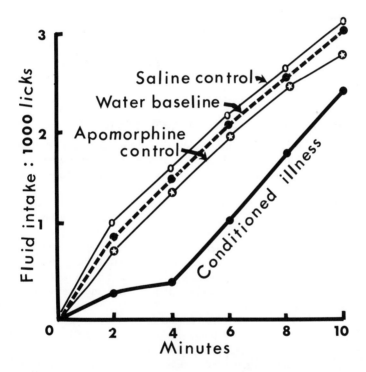

FIG. 6 Mean cumulative drinking of saccharin-flavored water for three groups of rats in a conditioned illness paradigm. The conditioned illness group had previously received a series of emetic (apomorphine) injections and on this occasion received a saline injection prior to drinking saccharin-flavored water for the first time. The saline controls received a similar saline injection, but no prior apomorphine injections. The apomorphine controls received prior apomorphine treatment but no saline injections prior to this test (Green, McGowan, & Garcia, unpublished data).

with saccharin for the first time. During the initial four minutes, the drinking curve resembles the saccharin-drinking rate of sick rats, i.e., rats injected with a noxious agent. Then the animals respond as if they made a sudden recovery. Control curves indicate that this effect cannot be attributed to the saline injection alone nor to the prior apomorphine injections alone. It seems that the animal associates the injection procedure with the gastrointestinal disturbance which follows immediately and continues for two hours. Later when it is injected with saline, the animal "anticipates" the malaise, rejecting the flavored solution for several minutes. When the disturbance does not occur in its usual temporal sequence, the rat begins to drink normally. Again the procedures are, strictly speaking, "nonassociative" as far as illness and taste are concerned but the propensity of the animal to adapt by rejecting a novel or distinctive fluid is revealed. We paraphrase Skinner:

> Classical, operant, pseudo, which is which? It doesn't matter. Of course these methods have training repertoires as different as their instrumentation. But once you make allowances for the differences in the ways in which they make contact with the animal, and in the ways they act upon criteria, what remains of behavior shows astonishingly organismic properties.

UNLOCKING THE ORGANISM FROM ITS NICHE

Robert B. Lockard (1971) in his pessimistically entitled paper "Reflections on the Fall of Comparative Psychology" has phrased the antithesis to Pavlov (see p. 21) and Skinner (see p. 22). Oddly enough his words have the same familiar ring:

> Pick any animal species at random, study its behavior in its normal habitat throughout its life cycle, and you will discover an intricate set of behaviors, many of them of almost incredible matching relationships to demands of the environment, like a lock and key. . . . You may also find that natural selection has produced special learning abilities such that some ecologically relevant task is learned at a much faster rate than an arbitrary task, or natural stimuli are much more effective than artificial stimuli.

The precise interlock that the organism achieves in handling environmental contingencies and illness is beautifully illustrated by the naturalistic studies of Lincoln Brower (1969) on the predation of the monarch butterfly by the bluejay. The butterfly in its larval state feeds on a milkweed plant containing a toxin which is apparently harmless to the insect but affects the vertebrate heart and causes emesis in the bird. Bluejays prey upon butterflys. The naive bird sees, pursues, and captures the toxic monarch butterfly. The bird tastes and consumes the insect; later it becomes ill and vomits. On the next encounter it pursues and captures the butterfly but it tends to reject the butterfly on the basis of taste. With further encounters the bluejay learns to recognize the now unpalatable butterfly on sight and no longer pursues the monarch or any other butterfly resembling the monarch.

However, the experimental laboratory studies of Wilcoxon, Dragoin, and Kral (1971), who employed artificial stimuli arbitrarily related to toxic injections, are equally revealing. Reasoning that the bobwhite quail is a diurnal feeder which uses its excellent visual system to direct its pecking responses, they demonstrated that the quail could learn to avoid drinking colored water on the basis of visual cues when illness was induced by a toxic injection one half hour after drinking. They verified that the rat, a nocturnal feeder with poor vision, dependent upon its excellent chemical analyzers, cannot accomplish this feat of directly associating visual cues with delayed illness.

In Brower's account the bluejay, like the rat, needs a two-step associative process, namely: taste (CS) is averted by illness (US) and then visual cues (CS) are then avoided by the aversive taste (US). The bluejay, like the rat, is an opportunistic predator, scavenger, and forager of animal and plant food sources. Adaptation to similar niches may lead to the similar associative mechanisms in both species. On the other hand, the bobwhite is able to associate visual cues (CS) directly (as well as flavors) to visceral illness (US) in a one-step process. This bird is much more dependent upon seeds and grains where the actual food and flavor is packaged in a tough and relatively tasteless seed coat. These speculations can only be tested by comparing these species in situations where the relevant ecological variables are experimentally manipulated.

It is inappropriate to critize the learning laboratory on the grounds that the stimulus sources and the apparatus are "artificial." Criticism should be directed at constricted experimental paradigms designed to control the animal. Such paradigms cannot lead to comprehensive behavioral laws, for so long as the plastic capacity of the organism far exceeds the demands of the test conditions, the data will reflect the limits of apparatus and experimental schedule rather than the nature of the beast. But this can be equally true of naturalistic paradigms, for so long as we observe the beast locked in his narrow ecological slot, we may never find out what he is able to learn, or, more importantly, what he is not able to learn. It is our task to derive hypotheses from field observations and to design experiments which truly test the limits of plasticity of the beast.

Konorski and his associates (Konorski, 1966; Konorski & Dobrzecka, 1967; Szwejkowska, 1967) have demonstrated what a dog can learn and what it cannot learn given apparently adequate signals and reinforcers. Dogs, given a bilateral motor task (left paw vs. right paw), easily learned when given acoustic signals differing in locus (front vs. rear). Remarkably, it was extremely difficult, if not impossible, for dogs to master this bilateral task when they were given two acoustic signals differing in quality (e.g., high pitch vs. low pitch) emanating from the same locus. However, dogs given a unilateral task (press vs. do not press with the same paw) easily learned on the basis of quality but they had difficulty with the directional cues.

Accurate auditory localization is a bilateral function and the authors conclude that orienting motor movements provide the potential pathways for utilization of the directional cues in the bilateral motor differentiation, but that no such potential pathways exist for the utilization of tonal quality. This latter cue, which can be handled unilaterally, is an effective cue for a unilateral (go-no go) differentiation indicating the existence of unilaterally organized pathways. No learning theory based on intensity, frequency, and recency could predict or explain these results. Only a neurological theory postulating potential pathways from centers integrating bilateral acoustic stimulation with bilateral motor movement can cope with these results.

TENTATIVE STEPS TOWARD A NEUROLOGY OF LEARNING

It has been suggested (Garcia & Ervin, 1968) that we examine anew the impliciations of the truism that all stimuli are not equivalent; that their specific nature depends upon the particular receptor which transduces the physical energy and the central mechanisms which handle the afferent volleys. Evolutionary explanations invoking natural selection are aversive to most psychologists because, as Skinner (1966) has recently pointed out, the evolutionary determinants appear to be lost in history and cannot be directly verified. But, the end-product of natural selection exists in the anatomical structure of the organism and there, theoretical learning propositions can be independently tested.

No comprehensive theory of learning is tenable without basic postulates on its neurology. Konorski (1966) sets forth an excellent example:

> The function of the afferent systems is to provide the brain with information concerning the external environment in which the organism is situated and the feedback generated by its own activity. The well-being of the organism requires that this information should be highly selective, picking up particular combinations of elements of the external world and neglecting the other ones ... this selectivity is provided by convergence of messages arising in particular elements of the receptive surface upon particular neurons (units) of higher levels of a given system, and by inhibition of those messages which are incongruent with the stimulus pattern represented by these units. ...
>
> Since the stimulus-patterns impinging upon each afferent system belong to various categories of various aspects of the events of the external world, each category having a different significance for the organism, these systems must be endowed with powerful sorting mechanisms distributing the messages delivered by the receptors to particular aggregates of units (centers or fields) for their proper utilization accomplished by associative systems. This is why each afferent system not only has a hierarchical structure but also is amply ramified, forming different hierarchies for different categories of stimuli.

Natural selection has designed the rat with distal and proximal defense perimeters to handle threats from the external environment. The animal localizes a distant event by sight and sound mediated by the head receptors and if that distant event is followed by an insult to the cutaneous surface it quickly learns defensive reaction. The distal and proximal afferent categories converge to a somatic center where potential pathways favor their integration. Other afferent categories are not so favored.

Natural selection has designed the rat with another distal-proximal system to cope with the internal environment. Foodstuffs are chemically analyzed by gustatory and olfactory receptors when sniffed and eaten. Later, as the food is absorbed, internal receptors report on the ultimate effects with the internal environment. These two afferent categories converge upon a visceral center which is relatively insulated from stimuli arising in the external environment. Since food absorption takes time, this system has become specialized to handle long interstimulus intervals.

Anatomical evidence for the existence of these two distinct systems has been described in the brain of the tiger salamander by C. Judson Herrick (1961) as two pools of interlaced fibers termed neuropil:

> One of these pools—the visceral sensory neuropil associated with the fasciculus solitarius—receives all fibers of gustatory and general visceral sensibility and discharges into the visceral motor mechanisms. The other pool—the somatic sensory neuropil—receives fibers of all types of cutaneous and deep sensibility that are concerned with adjustment to the external environment, i.e., the exteroceptive and proprioceptive systems of Sherrington's analysis (1948). This neuropil discharges into somatic motor apparatus that controls the movements of the skeletal muscles.

> This segregation of all sensory nerve fibers, except those of vision and olfaction, into only two receptive centers is the only well-defined localization of sensory functions present in the medulla oblongata. It corresponds with the fundamental difference in behavior between internal visceral activities and somatic sensorimotor activities that have an external reference. The visceral movements are for the most part of total pattern type. This is as true in men as in salamanders. Accordingly, there is little more specialization or separate localization of function in the fasciculus solitarius neuropil of men than of salamanders.

It may seem presumptuous to generalize from amphibia to man, but as the neural integration is similar, behavior should also be similar. Seligman (1970) has given a graphic account of how a man acquired an aversion for the distinctive taste of sauce *bearnaise* consumed prior to an attack of intestinal flu, yet did not acquire avoidance reactions to visual, auditory, and tactual cues more intimately associated in time and space with the illness. Nor did the fact that he knew the "true" viral cause of the illness alleviate the aversion for sauce *bearnaise*. The implications for behavior therapy in humans has been discussed by Wilson and Davison (1969). Gustatory conditioning in men, as in rats, is a matter of the visceral center, nucleus solitarius.

Herrick goes on, describing the much more complex evolutionary history of the somatic neuropil. In the salamander it is a mass-action system while in the high mammals it is a highly differentiated system of segregated nuclei which subserve complexly individuated behavioral patterns. Yet recent evidence indicates that some conditional pairings may be more appropriate than others. For example, it has been pointed out previously (Garcia & Ervin, 1968) that some units in the posterior nuclear group of the thalamus respond to both auditory and cutaneous stimulation (Poggio & Mountcastle, 1960; Rose & Woolsey, 1964). Behaviorally, Kamin and Schaub (1963) have demonstrated that rats can quickly associate an auditory CS with electrocutaneous shock even when CS-US intervals are one minute or more from onset to onset. When rat or man suffers electric shock he is most easily startled by a sharp sound. Such "pseudoconditioned" responses indicate the close relationship between these two afferent inputs.

Ramification is as common as convergence in the brain. Taste information apparently goes to both integrative centers in the brain but it is handled quite differently by these two centers. At one center taste information is integrated with visceral feedback over long CS-US intervals to adjust palatability; at the other center taste provides immediate reinforcement for motor approach-avoidance responses. In the rat, we found that taste could serve as an adequate signal, when associated with immediate peripheral pain presumably at the somatic center; but palatability was left unchanged because of the absence of requisite afferent (illness) volleys to the visceral center.

The nature of the conditioned response, as well as the CS-US duration, indicate which center is involved. With repeated trials and contiguity, visual cues can be associated with illness (Garcia, Kimeldorf, & Hunt, 1961; Rozin, 1969). In the shuttle box the animal moves away from the visual cues previously paired with illness indicating somatic integration. This response is relatively weak compared with shock-induced avoidance and extinguishes rapidly. If the rat is confined in the presence of these visual cues it will readily eat and drink (Garcia & Ervin, 1968); thus the shuttle box provides a test where the conditioned response (motor movement away from visual cues) is fundamentally different from the unconditioned response (inhibited ingestion to illness). Similarly conditioned illness (see Figure 6) which indicates some visceral integration of external cues with illness given contiguity, is also a transient phenomenon.

There is a mass of empirical evidence that, with CS-US contiguity and repeated presentations, the most improbable associations can be formed—see Bykov (1957) and more recently Miller (1969) for a wide variety of examples. Operant techniques employing immediate reinforcements have been used to manufacture wonderously complex habits indicating perhaps that, for a few seconds following the initial stimulation of a CS or the afferent feedback of the operant response, potential pathways are open to widely diverse integrative centers in the brain. But the associations which cannot be formed, given perceptible signals and effective reinforcers, may be more informative since they reveal the biased differentiated structure of the organism and call for neurological hypotheses which offer hope of independent anatomical verification.

Finally, we openly admit that we are experimental psychologists who spend a good deal of time studying the behavior of the rat, puzzling over the behavior of the human and writing about the behavior of the organism. We probe, insult, and deceive the robust, resourceful, and patient rat with all manner of artifice. We claim that much of what we learn from him is relevant for man. In defense we wish to cite in paraphrase yet another illustrious psychologist, Shakespeare:

> Hath not a rat eyes? hath not a rat hands, organs, dimensions, senses, affections, passions? fed with the same food, hurt with the same weapons, subject to the same diseases, healed by the same means, warmed and cooled by the same winter and summer, as a human is? If you prick them, do they not bleed? If you poison them, do they not die? and if they survive, will they not become averted to the flavor of the poison?

References

Barnett, S. A. *The Rat—A Study in Behavior.* Chicago, Aldine Press: 1963.

Beach, F. A. The snark was a boojum. *American Psychologist*, 1950, *5*, 115—124.

Bitterman, M. E. Techniques for the study of learning in animals—Analysis and classification. *Psychological Bulletin*, 1962, *59*, 81—93.

Borer, K. T. Disappearance of preferences and aversions for Sapid solutions in rats ingesting untasted fluids. *Journal of Comparative and Physiological Psychology*, 1968, *65*, 213.

Breland, K., and Breland, M. The misbehavior of organisms. *American Psychologist*, 1961, *16*, 681.

Brower, L. P. Ecological Chemistry. *Scientific American*, 1969, *220*, 22—29.

Bykov, K. M. *The Cerebral Cortex and The Internal Organs.* W. H. Gantt (trans. and ed.). New York: Chemical Publishing Co., 1957.

Dietz, M. N., and Capretta, P. J. Modification of sugar and sugar-saccharin preferences in rats as a function of electric shock to the mouth. New York: *Proceedings of the American Psychological Association*, September, 1966.

Estes, W. K. The statistical approach to learning theory. In S. Koch (ed.) *Psychology—A Study Of A Science.* New York: McGraw-Hill Book Co., 1959, 2.

Garcia, J., Buchwald, N. A., Bach-y-Rita, G., Feder, B. H., and Koelling, R. A. Electro-encephalographic responses to ionizing radiation. *Science*, 1963, *140*, 289—290.

Garcia, J., Buchwald, N. A., Feder, B. H., Koelling, R. A., and Tedrow L. Sensitivity of the head to x-ray. *Science*, 1964, *144*, 1470—1472.

Garcia, J., and Ervin, F. R. Appetites, aversions and addictions: A model for visceral memory. In J. Wortis (ed.) *Advances in Biological Psychiatry.* New York: Plenum, 1968.

Garcia, J., and Ervin, F. R. Gustatory-visceral and telereceptor-cutaneous conditioning—adaptation in internal and external milieus. *Communications in Behavioral Biology*, 1968, *1*, 389—415.

Garcia, J., Ervin, F. R., and Koelling, R. A. Learning with prolonged delay of reinforcement. *Psychonomic Science*, 1966, *5*, 121—122.

Garcia, J., Ervin, F. R., and Koelling, R. A. Toxicity of serum from irradiated donors. *Nature*, 1967, *213*, 682—683.

Garcia, J., Ervin, F. R., Yorke, C. H., and Koelling, R. A. Conditioning with delayed vitamin injections. *Science*, 1967, *155*, 716—718.

Garcia, J., Green, K. F., and McGowan, B. K. X-ray as an olfactory stimulus. In C. Pfaffmann (ed.) *Olfaction and Taste* III: *Proceedings of the Third International Symposium.* New York: Rockefeller University Press, 1969.

Garcia, J., and Kimeldorf, D. J. Temporal relationships within the conditioning of a saccharin aversion through radiation exposure. *Journal of Comparative and Physiological Psychology*, 1957, *50*, 180.

Garcia, J., Kimeldorf, J., and Hunt, E. L. The use of ionizing radiation as a motivating stimulus. *Psychological Review*, 1961, *68*, 383.

Garcia, J., Kimeldorf, D. J., Hunt, E. L., and Davies, B. P. Food and water consumption of rats during exposure to gamma radiation. *Radiation Research*, 1956, *4*, 33–41.

Garcia, J., Kimeldorf, D. J., and Koelling, R. A. A conditioned aversion towards saccharin resulting from exposure to gamma radiation. *Science*, 1955, *122*, 157–159.

Garcia, J., and Koelling, R. A. The relation of cue to consequence in avoidance learning. *Psychonomic Science*, 1966, *4*, 123–124.

Garcia, J., and Koelling, R. A. A comparison of aversions induced by x-rays, drugs and toxins. *Radiation Research*, 1967, Suppl. 7, 439–450.

Garcia, J., McGowan, B. K., Ervin, F. R., and Koelling, R. A. Cues—Their relative effectiveness as a function of the reinforcer. *Science*, 1968, *160*, 794–795.

Green, K. F., McGowan, B. K., Garcia, J., and Ervin, F. R. Onset of Bait-shyness. American Psychological Association Convention, 1968, 295–296.

Green, K. F., McGowan, B. K., and Garcia, J. Unpublished data.

Hebb, D. O. The American revolution. *American Psychologist*, 1960, *15*, 735–745.

Herrick, C. J. *The Evolution of Human Nature*. New York: Harper and Bros., 1961.

Hunt, E. L., Carroll, H. W., and Kimeldorf, D. J. Humoral mediation of radiation-induced motivation in parabiont rats. *Science*, 1965, *150*, 1747–1748.

Kamin, L. J., and Schaub, R. E. Effects of conditioned stimulus intensity on the conditioned emotional response. *Journal of Comparative and Physiological Psychology*, 1963, *56*, 502–507.

Kimble, G. A. *Foundations of Conditioning and Learning*. New York: Appleton-Century-Crofts, 1967.

Kimeldorf, D. J., and Hunt, E. L. Conditioned behavior and the radiation stimulus. In: *Response Of The Nervous System To Ionizing Radiation* (2nd International Symposium). Boston: Little, Brown and Co., 1964.

Konorski, J. Qualitative versus directional cues in two forms of differentiation. *Science*, 1966, *153*, 37–89.

Konorski, J. *Integrative Activity Of The Brain—An Interdisciplinary Approach*. Chicago: University of Chicago Press, 1967.

Konorski, J., and Dobrzecka, C. Qualitative versus directional cues in differential conditioning. *Acta Biologiae Experimentalis* (Warsaw), 1967, *22*, 163–168.

Lockard, Robert B. Reflections on the fall of comparative psychology: Is there a message for us all. *American Psychologist*, 1971, *25*, 168–179.

Lorenz, K. *Evolution And Modification Of Behavior*. Chicago: University of Chicago Press, 1965.

McLaurin, W. A. Postirradiation saccharin avoidance in rats as a function of the interval between ingestion and exposure. *Journal of Comparative and Physiological Psychology*, 1964, *57*, 316–317.

McLaurin, W. A., Farley, J. A., Scarborough, B. B., and Rawlings, T. D. Postirradiation saccharin avoidance with non-coincident stimuli. *Psychological Reports*, 1964, *14*, 507–512.

Miller, N. Learnable drives and rewards. In S. S. Stevens (ed.) *Handbook Of Experimental Psychology*. New York: Wiley and Sons, 1951.

Miller, N. Learning of Visceral and Glandular Responses. *Science*, 1969, *163*, 434–445.

Nachman, M. Learned aversion to the taste of lithium chloride and generalization to other salts. *Journal of Comparative and Physiological Psychology*, 1963, *56*, 343–349.

Pavlov, I. P. *Lectures On Conditioned Reflexes.* New York: International Publishers, 1928.

Perkins, C. C., Jr. An analysis of the concept of reinforcement. *Psychological Review*, 1968, *75*, 155—172.

Poggio, G. F., and Mountcastle, V. B. A study of the functional contributions of lemmiscal and spinothalamic systems to somatic sensibility. Central nervous mechanisms in pain. *Johns Hopkins Hospital Bulletin*, 1960, *106*, 266—316.

Rescorla, R. A. Pavlovian conditioning and its proper control procedures. *Psychological Review*, 1967, *74*, 71—80.

Revusky, S. H. Aversion to sucrose produced by contingent x-irradiation—Temporal and dosage parameters. *Journal of Comparative and Physiological Psychology*, 1968, *65*, 17—22.

Revusky, S. H., and Bedarf, E. W. Association of illness with prior ingestion of novel foods. *Science*, 1967, *155*, 219—220.

Rose, J. E., and Woolsey, C. N. Cortical connections and functional organization of the thalamic auditory system of the cat. In H. F. Harlow and C. N. Woolsey (eds.) *Biological and Biochemical Bases of Behavior.* Madison: University of Wisconsin Press, 1958.

Rozin, P. Central or peripheral mediation of learning with long CS-US intervals in the feeding system. *Journal of Comparative and Physiological Psychology*, 1969, *67*, 421—429.

Seligman, M. On the generality of the laws of learning. *Psychological Review*, 1970, *77*, 406—418.

Shakespeare, W. *The Merchant of Venice.* Act III, scene 1, lines 62—71.

Sherrington, C. S. *The Integrative Action Of The Nervous System.* 2nd edition (revision of 1906 edition). New Haven, Connecticut: Yale University Press, 1948.

Skinner, B. F. A case history in scientific method. In S. Koch (ed.) *Psychology—A study Of A Science.* New York: McGraw-Hill Book Co., 1959, *2*.

Skinner, B. F. The Phylogeny and Ontogeny of Behavior. *Science*, 1966, *153*, 1205—1213.

Smith, J. C., and Roll, D. L. Trace conditioning with x-rays as the aversive stimulus. *Psychonomic Science*, 1967, *9*, 11—12.

Spence, K. W. The role of secondary reinforcement in delayed reward learning. *Psychological Review*, 1947, *54*, 1—8

Szwejkowska, G. Qualitative versus directional cues in differential conditioning. *Acta Biologiae Experimentalis* (Warsaw), 1967, *27*, 169—175.

Tinbergen, N. *The Study of Instinct.* Oxford: Clarendon, 1951.

Wilcoxon, H. C., Dragoin, W. B., and Kral, P. A. Illness-induced aversions in rat and quail: Relative salience of visual and gustatory cues. *Science*, 1971, *171*, 826—828.

Wilson, G. T., and Davidson, G. C. Aversion Techniques in Behavior Therapy: Some theoretical and meta-theoretical considerations. *Journal of Consulting And Clinical Psychology*, 1969, *33*, 327—329.

A further mystery posed by the sauce Béarnaise phenomenon[1] is that only the taste of the sauce and not the filet mignon became vile. After all, both have distinctive flavors, and were eaten at the same time. Why are certain tastes selected above others? One possibility is that while I had eaten sauce Béarnaise a few times before, I had eaten beef very many times without getting sick. An Alan Funt Candid Camera Sequence seems parallel: A drinking fountain in a busy public place dispenses lemonade instead of water. Drinkers take a sip, startle, and then stare at the fluid. Drinkers who come up smoking cigarettes, however, take a sip, startle, and stare at their cigarettes. People seem to come prepared with hypotheses that some taste sources rather than others are responsible for alimentary consequences. In these two cases, the salient tastes are the more novel ones: Sauce Béarnaise is more novel than filet mignon, and cigarettes more novel than water.

Revusky and Bedarf demonstrate this principle experimentally by showing that novel tastes become aversive to rats more readily than familiar ones.

---

[1] We know of no experiments which deal with yet another mystery. The aversion waned over several years, rather than with trials—it was "forgotten" rather than "extinguished." This makes some evolutionary sense: Change of a food source from poisoned to nonpoisoned conditions in nature is a function of time, not of how often the animal eats from it.

4

ASSOCIATION OF ILLNESS
WITH PRIOR INGESTION
OF NOVEL FOODS

S. H. Revusky and E. W. Bedarf

Rats were permitted to ingest a novel food and a familiar food. One hour later they were x-irradiated. When they were subsequently allowed to choose between these foods, their preference for the novel food was less than that exhibited by appropriate controls.

If animals eat a particular food a few hours before they are x-irradiated, they will subsequently avoid that particular food because they associate the early symptoms of radiation sickness with it (1). Furthermore, injection of apomorphine, which like x-irradiation produces a gastrointestinal syndrome, also results in aversions to previously eaten foods (2). This ability to form associations between ingestion and and subsequent illness (3) is probably responsible, in part, for the avoidance by rats of slow acting poisons (2). However, another factor must also be involved. Since rats are likely to eat a number of foods over a long period of time, there must be a mechanism by which they can associate the poisoned food with the effects of the poison. A poisoned food is bound to be novel; otherwise the rat would probably already be dead. Our hypothesis is that rats associate radiation sickness with novel food rather than familiar food if they have eaten both types before they become sick. Conventional conditioning procedures suggest that association of a stimulus with a consequence is likely to be inhibited if there has been a number of earlier presentations of the stimulus in the absence of that consequence (4). Furthermore, neophobia, the hesitancy with which rats approach novel foods (5), seems to indicate the existence of an investigatory reflex (6) to novel foods which may predispose rats to associate novel illnesses with them.

Forty-eight male Sprague-Dawley rats were housed in individual cages (Hoeltge HB-11A) throughout the experiment and were given continual access to water and to ground rat chow for 1 hour each day. During days 1 through 8, half the rats were made familiar with milk (equal parts of condensed milk and water, by weight) by being allowed to drink it for 5 minutes per day, 17 hours after they had eaten their meal of chow; the remainder of the rats were allowed to

From *Science*, 155 (1967), 219–220.

45

drink sucrose solution (19.7 percent by weight) under the same conditions. The rats ate these foods in test cages similar to the home cages, except that the test cages had provisions for recording the number of times each rat licked the spout.

The conditioning trial was administered on day 9. Half the rats under each familiarization condition were allowed 100 licks of the familiar food in one test cage; they were then immediately transferred to a second test cage, where they were permitted 100 licks of the other (novel) food (termed the f→n procedure). The remaining rats received the novel food prior to the familiar food (n→f). After they had eaten both foods the rats were returned to their home cages, from which the water bottles had been removed. After 60 to 70 minutes, half the rats exposed to each of the four previous combinations of treatments were x-irradiated and half were not, so that there were eight groups with six rats in each group. Radiation consisted of 50 roentgens received in the course of 21.3 seconds from a GE Maxitron 250 KVP unit at 30 ma, 250 kv, filtered through 1 mm of aluminum and 0.5 mm of copper. The control rats were placed under the unenergized x-ray unit. The rats were given water at their regular feeding time, about 4½ hours after they were irradiated, and it was available for the remainder of the experiment.

Conditioning was tested on day 12. Each rat was deprived of food for 15 to 18 hours and then was placed in the test cage for 30 minutes with free access to both the novel and the familiar food. Preference for the novel food was defined as the number of licks to the novel food divided by the total number of licks.

TABLE 1   Mean   Preference   for   Novel
Food: Choice between Sucrose
and Milk

Conditioning procedure	Preferences	
	Irradiates	Controls
Novel food: sucrose		
f→n	0.534	0.948
n→f	.673	.904
Novel food: milk		
f→n	.004	.036
n→f	.005	.015

An F test (novel food by conditioning sequence by irradiation) shows the following factors had reliable effects: novel food ($p < .001$), irradiation ($p < .01$), and irradiation by novel food interaction ($p < .05$). All other effects had $p > .25$. Because of the significant interaction, separate F tests were used to analyze the irradiation effect for each novel food; the irradiation effect was reliable when sucrose was novel ($p < .01$), but not when milk was novel ($p = .18$). Preference expressed as ratio between number of licks to the novel food and total number of licks.

TABLE 2   Mean Preference for Novel Food: Choice between Grape Juice and Milk

Conditioning procedure	Preferences	
	Irradiates	Controls
Novel food: grape juice		
f→n	0.056	0.119
n→f	.010	.109
Novel food: milk		
f→n	.052	.350
n→f	.026	.267

The following effects were significant (F test): novel food ($p < .01$), irradiation ($p < .001$), and novel food by irradiation interaction ($p < .02$). All other effects had $p > .25$. The irradiation effect was significant when milk was novel ($p < .001$) but was marginal when grape juice was novel ($p < .08$). (In the context of the other results, this last probability, being two-tailed, may be considered evidence of reliability.) Preference expressed as in Table 1.

The irradiated rats showed a lower preference for the novel food than did the controls regardless of which earlier experimental procedures were used (Table 1). However this effect was not statistically reliable if only the rats for which milk was novel were considered. A probable reason is that there was a strong overall preference for sucrose, so that when milk was novel, the preference for it among the control rats was too small to permit a reliably smaller preference among the irradiated rats. Since rats prefer milk to grape juice (7), the procedure was repeated in a second experiment in which undiluted grape juice (Welch brand) was substituted for the sucrose solution used in the first experiment. In this

TABLE 3   Proportion of Rats Requiring More Time to Drink the Novel Fluid Than the Familiar Fluid on the Day of Conditioning (Both Experiments)

Novel food	Familar food	Proportion
Sucrose	Milk	0.417
Milk	Sucrose	.958
Grape juice	Milk	.958
Milk	Grape juice	.917

Except when sucrose was novel, each proportion shown was reliably greater than the chance level of .500 ($p < .001$, sign test).

second experiment, preference for thy novel food was reliably lower among the irradiated rats regardless of which food was novel (Table 2). When saccharin and water are presented to the rats before they are irradiated, their aversion to these fluids is attenuated if these fluids are already familiar to them (8). Thus the greater associative strength of novel foods in our experiment appears to be a general principle of conditioning.

The rats exhibited neophobia in both experiments. During the conditioning trial, the rats tended to drink the novel fluid more slowly than the familiar fluid (Table 3) except when sucrose was novel; this exception may be attributed to the greater palatability of sucrose solution (Table 1). Furthermore, during the test day of each experiment, the preference for milk among the controls was reliably greater if it was familiar than if it was novel. In view of this prominent role of neophobia, the radiation effect reported here may have been obtained not because of any selective association of the novel food with radiation effects but because a history of illness increases neophobia. This possibility may be discounted because a novel food presented more than a day after x-irradiation will not be avoided (9). Thus the apparent role of neophobia is to enhance the association of unusual gastrointestinal events with previously ingested novel foods. How it does so is unknown, but one possibility may be discounted. The increased time with which the animal is usually in contact with the animal food probably is not responsible for the selective association of illness with it; when sucrose was novel, the rats showed the radiation effect even though most of them drank the sucrose as quickly as the milk. Furthermore, among the individual irradiated rats in this category, there was no correlation between the time they took to drink sucrose divided by the time they took to drink milk and the later preference which they showed for sucrose ($p > .25$, Spearman r).

The rats were not fed or given water from the time they ate the test foods until 6 hours later. Therefore, if any aftertastes were present while the illness began, the aftertaste of the food last ingested should have been stronger. If such aftertastes help rats associate what they have eaten with later illness, the aversion for the novel food should be greater under f→n procedure than under n→f procedure. The fact that our experiments did not show this result (Tables 1 and 2), together with other findings (2) seems to indicate that aftertastes are not primarily responsible for the ability of rats to associate ingestion with later illness.

References and Notes

1. J. Garcia, D. J. Kimeldorf, E. L. Hunt, Psychol. Rev. 68, 383 (1961); D. J. Kimeldorf and E. L. Hunt, Ionizing Radiation: Neural Function and Behavior (Academic Press, New York, 1965).
2. J. Garcia, F. R. Ervin, R. A. Koelling, Psychonomic Sci., 5, 121 (1966).
3. Association of a cue with a consequence is usually considered impossible if their temporal separation is over a minute or so. For theoretical implications of association between ingestion and illness occurring hours later, see J. Garcia and R. A. Koelling, Psychonomic Sci. 4, 123 (1966); S. H. Revusky, "Hunger level during food consumption; effects on subsequent preference," ibid., 1967, 7, 109–110.
4. R. E. Lubow, J. Comp. Physiol. Psychol. 60, 454 (1965).
5. S. A. Barnett, The Rat: A Study in Behavior (Aldine, Chicago, 1963).

6. I. P. Pavlov, *Conditioned Reflexes* (Oxford Univ. Press, London, 1927).
7. S. H. Revusky, "Hunger level during food consumption; effects on subsequent preference," *Psychonomic Sci.*, in press.
8. W. A. McLaurin, J. A. Farley, B. B. Scarborough, *Radiation Res.* 18, 473 (1963); J. A. Farley, W. A. McLaurin, B. B. Scarborough, T. D. Rawlings, *Psychol. Rep.* 14, 491 (1964); J. Garcia and R. A. Koelling, *Radiation Res.*, in press.
9. B. B. Scarborough, D. L. Whaley, J. G. Rogers, *Psychol. Rep.* 14, 475 (1964); J. C. Smith, H. L. Taylor, D. D. Morris, J. Hendricks, *Radiation Res.* 24, 423 (1965).

Garcia's findings on preparedness in classical conditioning have helped solve a perennial problem in physiological psychology, that of specific hungers. Animals deficient in a given nutrient, such as thiamine or riboflavin, reliably seek out and eat substances containing that nutrient. Just how this is managed is a puzzle. The most obvious hypothesis, the "wisdom of the body," is that substances containing the needed nutrient somehow taste better, or that the threshold for detecting them is lowered. Such a hypothesis is unparsimonious and inelegant, for it requires that there be one mechanism to deal with each of the dozen or more nutrients for which specific hungers have been established. Thus, when calcium is lacking, calcium and not riboflavin-containing substances must come to taste better.

At about the time Garcia was working on poisoning, Paul Rozin and his colleagues independently made a breakthrough in specific hungers. In the next article, Rozin shows the symmetery between specific hungers and specific aversions. If being thiamine-deficient on one diet makes an animal sick, then this old diet should become aversive. If the old diet becomes aversive and the animal has a choice between it and a new diet, he will eat the new diet. In this way deficient animals seek out new foods. So thiamine-deficiency acts as a poison and animals are prepared to associate it with the taste of the diet they are becoming sick on. As with Garcia's phenomenon, this can be learned over long CS-US intervals and at the expense of such external CS's as the place in which the old diet sat. Rozin puts forward one elegant mechanism—paleophobia—to explain the seeking out of new foods in specific hungers.

5

SPECIFIC AVERSIONS AS A
COMPONENT OF SPECIFIC HUNGERS

Paul Rozin

Rats deficient in thiamine develop an aversion for the deficient diet, which may account for their potentiated feeding response to new foods. The specific aversion to their familiar deficient diet is demonstrated by (a) spillage of this diet (normal rats may spill highly unpalatable foods), (b) redirected feeding responses (chewing inedible objects) in the presence of deficient diets, and (c) after recovery on a new diet, an avoidance of the familiar deficient diet even when they are food deprived with no other food available. It is suggested that specific aversions play an important role in most specific hungers, and that specific hungers and adaptive responses to poisoning are two aspects of the same basic phenomenon.

Rodgers and Rozin (1966) have made some observations on thiamine-deficient rats that help to remove some of the traditional objections to a learning interpretation of thiamine-specific hunger. They reported that thiamine-deficient rats showed strong, often 100% preferences for any new diet offered to them, in opposition to the standard deficient diet. Furthermore, such typically anorexic rats avidly consumed the new diets. The exclusive, continued ingestion of a new diet over a period of many hours would facilitate the rat's identification of the recovery-producing diet. Ingestion of the new diet during the onset of recovery might bridge the delay of reinforcement "gap," because the rat would be continuing to eat the new diet for hours, and, in the meantime, recovering as a result of thiamine ingested in the initial meals. Rozin and Rodgers (1967)

From *Journal of Comparative and Physiological Psychology*, 64 (1967), 237–242.

This research was supported by National Science Foundation Grants GB 1489 and 4372. The author wishes to thank Willard Rodgers, Robert Rescorla, Martin Seligman, and Richard L. Solomon for their valuable comments and advice, and Barbara Marks and Deborah Donnelly for their technical assistance.

demonstrated novel-diet preferences in pyridoxine- or riboflavin-deficient rats, and Rodgers (1967) demonstrated the same phenomenon in rats deficient in a number of minerals, including calcium. In addition, Rozin and Rodgers (1967) showed that the preference for thiamine-rich foods by rats recovered from deficiency (Rozin, 1965) was nonspecific; recovered rats preferred any new food to the food on which they became deficient. In order to account for the appearance of a novelty response in the deficient or recovered rat, Rozin and Rodgers (1967) suggest that either the state of deficiency triggers an innate neophilia, or that the deficient rat develops an aversion to the deficient diet and thus shows a strong preference for any new food. It seems entirely reasonable to believe that the deficient diet could develop aversive properties, as its ingestion is most certainly associated with feelings of illness; in fact, the anorexia of thiamine deficiency could be considered a consequence of the aversion.

There appears to be a certain arbitrariness in debating whether the deficient diet is aversive or the new diet is highly desired. It is certainly unreasonable to assume that , in any choice of two diets, the less preferred is aversive, since obviously the choice may be between two highly desired substances. However, animals often show distinctive behaviors associated with conflict, withdrawal, and disgust when placed in aversive or noxious situations. Furthermore, if a food were aversive, one would expect that under most circumstances an animal would prefer nothing (no food) to eating it (see Irwin, 1961). If a hungry rat refuses to eat a nutritious, normally palatable food under normal caging conditions, it is reasonable to suggest that the food is aversive.

Because evidence for an aversion is dependent on the appearance of certain behaviors (e.g., spillage, redirected feeding, etc.), the behavior of rats in the presence of various foods prior to, during, and after recovery from thiamine deficiency was studied. Specifically, the responses of hungry recovered rats to the familiar deficient diet, a new diet, and a highly unpalatable (quinine adulterated) diet are compared.

METHOD

In the basic experiment, six Sprague-Dawley (COBS) weanling female rats were housed in large (18 x 15 x 9 in. Wahmann LC 27/A) cages, four singly and two together. A wooden barrier was placed in one corner of the cage, providing a partially visually isolated nest area. Water was continuously available, and food was offered from approximately 4:30 P.M. to 9:00 A.M. each day. For the singly housed Ss (318, 319, 357, 358), food was ordinarily offered in an uncovered 2-oz. glass cup which was securely mounted on one side of the cage. The two Ss housed together (320, 321) had food presented in a 3-in.-diameter metal cup. The two synthetic diets employed were nutritionally adequate and complete, except for the omission of thiamine during the deficiency period and in some tests. Diet 0^1 is a sweet (high-sucrose) granular diet, and Diet 4 (see Footnote 1) is a fine powdered high-starch diet.

All six Ss were raised and maintained on thiamine-deficient Diet 0 for 22-25 days. Two Ss, housed singly, were injected daily with thiamine and did not become deficient; the remaining four Ss became deficient. After clear signs of thiamine deficiency (anorexia and weight loss) had appeared in the deficient Ss, recovery was produced by offering all Ss a thiamine-enriched (10 μg/gm of thiamine) Diet 4. The experiment consisted of observing the feeding behavior of Ss during deficiency and recovery periods for the first 15 min. following presentation of food at approximately 4:30 P.M. each day. Since Ss were 7-8 hr. food deprived at this time, they typically showed great interest in and consumption of the food when it was presented. The E observed one or two Ss at a time, and recorded the behavior engaged in by each S every 5 sec. for a 15-min. period. Responses were classified, in a method similar to that used by Barnett (1963) and De Lorge and Bolles (1961), into the following categories: (a) eating, (b) grooming, (c) sniffing at food or food cup, (d) resting—lying, sleeping, or sitting, (e) exploring—sniffing, standing and sniffing, running, rearing, (f) drinking, and (g) chewing or mouthing objects other than food. A day's data consisted of 180 successive written entries describing the behavior.

The basic experiment consisted of a number of variations of the standard feeding procedure during the first 15 min. of feeding on some test days. On one or two occasions, during the final week of thiamine deficiency, the standard deficient Diet 0 was offered in a shallow furniture caster at the opposite end of the cage from the normal feeding site. This involved a major change in relation between the position of the cup and both the nest entrance and the water bottle. This cup and position change was instituted for the first 5 min. of a 15-min. period, and was followed by presentation of the familiar cup in the familiar position for the remaining 10-min. period and overnight. The procedure was designed to measure the effects of novel food-associated stimuli on the feeding behavior of the anorexic thiamine-deficient Ss and the controls. In the few days just prior to recovery (Days 22-24 of deficiency), Ss were exposed to deficient or enriched novel diets, in the familiar cups and familiar positions, for the middle 5 min. of a 15-min. test period. Throughout the deficiency period (first 22-24 days) Ss were always offered the standard familiar deficient diet in standard cup and position overnight, regardless of what they ate during the 15-min. test period. Then, during a 1-wk. recovery period, only the novel, thiamine-rich Diet 4 was offered, on the usual feeding schedule. At the end of this recovery period, when Ss were gaining weight rapidly, they were offered the original familiar deficient diet that they experienced during the deficiency period for the first 5 or 10 min. of the 15-min. test period. This was followed by the novel enriched diet that they had experienced for the last week. This procedure was designed to detect any retained aversion to the familiar deficient diet after recovery. The striking behavior shown by some Ss to the familiar deficient diet suggested that it would be useful to see the reactions of these same

---

[1] Diet 0 contained, in grams per kilogram: sucrose, 659; Mazola, 50; casein, 250; Hegsted salt mix, 40; choline, 1. Diet 3 contained, in grams per kilogram: sucrose, 20; starch, 434; Mazola, 5; Crisco, 250; casein, 250; Hegsted salt mix, 40; choline, 1. Diet 4 contained, in grams per kilogram: sucrose, 20; starch, 600; Mazola, 50; casein, 100; egg white solids, 189; Hegsted salt mix, 40; choline, 1. Each diet was supplemented with vitamins in the following amounts per kilogram: biotin, .5 mg.; folic acid, .5 mg.; nicotinic acid, 50 mg.; calcium pantothenate, 65 mg.; Vitamin A, 20,000 units; Vitamin D_2, 2,000 units; Vitamin E, 100 mg.; Vitamin K, 5 mg. Thiamine was added when necessary in the amount of 10 μg/gm.

Ss to a highly unpalatable diet. A few days following the tests with the familiar diet, Ss were offered the novel diet that they ordinarily avidly consumed, but adulterated with 1% quinine hydrochloride.

In order to confirm and extend the generality of the results of the initial experiment, a replication on four rats (three deficient, one control) was undertaken. Rats 446 (deficient) and 447 (control) were housed singly, with food in a standard 2-oz. glass cup, and Ss 448 and 449 (deficient) were housed together, and offered food in the metal cup. Conditions and procedure were essentially identical to those described above, except that a different combination of diets was used to ensure that the results from the initial experiment were not due to any special properties of Diet 0 as a deficient diet and Diet 4 as a recovery diet. In the replication, rats were raised on the highly palatable greasy Diet 3 (see Footnote 2). Novelty tests were performed with the normally less palatable Diet 0. Thus, in both experiments, the novel diet was less palatable to normal Ss than the deficient diet, and Diet 0 served as the deficient diet for the first experiment, but as the novel recovery diet in the second.

RESULTS

At the beginning of the experiment, all Ss approached the food cup as soon as it was placed in their cages and began to eat immediately and throughout most of the 15-min. observation period. Control Ss continued to behave in this manner throughout the experiment. As experimental Ss became deficient and their weight started to level off, they continued to approach the food on presentation, but after a cursory sniff and examination, left the vicinity of the food cup. They ate less and less as deficiency progressed.

Deficient Ss showed two responses during the observation period that are rarely seen in normal food-deprived rats in the presence of food. Some vigorously spilled the food by scooping it out of the cup with their paws, and occasionally emptied the entire 50 gm. of food in the cup during the 15-min. observation period. A few deficient rats also showed "redirected feeding"—vigorous chewing on the cage wire or wooden nest barrier when food was offered.

TABLE 1   Response of Thiamine-Deficient (D) and Control (C) Rats to Change in Food Cup and Location of Food

S	Responses to standard cup and position[a]							Responses to changed cup and position[a]						
	E	D	G	EX	SF	SP	RF	E	D	G	EX	SF	SP	RF
D-318	0	0	0	91	8	0	0	0	0	2	91	6	0	0
D-320	0	0	5	57	6	0	31	2	2	20	62	15	0	0
D-321	3	0	7	80↩	3	0	7	8	3	5	61	13	0	8
D-357	2	0	10	77	8	0	3	3	0	3	77	15	0	2
C-319	66	28	3	2	0	0	0	64	3	5	21	7	0	0
C-358	70	13	10	3	3	0	0	60	29	7	2	2	0	0

[a]Percentage of time spent in each of seven mutually exclusive and exhaustive activities during 5-min. test: E = eating, D = drinking, G = grooming, EX = exploring, SF = sniffing food, SP = spilling food, RF = redirected feeding.

TABLE 2   Responses of Thiamine-Deficient (D) and Control (C) Rats to Familiar and Novel Diets

S	Responses to familiar diet 0[a]							Responses to novel diet 4[a]						
	E	D	G	EX	SF	SP	RF	E	D	G	EX	SF	SP	RF
D-318	0	0	0	80	8	12	0	88	0	2	10	0	0	0
D-320	13	0	0	37	8	15	27	87	0	2	10	0	2	0
D-321	38	0	7	27	17	12	0	98	0	2	0	0	0	0
D-357	0	0	0	94	6	0	0	94	0	0	3	3	0	0
C-319	51	38	5	3	2	0	0	56	11	18	10	3	0	0
C-358	57	22	15	3	3	0	0	63	0	13	12	12	0	0

[a]Percentage of time spent in each of seven mutually exclusive and exhaustive activities during 5-min. test: E = eating, D = drinking, G = grooming, EX = exploring, SF = sniffing food, SP = spilling food, RF = redirected feeding.

The incidence of spillage and redirected feeding in the presence of familiar deficient diet during three 5-min. test periods is shown in Tables 1 and 2. Of course, these are three 5-min. sessions out of well over 200 that have been recorded on the 10 Ss of this study. In general only one S, 318, consistently spilled its food during the first 15 min., although the three other deficient Ss in the initial study showed spillage in the first 15 min. at least a few times during late deficiency. The three deficient Ss in the replication study did not spill their food, even overnight, but Diet 3 is rarely spilled because of its greasy, cohesive texture. Redirected chewing was common in deficient Ss; it appeared in four of the seven deficients and none of the controls. It is interesting that the one consistent spiller (318) virtually never showed redirected feeding.

On Day 20 or 21 of deficiency the standard diet was presented in the normal cup and position, and on the following day the standard diet was presented in a novel cup and markedly changed position. The responses of the six Ss raised on Diet 0 are shown in Table 1. It is clear that neither the two control Ss nor the four deficient Ss showed marked differences in their behavior patterns under the two sets of conditions. In the replication study, with Ss raised on Diet 3, one control and one deficient S showed no effects of the cup and position change, while two deficient Ss did show a clear potentiation of food intake. However, this potentiation of food intake was much smaller than that induced by a novel diet.

All deficient Ss in the initial study showed a marked, avid feeding response to novel diets, in contrast to their lack of interest in the familiar diet. The data presented in Table 2 represent the responses to a 5-min. presentation of the familiar deficient diet, followed immediately by a 5-min. presentation of a thiamine-supplemented novel diet. Responses to the novel-supplemented diet was essentially identical to responses made to the same novel diet without thiamine, when it was offered for 5 min. a day or two previously. The second test on a novel diet is presented here, because in this situation a 5-min. test with the familiar diet preceded presentation of the novel diet, and provides an effective comparison. The clear response to the novel diet was also seen in two of the three deficient Ss raised on Diet 3, in the replication (the deficient Ss that

TABLE 3   Responses of Rats Recovered from Thiamine-Deficient (D) and Control (C) Rats to Familiar and Novel Diets

S	Responses to familiar diet 0[a]							Responses to novel diet 4[a]						
	E	D	G	EX	SF	SP	RF	E	D	G	EX	SF	SP	RF
D-318	0	2	0	77	8	13	0	88	0	3	8	0	0	0
D-320	0	2	2	55	27	13	2	98	0	2	0	0	0	0
D-321	2	0	2	45	51	0	0	91	0	7	2	0	0	0
D-357	10	0	7	37	30	17	0	84	0	10	3	3	0	0
C-319	73	20	2	3	2	0	0	12	13	16	56	2	0	0
C-358	81	7	5	5	2	0	0	65	5	13	15	2	0	0

[a]Percentage of time spent in each of seven mutually exclusive and exhaustive activities during 5-min. test: E = eating, D = drinking, G = grooming, EX = exploring, SF = sniffing food, SP = spilling food, RF = redirected feeding.

did not show a clear novelty response also did not show marked anorexia), even though, in this case, Diet 0 was the novel rather than the familiar diet. Thus, this response has nothing to do with the specific properties of Diet 0. Control Ss showed no special response to the novel diet.

The avoidance of the familiar diet by Ss recovered from their deficiency is the most clear-cut and striking finding of this study. Data for the six Ss raised on Diet 0 are shown in Table 3. All seven deficient rats from both studies ate little if any of the familiar deficient diet when it was presented to them for the first 5 min. of a feeding session, following a 7-8-hr. food deprivation. Formerly deficient S 357 spent 10% of its time feeding, more than any deficient S, while the poorest feeding response seen among the controls was 52% (S 447 in the replication study). Three formerly deficient Ss (318, 320, and 448) did not eat the familiar deficient diet at all; three formerly deficient Ss spilled the familiar Diet 0 and one showed redirected feeding responses. It should be emphasized that these seven recovered Ss had no acute need for thiamine at the time of testing, so that the deficient familiar diet was an entirely adequate food source.

Eight rats (six recovered, two control) were offered a quinine (1%) adulterated diet[2] during the 15-min. test period a few days following the recovery tests. All showed some reluctance to eat this food, and four Ss clearly spilled it. No S showed redirected feeding. With the exception of the absence of redirected feeding, their behavior looked quite similar to the behavior of formerly deficient Ss offered the familiar deficient diet a few days before.

DISCUSSION

Observation of deficient rats strongly suggests that a specific aversion to a familiar deficient diet occurs and persists even after the rats have recovered. Such deprived rats spilled their familiar deficient diet just as they also spilled highly unpalatable quinine adulterated diets, and they showed redirected feeding (chewing wood or metal) in the presence of this food. Most important, the fact

[2] The qunine-adulterated diet consisted of 1% quinine hydrochloride, 99% Diet 4 (with 10 μg/gm of thiamine).

that hungry recovered rats avoided the familiar deficient diet, when no other foods were available (thus preferring no food to familiar deficient diet), strongly suggests that the familiar deficient diet is aversive. The marked similarity in behavior of some of the recovered rats, when presented with familiar deficient diet, to their behavior toward this same diet when they were actually deficient suggests that the aversion persists beyond the deficiency itself.

How does this specific aversion become established? Most likely it is a special and unusual case of classical conditioning, with the internal aversive events which result from vitamin deficiency as the US, and the deficient diet and its ingestion as the CS. The net effect of such conditioning would be cessation of ingestion of familiar deficient diet through a punishment or a conditioned aversion mechanism. There are three possible arrangements of the conditioning contingencies. (a) If one assumes that the deficient rat feels continuously ill, with a gradual intensification of discomfort as deficiency progresses, one is faced with the odd paradigm of a continuous US and occasional CSs (exposure to, eating, or sniffing food) superimposed on it. Under these circumstances, it is hard to imagine how conditioning could take place. (b) It is possible that all the conditioning takes place at the onset of deficiency symptoms: the rat experiences noticeable aversive consequences following ingestion of a few critical meals. Consistent with this position is the fact that rats show no novelty response after 8 days on a deficient diet, and show a full-blown novelty response after 12 days (Rozin, in press). There is no doubt that rats can learn about the aversive consequences of ingestion of poisons very rapidly (for a review, see Barnett, 1963) so that this mechanism is plausible. (c) It is possible that, following each meal consumed by a deficient rat, some of the aversive symptoms of deficiency (possibly nausea) temporarily increase, resulting in a pairing of CS and US, with a reasonably long time interval between them. This mechanism seems the most plausible of the three at this point. Both the second and third possibilities require learning with a very long CS-US interval (or a long delay of punishment). Garcia, Ervin, and Koelling (1966) have recently shown that rats can learn to associate distinctive tastes (CS) with specific aversive events occurring more than 1 hr. later.

The failure of novel, food-associated stimuli (cup and position) to potentiate feeding suggests that the rat develops an aversion specifically to the food, and not to other stimuli that are usually associated with it. This seems highly adaptive, since it is, after all, the food and not its container or location (or associated stimuli such as light and noise) that determines the nutritional value to the organism. The instrumental feeding behavior and proprioceptive feedback associated with it do not become aversive, as the animal readily feeds on new foods. This specificity of the acquired aversion to stimuli emanating directly from the food seems parallel to the remarkable specificity reported by Garcia and Koelling (1966) in X-radiated or poisoned rats. Chemical stimuli associated with the aversive consequences produced by these two manipulations developed much stronger secondary aversive properties than auditory-visual stimuli equally associated with the same events.

The neophilia of thiamine-deficient rats could be a direct consequence of a specific aversion for familiar deficient diet (paleophobia). On the other hand, it is also possible that a true neophilia exists along with the paleophobia. If this were the case, one might expect that the deficient or recovered rats might eat more novel diet than control rats of comparable hunger and size. The present data do not provide such a test, as the great differences in weight between control and deficient rats makes any direct comparison impossible.

If the novelty response is a manifestation of a specific aversion to a familiar deficient diet, then the thiamine-deficient rat is not really anorexic; rather, it has a strong aversion to the only food available, deficient food. It eats new foods readily. The specific aversion notion also suggests that the preferences for novel foods by rats recovered from deficiency simply represent a residue (failure to extinguish) of the specific aversion acquired during deficiency, thus dispelling much of the mystery about this recovery response.

It seems highly likely that specific aversions play a role in most, if not all, specific hungers, because novelty responses have been demonstrated for rats deficient in pyridoxine, riboflavin (Rozin & Rodgers, 1967), calcium, magnesium, and sodium (Rodgers, 1967). It is possible that neophilia, learned aversions, learned preferences based on beneficial effects of a particular diet, strong tendencies to connect chemical stimuli with internal events, and innate preferences for particular substances are all involved in any particular specific hunger. Such a strong "overdetermination" might be highly adaptive when one considers the importance of adequate nutrition to the organism.

The specific aversion component of specific hungers puts nutrient deficiencies in the same category as poisoning or punishment; thiamine-deficient diet can be considered to be a slow poison. The relationship and, in particular, the common properties shared by typical poisoning-aversion situations and nutrient-deficiency experiments should be explored. It may be that the highly developed poison-avoiding responses of the wild rat (for a review, see Barnett, 1963) and the well-investigated specific hunger behavior of the domestic rat are but two examples of the same general phenomenon.

References

Barnett, S. A. *The rat. A study in behaviour.* London: Metheun, 1963.

De Lorge, J., & Bolles, R. C. Effects of food deprivation on exploratory behavior in a novel situation. *Psychol. Rep.*, 1961, 9, 599—606.

Garcia, J., Ervin, F. R., & Koelling, R. A. Learning with prolonged delay of reinforcement. *Psychon. Sci.*, 1966, 5, 121—122.

Garcia, J., & Koelling, R. A. Relation of cue to consequence in avoidance learning. *Psychon. Sci.*, 1966, 4, 123—124.

Irwin, F. W. On desire, aversion and the affective zero. *Psychol. Rev.*, 1961, 68, 293—300.

Rodgers, W., & Rozin, P. Novel food preferences in thiamine-deficient rats. *J. comp. physiol. Psychol.*, 1966, 61, 1—4.

Rodgers, W. L. Specificity of specific hungers. *J. comp. physiol. Psychol.*, 1967, 64, 49—58.

Rozin, P. Specific hunger for thiamine: Recovery from deficiency and thiamine preference. *J. comp. physiol. Psychol.*, 1965, 59, 98—101.

Rozin, P. Thiamine specific hunger. In W. Heidel (Ed.), *Handbook of physiology.* Section, 6. *Physiology of the alimentary canal*, Vol. 1, Chap. 27. Washington, D. C.: American Physiological Society, 1967.

Rozin, P., & Rodgers, W. Novel-diet preferences in vitamin-deficient rats and rats recovered from vitamin deficiencies. *J. comp. physiol. Psychol.*, 1967, 63, 429—433.

An acquired aversion to the old diet accounts for the salient fact that in specific hungers, deficient animals seek out and eat new foods. But how is it that rats, having found new foods, will stick with the one that makes them better, even though there are other equally new foods around (Harris, Clay, Hargreaves, and Ward, 1933)? Zahorik and Maier provide evidence that the same mechanism which Rozin invokes to explain seeking out of the new food can be turned upside-down to explain the preference for one new food. Rats are prepared to associate taste with recovery from illness, and these tastes become preferred, just as tastes paired with the onset of illness become aversive. So, rather than the dozen odd mechanisms needed to explain the dozen odd specific hungers, we can now understand them with one mechanism—prepared association of tastes with gastrointestinal consequences.

6

APPETITIVE CONDITIONING WITH RECOVERY FROM THIAMINE DEFICIENCY AS THE UNCONDITIONAL STIMULUS

Donna M. Zahorik and Steven F. Maier

Pairing a taste with recovery from thiamine deficiency produced a preference for that flavor over tastes associated with deficiency and novel tastes in thiamine-deficient rats. The preference persisted after recovery from deficiency.

When a rat is presented a distinctively flavored diet paired with X-irradiation, apomorphine injection, or the production of thiamine deficiency, aversion to that diet flavor quickly develops (Garcia, Kimeldorf, & Hunt, 1961; Garcia, Ervin, & Koelling, 1966; Rozin, 1967). Procedurally, these experiments follow a Pavlovian conditioning paradigm: A taste CS is followed by an aversive UCS that produces an unpleasant internal state (nausea). However, the conditions under which learning occurs with a taste CS and an internal aversive UCS seem different from those under which Pavlovian conditioning ordinarily occurs. Aversions have been produced with only a few pairings and with delays between CS and UCS of as long as 6 h or 12 h (Revusky, 1968; Smith & Roll, 1967).

The above findings have led Garcia & Ervin (1968) to conclude that learning which involves gustatory CSs and gastrointestinal UCSs proceeds through a different mechanism than does learning that involves exteroceptive CSs (e.g., a tone) and external UCSs (e.g., an electric body shock). Both Garcia & Ervin (1968) and Rozin (1967) have argued that high sensitivity to the association

From *Psychonomic Science*, 17 (1969), 309–310.

between gustatory CSs and gastrointestinal UCSs is of great survival value to the rat in its natural habitat. Thus, a specialized mechanism may have evolved through natural selection. If this argument is correct, it seems likely that the use of a gustatory CS and a positive gastrointestinal UCS should also lead to rapid appetitive conditioning. However, all of the above studies have employed an aversive UCS. Only one study has been interpreted as evidence for appetitive conditioning with a gustatory CS and a gastrointestinal UCS (Garcia, Ervin, Yorke, & Koelling, 1967). Garcia et al., using a one-bottle test, found that rats which had become thiamine deficient while drinking water and had then recovered from deficiency while drinking a saccharin solution, drank more of the saccaharin solution than did rats that had become deficient while drinking saccharin and had recovered while drinking water. However, it is not entirely clear whether the rats developed a preference for the "recovery flavor," an aversion to the "deficiency flavor," or both, because only the recovery and deficiency flavors were tested. This distinction is important because it has been suggested (Rozin, 1967) that an aversion to the flavor associated with deficiency can account for all of the data on diet preference in thiamine-deficient animals. In order to determine whether or not a preference for the recovery flavor has developed, a preference test involving a "neutral" flavor is needed.

In addition, Garcia .et al. found that the above difference occurred only when the rats were deficient in thiamine. When the rats were in the nondeficient state, the rats that had experienced saccharin in combination with thiamine injection drank no more saccharin than did the rats that had experienced saccharin in combination with thiamine deficiency. It is possible that a more sensitive preference test might reveal an intake difference when S is nondeficient.

METHOD

Twenty male Sprague-Dawley rats, 6 months old at the beginning of the experiment, were fed a pelleted thiamine-deficient diet (Nutritional Biochemicals Corp.) ad lib. The Ss were given water for 30 min every 24 h. Each S's fluid consumption was measured to ±.5 ml during the daily drinking period. The Ss were randomly divided into four groups of five Ss each. Group 1 drank only water flavored with anise extract (.5 ml/100 ml), Group 2 drank only water flavored with banana extract (.3 ml/100 ml), Group 3 drank only water flavored with vanilla extract (.5 ml/100 ml) and Group 4 drank only tap water. The flavoring substances contained no thiamine.

After 20 days on this regimen, the mean fluid consumption had dropped to about 50% of consumption at the beginning of the experiment, indicating that the Ss were thiamine-deficient. On Day 21, each S was given a new flavor. As soon as S had consumed a few swallows of the new flavor, it was given an intramuscular injection of thiamine hydrochloride (200 µg/kg) and then allowed to complete its 30-min drinking period. The flavor paired with the injection for the various groups was: Group 1, vanilla; Group 2, anise, Group 3, banana; and Group 4, tap water. On Day 22, the animals were returned to the flavor originally paired with deficiency. The Ss were maintained on the "deficiency flavor" and the thiamine-deficient diet until their water intake again dropped to

TABLE 1   Experimental Design

	Group 1	Group 2	Group 3	Group 4
Paired with recovery	Vanilla	Anise	Banana	Tap water
				Vanilla
Novel	Banana	Vanilla	Anise	Anise
				Banana
Paired with deficiency	Anise	Banana	Vanilla	Tap water

50%, indicating deficiency. The injections were then administered a second time, paired with the "recovery flavor" for each group. The same procedure was followed for a third and a fourth injection.

When the Ss reached the criterion of deficiency after the fourth injection, all Ss were given the same three-flavor preference test. Bottles of anise-, banana-, and vanilla-flavored water were placed in random order on each cage, and the amount consumed from each bottle was measured after 30 min and again after 24 h. It may be seen that the design of the experiment was a simple Latin square, with three flavors and three conditions (paired with recovery, paired with deficiency, and novel flavor). The first three groups had each of the flavors paired with a different condition, with each combination of a flavor and a condition appearing in only one group (Table 1). The control animals had the same three-flavor test, but all three flavors were novel for the controls.

After being tested in the thiamine-deficient state, all Ss were given a diet of regular Purina chow and their "recovery flavor" of drinking water for the next 7 days, during which they recovered completely from vitamin deficiency. The same three-choice test was then administered to the recovered animals.

RESULTS

Figure 1 shows the outcome of the preference tests. The left portion depicts the mean intake of the fluid paired with recovery, the fluid paired with deficiency, and the novel fluid, after 30 min and after 24 h of testing during the deficient state. The right portion of Fig. 1 shows the identical data for the test conducted in the recovered state.

A separate analysis of variance (Lindquist Design VII for replicated Latin square) was performed on the 30-min and 24-h intake data. Since the two analyses revealed identical findings, only the analysis of the 30-min data will be presented. The effect of flavors (anise, vanilla, and banana) was significant ($F = 22.62$, df = 2/24, $p < .001$), indicating that the Ss preferred some flavors to others. However, flavors did not interact significantly with any of the other variables. The effect of deficiency was also significant ($F = 5.53$, df = 1/24, $p < .025$), indicating that Ss drank more in the recovered than in the deficient state. The effect of conditions (paired with recovery, paired with deficiency, novel) was also significant ($F = 8.08$, df = 2/24, $p < .005$). Duncan's multiple-range test revealed that the Ss drank more of the recovery flavor than either the deficiency or novel flavors ($p < .05$). There was no significant intake difference between the novel and deficiency flavors. Finally, conditions did not interact

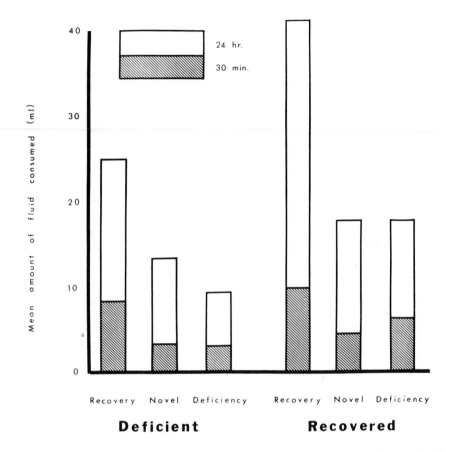

FIG. 1 Mean amount of fluid consumed after 30 min and after 24 h of preference testing in the deficient and recovered states, for the taste paired with recovery, the novel taste, and the taste paired with deficiency.

significantly with deficiency, indicating that the preference for the recovery flavor was as great in the nondeficient as in the deficient state.

DISCUSSION

This study demonstrates the development of a preference for a taste paired with recovery from thiamine deficiency. A large preference developed after only four pairings of the taste and injection of thiamine.

In contrast to the results of Garcia et al., the present experiment revealed a preference for the recovery flavor during both deficient and nondeficient states. This finding is important if one views the preference for the recovery flavor as a case of conditioned reinforcement. If the taste associated with recovery from thiamine deficiency acquires conditioned reinforcing properties, then S should show a preference for this taste in both the deficient and nondeficient states.

There were a number of differences between our procedure and that of Garcia et al. that could account for the above discrepancy. We employed a preference test, while Garcia et al. used an absolute intake measure. In addition, the test in the nondeficient state was here preceded by four recovery-flavor/thiamine-injection pairings *and* full recovery from deficiency in the presence of the recovery flavor. Garcia et al. used only four pairings. Hence, our procedures provided S with a greater opportunity to associate taste and recovery than did that of Garcia et al.

It should be noted that although a preference for the taste paired with recovery from thiamine deficiency did develop, an aversion to the taste paired with deficiency did not develop. This is consistent with the findings of Rozin, Wells, & Mayer (1964). These investigators found that an aversion developed to the taste of a solid diet paired with thiamine deficiency, but that an aversion did not develop to the taste of a liquid paired with thiamine deficiency.

References

Garcia, J., & Ervin, F. R. Gustatory-visceral and telereceptor-cutaneous conditioning: Adaptation in internal and external milieus. Communication in Behavioral Biology, 1968, 1 (Part A), 389—415.

Garcia, J., Ervin, F. R., & Koelling, R. A. Learning with prolonged delay of reinforcement. Psychonomic Science, 1966, 5, 121—122.

Garcia, J., Ervin, F. R. Yorke, C. H., & Koelling, R. A. Conditioning with delayed vitamin injection. Science, 1967, 155, 716—718.

Garcia, J., Kimeldorf, D. H., & Hunt, E. L. The use of ionizing radiation as a motivating stimulus. Psychological Review, 1961, 68, 383—395.

Revusky, S. H. Aversion to sucrose produced by contingent X-irradiation: Temporal and dosage parameters. Journal of Comparative & Physiological Psychology, 1968, 65, 17—22.

Rozin, P. Thiamine specific hunger. In C. Code (Ed.), Handbook of physiology. Vol. 1. Washington: American Physiological Society, 1967.

Rozin, P., Wells, C., & Mayer, J. Specific hunger for thiamine: Vitamin in water versus vitamin in food. Journal of Comparative & Physiological Psychology, 1964, 57, 78—84.

Smith, J. C., & Roll, D. L. Trace conditioning with X-rays as an aversive stimulus. Psychonomic Science, 1967, 9, 11—12.

In an overview of the findings on specific hungers, Paul Rozin and James Kalat spell out their theory of specific hungers and its implications for learning and comparative psychology. This article is not only comprehensive in its treatment of specific hungers, but theoretically intriguing in the breadth of material subsumed by their view. The authors treat a wide range of data: learning in the wild, development of language and reading in man, remembering, and forgetting. The overriding principle that they apply is that learning is only one of many ways that an animal adapts to its environment, and that the form learning takes will invariably reflect the real selective pressures that evolution has exerted on its species.

7

LEARNING AS A SITUATION—
SPECIFIC ADAPTATION

Paul Rozin and James W. Kalat

We propose that learning and memory are situation-specific adaptions, which have evolved as efficient solutions to particular types of environmental challenges. Learning and memory capacities should be best developed in situations and in species where other solutions to the problems at hand are less adaptive. Since these capacities evolve under the pressure of natural selection, they might well be shaped in evolution to match the particular situations in which they are manifested. Biologically speaking, we should expect a variety of different mechanisms or parameters of learning in different situations, rather than a uniform set of properties in all situations. There might indeed be some general laws of learning resulting from basic constraints and features of the operation of the nervous system, and perhaps reflecting general principles of causality in the physical world. However, if we look at learning within an adaptive-evolutionary framework, we should seek not only to uncover some of the common elements among the behaviors we study, but also to explore the plasticity of the mechanisms themselves, as they are shaped through selection to deal with particular types of problems. For many years, the leading ethologists (e.g., Tinbergen, 1951; Lorenz, 1965) have held a related position. They have emphasized the importance of considering learning within a naturalistic context; learning is viewed as being genetically programmed to occur at specific points in an ongoing behavior sequence. We wish to argue further that there are

This manuscript is based, in part, on an invited address by Rozin to A.P.A. Division 6 in 1969. A more extensive treatment of the material presented here, is available (Rozin and Kalat, 1971). The preparation of this article and some of the research reported in it were supported by National Science Foundation Grant GB 8013. We thank Henry Gleitman, Lila Gleitman, Willard Rodgers, Elisabeth Rozin, Martin E. P. Seligman, W. J. Smith, and Richard Solomon for their contributions to the formulation and clarification of the issues discussed here.

Supported by National Institute of Health Training Grant.

genetically determined differences in learning *mechanisms* themselves, as they are applied to different situations.

During the last 20 years, sensory psychologists and physiologists have accepted a similar position. There are spectacular species-and situation-specific adaptations in sensory systems, as illustrated by "bug detectors" in the frog retina (Lettvin et al., 1959) or "bat detectors" in the moth auditory system (Roeder, 1963). Needless to say, as in the case of learning and memory, there must be certain fundamental regularities or principles dictated by the basic properties of the units and connections in the nervous system. However, a wide range of important specializations such as those mentioned are clearly possible within these constraints.

The assumption of a single set of "general laws" appears still to be the predominant view in the field of learning and memory, though "imprinting" (Lorenz, 1957) appears to have gained some recognition as an exceptional specific adaptation. Imprinting is a mechanism of acquiring species recognition, particularly in some bird species. The newly hatched bird will follow any of a wide range of moving objects. In nature this object is almost certain to be its mother. It later accepts as its own species, and attempts to mate with, anything that looks like the object it actually followed during this early period. Unlike other types of learning, imprinting involves no apparent "reinforcer," requires no repetition, is unusually resistant to forgetting, and occurs only during a sharply limited "critical period" early in the bird's life. Imprinting appears to qualify as the kind of specifically adapted learning mechanism we are discussing, especially since it is difficult to imagine how the bird could solve its species-recognition problem if, for instance, its learning had to rely on positive reinforcement contingent on its social responses, or if exposure to a moving object were equally effective at all times of its life.

Recent research has demonstrated that food selection by the rat involves what appears to be another specialized learning mechanism. We shall argue that learning in this situation differs in several ways from learning in more traditional laboratory paradigms, that these differences represent evolutionary adaptations, and that to understand the role of learning and memory in food selection it is necessary to study the specific learning mechanisms involved and to integrate this with the animal's natural behavior patterns.

We shall first discuss specific hungers in order to illustrate the problem of adaptive specializations of learning. Second, we shall discuss taste-aversion learning and the specific learning mechanisms which seem to apply in this case. Finally, we shall describe some broader implications of our basic thesis.

SPECIFIC HUNGERS

Basic Phenomenon and Difficulties with a Learning Interpretation

Richter's (1943) classical work on specific hungers raised the question: When a rat is deficient in a particular nutrient, how can it select those foods which contain it? It is quite clear that sodium deficiency releases an *innate* preference for substances containing sodium (Richter, 1936; Nachman, 1962; Wilson and Stricker, 1970). However, it is unlikely that the rat has an innate recognition system for every other substance for which it can show a specific hunger. An alternative possibility is that rats learn "what makes them better" when they are ill (Harris et al., 1933; Scott and Quint, 1946). A rat would thus learn specific hungers for only those foods associated with recovery from deficiencies it has itself experienced. This notion has the distinct advantage of simplicity in that it accounts for all the specific hungers (except sodium) with one basic mechanism.

Scott and Verney (1947) reported evidence for a learning interpretation of specific hungers. Deficient rats ate flavored vitamin-supplemented food and an unflavored deficient food. After a preference developed for flavored, enriched food, the flavor was switched to the deficient food. Most rats now preferred the flavored deficient food, suggesting a learning mechanism.

Psychologists were reluctant to accept the learning interpretation, however, because of the long delay of reinforcement involved. The ingested nutrient could produce recovery (reward) effects only after many minutes or hours. There was no known precedent for learning with similar delays of reinforcement. If specific hungers were in fact learned, the learning must be of a new and unusual type.

The specific hunger phenomenon was first clearly demonstrated by Richter (1936, 1943) and Harris et al. (1933). Harris et al. found that, given a choice of three foods, one supplemented with B vitamins, rats deficient in vitamin B would quickly come to choose the enriched food (Fig. 1).

Rozin, Wells, and Mayer (1964) studied a simpler situation. They selected vitamin B_1 (thiamine), for which a clear specific hunger had been demonstrated (Richter, Holt, and Barelare, 1937; Scott and Quint, 1946). The basic design consisted of raising weanling rats on a thiamine-deficient diet for 21 days, at which time they showed clear signs of deficiency (anorexia and weight loss; for more details see Rozin, 1967a). They were then offered a choice between this deficient diet and the same diet supplemented with thiamine (see Fig. 2, panel 1). Control rats throughout the series of experiments to be described experienced the same diet and regime, but had thiamine in more than adequate amounts injected daily. Their food intake was restricted so that their weight curves matched the curves of the deficient rats; at the time of testing they had never ingested thiamine and were semistarved, but they were never thiamine-deficient.

As previously reported by Harris et al. (1933) and Scott and Quint (1946), thiamine-deficient animals strongly preferred the thiamine-enriched choice, while controls did not. A few rats with a choice between deficient and *highly enriched* diet showed no clear preference during the first few choice days, but in the meantime ingested great amounts of thiamine and showed marked recovery. Subsequently these rats developed a clear preference for the thiamine-rich diet. It seemed highly unlikely that a rat would show a preference for what it would have needed a few days ago, without showing that same preference when the thiamine presumably had reinforcing value. This anomalous observation was confirmed in an experiment in which rats were made deficient in thiamine, and were then injected with high amounts of thiamine while consuming the deficient diet (see Fig. 2, panel 2, for paradigm). After a period of recovery, the rats were

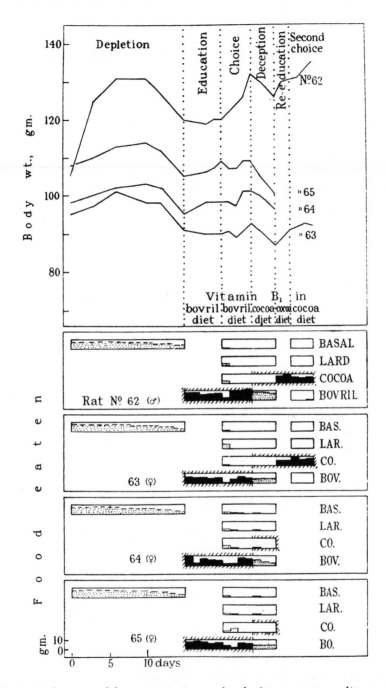

FIG. 1 Preferences of four vitamin-B-complex-depleted rats for a diet containing the vitamin B complex. Weight curves of each rat shown in upper panel. From Harris et al. (1933).

1. STANDARD—SPECIFIC HUNGER (Rozin, Wells, Mayer, 1964)

Ad	Ad vs Aθ
← 21 days →	

2. RECOVERY (Rozin. 1965)

Ad	Ad	Ad vs Aθ
← 21 days →	12 hr. – 10 days	

θ INJ

3. NOVELTY (Rodgers and Rozin, 1966)

Ad	Ad vs Bθ
← 21 days →	Aθ vs Bd

4. AVERSION (Rozin, 1967)

Ad	Bθ	Ad
← 21 days →	← 5 days →	

5. POISON vs VITAMIN DEFICIENCY (Rozin, 1968)

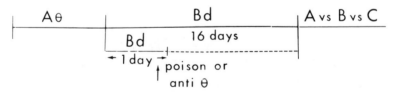

Aθ	Bd	A vs B vs C
	16 days	

Bd
← 1 day → ┆ poison or
↑ anti θ

FIG. 2 Paradigms for specific hunger experiments. Times run horizontally. Each capital letter refers to a different synthetic diet. θ indicates thiamine enriched; d indicates thiamine deficient. In paradigms 1—4, control groups had thiamine injected during the initial period on Ad. In the fifth paradigm, three different experimental groups are represented. One group became deficient slowly on diet B. A second group received diet B with a large amount of oxythiamine, a thiamine antagonist, producing thiamine deficiency in 1 day. The third group had LiCl, a poison, in diet B.

offered a choice of thiamine-enriched and -deficient diets. Preferences for the thiamine-enriched diets emerged at all the recovery intervals studied (Rozin, 1965).

This result raises a second problem for a learning interpretation of thiamine hunger: How could rats develop a learned preference for something that, at the time the preference appeared, had no known reinforcing effects? If the preference developed because of the initial reinforcing effects of the thiamine, why did it not appear until much later? We call this problem *preference after recovery*.

There are additional problems that could not be easily solved within the traditional learning framework. Given that a rat might learn with the delays of reinforcement that seem to hold here, how could the recovery be specifically associated with a particular food? In other words, if ingestion of two or more foods is followed by recovery, how does one of these foods acquire positive properties? We call this third problem, *which food?*

A logical extension of this notion raises the question of how food or the eating of food becomes associated with recovery, when many other potential candidates for association exist in the environment. Following ingestion of foods, including the vitamin-enriched food, and before recovery, the rat performs man acts, such as exploring, chewing, grooming, and sleeping, and experiences many stimuli. Why does the animal respond to food stimuli instead of other stimuli? We call this fourth problem *why food?*.

In summary, the four problems in the application of traditional learning principles to the explanation of specific hungers are (1) delay, (2) preference after recovery, (3) which food, and (4) why food.

Specific Hungers as Learned Aversions

A first step toward defining the role of learning in specific hungers was the appreciation of the importance of novelty as a determinant of food preferences (Rodgers and Rozin, 1966). Thiamine-deficient rats were offered the choice between new and old foods with thiamine in either the new or the old food (see Fig. 2, panel 3, for paradigm). Deficient rats offered the choice of new-enriched food vs. old-deficient food immediately and overwhelmingly preferred the new food, and maintained this preference over the 10-day testing period (Fig. 3). Rats offered thiamine in the old food also strongly preferred the *new* food for the first few days, and then switched to an old-enriched diet preference (Fig. 3). Therefore, for the first few days, these rats avoided the enriched food; novelty seemed more important than the presence of thiamine. Control groups (pair-weighed) showed no such phenomenon. These basic results were completely confirmed with other diets. It appears that the "specific hunger" for thiamine may simply reflect a novelty preference.

Rodgers (1967a) succeeded in demonstrating quite conclusively that there is no specificity to thiamine-specific hunger. Reasoning that the novelty response might mask an existing tendency to prefer the vitamin, he offered deficient rats the choice of a deficient novel diet or the same novel diet supplemented with thiamine. The usual strong specific hunger did not appear. When the choice was between two different novel diets, one enriched, preferences for the enriched

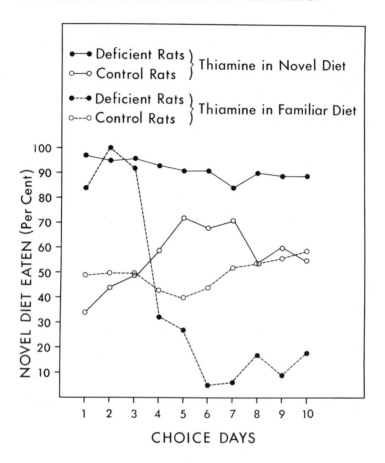

FIG. 3 Preferences for novel diets in thiamine-deficient and pair-weighed control rats. Each point represents the combined data for three rats.

source did not develop rapidly. Finally, separate groups of thiamine-deficient rats and pyridoxine-deficient rats were offered their basal diet in two forms: one supplemented with thiamine, the other with pyridoxine. If there were any specificity, one would expect each group to show a preference for the vitamin that would produce recovery. The groups did not differ significantly.

Two explanations for the novelty effect were considered. One is that the deficiency experience triggers an innately programmed neophilia. There is much independent evidence for the importance of the novel-familiar dimension in the rat and other organisms (Galef, 1970a), and that it controls much of rat behavior. The "neophilia" hypothesis would then state that deficiency increases the "positive valence" of the "new" category.

A more attractive hypothesis is that the novelty effect comes about through learning. The paradigms described all pit the new food against the familiar food that has been present during deficiency. The new food preference could be caused by an aversion to the old food. Put more colloquially, we could ask whether preferences for new foods appear because the rat "loves the new stuff or hates the old stuff." The issue can be settled by observing the behavior of control and deficient rats in the presence of novel and familiar foods (Rozin, 1967b; see Fig. 2, panel 4, for paradigm). Rats were placed in relatively large individual cages with a nesting area and a powdered food cup in a constant location. Their responses to food were observed during the first 15 min of an 8-hour food presentation each day. Every 5 sec their responses were recorded and classified into such categories as grooming, sleeping, eating, and chewing. The experimental rats were placed on a thiamine-deficient diet. As deficiency developed, the rats spent less time eating during the first 15 min. In addition to compensatory increases in grooming or varieties of exploratory behavior, two striking behaviors, quite rare in normals, appeared (see Fig. 4). One was spillage of the food. The rat would approach the food cup, sniff at the food, and then paw at the food in a scooping motion, spilling it out of the cup, so that it fell through the wire-mesh floor. The other new behavior was what we call "redirected feeding." Following an initial investigation of the food cup, rats would occasionally move over to the wooden barrier separating the nest area from the rest of the cage and begin to chew it vigorously. They might also chew on the cage wires. Spillage and redirected feeding suggest an aversion to the familiar diet. The redirected feeding suggests conflict between desire to eat and the aversiveness of the food available. Spillage is often seen in normal rats with highly unpalatable foods, such as quinine-adulterated diets.

When offered the old deficient food in a new container (metal instead of glass) in a new location, these deficient rats showed little potentiation of eating, and continued to show the behavior described above (see Fig. 4). Apparently the vessel and its location were not controlling the aversion. However, when a completely new deficient food was offered in the familiar vessel and location, uninterrupted avid eating ensued, suggesting that the aversion was specific to the food. The deficient rats were subsequently allowed to recover on a new, vitamin-enriched diet. Following 1 week of recovery, and after a 16-hour period of food deprivation, they were presented again with the familiar deficient food, for the first time since the onset of recovery. These food-deprived rats, showing no signs of deficiency at this time, responded to the familiar deficient food as they had before, with minimal ingestion and occasional spillage and redirected feeding (see Fig. 4). In this case, a nondeficient hungry rat prefers staying hungry to eating its original diet, which provides, in fact, perfectly adequate nutrition for him at the time, and is normally quite palatable. Preference of hunger (eating nothing) to ingestion in hungry rats and the similiarity in the rat's behavior toward deficient and highly unpalatable (quinine-adulterated) diets suggest strongly that we are dealing with an active aversion to the familiar food (Rozin, 1967b).

The learned-aversion interpretation places specific hungers in a new perspective. The instrumental learning paradigm that we have been using implicitly may not be appropriate. The aversion results seem more compatible with classical conditioning, with the diet as CS and nausea or other effects produced by its ingestion as the US. Presumably, the classically conditioned "ill effects" lead to avoidance of the familiar food. The mechanism suggested for the specific hunger phenomon, in the standard two-diet choice, would be that the rat learns an aversion to the familiar deficient food. Before the time of choice, he has already

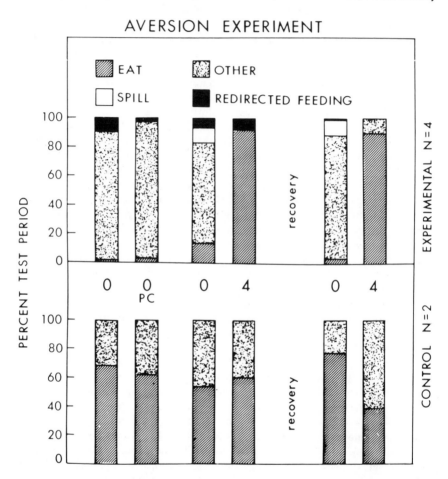

FIG. 4 Frequency distribution of behaviors sampled every 5 seconds for first 5 minutes of exposure to food on selected test days. Upper panel represents data from four thiamine deficient rats. Lower panel represents two control rats. First four bars in top panel represent samples taken during period of deficiency. First bar (O) indicates response to familiar deficient diet 0, in familiar environment. Second bar (O, PC) shows response to same diet 0 in new cup and new location. Third bar reproduces conditions for first bar, a few days later. Fourth bar represents response to novel, deficient diet 4. Last two bars show response of rats recovered (or sham recovered) on diet 4, to deficient diets O (bar 5) and 4 (bar 6).

done a significant part of his learning; he knows what not to eat. The initial preference for the new food follows. Its maintenance when the new food is enriched could be accounted for by an additional learned preference for the new food, or as a failure to develop an aversion to it (see section on learned preference).[1]

To the extent that specific aversions play a key role in specific hungers, there is an obvious parallel between specific hungers and poisoning. Both involve learned aversions; a vitamin-deficient diet is a slow-acting poison. The aversion experiment suggests that these two sets of phenomena are closely related. There is an impressive literature on poisoning, primarily in wild rats (Chitty and Southern, 1954). The same basic problems raised here (delay, which food, why food) arise with respect to poisoning. Since most poisons are designed and synthesized by man, innate aversions could hardly be involved. In comparing the literature on poisoning (see Barnett, 1963; Richter, 1953; Rzóska, 1953) to that on specific hungers, there is one apparent contrast. We have reported an increased "neophilia" in deficient white rats, while the poisoning literature on wild rats strongly indicates an exaggerated neophobia following poisoning. That is, wild rats, who show a much greater baseline tendency to avoid new objects or events than do domestic rats (e.g., see Galef, 1970), show a further exaggeration of this tendency, often to an extreme (Richter, 1953) following poisoning experiences. This disparity can be accounted for as a procedural difference, since the new-familiar choices we offered to our domestic rats were different from those usually offered poisoned wild rats. In particular, in the novelty experiments, which were done before we realized that specific aversions were involved, the rat was offered a choice between a familiar food associated with deficiency and a new food. The white rat may not have had an opportunity to demonstrate neophobia, since the alternative choice was a strongly aversive familiar diet.

A meaningful comparison between poisoning and specific hungers requires that both sets of phenomena be demonstrated under the same sets of conditions, and in the same strain of rats. In order to accomplish this, half-wild and domestic rats were raised on diet A, prior to induction of aversive consequences. Deficiency or poisoning (or neither in the case of controls) occurred in the presence of diet B. In the final test, rats were offered these two diets and a completely new one, diet C (Fig. 2, panel 5), thus allowing a fuller expression of

---

[1] For the remainder of this article, we shall continue to use the classical conditioning terminology to refer to the learning involved in food selection. We do this for convenience in exposition. We are not convinced that the classical conditioning paradigm is wholly appropriate. First, we do not know what the unconditioned stimulus is, and have some difficulty in defining conditioned and unconditioned response. More important, Gleitman (personal communication) has proposed that in taste-aversion learning, the CS itself acquires aversive properties: The rat avoids a poisoned food because it now tastes bad, rather than because it leads to a "conditioned sickness." We find support for this viewpoint in two observations: (1) deficient rats eagerly consume new or old safe foods, suggesting that "sickness" itself is not sufficient to inhibit eating (Rodgers and Rozin, 1966); (2) rats behave toward deficient or previously poisoned food in the same way as they behave toward bad tasting (quinine adulterated) foods (Rozin, 1967b).

the rat's neophobic or neophilic tendencies. Therefore, rats were faced with a choice among a familiar *safe* diet (A), a familiar aversive diet (B), and a completely new diet (C) (Rozin, 1968).

The single important result is that all rats suffering poisoning or deficiency showed an increased preference for the familiar safe food, i.e., a *neophobia* (Fig. 5). Half-wild rats showed a stronger neophobia following the aversive experience, but half-wild controls also showed a higher baseline neophobia. Experimental rats almost completely avoided the familiar aversive food (B) but ate some of the completely new food (Fig. 5). There were no major differences between the specific hunger and poisoning groups. Therefore, it appears that we can consider specific hungers as a parallel to poisoning. The behavior makes sense in an adaptive framework; following an unpleasant food-related experience, the rat tends to return to a known, *safe* food.

Resolution of the Difficulties with a Learning Interpretation

The specific aversion explanation of specific hungers, the realization of the importance of the familiarity-novelty dimension, and the appearance of two

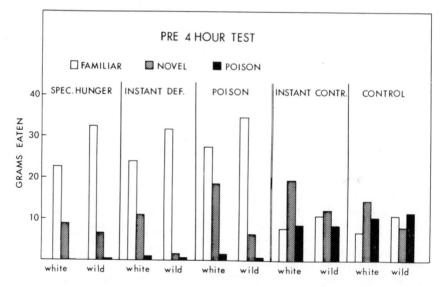

FIG. 5 Intake of familiar (safe), novel, and poisoned food in first 4-hour test, in white and half-wild rats. Spec. hunger refers to rats that gradually became deficient on diet B (see Fig. 2, panel 5). Instant def. refers to rats made thiamine deficient rapidly with antivitamin. Poison refers to rats poisoned with LiCl. Instant control rats were treated exactly like instant def. rats, but were given large amounts of thiamine with the antithiamine in diet "B." Controls received a standard vitamin-enriched diet B for one day. The data presented refer to the total intake of ten rats in each group. (Based on data from Rozin, 1968.)

articles of major significance by John Garcia and his colleagues enable us to resolve the four basic problems with a learning interpretation.

1. *Preference after recovery.* This can be accounted for as a retained aversion to the familiar food. Thiamine-deficient rats, recovered by injection for 12 hours or 5 days (while continuing to eat the same deficient diet), initially strongly prefer a novel food when offered a novel-familiar food choice, with thiamine *absent* from both choices (Rozin and Rodgers, 1967). In these experiments, recovery took place in the presence of the familiar food. The existence of a novelty effect suggests that the aversion had not fully extinguished by the time of testing. Significantly, in most of our experiments (some unpublished) the recovery effect showed some dimunution as time of recovery increased. The recovery effect should be maximal when recovery is associated with a new food, so that the old diet aversion does not extinguish. Strong "recovery" effects are in fact seen under such circumstances in the aversion experiment, with a single choice (Rozin, 1967b) and in typical two-choice experiments with long recovery periods (Rozin, unpublished data).

2. *Which food?* In the "standard" two-choice situation, the rat simply learns to avoid the deficient food when it is the only diet available. There is no "which food?" problem here.

The testing situations described up to this point, with the partial exception of the testing environment in the aversion experiment, have been very limited, well defined, and unnatural. Rats normally live in a relatively large area, have an elaborate social life, and seldom face simple binary food choices. It is reasonable to assume that one or only a few foods might be available to the rat during the deficiency period in nature, since a deficiency would be quite unlikely with a wide variety of foods available. However, one cannot seriously expect a one-by-one introduction of new foods into the natural environment.

In their classic work on B vitamin hungers, Harris et al. (1933) offered deficient rats a choice among a large variety (6–10) of foods, with only one containing B vitamins in significant amounts. Only a few of their rats preferred the enriched choice. How and under what circumstances can this be done? A solution to this problem should result from observation of the feeding patterns of rats faced with multiple food choices. A thiamine supplement was placed in one of four diet choices made available for 8 hours a day (Rozin, 1969a). Food intake from each cup was measured at hourly intervals. Four of 10 deficient rats developed clear preferences for the enriched choice within a few days, and 2 other rats developed strong preferences for two of the four choices, where one of the preferred choices was enriched. Analysis of the meals indicated a characteristic pattern, both on a daily and hourly basis. Meals, except for an initial daily sampling of many or all of the choices, tended to be restricted to one food each day (Fig. 6). In each case in Fig. 6, the portion of the record shown includes the time when the rat discovered the enriched food. The rat's feeding pattern seemed to maximize the possibility of associating each diet with its appropriate consequences, since meals tended to be isolated in time and to consist of a single food. The emergence of a strong preference for the enriched food was in each case preceded by a clearly defined meal of that food. Furthermore, no rat failed to develop a clear enriched food preference if it ate

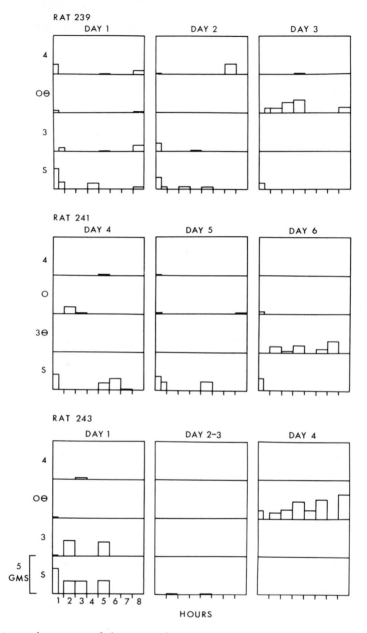

FIG. 6 Meal patterns of three rats showing a clear preference for the enriched choice. Each box represents the intake for one 8-hour session, broken down by the four diets and the nine measurement intervals (½ hour, 1 hour, and each additional hour). For each rat, the enriched diet is indicated by the symbol θ following the diet designation. The days selected for each rat lead up to and include the first day of clear selection of the enriched diet. Rat 243 ate virtually no food on days 2 and 3, so that these days have been combined into one box. Note calibration for all boxes in lower left-hand box. (Rozin, 1969b.)

an isolated meal of at least 1 gram from the enriched food. The rats that failed to show adaptive preferences in the initial part of the experiment failed to sample significant amounts of the enriched food. Similar, though less well defined, sampling patterns are seen in normal rats. Normals mix meals more, but this may be a direct consequence of the fact that their meals are larger. The anorexia of deficiency may, in and of itself, exaggerate in an adaptive way the normal feeding pattern of the rat. We have here another part of the answer to the "which food?" problem.

Social factors have become implicated in food selection, in some significant recent experiments. Galef and Clark (1971) studied responses to poisoning in colonies of wild rats observed in the laboratory under seminaturalistic conditions. A group of wild rats was offered two foods, one of which was poisoned. All rats promptly avoided this food. After the poison was removed, the rats still completely avoided the base. When a litter was born, the behavior of the young toward these new foods was observed. The parents and young were fed for 3 hours a day, and were under constant observation. During a 2-week period (days 14–28 of life in the pups), the pups came out to eat, but ate only the safe food (possibly because this was the only food being eaten by the parents). When the young were fully weaned and placed in a new cage, separated from their parents, they continued for 6 days to eat only the safe diet and to ignore the formerly poisoned diet. Further experiments (Galef and Clark, 1971; Galef, 1971) suggest that rat pups tend to approach and feed in proximity to adults. In this way they become familiar with the foods eaten by the adults, and avoid alternative diets as a result of their neophobia.

3. *Why food?* Rats in the aversion experiment (Rozin, 1967b) did not show an aversion to the container or the location of the deficient food. While introduction of a new food dramatically increased ingestion, change to a new location and container did not (Fig. 4). Apparently what the animal learned was specific to the food.

In a very important and much more compelling experiment, Garcia and Koelling (1966) provided evidence that there was a specific tendency for taste "CSs" to be associated with certain types of visceral "USs," while exteroceptive CSs such as light and sound were preferentially associated with exteroceptive USs, such as shock. They paired light, sound, and taste simultaneously with either electric shock or poisoning, in different groups of animals. The shocked animals developed an avoidance of the light and sound, but not of the taste. The poisoned animals, subjected to the same light-sound-taste pairing, avoided the taste and not the sound or light. This clearly establishes a principle of stimulus selectivity of which our "why food?" problem is one instance.

4. *Delay.* The reinterpretation of specific hungers, in itself, does not bring us much closer to solving the original problem. It does not seem to be possible to reinterpret what appeared to be long-delay learning in terms of short delays. However, a crucial experiment by Garcia, Ervin, and Koelling (1966) demonstrates that long-delay learning can occur in this system. They induced an aversion to saccharin in rats by injections of apomorphine, a drug that presumably produces gastrointestinal upset. Aversions were produced when the interval between termination of drinking and injection of the drug was ½ hour or

more. Only a few trials were necessary to establish a clear aversion. The adaptiveness of this capacity is clear. A learning mechanism that can bridge long delays is specifically adapted to the problems of taste-aversion learning and specific hungers; there is in the feeding system an inherent delay between ingestion and its metabolic consequences.

Learned Preferences

Specific hungers can be explained largely in terms of learned aversions; is there a positive side also? We have provided evidence for three categories of foods based on the animal's experience (Rozin, 1968). These are familiar-aversive, familiar-safe, and unexperienced or novel. Is there a fourth category, familiar-positive; that is, is the effect of positive consequences any different from the effect of neutral consequences, when these experiences are contingent upon ingestion of a particular substance?

Much evidence which appears to demonstrate positive preferences can be reinterpreted in terms of learned aversions. For example, Harris et al. (1933) found that when only one of a large number of diets contained adequate thiamine, most deficient rats were not successful in selecting it. However, if the rats were "educated" by being offered *only* the adequate food for several days, they showed a preference for this food when the larger number of diets was again offered. This preference could be explained as a combination of learned aversions and neophobia. That is, after "education" the rats have learned that the thiamine-containing diet is "safe," but it is not certain whether they have learned that it has any special "recovery from deficiency" properties which distinguish it from other safe diets, since we know that deficient rats prefer "old safe" foods to either old aversive or novel foods (Rozin, 1968). Similarly, in the sampling experiment (Rozin, 1969a), the rat's preference for the only enriched diet in a four-choice situation could be produced by aversions to the other choices.

Some recent experiments present more serious challenges to a pure aversion model. Garcia, Ervin, Yorke, and Koelling (1967) offered saccharin solution to thiamine-deficient rats just prior to thiamine injection. At all other times, water was the only fluid available. This procedure was repeated through a number of deficiency cycles. When thiamine deficient, the rats showed an increase in saccharin intake over trials (Fig. 7), both with respect to their own water intake and to the saccharin intake of controls (thiamine injection not contingent upon saccharin ingestion). Campbell (1969) has also demonstrated that thiamine-deficient rats show an increase in their absolute intake of a sucrose solution which has been associated with recovery from deficiency. Zahorik and Maier (1969) found that rats prefer the taste associated with recovery from thiamine deficiency to both the taste associated with deficiency and a novel taste. Furthermore, this preference was apparent in both deficient and recovered rats.

These experiments, which certainly provide evidence for learned preferences, can nevertheless be explained in terms of the three basic categories of food. A more decisive experiment would have to show that rats prefer a "recovery" solution to an old "safe" solution, i.e., one they drank without aversive consequences at a time when they were not vitamin deficient.

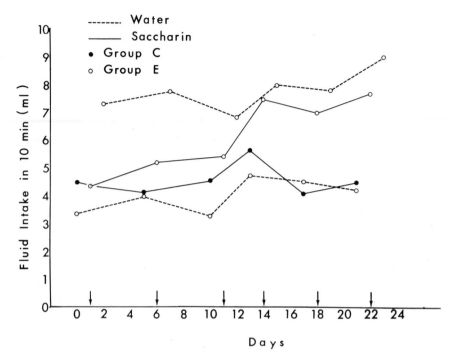

FIG. 7 Preferences for saccharin solution associated with recovery from thiamine deficiency. All one-bottle tests. Group E (*N* = 19): saccharin drink followed (2–17 minutes postdrinking) by injection of 20 μg of thiamine. Group C (*N* = 17): saccharin drink 24 hours prior, water drink immediately prior to injection. Bottom group E: water curve refers to water intake 24 hours prior to injection. Top group E: water curve refers to water intake 24 hours postinjection. Arrows indicate injection of thiamine. (Based on data from Garcia, Ervin, Yorke, & Koelling, 1967.)

Revusky (1967; Revusky and Garcia, 1970) demonstrated that food with clear positive consequences is preferred to foods with relatively neutral consequences. Rats drank one nutrient solution while hungry and another when satiated. Significant preferences appeared for the solution drunk while deprived in two bottle tests. This result is interpreted in terms of the greater (delayed) reinforcing effect of the solution drunk during deprivation. Since both solutions were equally familiar, and the satiated rats voluntarily drank the solution (so that an acquired aversion would be unlikely), this experiment meets the requirements for demonstrating a learned preference. The effect is clear, though not large, by comparison to the aversion data (see Revusky and Garcia, 1970 for additional data).

It is noteworthy that the positive preference effects reported have been rather small by comparison with learned aversions, and difficult to obtain (Kalat and Rozin, unpublished; Revusky and Garcia, 1970). We cannot satisfactorily explain this asymmetry. This remains, for the moment, an intriguing problem, with important implications for the regulation of food intake.

Summary and Extensions

We believe our theory of thiamine specific hunger holds for other learned specific hungers as well. Novel food preferences, which imply a learned aversion mechanism, have been demonstrated in calcium- and magnesium-deficient rats (Rodgers, 1967a) and in pyridoxine- and riboflavin-deficient rats (Rozin and Rodgers, 1967). The preference after recovery phenomenon appears in identical form in thiamine, pyridoxine, and riboflavin deficiency (Rozin and Rodgers, 1967).

The anorexia characteristic of most vitamin deficiencies seems to reflect, at least in part, a learned aversion to the deficient food. This is dramatically clear in the case of thiamine deficiency, where the anorexia symptom disappears precipitously when a new diet is offered. On the other hand, there is relatively little anorexia in vitamin A or vitamin D deficiency, and in both cases there has *not* been a clear demonstration of a specific hunger. Well-documented evidence on amino acid selection (Harper, 1967), where "deficiencies" are also characterized by anorexia, seem to fit into the scheme we have described. Furthermore, Rogers and Harper (1970) have reported positive preferences for a solution that corrects an amino acid imbalance.

We cannot complete this reconsideration of specific hungers without noting a particularly serious shortcoming of the mechanisms we have discussed. Although, in principle, they can account for most of the individual vitamin or mineral specific hungers, it is not clear how they can account for classic "cafeteria" self-selection of Richter (1943). Rats self-select a well balanced diet. Unless we assume that they develop incipient deficiencies of a variety of nutrients, and learn aversions and preferences on the basis of these minimal symptoms and their abatement, we have no explanation of this remarkable phenomenon. At this time, long-delay learning mechanisms appear inadequate to the task, since we cannot identify obvious candidates for unconditioned stimuli.

Our explanation of specific hungers is based on three fundamental points: (1) The contingencies in the feeding situation are not what they were thought to be; (2) new principles of learning are needed to account for the phenomenon; and (3) the novelty-familiarity dimension is of particular importance to the rat.

The shift from a preference to an aversion formulation resulted from observations of rats in a relatively naturalistic situation, and permits resolution of some of the problems raised. The "which food?" problem was solved by the discovery that the actual contingencies in a food-choice experiment are not what one might think them to be; both learned aversions and sampling patterns combine to simplify the situation. The preference after recovery effect is a special case of the novelty or aversion effect.

After understanding the contingencies involved and the importance of novelty, two of the original problems with a learning interpretation, "why food?" and "delay," were as puzzling as ever. It is remarkable that each of Garcia et al.'s two "classic" experiments (Garcia and Koelling, 1966; Garcia, Ervin, and Koelling, 1966) dealt directly with one of these problems at just the time that these two issues became *the* two problems in specific hungers.

These experiments were received with great skepticism by many, because of the radical nature of the conclusions; but in the context of the problems of specific hungers, it seemed clear that the basic principles demonstrated in these experiments must be essentially correct. Both belongingness and long-delay learning seem highly adapted to the problems of the feeding system. This suggests that specific learning mechanisms have evolved in response to specific problems. In the following section we shall consider these laws in greater detail, in order to elaborate the extensive ways in which learning mechanisms can be specifically adapted to particular problems.

UNIQUE ADAPTIONS OF LEARNING MECHANISMS IN THE FEEDING SYSTEM

In this section we shall consider learning about food. In considering whether it is a "new type" of learning, we examine the belongingness principle in some detail, and consider the importance of familiarity and novelty, and long-delay learning.

Principles of Stimulus Selection

When faced with a bewildering array of stimuli that could be associated with a gastrointestinal event, the rat has available principles by which to sort them out. One concerns his past experience with these stimuli, the novelty-familiarity dimension, and the other certain presumably built-in tendencies to associate certain categories of stimuli with certain relevant events (belongingness). We shall consider each in turn.

The Novelty-Familiarity Dimension. The novelty (or familiarity) of a stimulus is of particular importance for a rat (see Rozin, 1968; Galef, 1971). This distinction has special significance in determining the magnitude of a learned aversion to a given taste. Revusky and Bedarf (1967) (replicated by Wittlin and Brookshire, 1968) showed that rats learn aversions much more readily to novel solutions than to familiar solutions, even when they drink the familiar solution between the time they drink the novel solution and the time of poisoning. Almost the entire "familiarization" effect can occur in one 20-minute exposure to a solution (Kalat and Rozin, 1972). A robust familiarization effect (increased resistance to taste-aversion learning in familiar solutions) occurs even if the single exposure takes place 3 weeks prior to poisoning.

Belongingness. The "stimulus relevance" (Capretta, 1961) or "belongingness" (Garcia and Koelling, 1966) or "preparedness" (Seligman, 1970) phenomenon— i.e., the tendency to associate tastes with aversive internal consequences as opposed to associating either element with anything else—seems eminently sensible from an adaptive point of view. Gastrointestinal and related internal events are, in fact, very likely to be initiated or influenced by substances eaten. Taste receptors, by virtue of their location, provide information about these same substances. However, an equal ability to associate lights and sounds with gastrointestinal consequences would be far less adaptive; in fact, the common result would be "superstitious" learning. The belongingness phenomenon receives support not only from these adaptive arguments but also from neurological considerations. The gustatory receptors and the gut receptors are similarly classified as visceral sensory inputs, and show close neurological relationships in the medulla and possibly in the hypothalamus.

The notion of belongingness has been expressed in some form by prominent psychologists (Pavlov, 1927; Thorndike, 1911; Tolman, 1932; Kohler, 1947). In recent times, several authors have noted the phenomenon, though in a manner much less compelling than the work of Garcia and his colleagues. Braveman and Capretta (1965) found that a "nauseating" preload of 10 percent NaC1 was a more effective US than electric shock in producing a learned aversion to a sweet solution. They interpreted this result in terms of "stimulus-relevance." Rozin's (1967b) experiments showed that the aversion which developed during vitamin deficiency was specific to the food, and not to its location or container.

The evidence for a predisposition to associate tastes with subsequent gastrointestinal events is very convincing. Garcia and his colleagues (Garcia and Koelling, 1966; Garcia, McGowan, Ervin, and Koelling, 1968) have demonstrated it clearly in several different situations. The question arises whether and under what circumstances "unnatural" associations can be produced. Garcia, Kimeldorf, and Hunt (1961) and Rozin (1969b) have demonstrated clear aversions to exteroceptive (visual-spatial) cues, using X-ray or apomorphine as "US." However, such associations are relatively difficult to produce. Both experiments did not offer a distinctive chemical cue, and in both US administration overlapped exposure to CSs—i.e., there was close temporal contiguity. This feature appears to be critical in these unnatural associations. If a 30-minute delay between CS (drinking from a particular type of cup in a particular position, see legend of Fig. 8) and US is introduced, there is no evidence of an acquisition of an aversion (Fig. 8; Rozin, 1969b). The same interval supports clear aversions with a taste CS. Furthermore, "unnatural" associations may show relatively narrow generalization functions. Garcia, Kovner, and Green (1970) trained rats to avoid saccharin solution in one situation (shuttlebox) and tested in another (home cage). If "illness" was used as the US, the aversion generalized to the home cage without significant decrement. However, if the saccharin avoidance was conditioned with contingent electric shock as US, it did not generalize at all.

Salience. There is a demonstration of "intramodality" belongingness; rats tend to associate poisoning with some novel solutions more than with others (Kalat and Rozin, 1970). Rats drank one novel solution briefly, 15 minutes later drank a second novel solution, and another 15 minutes later were poisoned. The following day the rats were offered both solutions simultaneously. Certain "highly salient" solutions became more aversive than others under these conditions. The salience of a solution proved to be a more potent predictor of amount of acquired aversion than temporal proximity to poisoning. It was

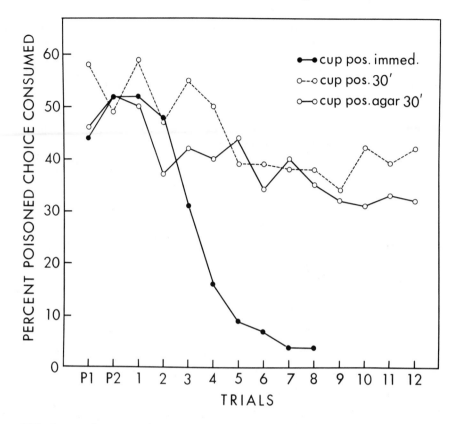

FIG. 8 Development of aversions to poisoned solutions with nongustatory cues. (Cup pos. imed: vessel and position cues, immediate apomorphine administration. Cup pos. 30': same as previous group, with 30-minute delay in drug administration. Cup pos. agar 30': vessel, position, texture, and temperature cues, with 30-minute delay in drug administration.) (Rozin, 1969a.)

possible to rank four novel solutions in a stable, transitive "salience" hierarchy, such that each solution proved more salient (associable with poisoning) than all "lower" solutions. Evidence for a salience effect on the "positive" side (recovery from thiamine deficiency) has been reported (Campbell, 1969).

As yet we do not know what the defining characteristics of the salience dimension are. It is probable that the "relative novelty" of these operationally novel solutions contributes to the effect; that is, more salient solutions may be more different from previously experienced solutions. There may also be factors associated with intrinsic properties of the solutions. Certain tastes (e.g., bitter?) may have a particular tendency to be associated with aversive consequences, so that different salience hierarchies might be produced with learned preferences as opposed to learned aversions.

A functional definition of belongingness. Some category of CSs, including tastes, preferentially associates with some category of USs, including "gastrointestinal distress." The unconditioned stimuli employed have been described as "poisoning," "nausea," and "gastrointestinal upset," but these ill-defined terms may not accurately describe the class of effective stimuli. Ingested foods produce significant internal effects outside the gastrointestinal system, so that the primary action of some of the USs presently employed may be outside the gastrointestinal system. On the other hand, it is hard to understand, from an adaptive point of view, why pain in the heart or lungs, for example, should be selectively associated with taste. In fact, it is not known whether gastrointestinal *pain* is selectively associated with taste. More research is needed to better define the range of visceral sensations with which tastes have high associability.

Belongingness may be related to the temporal parameters of the various CSs and USs. In the taste-visceral system, stimuli tend to have slow onsets and to last for long periods. Exteroceptive CSs and USs, in contrast, are characteristically brief and well defined in time. The importance of temporal factors and the visceral field for taste-aversion learning could both be determined by using experimentally controlled USs, such as electric shock to the stomach mucosa instead of the ill-defined poisoning procedures.

The category of effective CSs should differ from species to species. It is highly adaptive that an animal that identifies its foods by taste should have a specific ability to learn taste-poison associations, because foods are the usual cause of any aversive gastrointestinal stimulation. However, some species use other modalities as well. In particular, birds seem to put major emphasis on visual cues in the identification and selection of food. Experiments by Brower (1969) indicate that birds can readily learn aversions to the sight of food. Wilcoxon, Dragoin, and Kral (1969) report that Japanese quail learn poison-based aversions more readily to the color (or optical density) than to the taste of a solution.

We suggest that the critical dimension for poison-based aversion learning may not be "taste-vs.-other modalities" but "eating-related cues-vs.-other cues." This type of functional categorization of input is in harmony with J. J. Gibson's (1966) view of perceptual systems. Eating-related cues are whatever type of cue—gustatory, olfactory, visual, etc.—a particular species uses to identify food. Because of the intimate and relatively invariant relationship between taste receptors and food ingestion, and because of the neurological association between taste and visceral receptors, it is likely that taste cues would always be "eating-related" so that taste-poisoning belongingness should be practically universal.

A single sensory modality could include both eating-related and non-eating-related cues. Perhaps birds can form poison-based aversions to the sight of potential prey, but not to other sights. Also, it is known that odors are less effective than tastes in poison-based aversions in rats. Odors might be more effective when they emanate from a food source or when they are experienced simultaneously with a taste. It would be of interest to investigate the effective cues for poison-based aversion learning in other species in which food recognition is known to involve nongustatory cues. For instance, frogs have specific visual cells which respond maximally to flying insects and similar stimuli (Lettvin et al., 1959). The above analysis suggests that stimuli which excite these "bug detectors" might be more easily associated with poison than other types of visual stimuli.

Long-Delay Learning. The other major principle of taste-aversion learning is that learning occurs after long delays between taste and poison. This principle is also of clear adaptive value, and supports our contention that taste-aversion learning represents a specific learning ability evolved to meet the demands of a specific situation. Reliable taste-aversion learning occurs after a single trial with a delay of several hours between the taste and poisoning (Garcia, Ervin, and Koelling, 1966; Smith and Roll, 1967; Revusky, 1968); if it only occurred after delays no longer than a few seconds, as is characteristic of other known types of learning (Kimble, 1961), rat extermination would be an easy job indeed.

The alternative to viewing this as a specifically evolved learning mechanism is to assume that the long delays are mediated by a peripheral aftertaste, resulting in temporal contiguity between CS and US. However, there is no evidence to support this assumption, and an impressive amount of evidence incompatible with it. [This evidence is reviewed by Revusky and Garcia (1970) and Rozin and Kalat (1971).]

The main obstacle to rejecting the aftertaste hypothesis is not the lack of evidence against it, but the lack of an acceptable, clearly formulated alternative. One alternative theory (Revusky, 1971) attempts to derive the long-delay principle from the belongingness principle. It assumes that in any situation the rat associates a US with the most recent CS. For most USs, a wide variety of visual, auditory, and other cues are effective CSs; since such cues are constantly changing, any increase in the CS-US interval will greatly decrease the association of the US with the CS in question. But when poisoning is the US, only tastes are effective CSs. Since the rat experiences very few tastes during a long time period, learning can occur despite long CS-US delays.

There are problems with this attractive theory. It seems to predict that in the absence of taste interference, increases in the CS-US delay should be without effect. But with no tastes available in the interval, rats learn less aversion with longer delays, such that a 6-hour delay may produce no aversion (Kalat and Rozin, 1971). If this is to be explained in terms of interference from nontaste cues, which have little associability with poison, it should certainly be expected that the explicit introduction of novel tastes in the interval should produce great interference. Yet when a rat drinks three novel solutions between sucrose and poisoning, it still acquires a large aversion to sucrose (Kalat and Rozin, 1971). While it is clear that interference plays some role in determining the effects of CS-US delays, it is difficult to account for the above data in terms of interference as the sole determinant.

Another possibility (Kalat and Rozin, 1972; Rozin and Kalat, 1971) is that long-delay learning is a separate, independent principle of the taste-aversion learning system, evolutionarily adapted to the demands of the feeding system. In terms of the usual view of the CS-US delay function, one might argue that the CS "trace" decays more slowly for tastes than for other stimuli. A view we favor, however, is that the CS-US delay function does not represent "forgetting" of the CS, but *learning* that the CS is "safe." In these terms, we suggest that the rat learns that a novel taste is "safe" much more slowly than it learns that a light or sound is safe.

Summary: Learning About Foods

We can now describe how a rat handles some of the complex problems in food selection. The situation is probably less complex than it might appear. For example, the rat who gets sick in the garbage dump probably didn't recently sample all the choice delicacies available (Rozin, 1969a). His choice behavior itself will help to unconfound the situation. He *may* have eaten a *few* different foods. He "knows" that it was a *food* that made him sick (the belongingness principle) and can discount any familiar, safe foods (the novelty principle). He is likely to associate his illness with the last relevant (as defined above) thing or few things he ate over the last few hours (long-delay principle). Although some of these foods may become more aversive than others because of their intrinsic properties (salience effect), the rat will acquire a significant aversion to each of them (small interference effect), with those closer in time to the aversive event picking up somewhat more aversion (temporal "contiguity"). Similar mechanisms could be employed to account for important aspects of the regulation of food intake such as compensation for changes in caloric density of food.

GENERAL IMPLICATIONS FOR PSYCHOLOGY

On the Comparative Psychology of Learning

Given our general viewpoint that the laws of learning in a specific situation are shaped by the demands of that situation, it seems reasonable that an organism might have a capacity which manifests itself only in a small number of the total possible situations in which an experimenter might test for it. It is therefore, very difficult to describe the "intelligence" level of a species. For example, it is unlikely that salmon remember most things as well as homestream odors (Hasler, 1966) or that bees can learn complicated mazes as well as visual landmarks. We quote two eloquent voices from the past on this subject. "When we carry such an animal to the laboratory and experiment upon it there, it is like removing an organ from the body and studying it in a dissecting dish. We cannot understand its activities without knowing their relations to the rest of the body" (Jennings, 1906). "Unless the experimenter has wide experience with the animals that he studies and adapts his questions to their modes of behavior, the results give little information about their true capacities" (Lashley, 1949).

Let us consider some of the best comparative work in the area of learning to illustrate this point. Bitterman, Gonzalez, and their colleagues (Bitterman, 1964, 1968) have attempted to describe qualitative differences in learning capability among the major groups of animals, most notably fish and mammals.[2] They are aware that differences in sensory capacities, motivation, and motor capabilities can mistakenly lead one to attribute measured differences in performance in learning situations to differences in learning ability. As a result they are quite thorough in varying motivational level, and sensory and motor aspects of the situation. Furthermore, they look for qualitative differences in behavior, since

---

[2] We recognize, but shall not discuss here, the great problems in attempting to compare such large and diverse groups, particularly with a sampling of only a few more or less specialized species (see Hodos and Campbell, 1969).

differences such as rate of conditioning are so sensitive to parametric changes. Their assumption is that once a fish has been taught to press a lever for food reward, thereby demonstrating that he is capable of learning in the experimental situation, it should then be possible to demonstrate any learning capacity possessed by the fish and measurable in this type of apparatus. We question this assumption (see also Gleitman and Rozin, 1971).[3]

Two species of teleost fish (African mouthbreeders and goldfish), (in Skinner-box-type situations) fail to show habit reversal (Bitterman, Wodinsky, and Candland, 1958) or the partial reinforcement effect (PRE) (Gonzalez and Bitterman, 1969), while rats and other mammals clearly show such effects. However, to conclude that fish, or goldfish, do not have the capacity to improve on reversal tasks is equivalent to the claim that salmon have a poor memory, based on a visual discrimination experiment, when, to put it in the modern vernacular, visual memory might not be their "bag" (Hasler, 1966). Along these lines, there is evidence (Hogan, Kleist, and Hutchings, 1970) that the PRE appears in Siamese fighting fish with food rewards, but not with the reward of a visual conspecific male. This might be due to the existence of different learning capacities in different systems. At the least, *it would seem that before a capacity is denied to a species, it be tested for this capacity in those types of situations where its existence would have the greatest survival value.*

Habit reversal might be valuable to some fish in situations where the locale or availability of food varies cyclically. If food appears in abundance at particular places at particular times, then the presence of food yesterday at site Y is a good predictor of its presence today, while if the food was absent yesterday, it will almost certainly be absent today. Habit-reversal abilities here might aid the fish to abandon quickly a depleted area, but to return rapidly to it once it was discovered that food was again available. Simple seminaturalistic experiments of this type could easily be conducted. The regular tidal rhythms might also provide natural environmental stimuli that would foster habit reversal capabilities.

It is, of course, also quite possible that no fish possess any habit reversal capabilities. The data gathered by Gonzalez, Bitterman (1964, 1968), and Mackintosh (1965) suggest some interesting phylogenetic generalizations about learning capacities. Since the laboratory situations used to study rats and other mammals are often not ideally suited to *their* natural behavior, in the same way as the fish apparatus is not, it *is* interesting that the mammals show greater plasticity in these "unnatural" situations. One possible explanation for this, offered by Bitterman (1964), is that the rat possesses certain "higher" learning abilities that the fish studied do not. Another possibility is that rats (and

---

[3] It is not necessary to justify this work on the grounds that it leads to a meaningful description of the capabilities of a species or group, or of the evolution of behavior. In the hands of Bitterman, Gonzalez, and their colleagues and Mackintosh (1965) differences of the sort described have been very useful in analyzing the component abilities or processes in various types of learning tasks. It has led to potentially important insights into the nature of the PRE (Gonzalez and Bitterman, 1969) and attention (Mackintosh, 1965), for example. However, insofar as the work is considered comparative psychology, it must also be considered in the framework we are presenting.

probably most mammals) are "generalists," compared to most of the other vertebrates. That is, various specialized learning abilities, restricted to particular situations in other groups, have become more generally available in mammals and can be manifested in a wider variety of situations. Specialization across functional systems, though amply documented in the rat, may be much *less* apparent in the mammals than in other groups. Since psychologists have concentrated on mammalian behavior, this type of specificity may have eluded them.

The existence of situation-specific learning adaptations adds a new dimension to speculation about the evolution of intelligence. For instance, we can now consider the question; to what extent are what we call new capacities really new, and to what extent are they old ones reapplied or made more accessible? The "best" examples of learning and memory in the inframamalians are quite impressive. It may be that the "higher" abilities of the mammals are, at least to some extent, a broadened application of these, an "emancipation," as it were, to borrow a word from the ethologists, of a capacity from its original tight motivational system.

Acceptance of the notion of situation-specific capacities, or adaptive specializations, significantly widens the scope of phenomena to be included in a psychology of learning. In the past, psychologists have tended to use adherence to the conventional laws of learning as a criterion for classifying a behavior as learned, thus conveniently defining away many troubling naturalistic examples. The consequence has been rather systematic inattention to learning in nature. We can only speculate as to how many "general laws" of learning would require revision if more attention were given to such "unusual" examples of adaptive plasticity as the remarkable navigation abilities of bees (von Frisch, 1967), adaptation to displaced vision (Harris, 1965) or the development of bird song (Marler, 1970). [See Thorpe (1963), Gleitman and Rozin (1971), or Rozin and Kalat (1971) for further examples]. It would certainly seem that most learning that occurs in the world occurs under natural conditions. Furthermore, there is little justification for a bias which assumes that a possibly "plastic" behavior is innate until learning is proved. Given that a species has demonstrated learning abilities in one situation, there is no a priori reason to assume that it is unlikely to use learning abilities to solve problems in another situation.[4] A learned solution to a problem is not inherently more complex or sophisticated than a preprogrammed solution. The determining factors must be which solution is more efficient and which can evolve or develop more easily.

Adaptive Specialization and Cognitive Functions

It follows from the point of view presented here that an organism may have a capacity that manifests itself only in a small number of the total possible

---

[4] An interesting question concerns specific hunger for sodium, which appears to be innate in rats. Why, one might ask, should there be an innate mechanism for this specific hunger, when a learning ability exists which is adequate for other deficiencies? Two possible reasons have been suggested (Rodgers, 1967): (1) The great importance of sodium requires a more reliable, faster method of sodium detection; and (2) it is possible that the initial effects of sodium ingestion may be aversive to a sodium-deficient animal.

situations in which an experimenter might test for it. Such a "dissociation" may also be seen in the precocious development of language in humans. The remarkable linguistic abilities of young children seem to contrast sharply with their minimal conceptual capacities. Children who can form passive-negative sentences and create countless novel sentences that imply sophisticated cognitive structures show only the slightest traces of the elements of logic and symbol manipulation in some other situations. Partly for this reason, language has been described as a highly species-specific, "prestructured" system (Lenneberg, 1967).

The precocity of spoken language acquisition stands in contrast to the considerable difficulty often faced by children in the acquisition of reading. One might inquire as to why reading seems so much more difficult than speech. From our position, with its adaptive orientation, we would immediately note that reading is a relatively new acquisition of our species. Writing has been around for approximately 5000 years, and until this century, only a tiny portion of the population learned to read. In contrast to speech, which is associated with many impressive adaptations in the auditory system and brain, reading is new, and there has probably been little (or no) natural selection to facilitate this capacity or skill, which has come to be so critically important. The problem of learning to read is probably enhanced by the use of an alphabetic (phonemic) system, which, as far as we know, was invented only once (Gelb, 1963), and whose success is almost certainly due to its total long-term efficiency rather than accessibility or ease in initial learning.

Alphabets map into the sound pattern of language at the level of the phoneme. There is good reason to believe that phonemes are prime examples of highly abstract and inaccessible "concepts," specifically adapted to the language-speech system, but not necessarily easily available for use by other systems. Although there is evidence for the reality of the phoneme at some levels (Liberman, Cooper, Shankweiler, and Studdert-Kennedy, 1967), this unit is extremely difficult to define or comprehend. The work of Liberman and his colleagues (Liberman, Cooper, Shankweiler, and Studdert-Kennedy, 1967; Liberman, 1970) makes it clear how abstract the phoneme, is, since (1) many phonemes cannot be pronounced in isolation, and (2) the sound stream of speech cannot be segmented into successive units corresponding to phonemes. If we think of the phoneme as a specific adaptation in the auditory-speech-language area, relatively inaccessible to other systems, then a writing system which maps into language at this level might run into difficulty.

If the "inaccessibility" of the phoneme is a critical problem in reading, then children with serious reading backwardness should be able to learn to read if instruction is based on more natural or accessible units, such as words (morphemes) or syllables, which retain their identity in the sound stream. This has been demonstrated. Rozin, Poritsky, and Sotsky (1971) trained eight children who had failed to learn the elements of reading by the middle of the second grade, to read (in English) Chinese orthography, which maps into language at the morphemic level. Children were taught the appropriate English-word translation for 30 different Chinese characters and were capable of reading sentences and stories composed from this material with some fluency and comprehension (Fig. 9). Significant mastery of the material occurred with

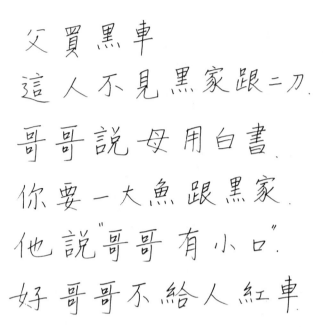

FIG. 9 Sample of Chinese material used in final test with disabled readers. The six sentences include all 30 symbols taught. The sentences read (from left to right, top to bottom): FATHER BUYS BLACK HOUSE. THIS MAN DOESN'T (NOT) SEE BLACK HOUSE AND TWO KNIVES. BROTHER SAYS MOTHER USES WHITE BOOK. YOU WANT ONE BIG FISH AND BLACK HOUSE. HE SAYS "BROTHER HAS SMALL MOUTH." GOOD BROTHER DOESN'T (NOT) GIVE MAN RED CAR. Eight subjects made a mean number of three errors on this 40-item test. The four subjects who were timed took a mean time of 1 minute 40 seconds to complete this task. (Rozin, Poritsky, and Sotsky, 1971.)

2½–5½ hours of tutoring, in children who had failed to learn the elementary phonetic principles of the English alphabetic system in 1½ years. Similarly, Gleitman and Rozin (1972), using more natural (pronounceable) syllable units instead of phonemes, have obtained some initial success in teaching English reading to children with a poor prognosis for reading acquisition. It may be useful to conceive a reading instruction as a recapitulation of the history of writing, beginning with symbols mapping into the morphemic level (logographs), and progressing through larger more accessible acoustic units, such as syllables, to phonemes (alphabetic units).

Another parallel to our point of view appears in the concept of decalage in the developmental psychology of Jean Piaget. He notes that at particular points in development, a cognitive structure may be applied in one situation but not another. With subsequent development, the cognitive structure becomes available in a wider variety of situations (Flavell, 1963, pp. 21–24.) For example, in the Piagetian scheme, both mass and weight conservation depend on the same cognitive structure, yet weight is conserved about 2 years after mass. We see a parallel to these ontogenetic phenomena in our suggestions about the phylogeny of intelligence. In both cases, a capacity is originally manifested in a narrow range of situations, and later in evolution or development becomes more generally available.

CONCLUSION

Psychologists have studied learning in a narrowly defined and rather arbitrary set of conditions. We have no assurance that the principles so derived are of general validity. In fact, by analogy with other biological systems we would expect a great variety of adaptive specializations in learning and memory. It remains debatable whether these specializations should be regarded as quantitative variations on basic laws of learning, or, in some cases, as qualitative differences. In either case, it is necessary for us to broaden our horizons beyond the limitations of the traditional learning laboratory. Learning and memory should be studied within an adaptive-evolutionary context.

References

Barnett, S. A. *The rat. A study in behaviour.* London: Methuen, 1963.

Bitterman, M. E. The evolution of intelligence. *Scientific American*, 1964, *212*, 92—100.

Bitterman, M. E. Comparative studies of learning in the fish. In D. J. Ingle (Ed.), *The central nervous system and fish behavior.* Chicago: University of Chicago Press, 1968. Pp. 257—270.

Bitterman, M. E.. Wodinsky, J., & Candland, D. K. Some comparative psychology. *American Journal of Psychology*, 1958, *71*, 94—110.

Braveman, N., & Capretta, P. J. The relative effectiveness of two experimental techniques for the modification of food preferences in rats. *Proceedings of the 73rd Annual Convention of the American Psychological Association*, 1965, *1*, 129—130.

Brower, L. P. Ecological chemistry. *Scientific American*, 1969, *220*, 22—29.

Campbell, C. Development of specific preferences in thiamine-deficient rats: Evidence against mediation by after-tastes. Unpublished master's thesis, library of the University of Illinois at Chicago Circle, 1969.

Capretta, P. J. An experimental modification of food preference in chickens. *Journal of Comparative and Physiological Psychology*, 1961, *54*, 238—242.

Chitty, D., & Southern, H. N. *Control of rats and mice.* Oxford: Clarendon Press, 1954.

Flavell, J. H. *The developmental psychology of Jean Piaget.* Princeton, N. J.: Van Nostrand, 1963.

von Frisch, K. *The dance language and orientation of bees.* Cambridge, Mass.: Belknap Press of Harvard University Press, 1967.

Galef, B. G. Aggression and timidity: Responses to novelty in feral Norway rats. *Journal of Comparative and Physiological Psychology*, 1970a, *70*, 370—381.

Galef, B. G. Social effects in the weaning of domestic rat pups. *Journal of Comparative and Physiological Psychology*, 1971, *75*, 358—362.

Galef, B. G., & Clark, M. M. Social factors in the poison avoidance and feeding behavior of wild and domestic rat pups. *Journal of Comparative and Physiological Psychology*, 1971, *75*, 341—357.

Garcia, J., Ervin, F. R., & Koelling, R. A. Learning with prolonged delay of reinforcement. *Psychonomic Science*, 1966, *5*, 121—122.

Garcia, J., Ervin, F. R., Yorke, C. H., & Koelling, R. A. Conditioning with delayed vitamin injection. *Science*, 1967, *155*, 716—718.

Garcia, J., Kimeldorf, D. J., & Hunt, E. L. The use of ionizing radiation as a motivating stimulus. *Psychological Review*, 1961, *68*, 383—385.

Garcia, J., & Koelling, R. A. Relation of cue to consequence in avoidance learning. *Psychonomic Science*, 1966, *4*, 123—124.

Garcia, J., Kovner, R., & Green, K. F. Cue properties vs. palatability of flavors in avoidance learning. *Psychonomic Science*, 1970, *20*, 313—314.

Garcia, J., McGowan, B. K., Ervin, F. R., & Koelling, R. A. Cues: Their relative effectiveness as a function of the reinforcer. *Science*, 1968, *160*, 794—975.

Gelb, I. J. *A study of writing*. Chicago: University of Chicago Press, 1963.

Gibson, J. J. *The senses considered as perceptual systems*. Boston: Houghton Mifflin, 1966.

Gleitman, H., & Rozin, P. Learning and memory. In Hoar and Randall (Eds.), *Fish physiology*. New York: Academic Press, 1971. Pp. 191—278.

Gleitman, L., & Rozin, P. Teaching reading by use of a syllabary. (Manuscript in preparation.)

Gonzalez, R. C., & Bitterman, M. E. The spaced-trials PRE as a function of contrast. *Journal of Comparative and Physiological Psychology*, 1969, *67*, 94—103.

Harper, A. E. Effects of dietary protein content and amino acid pattern on food intake and preference. In C. F. Code & W. Heidel (Eds.), *Handbook of physiology*, Alimentary Canal Vol. 1, Section 6, Chapter 29. Washington, D. C.: American Physiological Society, 1967, Pp. 399—410.

Harris, C. S. Perceptual adaptation to inverted, reversed, and displaced vision. *Psychological Review*, 1965, *72*, 419—444.

Harris, L. J., Clay, J., Hargreaves, F., & Ward, A. Appetite and choice of diet. The ability of the vitamin B deficient rat to discriminate between diets containing and lacking the vitamin. *Proceedings of the Royal Society, London*, Series B., 1933, *113*, 161—190.

Hasler, A. D. *Underwater guideposts*. Homing of salmon. Madison, Wisconsin: University of Wisconsin Press, 1966.

Hogan, J. A., Kleist, S., & Hutchings, C. S. L. Display and food as reinforcers in the Siamese fighting fish (*Betta splendens*). *Journal of Comparative and Physiological Psychology*, 1970, *70*, 351—357.

Jennings, H. S. *Behavior of the lower organisms*. New York: Columbia University Press, 1906.

Kalat, J. W., & Rozin, P. "Salience:" A factor which can override temporal contiguity in taste-aversion learning. *Journal of Comparative and Physiological Psychology*, 1970, *71*, 192—197.

Kalat, J., & Rozin, P. The role of interference in taste-aversion learning. *Journal of Comparative and Physiological Psychology*, 1971, *77*, 53—58.

Kalat, J., & Rozin, P. Learned safety as an explanation for taste-aversion delay of reinforcement gradients. *Journal of Comparative and Physiological Psychology, in press*.

Kimble, G. A. *Hilgard and Marquis' conditioning and learning*. New York: Appleton-Century-Crofts, 1961.

Kohler, W. *Gestalt Psychology*. New York: Liveright, 1947.

Lashley, K. S. Persistent problems in the evolution of mind. *Quarterly Review of Biology*, 1949, *24*, 28—42.

Lenneberg, E. *Biological foundations of language*. New York: John Wiley & Sons, Inc., 1967.

Lettvin, J. Y., Maturana, H. R., McCulloch, W. W., & Pitts, W. H. What the frog's eye tells the frog's brain. *Proceedings of the Institute of Radio Engineers*, 1959, *47*, 1940—1951.

Liberman, A., Cooper, F. S., Shankweiler, D. P. & Studdert-Kennedy, M. Perception of the speech code. *Psychological Review*, 1967, *74*, 431—461.

Lorenz, K. Companionship in bird life: Fellow members of the species as releasers of social behavior. In C. H. Schiller (Ed.), *Instinctive behavior*. New York: International Universities Press, 1957. Pp. 83—128.

Lorenz, K. *Evolution and modification of behavior*. Chicago: University of Chicago Press, 1965.

Mackintosh, N. J. Selective attention in animal discrimination learning. *Psychological Bulletin*, 1965, *64*, 124—150.

Marler, P. A comparative approach to vocal learning: Song development in white-crowned sparrows. *Journal of Comparative and Physiological Psychology*, Monograph, 1970, *71*, #2, Part 2, 1—25.

Nachman, M. Taste preferences for sodium salts by adrenalectomized rats. *Journal of Comparative and Physiological Psychology*, 1962, *55*, 1124—1129.

Pavlov, I. *Conditioned reflexes*. Oxford: Oxford University Press, 1927.

Revusky, S. H. Hunger level during food consumption: Effects on subsequent preference. *Psychonomic Science*, 1967, *7*, 109—110.

Revusky, S. H. Aversion to sucrose produced by contingent x-irradiation: Temporal and dosage parameters. *Journal of Comparative and Physiological Psychology*, 1968, *65*, 17—22.

Revusky, S. H. Role of interference in association over a delay. In W. Honig & H. James (Eds.), *2nd Annual Dalhousie Conference on Animal Memory*, 1971, in press.

Revusky, S. H., & Bedarf, E. W. Association of illness with prior ingestion of novel foods. *Science*, 1967, *155*, 219—220.

Revusky, S. H., & Garcia, J. Learned associations over long delays. In C. H. Bower & J. T. Spence (Eds.), *The psychology of learning and motivation: Advances in research and theory, IV*, in press, 1970.

Richter, C. P. Increased salt appetite in adrenalectomized rats. *American Journal of Physiology*, 1936, *115*, 155—161.

Richter, C. P. Total self-regulatory functions in animals and human beings. *Harvey Lectures Series*, 1943, *38*, 63—103.

Richter, C. P. Experimentally produced behavior reactions to food poisoning in wild and domesticated rats. *Annals of the New York Academy of Science*, 1953, *56*, 225—239.

Richter, C. P., Holt, L. E., Jr., & Barelare, B. Jr. Vitamin B_1 craving in rats. *Science*, 1937, *86*, 354—355.

Rodgers, W. L. Specificity of specific hungers. *Journal of Comparative and Physiological Psychology*, 1967, *64*, 49—58.

Rodgers, W., & Rozin, P. Novel food preferences in thiamine-deficient rats. *Journal of Comparative and Physiological Psychology*, 1966, *61*, 1—4.

Roeder, K. *Nerve cells and insect behavior*. Cambridge, Mass.: Harvard University Press, 1963.

Rogers, Q. R., & Harper, A. E. Selection of a solution containing histidine by rats fed a histidine-imbalanced diet. *Journal of Comparative and Physiological Psychology*, 1970, *72*, 66—71.

Rozin, P. Specific hunger for thiamine: Recovery from deficiency and thiamine preference. *Journal of Comparative and Physiological Psychology*, 1965, *59*, 98—101.

Rozin, P. Thiamine specific hunger. In *Handbook of Physiology*, Section 6, Alimentary Canal, Vol. 1, Chapter 30. Washington, D. C.: American Physiological Society, 1967a, 411—431

Rozin, P. Specific aversions as a component of specific hungers. *Journal of Comparative and Physiological Psychology*, 1967b, *64*, 237—242.

Rozin, P. Specific aversions and neophobia as a consequence of vitamin deficiency and/or poisoning in half-wild and domestic rats. *Journal of Comparative and Physiological Psychology*, 1968, *66*, 82—88.

Rozin, P. Adaptive food sampling patterns in vitamin deficient rats. *Journal of Comparative and Physiological Psychology*, 1969a, *69*, 126—132.

Rozin, P. Central or peripheral mediation of learning with long CS-US intervals in the feeding system. *Journal of Comparative and Physiological Psychology*, 1969b, *67*, 421—429.

Rozin, P., & Kalat, J. Specific hungers and poison avoidance as adaptive specializations of learning. *Psychological Review*, 1971, *78*, 459—486.

Rozin, P., Poritsky, S., & Sotsky, R. American children with reading problems can easily learn to read English represented by Chinese characters. *Science*, 1971, *171*, 1264—1267.

Rozin, P., & Rodgers, W. Novel diet preferences in vitamin deficient rats and rats recovered from vitamin deficiencies. *Journal of Comparative and Physiological Psychology*, 1967, *63*, 421—428.

Rozin, P., Wells, C., & Mayer, J. Thiamine specific hunger: Vitamin in water versus vitamin in food. *Journal of Comparative and Physiological Psychology*, 1964, *57*, 78—84.

Rzóska, J. Bait shyness, a study in rat behaviour. *British Journal of Animal Behaviour*, 1953, *1*, 128—135.

Savin, H., & Bever, T. The nonperceptual reality of the phoneme. *Journal of Verbal Learning and Verbal Behavior*, 1970, *9*, 295—302.

Scott, E. M., & Quint, E. Self selection of diet. III. Appetites for B vitamins. *Journal of Nutrition*, 1946, *32*, 285—291.

Scott, E. M., & Verney, E. L. Self selection of diet. VI. The nature of appetites for B vitamins. *Journal of Nutrition*, 1947, *34*, 471—480.

Seligman, M. E. P. On the generality of the laws of learning. *Psychological Review*, 1970, *77*, 406—418.

Smith, J. C., & Roll, D. L. Trace conditioning with x-rays as an aversive stimulus. *Psychonomic Science*, 1967, *9*, 11—12.

Thorndike, E. L. *Animal intelligence*. New York: Hafner, 1911.

Thorpe, W. H. *Learning and instinct in animals*. 2nd edition. London: Metheun, 1963.

Tinbergen, N. *The study of instinct*. Oxford: Clarendon Press, 1951.

Tolman, E. C. *Purposive behavior in animals and men*. New York: Appleton-Century-Crofts, 1932.

Wilcoxon, H. C., Dragoin, W. B., & Kral, P. A. Differential conditioning to visual and gustatory clues in quail and rat: Illness induced aversions. Paper read at Psychonomic Society, 1969.

Wilson, N. E., & Stricker, E. M. Salt seeking behavior in rats following acute sodium deficiency. *Journal of Comparative and Physiological Psychology*, 1970, *72*, 416—420.

Wittlin, W. A., & Brookshire, K. H. Apomorphine-induced conditioned aversion to a novel food. *Psychonomic Science*, 1968, *12*, 217—218.

Zahorik, D. M., & Maier, S. F. Appetitive conditioning with recovery from thiamine deficiency as the unconditioned stimulus. *Psychonomic Science*, 1969, *17*, 309—310.

We have seen so far that the equipotentiality premise does not hold for classical conditioning and that preparedness helps to organize the data. At this point the reader might accuse preparedness of being a merely descriptive device which is theoretically empty. But preparedness can take on a truly explanatory role. Operationally, if an animal is prepared for one contingency he learns about it with minimal input, and if unprepared for another he learns about it painstakingly. Preparedness moves from a description to an explanation if any or all of three empirical questions can be answered affirmatively:

1. Do different physiological properties and neural substrata underlie different regions of the dimension; e.g., does elaborate prewiring mediate prepared associations to ensure their being made, while more plastic structures mediate unprepared associations?

2. Do different cognitive mechanisms underlie different regions of the dimension; e.g., do such processes as conscious expectations, attention, "information-seeking," hypotheses, and beliefs accompany relatively unprepared associations, while "blind" mechanisms not involving cognition accompany prepared associations?

3. Do different laws of learning hold in different regions of the continuum; e.g., is the family of extinction functions for prepared associations relatively flat, the family for rather unprepared ones gradual, and the family for very unprepared ones precipitous? If it were the case that the neurological substrata, cognitive processes, and laws of learning all varied systematically with preparedness operationally defined, we would have a powerful theoretical system.

The next two articles are concerned with the first of the three questions: Are the physiological properties of highly prepared associations different from those of more arbitrary, unprepared associations? Garcia, McGown, and Green (this volume, p. 21) discussed the possibility of highly specialized neuroanatomical structures as mediators of taste aversions. In the next study Roll and Smith find that rats can form taste-poisoning associations even under deep anesthesia. This dramatic finding, which to our knowledge has not been reported in unprepared Pavlovian conditioning, suggests that the physiological basis of prepared associations may be more robust than that for unprepared associations.

8

CONDITIONED TASTE AVERSION
IN ANESTHETIZED RATS

David L. Roll and James C. Smith

Avoidance of a saccharin solution was produced in rats by pairing the injestion of that solution with ionizing radiation. The brief radiation exposure was presented early during a deep surgical anesthesia which lasted for 8 hours. Some aversion was also seen in animals that were not irradiated but only anesthetized. Extinction of the aversion in these control animals was complete after 5 days, while extinction in the irradiated subjects was not observed for the 7 days of the postirradiation preference test.

Avoidance of a normally preferred solution of saccharin-flavored water can be produced in rats by pairing the ingestion of that solution with ionizing radiation (see Kimeldorf and Hunt, 1965). The phenomenon has been described as conditioning, with the saccharin solution serving as the CS and radiation as the US (Garcia et al., 1955; Rozin, 1969). Both stimuli in this situation are somewhat unusual in that they maintain their effectiveness for extended durations after termination of the subject's contact with them. Saccharin-flavored water is an effective CS when presented as much as 6 hours prior to the onset of ionizing irradiation in a trace conditioning design (Smith and Roll, 1967). In addition, a postexposure conditioning design has been used to demonstrate that X-irradiation is effective in motivating avoidance of saccharin when the first contact with the saccharin is made as much as 6 hours after the irradiation period (Scarborough, Whaley, and Rogers, 1964).

In attempting to delineate the sources of radiation-induced motivation, Hunt and Kimeldorf (1967) rejected neural stimulatory effects during irradiation as a critical factor in the conditioning process. They demonstrated that rats irradiated under deep surgical anesthesia and given saccharin to drink immediately thereafter avoided a saccharin solution in a subsequent postexposure test to as great a degree as nonanesthetized subjects.

Supported by Contracts AT-(40-1)-2903 and AT-(40-1)-02690 with the Division of Biology and Medicine, United States Atomic Energy Commission.

In the Hunt and Kimeldorf (1967) experiment, the rats were anesthetized with ethyl ether, a quick-acting anesthetic. They were irradiated while under anesthesia for a total dose of 90 roentgens administered in 90 seconds. Approximately 40 minutes after the initiation of the anesthesia, the S's were allowed to drink the saccharin.

Evidence is quite good that the aversion property of the irradiation does not cease with the offset of the exposure (Scarborough et al., 1964; Smith, 1971). The sampling of saccharin during the 6 hours following a 100-roentgen exposure of X-rays will likely result in a subsequent aversion to the flavored solution. If one wants to demonstrate that this conditioned aversion to taste solutions can occur in rats under anesthesia, the animal should not only be anesthetized during the radiation exposure (as in the Hunt and Kimeldorf study), but maintained in this sleep state for at least 6 hours after the X-ray exposure.

The present experiment was an attempt to demonstrate conditioned aversion to saccharin by presenting the saccharin, anesthetizing the rat for 8 hours, and presenting the brief radiation exposure early during the sleep state.

METHOD

The S's for this experiment were 20 male Sprague-Dawley rats approximately 100 days old. They were individually housed and given free access to food at all times except during irradiation or sham exposures and the 8-hour period of anesthetization.

The X-rays were generated by a GE Maxitron operated at 250 kV, 20 mA through a 3-mm Al filter at a subject to target distance of 47 inches. The S's were irradiated in Plexiglas chambers on a rotating turntable at a dose rate of 30 R/min for a total dose of 100 roentgens.

Two days of habituation training were given prior to the X-ray saccharin pairing. This training consisted of a 20-minute period of access to a water bottle each day following 24 hours of water deprivation. The S's were placed in the Plexiglas boxes and given a sham exposure under the X-ray machine for 200 seconds.

Following a third 24-hour water-deprivation period, the S's received a 20-minute period of access to a 0.1 percent solution (by weight) of saccharin-flavored water. Immediately after the saccharin ingestion period all S's were given an IP injection of chloroprothixene[1] followed 20 minutes later by an IP injection of Nembutal (40 mg/kg). Dosages were determined by the dose-weight chart provided by Rye and Elder (1966). Chloroprothixene is recommended for long-term anesthetization since it aids in central-nervous-system depression, but has a stimulatory effect on the respiratory system. Sixty minutes after the beginning of the saccharin ingestion period the 10 experimental S's were placed in the Plexiglas chambers and irradiated for 200 seconds. The 10 control S's were then placed in the Plexiglas chambers and given a third sham exposure with the noise of the X-ray machine present, but no current applied to produce irradiation. The S's were irradiated or given a sham exposure only when

---

[1] Manufactured by Hoffman-La Roche, Inc., under the trade name Taractan.

they failed to exhibit a corneal reflex and showed no response to a sharp tail pinch.

Following irradiation or sham exposure the S's were returned to individual cages and tested for wakefulness every 10 minutes. When a weak corneal reflex was observed, the subject was given a 0.5-cc injection (IP) of Nembutal. This deep anesthesia was maintained for a minimum of 8 hours. No subjects showed reaction to a sharp tail pinch during the 8-hour period.

A two-bottle preference test between water and the 0.1 percent saccharin solution was started 24 hours after irradiation or sham exposure. The test was continued for 7 days. Each day the bottles were weighed and reversed in position.

RESULTS

Two control S's and one experimental S died under anesthesia. The remainder of the subjects responded to a tail pinch for the first time between 8½ and 10 hours after irradiation. Figure 1 shows the median preference score for the two

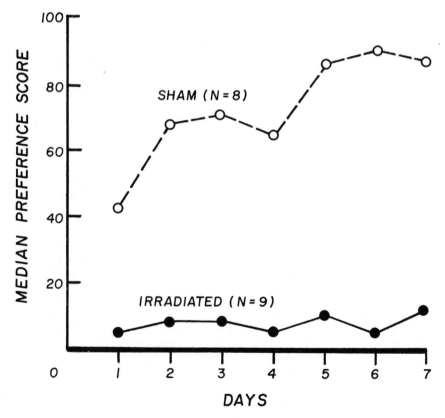

FIG. 1

groups on each day of testing. The preference score represents the percentage of total fluid intake which was saccharin solution. It is obvious that a relatively long-term aversion to the sweetened water was produced in the irradiated S's. The fact that long-term anesthesia alone paired with saccharin ingestion did not produce the aversion was demonstrated by the sham-irradiated S's. A temporary depression in saccharin preference was observed in the sham group on the first day, but normal drinking behavior was observed by test day 5. This recovery was not observed in the irradiated S's.

The Mann-Whitney test for difference in location showed that the preference scores of the two groups were statistically significant ($P < .05$ for each day).

DISCUSSION

The fact that conditioning occurred when S's were under deep anesthesia lends support to Hunt and Kimeldorf (1967) in that humoral changes rather than immediate neural stimulatory effects are responsible for the motivating properties of X-irradiation. This conditioning occurred even when the animals were in this sleep state during the postexposure period, a time when X-irradiation is known to be an effective motivating stimulus as well as during the irradiation period.

Evidence is growing that a humoral change produced by irradiation may be the critical determinant of the motivational properties of that stimulus. In experiments reported by Hunt et al. (1965, 1966, 1968, 1969) sham-irradiated members of a parabiont pair of rats avoided saccharin after the partner was exposed to X-rays. These authors suggested that if a humoral change is a factor in the motivation process, the change must "differentially affect (inform) the central nervous system, either indirectly, as through a peripheral receptor, or directly, perhaps by acting on a differentially sensitive region ('receptor') within the central nervous system" (Hunt and Kimeldorf, 1967, p. 414).

References

Garcia, J., Kimeldorf, D. J., & Koelling, R. A. Conditioned aversion to saccharin resulting from exposure to gamma radiation. *Science*, 1955, *122*, 157–158.

Hunt, E. L., Carroll, H. W., & Kimeldorf, D. J. Humoral mediation of radiation-induced motivation in parabiont rats. *Science*, 1965, *150*, 1747–1748.

Hunt, E. L., Carroll, H. W., & Kimeldorf, D. J. Some characteristics of the humoral motivating factor induced by radiation in parabiont rats. *Radiation Research*, 1966, *27*, 511–512.

Hunt, E. L., Carroll, H. W., & Kimeldorf, D. J. Effects of dose and of partial body exposure on conditioning through a radiation induced humoral factor. *Physiol. & Behav.*, 1968, *3*, 809–813.

Hunt, E. L., & Kimeldorf, D. J. The humoral factor in radiation-induced motivation. *Radiation Research*, 1967, *30*, 404–419.

Hunt, E. L., & Carroll, H. W. Saccharin aversion conditioning with X-irradiation in gastrectomized rats. *Radiation Research*, 1969.

Kimeldorf, D. J., & Hunt, E. L. *Ionizing Radiation: Neural Function and Behavior*. New York: Academic Press, 1965.

Rozin, P. Central or peripheral mediation of learning with long CS-US intervals in the feeding system. *J. Comp. Physiol. Psychol.*, 1969, *67*, 421–429.

Rye, M., & Elder, S. A suggestion concerning the anesthetization of the rat. *Journal of the Experimental Analysis of Behavior*, 1966, *9*, 243–244.

Scarborough, B. B., Whaley, D., & Rogers, J. G. Saccharin avoidance conditioning instigated by X-irradiation in backward conditioning paradigms. *Psychological Reports*, 1964, *14*, 475–481.

Smith, J. C. Radiation: Its detection and its effect on taste preferences. In *Progress in Physiological Psychology IV*, E. Stellar, and J. Sprague, editors. New York: Academic Press, 1971.

Smith, J. C., & Morris, D. D. The effects of atropine sulfate and physostigmine on the conditioned aversion to saccharin solution with X-rays as the unconditioned stimulus. In *Response of the Nervous System to Ionizing Radiation*, T. J. Haley and R. S. Snider, editors, pp. 662–672. Little, Brown & Co., Boston, 1964.

Smith, J. C., & Roll, D. L. Trace conditioning with X-rays as an aversive stimulus. *Psychonomic Science*, 1967, *9*, 11–12.

Marvin Nachman presents a second line of evidence that different physiological substrata may underlie taste-aversion learning than underlie less-prepared conditioning in the next article. Electroconvulsive shock commonly disrupts the learning of such an unprepared contingency as a tone predicting foot shock. Nachman has found, however, that ECS-induced amnesia does not develop for taste aversion. Best and Zuckerman (1971) provide yet another line of evidence: Cortical spreading depression, which disrupts ordinary fear conditioning, also fails to disrupt taste-aversion learning.

9

LIMITED EFFECTS OF ELECTROCONVULSIVE SHOCK ON MEMORY OF TASTE STIMULATION

Marvin Nachman

Rats which drank saccharin for 5, 10, or 30 sec. and were made sick 5 min. later by an injection of LiCl learned to avoid drinking saccharin again. An ECS given immediately after 30 sec. of saccharin drinking had no effect on the learned saccharin aversion while ECS given immediately after 5 or 10 sec. of saccharin drinking produced some amnesic effects. The results were consistent with the idea of a brief temporal gradient for ECS effects although, even at short temporal intervals, amnesic effects occurred in only a small percentage of subjects. The relatively limited effects of ECS were interpreted to be a result of the particularly strong type of learning used. In a second experiment, ECS was found to be ineffective as a US in producing learned taste aversion.

In order to study the temporal effects of ECS on memory storage, most contemporary investigators have used a one-trial learning task in which the learning trial is limited to a few seconds. Since the time of learning can be relatively precisely specified, this procedure permits the study of various learning-ECS intervals and it also avoids the complications due to multiple-trials and multiple-ECS treatments. However, the amount of learning shown by animals after one trial is often difficult to measure and investigators have therefore concentrated on shock conditioning to produce readily measurable and reliable one-trial learning. In recent years, the passive-avoidance form of shock conditioning has been most widely used because this technique has the additional advantage of minimizing the confounding of aversive and amnesic

From *Journal of Comparative and Physiological Psychology*, 73 (1970), 31—37.

This report was supported in part by Special Fellowship 7 F03 MH14939-01A1 from the National Institutes of Health. The author wishes to thank Jacques Le Magnen and the College de France for their gracious hospitality.

effects of ECS since these two effects have opposite influences on the response to be avoided.

These considerable advantages of the one-trial passive-avoidance learning task using shock are greatly offset, however, by the concurrent effects produced by the learning of a conditioned emotional response. A rat receiving a shock in a certain place is likely to "freeze" on subsequent trials and its passive avoidance, i.e., freezing, may be, in part, a result of the CER rather than a discriminated inhibition of a particular response. Spevack and Suboski (1969) and Chorover and Schiller (1965, 1966) have suggested that the amnesic effects of ECS are limited to a brief time interval of several seconds and that the often-reported longer effects of ECS, extending over minutes or hours, are due to the interference of ECS with a CER.

The present experiment was designed to investigate the temporal effects of ECS on a learned taste aversion, a learning task which has many of the same advantages as passive-avoidance conditioning but in addition does not employ shock and does not result in a confounding CER. Rats which drink a distinctive tasting solution and then become sick readily learn to avoid drinking that solution subsequently (Garcia & Ervin, 1968; Nachman, 1963, 1970). A strong learned taste aversion occurs after a single trial, is long lasting, and is extremely reliable. The fact that the aversion is relatively specific to the solution which the animal drank before it became sick suggests that the animal must remember what it drank at the time it became sick. The present experiment, by giving rats an ECS after they drink, and then making the sick, investigated whether the ECS would produce amnesia for the solution which the animal drank.

Preliminary experimentation was first done to determine the range of the temporal gradient of ECS to be explored in greater detail. In this preliminary work, it was established that rats could learn a saccharin aversion if they were made sick with LiCl after drinking saccharin for only a matter of seconds and that if the drinking occurred for 20 sec. or more, ECS did not produce any apparent amnesia. The experiment reported here studied ECS effects, in greater detail, after 5–30 sec. of saccharin drinking.

EXPERIMENT 1

Method

The subjects were 88 male 50-day-old 200–220 gm. Sprague-Dawley rats from the Holtzman Co. They were housed in wire-mesh cages and throughout the experiment received Purina chow ad lib in these home cages. The procedure for producing learned saccharin aversions was almost identical to that previously described (Nachman, 1970). The rats were water deprived, and beginning the next day they received as their sole water supply a daily single-bottle 10-min. drinking test with tap water for 5 days in a wooden, with wire-mesh floor, drinking box, 30 x 17 x 17 cm. The animals were adapted to the drinking boxes for 3–5 min. before each 10-min. test and the tests were started by the raising of a guillotine door. On the second of these 5 days, all subjects were fitted with snap connectors ("Starlet-Dot fasteners") for the administration of ECS. The snap connectors were set in the pinnae under light ether anesthesia.

The rats were randomly assigned to 11 groups of eight rats each. On Day 6, the treatment day, each animal was placed in the wooden drinking box with its ear snaps attached by suspended wires to the ECS apparatus. Lightweight counterbalanced wires were used and, in most cases, the rats ignored the suspended wires. The treatments began after the rats were in the drinking boxes for 30 sec.

The 11 groups were treated as follows in the drinking boxes (see Table 1). Groups 1 and 2, control groups, were simply kept in the boxes for 30 sec. and then removed to their home cages without having had access to fluid. Group 3, another control group, similarly did not have access to fluid but, at the end of 30 sec. in the drinking boxes, they were given an ECS automatically by the experimenter pressing a button, and then returned immediately to their home cages. For Groups 4, 5, and 6, the guillotine door was raised and these groups were allowed to drink a .25% sodium saccharin solution for 5 sec., 10 sec., and 30 sec., respectively. At the end of the specified time, the guillotine door was immediately lowered and the animals were rapidly removed from the drinking boxes (within 10 sec.) and returned to their home cages. Groups 7, 8, and 9 similarly received 5, 10, and 30 sec., respectively, of .25% saccharin, but at the end of these time intervals an ECS was administered by the experimenter pressing a button at the same time as the guillotine door was lowered. The lowering of the guillotine door was included so that if any possible cues arose from the start of the door coming down, they would be the same in Groups 7, 8, and 9 as in Groups 4, 5, and 6.

Group 10 was used to study the effects of ECS delay. This group received 5 sec. of saccharin and this drinking was terminated by the lowering of the guillotine door. Then, after a 25-sec. delay in the wooden box, an ECS was administered. Thus, Group 10 drank for only 5 sec. but received an ECS 30 sec. after the beginning of the drinking.

Special precautions were taken to insure that the drinking-time intervals and ECS delays were accurate. A Grason-Stadler drinkometer was used and wired so that the rat's first lick started a 1/100-sec timer with a sweep second hand. The experimenter watched the timer and, after a little practice, could accurately close the guillotine door and give an ECS at the end of the 5-, 10-, or 30-sec. intervals. Further wiring was arranged to indicate whether any licks had occurred more than .5 sec. after the specified time interval. This event never happened. Because the drinking tests were conducted in wooden boxes, the animals were not seen by the experimenter and all treatments were done without seeing the rat. Amounts drunk in the 5-, 10-, and 30-sec. periods were recorded to the nearest .1 ml. using graduated centrifuge tubes. The mean intake in the 5-, 10-, and 30-sec. periods was .18 ml., 39 ml., and 102 ml., respectively, and there were no significant differences in intake between the ECS and the no-ECS groups.

Rats receiving saccharin for 5, 10, or 30 sec. and then receiving an ECS may have some residual saccharin taste in their mouths as they recover from the convulsion. Thus, if they were to show memory for saccharin drinking, it could conceivably be due to the taste of saccharin after the convulsion rather than to the saccharin drinking before the convulsion. To control for this possibility,

Group 11 was included. Group 11 was placed in the drinking box and, at the end of 30 sec., received an ECS without receiving any access to fluid. In this respect, it was treated exactly the same as Group 3. However, Group 11 was then given a mouth rinse with saccharin in order to give the rats an aftertaste which would be roughly comparable to the aftertaste of rats which had drunk saccharin. This rinse was done as follows: Within a few seconds after the beginning of the convulsion, and as soon as it was possible to open the convulsing rat's mouth, the mouth and tongue were thoroughly rinsed, using a 1-ml. syringe, with 1 ml. of .25% saccharin. Care was taken not to force any fluid down the rat's throat but, at the same time, every attempt was made to thoroughly soak the mouth with the saccharin. As the rat slowly recovered from the convulsion in its home cage, it usually had saccharin solution dripping or frothing at the mouth.

To make the rats sick for the learned saccharin aversion, rats were given a 2% of body weight ip injection of .15 M LiCl. The injections were given 5 min. after the rats had been removed from the drinking boxes and they were simply removed from their home cages, injected, and returned to their home cages. All subjects from Groups 2–11 were injected with LiCl; Group 1 did not receive any injection. Previous work has indicated that control injections with .15 M NaCl are without effect.

The ECS was administered by the passage of 2,500-v. ac through a 45,000 ohm resistor in series with the rat, resulting in approximately 50 mA. The ECS was given for .2 sec. by a Hunter timer and current monitored with an oscilloscope.

The rats received no other fluid on the treatment day apart from the 5, 10, or 30 sec. of saccharin drunk by some of the groups. On each of the next 2 days, Days 7 and 8, all animals again received a 10-min. water test in the drinking boxes. These tests were included to be sure that all groups were fully recovered from the LiCl illness and the ECS effects and that any decreased intake would therefore be attributable to a learned aversion to the saccharin solution.

On Day 9, the test day, each rat was given a 10-min. test with .25% saccharin. In the tests of Days 7-9, the rats did not have any wires attached to their pinnae and the 10-min. tests were timed from the raising of the guillotine door. Amounts drunk were recorded using 25-ml. cylinders, graduated in units of .2 ml.

Results

Table 1 contains the group mean intakes of saccharin on the test day and of water on the day before, and 2 days after, the treatment day.

The 11 groups were very similar in their water intake both before and after the treatment day indicating that the various treatment combinations of sickness, ECS, and drinking of saccharin did not affect the water intake of the next 2 days. On Days 5, 7, and 8 there were no significant differences among groups in water intake ($F = 1.33$, $df = 10/77$, $p > .1$; $F = 1.20$, $df = 10/77$, $p > .1$; $F = .58$, $df = 10/77$, $p > .1$, respectively).

The effects of the various treatments were clearly evident on the 10-min. saccharin-intake test of Day 9 and differences among groups were highly significant ($F = 23.07$, $df = 10/77$, $p < .001$).

TABLE 1   Mean Intake (ml.) of Water on Days 5, 7, and 8 and of .25% Saccharin on Day 9 of 11 Groups Receiving Different Treatments on Day 6

| | Treatments | | | | | | |
| | Drank | | LiCl | Pretreat-ment (Day 5) | Posttreat-ment 1 (Day 7) | Posttreat-ment 2 (Day 8) | Test (Day 9) |
Group	saccharin	ECS	sick				
1	No	No	No	12.3	12.6	13.9	13.1
2	No	No	Yes	13.8	13.2	14.2	13.0
3	No	Yes	Yes	14.1	13.7	14.7	14.9
4	5 sec.	No	Yes	12.3	13.3	14.3	3.8
5	10 sec.	No	Yes	13.1	13.1	13.8	.7
6	30 sec.	No	Yes	12.5	12.9	14.4	1.4
7	5 sec.	Yes	Yes	13.6	12.7	14.4	8.6
8	10 sec.	Yes	Yes	14.3	13.4	15.0	6.3
9	30 sec.	Yes	Yes	13.7	15.2	15.2	1.7
10	5 sec.	Delayed ECS	Yes	13.2	13.5	14.4	8.6
11	No	ECS and saccharin rinse	Yes	14.4	14.9	15.6	16.5

Control Groups 1, 2, and 3 did not differ from each other in saccharin intake of Day 9 ($F = .86$, $df = 2/21$, $p > .1$). All three groups had not received saccharin on the treatment day and the lack of differences among groups on the test day was indicative of the fact that the LiCl sickness or the combination of ECS and LiCl sickness did not have any negative influence on saccharin intake.

In contrast to the control groups, Experimental Groups 4–10, which drank some saccharin before being made sick on the treatment day, all showed clear evidence of saccharin aversion on the test day. Groups 4, 5, and 6, which had drunk saccharin for 5, 10, and 30 sec., respectively, and had not received an ECS, all showed a large degree of saccharin aversion on Day 9 and did not differ significantly from each other in their intake ($F = 1.82$, $df = 2/21$, $p > .1$). The lack of difference in the amount of aversion shown by Groups 4, 5, and 6 is further seen by an examination of the intakes of individual rats. Of the 24 rats in these three groups, 23 showed strong saccharin aversion on Day 9 with a mean intake of 1.3 ml. and a range of 0–4.0 ml. The twenty-fourth rat, in the 5-sec. group (Group 4), showed no saccharin aversion and drank 14.6 ml which inflated the mean of that group to 3.4 ml. from 1.8 ml. without that rat. There is nothing in the data which reveal why that rat did not learn the aversion. It apparently received a typical LiCl injection to make it sick and in 5 sec. had drunk .1 ml. of saccharin which, while low, was an amount drunk by some other rats in the 5-sec. groups. Perhaps the minimal amount drunk was responsible for the lack of learning since in other experiments, using longer drinking periods, learned aversions have always been found to occur.

The saccharin-intake data of Groups 7, 8, and 9 on Day 9 reveal that ECS had an effect on the learned saccharin aversion and that the effect was a function of the amount of saccharin drinking which had occurred prior to the ECS. Groups 7, 8, and 9, which drank saccharin for 5, 10, and 30 sec., respectively, and received an immediate ECS at the end of their drinking, differed significantly in their intake of saccharin on the test day ($F = 3.99$, $df = 2/21$, $p < .05$). The 5-sec. (Group 7) and 10-sec. (Group 8) groups did not differ from each other ($t = .89$, $df = 14$, $p > .1$) but each of these groups showed less of an aversion than the 30-sec. group, Group 9 ($t = 2.46$, $df = 14$, $p < .05$; $t = 3.67$, $df = 14$, $p < .01$, respectively).

The effects of ECS after 5, 10, and 30 sec. of drinking are even more evident by comparing the groups which had an ECS after 5, 10, or 30 sec. of saccharin drinking with those which did not have an ECS after these same drinking times. The 30-sec. groups (Groups 6 and 9) did not differ in their test-day saccharin intake, indicating that ECS after 30 sec. of drinking did not produce amnesia for the saccharin experience ($t = .40$, $df = 14$, $p > .1$). In contrast, the 10-sec. ECS animals (Group 8) showed significantly less saccharin aversion than the 10-sec. no-ECS group (Group 5; $t = 3.14$, $df = 14$, $p < .01$) and, similarly, the 5-sec. ECS rats (Group 7) showed less saccharin aversion than the 5-sec. no-ECS rats (Group 4; $t = 2.12$, $df = 14$, $p < .05$, one-tailed; if the one discrepant rat from Group 4 which did not learn the saccharin aversion is eliminated, the $t = 3.41$, $df = 13$, $p < .01$).

Although the ECS given to Groups 7 and 8 after 5 and 10 sec. of saccharin, respectively, produced some apparent amnesia for the taste of saccharin, it is equally evident that the amount of amnesia was very limited and that both of these groups still showed considerable saccharin aversion, i.e., the 8.6 ml. drunk by Group 7 and the 6.3 ml. drunk by Group 8 were significantly less than the amount drunk by their comparable control, Group 3 ($t = 2.99$, $df = 14$, $p < .01$; $t = 4.04$, $df = 14$, $p < .01$, respectively). Since it is of considerable theoretical interest that relatively little amnesia of saccharin was produced after only 5 or 10 sec. of drinking, it is worth examining individual rats, particularly since in retrograde amnesia studies, medians are often reported instead of means. Of the 24 control animals in Groups 1–3, the lowest saccharin intake on Day 9 was 8.0 ml. Five of the 8 subjects in each of Groups 7 and 8 took less than 8.0 ml. which is clearly indicative of a saccharin aversion and 2 additional rats in Group 8 drank relatively low amounts of 9.4 ml. and 10.0 ml., which, when compared to their water intake, was less than the comparable intake of 22 of the 24 control animals. Thus, it appears probable that only three of the eight rats in the 5-sec. ECS group and one of the eight in the 10-sec. ECS group showed an absence of saccharin aversion on the test day and drank amounts which were comparable to the control groups.

The findings that the 5-sec. ECS rats (Group 7) showed some amnesia and the 30-sec. ECS rats (Group 9) did not show amnesia could have been due either to different amounts of learning which occurred with 5-sec. and 30-sec. saccharin drinking or to the different delay times of ECS administration. The results of Group 10, which drank saccharin for only 5 sec. but received its ECS 30 sec. from the beginning of drinking, clearly indicate that the amount of saccharin drinking before the ECS was the important factor and not the ECS delay time. The mean of 8.6 ml of saccharin drunk by Group 10 was identical to the amount drunk by the 5-sec. ECS animals (Group 7) and was significantly different from the 1.7 ml. drunk by the 30-sec. ECS rats (Group 9; $t = 5.75$, $df = 14$, $p < .001$).

Group 11, the control group which did not drink saccharin but was given a saccharin rinse after the ECS, showed absolutely no indication of any saccharin aversion. All eight rats in this group drank between 11.8 ml. and 19.0 ml. on Day 9 and the mean of 16.5 ml. was actually somewhat higher than the mean of 13.7 ml. drunk by Control Groups 1–3 (t = 2.25, df = 30, p < .05), although this was probably because Group 11 consisted of rats which drank slightly more as evidenced by their higher water-intake scores before and after the treatment.

Discussion

The one-trial learning task used in the present experiment was highly suitable for the study of ECS amnesic effects. There was little variability in the degree to which rats learned the saccharin aversion and drinking periods as brief as 5 sec. were sufficient to produce a strong learned aversion. In addition, the data of Group 11 showed that the "aftertaste" of saccharin given by mouth rinse following an ECS was not sufficient by itself to produce a learned aversion.

The major experimental results showed that ECS exerted very limited amnesic effects on the memory of saccharin drinking and are in contrast to the large majority of studies which have found significant amnesic effects at various temporal intervals, often extending over many minutes or hours. Even in those studies which have reported relatively short temporal gradients, significant ECS amnesic effects have been found at delay times ranging from 20 sec. to several minutes (Pfingst & King, 1969; Pinel, 1969; Quartermain, Paolino, & Banuazizi, 1968; Quartermain, Paolino, & Miller, 1965; Spevack & Suboski, 1969; Suboski, Black, Litner, Greenner, & Spevack, 1969).

In the present experiment, there was no evidence of any amnesic effect of ECS after 30 sec. of saccharin drinking, and, in pilot work, there was a similar lack of ECS effect after 20 sec. of drinking. More important, perhaps, is the fact that immediate ECS produced amnesia in only a small percentage of the animals that drank saccharin for as little as 5 or 10 sec. It would be of interest to know whether rats would learn a saccharin aversion with drinking times less than 5 sec. and whether ECS would produce higher amnesia rates after the shorter drinking times. The results of the present study are in agreement with those of Chorover and Schiller (1965) who also found that the amnesic effects of ECS were limited to a 10-sec. delay period and that, at 5- and 10-sec. delays, ECS produced only a partial amnesic effect. Sprott and Waller (1966) used a very well-learned operant task and similarly found, using repeated treatments with two rats, that ECS was effective within 9 sec. of a grid shock but not after 12.5 sec.

In recent years, the experimental work with ECS has tended to support the findings of a short temporal gradient for ECS amnesic effects (Spevack & Suboski, 1969). While the present results are in agreement with this conclusion, it should also be emphasized that in the present experiment the majority of rats which drank for 5 or 10 sec. and then received an immediate ECS showed no evidence of amnesia for the drinking. Any theory which suggests that ECS interferes with "neural consolidation" must either postulate an extremely short gradient of a few seconds or in some way account for numerous "exceptions."

It is not clear why the memory of taste stimulation should be more resistant to ECS-induced amnesia than are other learning tasks, although it seems reasonable to assume that it may be related to the fact that learning involving taste stimulation and sickness occurs very readily and is extremely durable. In the course of various experiments in the laboratory, the present author has tested over 500 rats which have had a single several-minute drinking trial with any of several solutions and then been made sick with LiCl. In every case, without exception, a strong learned aversion has been found to occur and such learned aversions have also been found to persist for months.

The data of Groups 7, 9, and 10 provide some support for the idea that the amount of learning may influence the ECS amnesic effect and, under some conditions, may be relatively more important than the ECS delay times. Groups 7 and 9 which each drank saccharin for 5 sec. did not differ in their amount of learned aversion although they had been given ECS at different delays. In contrast, Groups 9 and 10, which differed in the amount of time they were allowed to drink saccharin, differed in their amount of aversion, even though ECS was given at the same time for both groups. The fact that longer drinking times produce greater resistance to ECS-induced amnesia appears to be highly similar to results which show that the amount of ECS-induced amnesia is a function of the duration (Chorover & Schiller, 1965) or strength (Ray & Bivens, 1968) of a footshock in passive-avoidance tasks.

EXPERIMENT 2

Experiment 2 was a brief investigation of whether an ECS given after saccharin drinking would produce any learned aversion comparable to that produced by a LiCl injection given after saccharin drinking. In this experiment, the interest was in any possible sickness-like effects of ECS rather than in any potential amnesic effects. Therefore, the design used was to allow rats to learn by drinking saccharin for 10 min. before an ECS treatment.

Method

The procedure of Experiment 2 was a direct continuation of Experiment 1. The subjects used were the 24 control rats of Groups 1, 2, and 3 which had not previously tasted saccharin. The 10-min. saccharin test of Day 9 which concluded Experiment 1 was used as the treatment day of Experiment 2 as follows. Immediately following the 10-min. saccharin test of Day 9, eight rats (four from Group 1 and four from Group 2, randomly chosen) became Group 12 and were given an ECS. The ECS was administered within 15 sec. of the end of the 10-min. saccharin tests; rats were removed from the drinking boxes, ear-snap wires were attached, and the ECS given while the rats were held by the experimenter. The other eight rats from Groups 1 and 2 became Group 13 and, at the end of the 10-min. test of Day 9, these animals were returned to their home cages and then, 5 min. later, given a 2% of body weight ip injection of .15 M LiCl. The eight rats, formerly of Group 3, all became Group 14, a control group, since these rats had an ECS in Experiment 1 and it was desirable to avoid the complications of giving some of them a second ECS treatment. Group 14 was returned to their home cages after the 10-min. saccharin test of Day 9. On Days 10 and 11, all rats received a 10-min. water test and on Day 12, a 10-min. saccharin test.

Results and Discussion

The mean intake of Groups 12, 13, and 14 appears in Table 2. The results are very clear in indicating that ECS as a treatment does not produce an aversion. All rats of Group 13, given LiCl, avoided saccharin with a mean intake of .3 ml. of a range of 0—.8 ml. and none of the rats of Group 12, given an ECS, showed any signs of saccharin aversion. Group 12 had a mean intake of 14.1 ml. and a range of 10.2—16.0 ml. Group 14, however, did drink more saccharin than Group 12 on Day 12 ($t = 2.91$, $df = 14$, $p < .05$) which may have been due to initial differences in saccharin intake since the change in saccharin intake from Day 9 to Day 12 was not significantly different between the two groups ($t = 1.02$, $df = 14$, $p > .10$).

The results give additional support to the idea that learned taste aversions are a result of associations formed between gustatory stimuli and consequent visceral sickness effects (Garcia & Ervin, 1968).

TABLE 2   Mean 10-Min. Intake (ml.) of .25% Saccharin on Days 9 and 12 and of Water on Days 10 and 11 of Groups Given ECS, LiCl, or No Treatment Following the 10-Min. Saccharin Intake of Day 9

Group	Treatment	Pretreatment (Day 9)	Posttreatment 1 (Day 10)	Posttreatment 2 (Day 11)	Test (Day 12)
12	ECS	13.8	15.3	14.0	14.1
13	LiCl	12.3	14.1	13.2	0.3
14	None	14.9	14.2	13.3	16.9

References

Chorover, S. L., & Schiller, P. H. Short-term retrograde amnesia (RA) in rats. *Journal of Comparative and Physiological Psychology*, 1965, *59*, 73—78.

Chorover, S. L., & Schiller, P. H. Reexamination of prolonged retrograde amnesia in one-trial learning. *Journal of Comparative and Physiological Psychology*, 1966, *61*, 34—41.

Garcia, J., & Ervin, F. R. Gustatory-visceral and telereceptor-cutaneous conditioning—adaptation in internal and external milieus. *Communications in Behavioral Biology*, 1968, *1*, 389—415.

Nachman, M. Learned aversion to the taste of lithium chloride and generalization to other salts. *Journal of Comparative and Physiological Psychology*, 1963, *56*, 343—349.

Nachman, M. Learned taste and temperature aversions due to lithium chloride sickness after temporal delays. *Journal of Comparative and Physiological Psychology*, 1970, *73*, 22—30.

Pfingst, B. E., & King, R. A. Effects of posttraining electroconvulsive shock on retention-test performance involving choice. *Journal of Comparative and Physiological Psychclogy*, 1969, *68*, 645—649.

Pinel, J. P. J. A short gradient of ECS-produced amnesia in a one-trial appetitive learning situation. *Journal of Comparative and Physiological Psychology*, 1969, *68*, 650—655.

Quartermain, D., Paolino, R. M., & Banuazizi, A. Effect of electroconvulsive shock on retention of a one-trial-approach and a one-trial-avoidance response in a T-maze. *Communications in Behavioral Biology*, 1968, *2*, 121—127.

Quartermain, D., Paolino, R. M., & Miller, N. E. A brief temporal gradient of retrograde amnesia independent of situational change. *Science*, 1965, *169*, 1116—1118.

Ray, O. A., & Bivens, L. W. Reinforcement magnitude as a determinant of performance decrement after electroconvulsive shock. *Science*, 1968, *160*, 330—332.

Spevack, A. A. & Suboski, M. D. Retrograde amnesic effects of electroconvulsive shock on learned responses. *Psychological Bulletin*, 1969, *72*, 66—76.

Sprott, R. L., & Waller, M. B. The effects of electroconvulsive shock on the action of a reinforcing stimulus. *Journal of the Experimental Analysis of Behavior*, 1966, *9*, 663—669.

Suboski, M. D., Black, M., Litner, J., Greenner, R. T., & Spevak, A. A. Long and short-term effects of ECS following one-trial discriminated avoidance conditioning. *Neuropsychologia*, 1969, *9*, 349—356.

So we have some evidence that the physiology of prepared classical conditioning may differ from that of unprepared conditioning. In the last ten years there has been a resurgence of interest in cognitive mechanisms in learning, in particular information seeking and attention. Beginning with the provocative work of David Egger and Neal Miller (1962) on information and redundancy in secondary reinforcment, this research demonstrates that the amount of information that a CS provides about the occurrence of a US determines the degree of conditioning. Over the last five years, Leo Kamin (1969), and Robert Rescorla and Alan Wagner (1972), have extended and systematized these findings. One fundamental and consistent result is that redundant CS's which do not give the animal any more information about the US than he already has show little or no conditioning. These findings, however, are based on research using relatively arbitrary CS's and US's such as tones and foot shocks, or lights and puffs of air to the eye. James Kalat and Paul Rozin treat the cognitive question in the next reading and suggest a primitive mechanism behind taste-illness conditioning, one which does not involve information-seeking.[1] They find that taste-nausea conditioning occurs even when the CS does not provide new information. This finding suggests that highly prepared associations are not readily blocked by informational factors, and even helps to illuminate why sauce Béarnaise came to taste awful to me even though I knew that the stomach flu and not the sauce had caused my illness.

[1] The readings by Lennenberg, by Furth and Piaget, and by Garcia, Kovner, and Green will also consider cognitive correlates of preparedness. The third question, that of different laws of learning, will be treated in connection with the Williams and Williams, Stimbert, and Breland and Breland readings in the next section of this volume.

10

YOU CAN LEAD A RAT TO POISON
BUT YOU CAN'T MAKE HIM THINK

James W. Kalat and Paul Rozin

Rats were given an ambiguous experience: they drank two solutions prior to a single poisoning. The question was: Could the rats use their previous or subsequent experience with one of the solutions to decrease the ambiguity, and thereby raise or lower their aversion to the other solution? The rats consistently failed to do so. This suggests that taste-aversion learning is not a relatively advanced or "cognitive" type of learning, and that it may in fact be a relatively primitive, noncognitive type.

We are interested in considering whether taste-aversion learning represents a highly advanced "cognitive" form of learning or a relatively "primitive" one. On one hand, the long delays with which taste aversions can be learned suggest a more "complex" type of learning, with some type of "cognitive" mediation of the long delays. On the other hand, it is possible that taste-aversion learning represents what we might call a "more primitive" type of learning (Seligman, 1970; Rozin and Kalat, 1971). We mean this in the sense of phylogeny and in the sense of relative absence of "higher," "cognitive," "information seeking," or cerebral influences. In the phylogenetic sense, we suggest that taste aversion and related types of learning are probably widespread, at least among the vertebrates. Selection of nutritious food and avoidance of harmful foods is of great importance to almost all animals. Except for those species whose diet is limited to so few reliably safe foods that their choices could feasibly be programmed genetically, learning must play a significant role in the selection of foods. In the second ("less cognitive") sense, there is supporting evidence from human anecdotal reports that acquired food aversions are not affected by conscious knowledge that the food is not toxic. Furthermore, taste-aversion learning can occur even if the poison is administered to a rat which is under anesthesia at the

Supported by grant from NSF-GB 8013. We thank Martin E. P. Seligman for advice on the manuscript. J. W. K. was supported by a National Institutes of Health Training Grant.

time, and kept under anesthesia for several hours after the poisoning (Berger, 1972; Roll & Smith, 1972). It can also occur while the cerebral cortex is inactivated by cortical spreading depression (Best and Zuckerman, 1971). Evidently the learning takes place in subcortical areas not fully suppressed by the anesthetic.

In the first experiment of this paper, we test the ability of the rat to reconsider an ambiguous experience in light of a *subsequent* experience. So far as we know, this ability has not been demonstrated for the rat in any other form of learning; if it were confirmed it would suggest a complex, "insightful" mechanism for taste-aversion learning. In the second experiment we test the rat's ability to unconfound an ambiguous experience in light of a *previous* experience—an ability which has already been demonstrated in other types of learning [Kamin's (1969) blocking effect]. Negative findings in this experiment would imply that taste-aversion learning differs from other types of learning in the direction of being *less* "complex."

PART ONE: "RETROSPECTION"

Rats were poisoned after drinking two solutions. Subsequently one group underwent extinction on one of the solutions. The question was whether this subsequent extinction would retrospectively produce a reevaluation of the original poisoning, leading to the "conclusion" that "it must have been the other solution that made me sick." If so, the extinction group should show more aversion to the test solution.

Method

Two versions of this experiment, "1A" and "1B," differing only slightly, were conducted at separate times and with different rats. In both versions, subjects were 17 female white rats, obtained from Charles River Laboratories. They had previously been used in an experiment in which they were poisoned once after drinking two familiar solutions, 1 percent vanilla and 5 percent casein hydrolysate; experimental groups in the present experiments were balanced for previous experience. In experiment 1A rats were of age 65–70 days; in 1B ages were about 80 days.

For all experiments in this paper, rats were kept in individual wire-mesh cages (Wahmann LC-75/A) having two openings for insertion of 30-ml graduated "Richter" tubes (±0.5 ml). Prior to each experiment, each rat was given 20 min access to tap water once a day until all rats were consistently drinking from the tube within seconds after it was presented. No other water was ever available. The rats had ad lib access to Purina Laboratory Chow at all times. For further details of general procedure, see Kalat & Rozin (1970).

On the first day of experiment 1A, all rats were presented with a 0.15 M solution of NaCl in tap water for 2½ min. Fifteen min later,[1] the rats were presented with a 10 percent (w/w) sucrose solution, also for 2½ min. Another

---

[1] Throughout this paper, "x min later" means X min after presentation of the solution, not after its removal.

15 min later the rats were intubated with 6 ml of 0.15 M LiCl, which has previously been found to produce reliable learned aversions. Experiment 1B followed the same procedure, except that the first solution was 1 percent (w/w) Food Club Instant Coffee, and the second solution was 0.15 M NaCl.

In experiment 1A, the "sucrose-extinction" group (N = 9) received the sucrose solution three times, 20 min each time, in the two days following poisoning.[2] The control group (N = 8) received water each time. Neither group was poisoned. On the fourth day both groups received water for 20 min. On the fifth day both groups were presented with two tubes simultaneously, one containing 0.15 M NaCl, the other containing water, for 20 min. Intakes of each solution were recorded to the nearest 0.15 ml.

In experiment 1B, on the day following poisoning all rats received the NaCl solution for 2½ min, during which time they drank a mean of 2.9 ml. The "NaCl-extinction" group (N = 8) was not poisoned; the "NaCl-re-poison" group (N = 9) was intubated with LiCl solution 15 min after drinking. On the third day both groups received water for 20 min. On the fourth day both groups were presented with two tubes simultaneously, one containing 1 percent coffee solution, the other containing water, for 20 min. Intakes were again recorded to the nearest 0.5 ml.

Results

A "retrospection" hypothesis would predict that extinction on one of the two solutions which preceded poisoning would cause an increase in aversion to the other, while a second poisoning on one solution (as in experiment 1B) should decrease aversion to the other. Thus in both experiments the extinction group should drink less of the test solution (show more aversion) than the other group. Table 1 presents the median intakes for the 20-min presentation on the test day. In both experiments the differences between the two groups were very small and did not approach statistical significance.[3] Apparently you can lead a rat to poison, but you can't make it *think*.

TABLE 1   Results of Part 1

Expt.	Group	Test Soln.	Median volume of Test soln. in ml	Median volume water in ml
1A	Sucrose-extinction	NaCl	1	10
	Control	NaCl	1.25	9.5
1B	NaCl-extinction	Coffee	0.5	11.75
	NaCl-re-poison	Coffee	1	10

[2] This group's intake of sucrose increased from a mean of 7.1 ml on the first post-poisoning presentation to 18.8 ml on the third, indicating that considerable extinction had occurred.

[3] Throughout this paper, all statements regarding statistical significance refer to a two-tail Mann-Whitney U-test.

PART TWO: "BLOCKING"

When rats drank two solutions prior to poisoning, the learned aversiveness of one of those solutions was not measurably affected by subsequent experience with the other solution. The question arises: Would there be any effect from *previous* experience with the other solution? That is, the retrospection design *assumed* that using the paradigm A-B-poison, the aversion to A would be greater if B had previously been experienced without negative consequences or less if B had been previously followed by poison. Kamin (1969) has explored this question in classical conditioning with shocks as the US. He finds that if CS_1 is paired many times with shock, and then a compound of CS_1 and CS_2 is paired with shock, rats acquire only a small conditioned response to CS_2. In some manner the CS_1 has protected the CS_2 from conditioning. If an analogous principle applies in taste-aversion learning, it would be expected that if poisoning follows two solutions, one of which had already become aversive by association with poisoning, the other solution should not become very aversive.

Method

Four versions of this experiment were conducted (2A-2D). Subjects were experimentally naive female white rats, kept under the conditions described above. Ages were as follows: experiment 2A, 55–60 days; experiment 2B, 70–75 days; experiment 2C, 55–60 days; experiment 2D, 65–70 days. In each experiment rats were divided into two groups of 10. The variations among the four experiments are illustrated in Table 2. On day 1, both groups drank the "blocking" solution for 2½ min; the "blocking" group was poisoned 30 min later with 6 ml of 0.15 M LiCl. The "nonblocking" group was not poisoned. On days 2 and 3 all rats were given water for 20 min; the "nonblocking" group was poisoned on day 2, about 6 hours after drinking water, to equalize groups on experience with poisoning. On day 4, all rats drank the interfering solution and the test solution, each for 2½ min, followed by poisoning. The experiments differed in the solutions used, the order of test and blocking solutions, and the length of the delays between the two solutions and between the second and poisoning, as illustrated in Table 2. Care was taken to match the amounts the two groups drank of the interfering solution: the blocking group, which would normally drink less, since this solution has become aversive to them, was given this solution for 2½ min; each member of the nonblocking group was given the solution only until its intake approximated that of a paired member of the blocking group. On day 5 all rats were again given water for 20 min; on day 6 rats were given two bottles for 20 min, one containing the test solution and the other containing water. Each rat's intake of each solution was measured to the nearest 0.5 ml. The solutions used were 5 percent casein hydrolysate (w/v, enzymatic, extra-soluble), 10 percent (w/v) sucrose, 0.15 M NaCl, and 1 percent French's vanilla extract, all prepared in tap water at room temperature.

On the basis of previous data (some unpublished) it seemed safe to assume that the procedures of experiments 2A–2C, independent of prior experience with one of the solutions, would produce significant aversions to the test solution (Kalat & Rozin, 1970). Since the issue under consideration was whether the blocking and nonblocking groups would differ in aversion to the test solution, no control group for nonaversion was felt necessary. However, experiment 2D involved aversion to vanilla. Since previous data (Kalat & Rozin, 1970) indicated that it was difficult to establish a learned aversion to a less concentrated (0.17 percent) vanilla solution, experiment 2D included a control group to permit demonstration that some aversion to the 1 percent vanilla solution occurred. This control group's treatment was identical to that of the nonblocking group except that it was not poisoned following consumption of sucrose and vanilla.

Results

The results are presented along with the procedure in Table 2. If a previously established learned aversion to a solution causes it to have a larger blocking effect in a subsequent two-solution poisoning situation, the blocking group should learn less aversion to a novel solution than the nonblocking group. Alternatively, if an animal ingests a solution without unfavorable consequences, and if this solution is later presented along with a novel solution in a poisoning paradigm, such a familiar solution should have a minimal interfering effect.

In none of the experiments did rats drink a substantial amount of the test solution. Although a control group was included in only one experiment, previous data make it clear that all the experimental groups were showing a considerable aversion to the test solution. In experiment 2D, both the blocking and nonblocking groups showed a significant ($p < 0.01$) aversion to vanilla, relative to controls.

The differences between the blocking and nonblocking groups are small and inconsistent. In two experiments the difference was in the direction predicted by the blocking hypothesis, but in the other two experiments the difference was in the opposite direction. Only in one of the latter cases did the difference approach statistical significance. Considering the four experiments together, it is not possible to discern any systematic difference between the blocking and nonblocking groups.

Discussion

It has been demonstrated (Revusky & Garcia, 1970; Kalat & Rozin, that if a second solution is presented between a test solution and poison it produces some interference with learned aversion to the first. In the four experiments of part 2, in which we varied several parameters, there was no evidence that a prior learned aversion to a solution affects the amount of interference it produces; i.e., there was no blocking effect.

A significant but incomplete blocking effect has, however, appeared in a taste-aversion experiment by Revusky (1971). Revusky's procedure differed from ours in several ways, including number of poisonings on the blocking solution, solutions and time intervals used, and duration of the test. However, he presented the blocking solution between the test solution and poisoning, as we did in three of our four experiments. We have replicated Revusky's procedure with a small number of animals and have obtained a small effect in the direction

TABLE 2 Procedure and Results of Part 2

	Day 4 Procedure				Test results			
Experiment	Solution 1	Intersolution Delay	Solution 2	Solution 2 Poison Delay	Median volume Test Solution	Median volume Water	Direction of Difference	Significance level of Difference
2A	Sucrose (test)	15 min.	Casein hydrolysate (interfering)	15 min.	Block: 0.25 ml	Block: 11.5 ml	Counter to hypothesis	Suc: p=.53
					Non-block: 0.75	Non-block: 11.75		H$_2$0: p=.80
2B	NaCl (test)	15 min.	Casein hydrolysate (interfering)	15 min.	Block: 0.75	Block: 11.75	Agrees with hypothesis	NaCl: p=.80
					Non-block: 0.5	Non-block: 11.25		H$_2$0: p=.68
2C	Casein Hydrolysate (test)	2 hrs.	Sucrose (interfering)	30 min.	Block: 3.25	Block: 10.75	Agrees with hypothesis	Cas: p=.68
					Non-block: 2.75	Non-block: 9.75		H$_2$0: p=.74
2D	Sucrose (interfering)	7 min.	Vanilla (test)	15 min.	Block: 0.25	Block: 15.25	Counter to hypothesis	Van: p=.08
					Non-block: 1.75	Non-block: 9.25		H$_2$0: p=.05
					Control: 7.5	Control: 7.0		

Revusky reports. It is not clear at this point which parametric differences are decisive in obtaining any blocking effect.[4]

Our inability to obtain a blocking effect under a number of different conditions contrasts with the apparent ease of obtaining large, robust blocking effects with the CER and other types of learning (Kamin, 1969; Wagner, 1969).[5] Our retrospection and blocking experiments, taken together, offer no support to the position that taste-aversion learning is an advanced, unusually cognitive type of learning. The rat's ability to modify its interpretation of an ambiguous poisoning experience in terms of previous or subsequent experience appears meagre. It would seem a reasonable hypothesis based on our results and the evidence cited in the introduction that taste-aversion learning involves a mechanism in some respects more "primitive" than the mechanism involved in certain other types of learning. The absence of blocking suggests that the rat is not acting as an "information seeker" in taste-aversion learning, and possibily that the "CS" does not become a *signal* for the US. Rather, the "CS" might be better described as taking on the negative emotional properties of the US. For instance, the rat might be avoiding a taste not because it predicts poisoning, but because it now tastes unpleasant.

As yet, taste-aversion learning has been investigated in only a few species. It may be that the ability to learn about tastes is widespread, and occurs even in species whose learning abilities in other situations are most unimpressive. The great importance of selecting adequate foods might favor evolution of this ability in a species with little or no other learning abilities.

References

Berger, B. Learning in the anesthetized rat. Manuscript in preparation, 1971.

Best, P. J., & Zuckerman, K. Subcortical mediation of learned taste aversion. *Physiology & Behavior*, 1971, 7, 317–320.

Garcia, J., & Koelling, R. A. Relation of cue to consequence in avoidance learning. *Psychonomic Science*, 1966, 4, 123–124.

Kalat, J. W., & Rozin, P. "Salience:" a factor which can override temporal contiguity in taste-aversion learning. *Journal of Comparative and Physiological Psychology*, 1970, 71, 192–197.

Kalat, J. W., & Rozin, P. The role of interference in taste-aversion learning. *Journal of Comparative and Physiological Psychology*, 1971, 77, 53–58.

[4] We are puzzled that Revusky's procedure is apparently more effective than ours in obtaining a blocking effect. Our animals had been poisoned only once on the blocking solution, and most of them drank at least 1–2 ml of the blocking solution on the day when it was supposed to do the blocking. With Revusky's procedure, however, the rats were poisoned twice on the blocking solution; in our replication we found that most rats did not drink a measurable amount of the blocking solution (and appeared merely to sniff at it). It seems strange that the blocking solution would be more effective in the condition under which rats drank less (and possibly none) of it.

[5] Our procedure is not, of course, strictly analogous to Kamin's. The one-trial learning and long delay of reinforcement are inherent characteristics of taste-aversion learning; thus these parameters necessarily differ from Kamin's. Furthermore, Kamin presented the two CSs simultaneously, while we felt it advisable to present the two solutions successively rather than as a mixture.

Kamin, L. J. Predictability, surprise, attention, and conditioning. In B. A. Campbell & R. M. Church (Eds.), *Punishment and aversive behavior*. New York, Appleton-Century-Crofts, 1969, 279—296.

Revusky, S. H. Role of interference in association over a delay. In W. Honig & H. James (Eds.), *2nd Annual Dalhousie Conference on Animal Memory*. New York: Academic Press, 1971.

Revusky, S. H., & Garcia, J. Learned associations over long delays. In Gordon H. Bower (Ed.), *The psychology of learning and motivation*, vol. 4, 1970, pp. 1—84.

Roll, D. L., & Smith, J. C. Conditioned taste-aversion in anesthetized rats. In M. E. P. Seligman & J. Hager, *Biological Boundaries of Learning*. New York: Appleton-Century-Crofts, 1972.

Rozin, P., & Kalat, J. W. Specific hungers and poison avoidance as adaptive specializations of learning. *Psychological Review*, 1971, 78, 459—486.

Seligman, M. E. P. On the generality of the laws of learning. *Psychological Review*, 1970, 77, 406—418.

Wagner, A. R. Incidental stimuli and discrimination learning. In R. M. Gilbert & N. S. Sutherland (Eds.), *Animal Discrimination Learning*. New York, Academic Press, 1969, 83—111.

II
INSTRUMENTAL LEARNING

We begin the section on preparedness in instrumental learning with excerpts from Edward L. Thorndike's doctoral dissertation written in 1898. It is a shame that Animal Intelligence *is now read only rarely in the original by students of psychology. Published when Thorndike was only 24, this work may be the most significant doctoral dissertation ever done in psychology. In it can be found not only the well-known beginnings of the instrumental learning tradition but also the discovery of learning set, the first experimental work in comparative psychology, the first experiments on forgetting and discriminative control in animals, experiments separating cognitive from noncognitive learning, and many other gems. These excerpts are presented not as a historical curiosity, however, but as evidence that the father of general-process learning theory recognized and experimented on associations of greater and lesser preparedness.*

It is commonly known that Thorndike put cats in large boxes and investigated the course of learning to pull strings to escape. What is less widely known is that he put his cats in not just one puzzle box but a whole series of different ones (incidentally, it was here that he seems to have discovered learning set) (Thorndike, 1898, pp. 27–31). In one box the cats had to pull a string to get out, in another a button had to be pushed, in another a lever had to be pressed, etc. One of his boxes—box Z—was truly puzzling: It was just a large box with nothing but a door which the experimenter could open. Thorndike opened the door in box Z whenever cats licked themselves or scratched themselves. The cat uses both of these frequently occurring responses instrumentally: It scratches itself to stop itches, and licks itself to remove dirt. Thorndike had established that getting out of a puzzle box was a sufficient reward (satisfier) for reinforcing string pulling, button pushing, and lever pressing. However, Thorndike's cats had trouble with box Z, as this selection shows. A reanalysis of the individual learning curves presented by Thorndike for each of the seven cats tested in box Z documents the impression: Of the 28 individual learning curves (for boxes other than Z) presented for these seven cats, 22 show faster learning than in Z, three show approximately equal learning, and only three show slower learning. While every cat eventually got better at licking or scratching to escape, such learning was neither easy nor smooth. Moreover, these acts were labile and eventually degenerated to mere vestiges of the natural act.

In addition to thus demonstrating contrapreparedness in instrumental learning, Thorndike also hinted at the importance of preparedness in classical conditioning or "associative shifting" (Thorndike, 1935, pp. 192–197). One of his students (Bregman, 1934) tried to replicate the results of Watson and Rayner (1920), who found that little Albert became afraid of a white rat, rabbit, and dog which had been paired with a startling noise. Bregman was unable to show any fear conditioning when she paired more conventional CSs, such as the sight of blocks or curtains, with startling noise. Thorndike speculated that infants at the age of locomotion are more prepared to manifest fear to objects that wiggle and contort themselves than to motionless CSs. So although he is remembered as the founder of general process learning theory, he was aware that his subjects were not empty organisms devoid of evolutionary history and genetic makeup.

II

ANIMAL INTELLIGENCE

Edward L. Thorndike

After considerable preliminary observation of animals' behavior under various conditions, I chose for my general method one which, simple as it is, possesses several other marked advantages besides those which accompany experiment of any sort. It was merely to put animals when hungry in enclosures from which they could escape by some simple act, such as pulling at a loop of cord, pressing a lever, or stepping on a platform. (A detailed description of these boxes and pens will be given later.) The animal was put in the enclosure, food was left outside in sight, and his actions observed. Besides recording his general behavior, special notice was taken of how he succeeded in doing the necessary act (in case he did succeed), and a record was kept of the time that he was in the box before performing the successful pull, or clawing, or bite. This was repeated until the animal had formed a perfect association between the sense-impression of the interior of that box and the impulse leading to the successful movement. When the association was thus perfect, the time taken to escape was, of course, practically constant and very short. . . .

Furthermore, although the associations formed are such as could not have been previously experienced or provided for by heredity, they are still not too remote from the animal's ordinary course of life. They mean simply the connection of a certain act with a certain situation and resultant pleasure, and this general type of association is found throughout the animal's life normally. The muscular movements required are all such as might often be required of the animal. . . .

The starting point for the formation of any association in these cases, then, is the set of instinctive activities which are aroused when a cat feels discomfort in the box either because of confinement or a desire for food. This discomfort, plus the sense-impression of a surrounding, confining wall, expresses itself prior to any experience, in squeezings, clawings, bitings, etc. From among these movements one is selected by success. But this is the starting point only in the case of the first box experienced. After that the cat has associated with the feeling of confinement certain impulses which have led to success more than others and are thereby strengthened. A cat that had learned to escape from A by clawing [a wire loop] has when put into C [button] or G [thumb latch] a

These excerpts, from E. L. Thorndike's *Animal Intelligence* (New York: Columbia University, 1898, pp. 6–28), were selected by the editors, whose additions to the text are enclosed in brackets.

greater tendency to claw at things than it instinctively had at the start, and a less tendency to squeeze through holes. A very pleasnt form of this decrease in instinctive impulses was noticed in the gradual cessation of howling and mewing. However, the useless instinctive impulses die out slowly, and often play an important part even after the cat has had experience with six or eight boxes. And what is important in our previous statement, namely, that the activity of an animal when first put into a new box is not directed by any appreciation of *that* box's character, but by certain general impulses to acts, is not affected by this modification. Most of this activity is determined by heredity; some of it, by previous experience. . . . Starting, then, with its store of instinctive impulses, the cat hits upon the successful movement, and gradually associates it with the sense-impression of the interior of the box until the connection is perfect, so that it performs the act as soon as confronted with the sense-impression. The formation of each association may be represented graphically by a time-curve. In these curves lengths of one millimeter along the abscissa represent successive experiences in the box, and heights of one millimeter above it each represent ten seconds of time. The curve is formed by joining the tops of perpendiculars erected along the abscissa 1 mm. apart (the first perpendicular coinciding with the y line), each perpendicular representing the time the cat was in the box before escaping. . . .

In boxes A [wireloop], C [button], D [string inside], E [string outside], I [lever], 100% of the cats given a chance to do so hit upon the movement and formed the association. The following table shows the results where some cats failed.

	No. cats tried	No. cats failed
F [loose string outside]	5	4
G [thumb latch]	8	5
H [swinging door]	9	2
J [loop plus stick]	5	2
K [loop plus bolts]	5	2

The time-curves follow. By referring to the description of apparatus they will be easily understood. Each mm. along the abscissa represents one trial. Each mm. above it represents 10 seconds.

These time-curves show, in the first place, what associations are easy for an animal to form, and what are hard. The act must be one which the animal will perform in the course of the activity which its inherited equipment incites or its previous experience has connected with the sense-impression of a box's interior. The oftener the act naturally occurs in the course of such activity, the sooner it will be performed in the first trial or so, and this is one condition, sometimes, of the ease of forming the association. . . .

The following curves showing the history of cats 1, 5, 13 and 3, which were let out of the box Z when they licked themselves, and of cats 6, 2, and 4, which were let out when they scratched themselves, are interesting because they show associations where there is no congruity (no more to a cat than to a man) between the act and the result. One chick, too, was thus freed whenever he pecked at his feathers to dress them. He formed the association, and would whirl

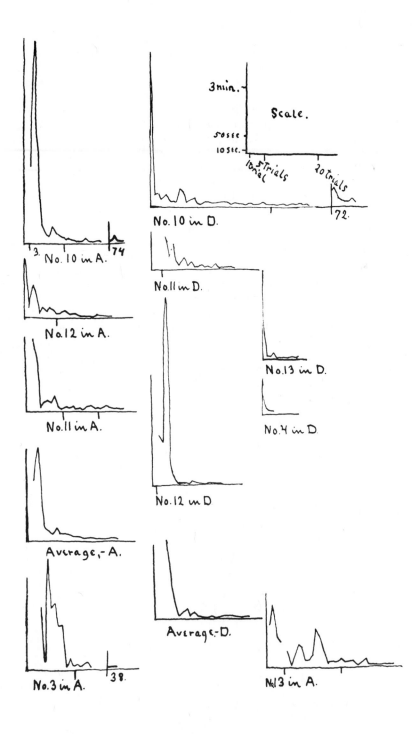

No. 10 in A.

No. 12 in A.

No. 11 in A.

Average,- A.

No. 3 in A.

3 min.

Scale.

50 sec.
10 sec.

10 trial
5 trials

20 trials

No. 10 in D.

72.

No. 11 in D.

No. 13 in D.

No. 4 in D.

No. 12 in D.

Average,- D.

No. 3 in A.

74

38.

his head round and poke it into the feathers as soon as dropped in the box. There is in all these cases a noticeable tendency, of the cause of which I am ignorant, to diminish the act until it becomes a mere vestige of a lick or scratch. After the cat gets so that it performs the act soon after being put in, it begins to do it less and less vigorously. The licking degenerates into a mere quick turn of the head with one or two motions up and down with tongue extended. Instead of a hearty scratch, the cat waves its paw up and down rapidly for an instant. Moreover, if sometimes you do not let the cat out after this feeble reaction, it does not at once repeat the movement, as it would do if it depressed a thumbpiece, for instance, without success in getting the door open. Of the reason for this difference I am again ignorant. . . .

Another reason for allowing animals representations and images is found in the longer time taken to form the association between the act of licking or scratching and the consequent escape. If the associations in general were simply between situation and impulse and act, one would suppose that the situation would be associated with the impulse to lick or scratch as readily as with the impulse to turn a button or claw a string. Such is not the case. By comparing the curves for Z with the others one sees that for so simple an act it takes a long time to form the association. This is not a final reason, for lack of attention, a slight increase in the time taken to open the door after the act was done, or an absence of preparation in the nervous system for connections between these particular acts and definite sense-impressions, may very well have been the cause of the difficulty in forming the associations. Nor is it certain that *ideas* of clawing loops would be easier to form than ideas of scratching or licking oneself.

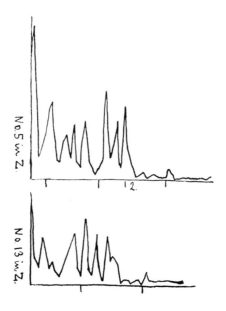

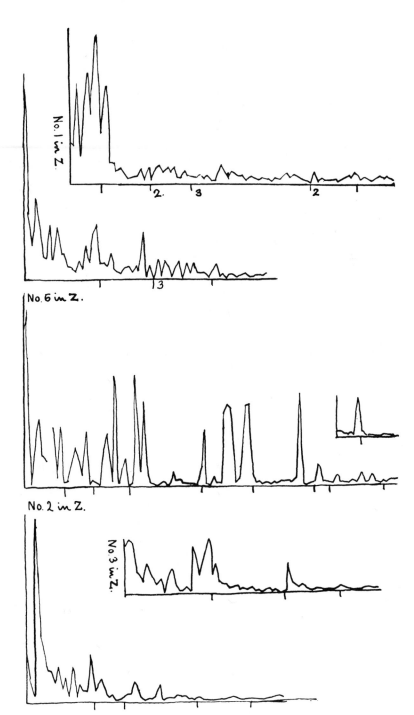

No. 1 in Z.

No. 6 in Z.

No. 2 in Z.

No. 3 in Z.

No. 4. in Z.

Other prominent learning theorists following Thorndike have mentioned concepts allied to preparedness. Clark Hull's habit family hierarchy and sUr (unconditioned connection between stimulus and response) and E. C. Tolman's field-cognition modes are examples. Unfortunately, little further theorizing or empirical work was generated by these notions. More recently Jerzy Konorski, director of the Nencki Institute in Warsaw, Poland, has theorized extensively and performed experiments on preparedness. Like Thorndike, he has worked on the instrumentalization of reflex movements. In contrast to Thorndike, Konorski (1967) reports that such reflexes as scratching and licking in cats are easy to reinforce with food. He too has found, however, that these responses tend to become reduced, simplified, and arhythmic, but attributes this to response differentiation. In addition, he has great difficulty in reinforcing yawning and sneezing in dogs with food, and suggests that these associations may be what we would call "contraprepared."

Konorski and his colleagues have extended these findings to the discriminative control of instrumental responding. Dobrezecka, Szwejkowska, and Konorski in the next selection find that dogs are almost unable to learn to move one paw rather than another for food when different qualities of sound tell the dog which paw is correct, but learn this easily when the sounds come from different places. Like Garcia and Koelling, they also perform the complementary experiment and find that dogs have trouble learning to move a paw or not to move it when auditory cues come from different places, but learn readily when the cues are different in quality and come from the same place. Direction of auditory cue, therefore, is more prepared to control direction of responding than quality, and quality more prepared to control "go-no go" responding than direction.

12

QUALITATIVE VERSUS DIRECTIONAL CUES IN TWO FORMS OF DIFFERENTIATION

Czeslawa Dobrzecka, Genowefa Szwejkowska, and Jerzy Konorski

Dogs given opportunities to base their instrumental conditioned responses in differentiation learning on either the quality of the auditory conditioned stimulus (for example, metronome versus buzzer) or the direction of its source (in front or behind) choose different cues in different tasks. In $S_1 \to R_1$, $S_2 \to R_2$ (left leg–right leg) differentiation they exclusively use directional cues and are almost unable to learn this task when only quality cues are available. When confronted with Pavlovian $S + \to R$, $S - \to$ no R (go–no go) differentiation, however, they generally learn on the basis of quality cues, although some animals also attend to the directional cues. Thus an animal's success or failure in a given differentiation procedure depends not only on its ability to discriminate the stimuli but also on the task with which it is confronted.

Lawicka (*1*) has shown that, in a free-moving situation, success or failure of training in go left–right differentiation or go–no go differentiation depends on the character of auditory cues used for the particular task. While for go left–go right differentiation the adequate cues are provided by auditory stimuli presented from *different directions*, for go–no go differentiation they are provided by stimuli of *different quality*. We have now further investigated the same problem, using a different technique.

We used 29 dogs in a Pavlovian soundproof conditioned-reflex (CR) chamber. An animal, placed on a stand, was given food by remote control from a feeder

From *Science*, 153 (1966), 87–89.
We thank Mortimer Mishkin for assistance with the manuscript.

situated before him. An instrumental CR consisted in placing the left or right foreleg on the feeder in response to a conditioned stimulus (CS); intertrial intervals were about 1 minute.

In experiment 1, 11 dogs were trained to place their right forelegs on the feeder in response to the sound of a metronome situated in front of them (Ma) and to place there their left forelegs in response to a buzzer situated behind them (Bp). During training the two stimuli were presented randomly; 5 seconds after presentation of the stimulus the appropriate leg was passively placed on the feeder and food was immediately delivered. Passive placement was remotely controlled by a system of ropes and pulleys. After a few sessions the animals started to execute the trained movements actively in response to the CS's. If the response was correct, food was immediately presented; if incorrect, the CS was discontinued and food was not delivered. If a dog did not respond to 5 seconds of CS, it was prompted by a tug on the proper leg. Eight reinforced trials were given per session, each CS being presented four times in random order.

The task was mastered to a criterion of 80 consecutive correct responses in an average of 230 (range, 120 to 360) trials; these scores include the trials with passive movements. During each of the ten test sessions that followed, interspersed among the regular trials were two trials with (i) a buzzer presented in front of the animal (Ba) and (ii) a metronome presented behind it (Mp). In all trials either movement was reinforced by food. The results (Table 1) show that in eight dogs at least 90 percent of the responses were determined by the direction of the CS, with total neglect of its quality; that is, the metronome presented from behind evoked the same movement as the buzzer from behind, while the buzzer presented in front evoked the same movement as the

TABLE 1   Results of Test Trials in $S_1 \rightarrow R_1, S_2 \rightarrow R_2$ Differentiation with 11 Dogs

Responses (No.)					
Mp			Ba		
To quality (M)	To direction (p)	None	To quality (B)	To direction (a)	None
0	9	1	0	10	0
0	10	0	0	10	0
1	8	1	0	10	0
0	10	0	0	10	0
0	10	0	1	9	0
0	10	0	0	10	0
0	10	0	2	8	0
5	5	0	1	9	0
2	8	0	2	8	0
0	10	0	0	10	0
4	1	5	0	10	0
		Totals (%)			
10.9	82.7	6.4	5.5	94.5	0

The metronome was shifted behind (Mp) and the buzzer in front of (Ba) the animals.

metronome in front. In three other dogs the responses were mixed. In no dog, however, did the quality cue prevail over the directional cue.

Further evidence indicating the significance of the directional cues for right leg—left leg differentiation is provided by the results of a control procedure. Six dogs were similarly trained except that both CS's sounded from the same point in front of the animal, so that the directional cue was absent; three of them eventually mastered the task after 1000 to 1500 trials, while the other three could not learn even after longer training. In all six dogs symptoms of neurosis developed from time to time. In contrast, when two CS's of different modalities (visual versus auditory) were presented in front of two dogs, the task of right leg—left leg differentiation was quickly learned within about 250 trials.

In experiment 2, ten dogs were trained in go—no go differentiation, the instrumental response being movement of the right foreleg. Response by this movement to the positive CS was always reinforced by food, while the negative CS never brought food. Either the buzzer or a 900-cy/sec tone was the positive CS, while the metronome or a 600-cy/sec tone was the negative CS. For five dogs the positive CS was in front of the animal and the negative one was behind; for the other five these positions were reversed. The dogs learned the buzzer-metronome differentiation almost immediately; the high tone—low tone differentiation required a few hundred trials.

When the animals were responding correctly in 100 percent of the trials, 20 test trials were given in the same way as in experiment 1—but always without reinforcement, so as not to teach the animal to respond with the movement to the new stimulus combination. The results (Table 2) show that for every dog but one the negative CS placed in the position of the positive CS completely preserved its negative significance—that is, the animals never performed the

TABLE 2   Results of Test Trials in $S_1 \rightarrow R_1$, $S_2 \rightarrow$ No R Differentiation with 10 Dogs

		Responses (No.) to				Responses (No.) to	
CS+	Reverse location	Quality	Direction	CS−	Reverse location	Quality	Direction
Ba	Bp	0	10	Mp	Ma	10	0
Ba	Bp	3	7	Mp	Ma	9	1
Ba	Bp	9	1	Mp	Ma	10	0
Bp	Ba	4	6	Ma	Mp	10	0
Bp	Ba	10	0	Ma	Mp	10	0
Bp	Ba	7	3	Ma	Mp	10	0
T_1a	T_1p	9	1	T_2p	T_2a	10	0
T_1a	T_1p	8	2	T_2p	T_2a	0	10
T_1p	T_1a	10	0	T_2a	T_2p	10	0
T_1p	T_1a	10	0	T_2a	T_2p	10	0
				Totals (%)			
		70	30			89	11

Symbols B, buzzer; M, metronome; T_1, 900-cy/sec tone; T_2, 600-cy/sec tone; a, presented in front; p, presented behind.

taught movement in response to it. As for the positive CS placed in the position of the negative CS, it maintained its positive significance in the majority of trials with seven dogs, while negative responses prevailed iñ three dogs. In all, the animals reacted according to the quality of the CS in 80 percent of the trials and to the direction of the CS in only 20 percent.

So, as Lawicka discovered, animals trained in a differentiation procedure requiring two different instrumental responses to two auditory stimuli mainly use directional cues; they are almost unable to learn the task when confronted with purely qualitative cues. On the other hand, in a go—no go differentiation procedure based on reinforcement-versus-nonreinforcement of responses to two auditory stimuli mainly utilize qualitative cues.

These facts have been tentatively interpreted in detail (2). It is notable that monkeys (3) also can establish without difficulty a go—no go differentiation between two different tones emanating from the same point, while there go left—go right differentiations between these stimuli are as difficult as they are for dogs; in contrast, the go right—go left differentiation between directional cues is easy.

References and Notes

1. W. Lawicka, *Bull. acad. Polon. sci. Classe II*, 12, 35 (1964).
2. J. Konorski, in *Excerpta Med. Intern. Congr. Ser. 49 Leiden* (1962), pp. 318—29; *Acta Biol. Exp.* 24, 59 (1964).
3. W. Lawicka, unpublished.

While Thorndike attributed the difficulty of some instrumental learning to a simple absence of preparation, Konorski (1967) attributes it to the presence of a competing innate or prepared association, contrapreparedness in the literal sense. In the next article, Robert Bolles and Sally Seelbach provide systematic evidence of contrapreparedness, which they too attribute to response competition. They try to reward rearing, exploration, and grooming with noise offset and punish these three responses with noise onset. Rearing, grooming, and exploration are frequently occurring responses in the rat. This frequency or "operant level" should not be confused with preparedness. In this study we see that responses all having high operant levels are differentially prepared in that whereas some of these responses could be rewarded or punished in this way, others could not.

13

PUNISHING AND REINFORCING EFFECTS OF NOISE ONSET AND TERMINATION FOR DIFFERENT RESPONSES

Robert C. Bolles and Sally E. Seelbach

Onset or termination of an intense white noise was made contingent upon the occurrence of certain responses in the rat's repertory in order to determine the extent to which the probabilities of these responses can be reduced by noise onset (punishment training) and increased by noise termination (escape training). Comparison with the appropriate controls indicated that rearing was affected by escape training but not punishment, certain exploratory responses were affected by both kinds of training, and that grooming was affected by neither. The results are interpreted in terms of response competition.

It has been reported that rats will learn to press a bar in order to terminate a loud noise (Harrison & Tracy, 1955). Campbell (1955) also found that rats would learn to go to that side of a tilting cage which resulted in the reduction of the intensity of a loud noise. In both of these situations, however, only modest levels of performance were attained; even with quite high noise levels the reinforced response gained in strength only gradually. On the other hand, Barnes and Kish (1957) have reported much more impressive learning effects in mice using both noise termination and noise onset. Barnes and Kish obtained what appeared to be rapid escape learning reinforced by noise termination and rapid learning through punishment with the onset of noise; the criterion response involved standing on a marked platform in one corner of the test apparatus. These apparently contradictory findings about the efficacy of loud noise as a

From *Journal of Comparative and Physiological Psychology*, 58 (1964), 127–131.
Supported in part by Research Grant G-24245 from the National Science Foundation.

reinforcer suggest that the facility with which a response is learned or inhibited depends upon what the response is. The present study shows that this is indeed the case.

EXPERIMENT 1

Method

Subjects. The Ss were 28 male rats, Sprague-Dawley strain, approximately 70 days old. They were maintained on ad-lib. food and water but no food or water was available in the test situation. The Ss had never been deprived or handled prior to testing.

Apparatus. The test chamber was a wooden box 14 x 9 in., 10 in. high, painted gray all over except for the front wall which was glass so Ss could be observed, and the top which was hardware cloth so that sound could enter. The sound source was a wide range white noise generator built by Scientific Prototype Company. The speaker was a Goodmans in a base reflex box supplemented by a University Tweeter (Model T-202) which is advertised to have a frequency range extending to 40,000 cps. The speakers and the test box were located in a sound isolating room with a one-way window through which Ss were observed. Speakers were located above and somewhat to one side of the test box. The average sound level in the test box as measured by a General Radio 1551-C sound level meter was about 95 db. It would be expected that there would be some standing wave patterns and sound shadows within the test box. The S's behavior indicated that there were differential sound fields, i.e., more time was spent in some corners of the box than others, but these effects were of secondary importance and did not obscure the principal behavioral effects of sound onset and termination. The minimal effect of these secondary effects can be attributed to the use of wide range white noise.

Procedure. The S was put into the test box for a 30-min. test session and the acquisition training begun immediately. The E watched S continually during the session and pressed a button whenever and as long as the criterion response occurred. The criterion response in Experiment 1 was "rearing," standing up on the hindlegs. Pressing the button recorded the response and could change the noise intensity 40 db. Four groups of 7 Ss each were run. One group was run under escape conditions: whenever S reared, the sound intensity was reduced from 95 to 55 db. and it stayed reduced until S dropped down on all four feet. Simultaneously with the reduction in sound a 1-sec. pulse generator was connected to a cumulative recorder so that the recorder pen advanced one step each second that the criterion response occurred. A second group was run under punishment conditions: whenever S reared, the sound intensity was increased from 55 to 95 db. Cumulative records of the time spent rearing were again obtained. Two control conditions were run, one with the sound level set at a constant 95 db. (loud control) and one with the sound level set at a constant 55 db. (soft control).

Results

The cumulative response data were translated into probability measures by determining the proportions of successive 3-min. intervals during which the rearing response occurred. The results of this analysis for each of the four experimental conditions are shown in Figure 1.

It is clear that under escape conditions there was learning to escape by rearing and that rearing came to dominate S's behavior in the test situation. After 15 min. there was no overlap between the scores of Ss in the escape group and Ss in any other group. Three of the seven Ss in the escape group met a 5-min. criterion of continuous rearing during the 30-min. test session. Under the control conditions, by contrast, rearing rapidly dropped out. It would seem from Figure 1 that punishment is likewise effective in altering the probability of the rearing response. But there are difficulties with this interpretation, as we will see in Experiment 2.

Observing Ss in the test situation it was evident that the total pattern of behavior occurring under loud noise is very little different from that occurring under soft noise conditions. Thus it appears as though noise level per se has little or no effect upon behavior and that whatever reinforcing effects are present in the escape and punishment groups are a consequence of events occurring when the noise level is shifted. This situation is thus considerably different from the

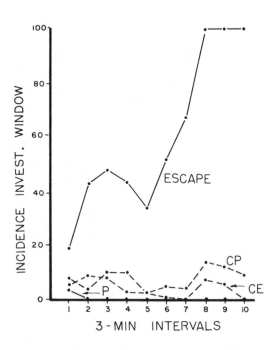

FIG. 1 Median percentage occurrence of rearing during successive 3-min. intervals for Ss reinforced or punished for rearing and for control Ss.

situation with shock in which a variety of responses—squealing, jumping, and running around—continue in the presence of shock. The only overt response to loud noise is a momentary startle-type of reaction which occurs when the sound level is increased. Whatever unauthorized escape responses from sound may have occurred when the sound was at a constant high level, they escaped detection, and evidently failed to interfere with the usual sorts of behavior that occur in novel situations such as exploring and grooming.

The results shown in Figure 1 are strikingly similar to those reported by Barnes and Kish (1957). Using a spatially defined response, they found a similar rate and asymptote of learning under their escape conditions and a similar depression of response probability with their punishment conditions.

EXPERIMENT 2

There remains a question whether what appears to be a punishment effect is most appropriately interpreted as a punishment effect. The question is whether the depression of rearing represents an inhibition of that specific response or is the result of some diffuse "emotional" reaction to the changing sound intensities. Experiment 2 was an attempt to answer this question.

Method

Fourteen naive Ss of the same description as before were run in two test boxes like that used before.

Pairs of Ss were run simultaneously. One E ran one of a pair under the punishment condition in precisely the same manner as in Experiment 1. The behavior of the punishment S was used to determine the sound level for both itself and the control S. The second E recorded behavior of the yoked control Ss in the second box.

Results

The results shown in Figure 2, were again analyzed in terms of the proportion of time spent making the criterion response, rearing, in successive 3-min. intervals under the different conditions. Note that performance under the punishment condition was very similar to that obtained in Experiment 1 under the comparable conditions. The response probability was initially about .15 and declined gradually to near zero in about 25 min. The probability of rearing was markedly lower for the yoked control Ss, however, than for either the constant loud or constant soft Ss of Experiment 1. The yoked controls spent less time rearing than Ss that were punished for rearing, although this difference was not statistically significant (Mann-Whitney test).

This finding suggests that occasional sudden sharp increases in noise level for brief periods of time produce a generalized emotional reaction in the rat and that this emotional reaction competes not only with the criterion response, rearing, but competes to the same degree with other behaviors such as exploring and grooming. Considering this base line of below normal incidence of rearing, it is apparent that making the onset of sound contingent upon S's behavior does not provide any greater depressing effect than it does when it is not contingent

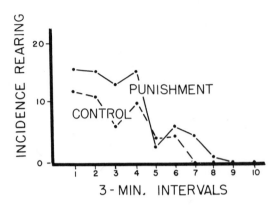

FIG. 2 Median percentage occurrence of rearing during successive 3-min. intervals for punished and yoked control Ss.

upon S's behavior. In short, noise does not seem to have a specific punishment
effect on the rearing response.

EXPERIMENT 3

Experiment 3 is concerned with the effects of noise onset and termination
upon a different class of responses.

Method

Subjects and Apparatus. Four groups of 6 Ss of the same description as before
were run. The apparatus was the same as before except that a 1-in. round
window was cut in the center of one end of the box, centered 2 in. above the
floor.

Procedure. The procedure was the same as before except in two respects.
First, two boxes were used throughout to make use of the yoked control
procedure so that pairs of Ss were run under escape and yoked escape control
conditions and under punishment and yoked punishment control conditions.
Second, the criterion response was no longer rearing but was investigating the
window. This generic term included poking the nose through the window,
sniffing or chewing the rim of the window, and any other behavior that brought
S's nose within .25 in. or so of the edge or aperture of the window. For the
escape and escape control Ss the sound was reduced from 95 to 55 db. whenever
and for as long as the escape S made the criterion response. For the punishment
and punishment control Ss the sound was increased from 55 to 95 db. whenever
and for as long as the punishment S made the criterion response.

Results

The incidence of the criterion response for successive 3-min. periods for the
four experimental conditions is shown in Figure 3. We may note that the

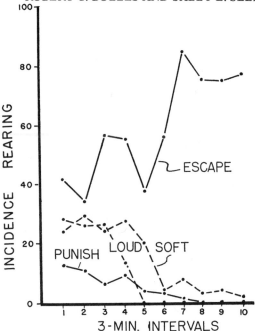

FIG. 3 Median percentage occurrence of window investigation during successive 3-min. intervals for Ss reinforced or punished for investigating the window and for yoked control Ss.,

incidence of investigating the window is somewhat lower than the incidence of the rearing response; the yoked control Ss showed an over-all mean incidence of window investigation of .06 throughout the test. With this class of responses escape learning occurred about as rapidly as with the rearing response, but reached a higher asymptote. The median S met a 5-min. criterion of continuous window investigating under the escape condition. This was usually accomplished while S froze or, in one case, slept with his nose propped on the front edge of the window. In contrast to the findings with the rearing response, the punishment condition was effective in inhibiting window investigating. A Mann-Whitney test showed that punishment Ss spent significantly less time in making the criterion response than did the yoked punishment control Ss $(p < .01)$.

One interesting feature of the behavior under the punishment condition was that there was little evidence of any generalized immobilizing emotional response. The animals continued predominantly to explore the test box, especially that side of it opposite the window. After a few minutes the box had become rather thoroughly explored (this was true for all groups) except for the window and the area immediately around it. Typically there then ensued a period in which there was overt evidence of conflict between exploratory tendencies to approach the window and withdrawal tendencies conditioned by punishment. The S would stretch out in the manner characteristic of the rat and make vacillatory approach and withdrawal reactions. Typically these periods of conflict ended with S coming too close to the window, getting a burst of noise and immediately retreating. Thus it seems that withdrawal from the window had been conditioned not only to the loud noise itself but to environmental stimuli in the vicinity of the window. During the course of 30-min. punishment Ss made a median of eight contacts with the window as opposed to 24 for the yoked punishment control Ss; this difference is significant (Mann-Whitney, $p < .01$).

EXPERIMENT 4

Experiment 4 was a replication of Experiment 3 except that a different criterion response was used, viz., grooming.

Method

Four groups of 6 Ss of the same description as before were run in the two test boxes with windows.

The Ss were again run in pairs under escape and yoked escape control conditions and punishment and yoked punishment control conditions. For the escape and escape control Ss, the sound was reduced from 95 to 55 db. whenever and for as long as the escape S engaged in any form of grooming, namely, washing the face, licking the fur, or scratching. For the punishment and punishment control Ss the sound was increased in intensity from 55 to 95 db. whenever and for as long as the punishment S engaged in any form of grooming.

Results

The incidence of grooming for successive 3-min. periods for each of the four experimental conditions is shown in Figure 4. Figure 4 indicates that the termination of intense noise fails to reinforce grooming and that punishment for grooming fails to inhibit it. There was, however, a marked difference between the escape and punishment conditions; the two upper curves are significantly higher than the two lower curves (Mann-Whitney, $p < .01$). This demonstrates first of all the methodological importance of running yoked controls; had Ss just been tested under the escape and punishment conditions it would have been easy to conclude that escape training failed but that punishment training was effective. This pattern of findings also demonstrates that brief bursts of intense sound from time to time produce a greater generalized inhibition of grooming than brief periods of relative quiet from time to time.

DISCUSSION

Taking the results of the four experiments together we have the following pattern of findings: under the present conditions termination of loud noise is reinforcing (S will learn to escape it) for the rearing and window investigating responses but not for grooming, and the onset of noise is punishing (S will learn to avoid it) for the window investigating response but not for rearing or

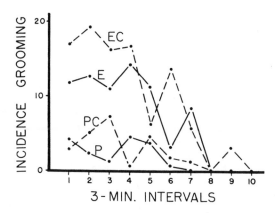

FIG. 4 Median percentage occurrence of grooming during successive 3-min. intervals for Ss reinforced or punished for grooming and for yoked control Ss.

grooming. Put another way, rearing is subject to conditioning by negative reinforcement but not by punishment, investigating the window is subject to both negative reinforcement and punishment, and grooming is subject to neither negative reinforcement nor punishment. Thus the simple question, "is loud noise a negative reinforcer?" does not seem to have a simple answer; it appears to have different effects upon different responses.

Thorndike had called our attention to the fact that whether or not a punishing state of affairs results in the inhibition of a particular response depends in part upon what the punisher in question makes the organism do (Thorndike, 1932, p. 276). This response competition interpretation of punishment has been accepted within a wide range of theoretical positions, e.g., Guthrie (1935), Skinner (1938), Miller and Dollard (1941), and Dinsmoor (1954). The present findings not only support this general interpretation of punishment and the specific role of loud noise as a punisher, but suggest that the same considerations may be applicable to escape training as well. Thus, it may be the whether or not an organism will learn to escape from a "noxious stimulus" depends in part upon what the particular stimulus makes the organism do. If the elicited response, or respondent, competes successfully with the criterion response and if this response can be generalized to other stimuli in the situation, then escape training will be effective. But if, as in the case of grooming, the termination of loud noise elicits an orienting response which interrupts grooming, then grooming cannot be reinforced by the termination of noise. Similarly, if the startle reaction to sound does *not* interrupt grooming, then the onset of noise cannot inhibit grooming.[1] What distinguishes loud noise from electric shock in this respect is that the behavior elicited both by the onset and termination of shock is so very apt to interrupt whatever behavior was just previously occurring.

[1] What we are proposing is a variation of Denny and Adelman's (1955) elicitation hypothesis of reinforcement.

References

Barnes, G. W., & Kish, G. B. Reinforcing properties of termination of intense auditory stimulation. *J. comp. physiol. Psychol.*, 1957, *50*, 40–43.

Campbell, B. A. The fractional reduction in noxious stimulation required to produce "just noticeable" learning. *J. comp. physiol. Psychol.*, 1955, *48*, 141–148.

Denny, M. R., & Adelman, H. M. Elicitation theory: I. An analysis of two typical learning situations. *Psychol. Rev.*, 1955, *62*, 290–296.

Dinsmoor, J. A. Punishment: I. The avoidance hypothesis. *Psychol. Rev.*, 1954, *61*, 34–46.

Guthrie, E. R. *The psychology of learning.* New York: Harper, 1935.

Harrison, J. M. & Tracy, W. H. The use of auditory stimuli to maintain lever pressing behavior. *Science*, 1955, *121*, 273–274.

Miller, N. E., & Dollard, J. *Social learning and imitation.* New Haven: Yale Univer. Press, 1941.

Skinner, B. F. *The behavior of organisms.* New York: Appleton-Century, 1938.

Thorndike, E. L. *The fundamentals of learning.* New York: Teachers College, 1932.

The next two articles deal with highly prepared instrumental learning. The key peck for grain in the pigeon is often thought of as an operant which is parallel to the lever press for food in the rat. But one important difference should be noted: In nature, lever pressing is only arbitrarily related to eating for the rat, while pecking is the response pigeons make to eat grain. Paul Brown and Herbert Jenkins find the key peck for grain to be prepared, so prepared in fact that the pigeon acquires the response even when it has no effect on producing grain. Simply presenting a lit key followed by grain causes the pigeon to begin key pecking, and he will continue to peck even if this does not increase the probability of grain.

14

AUTO-SHAPING OF THE PIGEON'S KEY-PECK

Paul L. Brown and Herbert M. Jenkins

Reliable acquisition of the pigeon's key-peck response resulted from repeated unconditional (response-independent) presentations of food after the response key was illuminated momentarily. Comparison groups showed that acquisition was dependent upon light—food pairings, in that order.

In the usual arrangement for discriminative operant conditioning, reinforcement is conditional on a stimulus and on a response. Food may be delivered to a hungry pigeon only when it pecks a key and only when the key is lighted. By relaxing, in different ways, the conditionality in the rule for delivering food, three other conditioning arrangements of interest can be generated. The delivery of food may be entirely unconditional, *i.e.*, without regard to the stimulus that is present or to behavior; the delivery of food may be conditional on behavior (e.g., the pigeon must peck a key) but unconditional with respect to stimuli; or the delivery of food may be conditional on the stimulus (*e.g.*, food is delivered only when the key is lighted) but unconditional with respect to responses. Following Skinner, behavior acquired under these arrangements may be characterized as superstitious.

In the classic experiment on superstitious conditioning (Skinner, 1948), the rule of reinforcement was entirely unconditional. The delivery of food was governed only by a temporal schedule and was therefore without regard to behavior. Since food was delivered in an unchanging environment, it can be regarded as unconditional with respect to stimuli, although holding the stimulus constant yields a special case of unconditionality. It would more closely parallel the sense in which food delivery is unconditional on behavior had a stimulus been switched between two or more values independently of food delivery. In

From *Journal of the Experimental Analysis of Behavior*, II (1968), 1—8.

Supported by Grants MH 08442-03 from the National Institute of Mental Health and APT-103 from the National Research Council of Canada held by the second author. The first author holds a United States Public Health Service Predoctoral Fellowship from the National Institute of Mental Health. Parts of this research were presented at the annual meeting of the Eastern Psychological Association, April 1967.

any case, the well known result of Skinner's experiment was the development of stereotyped, although idiosyncratic, movement patterns.

An arrangement of the second type, in which reinforcement is conditional on responses but unconditional on stimuli, was investigated by Morse and Skinner (1957). The pigeon's key-peck was reinforced at variable intervals (reinforcement conditional on responses). Once during each hour the color of the key was changed for a 4-min period independently of the program of reinforcement (reinforcement unconditional on stimuli). Some birds developed an especially high rate during the 4-min stimulus while others developed an especially low rate. The direction of change in rate reversed for some birds in the course of long exposure to the procedure. Although the key-peck was conditioned before the stimulus changes were introduced in the Morse and Skinner experiment, that is not an essential feature of the second type of superstitious conditioning. Had a response with an appreciable operant level been chosen, the strengthening of the response through conditional reinforcement, and the acquisition of control by stimuli programmed independently of reinforcement, might have proceeded together. The essential feature of an arrangement of the second type is independence of the program of stimulus changes from the program of reinforcement, coupled with the dependence of reinforcement on responses.

An arrangement of the third type, in which reinforcement is conditional on stimulus values but not on responses, was used in the present experiment. A standard pigeon key was lighted just before food was delivered. The repeated pairing of light with food conditioned a variety of movements to the lighted key. Among these movements was a peck at the lighted key. Because the key-peck is normally shaped by the use of response conditional reinforcement, its emergence under the present circumstances is especially interesting. We have therefore concentrated on analyzing the conditions responsible for the emergence of the first key-peck rather than on other movements that develop in the presence of the stimulus that precedes reinforcement.

Types of superstitious conditioning are classified in terms of procedures, not in terms of behavioral outcomes. The classification does not imply that the behavioral effects observed in each case arise from the same conditioning process. To say that all three procedures produce superstitious conditioning points only to their common feature; namely, that they entail certain unconditional relations among stimuli, responses, and reinforcements. The present experiments show that the emergence of the key-peck when a key-light is repeatedly paired with food presentation is the result of a conditioning process of some sort. Critical questions remain, however, as to what kind of conditioning is at work.

METHOD

The following features were common to the several experiments.

Subjects

Experimentally naive male White King pigeons, 5 to 6 yr old upon arrival in the laboratory, were maintained at 80% of their free-feeding weight.

Apparatus

A single-key operant conditioning box for pigeons (Lehigh Valley Electronics Model 1519C) was used. The center of the translucent plastic disc that served as the key was located in the center of the working panel 10 in. above the floor. The center of the opening to the food tray was located 5 in. directly below the key. Reinforcement was 4-sec. access to the grain tray. The general illumination of the box, backlighting of the key, and lighting of the food-tray opening during reinforcement were provided by supplying 25 v ac to miniature lamps (No. 1820). The compartment light was mounted in a housing, above the key, which directed the light toward the ceiling. It remained on throughout all sessions. A steady masking noise was used in the box. Automatic programming and recording equipment was located in a separate room.

Recording

The basic datum was the occurrence of the first key-peck. An Esterline-Angus operations recorder provided a continuous record of stimulus presentations and responses.

Pretraining

Subjects were trained to approach quickly and to eat from the lighted food tray. Initially the tray was held in the up position and the food-tray opening was filled to the brim with grain. After the pigeon had eaten for 10 to 15 sec, the tray was lowered. On subsequent presentations, the tray was held until the pigeon ate from it. By the end of 10 tray operations all pigeons were reaching the tray and eating within a 4-sec tray-up interval. The key was unlighted during this phase. The tray was raised without knowledge of the bird's position.

EXPERIMENT 1

The basic paradigm consisted of the repeated pairing of a stimulus with the delivery of food. If the emergence of a key-peck under this regime were the result of some form of conditioning, the order in which stimulus and food appeared should be critical. In Exp. 1 the results of forward pairings (stimulus then food) were compared with the result of reverse pairings (food then stimulus).

Procedure

Forward Pairing. Thirty-six subjects received two sessions, each consisting of 80 pairings of an 8-sec white key-light followed immediately, at the offset of the key-light, by a 4-sec tray operation. Between trials the key was unlighted. The intertrial intervals varied randomly from 30 to 90 sec in 5-sec steps. All values were equally represented, yielding a mean intertrial duration of 60 sec. Two other conditions that had no effect on the emergence of the *first* key peck were introduced to maintain the peck to the lighted key for use in subsequent experiments. A peck during the 8-sec light-on period turned the light off and operated the tray immediately. A peck in an intertrial period prevented the appearance of a trial for the next 60 sec.

Reverse Pairing. Twelve subjects received the same treatment except that the order of tray operation and key-light was reversed. The tray operated for 4 sec and then the key-light came on for 8 sec. As in the forward pairing case, although irrelevant to the emergence of the first key-peck, a response on the trial turned the light off and operated the tray.

Results

A schema of the experimental arrangements and summary results are shown for the two groups of Exp. 1 and for those in subsequent experiments in Table 1.

TABLE 1 Summary of Results

PROCEDURE	NUMBER OF Ss	NO. & % OF Ss EMITTING A PECK WITHIN 160 TRIALS	MEAN TRIAL OF 1st PECK	RANGE
(FORWARD PAIRING)	36	36·100 %	45	6-119
(REVERSE PAIRING)	12	2-17 %	54	50-57
(TRIALS ONLY)	6	0·0 %	—	—
(TRAY ONLY-CONSTANT LIGHT)	12	4-33 %	NOT APPLICABLE	
(FORWARD PAIRING-3 SEC,TRIAL)	22	21-95 %	47	10-112
(FORWARD PAIRING-DARK KEY)	6	2-33 %	141	140-142
(FORWARD PAIRING-RED KEY)	6	6-100 %	33	14-66
(FORWARD PAIRING-FIXED TRIAL)	12	11-92 %	55	26-133

All 36 subjects in the forward-pairing group made a key-peck during the 8-sec trial at some point within the series of 160 trials. The mean and the range of the trial number of first peck are given in Table 1. For all but one subject, the first peck was made during the trial. An average of only 3.8 intertrial responses were made per session. Discriminative control by the key-light was unmistakable.

Direct observation and a study of motion pictures made of pigeons that were not part of the present group showed the following gross stages in the emergence of the key-peck: first, a general increase of activity, particularly during the trial-on period; second, a progressive centering of movements around the area of the key when lighted; and, finally, pecking movements in the direction of the key. As would be expected, the conditioning of recognizable movement patterns to the light occurred well before the key-peck. In almost all cases it became evident after 10 to 20 pairings that the lighted key occasioned specific movements, oriented to the key, that did not appear in the intertrial interval.

In the reverse-pairing condition only two of the 12 subjects struck the key within 160 trials; far less activity was directed toward the key. After two sessions, the 10 pigeons which failed to peck under the reverse-pairing procedure were placed on the forward-pairing procedure. Eight acquired the key-peck within an average of 59 trials (range of 13 to 88 pairings). The remaining two showed clear conditioning of some form of response occasioned by the lighted key but did not peck within a total of 160 forward-pairings.

EXPERIMENT 2

The results of the previous experiment demonstrate the importance of the order of the pairings. It is possible, however, that the comparison of the two orders exaggerates the efficacy of the forward-pairing arrangement because the reverse-pairing may work against the occurrence of movements toward the lighted key (cf. Rescorla, 1967). A group of subjects was therefore run with trial presentations but no tray operations in order to estimate the operant level of response to brief key-lights. There is also a practical question. If one is simply interested in conditioning a key-peck, is it helpful to use a momentary illumination of the key in conjunction with tray operations or would steady illumination of the key do as well in producing the first peck? To answer that question, a group was run with a steady key-light and intermittent tray operations.

Procedure
Trials Only. Six subjects received a program identical to that in the forward-pairing condition of Exp. 1 except that the tray did not operate.

Tray Operation Only. Twelve subjects received tray operations on the same schedule as in the forward-pairing condition of Exp. 1. The key-light, however, remained on throughout the sessions.

Results
From the summary data for these conditions in Table 1, it can be seen that no animal pecked the lighted key under the trials-only condition. All were

subsequently placed on the forward-pairing procedure and all acquired the key-peck within an average of 23 trials and a range of 6 to 45 trials.

The time available to make a peck at the constantly lighted key in the tray-only condition was about seven times longer than in the forward-pairing condition, but only four of the 12 subjects in the tray-only condition made a peck at any time. This proportion is very significantly less than the 36 of 36 animals that made a first peck in the forward-pairing procedure. The tray-only procedure did produce superstitious movement patterns of the kind described by Skinner (1948) but the movements were not as a rule oriented to the key.

The results attest to the efficacy of the forward-pairing procedure and show it to be superior to the use of a constantly lighted key with intermittent food presentations for the practical purpose of establishing a key-peck.

EXPERIMENT 3

The effects of three variations on the key-light stimulus were examined in the forward-pairing procedure.

If orienting toward and looking at the key is concentrated at the onset of the light, a shorter time between onset and food delivery might produce more rapid acquisition of the peck. A group was therefore run with a shorter trial stimulus.

The similarity of the white-lighted food-tray opening, in which the bird pecks at grain, to the white-lighted key might contribute to the occurrence of the key-peck through stimulus generalization. It should be noted, however, that the presumed effect of stimulus generalization would apply equally to the forward-pairing and to the reverse-pairing condition. Conceivably, however, similarity and forward-pairing interact to produce the result in the forward-pairing condition. The similarity of the trial stimulus to the tray light was reduced in different ways in two separate groups in order to examine the contribution of stimulus generalization.

Procedure

Forward Pairing—3-Sec Trial. Twenty-two subjects were trained under the forward-pairing procedure with a 3-sec trial rather than the 8-sec trial used in the previous forward-pairing groups.

Forward Pairing—Dark Key. Six subjects received the standard forward-pairing program except that the key was lighted (white) during the intertrial period and was turned off on the 8-sec trial that preceded tray operation.

Forward Pairing—Red Key. Six subjects received the same program as the previous group except that the key changed from white, during the intertrial period, to red on the trial, rather than from white to off.

Results

Results for the group that received forward pairings with a 3-sec trial are shown in Table 1. All but one of the 22 subjects pecked the key. However, acquisition was not faster than with the 8-sec trial. The shorter trial does reduce the opportunity for the peck to occur and this may balance out the advantage, if any, of a shorter interval from trial onset to reinforcement.

When the key-light was turned off on the trial (forward-pairing—dark-key condition in Table 1) two of the six subjects made a peck on the trial, and in both cases this occurred late in the second session. An additional two sessions were carried out. Two more birds pecked the dark key, one on the 195th pairing, the other on the 249th pairing. In all four cases, the first peck was made on the trial.

Direct observation showed that a special movement was conditioned on the dark-key trial, but the key-peck was clearly less likely to emerge, or at least required more pairings, in this arrangement than when the trial was marked by the lighting of the key. It is perhaps remarkable that the dark key was pecked at all, since during the trial the key had the same general appearance as the remainder of the panel. In the dim illumination of the enclosure there was little to contrast the key with the background.

The use of a red key on the trial made it stand out from the background on the trial, but still made the trial stimulus dissimilar to the white-lighted tray opening. All six subjects in the forward-pairing—red-key group acquired the peck. In every case the first peck occurred during the trial period. Subsequently an average of 41 intertrial responses per session occurred, a higher rate than was found with the standard forward-pairing arrangement (Exp. 1). The increase in intertrial responding is probably the result of greater generalization between a red trial stimulus and the white intertrial stimulus than is found with a white trial stimulus and a dark key between trials. The important point to note, however, is that the first peck occurred to the red key, not to the white intertrial stimulus which was more similar to the tray light. Further, acquisition with red key-light was no less rapid (average of 33 trials) than with a white key-light. Stimulus generalization from the tray-light to the key-light does not appear to contribute significantly to the present result.

EXPERIMENT 4

In the previous experiments the first key-peck brought an immediate operation of the food tray. Consequently the routine maintenance of responding after the first peck was not of special interest. In the present experiment key-pecks did not affect the trial duration nor the operation of the tray. It is of interest to examine the course of responding beyond the first peck for this arrangement.

Procedure

Forward Pairing—Fixed Trial. Twelve subjects received the standard forward-pairing procedure with an 8-sec trial which now remained fixed in duration throughout 160 pairings in two sessions.

Results

As shown in Table 1, all but one of the 12 subjects made at least one key-peck. One pigeon made only a single key-peck. Cumulative response curves for the remaining 10 birds are shown in Fig. 1. Five subjects developed and maintained a high rate throughout the 8-sec trial. The others showed an

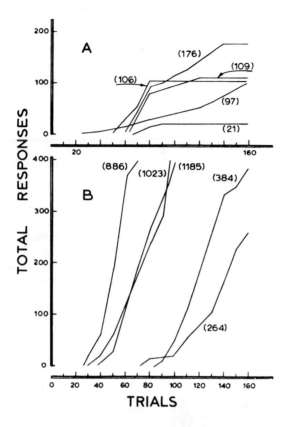

FIG. 1   Cumulative responses for individual birds in Exp. 4 in which a key-peck did not terminate the trial. Numbers in parentheses indicate total key-pecks by the 160th trial. For purposes of presentation the five subjects with a low rate of responding are shown in Panel A and the five with a high rate of responding are shown in Panel B.

appreciably lower level of responding and several stopped pecking the key before the end of the second session. One animal continued pecking during the trial but the location of the peck drifted away from the key. As would be expected, the arrangement does not guarantee a stable performance, but it is capable of generating a surprisingly high level of maintained key-pecking in a substantial percentage of cases. Again, intertrial key responses were infrequent (mean of 5.8 per session for the 11 subjects represented in Fig. 1).

In terms of the appearance of the first key-peck, the results for the fixed-trial group were similar to those obtained in the standard forward-pairing condition and in the forward-pairing—3-sec trial condition.

COLLECTED RESULTS FOR ACQUISITION

A frequency distribution of trial number on which the first peck occurred is shown in Fig. 2 for the 70 pigeons run under the three forward-pairing—3-sec trial group in Exp. 3 and the forward-pairing—fixed-trial group in Exp. 4. The mode of the distribution lies between the 21st and the 40th pairings.

DISCUSSION

The experiments have shown the reliable emergence of a key-peck as the result of unconditional forward pairings of a key-light stimulus and food. Some of the conditions for the occurrence of this response have been explored, but the present arrangement contains other features whose contribution to the result is unknown. Experiments in progress show that the location of the key near the food tray is not a critical feature, although it no doubt hastens the process. Several birds have acquired the peck to a key located on the wall opposite the tray opening or on a side wall. On the other hand, the use of a key-light as a stimulus is undoubtedly a critical feature. It could hardly be expected that an auditory stimulus or variations in overall illumination would yield a key-peck with the present procedure. For reasons shortly to be discussed, a question of particular interest is whether the use of grain as a reinforcer is essential to the emergence of the peck.

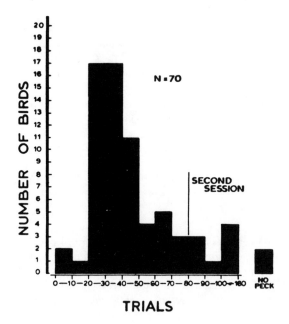

FIG. 2 Frequency distribution showing trials on which birds in certain forward-pairing groups (see text) emitted the first peck.

In our present view, the emergence of the key-peck may be characterized as a process of auto-shaping on which a direction is imposed by the species-specific tendency of the pigeon to peck at the things it looks at. The bird notices the onset of the light and perhaps makes some minimal motor adjustment to it. The temporal conjunction of reinforcement with noticing leads to orienting and looking toward the key. The species-specific look-peck coupling eventually yields a peck to the trial stimulus.

An appeal to some species-specific predispositions with respect to the stimulus is made necessary by the progressive change in behavior that leads up to the peck. It is not the initial behavior to the lighted key that is established by reinforcement. The progression would appear to be toward more rather than less effortful forms.

With the exception of the species-specific component, our account essentially parallels the accounts offered by Skinner (1948) and by Skinner and Morse (1957) for the first and second types of superstitious behavior. It relies on the shaping action of reinforcement and on the acquisition of discriminative control over the shaped response as a result of the joint presence of the stimulus and the reinforced response. However, what we have called a third type of superstition is also the standard arrangement for classical conditioning and that suggests the possibility of classically conditioned effects arising directly from the repeated pairing of a stimulus with food. Although we agree completely with Kimble's comment (1964) on a paper by Longo, Klempay, and Bitterman (1964) that the use of a classical conditioning procedure in no way guarantees that any response that becomes conditioned is a classically conditioned response, we nevertheless think it unwise to ignore the possibility that some form of classical conditioning contributes to the result.

There are two ways in which this might occur. First, classical conditioning could produce the response through stimulus substitution. The CS (lighted key) comes to evoke the response (peck) elicited by the UCS (grain). That seems unlikely because the peck appears to grow out of and depend upon the development of other motor responses in the vicinity of the key that do not themselves resemble a peck at grain. Even so, it will be of interest to see whether the use of water as a reinforcer, at which birds do not peck, will also condition the key peck.

Second, there is now a considerable number of experiments showing that classical pairings of a stimulus with food make the stimulus capable of affecting operant responses that were not occurring and could not have been shaped or specifically reinforced during the pairings (Bower and Grusec, 1964; Bower and Kaufman, 1963; Estes, 1943; Estes, 1948; Morse and Skinner, 1958; Trapold and Fairlie, 1965; Trapold and Odom, 1965; Walker, 1942). Clearly, there are stimulus effects resulting from pairing that are not specific to whatever responses may be concurrent with the pairing. Would not the same type of effect be involved in the acquisition of responses that are being made concurrently with the pairings as in the present arrangement? A general excitatory effect of the key-light resulting from the pairing of light and food may facilitate the general activity out of which the shaping produces a particular form of movement. While it is hard to see how an effect of this sort could not be involved, untangling a classical component from the response-specific action of reinforcement is extremely difficult, as the literature on the distinction between classical and operant conditioning so amply demonstrates.

Although the emergence of the key-peck as the result of response-independent pairings of the key-light with food raises several as yet unanswered questions about underlying processes, it does produce the key-peck with surprising regularity. When a large number of birds is to be used, the procedure saves time and labor. It no doubt results in idiosyncratic movement patterns associated with the peck itself, but is probably no worse in this respect than is hand-shaping. The procedure is easier to specify and to standardize. Further, it is free from the systematic effects that might be expected to result from individual differences among experimenters in the art of handshaping.

References

Bower, G. and Grusec, T. Effect of prior Pavlovian discrimination training upon training an operant discrimination. *J. exp. Anal. Behav.*, 1964, 7, 401—404.

Bower, G. and Kaufman, R. Transfer across drives of the discriminative effect of a Pavlovian conditioned stimulus. *J. exp. Anal. Behav.*, 1963, 6, 445—448.

Estes, W. K. Discriminative conditioning I. A discriminative property of conditioned anticipation. *J. exp. Psychol.*, 1943, 32, 152—155.

Estes, W. K. Discriminative conditioning II. Effects of a Pavlovian conditioned stimulus upon a subsequently established operant response. *J. exp. Psychol.*, 1948, 38, 173—177.

Kimble, G. A. Comment. *Psychon. Sci.*, 1964, 1, 40.

Longo, N., Klempay, S., and Bitterman, M. E. Classical appetitive conditioning in the pigeon. *Psychon. Sci.*, 1964, 1, 19—20.

Morse, W. H., and Skinner, B. F. A second type of superstition in the pigeon. *Amer. J. Psychol.*, 1957, 70, 308—311.

Morse, W. H. and Skinner, B. F. Some factors involved in the stimulus control of behavior. *J. exp. Anal. Behav.*, 1958, 1, 103—107.

Rescorla, R. A. Pavlovian conditioning and its proper control procedures. *Psychol. Rev.*, 1967, 74, 71—80.

Skinner, B. F. "Superstition" in the pigeon. *J. exp. Psychol.*, 1948, 38, 168—172.

Trapold, M. A. and Fairlie, J. Transfer of discrimination learning based upon contingent and non-contingent training procedures. *Psychol. Rep.*, 1965, 17, 239—246.

Trapold, M. A. and Odom, P. B. Transfer of a discrimination and a discrimination reversal between two manipulandum-defined responses. *Psychol. Rep.*, 1965, 16, 1213—1221.

Walker, Katherine C. The effect of a discriminative stimulus transferred to a previously unassociated response. *J. exp. Psychol.*, 1942, 31, 312—321.

We now return to the question of whether the laws of learning may vary with preparedness. David and Harriet Williams take the prepared key pecking response for grain and arrange the contingencies so that pecking the lighted key "costs" the pigeon grain. Such a procedure produces extinction in less prepared operants such as bar pressing for food in the rat. But Williams and Williams find that key pecking is maintained even when it prevents reinforcement. Their results suggest that extinction in prepared situations may be qualitatively different from extinction in unprepared ones.

15

AUTO-MAINTENANCE IN THE PIGEON: SUSTAINED PECKING DESPITE CONTINGENT NON-REINFORCEMENT

David R. Williams and Harriet Williams

If a response key is regularly illuminated for several seconds before food is presented, pigeons will peck it after a moderate number of pairings; this "auto-shaping" procedure of Brown and Jenkins (1968) was explored further in the present series of four experiments. The first showed that pecking was maintained even when pecks turned off the key and prevented reinforcement (auto-maintenance); the second controlled for possible effects of generalization and stimulus change. Two other experiments explored procedures that manipulated the tendency to peck the negatively correlated key by introducing alternative response keys which had no scheduled consequences. The results indicate that pecking can be established and maintained by certain stimulus-reinforcer relationships, independent of explicit or adventitious contingencies between response and reinforcer.

Brown and Jenkins (1968) reported a method for automatically and rapidly establishing key pecking in pigeons. Although their "shaping" procedure was carried out without reference to the birds' behavior, it led uniformly to the development of key pecking. Brown and Jenkins suggested that adventitious reinforcement of key-orienting behavior, aided by a tendency for birds to peck at things they look at, might provide a full account of their findings. The

From *Journal of the Experimental Analysis of Behavior*, 12 (1969), 511–520.

Dedicated to B. F. Skinner in his sixty-fifth year. This research was supported by a grant, NSF GB 5418, from the National Science Foundation. The authors are grateful to Thomas Allaway, Joseph Bernheim, and Elkan Gamzu for comments as helpful as they were astute.

consistent success of their procedure with a large number of subjects, however, suggests the operation of a more deterministic mechanism than one based primarily on adventitious reinforcement. The present experiments were carried out to explore the possibility that the auto-shaping procedure directly and actively engenders pecking.

The basic procedure of the present experiments was a variant of Brown and Jenkins' procedure in which pecks prevented reinforcement. As in their method, a response key was illuminated for several seconds before grain was presented. In the present experiment, key pecking turned off the key and blocked presentation of the reinforcer, so that pecking actually prevented the reinforcing event. Because the effect of key pecking under this procedure was not irrelevant to reinforcement but rather reduced it, persistent responding would raise a strong presumption that key pecking can be directly maintained by variables which do not involve response-reinforcer relationships of either deliberate or accidental origin.

EXPERIMENT 1

Method

Subjects. Thirteen naive Silver King pigeons, deprived to 80% of their free-feeding weight, served.

Apparatus. The pigeon chamber was 13 by 13 by 12 in.; one wall housed a standard three-key Lehigh Valley pigeon panel with keys which could be transilluminated by colored lights and vertical and horizontal striped patterns. The house-light and the keys used #1829 bulbs operated at 20 v dc. The keys were 8.5 in. above the floor of the compartment, and the grain hopper was centered 5 in. below the middle key.

Procedure. Upon initial placement in the experimental space, an experimentally naive bird was confronted by a raised grain hopper filled to the top with grain. The bird was allowed to eat for about 20 sec, after which the hopper was withdrawn. Over the course of several further presentations, which took place without reference to the bird's behavior, eating time was reduced to 4 sec. After these initial unsignalled presentations, birds were either placed directly on the negative procedure or first treated as described in Table 1, and then placed on the negative procedure.

TABLE 1   Number of Sessions During Which the Procedures Indicated Were in Force

Bird	Hand-Shaping	Auto Shaping	FR 1 Timeout
P-16	1	0	1
P-17	0	2	1
P-18	0	4	2

Procedures to the left were carried out first.

Auto-shaping: positive response contingency. Trials consisted of a 6-sec illumination of the center key, after which the key and the houselight were turned off, and the hopper was presented for 4 sec. Trials were separated by an intertrial interval averaging 30 sec, and ranging from 3 to 180 sec. Each peck on the lighted key turned off the key and the houselight, and presented the feeder directly. Intertrial pecks were recorded but had no scheduled consequences.

Auto-shaping: negative response contingency. The negative auto-shaping procedure exactly duplicated the positive auto-shaping procedure described above, except on trials where the lighted key was pecked. On those trials, the peck turned off the key, but the grain hopper was not presented. Neither the intertrial interval nor the onset of the next trial was altered by a peck; the key was simply darkened and the grain hopper was not presented. Intertrial pecks had no scheduled consequences.

Hand-shaping. After the general pretraining trials, the magazine was presented 50 additional times without warning on each of two successive days. The times between presentations were similar to the intertrial intervals in the auto-shaping procedure, but the response key was never illuminated. On the third experimental day, the key was illuminated on a trials basis, as in the auto-shaping procedure. The key remained on until the reinforcer was presented according to the method of successive approximations described in Ferster and Skinner (1957). A total of 50 reinforcers was presented on this day.

FR 1 Timeout. Under this procedure, the key was illuminated for a 6-sec period, unless a peck occurred. If a peck occurred, the house-light and key light were turned off and the reinforcer was presented. If the key was not pecked, it was turned off and no reinforcer was presented. Intertrial intervals were the same as in the positive auto-shaping procedure.

Results

Figure 1 shows results from four birds trained under auto-shaping with a negative response contingency. P-12 and P-19 received no prior training, whereas P-16 and P-17 had previously been trained on FR 1 Timeout. The ordinate of each panel represents the cumulative number of trials within each daily session on which a peck occurred, while the abscissa marks successive trials. A high slope indicated a high frequency of pecks on the negatively correlated key, and therefore a low frequency of reinforcement. Substantial responding clearly took place despite the negative correlation between pecking and reinforcement. Although P-12 did not begin pecking until 220 trials had been administered (and, therefore, 220 reinforcers presented), pecking was maintained at a remarkably high level for the next 18 days until another procedure (to be described in Exp. III) was instituted. Once pecking commenced, it persisted at a level such that only five to 20 reinforcers per day were presented out of a possible 50. P-19 began substantial pecking on the second day of training but did not maintain a high rate after Trial 150. Over the next 12 experimental sessions, pecking by this bird did not disappear but occurred only on a small percentage of the trials.

Because of prior training with a positive response contingency, P-16 and P-17 began the procedure with a high frequency of pecking. Over the first five

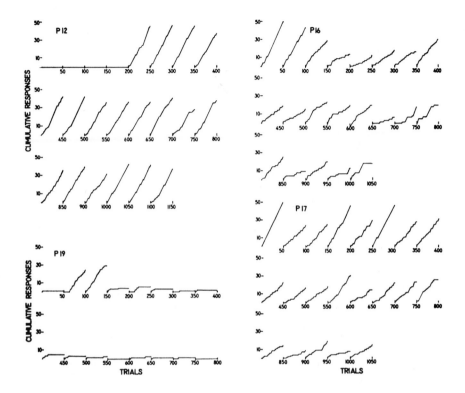

FIG. 1 Cumulative responses of four birds within daily sessions of 50 trials each. Pecking of P-16 and P-17 had previously been reinforced, while that of P-12 and P-19 had not. Throughout these sessions, each peck terminated the trial and prevented reinforcement.

sessions, the tendency of P-16 to peck decreased in a regular fashion. Some recovery took place after the fifth day, however, and substantial pecking continued throughout the next 15 days, waxing and waning over periods of several sessions. P-17 produced a similar overall pattern: during the first few days of the experiment the frequency of pecking declined markedly, but a series of recoveries and regressions characterized subsequent experimental days.

Results from the first 13 birds trained on auto-shaping with a negative response contingency are summarized in Fig. 2. It is evident that the procedure typically supported significant levels of responding whether or not key pecking had previously been reinforced (see Table 1 for particulars), and that the key pecking response could be established and maintained even though reinforcement was contingent on a failure to peck the key. Only one bird (P-19) regularly responded on less than 10% of the trials once pecking had begun.

The negative contingency was not wholly without effect. Two birds (P-019 and P-020) were changed from the negatively contingent procedure to FR 1

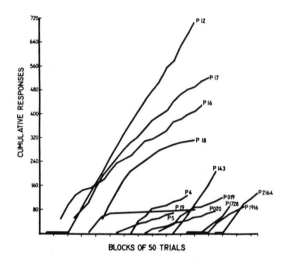

FIG. 2 Cumulative responses per session for the first 13 pigeons run with contingent non-reinforcement. Curves for the various birds are displaced along the abscissa.

Timeout with percentage reinforcement immediately after the sessions shown in Fig. 2. Under this new procedure, reinforcement was available on the same proportion of trials as had actually included reinforcement on the final three days with the negative contingency. Latency distributions from the last three days of contingent nonreinforcement, and from the last three sessions under percentage reinforcement, are compared in Fig. 3. Two changes are evident: under percentage reinforcements, pecking took place on a greater proportion of trials than before, and the pecks were generally of shorter latency. The longer latencies that characterized the distributions under the negative procedure were also a conspicuous feature of latency distributions from other birds trained with the negative procedure.

EXPERIMENT II

The persistent pecking observed under the negative contingency might be attributed to generalization of feeder-oriented pecking or to reinforcement from stimulus change. A successive discrimination experiment carried out in a parametrically similar framework permitted assessment of these possibilities. On trials where the key was illuminated with the positive discriminative stimulus (S^D), a peck turned off the key and was reinforced; trials of this sort maintain feeding and feeder-oriented pecking in the situation. On trials where the other stimulus (S^Δ) was presented, no grain reinforcers could be produced but pecks did turn off the stimulus. Observation of pecking at S^Δ thus provided a means of assessing both the level of generalized pecking and the level of pecking

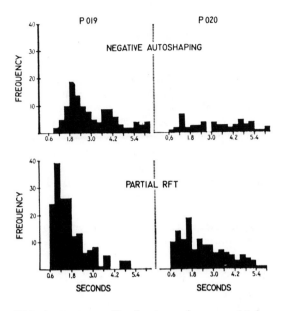

FIG. 3 Latency distributions for two birds (left and right columns) under contingent non-reinforcement and subsequent partial reinforcement. Latencies are indicated only for trials where pecks actually occurred.

maintained by the stimulus change itself. The main difference between discrimination training and auto-shaping with a negative contingency is that S^Δ is never paired with grain, but the negatively contingent key does receive such pairing on trials where pecks are not made. Differences between pecking S^Δ and pecking the negative key therefore indicate the effectiveness of the pairing procedure itself.

Method

Subjects. Six experimentally naive Silver King pigeons were deprived to 80% of their free-feeding weight.

Procedure. The apparatus and general procedures were identical to those described for Exp. I. Three birds (P-20, P-21, P-2) were trained initially by positive auto-shaping, and three (P-7, P-8, P-9) by the hand-shaping procedure. After pecking commenced, all birds were trained on the FR 1 Timeout procedure for two days. Discrimination training was then introduced and consisted of 100 trials per day, of which half were positive and half were negative. The intertrial intervals were as in Exp. I. For birds P-7, P-8, and P-2 the discriminanda were red *vs.* green keys and for birds P-9, P-20, and P-21 they were horizontal *vs.* vertical stripes presented against a green background. On any trial the key was illuminated for 6 sec if no peck occurred. When a peck occurred, the key was turned off. On positive trials, 4-sec access to grain followed immediately, but no access to grain was provided on negative trials. The rate of trial presentation could not be influenced by pecking.

Results and Discussion

Because all birds pecked on virtually every positive trial, those results are not presented. Figure 4 summarizes the data from S^Δ trials for all six birds, plotted on coordinates similar to those of Fig. 2 to facilitate comparison. Training was terminated for each bird after a session in which no pecks were made to S^Δ; those sessions are included in the figure.

After responding on virtually all of the 50 S^Δ trials of the first session, birds with a hue discrimination ceased responding after one or two additional sessions; birds with the horizontal-vertical discrimination persisted somewhat longer, but did not show the sustained responding typical of the auto-maintenance performances shown in Fig. 2.

Since the persistent responding that characterizes auto-maintenance was not sustained by S^Δ, generalized pecking and reinforcement of pecking by stimulus change as such, seem inadequate to account for the auto-maintenance phenomenon. The main difference between S^Δ and a negatively correlated key is

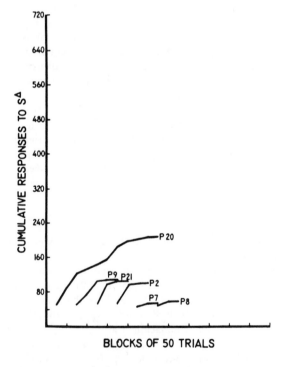

FIG. 4   Cumulative responses per session to S^Δ. Curves for the various birds are displaced along the abscissa; the scale is the same as that used in Fig. 2.

the pairing of the latter with grain on trials where pecks do not occur: this aspect of the procedure, then, appears to be responsible for the sustained pecking observed under the negative contingency.

The uniformly high tendency of all birds to peck S^D even while S^Δ responses declined and disappeared, demonstrates that some visual information from the key was received on every trial. If "noticing the key", followed by an automatic "look-peck coupling" were sufficient to sustain continued responding, pecking of S^Δ would have persisted, just as pecking to the response key did in Exp. I. It is clear that noticing a stimulus that is never followed by grain does not lead to pecking.

EXPERIMENT III

The previous experiments indicated that pairing a response key with grain sustains pecking at the key, even though the key peck prevents reinforcement. The phenomenon of auto-maintenance is both surprising and difficult to pursue because of the failure of the negative contingency to exert a strong suppressive effect. In this experiment, a procedure designed to abolish pecking on the negative key was explored. Two differently colored keys were simultaneously illuminated and darkened on every trial. The negative contingency was in force on one key, but the other key was functionally irrelevant: pecks there had no scheduled consequence or greater significance than, for example, pecks on the floor or houselight. The development of responding on the functionally irrelevant key in preference to the negative key would indicate behavioral sensitivity to some aspect of the negative contingency, and would thereby provide a means of identifying more clearly the circumstances that sustain pecking on the negative key.

Method

Subjects. Two experimentally naive birds, and four others shifted directly from Exp. I, were maintained at 80% of their pre-experimental weights.

Procedure. The negatively contingent procedure of Exp. I was carried out exactly as described there except that a second key was illuminated and darkened along with the negative key. The two keys were distinguished by color—red or green—and the color correlated with the negative contingency was counterbalanced across birds. The center and right key positions were used, and position of the two key colors reversed in an unpredictable manner during all sessions, so that key color and not position was correlated with the contingency.

Results

Results of two birds trained from the beginning of the experiment with both negatively correlated and irrelevant keys are shown in Fig. 5. P-23 began pecking on the third day of training, and emitted substantial numbers of pecks on both the irrelevant and the negatively contingent key. The frequency of pecking the negative key declined during the next several sessions, and the significance of the key colors was reversed after a session in which the negatively contingent key was never pecked. On the day following reversal, no pecks were made on the irrelevant key (which had previously been negatively contingent) and the other

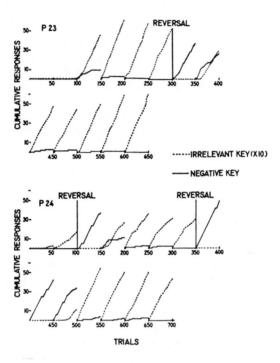

FIG. 5 Cumulative responses per trial to the negative and (on a reduced scale as indicated) the irrelevant key. The heavy vertical lines indicate when the significance of the key colors was reversed.

key (previously irrelevant) was pecked on virtually every trial. During the next few days, however, this pattern reversed and by the end of the sessions shown, all pecking was again directed at the irrelevant key. Similar results were obtained for P-24; whenever the significance of the key color was reversed, pecking changed from the negatively contingent to the irrelevant key during the course of several sessions.

This bird showed a marked preference for the key that was initially irrelevant; so the first shift was made after two sessions during which the irrelevant key sustained substantial pecking and no pecks were made on the negatively contingent key. It is evident that the contingency exerted stronger control than the marked bias for pecking a particular key color, and that the locus of pecking shifted from the negatively contingent to the irrelevant key after all reversals of conditions.

The irrelevant key was similarly effective in birds that had previously been trained only on the negative key. Figure 6 shows the development of control by the irrelevant key in two birds that served as subjects in Exp. I. In both cases the irrelevant key gradually gained control during a series of sessions and, as with the

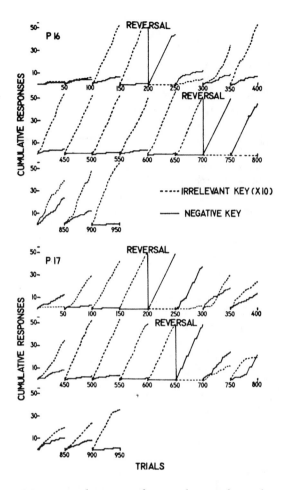

FIG. 6 Development of responding to the irrelevant key by two birds with a prior history of contingent non-reinforcement. The heavy vertical lines indicate where the significance of the key colors was reversed.

naive birds, ultimately extinguished responding on the negatively contingent key. These results are typical of those of all four birds in which this procedure was carried out: in every case responding on the negatively contingent key ceased, and after reversal of stimuli, behavior shifted from the negatively contingent to the irrelevant key.

The continuing importance of the irrelevant key is suggested by the vigorous but gratuitous responding directed to it. It appears that the irrelevant key directs responding away from the negatively contingent key but does not produce an overall suppression. Direct evidence on this point was obtained by alternatively providing and omitting the irrelevant key in five-trial blocks. The negative contingency was effective only when the irrelevant key was present. When it was absent, the negative key was frequently pecked, though such responses prevented reinforcement. Apparently the irrelevant key provided a stronger stimulus for pecking than did the negative key. Even though it did not make the negative contingency effective by itself, the irrelevant key effectively demonstrated behavioral sensitivity to some aspect of the negative contingency.

EXPERIMENT IV

The only difference between the negative and irrelevant keys was the contingency scheduled on one and omitted on the other; as stimuli, both bore identical relationships to the grain reinforcer. The final experiment was carried out to determine whether intrinsic stimulus properties of the irrelevant key (as contrasted with those of other ostensibly suitable stimuli for pecking, such as the houselight) were responsible for its effectiveness, or whether the temporal relationship between the irrelevant key and the reinforcer was critical. In this experiment, a continuously illuminated but irrelevant key was substituted for the intermittent irrelevant key of Exp. III. As in the previous experiment, two keys were available on every trial, one scheduled with the negative contingency, the other with no contingency at all. The irrelevant key was also present between trials; it was darkened only during feeder presentations, and its location among the three key positions was changed at the start of each trial. If the mere availability of an irrelevant key is sufficient to support control by the negative contingency, a continuous key should substitute effectively for an intermittent one. However, if temporal relations between the irrelevant key and the reinforcer are important, the continuous key would not be an effective substitute. To assess the relative effectiveness of the continuous and intermittent irrelevant keys, additional birds received both continuous and intermittent irrelevant keys, while other birds were exposed only to the continuous key.

Method

Subjects. Four experimentally naive birds, and four others shifted directly from Exp. I, were maintained at 80% of their pre-experimental weight.

Procedure. The negatively contingent procedure of Exp. I was carried out exactly as described there with the addition of one or two other keys, distinguished by color from each other and from the negative key. For P-1916, P-2164, P-1909, and P-2096, a second key with no scheduled consequences was continuously illuminated except during feeder presentations. The position of this second key and the position of the negatively contingent key shifted at the start of each trial (defined by the presentation of the negatively contingent key). Both keys were distinctively colored and colors were counterbalanced for the four subjects. All three possible key locations were used, with two of the three being illuminated on any trial until a peck occurred or the reinforcer was presented. The negative key was darkened when pecked, but the continuous key did not go out. For P-1543, P-1728, P-1446, and P-1649, the procedure was exactly the same except that an intermittent irrelevant key was also present, and operated as in Exp. III. The intermittent irrelevant key had a third distinctive color, which was the same for all four birds, but the colors of the continuous and negative keys were counterbalanced. The location of all three key colors was shifted at the start of every trial, and following a peck or a reinforcement, the continuous key stayed in the same place until the onset of the next trial.

Results

The two left panels (A and B) of Fig. 7 show responding over the course of the entire experiment for two birds trained first with the negative contingency alone; the right panels (C and D) show performance of two birds trained with a continuous key present from the start of the experiment. The two birds with only a continuous irrelevant key responded on the negative key for more than 30 sessions, and pecked far less on the continuous irrelevant key (Panels A and C). As in Exp. III, pecking on the negative key was controlled by the parallel presentation of an intermittent irrelevant key. Data from the other birds were entirely consistent with the results shown here: an irrelevant key presented along with the negative key enabled the contingency to gain control, but an irrelevant key that was continuously available did not.

The continuous key did not go entirely unpecked; P-1649, in fact, pecked more frequently on the continuous than on the intermittent key for the first four days after it was introduced. The timing of the pecks on the continuous key is of interest: not once during the experiment did a peck occur on the continuous key while the negatively correlated key was illuminated. Pecking was directed to the continuous key solely during the intertrial interval when it was the only key available.

Following the experiment proper, six birds were given additional training with the continuous key alone. The procedure was exactly as before except that the negative and intermittent irrelevant keys were never turned on. Because the location of the continuous key shifted when the trial began, it continued to signal the forthcoming presentation of grain; now, however, it was the only event to do so. Data from these sessions are shown to the right of the solid bars in Fig. 7. In all, four of the six birds trained under this procedure developed substantial pecking on the continuous key. Although pecking occurred throughout the session, it was concentrated in the 6 sec following a shift in the location of the key, when the presentation of grain was imminent.

The continuous key was not functionally similar to the intermittent key: it did not compete successfully with the negative key, nor was it pecked as often as the intermittent irrelevant key. The ineffectiveness of the continuous key is clearly consistent with the failure of other stimulus alternatives, such as the houselight, to substitute in function for the intermittent irrelevant key. If any of the effects reported in Exp. I and III were related to special characteristics of illuminated keys, the findings of those experiments would presumably have been disturbed by the presence of a continuously available key of similar appearance. The inability of the continuous key to compete with the negative key is particularly significant in light of the fact that responding finally developed, even in birds for which no key peck had ever been reinforced, when the continuous key was ineffective because it was a weaker stimulus for pecking, not

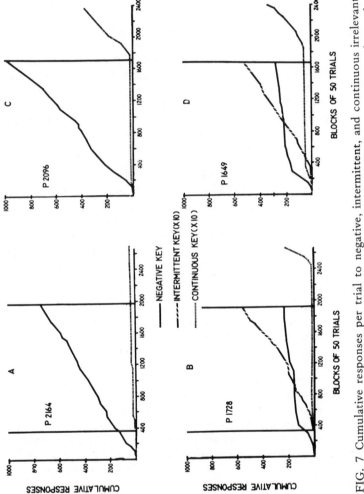

FIG. 7 Cumulative responses per trial to negative, intermittent, and continuous irrelevant keys. Panels A and B show cases where birds were trained first on the negative key only. Panels B and D show cases where three keys were present during the main part of the experiment. The heavy vertical lines within panels indicate changes in the variety of keys presented on each trial.

because it was a wholly inadequate one. It could not have been weaker than the negative key because of extinction of pecking during the intertrial interval: due to the negative contingency, responses on the continuous key were inevitably more closely related to reinforcement than those on the negative key. On the other hand, the relative effectivenss of the negative key, compared to the continuous key, would seem also to be due to its association with the reinforcer: pairing of the negative key and the reinforcer established a relatively strong and directed tendency to peck on the negative key. Finally, the success of the intermittent irrelevant key in competing with the negative key would appear to depend in part on the fact that it bore the same stimulus-reinforcer relationship as the negative key, and to some consequence of the fact that reinforcement was never withheld in its presence.

GENERAL DISCUSSION

Successful auto-maintenance—persistent, directed key pecking despite contingent non-reward—does not seem to be a natural implication of either operant or respondent principles. Because actual pecking of the negative key produces nonreinforcement, it cannot be directly maintained by adventitious relationships. If it is supposed that unobserved behaviors preceding the actual striking of the key are adventitiously maintained, then either (a) one must assume that these adventitiously maintained precursors are inflexibly linked to pecking and account for why they are not extinguished or replaced by precursors for other responses, or (b) one must suppose that the precursors do not invariably lead to pecking but can precede other behaviors as well. If the latter assumption is made, then it is difficult to see why, by operant principles, the precursors do not become closely linked to some other behavior because of the consistent reinforcement such linkage would produce. Even if attention—heightened and directed by adventitious reinforcement and giving rise to behavior through a look-peck coupling—is assumed to be responsible for the initial pecks (Brown and Jenkins), it is difficult to see why the continual extinction of a specific response component would not lead to an operant shift in attention and inconsequential responding (when the negative key comes on, look at the continuous key and peck it). It is, for example, very difficult to see how the continuous key could ultimately control pecking but not compete with the negative key. It seems clear that stimulus-reinforcer relationships, and not only response-reinforcer interactions, play a special role in this phenomenon. Such a conclusion, of course, takes the phenomenon out of reach of a standard operant analysis, where the influence of stimuli depends on their discriminative function with regard to experimental contingencies.

Similarities to the respondent domain are easy to recognize: indeed, the auto-maintenance procedure is formally identical to the "omission training" procedure of Sheffield (1965) except that a key peck substitutes for a saliva drop. In the present case, the response at issue is topographically similar to the response made to food. However, even if one ignores the usual application of respondent analyses to autonomic rather than skeletal behahvior, the directed quality of the induced pecking does not follow naturally from respondent principles (see also Brown and Jenkins, 1968). It is unclear, for example, why pecking would be directed at the key rather than the feeder, or indeed why it would be directed anywhere at all. Although respondent laws (which deal with laws of stimulus-reinforcer pairings) are no doubt pertinent to the present phenomenon, a detailed account of this phenomenon would seem to demand a serious augmentation of respondent principles to account for the directed quality of the response.

The most direct empirical precedent for the present phenomena is provided by the work of Breland and Breland (1961), who found, in several species, that response patterns that were related to a reinforcer could "drift" into a situation even though they delayed and interfered with actual production of the reinforcer. As in the present case, such behaviors were intrusive, counterproductive, and uncontrolled by their contingencies. In addition, it has been shown that pigeons trained to peck at other pigeons develop far more elaborate patterns of "aggressive" behavior than the actual contingency demands; the behavior is sometimes so vigorous that it continues into the period when reinforcement is available (Skinner, 1959; Reynolds, Catania, and Skinner, 1963; Azrin and Hutchinson, 1967). Similar effects have been reported in rats (Ulrich, Johnston, Richardson, and Wolff, 1963). When rats' running is reinforced, the speed at which they run is governed directly by the magnitude of the reinforcer, and fast running develops whether or not it produces more rapid reinforcement (Williams, 1966). These examples make it clear that contingencies of reinforcement alone do not determine when or how strongly some behaviors occur, even if the behaviors appear to be skeletal or "voluntary". As an instance of such direct control, the present phenomenon does not appear to be an isolated curiosity.

The place of this phenomenon in the general operant framework deserves explicit consideration. While it has always been recognized that many aspects of experiments, such as deprivation or physical details of the experimental space, influence the "operant level" of some responses, it now appears that many other variables, such as stimulus-reinforcer relationships, can also have an important influence on the unreinforced level of occurrence of some responses. That the stimulus-reinforcer pairing overrode opposing effects of differential reinforcement indicates that the effect was a powerful one, and demonstrates that a high level of responding does not imply the operation of explicit or even adventitious reinforcement. This point should be taken into careful account when effects of reinforcing contingencies *per se* are under investigation (see, for example, Herrnstein, 1966).

To relate the present work to the concept of "operant level" furnishes a context but does not provide an account. In further work, the concept of "arbitrariness", which is so frequently claimed for operants, will require close attention: is the action of reinforcement—direct or contingent—different when a response is "naturally" in the organism's repertoire, or when it bears a special relationship to the reinforcer? More broadly, consideration should be given to ascertaining how frequently direct, as opposed to contingent, influences of reinforcers enter into the determination of "skeletal" or "voluntary" behavior in natural environments.

References

Azrin, N. H. and Hutchinson, R. R. Conditioning of the aggressive behavior of pigeons by a fixed-interval schedule of reinforcement. *Journal of the Experimental Analysis of Behavior*, 1967, *10*, 395—402.

Breland, K. and Breland, M. The misbehavior of organisms. *American Psychologist*, 1961, *16*, 681—684.

Brown, P. L. and Jenkins, H. M. Auto-shaping of the pigeons's key-peck. *Journal of the Experimental Analysis of Behavior*, 1968, *11*, 1—8.

Ferster, C. B. and Skinner, B. F. *Schedules of reinforcement*. New York: Appleton-Century-Crofts, 1957.

Herrnstein, R. J. Superstition: a corollary of the principles of operant conditioning. In W. K. Honig (Ed.), *Operant behavior: areas of research and application*. New York: Appleton-Century-Crofts, 1966, pp. 33—51.

Reynolds, G. S., Catania, A. C., and Skinner, B. F. Conditioned and unconditioned aggression in pigeons. *Journal of the Experimental Analysis of Behavior*, 1963, *6*, 73—74.

Sheffield, F. D. Relation between classical conditioning and instrumental learning. In W. F. Prokasy (Ed.), *Classical conditioning*. New York: Appleton-Century-Crofts, 1965. Pp. 302—322.

Skinner, B. F. An experimental analysis of certain emotions. *Journal of the Experimental Analysis of Behavior*, 1959, *2*, 264. (Abstract).

Ulrich, R., Johnston, M., Richardson, J., and Wolff, P. The operant conditioning of fighting behavior in rats. *Psychology Records*, 1963, *13*, 465—470.

Williams, D. R. Relation between response amplitude and reinforcement. *Journal of Experimental Psychology*, 1966, *71*, 634—641.

What are we to make of the failure of the key peck to extinguish even when it is counterproductive? One likely possibility is that once prepared instrumental responses take hold, it is not easy to stop them. There is another possibility: that the autoshaped key peck is not an instrumental response, but a classically conditioned response. We have considered it operant and included it in this section simply because it is the response most commonly used in instrumental learning studies of reinforcement schedules. But in autoshaping, a CS (lit key) is paired with delivery of grain (US), which elicits a pecking response (UR). Soon the lit key comes to control pecking (CR). If this is so, the reason extinction is not observed in negative autoshaping may be that the classical contingency is not broken; the lit key-grain pairing would have to be broken, not the pecking-grain contingency. Barry Schwartz in a personal communication claims that such a procedure extinguishes the key peck. He has also (1971) provided related evidence: Autoshaped and CRF key pecks have a response duration of 10−20 milliseconds, while fixed-interval and ratio pecks have a duration of 30−40 milliseconds. These data might indicate that the longer pecks are truly voluntary, deliberate, and instrumental, while the autoshaped pecks are involuntary and reflexive, and thus subject to classical conditioning.

Be that as it may, there is other evidence that prepared learning may be qualitatively more resistant to extinction than unprepared learning. In the following study of the discriminative control of instrumental responding Vaughn Stimbert trains rats to choose a water reward in the goal box either with an inanimate object as the cue which indicates the correct box or with another rat as the cue. Using a conspecific cue his rats learn rapidly and show great resistance to extinction. With the inanimate cue, learning is painstaking and extinction precipitous. So rats seem prepared to learn which way to go on the basis of what other rats do, and to hold on more tenaciously to this learning than to learning controlled by more arbitrary cues.

16

A COMPARISON OF LEARNING BASED
ON SOCIAL OR NONSOCIAL
DISCRIMINATIVE STIMULI

Vaughn E. Stimbert

Two groups of six rats each were trained to run across an open-field maze with four choice-point alternatives. For one group the correct response was based upon a social discriminative stimulus and for the other it was based upon a nonsocial discriminative stimulus. Results indicated that social responses were learned faster and were more durable under extinction conditions than were responses based on nonsocial stimuli.

Previous studies in the area of animal social learning (Nakamura, Smith, & Schwartz, 1963; Stimbert, 1970) have suggested that responses based on social cues may be acquired faster and be more durable than responses to nonsocial cues. Although numerous investigations (Daniel, 1942; Husted & McKenna, 1966; Miller, Banks, & Ogawa, 1962; Murphy, Miller, & Mirsky, 1955; Skinner, 1962; Wiest, 1969) have shown the feasibility of using social cues in learning studies, apparently no direct comparisons have been made between social and nonsocial discriminative stimuli utilizing identical apparatus and similar response topographies. Since a large part of the adaptive behaviors of animals requires responses based on social learning, it is of some concern to determine how this learning differs, if at all, from that based on nonsocial stimuli. The present study was designed to determine *if* such differences exist, and no attempt was made to identify the specific components of social and inanimate stimuli that might produce such differences.

From *Psychonomic Science*, 20 (1970), 185—186.

SUBJECTS

The experimental Ss were 12 experimentally naive Sprague-Dawley female albino rats about 126 days old at the beginning of the study. Six Ss were assigned randomly to the social group and six to the nonsocial group. Twelve female Sprague-Dawley rats, approximately 300 days old, were used as stimulus (leader) Ss. These rats had been used in two previous studies and were highly proficient in traversing an open-field apparatus with other Ss present.

APPARATUS

The apparatus was an open-field maze with double startboxes in tandem on one side and four double-compartment goalboxes on the other side. Photocells were located 1 in. in front of the rear startbox and at the entrance to each goalbox. They were programmed through relays and timers to record the latencies of experimental Ss leaving the startbox and the running times of all Ss. Running times included both start times and time to enter the goalbox. Other features of the apparatus and the training procedures have been previously described in detail (Stimbert, 1969).

PROCEDURE

The social response to be acquired by the social group in this study was following behavior. A leader S previously trained to a specific goalbox (three leader Ss per box) was released from the front startbox and simultaneously a follower S was released from the rear startbox. The follower was reinforced with .5 ml of water for entry into the same goalbox as the leader. The double-compartment goalboxes separated leader and follower Ss and precluded viewing of the other S being reinforced. Leaders were alternated randomly so that on any one trial each goalbox had an equal probability of being correct.

For the nonsocial group Ss were also released from the rear startbox; however, they were trained to run down a black strip of cloth tape, 1 in. wide, which began at the front startbox and ended at one of the four goalboxes containing .5 ml of water. The tape was alternated from goalbox to goalbox in the same random fashion as the leader Ss in the social group. This arrangement produced nearly identical behavioral topographies in both groups.

Extinction sessions were identical to acquisition sessions, with the exception that water was unavailable for any experimental S. Each experimental S performing without error during one acquisition session (10 trials) was placed on extinction the subsequent session. All S were run under 24-h water deprivation.

RESULTS

The accuracy of rats learning a social cue vs an inanimate cue is displayed in Fig. 1. During acquisition all Ss in the social group learned to follow other Ss in a maximum of 80 trials, whereas after 200 trials, the nonsocial group was running with only 72% accuracy and only two Ss in the group had reached the 100% criterion level. Based on the number of trials to criterion, these differences were

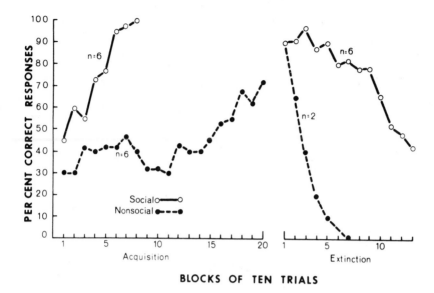

FIG. 1 Percentage correct in acquisition and extinction by blocks of 10 trials.

statistically significant ($t = 269$, $df = 10$, $p < .001$). Due to time limitations, the acquisition phase was discontinued after 200 trials and extinction sessions were run on those Ss having reached criterion.

It can also be seen in Fig. 1 that during extinction nonsocial Ss reached a chance level (25%) of performance after 40 trials, while social Ss were following above 40% after 130 trials. Based on trials to criterion for those Ss reaching an extinction criterion of 0% following for one session, these differences were statistically significant ($t = 10.95$, $df = 2$, $p < .01$)

Differences in running speeds during acquisition and extinction are shown in Fig. 2. Again, the performance of the social group is consistently superior to that of the nonsocial group. In acquisition, group differences are not as marked as in extinction, where, after 20 trials, the running speeds in the nonsocial group dropped to less than .2 ft/sec. On the other hand, social Ss maintained speeds consistent with their terminal acquisition performance of about 1 ft/sec.

DISCUSSION

The present findings support the hypothesis that a response to an animate, social discriminative stimulus is learned faster and is more durable than a response to an inanimate, nonsocial discriminative stimulus. Even after reaching the same asymptotic level of performance in acquisition, differences between the groups during extinction are striking and favor the social response. Individual social Ss have been observed to follow at an 80% level of accuracy after as many as 150 extinction trials.

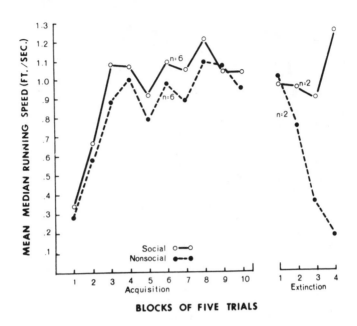

FIG. 2 Running times in acquisition and extinction by blocks of five trials.

Informal comparisons of previous studies on following behavior in rats with other studies involving nonsocial situations lead to conclusions that are consistent with the extinction data from this experiment. For example, it appears that approximately 150 trials are required to reduce social following behavior to a chance (25%) level once acquired under continuous reinforcement. With partial reinforcement experience, 150 trials only reduces following to 60% (Stimbert, 1970). Using counterconditioning procedures during extinction, whereby nonfollowing responses are reinforced, the number of extinction trials required to obtain a chance performance is approximately 75 (Stimbert, 1969) or one-half that of extinction procedures making reinforcement unavailable for any response. In contrast, studies of extinction in straight runways or T-mazes frequently show Ss reaching criterion in 25 trials or less. In fact, it is unusual to find extinction data reported on more than 30 trials, which suggests extinction is essentially complete at that point. Thus, the fastest extinction obtained in studies of social following behavior indicates more durability than extinction in nonsocial situations.

At this time it is difficult to identify the specific factors responsible for the superiority of social discriminative stimuli. Even though the social stimulus is typically available for viewing less than 2 sec, the response is acquired more rapidly than one based on a nonsocial, fixed and, what would seem to be, a more discriminable visual stimulus. Using present procedures, assessment of the importance of olfactory, auditory, and movement cues in facilitating what is primarily a visually controlled response might be accomplished. For example, it may be productive to study following behavior in anosmic rats or to compare social learning based on moving vs fixed social stimuli. Following behavior could also be investigated by systematically changing the leader S so as to include other strains of rats or possibly a different species. This methodology provides an additional approach for determining the variables relevant to animal social behavior.

References

Daniel, W. J. Cooperative problem solving in rats. *Journal of Comparative Psychology,* 1942, *34,* 361—369.

Husted, J. R., & McKenna, F. S. The use of rats as discriminative stimuli. *Journal of the Experimental Analysis of Behavior,* 1966, *9,* 677—679.

Miller, R. E., Banks, J. H., Jr., & Ogawa, N. Communication of affect in "cooperative conditioning" of rhesus monkeys. *Journal of Abnormal & Social Psychology,* 1962, *64,* 343—348.

Murphy, J. V., Miller, R. E., & Mirsky, I. A. Interanimal conditioning in the monkey. *Journal of Comparative & Physiological Psychology,* 1955, *48,* 211—214.

Nakamura, C. Y., Smith, J. C., & Schwartz, F. W. Establishment of a lasting discriminative stimulus in rats by competition training. *Journal of Comparative & Physiological Psychology,* 1963, *56,* 852—856.

Skinner, B. F. Two "synthetic social relations." *Journal of the Experimental Analysis of Behavior,* 1962, *5,* 531—533.

Stimbert, V. E. Effects of early experience on social learning in rats. *Journal of Comparative & Physiological Psychology,* 1969, *69,* 640—643.

Stimbert, V. E. Partial reinforcement of social behavior in rats. *Psychological Reports,* 1970, *26,* 723—726.

Wiest, W. M. Socially mediated stimulus control in pigeons. *Psychological Reports,* 1969, *25,* 139—148.

Brown and Jenkins really started something. Investigations of the preparedness of keypecking in the pigeon are mushrooming. Differential reinforcement of low rates (DRL) is a schedule which forces the animal to refrain from responding for a time so that a later response will produce food. If he responds during the waiting period, he loses the reinforcer. Rats do well on a bar-press DRL, but pigeons do very poorly on a key-peck DRL. Barry Schwartz and David Williams (1971) reported that if pigeons can peck at an irrelevant "bleeder" key which is lit whenever the DRL key is lit, they can allocate their responses adaptively by pecking at high rates on the bleeder key until the waiting period is up, and then pecking the DRL key. Nancy Hemmes (1970) has reported that if pigeons are required to step on a treadle as the DRL response, they learn rapidly. So it appears that highly prepared responses are hard to inhibit and can disrupt behavior which requires their inhibition. If more arbitrary responses are used in schedules requiring the inhibition of responding, learning proceeds readily.

The last article in the instrumental learning section, by the late Keller Breland and his wife, Marian Breland, demonstrates such intrusion of prepared responses onto arbitrary operants. Trained as experimental psychologists, the Brelands made their living by training many species to perform theatrical and commercially appealing responses. Out of their broad experience, they made a signal contribution to the experimental analysis of behavior by bringing "instinct" back into the empty organism. In the previous article Williams and Williams showed that a response highly prepared for food getting is maintained even under conditions which prevent reinforcement. Breland and Breland find that pigs, raccoons, and chickens readily learn a large number of quite arbitrary responses to get food, but occasionally, just when acquisition is going smoothly, behaviors which postpone or prevent reinforcement intrude increasingly. These behaviors are from the species' natural food-getting repertoire. So highly prepared responses, like the one investigated by Brown and Jenkins, and Williams and Williams, may not only fail to extinguish, but also crop up unexpectedly and compete with the learning of less-prepared operants. The intrusion of prepared responses may be the mechanism of some or even all contrapreparedness.

17

THE MISBEHAVIOR OF ORGANISMS

Keller Breland and Marian Breland

There seems to be a continuing realization by psychologists that perhaps the white rat cannot reveal everything there is to know about behavior. Among the voices raised on this topic, Beach (1950) has emphasized the necessity of widening the range of species subjected to experimental techniques and conditions. However, psychologists as a whole do not seem to be heeding these admonitions, as Whalen (1961) has pointed out.

Perhaps this reluctance is due in part to some dark precognition of what they might find in such investigations, for the ethologists Lorenz (1950, p. 233) and Tinbergen (1951, p. 6) have warned that if psychologists are to understand and predict the behavior of organisms, it is essential that they become thoroughly familiar with the instinctive behavior patterns of each new species they essay to study. Of course, the Watsonian or neobehavioristically oriented experimenter is apt to consider "instinct" an ugly word. He tends to class it with Hebb's (1960) other "seditious notions" which were discarded in the behavioristic revolution, and he may have some premonition that he will encounter this bete noir in extending the range of species and situations studied.

We can assure him that his apprehensions are well grounded. In our attempt to extend a behavioristically oriented approach to the engineering control of animal behavior by operant conditioning techniques, we have fought a running battle with the seditious notion of instinct.[1] It might be of some interest to the psychologist to know how the battle is going and to learn something about the nature of the adversary he is likely to meet if and when he tackles new species in new learning situations.

Our first report (Breland & Breland, 1951) in the *American Psychologist*, concerning our experiences in controlling animal behavior, was wholly affirmative and optimistic, saying in essence that the principles derived from the laboratory could be applied to the extensive control of behavior under

From *American Psychologist*, 61 (1961), 681–684.

[1] In view of the fact that instinctive behaviors may be common to many zoological species, we consider *species specific* to be a sanitized misnomer, and prefer the possibly septic adjective *instinctive*.

nonlaboratory conditions throughout a considerable segment of the phylogenetic scale.

When we began this work, it was our aim to see if the science would work beyond the laboratory, to determine if animal psychology could stand on its own feet as an engineering discipline. These aims have been realized. We have controlled a wide range of animal behavior and have made use of the great popular appeal of animals to make it an economically feasible project. Conditioned behavior has been exhibited at various municipal zoos and museums of natural history and has been used for department store displays, for fair and trade convention exhibits, for entertainment at tourist attractions, on television shows, and in the production of television commercials. Thirty-eight species, totaling over 6,000 individual animals, have been conditioned, and we have dared to tackle such unlikely subjects as reindeer, cockatoos, raccoons, porpoises, and whales.

Emboldened by this consistent reinforcement, we have ventured further and further from the security of the Skinner box. However, in this cavalier extrapolation, we have run afoul of a persistent pattern of discomforting failures. These failures, although disconcertingly frequent and seemingly diverse, fall into a very interesting pattern. They all represent breakdowns of conditioned operant behavior. From a great number of such experiences, we have selected, more or less at random, the following examples.

The first instance of our discomfiture might be entitled, What Makes Sammy Dance? In the exhibit in which this occurred, the casual observer sees a grown bantam chicken emerge from a retaining compartment when the door automatically opens. The chicken walks over about 3 feet, pulls a rubber loop on a small box which starts a repeated auditory stimulus pattern (a four-note tune). The chicken then steps up onto an 18-inch, slightly raised disc, thereby closing a timer switch, and scratches vigorously, round and round, over the disc for 15 seconds, at the rate of about two scratches per second until the automatic feeder fires in the retaining compartment. The chicken goes into the compartment to eat, thereby automatically shutting the door. The popular interpretation of this behavior pattern is that the chicken has turned on the "juke box" and "dances."

The development of this behavioral exhibit was wholly unplanned. In the attempt to create quite another type of demonstration which required a chicken simply to stand on a platform for 12–15 seconds, we found that over 50% developed a very strong and pronounced scratch pattern, which tended to increase in persistence as the time interval was lengthened. (Another 25% or so developed other behaviors—pecking at spots, etc.) However, we were able to change our plans so as to make use of the scratch pattern, and the result was the "dancing chicken" exhibit described above.

In this exhibit the only real contingency for reinforcement is that the chicken must depress the platform for 15 seconds. In the course of a performing day (about 3 hours for each chicken) a chicken may turn out over 10,000 unnecessary, virtually identical responses. Operant behaviorists would probably have little hesitancy in labeling this an example of Skinnerian "superstition" (Skinner, 1948) or "mediating" behavior, and we list it first to whet their explanatory appetite.

However, a second instance involving a raccoon does not fit so neatly into this paradigm. The response concerned the manipulation of money by the raccoon (who has "hands" rather similar to those of the primates). The contingency for reinforcement was picking up the coins and depositing them in a 5-inch metal box.

Raccoons condition readily, have good appetites, and this one was quite tame and an eager subject. We anticipated no trouble. Conditioning him to pick up the first coin was simple. We started out by reinforcing him for picking up a single coin. Then the metal container was introduced, with the requirement that he drop the coin into the container. Here we ran into the first bit of difficulty: he seemed to have a great deal of trouble letting go of the coin. He would rub it up against the inside of the container, pull it back out, and clutch it firmly for several seconds. However, he would finally turn it loose and receive his food reinforcement. Then the final contingency: we put him on a ratio of 2, requiring that he pick up both coins and put them in the container.

Now the raccoon really had problems (and so did we). Not only could he not let go of the coins, but he spent seconds, even minutes, rubbing them together (in a most miserly fashion), and dipping them into the container. He carried on this behavior to such an extent that the practical application we had in mind—a display featuring a raccoon putting money in a piggy bank—simply was not feasible. The rubbing behavior became worse and worse as time went on, in spite of nonreinforcement.

For the third instance, we return to the gallinaceous birds. The observer sees a hopper full of oval plastic capsules which contain small toys, charms, and the like. When the S_D (a light) is presented to the chicken, she pulls a rubber loop which releases one of these capsules onto a slide, about 16 inches long, inclined at about 30 degrees. The capsule rolls down the slide and comes to rest near the end. Here one or two sharp, straight pecks by the chicken will knock it forward off the slide and out to the observer, and the chicken is then reinforced by an automatic feeder. This is all very well—most chickens are able to master these contingencies in short order. The loop pulling presents no problems; she then has only to peck the capsule off the slide to get her reinforcement.

However, a good 20% of all chickens tried on this set of contingencies fail to make the grade. After they have pecked a few capsules off the slide, they begin to grab at the capsules and drag them backwards into the cage. Here they pound them up and down on the floor of the cage. Of course, this results in no reinforcement for the chicken and yet some chickens will pull in over half of all the capsules presented to them.

Almost always this problem behavior does not appear until after the capsules begin to move down the slide. Conditioning is begun with stationary capsules placed by the experimenter. When the pecking behavior becomes strong enough, so that the chicken is knocking them off the slide and getting reinforced consistently, the loop pulling is conditioned to the light. The capsules then come rolling down the slide to the chicken. Here most chickens, who before did not have this tendency, will start grabbing and shaking.

The fourth incident also concerns a chicken. Here the observer sees a chicken in a cage about 4 feet long which is placed alongside a miniature baseball field.

The reason for the cage is the interesting part. At one end of the cage is an automatic electric feed hopper. At the other is an opening through which the chicken can reach and pull a loop on a bat. If she pulls the loop hard enough the bat (solenoid operated) will swing, knocking a small baseball up the playing field. It it gets past the miniature toy players on the field and hits the back fence, the chicken is automatically reinforced with food at the other end of the cage. It it does not go far enough, or hits one of the players, she tries again. This results in behavior on an irregular ratio. When the feeder sounds, she then runs down the length of the cage and eats.

Our problems began when we tried to remove the cage for photography. Chickens that had been well conditioned in this behavior became wildly excited when the ball started to move. They would jump up on the playing field, chase the ball all over the field, even knock it off on the floor and chase it around, pecking it in every direction, although they had never had access to the ball before. This behavior was so persistent and so disruptive, in spite of the fact that it was never reinforced, that we had to reinstate the cage.

The last instance we shall relate in detail is one of the most annoying and baffling for a good behaviorist. Here a pig was conditioned to pick up large wooden coins and deposit them in a large "piggy bank." The coins were placed several feet from the bank and the pig required to carry them to the bank and deposit them, usually four or five coins for one reinforcement. (Of course, we started out with one coin, near the bank.)

Pigs condition very rapidly, they have no trouble taking ratios, they have ravenous appetites (naturally), and in many ways are among the most tractable animals we have worked with. However, this particular problem behavior developed in pig after pig, usually after a period of weeks or months, getting worse every day. At first the pig would eagerly pick up one dollar, carry it to the bank, run back, get another, carry it rapidly and neatly, and so on, until the ratio was complete. Thereafter, over a period of weeks the behavior would become slower and slower. He might run over eagerly for each dollar, but on the way back, instead of carrying the dollar and depositing it simply and cleanly, he would repeatedly drop it, root it, drop it again, root it along the way, pick it up, toss it up in the air, drop it, root it some more, and so on.

We thought this behavior might simply be the dilly-dallying of an animal on a low drive. However, the behavior persisted and gained in strength in spite of a severely increased drive—he finally went through the ratios so slowly that he did not get enought to eat in the course of a day. Finally it would take the pig about 10 minutes to transport four coins a distance of about 6 feet. This problem behavior developed repeatedly in successive pigs.

There have also been other instances: hamsters that stopped working in a glass case after four or five reinforcements, porpoises and whales that swallow their manipulanda (balls and inner tubes), cats that will not leave the area of the feeder, rabbits that will not go to the feeder, the great difficulty in many species of conditioning vocalization with food reinforcement, problems in conditioning a kick in a cow, the failure to get appreciably increased effort out of the ungulates with increased drive, and so on. These we shall not dwell on in detail, nor shall we discuss how they might be overcome.

These egregious failures came as a rather considerable shock to us, for there was nothing in our background in behaviorism to prepare us for such gross inabilities to predict and control the behavior of animals with which we had been working for years.

The examples listed we feel represent a clear and utter failure of conditioning theory. They are far from what one would normally expect on the basis of the theory alone. Furthermore, they are definite, observable; the diagnosis of theory failure does not depend on subtle statistical interpretations or on semantic legerdemain—the animal simply does not do what he has been conditioned to do.

It seems perfectly clear that, with the possible exception of the dancing chicken, which could conceivably, as we have said, be explained in terms of Skinner's superstition paradigm, the other instances do not fit the behavioristic way of thinking. Here we have animals, after having been conditioned to a specific learned response, gradually drifting into behaviors that are entirely different from those which were conditioned. Moreover, it can easily be seen that these particular behaviors to which the animals drift are clear-cut examples of instinctive behaviors having to do with the natural food getting behaviors of the particular species.

The dancing chicken is exhibiting the gallinaceous birds' scratch pattern that in nature often precedes ingestion. The chicken that hammers capsules is obviously exhibiting instinctive behavior having to do with breaking open of seed pods or the killing of insects, grubs, etc. The raccoon is demonstrating so-called "washing behavior." The rubbing and washing response may result, for example, in the removal of the exoskeleton of a crayfish. The pig is rooting or shaking—behaviors which are strongly built into this species and are connected with the food getting repertoire.

These patterns to which the animals drift require greater physical output and therefore are a violation of the so-called "law of least effort." And most damaging of all, they stretch out the time required for reinforcement when nothing in the experimental setup requires them to do so. They have only to do the little tidbit of behavior to which they were conditioned—for example, pick up the coin and put it in the container—to get reinforced immediately. Instead, they drag the process out for a matter of minutes when there is nothing in the contingency which forces them to do this. Moreover, increasing the drive merely intensifies this effect.

It seems obvious that these animals are trapped by strong instinctive behaviors, and clearly we have here a demonstration of the prepotency of such behavior patterns over those which have been conditioned.

We have termed this phenomenon "instinctive drift." The general principle seems to be that wherever an animal has strong instinctive behaviors in the area of the conditioned response, after continued running the organism will drift toward the instinctive behavior to the detriment of the conditioned behavior and even to the delay or preclusion of the reinforcement. In a very boiled-down, simplified form, it might be stated as "learned behavior drifts toward instinctive behavior."

All this, of course, is not to disparage the use of conditioning techniques, but is intended as a demonstration that there are definite weaknesses in the philosophy underlying these techniques. The pointing out of such weaknesses should make possible a worthwhile revision in behavior theory.

The notion of instinct has now become one of our basic concepts in an effort to make sense of the welter of observations which confront us. When behaviorism tossed out instinct, it is our feeling that some of its power of prediction and control were lost with it. From the foregoing examples, it appears that although it was easy to banish the Instinctivists from the science during the Behavioristic Revolution, it was not possible to banish instinct so easily.

And if, as Hebb suggests, it is advisable to reconsider those things that behaviorism explicitly threw out, perhaps it might likewise be advisable to examine what they tacitly brought in—the hidden assumptions which led most disastrously to these breakdowns in the theory.

Three of the most important of these tacit assumptions seem to us to be: that the animal comes to the laboratory as a virtual *tabula rasa*, that species differences are insignificant, and that all responses are about equally conditionable to all stimuli.

It is obvious, we feel, from the foregoing account, that these assumptions are no longer tenable. After 14 years of continuous conditioning and observation of thousands of animals, it is our reluctant conclusion that the behavior of any species cannot be adequately understood, predicted, or controlled without knowledge of its instinctive patterns, evolutionary history, and ecological niche.

In spite of our early successes with the application of behavioristically oriented conditioning theory, we readily admit now that ethological facts and attitudes in recent years have done more to advance our practical control of animal behavior than recent reports from American "learning labs."

Moreover, as we have recently discovered, if one begins with evolution and instinct as the basic format for the science, a very illuminating viewpoint can be developed which leads naturally to a drastically revised and simplified conceptual framework of startling explanatory power (to be reported elsewhere).

It is hoped that this playback on the theory will be behavioral technology's partial repayment to the academic science whose impeccable empiricism we have used so extensively.

References

Beach, F. A. The snark was a boojum. *Amer. Psychologist*, 1950, *5*, 115—124.

Breland, K., & Breland, M. A field of applied animal psychology. *Amer. Psychologist*, 1951, *6*, 202—204.

Hebb, D. O. The American revolution. *Amer. Psychologist*, 1960, *15*, 735—745.

Lorenz, K. Innate behaviour patterns. In *Symposia of the Society for Experimental Biology. No. 4. Physiological mechanisms in animal behaviour.* New York: Academic Press, 1950.

Skinner, B. F. Superstition in the pigeon. *J. exp. Psychol.*, 1948, *38*, 168—172.

Tinbergen, N. *The study of instinct.* Oxford: Clarendon, 1951.

Whalen, R. E. Comparative psychology. *Amer. Psychologist*, 1961, *16*, 84.

III

AVOIDANCE
LEARNING

The interest of general-process learning theorists has centered increasingly on avoidance learning in recent years. In a typical avoidance procedure, a signal predicts food shock. If the animal, usually a white rat, makes the avoidance response before the shock comes on, shock does not occur and the signal goes off. If he fails to make the avoidance response and shock comes on, he can turn it off by making an escape response. When an animal has acquired avoidance, he is engaging in a complex behavior which has the appearance of being purposeful; i.e., he responds to prevent a noxious event in the future. One reason this is of strong interest to theorists is that it is an example of a complex, forward-looking act which can apparently be explained by simpler principles. The most prominent current hypothesis, two-factor theory, explains avoidance as the interaction of classical conditioning and instrumental training: The animal learns to fear the signal by classical pairing with shock, and learns to avoid by escaping fear because the "avoidance" response is instrumentally reinforced by termination of the fear-evoking stimulus. So the "forward-looking" avoidance response is merely escape from already present fear. In the first two sections of the book, we have seen that preparedness is needed to supplement the principles of classical and instrumental learning, so it is not surprising that preparedness should be relevant to avoidance learning, if it is a combination of the two.

In the first reading, Robert Bolles stresses the importance of the natural history of the animal and its response repertoire in its ability to learn avoidance in the laboratory. He presents evidence which shows that equipotentiality does not hold in avoidance, and argues that a trainable avoidance response must be chosen from the species-specific defensive repertoire of the animal—learning for which evolution has prepared the species.

18

SPECIES — SPECIFIC DEFENSE REACTIONS AND AVOIDANCE LEARNING

Robert C. Bolles

The prevailing theories of avoidance learning and the procedures that are usually used to study it seem to be totally out of touch with what is known about how animals defend themselves in nature. This paper suggest some alternative concepts, starting with the assumption that animals have innate species-specific defense reactions (SSDRs) such as fleeing, freezing, and fighting. It is proposed that if a particular avoidance response is rapidly acquired, then that reponse must necessarily be an SSDR. The learning mechanism in this case appears to be suppression of nonavoidance behavior by the avoidance contingency. The traditional approaches to avoidance learning appear to be slightly more valid in the case of responses that are slowly acquired, although in this case, too, the SSDR concept is relevant, and reinforcement appears to be based on the production of a safety signal rather than the termination of an aversive conditioned stimulus.

Avoidance learning as we know it in the laboratory has frequently been used to "explain" how animals survive in the wild. The purpose of this paper is to turn this inferential process around and use the limited knowledge of natural defensive behavior to help account for some of the anomalies that have been found in laboratory studies of avoidance learning. Let us begin by recalling a little fable. It is a very familiar fable. It was already part of our lore when Hull gave his version of it in 1929, and the story has been told again many times since then. It goes something like this: Once upon a time there was a little animal who ran around in the forest. One day while he was running around, our hero was suddenly attacked by a predator. He was hurt and, of course, frightened, but he was lucky and managed to escape from the predator. He was able to get away

From *Psychological Review*, 77 (1970), 32—48.

The research reported here was supported by National Science Foundation Research Grant GB-5694.

and safely back to his home. The fable continues: Some time later our furry friend was again running around in the forest, which was his custom, when suddenly he perceived a conditioned stimulus. He heard or saw or smelled some stimulus which on the earlier occasion had preceded the attack by the predator. Now on this occasion our friend became frightened, he immediately took flight as he had on the previous occasion, and quickly got safely back home. So this time our hero had managed to avoid attack (and possibly worse) by responding appropriately to a cue which signaled danger; he did not have to weather another attack. And from that day hence the little animal who ran around in the forest continued to avoid the predator because the precariousness of his situation prevented, somehow, his becoming careless or forgetful.

The moral of this tale, we are told, is that little animals survive in nature because they learn to avoid big dangerous animals. The ability to learn to avoid has such obviously great survival value, we are told, that we should surely expect the higher animals to have evolved this ability. We should also expect animals to be able to learn to avoid in the laboratory, and we should expand our theories of behavior to encompass such learning.

I propose that this familiar fable with its happy ending and plausible moral is utter nonsense. The parameters of the situation make it impossible for there to be any learning. Thus, no real-life predator is going to present cues just before it attacks. No owl hoots or whistles 5 seconds before pouncing on a mouse. And no owl terminates his hoots or whistles just as the mouse gets away so as to reinforce the avoidance response. Nor will the owl give the mouse enough trials for the necessary learning to occur. What keeps our little friends alive in the forest has nothing to do with avoidance learning as we ordinarily conceive of it or investigate it in the laboratory.

SPECIES-SPECIFIC DEFENSE REACTIONS

What keeps animals alive in the wild is that they have effective *innate* defensive reactions which occur when they encounter any kind of new or sudden stimulus. These defensive reactions vary somewhat from species to species, but they generally take one of three forms: Animals generally run or fly away, freeze, or adopt some type of threat, that is, pseudo-aggressive behavior. These defensive reactions are elicited by the appearance of the predator and by the sudden appearance of innocuous objects. These responses are always near threshold so that the animal will take flight, freeze, or threaten whenever any novel stimulus event occurs. It is not necessary that the stimulus event be paired with shock, or pain, or some other unconditioned stimulus. The mouse does not scamper away from the owl because it has learned to escape the painful claws of the enemy; it scampers away from anything happening in its environment, and it does so merely because it is a mouse. The gazelle does not flee from an approaching lion because it has been bitten by lions; it runs away from any large object that approaches it, and it does so because this is one of its species-specific defense reactions. Neither the mouse nor the gazelle can afford to *learn* to avoid; survival is too urgent, the opportunity to learn is too limited, and the parameters of the situation make the necessary learning impossible. The animal which survives is one which comes into its environment with defensive reactions already a prominent part of its repertoire.

There is, of course, a considerable gulf between the wild animal of the field and forest and the domesticated animal of the laboratory. Our laboratory rats and dogs and monkeys are relatively approachable and are on relatively friendly terms with us. However, this good relationship changes as soon as the animal is placed in a box and given a few electric shocks. When shocked, the normally friendly, inquisitive laboratory animal shows a dramatic change in behavior. Exploration and grooming drop out; so does all of its previously acquired appetitive behavior—bar pressing, etc. Instead of its normal range of highly flexible, adaptive, and outgoing behavior, its behavior is severely restricted to those defensive reactions that characterize the wild animal. It is furtive, hostile, and will flee if given the opportunity to do so.

In short, I am suggesting that the immediate and inevitable effect of severe aversive stimulation on a domesticated animal is to convert it, at least temporarily, into a wild animal by restricting its response repertoire to a narrow class of species-specific defense reactions (SSDRs). I am suggesting further that this sudden, dramatic restriction of the subject's (Ss) behavioral repertoire is of the utmost importance in the proper understanding of avoidance learning.

The concept of the SSDR repertoire enables one to make sense of what is one of the most challenging problems in avoidance learning, namely, that some responses either cannot be learned at all, or are learned only occasionally after extensive training. A particular S may be able to learn one avoidance response (R_a) with great facility and be quite unable to learn another R_a. In the latter case, the response may occur frequently, the presumed reinforcement contingencies may be regularly applied, and yet R_a fails to gain in strength. Such failures of learning indicate either that some responses are not acquirable, or that the reinforcement contingencies are not what they were thought to be.

These failures of Ss to learn in situations where the theories require them to, pose a serious challenge to contemporary behavior theory. Is it possible that some responses in S's repertoire actually are not acquirable as R_as? Such a conception defies one of the principal tenets of operant conditioning theory. The present paper argues for just this conclusion. I suggest that there is a restricted class of behaviors that can be readily acquired as R_as? Specifically, I am proposing that an R_a can be rapidly acquired only if it is an SSDR.

Is it possible, on the other hand, that the events which are ordinarily assumed to reinforce R_a actually are not effective in that capacity? I will argue that this is indeed the case, and that an R_a is rapidly acquired only by the suppression of other SSDRs. In other words, I propose that the primary effect of avoidance training is to get rid of competing behavior, and that this is accomplished mainly by the avoidance contingency.

The frequently reported failures of rats to learn certain R_as, such as wheel turning and bar pressing (e.g., D'Amato & Schiff, 1964; Meyer, Cho, & Wesemann, 1960; Smith, McFarland, & Taylor, 1961), should not be regarded as peculiar or as exceptions to the general applicability of operant conditioning principles, but rather as one end of a continuum of difficulty of learning. Learning the R_a in a shuttle box is likely to require about 100 trials, and a few rats apparently never acquire the response (Brush, 1966). Learning to run in a wheel proceeds considerably faster and more surely. All Ss learn the R_a within 40 trials (Bolles, Stokes, & Younger, 1966). But if we let the rat run down an alley to avoid shock, it may learn to do so in half a dozen trials (Theios, 1963). At the other extreme, if we place a rat in a box and shock it there, it may learn in one trial to jump out of the box (e.g., Maatsch, 1959). There is a continuum of difficulty here, and the parameter that is involved, what R_a the situation requires, is an enormously important one which accounts for more of the variance than any other so far discovered in avoidance learning. Indeed, the response requirement is the only really impressive parameter we know of, and it is a serious indictment of our major behavior theories that they pay no systematic attention to it.

By contrast, the SSDR hypothesis takes the fact that there are great differential rates of learning as its first principle. If we assume that the rat's SSDR repertoire consists of freezing, fleeing, or fighting (threat behavior), then it is clear why the jump-out box and the one-way apparatus should lead to such rapid acquisition. First, these situations provide abundant stimulus support for fleeing; more importantly, since freezing and aggressive behavior lead only to shock (because they fail to avoid it), these behaviors will be rapidly suppressed and the remaining SSDR, fleeing, will rapidly emerge as the most likely response in the situation. Running in the wheel and in the shuttle box are similar in that again freezing and fighting are punished by the nonavoidance of shock, but there is the difference that S cannot flee the situation. The S can make the right kind of response, but its effectiveness is compromised by the fact that in the wheel S does not actually change its environment, while in the shuttle box S must return to a place it has just left.

Bar pressing is certainly not an SSDR and, accordingly, we would have to predict that it cannot be learned as an R_a. The truth is that it frequently is not learned. It is also true, however, that it sometimes is learned, and this fact has to be dealt with. I suggest that when bar pressing is learned, the course of learning must necessarily be slow and uncertain because the processes involved are slow and uncertain. What is involved apparently, is a stage of acquisition in which S freezes while holding onto the bar. Bolles and McGillis (1968) measured the latency of the bar-press escape response (R_e), and found that within 40 trials it fell to values in the order of .05 second. Such short shocks appear to be the result of very fast, "reflexive" presses which occur, and which can only occur, if S is freezing on the bar. This behavior then has the effect of limiting the total amount of shock received to a value which does not disrupt S's ongoing behavior. Freezing anywhere else in the box or in any other posture will be disrupted by unavoided shocks, and punished by these shocks, and so too will any consistent efforts to get out of the box. In effect, the rat must end up freezing on the bar because that is the only response which on the one hand is an SSDR, and on the other hand can continuously survive the avoidance contingency. The observation of rats in this situation indicates that this is what happens. Even the attempts to "shape" the bar-press R_a in the manner that pressing for food is commonly shaped must start with S freezing on the bar (D'Amato, Fazzaro, & Etkin, 1968; Feldman & Bremner, 1963; Keehn &

Webster, 1968). Thus, freezing on the bar appears to be a necessary stage in the acquisition of the bar-press R_a, just as the SSDR hypothesis suggests. How operant R_as can sometimes gradually emerge from this stage of respondent R_es is another story which will have to be considered later. The present discussion merely establishes that the SSDR hypothesis makes sense of the fact that some R_as are trivially easy to acquire while others evidently tax the limits of a particular species, and it provides, as far as I know, the first systematic account of these huge differences.

There is a trivial sense in which the SSDR hypothesis must be true, namely, that if the SSDR repertoire includes all of S's behavior in the aversive situation, then no other responses will occur there so no other responses can be reinforced there. The SSDR hypothesis is intended to mean something much more subtle and important than the obvious truth that a response must occur before it can be reinforced, however. When appetitive behavior is reinforced with food, it is profitable and convenient to define specific responses in terms of the movements involved, for example, when we "shape" the bar-press response. It is also convenient to define specific responses in terms of their effects on the environment, for example, whether or not it causes a bar to be depressed. These response-class definitions are serviceable because food reinforcement appears to have equivalent effects on all members of these classes. But we will shortly turn to data which indicate that neither of these kinds of response classes, equivalent movements or equivalent environmental effects, holds together in the case of avoidance learning, at least not with respect to the reinforcement operation. Consider the acquisition of a jumping R_a. It appears to be relatively difficult to establish a particular jump topography, and relatively difficult to train the rat to jump if jumping avoids shock and terminates the conditioned stimulus (discussed subsequently), but it is very easy to teach the rat to jump out of a box where it has been shocked (Maatsch, 1959). The critical feature of jumping as a flight response appears to be whether it is *functionally effective* in the sense that it actually makes flight possible. The possibility of flight appears to be much more important in establishing a flight response than either its topographical features or even whether it is effective in avoiding shock.

Consider running, which is also sometimes rapidly learned and sometimes is not. We must classify running as an SSDR because we observe that the rat runs in aversive situations (and out of them if it can). We can arrange aversive situations that provide different amounts of stimulus support for running, that is, we can change its operant rate and alter the whole SSDR repertoire by varying the situation. We can also arrange to make running effective in the sense that its occurrence prevents shock. But I contend that no matter how we arrange the situation, running will not be acquired as an R_a, at least not very readily, unless the running response is effective for flight, that is, effective in the functional sense that it takes the rat out of the situation. With other animals we should expect the case to be different if flight is functionally different. For example, whereas the rat and other small rodents flee from predators by getting completely away from them, an animal such as the dog needs to, and typically does, only stand off at some distance. From such observations the SSDR hypothesis suggests the inference that dogs might be much better than rats at learning to run in the shuttle box. Under some circumstances they are evidently quite good at it (e.g., Solomon & Wynne, 1953).

The argument so far can be summarized by giving an explicit statement of the SSDR hypothesis: For an R_a to be rapidly learned in a given situation, the response must be an effective SSDR in that situation, and when rapid learning does occur, it is primarily due to the suppression of ineffective SSDRs.

THE ESCAPE CONTINGENCY

One implication of the SSDR hypothesis is that the contingencies which have traditionally borne the theoretical burden of reinforcing avoidance behavior, namely, the escape contingency and the conditioned stimulus (CS) termination contingency, are relatively ineffectual. There is now considerable evidence suggesting that this is the case and indicating that neither of these familiar aspects of the normal avoidance training procedure is crucial for the establishment of avoidance behavior. Let us look briefly at some of this evidence.

At first, the phenomenon of defensive learning was viewed as an example of Pavlovian conditioning, and the earliest experimental procedures reflected this kind of theoretical orientation. Thus, there was no escape contingency; it was the unconditioned response (UCR) that was *elicited* by a brief inescapable shock that was supposed to become conditioned to the CS. Instrumental avoidance learning procedures arose from the discovery that Pavlovian techniques only seemed to work with autonomic responses and with reflexes. Other techniques had to be developed to train instrumental or operant defensive behavior. The Pavlovian heritage was still apparent, however. An avoidance response was first conditioned to the shock as an escape response (R_e), and it was called a UCR at this stage. Then, as it became conditioned to the CS, as it "gradually emerged," it was called a conditioned response (CR) (Solomon & Brush, 1956). In this view the escape contingency was a necessary part of the avoidance training procedure; it was essential for the maintenance of the UCR. This interpretation prevailed until Brogden, Lipman, and Culler (1938) and Mowrer (1939) began to demonstrate its inadequacy. Then, although a pure contiguity account of avoidance could no longer be defended, a semicontiguity or compromise position began to prevail. According to this view, which is still probably the predominant view today, R_a gains *some* of its strength by generalization, or through conditioning, from the strength of R_e. In practical terms, the escape contingency was supposed to help establish R_a and accordingly, it became a regular part of the avoidance training procedure.

The simplest and methodologically most elegant way to assess the actual importance of the escape contingency is to permit shock escape to occur but to make its occurrence contingent on some response other than R_a. The first such study was conducted by Mowrer and Lamoreaux (1946), who demonstrated the possibility of training rats to make an R_a which was different from R_e. Some Ss were required to run to avoid shock and to jump in the air to escape shock following a failure to avoid. Other Ss were required to jump to avoid and to run to escape. Controls were required to learn identical escape and avoidance responses which were either jumping or running. The reported results indicated that the homogeneous groups, for which R_a and R_e were the same, showed a marked superiority over the heterogeneous groups, for which R_a and R_e were different. However, the important finding, according to Mowrer and Lamoreaux, was that the heterogeneous groups acquired R_a at all. The fact that the heterogeneous groups suffered a decrement relative to the homogeneous groups suggested to Mowrer and Lamoreaux that while the escape contingency was not essential, it did make a contribution to the strength of R_a.

This study and the few subsequent studies have left several basic theoretical questions unanswered, however. For example, it is not possible to say on the basis of the available evidence if independent R_as and R_es can be obtained as a general rule, or only under rather special circumstances. It is not known if independence of R_a and R_e can be shown for any selected pair of responses, or whether this independence is restricted just to certain responses. In an attempt to answer this question, a larger study which involved three different responses was made. Rats were trained in a running-wheel situation and different groups were required either to run (resulting in a quarter turn of the wheel), to turn (an about-face without moving the wheel), or to rear (stand up on the hind legs). For different groups the nonoccurrence of shock was made contingent on one of these responses and, following a failure to avoid, the termination of shock was made contingent on either the same response or one of the other two responses. Thus there were three homogeneous groups and six heterogeneous groups.

The results of this experiment (Bolles, 1969) are summarized in Figure 1. It is apparent, first, that some R_as are much more rapidly acquired than others, regardless of the R_e requirement. It is also apparent that whether there is a difference between homogeneous conditions, which permit generalization from R_e, and heterogeneous conditions, which preclude such generalization, depends entirely on what the R_a is. Thus, if R_a is chosen to be running, then it will be rapidly acquired more or less independently of other experimental conditions, including the escape contingency. Rearing, on the other hand, is not learned as an R_a, even with the escape contingency, at least not within 80 trials. Turning may be thought of an intermediate; it is not a flight response, but when other conditions are optimized it can be acquired through the joint action of the escape contingency and the avoidance contingency. It should be emphasized, however, that when the turning R_a is learned, the learning proceeds rather slowly.

These results indicate that the escape contingency does not play a consistent part in the acquisition of R_a, and that only in the case of one response, turning, did it make an appreciable contribution to avoidance learning. It is interesting to note that Mowrer and Lamoreaux's results also showed this type of specificity. They found that running in the shuttle box was as readily acquired as an R_a by homogeneous and heterogeneous groups, but that jumping in the shuttle box was not acquired as an R_a unless the R_e was also jumping. The usual conclusion drawn from their results, that is, that heterogeneous groups can learn to avoid but not as effectively as homogeneous groups, is obtained as a statistical artifact of lumping the different results for different R_as. Mowrer and Lamoreaux's data, as well as those shown in Figure 1, also belie the frequently drawn conclusion that R_a can be any response drawn from S's repertoire. This simply is not true.

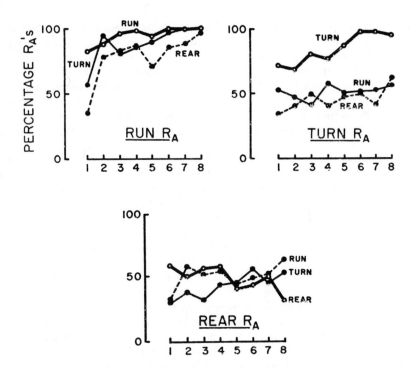

FIG. 1 Mean percentage of avoidance (R_as) on 10-trial blocks for rats required to run, turn, or rear to avoid shock and to run, turn, or rear to escape shock. (Labels on individual curves refer to the R_e requirement. Adapted from Bolles, 1969.)

In the case of rearing, the response occurred on about 40% of all trials. Its occurrence always avoided shock and terminated the CS, and for one group it also escaped shock on nonavoidance trials, but it never gained in strength. Rearing occurred, although it is not a flight response itself, in the context of flight, that is, in the attempt to climb the walls. But in this context it was ineffective because S was never able to climb out of the situation. This behavior persisted because all other behavior, that is, other attempts to escape, and freezing and aggressive reactions, were also punished. As noted in the previous section, for a flight response to be an effective SSDR for the rat, it must take S out of the situation (as in a one-way apparatus). It is not sufficient that the response has a high operant rate, or even that it might be effective in getting away in another situation.

It might be argued that running in the wheel also fails to get the animal away, so that this response should not have been learned either, according to the SSDR hypothesis. Perhaps this is the proper interpretation, and perhaps we have managed to discredit the SSDR hypothesis right at its inception. It cannot be argued that running in the wheel constitutes an effective SSDR while running in the shuttle box is marginally effective merely because the former is more rapidly acquired than the latter. From the viewpoint of the SSDR hypothesis, both situations are ambiguous in that they permit only limited or compromised flight. The running wheel has been recognized as a peculiar piece of apparatus by many investigators who have used it in general activity studies, however, and perhaps it does permit the rat to "get away" in some meaningful sense. Certainly it permits the rat to run continuously, to change cues in the immediate environment, including the ground underfoot, and to get away from the accumulation of its own odors. It may be immaterial that running in the wheel does not change extra-apparatus cues or the rat's location with respect to them. Further investigation is needed with various modifications of both the wheel and the shuttle box to pinpoint the critical factors and provide a real test of the SSDR hypothesis. The issue should be further illuminated by additional investigation in more naturalistic settings as well as with other kinds of animals to obtain a better idea of what constitutes effective flight in nature. The rat's facility with the running wheel may be relatively specific to the rat.

To return to the escape contingency, there have been a number of studies in which it has been eliminated in other ways. Bolles et al. (1966) trained Ss with shocks of .1-second duration, that is, too short to be response terminated, and found very little decrement relative to Ss that were required to terminate shock in the usual manner. Similar results have been reported by D'Amato, Keller, and DiCara (1964), Hurwitz (1964), and Sidman (1953) in the bar-press situation, although there is some question about whether there may still be some possibility of escape with the short shocks that were used. There are also a few instances in which negative transfer from R_e to R_a has been reported (Turner & Solomon, 1962; Warren & Bolles, 1967).

So much for the escape contingency. Knowledge about the escapability of shock does not permit us to predict how fast an animal will learn a particular R_a, or whether R_a will be learned at all. Other considerations are much more important, and one of the most important of these appears to be what the R_a is. The data suggest that R_a will be rapidly acquired if and only if it permits S to flee, freeze, or fight, and that whether there is an escape contingency is relatively inconsequential.

THE CS-TERMINATION CONTINGENCY

Another regular part of most avoidance experiments is the warning stimulus, or CS. Both its name and part of its assumed function derive from the Pavlovian tradition. The CS was assumed to be the stimulus to which the R_a (or CR) became conditioned. It has become fairly common in recent years to incorporate various control procedures for sensitization effects in order to determine if R_a is under the associative control of the CS. "Real" avoidance is attributed to performance beyond that displayed by sensitization control Ss. There is some irony in the fact that what counts in nature is not an animal's ability to learn this kind of discrimination but rather that it be subject to these sensitization effects! As observed in the introductory section, what keeps animals alive in nature is that they display SSDRs whenever there is any stimulus change in the environment. Some investigators have begun to suggest that perhaps in the laboratory, too, the stuff of which avoidance behavior is really made is rather indiscriminant defensive behavior (Bolles et al., 1966; D'Amato, 1967).

The major theoretical emphasis on the CS, of course, is not its discriminative function but the reinforcement that is widely assumed to result from its termination. Some theorists introduce the additional element of fear; termination of the CS is assumed to lead to a reduction of fear which is reinforcing (e.g., Miller, 1951; Mowrer, 1939). Others contend that the fear construct is gratuitous here, and that it is sufficient to assume that because the CS is paired with shock it will become a conditioned negative reinforcer (e.g., Dinsmoor, 1954; Schoenfeld, 1950). According to either version of the story, however, termination of the CS is held to be an essential ingredient in avoidance learning. Hence, the termination of the CS is usually made contingent on the occurrence of R_a, and under these circumstances it is easy to point to CS termination as the source of reinforcement when learning occurs.

The argument gained considerable support from Mowrer and Lamoreaux's (1942) early demonstration that making CS termination coincident with the occurrence of R_a led to much faster acquisition than having it go off automatically before R_a occurred or having its termination delayed for some seconds after R_a occurred. There was a little room for concern that any learning was found under the latter conditions, but Kamin (1956) was able to account for it in terms of delay of reinforcement effects, and at this point the CS-termination hypothesis appeared to be quite secure.

There were still a few lines of evidence, however, that stubbornly resisted falling into line with the CS-termination hypothesis, and some of them suggested that the efficacy of CS termination might depend on what R_a was required of the animal (e.g., Mogenson, Mullin, & Clark, 1965). Bolles et al. (1966) attempted to extend the Mowrer and Lamoreaux and the Kamin design, first, by studying the effectiveness of the CS-termination contingency in two different situations, and, second, by experimentally separating all three of the potential reinforcement contingencies: CS termination, avoidance of shock, and escape from shock. This was a factorial study in which shock was either escapable or not (because it was too short), avoidable or not, and the CS either terminated with the R_a or was continued for some seconds after it. The Ss were trained either in a shuttle box or a running wheel. The results are summarized in Table 1.

An analysis of variance shows that in the shuttle-box avoidance, escape and CS termination accounted for, respectively, 39%, 22%, and 19% of the variance among groups. Thus the three contingencies contributed roughly equally to the performance in the shuttle box (also see Kamin, 1956). There was also a significant interaction which took the form that no one contingency by itself was able to produce learning. In the running wheel the pattern was quite different. Here, avoidance, escape, and the CS termination accounted for, respectively, 85%, 0%, and 9% of the variance among groups. Thus, the avoidance contingency was vastly more important than the other two. Moreoever, there was no interaction among the contingencies, and avoidance alone led to quite creditable acquisition. In short, the relative importance of the three contingencies depends on the situation, and, more specifically, on what

TABLE 1 Percentage of R_aS in Two Different Situations as a Function of Whether S Could Avoid Shock (A), Escape Shock (E), or Terminate the CS (T)

Available contingencies	Apparatus	
	Shuttle box	Wheel
AET	70	85
AE	40	75
AT	37	79
ET	31	38
A	15	62
E	9	26
T	10	48
None	15	28

Adapted from Bolles et al. (1966).

response is required of S. When R_a is running in the wheel, which I believe is an effective SSDR, the avoidance contingency itself is the big factor and the CS termination is relatively unimportant. But in the shuttle box, where the effectiveness of R_a is more doubtful, the avoidance of shock and the termination of the CS assume more nearly equal importance.

Bolles and Grossen (1969) have subsequently expanded this procedure by using situations in which the status of R_a is still more varied, namely, a one-way runway and a bar-press situation. These investigators also sought to analyze further the role of CS termination in those situations such as the bar press and the shuttle box where it does appear to be important. Is the critical function of CS termination in these situations really reinforcement? It seems possible that when CS termination is made contingent on R_a, it is not reinforcing R_a in the usual sense but rather providing S with information, or feedback. CS termination may merely be a stimulus change which signals that the environment has been altered in some way. To test this possibility, groups of Ss were trained with no CS-termination contingency but with a feedback stimulus contingency. For these Ss a brief change in illumination conditions was made contingent on R_a. This feedback stimulus (FS) was presented only on avoidance trials, that is, it was never contiguous with shock. The important comparisons are among groups which had the normal CS-termination contingency, groups which had neither CS termination nor FS presentation, and groups which had no CS termination but did have the FS presentation. The results for rats trained under these conditions in three different avoidance situations are shown in Figure 2. The black data points indicate the results for Ss run in a partial replication in which the CS-termination contingency was eliminated by using a trace conditioning procedure, that is, by using a short CS rather than one which continued for 5 seconds after the R_a. The generally inferior performance of the trace Ss can presumably be attributed to the loss of the discriminative function of the CS.

In the one-way avoidance situation, learning proceeded very rapidly. There was no appreciable decrement in performance for Ss which lacked the

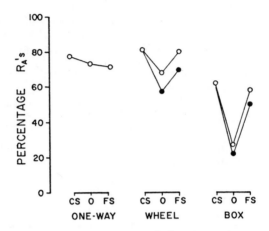

FIG. 2   Mean percentage of R_as for rats trained with either CS termination (CS), FS presentation (FS), or neither (O). (Training comprised 20 trials in the one-way situation, 40 trials in the running wheel, and 80 trials in the shuttle box. Adapted from Bolles & Grossen, 1969.)

CS-termination contingency, nor was there any improvement in performance for Ss which received the response-contingent FS. There were, in short, no differences among the three groups. In the running-wheel situation, acquisition was not as fast as in the one-way apparatus, but it was still quite fast. There was a small but statistically significant decremental effect of withholding the CS-termination contingency, and the introduction of the FS contingency returned performance nearly to the normal level. Then in the shuttle-box situation, where acquisition was considerably slower, the loss of the CS-termination contingency led to a serious decrement in acquisition, and the use of the FS again virtually eliminated this decrement. Sidman's (1953) procedure was used in the bar-press situation, which prevents a direct comparison of the results in terms of percentage of R_as, and these results are therefore not shown in the figure. But the bar-press results can easily be described. In the absence of a CS, and the CS-termination contingency, the median S failed to learn the response when there was no R_a-contingent feedback (a special bar was used which provided minimum auditory and kinesthetic feedback). By contrast, all Ss eventually learned the bar-press R_a when it produced a click and a brief change in illumination. Thus, in the bar-press situation, the FS made the difference between the group as a whole being able or not being able to learn the response. Bolles and Popp (1964) had earlier indicated the necessity of having some stimulus event contingent on the bar-press R_a.

There appears to be a striking parallel between the effectiveness of the CS-termination and the FS-presentation contingencies as the response requirement is varied. When learning is very rapid, that is, when R_a is an SSDR, neither contingency makes much difference. But when learning is slow and uncertain, that is, when R_a is not an SSDR, then learning depends on there being some response-contingent event, and it seems to make little difference whether it is CS termination or FS presentation. That these two procedures have such equivalent effects on performance strongly suggests that they may be functionally equivalent. Indeed, it is tempting to suppose that CS termination leads to avoidance learning, not because it causes a reduction in fear, nor because it reduces aversiveness, but merely because it provides response feedback. CS termination may merely tell the animal that it has responded; it has done something to affect the environment.

This interpretation is entirely consistent with the results of Bower, Starr, and Lazarovitz (1965), who found a direct relationship between the rate of acquisition of R_a and the amount of change in the CS which was made contingent on R_a. This kind of interpretation takes the problem of avoidance learning out of its traditional niche among reinforcement phenomena and puts it more into the realm of discrimination learning. D'Amato et al. (1968) have already urged such a move and these investigators, it should be noted, had previously obtained results in the bar-press situation very much like those of Bolles and Grossen (1969). The main difference was that D'Amato et al. used a discrete trial procedure, whereas Bolles and Grossen used Sidman's procedure. The fact that the introduction of an FS restores performance in both cases attests to the generality of the FS effect.

So much for the CS-termination contingency. It is clear that while the CS-termination contingency is of some importance in some situations, it is of little consequence in situations such as the one-way runway and the running wheel where R_a is very rapidly acquired. If we wish to predict whether R_a will be acquired or how fast it will be acquired, then knowledge about the CS-termination contingency will not give us nearly as much information as knowing what the R_a is. Moreover, even in those situations where CS termination is important, it turns out that it can be replaced by an entirely different kind of response contingency which produces learning just as effectively. It is becoming increasingly difficult to believe that avoidance learning occurs because the CS elicits fear or because it is aversive.[1] Let us look briefly at an alternative view of the role of the CS.

THE SAFETY SIGNAL EFFECT

The previous section suggested one interpretation of the CS-termination effect, namely, that termination of the CS serves as a source of feedback, or stimulus change. This is an attractive hypothesis and it is supported by some evidence (Bolles & Grossen, 1969; Bower et al., 1965; D'Amato et al., 1968). Bolles and Grossen have suggested that the reason some situations lead to such

---

[1] For example, Cole and Wahlsten (1968), Lockard (1963), and Sidman (1955) all show in different ways that the discriminative function of the CS can be much more important than its aversiveness.

rapid avoidance learning may be that they furnish S with a great deal of *intrinsic* feedback. Accordingly, the addition of *extrinsic* feedback provided by the experimenter in the form of lights out or tone termination contributes relatively little to that already resulting from the occurrence of R_a. As we move on to situations which involve little intrinsic feedback, for example, the bar press, which requires little effort and which does not change S's environment, the acquisition of the response may depend on there being some extrinsic feedback. With the assumption that intrinsic feedback has greater weight (or a higher sampling probability) than extrinsic feedback, we would be in a good position to explain many of the findings that have been discussed above. The rate-of-learning effect, the CS-termination effect, and the FS-presentation effect would all fall neatly into line.

There are, however, some difficult problems with this interpretation, and some of the evidence does not fall into line so readily: (*a*) Why should intrinsic feedback be inherently more important than an arbitrarily selected external stimulus change, such as the termination of a tone? It is easy to argue that flight reactions necessarily produce a lot of stimulus change, but flight is not the only SSDR, and there is reason to believe that other SSDRs are also very rapidly acquired. For example, the author's observations, as well as those of Keehn (1967), indicate that freezing is acquired in very few trials, even though it is not a vigorous kind of behavior and does not change the situation. The rapid learning of the pseudo-flight response in the running wheel also indicates that the character of the response may be much more important than the simple quantity of stimulus change it produces. (*b*) Why does the rate of acquisition depend on the direction of stimulus change, that is, whether the stimulus goes on or off, and on its quality and modality (e.g., Myers, 1960, 1964)? Why is a change in geographical location such a particularly effective stimulus change? (*c*) Why does FS presentation or CS termination appear to be effective only with extended training? That is, if stimulus change is the critical factor, then why doesn't it seem to have an effect in a rapidly acquired R_a or in the early trials of a slowly acquired R_a?

This last point needs some illustration. The data shown at the far right in Figure 2 represent the performance of rats with an FS in the shuttle box. Over the course of 80 trials, these Ss avoided nearly as well as those under the usual CS-termination condition. But the learning curves for the two groups were markedly different; the FS group showed a serious decrement during the first 40 trials, but then caught up with the CS group and eventually surpassed it. In short, the FS condition is not completely equivalent to the CS condition, it only produces the same mean performance over the course of the right number of trials. There seems to be a delay in the action of the FS contingency, such that it begins to be effective only after S has been in the situation for a number of trials, perhaps 40 or 50. D'Amato et al. (1968) found in their bar-press study that there was no FS effect during the first several hundred trials; it materialized only with continued training. One possibility is that the CS has functions beyond those it shares with the FS. It certainly has a discriminative function, and it may have others, including even an acquired aversiveness function.

A second possibility that is more interesting and more compelling is that the

FS does more than provide information. Perhaps it actively reinforces R_a, and perhaps 40 or 50 trials (or more depending on the situation) are required for its reinforcing powers to be established. What I am suggesting is that the response-contingent FS acts as a *safety signal* of the sort that Rescorla and LoLordo (1965) have described.

Rescorla and LoLordo gave dogs a number of sessions in which one stimulus was repeatedly paired with unavoidable shock independently of the dogs' behavior, and a second, contrasting stimulus was explicitly paired with the absence of shock. The one stimulus thus became a danger signal (DS) while the second became a safety signal (SS). (It is difficult to know how to label these stimuli without begging the question of how they function; there is no intention to imply anything by the designation DS and SS beyond the procedural fact that the one stimulus is correlated with shock while the other is correlated with the absence of shock.) Several procedures were used in these sessions, and it seemed to make little difference precisely how the DS-SS contrast was made as long as the SS consistently predicted the absence of shock. Following this training, the stimuli were introduced momentarily while S was performing a previously well-established shuttle-box R_a. The DS was found to produce a short-term elevation in the rate of the R_a, whereas the SS was found to depress the rate of the R_a.

These dramatic results lend themselves to a variety of possible interpretations, but the one favored by Rescorla and LoLordo is that (a) the SS and DS acquire their behavioral effects through Pavlovian conditioning processes, and (b) the DS increases S's fear motivation, whereas the SS inhibits fear. They propose that fear is conditioned to the DS by a Pavlovian excitatory mechanism, and that in the test situation the momentary DS provides additional short-term motivation for the previously learned R_a. Similarly, the inhibition of fear by SS is assumed to be produced by a Pavlovian inhibitory mechanism so that brief presentation of the SS in the test situation provides a momentary reduction in S's prevailing fear motivation (also see Rescorla & Solomon, 1967).

Without necessarily denying the validity of this interpretation, I want to call attention to other potential properties of these DS and SS stimuli. I would emphasize that the presentation of a DS may be punishing and that the presentation of an SS may be positively reinforcing. Rescorla and LoLordo could not find such effects because their experimental situation was set up to demonstrate motivational (and de-motivational) effects. But Rescorla (1969) has subsequently found that an SS established in the same noncontingent manner can serve to reinforce an R_a when it is later introduced as a consequence of that R_a, that is, when it is made contingent on it. Similarly, Weisman and Litner (1968) have shown that an SS can be used as a reinforcer to produce either a high or a low rate of responding by making its occurrence differentially contingent on a high or low rate. Hendry (1967) has reported a related reinforcement effect in a conditioned suppression situation.

Let us make a logical extension: think of the R_a-produced feedback stimulus in the avoidance learning situation as gradually acquiring safety signal properties. Include among these properties the ability to reinforce R_a. A number of parallels may already be noted between the FS and the SS. For example, if there is an instrumental avoidance contingency, then the FS is surely correlated with the absence of shock, just as the SS is in Rescorla and LoLordo's noncontingent training sessions. The main difference is that the FS is by definition contingent on the occurrence of the response, while (at least so far) the SS is established independently of S's behavior. The noncontingent procedure provides a vivid demonstration that the DS and SS stimuli can acquire their behavioral powers independently of S's behavior. DiCara and Miller (1968) have reported an even more vivid demonstration of what appear to be SS and DS effects by using rats that were deeply curarized. But the possibility of establishing an SS independently of S's behavior does not mean that an SS cannot be established when it is response contingent. Indeed, a response-produced SS might be more discriminable and more readily established than if the stimulus was scheduled to appear intermittently without any antecedents. There have been no direct comparisons of SS and FS effects, but a comparison across studies using SS and FS techniques is suggestive. Thus, we have seen that establishing an effective FS seems to require 40 or 50 trials or perhaps more in some situations, while from the fact that the SS effect is typically reported in studies that involve 90 or so pairings of the SS with the absence of shock, we may presume that the effect requires approximately the same number. Hammond (1966) has claimed to have shown a more rapidly established SS effect in a conditioned suppression situation, but this interpretation seems doubtful in view of the transitory nature of the effect.

The author and his colleagues have recently conducted a series of studies with SS and DS procedures to determine if the SS and DS effects vary across situations with different R_a requirements in the same manner as we had previously found the FS and CS effects to vary. The results have been rather encouraging. Thus, in the one-way runway, where there was no CS-termination or FS-presentation effect, a total absence of SS and DS effects was found. In the running wheel, where the former effects had been found to be small (see Figure 2), the latter were found to be small too, and unimpressive statistically. Then with the shuttle box, in the only one of these studies that has been published (Grossen & Bolles, 1968), large and highly reliable effects which mirrored the size of the CS and FS effects in that situation were found. In all of these studies, procedures like those of Rescorla (1966) were used, including 90 noncontingent pairings. The chief difference in procedure was that we used rats, whereas Rescorla used dogs.

So far, then, the parallel between FS and SS effects suggests that they may be equivalent. The bar-press situation is critical, however, and our results there have unfortunately been largely negative. However, Weisman and Litner (1968) obtained impressive SS effects with a wheel-turn R_a, which is comparable to the bar-press R_a in a number of other respects. Perhaps there are unique features of the bar-press R_a that we have not sufficiently allowed for; perhaps its initial dependence on freezing is relevant; or perhaps there is a critical element of the SS-DS procedure that remains to be isolated. For example, it is not clear why SS effects have been reported thus far only in free-operant situations where the rate of responding is measured. We do not know if the effect is limited to rate measures of nondiscriminated avoidance or whether it can be obtained as well with other response measures in discriminated avoidance situations.

In spite of a number of such unanswered questions, it is tempting to hypothesize that the CS-termination effect, the FS-presentation effect, and the SS-reinforcing effect are all functionally equivalent. I propose that this is indeed the case, and further, that in those situations where CS termination is effective in strengthening an R_a, it is effective because it serves as response feedback, and that such feedback is positively reinforcing because it functions as a safety signal. CS termination tells the animal, in effect, that shock is not going to occur.

It should be emphasized that this SS mechanism appears to be limited to learning situations in which the R_a is acquired relatively slowly, for example, in 40 trials or more. The reason for this limitation is evidently that to become established, the SS mechanism requires a number of the pairings of the SS with the absence of shock. The implication of this limitation is that whenever an R_a is rapidly acquired, for example, in 40 trials or less, its acquisition must be based on mechanisms that have little to do with the SS, the response-contingent FS, or the CS-termination contingency.

RELATION TO OTHER ACCOUNTS OF AVOIDANCE LEARNING

The arguments that have been advanced here have been based in part on the finding that the escape contingency is not essential for the acquisition of avoidance learning. This finding is not new, of course; it has been known and widely accepted ever since Mowrer and Lamoreaux's (1946) classic study, and a purely Pavlovian or contiguity interpretation of avoidance has not been seriously advocated for some years. The prevailing accounts of avoidance learning appear to cast the escape contingency in the simple but not altogether bad role of increasing the operant rate of R_a. The question of choosing the right R_a involves much more than obtaining a suitably high operant rate, however. Thus, the data shown in Figure 1 indicate what happened with three R_as with nearly equal operant rates. With one the escape contingency was apparently an essential ingredient in learning, with a second R_a it was unimportant because learning was so rapid without it, but with the third R_a the escape contingency was unimportant because neither it nor any other contingency produced learning. Meyer et al. (1960) suggested the appropriate conclusion some years ago: "However inconvenient the general implication, operants are *not* arbitrary; in avoidance learning, their selection is perhaps the most important of considerations [p. 227]."

The argument with regard to the CS-termination contingency is similar, but in the case of CS termination, it is nearly always cast in the leading role in avoidance learning. Fear-reduction theorists and operant theorists alike usually attribute the learning of R_a to response-contingent CS termination. The situation is only slightly complicated by the fact that some theorists attribute reinforcement to the reduction of the fear that is commonly assumed to become classically conditioned to the CS; CS termination is still assumed to be a critical agent in reinforcing R_a. The situation is complicated just a little more by the necessity to invent (or, more politely, to hypothesize the existence of) suitable CSs to explain the acquisition of avoidance when there is no observable CS. Sidman (1953) showed that rats could learn to avoid unsignaled shock, and it therefore became necessary to hypothesize that there were *implicit* CSs, the termination of which could be said to reinforce the R_a. This need was all the more urgent because, presumably, Sidman's situation provided S with no escape contingency.

The argument is now quite familiar: the proprioceptive and kinesthetic feedback from nonavoidance behavior serves as the needed CS. If S persists in some response, R_1, which fails to avoid shock, then the feedback from this behavior, S_1, will be paired with shock. After a number of such trials, S_1 will acquire conditioned, or secondary, aversiveness so that the subject will be reinforced for discontinuing R_1 and initiating some alternative response, R_2. If R_2 also fails to avoid shock the story will be repeated. Only R_a is exempt from the action of the avoidance contingency. The stimuli which earlier occasioned R_1, R_2 ... must gradually gain discriminative control over R_a as the repeated transitions from the various R_i to R_a and the consequent terminations of the various S_i reinforce R_a. This theoretical mechanism, originally proposed by Schoenfeld (1950), Sidman (1953), and Dinsmoor (1954), has been subsequently elaborated by Anger (1963). Anger noted that while one stage of acquisition may depend on the aversiveness of S_1, S_2 ..., there must come a point at which the principal discriminative control and the principal source of reinforcement for R_a is the lapse of time since the last preceding R_a. Only in this way Anger argued, can one explain the temporal distribution of R_as, or the continued improvement in performance as the subject becomes more proficient. So although there may be some question regarding just which implicit CSs are involved, there is rather widespread agreement that there are some implicit, response-produced stimuli, the termination of which reinforces avoidance learning.

I have no basic fault to find with the postulation of implicit CSs, but I think it important to point out that this conceptual scheme leads to some logical and empirical difficulties. One difficulty is that this account of avoidance involves a peculiar superfluity of explanatory mechanisms. The most common interpretation (e.g., Dinsmoor, 1954) involves what is basically an escape paradigm. While the avoidance contingency is clearly implicated as the principal contact of the situation with S's behavior, the S is not usually assumed to be avoiding in any real sense, but escaping. The assumed reinforcement mechanism is the termination of implicit CSs, the stimuli, S_1, S_2 ..., that have been paired with shock.

Alternatively, we can think in terms of a punishment paradigm. We might suppose that the avoidance contingency is effective, not because it permits S to escape from the various S_i, but because it directly punishes, or suppresses, the various R_i. Dinsmoor (1954) has argued quite rightly that the punishment effect itself needs explication. He has attempted to reduce the phenomena of punishment to avoidance terms, and then to reduce the avoidance to escape from S_1. This tactic is certainly defensible, but is it superior to taking the phenomena of punishment as primary and using them to explain those of avoidance, and perhaps even escape? I have tried to show that in the special case of a very rapidly acquired R_a, that is, when R_a is an effective SSDR, the punishment paradigm is uniquely able to handle the facts. In the case of a rapidly acquired R_a, there hardly seems time to make all the necessary S_i aversive, especially if we cannot show that an environmental CS affects the behavior in the same amount of time! A much faster and more direct mechanism is needed in this case, and the punishment of competing SSDRs is such a mechanism.

The agreed upon importance of the avoidance contingency in unsignaled avoidance suggests another interpretation: an avoidance paradigm. We might suppose that S really is avoiding shock. Although recognizing that it is difficult to put such a concept into precise behavioral terms, some writers have argued that this is the best conception of the problem (e.g., D'Amato et al., 1968; Keehn, 1966). Other theorists (e.g., Herrnstein & Hineline, 1966; Sidman, 1966) have recently come to the similar conclusion that what really reinforces avoidance behavior is the overall reduction in shock·density it produces. In the situations that are described, S is not able to avoid shock, or escape it, or to terminate CSs; S merely receives fewer shocks when R_a occurs. Under these conditions the rate of R_a increases. It should be emphasized, however, that the effects described by Herrnstein and Hineline and by Sidman are found after very extensive training. When Herrnstein and Hineline (1966) carefully eliminated all other sources of reinforcement besides reduction in shock density, the bar-press R_a only *began* to emerge after tens of thousands of shocks had been administered. Are we to believe then that this is the source of the reinforcement by which rats can learn other R_as in 100 trials, or 10 trials, or by which they learn to survive in nature? What Herrnstein and Hineline seem to have shown, quite to the contrary, is that avoidance itself, or response-contingent shock density reduction, *cannot* be the mechanism that produces the faster acquisition of R_a generally found under other conditions. We may marvel that such subtle control of the rat's behavior is possible, and we must admire the diligence of the experimenters who brought it about. But just because behavior can eventually be brought under the control of some stimulus and maintained by some contingency, it certainly does not follow that this stimulus controls the behavior under other circumstances or that the contingency is effective when others are available. Nor is there any reason to believe that the factors which can ultimately be used to govern some behavior are necessarily the same as those that were important in establishing it originally. We must look elsewhere for mechanisms to explain how the rat does most of its avoidance learning.

As a final alternative to the CS-termination hypothesis, we can consider an appetitive paradigm: The S learns to avoid shock, not because termination of S_i (or an explicit CS) is negatively reinforcing, but because R_a and the production of its feedback, S_a, is positively reinforcing. Denny and his students are among the few who have defended an appetitive paradigm (e.g., Denny & Weisman, 1964). Although Denny's relaxation theory emphasizes the response which becomes conditioned to the safety signal, whereas I am more concerned with the safety signal itself, there are many striking points of similarity between relaxation theory and the SSDR hypothesis, and both accounts generate similar predictions about avoidance behavior.

I have tried to show that the safety signal interpretation is especially able to handle the data in those cases where R_a is relatively slowly acquired, that is, when R_a is not an SSDR. In this case I assume that during the initial trials, S's behavior is restricted to a small set of SSDRs, and that learning will occur only if a number of rather delicate conditions are fulfilled. The first is that one of S's SSDRs (e.g., freezing) must be topographically compatible with the required R_a (e.g., bar pressing). Then shock must elicit enough reflexive bar presses so that S can either avoid some shocks (the postshock burst in Sidman's situation) or minimize their duration (when there is an escape contingency). With the minimization of shock, we may expect a gradual return of S's normal response repertoire, so that it is no longer restricted to SSDRs. This recovery process may be facilitated in the manner that Rescorla and LoLordo have suggested, that is, the R_a-contingent FS may become a safety signal and inhibit fear.[2] Finally, I assume that the safety signal actively reinforces R_a, and that eventually R_a may come under the control of still other, more subtle stimuli as their safety-signal properties gradually become discriminated. At this point we may be able to find S quite proficiently performing an R_a which is as unlikely and as unnatural as pressing a bar.

It is clear that an animal's defensive repertoire can be extended beyond the narrow limits set by its SSDRs. But it is unfortunate that our theoretical predilections have led us to be preoccupied with the ultimate limits to which this extension can be carried and with defending CS termination as the reinforcement mechanism. In retrospect, it hardly seems possible that the acquisition of the bar-press R_a could ever have been seriously attributed simply to the action of CS termination, but it was. These preoccupations have not really advanced our understanding of how such extensions occur, how other, more natural R_as are learned, or for that matter how animals survive in nature.

References

Anger, D. The role of temporal discrimination in the reinforcement of Sidman avoidance behavior. *Journal of the Experimental Analysis of Behavior*, 1963, *6*, 477–506.

Bolles, R. C. Avoidance and escape learning: Simultaneous acquisition of different reponses. *Journal of Comparative and Physiological Psychology*, 1969, *68*, 355–358.

Bolles, R. C., & Grossen, N. E. Effects of an informational stimulus on the acquisition of avoidance behavior in rats. *Journal of Comparative and Physiological Psychology*, 1969, *68*, 90–99.

Bolles, R. C., & McGillis, D. B. The non-operant nature of the bar-press escape response. *Psychonomic Science*, 1968, *11*, 261–262.

[2] I have been careful to say nothing here about fear because I suspect we should let that tortured concept rest awhile and try to get along without it. However, if it is felt necessary to introduce the term, I would like to see it used as Rescorla and Solomon (1967) used it, that is, to refer to some observed feature of instrumental behavior. The restriction of the animal's behavioral repertoire to a narrow set of SSDRs might just be an appropriate feature.

Bolles, R. C., & Popp, R. J., Jr. Parameters affecting the acquisition of Sidman avoidance. *Journal of the Experimental Analysis of Behavior*, 1964, 7, 315–321.

Bolles, R. C., Stokes, L. W., & Younger, M. S. Does CS termination reinforce avoidance behavior? *Journal of Comparative and Physiological Psychology*, 1966, 62, 201–207.

Bower, G., Starr, R., & Lazarovitz, L. Amount of response-produced change in the CS and avoidance learning. *Journal of Comparative and Physiological Psychology*, 1965, 59, 13–17.

Brodgen, W. J., Lipman, E. A., & Culler, E. The role of incentive in conditioning and learning. *American Journal of Psychology*, 1938, 51, 109–117.

Brush, F. R. On the differences between animals that learn and do not learn to avoid electric shock. *Psychonomic Science*, 1966, 5, 123–124.

Cole, M., & Wahlsten, D. Response-contingent CS termination as a factor in avoidance conditioning. *Psychonomic Science*, 1968, 12, 15–16.

D'Amato, M. R. Role of anticipatory responses in avoidance conditioning: An important control. *Psychonomic Science*, 1967, 8, 191–192.

D'Amato, M. R., Fazzaro, J., & Etkin, M. Anticipatory responding and avoidance discrimination as factors in avoidance conditioning. *Journal of Experimental Psychology*, 1968, 77, 41–47.

D'Amato, M. R., Keller, D., & DiCara, L. Facilitation of discriminated avoidance learning by discontinuous shock. *Journal of Comparative and Physiological Psychology*, 1964, 58, 344–349.

D'Amato, M. R., & Schiff, D. Long-term discriminated avoidance performance in the rat. *Journal of Comparative and Physiological Psychology*, 1964, 57, 123–126.

Denny, M. R., & Weisman, R. G. Avoidance behavior as a function of length of nonshock confinement. *Journal of Comparative and Physiological Psychology*, 1964, 58, 252–257.

DiCara, L. V., & Miller, N. E. Changes in heart rate instrumentally learned by curarized rats as avoidance responses. *Journal of Comparative and Physiological Psychology*, 1968, 65, 8–12.

Dinsmoor, J. A. Punishment: I. The avoidance hypothesis. *Psychological Review*, 1954, 61, 34–46.

Feldman, R. S., & Bremner, F. J. A method for rapid conditioning of stable avoidance bar pressing behavior. *Journal of the Experimental Analysis of Behavior*, 1963, 6, 393–394.

Grossen, N. E., & Bolles, R. C. Effects of a classical conditioned "fear signal" and "safety signal" on nondiscriminated avoidance behavior. *Psychonomic Science*, 1968, 11, 321–322.

Hammond, L. J. Increased responding to CS⁻ in differential CER. *Psychonomic Science*, 1966, 5, 337–338.

Hendry, D. P. Conditioned inhibition of conditioned suppression. *Psychonomic Science*, 1967, 9, 261–262.

Herrnstein, R. J., & Hineline, P. N. Negative reinforcement as shock-frequency reduction. *Journal of the Experimental Analysis of Behavior*, 1966, 9, 421–430.

Hull, C. L. A functional interpretation of the conditioned reflex. *Psychological Review*, 1929, 36, 498–511.

Hurwitz, H. M. B. Method for discriminative avoidance training. *Science*, 1964, 145, 1070–1071.

Kamin, L. J. The effects of termination of the CS and avoidance of the US on avoidance learning. *Journal of Comparative and Physiological Psychology*, 1956, 49, 420–424.

Keehn, J. D. Avoidance responses as discrminated operants. *British Journal of Psychology*, 1966, 57, 375–380.

Keehn, J. D. Running and bar pressing as avoidance responses. *Psychological Reports*, 1967, 20, 591–602.

Keehn, J. D., & Webster, C. D. Rapid discriminated bar-press avoidance through avoidance shaping. *Psychonomic Science*, 1968, *10*, 21—22.

Lockard, J. S. Choice of a warning signal or no warning signal in an unavoidable shock situation. *Journal of Comparative and Physiological Psychology*, 1963, *56*, 526—530.

Maatsch, J. L. Learning and fixation after a single shock trial. *Journal of Comparative and Physiological Psychology*, 1959, *52*, 408—410.

Meyer, D. R., Cho, C., & Wesemann, A. F. On problems of conditioning discriminated lever-press avoidance responses. *Psychological Review*, 1960, *67*, 224—228.

Miller, N. E. Learnable drives and rewards. In S. S. Stevens (Ed.), *Handbook of experimental psychology*. New York: Wiley, 1951.

Mogenson, G. J., Mullin, A. D., & Clark, E. A. Effects of delayed secondary reinforcement and response requirements on avoidance learning. *Canadian Journal of Psychology*, 1965, *19*, 61—73.

Mowrer, O. H. A stimulus-response analysis of anxiety and its role as a reinforcing agent. *Psychological Review*, 1939, *46*, 553—565.

Mowrer, O. H., & Lamoreaux, R. R. Avoidance conditioning and signal duration—a study of secondary motivation and reward. *Psychological Monographs*, 1942, *54*(5, Whole No. 247).

Mowrer, O. H., & Lamoreaux, R. R. Fear as an intervening variable in avoidance conditioning. *Journal of Comparative Psychology*, 1946, *39*, 29—50.

Myers, A. K. Onset vs. termination of stimulus energy as the CS in avoidance conditioning and pseudoconditioning. *Journal of Comparative and Physiological Psychology*, 1960, *53*, 72—78.

Myers, A. K. Discriminated operant avoidance learning in Wistar and G-4 rats as a function of type of warning stimulus. *Journal of Comparative and Physiological Psychology*, 1964, *58*, 453—455.

Rescorla, R. A. Predictability and number of pairings in Pavlovian fear conditioning. *Psychonomic Science*, 1966, *4*, 383—384.

Rescorla, R. A. Establishment of a positive reinforcer through contrast with shock. *Journal of Comparative and Physiological Psychology*, 1969, *67*, 260—263.

Rescorla, R. A., & LoLordo, V. M. Inhibition of avoidance behavior. *Journal of Comparative and Physiological Psychology*, 1965, *59*, 406—412.

Rescorla, R. A. & Solomon, R. L. Two-process learning theory: Relationships between Pavlovian conditioning and instrumental learning. *Psychological Review*, 1967, *74*, 151—182.

Schoenfeld, W. N. An experimental approach to anxiety, escape and avoidance behavior. In P. H. Hock & J. Zubin (Eds.), *Anxiety*. New York: Grune & Stratton, 1950.

Sidman, M. Two temporal parameters of the maintenance of avoidance behavior by the white rat. *Journal of Comparative and Physiological Psychology*, 1953, *46*, 253—261.

Sidman, M. Some properties of the warning stimulus in avoidance behavior. *Journal of Comparative and Physiological Psychology*, 1955, *48*, 444—450.

Sidman, M. Avoidance behavior. In W. K. Honig (Ed.), *Operant behavior: Areas of research and application*. New York: Appleton-Century-Crofts, 1966.

Smith, O. A., Jr., McFarland, W. L., & Taylor, E. Performance in a shock-avoidance conditioning situation interpreted as pseudoconditioning. *Journal of Comparative and Physiological Psychology*, 1961, *54*, 154—157.

Solomon, R. L., & Brush, E. S. Experimentally derived conceptions of anxiety and aversion. In M. R. Jones (Ed.), *Nebraska Symposium on Motivation*, 1956, *4*, 212—305.

Solomon, R. L., & Wynne, L. C. Traumatic avoidance learning: Acquisition in normal dogs. *Psychological Monographs*, 1953, *67*(4, Whole No. 354).

Theios, J. Simple conditioning as two-stage all-or-none learning. *Psychological Review*, 1963, *70*, 403—417.

Turner, L. H., & Solomon, R. L. Human traumatic avoidance learning: Theory and experiments on the operant-respondent distinction and failures to learn. *Psychological Monographs*, 1962, 76(40, Whole No. 559).

Warren, J. A., Jr., & Bolles, R. C. A reevaluation of a simple contiguity interpretation of avoidance learning. *Journal of Comparative and Physiological Psychology*, 1967, *64*, 179–182.

Weisman, R. G., & Litner, J. S. Positive conditioned reinforcement of Sidman avoidance behavior in rats. *Journal of Comparative and Physiological Psychology*, 1969, *68*, 597–603.

Rats learn readily to press bars to get food pellets. Rats also learn very readily to jump (Baum, 1969) and readily to run (Miller, 1951) from a dangerous place to a safe place to avoid shock. From this, equipotentiality deduces that rats should learn readily to press bars to avoid shock. But this isn't so (D'Amato and Schiff, 1964). Very special procedures must be instituted to train rats to press levers to avoid shock reliably (D'Amato and Fazzaro, 1966; Fantino, Sharp, and Cole, 1966). Similarly, pigeons learn very readily to peck lighted keys to obtain grain—so readily, in fact, that we cannot consider it an arbitrary response (see Brown and Jenkins, this volume, p. 146). The next article, by Philip Hineline and Howard Rachlin, shows the lengths that clever experimenters must to go in order to train even two out of three pigeons to avoid by key-pecking. The ingenuity required does not attest to pigeons' being too dumb to learn about avoidance contingencies; ask anyone who has tried to kill them by throwing rocks how good pigeons are at avoiding. Moreover, Emlen (1969), Bedford and Anger (1968), and MacPhail (1968) have shown that birds learn easily to jump, to fly, and to run to avoid shock. More probably, as Bolles suggests, the problem is training a primarily appetitive response—pecking—for defense.

It should be noted here that the notion of "Species Specific Defense Response" proposed by Bolles is somewhat circular as it stands. For if Hineline and Rachlin had easily trained key-pecking for avoidance, the reader would have been free to conclude that it was really an SSDR after all, and the hypothesis would remain intact. It is necessary to set up criteria independent of successful avoidance which establish that a response is an SSDR. Systematic observation of the reactions of a species to its natural predators might help break the circularity.

19

ESCAPE AND AVOIDANCE OF SHOCK BY PIGEONS PECKING A KEY

Philip N. Hineline and Howard Rachlin

Pigeons had been trained to peck a key when each peck removed a slowly increasing series of electric shocks. Without loss of the established key-pecking response, the birds were gradually weaned from this procedure to one where intense shocks were presented suddenly, duplicating features that had proved ineffective for initial shaping of the response. Finally, a procedure was introduced in which key pecks could avoid shock. Avoidance responding was maintained in two of three pigeons.

Much of the work reported in this Journal has shown that when on schedules of positive reinforcement, pigeons behave much like other animals. A pigeon's key peck is a convenient analog to a rat or monkey's lever press. Pigeons have also been frequently used in studies where electric shocks are used to punish appetitively maintained responses (*e.g.*, Azrin, 1960; Azrin and Holz, 1961; Holz, Azrin, and Ulrich, 1963). The punished behavior of pigeons appears similar to comparable behavior of rats and monkeys (Appel and Peterson, 1965; Hake, Azrin, and Oxford, 1967). But pigeons have been neither convenient nor typical subjects for escape or avoidance schedules of shock. Undocumented personal communications report failures of pigeons to avoid; a brief reference by Dinsmoor (1967) suggests that this has been a general finding. Even without these one could predict, from the conspicuous scarcity of systematic studies of pigeons on these schedules, that standard escape and avoidance procedures are ineffective when applied to pigeons. We have discovered only four published reports of escape or avoidance in pigeons: Azrin (1959b) shaped key pecking in one pigeon, using manual control of shock intensity. Hoffman and Fleshler (1959) failed to get key pecking, but did shape and maintain head-lifting

From *Journal of the Experimental Analysis of Behavior*, 12 (1969), 533–538.

This work was supported by Research Grants Number GB-7334 from the National Science Foundation, and Number 1 RO 1 MH 14648 from the National Institute of Health.

responses with escape contingencies and, in one bird, maintained head-lifting with avoidance contingencies. MacPhail (1968) trained pigeons to escape and avoid shock with an ambulatory response in a shuttle box. The only study that maintained key pecking extensively was one by Azrin, Hake, Holz, and Hutchinson (1965), who arranged for a peck on one key to remove a punishment contingency from positively reinforced responding on a second key, thus, in a sense, avoiding shocks. The first three of these experiments suggest possible sources for the difficulty in conditioning pigeons' responses with shock removal. The study by Azrin, and that by Hoffman and Fleshler, suggest that the pigeon's sensitivity to shock must fluctuate, for in both of these studies shock intensity was adjusted frequently. Another likely source of difficulty is shock-produced behavior incompatible with the response to be shaped.

The present authors have reported a procedure designed to minimize these two problems; stable key pecking was shaped and maintained by response-contingent shock removal when the shock was a slowly increasing series of pulses (Rachlin and Hineline, 1967). This basic procedure supported responding on both fixed-interval and fixed-ratio schedules of shock removal (Hineline and Rachlin, 1969). In the present experiments, responding was maintained while the gradually increasing shock was transformed into sudden and intense shock. The pigeons were subsequently trained to avoid shock by pecking the key during periods when the shock was not present.

METHOD

Subjects

Three adult male White Carneaux pigeons, whose early performance on aversive schedules has been reported previously (Rachlin and Hineline, 1967), were used. Birds 270 and 319 had been trained to peck for food; this pecking had subsequently been extinguished. Bird 499 was experimentally naive at the beginning of the experiment. In all birds, gold wires were implanted under the pubis bones (Azrin, 1959a), and the birds were given free access to food and water in their home cages.

Apparatus

The experimental chamber of standard dimensions (Ferster and Skinner, 1957) was made of wire mesh coated with an insulating spray. The shock was 110 v ac transformed by a 0 to 110 v variable transformer, then stepped up by a 400-v transformer, and run through a 25 K or larger resistor, through relay contacts which closed to produce a 35-msec pulse every second, and through a Gerbrands mercury swivel mounted on the ceiling of the chamber. The variable transformer was driven by a motor and gear changer (or by a stepping device, in some of the later work) with a clutch arrangement. This apparatus provided for trains of shock pulses, with intensity linearly increasing in time, and for sudden reset of the intensity to zero. In all of the following experiments, the maximum shock was 8.5 ma. If the shock reached 8.5 ma, it remained at that value until reset. The experimental chamber was contained in a sound-resistant chest; white noise was supplied throughout. There was a houselight on the roof of the experimental chamber, and a transilluminated key was mounted on the wall, 10 in. above the floor.

Preliminary Procedures and Results

As described previously, for initial conditioning, trains of 2-per-sec pulses were presented, shock intensity increasing very slightly with each pulse, in the presence of a dim and diffuse houselight and the transilluminated response key. Successive approximations to key pecking were reinforced by resetting the shock suddenly to zero for 5 sec during which all lights were off. When the lights came back on, the shock again increased linearly from zero intensity. Key pecks automatically produced the blackout and shock reset. It was found helpful to mount a transparent hemispherical extension on the response key during training; the extension could be removed after initial training. These procedures produced reliable key pecking in five of seven birds, but several hours of shaping were required for four of the five. A procedure for automatically shaping key pecking with negative reinforcement similar to Brown and Jenkins (1968) "autoshaping" procedure was also somewhat successful (Rachlin, 1969).

Once established, key pecking was easily manipulated with a wide range of rates of shock increase (0.0374 ma/min to 37.4 ma/min). At the highest and lowest rates of increase, pecking was erratic; within the extremes, responding was systematically related to the controlling conditions; when shock intensity increased rapidly, the pigeons pecked at higher intensities than when shock increased slowly.

After these experiments the pigeons were exposed to several procedural variations intended to produce avoidance responding. These variations entailed removal of shock for short periods during shock increase, and replacing the shock by a signal. Pecking during the signal would have avoided the more intense shock to come. These variations were unsuccessful. The pigeons generally did not peck during the short shock-free periods even though these periods were inserted at times during the course of shock increase when the pigeons had previously pecked frequently. The pigeons were also exposed to fixed-interval and fixed-ratio escape conditioning reported elsewhere (Hineline and Rachlin, 1969).

Procedure A. Escape from Sudden Shock

The basic escape procedure was modified as diagrammed in Fig. 1. In the first session, the 5-sec blackout was followed by an additional 25 sec of shock-free time; the shock-intensity programmer increased at its usual rate (indicated by the dashed line in the figure), but shocks were not delivered. During this shock-free time, only the houselight was illuminated and key pecks were ineffective. At the end of the 25 sec, the key was illuminated and shocks were delivered as if there had been no additional shock-free time. Pecks from then on were effective. On the following day, the shock-free period was 50 sec; the shock intensity at onset was 0.62 ma. For each successive session, this shock-free period was increased by 25 sec with a corresponding increase in the intensity of shock at its onset (in Fig. 1, the duration of shock-free time is indicated by the variable X) until it reached a value of 575 sec. On this final session, the intensity

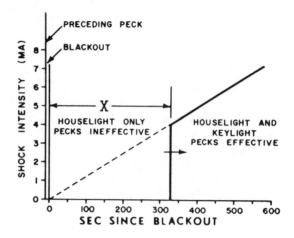

FIG. 1 Diagram of procedure for developing escape from shock with sudden shock onset. The heavy line indicates shock intensity; time since blackout is indicated on the abscissa. As indicated by the arrow, the time from blackout to shock onset was varied (from day to day). The diagonal line describes the intensity of shock at its onset as a function of time until that onset; the diagonal also describes the growth in intensity of the shocks after onset of the train of shocks.

of shock at its onset was 7.15 ma. Birds 270, 319, and 499 were run on this procedure.

Results of Procedure A

All three birds responded throughout this procedure. Figure 2 shows the median latency of response, measured from end of blackout, for each bird as a function of time from end of blackout to onset of shock. The points corresponding to zero on the abscissa represent median latencies for these subjects in a previous experiment, where shock increase was gradual from its beginning. As the time to shock onset was increased from zero, the median latency decreased for two of the three birds. The third bird, 270, began with an extremely small median latency and had little room for decrease. The median latencies of the two continued on a generally decreasing trend until they approached the time of shock onset. Thereafter, as the intensity of shock at onset increased from session to session, the median latencies followed closely along the 45-degree line that corresponds to responding immediately upon the onset of shock. The dispersion of response latencies (not shown) tended at first to increase as the median latency decreased. But this dispersion decreased markedly as soon as the median latency approached the time of shock onset.

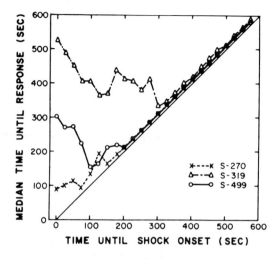

FIG. 2 Median time until response as a function of the interval between blackout and shock onset for Pigeons 270, 319, and 499. The diagonal line describes the locus where data points would lie if the birds always responded immediately at shock onset. Each data point is based on a single session.

Procedure B. Avoidance

The sudden shock procedure was changed to resemble standard discriminated avoidance procedures (Hoffman, 1966). The 5-sec blackout was always followed by a 475-sec shock-free ("intertrial") interval during which key pecks were ineffective and only the houselight was illuminated (see Fig. 3). At 475 sec, the keylight was illuminated ("warning stimulus"), and the response key was made effective, but no shocks were delivered. If no response had occurred by the five-hundredth second, shock was introduced, beginning at an intensity of 6.20 ma and increasing at the rate of 0.745 ma/min until a peck occurred. Thus, a peck between the four hundred seventy-fifth and five-hundredth sec turned off the "warning stimulus" and prevented the occurrence of shock; a peck after the five-hundredth second resulted in escape from shock.

Results of Procedure B

This procedure produced appreciable avoidance responding in two of the three birds. Figure 4 shows per cent avoidance as a function of sessions. "Per cent avoidance" is equal to the number of avoidance responses divided by the total number of trials, expressed as a per cent. Bird 270 quickly came to avoid on approximately 90% of all trials. Bird 499 avoided between 30% and 70%, with considerable day-to-day fluctuation, and Bird 319 emitted some avoidance responses during the first 18 sessions of the procedure, but eventually reverted

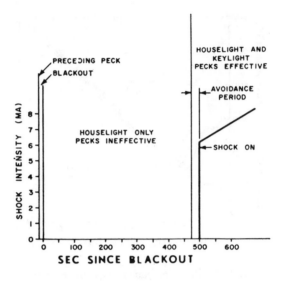

FIG. 3 Diagram of avoidance procedure. Time since blackout (or since the beginning of the session, for the first trial) is represented on the abscissa. The heavy line describes shock intensity. As indicated, pecks during the 25-sec "avoidance period" produced a blackout and prevented the onset of shock.

to escape responding. It may be significant that this bird had a considerably shorter conditioning history than the other two. It had been omitted from some of the procedures mentioned previously.

DISCUSSION

With the procedure used for initial shaping and maintenance of key pecking, it was not clear whether a response was reinforced by the removal of shock that was scheduled at the time of the response, or by the prevention of more intense shocks to come. In one case we would say that the response was maintained by escape contingencies; in the other, that the response was maintained by avoidance contingencies. Mowrer (1940) used a similar procedure with rats and found that they came to respond at low shock intensities—in the word of Kimble (1961, p. 69): "as soon as they could feel the shock." Kimble concluded that the rats' responding was maintained as avoidance rather than as escape. The pigeons in the present experiments did not confine their responses to low shock intensities, but avoidance contingencies could have been operative here, too.

Whether the birds were avoiding or escaping on Procedure A, performance on this procedure was closely correlated with that on Procedure B, the *bona fide* discriminated avoidance procedure. Bird 270, which avoided best on Procedure

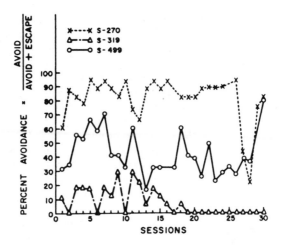

FIG. 4 Per cent avoidance as a function of sessions of exposure to the avoidance procedure, for Pigeons 270, 319, and 499. Per cent avoidance was computed by dividing the number of avoidance responses in a session by the total number of trials in that session. This latter was also equal to the sum of avoidance and escape responses.

B, had responded most at low intensities on Procedure A and on earlier procedures. Bird 319, which avoided least well on Procedure B, had responded only at high intensities on Procedure A and on earlier procedures. This correlation between performances on different procedures may be based directly on differing sensitivies to shock that perhaps stem from differing electrode implants. On the other hand, the correlation may mean that some birds (270 in particular) were indeed avoiding on all the procedures. If sensitivity to shock, as measured by the intensities at which a given pigeon responded on Procedure A, determined whether a given pigeon would avoid on Procedure B, it should follow that higher intensities of shock onset in Procedure B would have increased the avoidance responding of those pigeons that avoided infrequently. Unfortunately this notion has not yet been tested.

Through this and previous work there have been hints that exposure to shock reduces the subsequent effective intensity of shock; with continued exposure, strong shocks come to resemble weaker ones in their effects on behavior. Evidence for such adaptation or habituation to shock is supplied by the results of Procedure A, where sudden onset of shock replaced the gradual increase from zero. Responding shifted systematically to lower shock intensities when the shock no longer increased gradually from zero, suggesting that the shock was made effectively more intense by its sudden onset or by the interpolated intervals of shock-free time. Elsewhere, pigeons' adaptation to electric shock has been observed when mild shock is used to punish appetitively maintained key pecking (Azrin, 1959c; Rachlin, 1966). The punishment produces most suppression at the beginnings of sessions, except when a timeout is inserted in mid-session, producing renewed potency of the punishing shock (Azrin, 1960). The interpolation of shock-free intervals in some of our preliminary procedures was accompanied by shifts of responding to lower intensities. Also, there were hints of adaptation during an initial, abortive attempt to produce escape responding in pigeons, where we used continuous shock instead of pulsing shock. The shock was somewhat effective at the beginnings of sessions, but the birds appeared quickly to become insensitive as sessions continued. Whether such changes in effectiveness of shock with exposure are based on sensory adaptation or on some more obscure process, remains an open question. Certainly they are worthy of specific study instead of being observed only as by-products or secondary effects in studies on other topics.

The present experiments have introduced procedures that produce, in the pigeon, negatively reinforced behavior somewhat comparable to that observed in other species. Some features of these experiments, such as the gradual shock increase during shaping of a new response, and transitional procedures for changing from gradual shock increase to sudden shock onset, may prove necessary for negative reinforcement with pigeons and other species that are refractory to standard negative reinforcement procedures. In addition, it is likely that some of these features could make negative reinforcement more effective for animals that respond relatively well on the present standard procedures.

References

Appel, J. B. Punishment and shock intensity. *Science*, 1963, *141*, 528–529.

Appel, J. B. and Peterson, N. J. Punishment: effects of shock intensity on response suppression. *Psychological Reports*, 1965, *16*, 721–730.

Azrin, N. H. A technique for delivering shock to pigeons. *Journal of the Experimental Analysis of Behavior*, 1959, *2*, 161–163. (a)

Azrin, N. H. Some notes on punishment and avoidance. *Journal of the Experimental Analysis of Behavior*, 1959, *2*, 260. (b)

Azrin, N. H. Punishment and recovery during fixed-ratio performance. *Journal of the Experimental Analysis of Behavior*, 1959, *2*, 301–305. (c)

Azrin, N. H. Effects of punishment intensity during variable-interval reinforcement. *Journal of the Experimental Analysis of Behavior*, 1960, *3*, 123–142.

Azrin, N. H. and Holz, W. C. Punishment during fixed-interval reinforcement. *Journal of the Experimental Analysis of Behavior*, 1961, *4*, 343–347.

Azrin, N. H., Hake, D. F., Holz, W. C., and Hutchinson, R. R. Motivational aspects of escape from punishment. *Journal of the Experimental Analysis of Behavior*, 1965, *8*, 31–44.

Brown, P. L. and Jenkins, H. M. Auto-shaping of the pigeon's key-peck. *Journal of the Experimental Analysis of Behavior*, 1968, *11*, 1–8.

Dinsmoor, J. Escape from shock as a conditioning technique. In Marshall R. Jones (Ed.), *Miami Symposium on the Prediction of Behavior, 1967. Aversive Stimulation.* Coral Gables, Florida: University of Miami Press.

Ferster, C. B. and Skinner, B. F. *Schedules of reinforcement.* New York: Appleton-Century-Crofts, 1957.

Hake, D. F., Azrin, N. H., and Oxford, R. The effects of punishment intensity on squirrel monkeys. *Journal of the Experimental Analysis of Behavior*, 1967, *10* 95–107.

Hineline, P. N. and Rachlin, H. C. Notes on fixed-ratio and fixed-interval escape responding in the pigeon. *Journal of the Experimental Analysis of Behavior*, 1969, *12*, 129—133.

Hoffman, H. S. Discriminated avoidance. In W. K. Honig (Ed.), *Operant conditioning: areas of research and application*. New York: Appleton-Century-Crofts, 1966, Pp. 499—530.

Hoffman, H. S. and Fleshler, M. Aversive control with the pigeon. *Journal of the Experimental Analysis of Behavior*, 1959, *2*, 213—218.

Holz, W. C., Azrin, N. H., and Ulrich, R. E. Punishment of temporally spaced responding. *Journal of the Experimental Analysis of Behavior*, 1963, *6*, 115—122.

Kimble, G. A. *Hilgard and Marquis' Conditioning and Learning*. New York: Appleton-Century-Crofts, 1961. Pp. 68—91.

Macphail, E. M. Avoidance responding in pigeons. *Journal of the Experimental Analysis of Behavior*, 1968, *11*, 625—632.

Rachlin, H. C. Recovery of responses during mild punishment. *Journal of the Experimental Analysis of Behavior*, 1966, *9*, 251—263.

Rachlin, H. C. and Hineline, P. N. Training and maintenance of key pecking in the pigeon by negative reinforcement. *Science*, 1967, *157*, 954—955.

Rachlin, H. C. Autoshaping of key pecking in pigeons with negative reinforcement. *Journal of the Experimental Analysis of Behavior*, 1969, *12*, 521—531.

Just as Dobrezecka, Szwejkowska, and Konorski (this volume, p. 131) showed that the discriminative control of instrumental responding is not equipotential, so the next study, by James Allison, Daniel Larson, and Donald Jensen, shows that the discriminative control of avoidance is also differentially prepared. In the classic demonstration of avoidance learning, Neal Miller (1951) trained rats to run and to turn a wheel to get from an electrified white side of a box to a safe black side. Allison, Larson, and Jensen show that Miller hit on a prepared choice of contingencies: They find that rats prefer black to white, particularly when afraid, and have trouble learning to flee black to get to white. The natural history of a nocturnal, cavity-dwelling animal like the rat suggests that they may be prepared to learn that white is dangerous and dark safe, and so contraprepared to learn the reverse.

20

ACQUIRED FEAR, BRIGHTNESS PREFERENCE, AND ONE-WAY SHUTTLEBOX PERFORMANCE

James Allison, Daniel Larson, and Donald D. Jensen

Rats choosing between black and white showed an unlearned preference for black which was strengthened by previous shock in white, and weakened but not reversed by equivalent shock in black. Congruous findings were obtained with a one-way shuttlebox: escape from white to black occurred more readily than escape from black to white, whether S had or had not been shocked in the start compartment. Incongruously, fear conditioning did not facilitate escape performance, but rather impaired it early in training.

In the classic demonstration of an acquired fear drive, rats shocked in the white side of a shuttlebox later learned to escape from the white to the black side, although both sides were then free of shock (Miller, 1948). Those data suggest that rats previously shocked in white would prefer black to white, given a choice between the two—as do rats with no history of shock (Douglas, 1966; Freedman, 1965). Further, it seems likely that the unlearned preference for black would be strengthened by shock in white, and weakened or even reversed by shock in black, but Miller's data provide no basis for these predictions. There was no nonshocked control group, and no group run from black to white. Later work with the Miller shuttlebox does not seem to include any factorial experiment using the four relevant conditions: escape from white to black or from black to white after preliminary experience in the start compartment with or without shock. The two experiments reported here were done (a) to confirm

From *Psychonomic Science*, 8 (1967), 269–270.

This work was supported in part by Grant MH 11470 from the National Institute of Mental Health, United States Public Health Service, to J. A. The participation of D. L. was supported by NSF Undergraduate Research Participation Program Grant GY 878. We thank William C. Leonard for his assistance.

the preference for black over white among rats with no history of shock, (b) to study the extent to which the preference could be increased by previous shock in white, and decreased by previous shock in black, and (c) to examine the relationship between brightness preference and instrumental performance in the Miller shuttlebox.

The preference tester was a wooden enclosure 14 in. high, with a 25 x 25 in. grid floor and a frosted Plexiglas ceiling. Partition walls divided it into a start compartment, 12 x 25 in., and two alternative goal compartments, 12 x 12 in. each. Start and goal compartments were separated by a guillotine door, 9 x 14 in. An open passageway between the two goal compartments allowed S to move back and forth between them after the initial choice had been made. Wall and floor colors were manipulated by means of interchangeable wall inserts and floor pans painted black or white, and interchangeable guillotine doors were painted appropriately. S chose between a white and a black goal compartment after preliminary experience in the start compartment, white or black, with or without shock.

A total of 40 male Long-Evans rats, 90–150 days old, were assigned randomly to four groups of 10: WNS (white start compartment, no shock), WS (white start compartment, shock), BNS (black start compartment, no shock), or BS (black start compartment, shock). On Day 1, S either was or was not shocked while confined for 7 min in the start compartment with the guillotine door closed. The shock treatment consisted of 24 1-sec, 1-mA scrambled shocks at one every 15 sec, beginning with the second minute of confinement. Shock invariably elicited vocalization and startle. S was then removed to a holding cage for 10 min, and returned to the home cage. On Day 2, 24 h later, S got five choice trials with an intertrial interval of 4 min. Half of each group had the black goal compartment on the right, half on the left. E began each trial by placing S in the start compartment through a doorway centered laterally in its long wall. E raised the guillotine door after a 15-sec delay, closed it when S entered either goal compartment, and removed S to the holding cage 100 sec later. On each trail, E recorded initial choice and time spent in each goal compartment.

As Table 1 shows, nonshocked Ss chose the black goal compartment more often than the white (two-tailed, $p = .04$ by the binomial test). The preference for black over white was increased by previous shock in white, and decreased but not reversed by previous shock in black, producing a significant interaction ($F = 5.64$, $df = 1/36$, $p < .025$). Time spent data agreed closely with initial choice data. Nonshocked Ss spent a greater proportion of time in the black than the white goal compartment (two-tailed, $p = .02$). The preference for black over white was increased by shock in white, and decreased by shock in black ($F = 7.96$, $df = 1/36$, $p < .01$). There were no significant effects involving the trials variable.

Four corresponding groups were trained in a shuttlebox to escape from white to black or from black to white after preliminary experience in the start compartment with or without shock. Since rats with no history of shock preferred black to white, we expected Group WNS to perform better than Group BNS. Since previous shock in white increased the preference for black over white, and equivalent shock in black decreased it by a comparable amount,

TABLE 1 Initial Choice of Black Rather Than White, and Time Spent in Black Rather Than White

Start box	Initial choice Treatment		Time spent Treatment	
	No shock	Shock	No shock	Shock
White	.66	.84	.66	.86
Black	.66	.50	.71	.57

The tabular entries are mean proportions based on all five trials.

Group WS was expected to perform better than Group BS. Similarly, Group WS was expected to perform better than WNS, and BS better than BNS.

The Ss were male Long-Evans rats, 90–150 days old, assigned randomly to four groups of nine. The shuttlebox was patterned closely after Miller's, except that ours had a grid floor on each side, with a black or white floor pan. On Day 1, S was confined in the black or white side for 7 min, with or without 24 1-sec, 1-mA scrambled shocks. On Day 2, 24 h later, S was trained to escape from the appropriate start to the appropriate goal compartment by touching the paddlewheel just above the guillotine door, with either forepaw. When the wheel was touched the door was opened, and S spent 30 sec in the goal compartment before being removed to the holding cage. Each S got 10 trials, with an intertrial interval of 2 min.

Two procedural differences between our experiment and Miller's should be pointed out. First, Miller's Ss received both escapable shock and inescapable shock during the fear conditioning phase. We did not use escapable shock because we were unable to adapt an escape procedure to our nonshocked controls without introducing other contaminating differences between their treatment and the shock treatment. Second, Miller discarded several Ss for failing to respond within a 100-sec cutoff early in escape training. We discarded none.

As expected, Group WNS performed better than Group BNS (see Fig. 1). Group WNS showed no consistent trend as training progressed ($F = 1.16$, $df = 4/64$, $p > .25$), while BNS responded progressively slower across trial blocks ($F = 3.90$, $df - 4/64$, $p < .01$). As expected WS performed better than BS. Group WS responded progressively faster as training progressed ($F = 3.77$, $df = 4/64$, $p < .01$), confirming Miller's findings, while BS showed no consistent trend ($F = 1.26$, $df = 4/64$, $p > .25$).

According to acquired drive theory, and according to our preference data, WS should have performed better than WNS, and BS better than BNS. These predictions could not be evaluated unambiguously. At the outset of escape training, WS performed worse than WNS ($t = 2.13$, $df - 16$, two-tailed, $p. < .05$), and BS worse than BNS ($t = 3.55$, $df = 16$, two-tailed, $p < .01$). At the end of training WS did not differ from WNS, nor BS from BNS. Thus, the fear conditioning procedure may simply have produced a temporary depression of

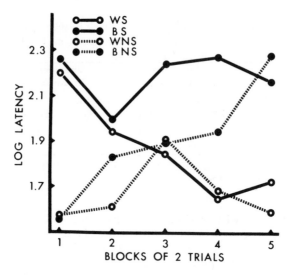

FIG. 1   Mean log latency (see) in blocks of two trials.

performance among WS and BS, and no effect upon the reinforcing properties of escape from white to black or from black to white, respectively.

We conducted a separate analysis after excluding five Ss that would have been discarded had we adopted Miller's cutoff criterion (Miller, 1948, pp. 92–93). The analysis required no change in the conclusions presented above.

Most textbooks attribute Miller's results—the progressive improvement in escape performance—to acquired reinforcing properties of escape from white to black. This work suggests that such an interpretation is misleading and oversimplified in two respects. First, it seems clear that fear conditioning depresses initial performance in the shuttlebox. Consequently, it is uncertain how much of the subsequent improvement in escape performance can be attributed to reinforcement. Second, it seems clear that the fear conditioning procedure operates upon an unlearned preferences for black over white. Consequently, if Miller's rats were reinforced by escape from white to black, its reinforcing properties were probably not entirely acquired.

References

Douglas, R. J. Cues for spontaneous alternation. *J. comp. physiol. Psychol.*, 1966, *62*, 171–183.

Freedman, P. E. Habituation of alternation behavior. *J. exp. Psychol.*, 1965, *69*, 613–617.

Miller, N. E. Studies of fear as an acquirable drive: I. Fear as motivation and fear-reduction as reinforcement in the learning of new responses. *J. exp. Psychol.*, 1948, *38*, 89–101.

So the discriminative control of avoidance is differentially prepared in rats. Sara Shettleworth, trained in both ethology and experimental psychology, shows that aversive learning is also differentially prepared in domestic chicks. Chicks learn to refrain from drinking during a visual stimulus, when punished by shock to the beak, but not when punishment is signaled by an auditory stimulus. When fear conditioning is carried out with shock to the feet, however, fear is controlled by sound, but not by light. The fact that aversive control of drinking in the chick is primarily visual may be related to the fact that feeding is a primarily visual activity in almost all birds.

21

CONDITIONING OF DOMESTIC CHICKS TO VISUAL AND AUDITORY STIMULI: CONTROL OF DRINKING BY VISUAL STIMULI AND CONTROL OF CONDITIONED FEAR BY SOUND

Sara J. Shettleworth

Psychologists usually assume that animals have a generalized ability to acquire arbitrary associations. In the area of the control of behavior by external stimuli, for example, it is implicitly assumed that any suprathreshold stimulus can be brought to control any behavior, at least when it is the only event that predicts reinforcement of that behavior. More biologically oriented students of behavior, on the other hand, readily assert that individuals of each species are predisposed to modify only certain aspects of their behavior, and to do so only in ways that are relevant to survival in natural conditions for the species. Many observations suggest that this is so (Tinbergen, 1951; Eibl-Eibesfeldt, 1970, chap. 13), and

This report is a slightly expanded version of a paper presented at the meetings of the Eastern Psychological Association, April, 1970. It is based on a thesis submitted to the Department of Psychology, University of Toronto, in partial fulfillment of the requirements for the Ph.D. degree and was prepared while the author was an Ontario Mental Health Foundation Research Fellow. A fuller report will be published elsewhere (Shettleworth, in press). This work was supported by grant APA-116 from the National Research Council of Canada to G. E. Macdonald. The author thanks J. A. Hogan, G. E. Macdonald, and N. Mrosovsky for their helpful comments on the manuscript.

now experimental support for this idea has begun to appear from within the psychology of learning itself (reviews by Seligman, 1970, and Shettleworth, 1972).

The experiments in this paper were suggested by reports that a large number of animals learn very readily to discriminate on sight between edible and inedible or unpalatable objects. Rapid acquisition of visual-taste associations is important in various insectivirous predators' learning to avoid eating unpalatable insects and their mimics (see Rettenmeyer, 1970, for a review), and it is equally important in young animals' learning what to eat and drink. For example, right after hatching, domestic chicks peck indiscriminately at a wide variety of objects, but within 2 or 3 days they come to peck predominantely at edible objects, they recognize water, and they avoid pecking at their own feces and other things that are distasteful to them. This discrimination is clearly visual. Because it is so important for chicks to make it rapidly, they might be specifically prepared to do so. It would not be much use for them to use auditory stimuli in this situation since sounds are not in general a distinguishing feature of their food. This suggests that chicks might selectively associate visual rather than auditory stimuli with an immediate consequence of pecking or—as in these experiments—drinking.

This idea was investigated by training domestic chicks on various successive auditory and visual discriminations using shocked or quinine-flavored water. Figure 1 shows the apparatus. It had a grid floor, a houselight behind diffusing Plexiglas, and a speaker in the ceiling above the water dish. A one-way mirror covered one wall. When the guillotine door was raised, the chick could drink from the water dish. Eight-day-old chicks were water-deprived and trained to drink in the apparatus for several sessions. Then they had three daily successive discrimination-training session of 11 trials each while 18 hours (± 1 hour) water-deprived. On each trial water was available for 1 minute or until the chick took four drinks, whichever came sooner. The intertrial interval was about 10 seconds.

In the first experiment, three groups of six to eight chicks were trained with a compound visual-auditory discriminative stimulus. The visual component was the houselight flashing from white to blue three times a second. The sound was an 90-dB clicking sound interrupted five times a second. This was about 25 dB above the background noise level. Shocks (370 V ac through a 470-Kohm resistor in series with the chick, or about 0.7 mA) were given via the water when the chick's beak completed a circuit between the water and the floor. One group ($N = 8$) was shocked for drinking in the presence of the compound stimulus, one ($N = 8$) in its absence, and a control group ($N = 6$) had stimuli but no shocks. After two sessions of training, or three for the absence-of-stimulus shocked group, there was a test session in which the flashing light and the clicks were each presented once alone unreinforced to each bird while the usual trials with compound and no stimulus were continued. The order of testing was balanced across subjects.

Figure 2 shows the median latencies in each stimulus condition on the test day. By the time of the test, the two groups that had discrimination training had learned the discrimination quite well. They seldom tried to drink at all in the

FIG. 1 Appartus in which chicks were trained on discriminations between palatable and unpalatable water and in which CER experiments were carried out. It is shown as it appeared during trials of the drinking experiments.

shocked condition, and drank readily in its absence. (Failures to drink were counted as 60-sec latencies.) The test trials with flash and clicks alone showed that the behavior of both these groups was completely controlled by the presence or absence of the visual stimulus. There was no control by the sound. Behavior in its presence was the same as that in the absence of the compound stimulus. This was true of each individual bird. The control birds drank readily in all the stimulus conditions.

Of course this result is not very impressive by itself. The sound could just be a weak stimulus for chicks. Or it could be overshadowed by the flashing light when they are presented together. But this does not seem to be so. In further experiments, chicks were trained in the same way with a slightly weaker shock (300 V ac) but with the clicks or the flashing light alone. Other groups had a different visual stimulus—the color of the water—and others had a different sound—a 500-Hz a 112-dB tone interrupted 5 times a second. Now, one thing we can look at here is whether each of the stimuli disrupts drinking the first time it is presented, i.e., on the first discrimination training day following pretraining. This provides an index of whether a stimulus is being seen or heard and attended to in the situation. These data for each of the four stimuli and for the compound

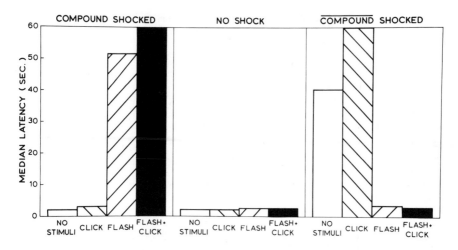

FIG. 2 Median latencies to contact the water on the test day in the presence of the compound of flashing light and clicks, flash or clicks alone, or no stimulus, for groups of chicks shocked for drinking in the presence of the compound, in its absence, or not shocked at all.

of flash and clicks are shown in Fig. 3. Each mean is from a number of birds in various experiments with the same pretraining experience. All the stimuli significantly increased the latency to drink relative to the no-stimulus condition. Latencies on the first daily no-stimulus trial were about the same in all groups. Two things here show that the clicks which failed to acquire conditioned control over drinking in the first experiment were being heard. First, clicks alone significantly increased the latency to drink. Second, the latency with the compound of clicks and flash was significantly longer than that with flash alone (Mann-Whitney U-tests, $p < 0.05$). So either alone or in combination with the flashing light, the clicks were heard initially. The tone was clearly heard, too. In fact, it had considerably more effect on the chicks' behavior than either visual stimulus alone.

This suggests that chicks should learn in this situation with the clicks—or the tone—as the only available discriminative stimulus. But this did not happen. Figure 4 shows the results of an experiment in which four groups of six chicks had flash, blue water, clicks, or tone paired with shock to the water. The data are presented as the differences between latencies on pairs of shocked and unshocked trials. That is, the latency on an unshocked trial is subtracted from the latency on the corresponding shocked trial. With either of the visual stimuli this difference quickly became large and positive. The chicks suppressed drinking almost completely in the presence of the stimulus signaling shock, while they drank readily in the absence of the stimulus. Each animal in these two groups showed clear evidence of learning. But with the clicks or the tone, the difference hovered around zero throughout training. No animal in these groups developed a consistent discrimination. Results were similar when the stimuli signaled the

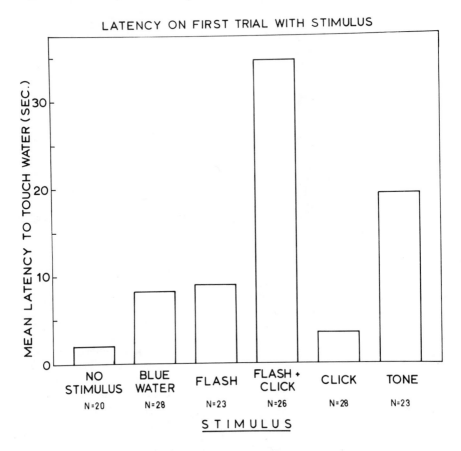

FIG. 3 Mean latency to touch the water on the first trial with each of four different stimuli and for the analogous trial in a control condition with no stimulus. Latencies in the absence of stimuli were about the same for all groups.

absence of shock rather than its presence or when a percent quinine solution was used instead of shock. With the stronger shock there was still little or no difference between latencies to drink in the shocked and unshocked conditions if clicks or absence of clicks was paired with shock, although here some birds did begin to discriminate. But discrimination was always rapid and consistent when the flash-click compound was used.

These data all suggest that indeed chicks are specialized to associate visual stimuli with some immediate consequence of drinking or pecking. The relative failure of sounds to acquire control of drinking seems to be due specifically to a failure of association and not a failure of attention—at least in the sense of noticing the stimuli—since the sounds initially had some unconditioned control. This interpretation implies that the relative failure of conditioning to sounds is specific to drinking—and probably to feeding as well. But it is also possible that

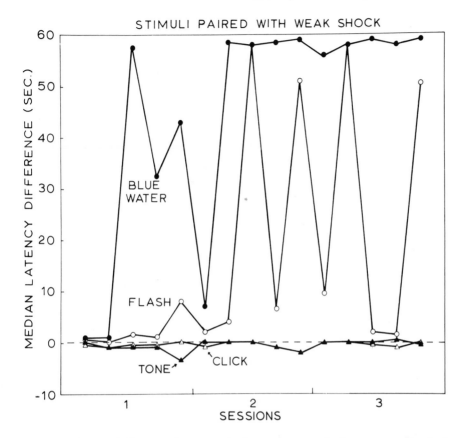

STIMULI PAIRED WITH WEAK SHOCK

FIG. 4 Median differences between the latency to touch the water on shocked trials and the latency on corresponding unshocked trials for groups of six chicks which had shock paired with each of four different stimuli.

chicks simply do not condition to sounds in any situation. The final experiment tests this notion by using the clicking sound and the flashing light in a different conditioning paradigm.

Chicks of the same age and preexperimental history as before had fear conditioning in the same apparatus with the same stimuli. The compound of flashing and clicking was presented for 21 sec, with a 1-mA foot-shock during the last second. Control subjects had shocks explicitly unpaired with the stimulus. The time a chick spent moving and the number of calls it made were recorded continuously. Then behavior in the 20 sec preceding the stimulus was compared to behavior during the first 20 sec of the stimulus.

After two sessions of habituation to the test chamber, 11 experimental and 11 control chicks had 12 trials on each of two successive days. Trials were initiated every 90 sec on the average. During the second session, the clicks and the flashing light were each presented twice alone, unreinforced, to each bird with order balanced across subjects. Figure 5 shows the results from all trials on the test day. First of all, birds in the paired or conditioning group significantly increased moving and calling when the compound stimulus was on. The controls did not change their behavior consistently in the presence of this stimulus. When

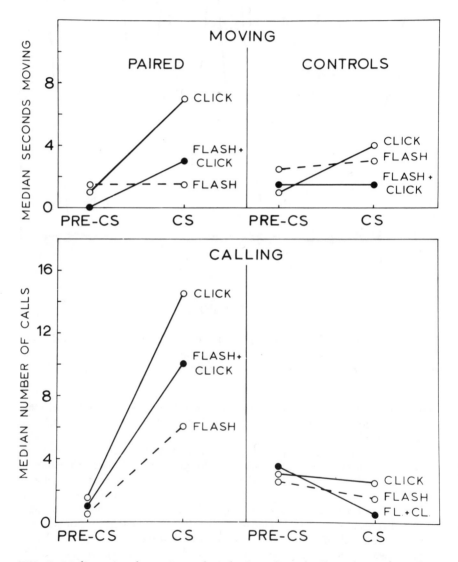

FIG. 5   Median seconds moving and median number of calls in the 20 sec before and during a 20-sec presentation of the compound of flash and clicks and each of its elements alone for the group that had the compound paired with shock in a CER procedure and for the explicitly unpaired control group.

the flash and click was presented alone to the conditioned birds, moving was completely controlled by the sound. The flashing light had no control over moving. It did have some control over calling, but the sound had more. The behavior of the controls did not change consistently with any of the stimuli. So in this conditioning situation, the sound which had little or no acquired control over drinking actually predominated over the flashing light in gaining control of behavior.

These experiments clearly demonstrates a nonarbitrary relationship between the stimuli which come to control behavior and the situation in which they appear. However, there remain a number of unsolved problems. For example, it appears that the important difference between stimuli that are readily associated with punishment for drinking and those that are not is one of modality. This is especially so because the flashing light, which readily controlled drinking, was diffuse, as were the sounds, which controlled drinking only weakly. Yet a visual stimulus explicitly removed from the water—colored stripes on the tray beside the water dish—did not gain as good control as either blue water or the flashing light, although it was more effective than the sounds. This suggests that a sound emanating from the water might be associated with punishment for drinking more readily than the diffuse sounds used so far. However, this point does not detract from the finding that the chicks learned only very slowly, if at all, to suppress drinking to sounds they could clearly hear. In fact, under some conditions their unconditioned, or pseudoconditioned, response to the clicks persisted for many trials and was finally replaced by no detectable discrimination at all.

The results of the fear-conditioning experiments are not entirely unambiguous, either, since some aspects of behavior during training with the compound and testing with the elements were inconsistent with data from training with each of the stimuli alone. There was some suggestion that the flashing light had an unconditioned or pseudo-conditioned suppressive effect on activity. It would be instructive to use the same stimuli in a different fear-conditioning situation to determine how far the results represent a special propensity of sounds to selectively control the chicks' fear responses.

More important for interpretation of the overall results of these experiments are the many differences between the two experimental paradigms. Among them are the difference in duration, distribution, and temporal relationship of stimuli and shocks and the almost certain differences in psychological intensity of the aversive stimuli. Moreover, in the drinking experiments, aversive stimulation was contingent on the chicks' behavior, while in the CER experiments, shock was unavoidable and inescapable. While any or all of these differences may have been responsible for the profound differences in behavior from one situation to the other, there appears to be no reason why any of them would produce a complete reversal in the stimuli controlling behavior. A further important difference in the two paradigms is in where the aversive stimulation was applied. Garcia and Ervin (1968) and Konorski (1964) have suggested that their similar findings have an anatomical basis in specialized neural circuits. The present results for the control of drinking may have a similar basis in a specialized central integration of visual stimuli with stimuli received via the beak. The fact that results with quinine and beak shock were similar supports this idea, and it is currently being tested.

These experiments were originally suggested by the idea that a specialized ability to selectively associate visual stimuli with an immediate consequence of drinking or pecking might play a role in how chicks originally learn what to eat and drink. Strictly speaking, the present experiments do not provide any conclusive evidence on this point, since they were done when the chicks were about 10 days old and had already learned to recognize food and water. Earlier experience of certain stimulus-stimulus relations may play some role in the development of the associative predisposition which is present by this age, or it may be present at hatching.

References

Eibl-Eibesfeldt, I. *Ethology: The biology of behavior.* New York: Holt, Reinhart and Winston, 1970.

Garcia, J. and Ervin, F. R. Gustatory—visual and telereceptor—cutaneous conditioning—adaptation in external and internal milieus. *Communications in Behavioral Biology,* 1968, part A, 389—415.

Konorski, J. Some problems concerning the mechanism of instrumental conditioning. *Acta Biologiae Experimentalis (Warsaw),* 1964, *24,* 59—72.

Rettenmeyer, C. D. Insect mimicry. *Annual Review of Entomology,* 1970, *15,* 43—74.

Seligman, M. E. P. On the generality of the laws of learning. *Psychological Review,* 1970, 77, 406—418.

Shettleworth, S. J. Constraints on learning. *Advances in the Study of Behavior,* 1972, 4.

Shettleworth, S. J., Stimulus relevance in the control of drinking and conditioned fear responses in domestic chicks, *Gallus gallus. Journal of Comparative and Physiological Psychology,* in press.

Tinbergen, N. *The study of instinct.* London: Oxford University Press, 1951.

The final paper in the avoidance section considers whether the same cognitive or learning mechanisms are at work in both prepared and unprepared avoidance. John Garcia, Richard Kovner, and Kenneth Green demonstrate that rats can use taste cues to avoid shock in a shuttlebox, but the taste which signals shock is not avoided in the home cage. If rats learn to "avoid" taste in a T-maze because it has been paired with illness, they shun it both in the T-maze and in the home cage. The rats act as if what they learn is that taste merely signals shock while it "causes" illness. So, in spite of the fact that the avoidance conditioning is operationally parallel in the two cases, a more robust learning mechanism may be at work in the taste-illness association than in the unnatural taste-shock one.

22

CUE PROPERTIES VERSUS PALATABILITY OF FLAVORS IN AVOIDANCE LEARNING

John Garcia, Richard Kovner, and Kenneth F. Green

When a flavor is immediately followed by peripheral electric shock, rats learn to use the flavor cue to avoid shock, but ingestion of that flavor is not reduced outside the shock apparatus. In contrast, when a flavor is followed by internal illness, rats will reject that fluid in or out of the situation where illness occurred. However, motor approach to visual cues previously associated with that flavor is not immediately affected. Thus flavor, used as a cue, acquires generalization properties depending upon the subsequent reinforcer and reflecting differential specialization in mechanisms controlling palatability and locomotor responses.

Not all combinations of signals and punishments are effective in avoidance training of animals. Rats will maintain or increase their intake of a distinctively flavored food previously paired with electrocutaneous shock, but will markedly decrease their consumption if this flavor has been paired with illness induced by injections or X-rays. Conversely, when flavor is held constant, they will hesitate to approach a visually distinctive food that has been previously paired with shock, but will approach and eat this food readily if it has been followed by illness (Garcia & Koelling, 1966; Garcia et al., 1968). These results suggest that central mechanisms controlling palatability, ingestion, and malaise differ from those integrating external signals, locomotion, and cutaneous insults, and that it may be difficult to reduce palatability with contingent shock. However, it may be possible to use a flavor to signal locomotor avoidance of shock without depressing its palatability. Furthermore, if a flavor is suddenly made unpalatable,

From *Psychonomic Science*, 20 (1970), 313–314.
Research supported by NIH Grant EC 00132.

ingestion may be depressed without immediate inhibition of locomotor approach towards cues leading to that flavor.

METHOD

Two experiments were conducted to test these implications. Young adult male rats (approximately 400 g) maintained in individual cages, were habituated to handling and drinking once each day for 2 weeks before training began. Flavor stimuli consisted of saccharin water (1.0 g saccharin per liter) or salty water (7.0 g NaCl per liter). These solutions were about equally preferred to each other and both were preferred to unflavored water. After training, posttests of fluid intake were conducted in the usual balanced order; half the animals were tested first in the apparatus and then in their home cages, and the other half were treated conversely.

Experiment A was conducted to determine if an animal could be taught to avoid electric shock to the paws in a gray shuttlebox (5 x 36 in., with 8-in. walls) where flavors provided the only available cues, and if so, to determine what effect the flavor-shock association would have upon preference for those flavors outside of the shuttlebox. For six rats, salty water was the shock fluid and saccharin was the safe fluid, while five rats were treated conversely. Each thirsty rat was placed in the center of the shuttlebox and allowed to select a drinking spout at either end. When the rat selected the shock fluid, he was shocked within 2.0 sec of his first lick at the spout with a single pulse to the paws via the floor grid and a constant current source at a minimal intensity (about 0.2 sec at 2.0 mA) sufficient to interrupt drinking without producing excessive fear. If a rat persisted in drinking the shock fluid, shocks were repeated and, if necessary, intensity was increased until the rat "corrected itself" by going to the other end, where it was allowed to drink the safe fluid for at least 2 min. If the rat initially chose the safe fluid, it was allowed to drink undisturbed for a similar period. Two to four trials were given daily. Between trials flavors were switched according to a random schedule, given that the shock fluid appeared no more than three consecutive times at the same end and an equal number of times at both ends in a run of 20 trials. After training, preference tests for the two fluids were tested in (1) four 3-min shock-free trials in the shuttlebox and (2) one 20-min trial in the home cage with two bottles, after animals were allowed to sample both fluids.

Experiment B was conducted to test approach reactions to visual cues previously associated with a preferred (saccharin) solution after that flavor was made aversive by pairing it with illness in another situation. Animals were trained in a T-maze composed of narrow (5-in.) alleys and high (18-in.) walls. The 18-in. gray stem led to a choice point with a black right and white left arm, each 18 in. long. Our rats displayed the well-known preference for black over white; thus all animals were rewarded with the preferred saccharin in the nonpreferred white left arm of the maze. Water was always provided in the black arm. During the first part of training (Trials 1 to 40) each thirsty rat was given a free choice between the black (water) arm and the white (saccharin) arm, followed by a forced-choice trial to the opposite side to insure that it sampled both fluids. Only the free-choice responses were scored as a measure of learning. Initially the animals were given two trials per day with a 30-sec drink and later four trials with a 10-sec drink.

After all animals had learned to select the white arm for saccharin, maze trials were suspended for 8 days of aversion conditioning. On Day 1 all rats received water in their home cages for their 10-min drinking period. On Day 2 they received saccharin and 10 min later they were given a toxic injection (8.0 ml of .12 M LiCl IP) which produces a mild illness (inactivity, anorexia). On Day 7 the treatment was repeated. Water was provided on all other days. On Day 9 maze trials were resumed. After the toxic treatment and maze training, the animals' ingestion of saccharin water and tap water were tested in 10-min single-bottle tests in the maze goalbox and in the home cages.

RESULTS AND DISCUSSION

These experiments indicate that flavors, when used as cues, acquire generalization properties that reflect the nature of the reinforcer and the performance required of the animal. In Experiment A (Fig. 1), the animals learned to use flavor to avoid the peripheral insult of shock in 20 to 28 trials, a performance that compares favorably with shuttlebox avoidance when visual or acoustical cues are used.[1] The rats learned to approach the spout cautiously, stretch their

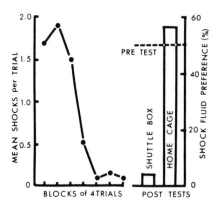

FIG. 1 Experiment A. The graph (left) illustrates mean shocks per trial as rats learned to use a flavor cue to avoid shock in a shuttlebox. The bars (right) indicate their preference for the shocked fluid in two places after flavor-shock training. [This difference is significant (p < 0.01).]

[1] A brief discussion of Experiment A will appear in Revusky, S. H., & Garcia, J., Learned associations over long delays. In G. Bower and J. T. Spence (Eds.), *The psychology of learning and motivation*. Vol. 4. New York: Academic Press 1970.

necks, sniff, and lick gingerly. If the bottle contained the shock fluid, they quickly turned and went to the bottle at the other end of the box; if it contained the safe solution, they drank steadily. Under these conditions, the flavor cues, like external signals, apparently require immediate reinforcement and are probably subject to the same contextual and distractive influences that affect external signals.

However, ingestion of the shocked fluid is not reduced outside of the spatiotemporal context of the shock. This is supported by preference tests outside the apparatus in Experiment A (Fig. 1) and in the previous experiments in which the animals were tested in the apparatus but under extinction conditions, i.e., when shock was not applied in its usual temporal sequence (Garcia et al., 1968).

In contrast, when a flavor is followed by internal malaise, the animals' ingestion of that flavor is reduced even in situations where the illness was not induced. Although training was prolonged in Experiment B (Fig. 2) due to the high initial preference for the black arm of the T-maze with its unsweetened water, the thirsty rats eventually learned to select the white arm for saccharin. They persisted in selecting the white (saccharin) arm even after the conditional pairing of saccharin illness, whether the white arm now contained water which.

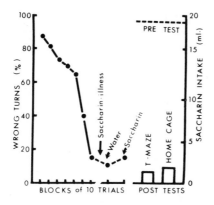

FIG. 2 Experiment B. The graph (left) illustrates mean errors per 10-trial block as rats learned to obtain saccharin-water in the right (white) arm of a T-maze. The "water" and "saccharin" points indicate turns in two test blocks, where water then saccharin was available in that arm following flavor-illness pairing. The bars (right) indicate ingestion in two places after that pairing. [This difference is not significant (p. < 0.05).]

they drank or saccharin which they merely sampled. Apparently, prolonged "reversal training" would be required to teach the animals that the visual-spatial cues of the white arm now led to an aversive flavor.

Furthermore, postillness tests (Fig. 1) revealed a marked decrement in saccharin intake in the T-maze, where they had never been made ill, as well as in the home cages. This substantiates previous studies which demonstrated that contextual place cues associated with illness have little effect upon ingestion or preference (Garcia & Ervin, 1968; Rozin, 1969) and that immediate reinforcement is not required when toxic agents are used to establish changes in palatability of flavors (Garcia, Ervin, & Koelling, 1966; Smith & Roll, 1967; Revusky, 1968).

Rats act as if they inferred that flavors might be "merely associated" with peripheral pain in space and time but could "actually cause" illness. Similar behavior has been reported by Brower (1969) for bluejays that became ill after eating toxic monarch butterflies. We believe that this reflects differential specialization in the adaptive mechanisms for the external and internal environments. In a previous paper (Garcia & Ervin, 1968) convergence of the taste and visceral afferents to the nucleus of the tractus solitarius was proposed as the integrative mechanism by which flavors and visceral illness are specifically associated over long interstimulus intervals to adjust palatability. The present data suggests that the taste information must also diverge to other integrative centers where it can be used, under the same spatiotemporal constraints as external stimuli, to guide locomotor avoidance responses.

References

Brower, L. P. Ecological chemistry. *Scientific American*, 1969, *220*, 22—29.

Garcia, J. & Ervin, F. R. Gustatory-visceral and telereceptor-cutaneous conditioning, adaptation in internal and external milieus. *Communications in Behavioral Biology*, 1968, *1*, 389—415.

Garcia, J., Ervin, F. R., & Koelling, R. A. Learning with prolonged delay of reinforcement. *Psychonomic Science*, 1966, *5*, 121—122.

Garcia, J., & Koelling, R. A. The relation of cue to consequence in avoidance learning. *Psychonomic Science*, 1966, *4*, 123—124.

Garcia, J., McGowan, B. K. Ervin, F. R., & Koelling, R. A. Cues—their relative effectiveness as a function of the reinforcer. *Science*, 1968, *160*, 794—795.

Revusky, S. H. Aversion to sucrose produced by contingent X-irradiation—temporal and dosage parameters. *Journal of Comparative & Physiological Psychology*, 1968, *65*, 17—22.

Rozin, P. Central or peripheral mediation of learning with long CS-US intervals in the feeding system. *Journal of Comparative & Physiological Psychology*, 1969, *67*, 421—429.

Smith, J. C., & Roll, D. L. Trace conditioning with X-rays as the aversive stimulus. *Psychonomic Science*, 1967, *9*, 11—12.

IV

ETHOLOGY AND COMPARATIVE PSYCHOLOGY

A great deal of ethological work has preceded the research presented in the previous sections. Having no preoccupation with general laws of learning, ethologists have held nothing resembling an equipotentiality premise. On the contrary, Konrad Lorenz and Niko Tinbergen, the modern initiators of this tradition, have been scrupulous in their attention to species-specific behaviors, among them learning. Their awareness of the nonequipotentiality of learning had an impact upon such comparative psychologists as Daniel Lehrman and his colleagues, but little on general-process learning theorists. The growing awareness of learning theorists has been more a product of such experimental anomalies as we have looked at, generated by their own assumptions within their own laboratories. But as a result they are increasingly open to the original ethological literature and to the experimental results of a second wave of comparative psychology and ethology, characterized by research such as we include here.

Niko Tinbergen's The Study of Instinct (1951) represents the culmination of the original European ethological endeavor. In the selection from the landmark work which follows, he discusses several ethological instances of the "predisposition" to learn certain specific things and the failure to learn seemingly comparable ones—predispositions which characterize species and appear to be genetically determined. For example, herring gulls learn immediately to recognize their own chicks but never their own eggs. It is worth noting that the bulk of the observations and experiments cited by Tinbergen in support of preparedness were done in the 1930s; the learning-theory implications of these data are only now beginning to be fully appreciated by psychologists of learning.

23

THE INNATE DISPOSITION TO LEARN

Niko Tinbergen

'LOCALIZED LEARNING'

The student of innate behaviour, accustomed to studying a number of different species and the entire behaviour pattern, is repeatedly confronted with the fact that an animal may learn some things much more readily than others. That is to say, some parts of the pattern, some reactions, may be changed by learning while others seem to be so rigidly fixed that no learning is possible. In other words, there seem to be more or less strictly localized 'dispositions to learn'. Different species are predisposed to learn different parts of the pattern. So far as we know, these differences between species have adaptive significance.

Some instances may illustrate this important fact of localized dispositions.

Herring gulls have a number of innate reactions to the young: they brood them, feed them, and rescue them if attacked by strangers or predators. Interchanging the young of two nests of the same age has very different effects, depending on the age of the young. When they are only a few days old they will be accepted by their 'foster parents.' But if the same test is made when the young are more than 5 days old, they will not be accepted. This means that after a period of about 5 days, during which a parent herring gull is willing to take care of any young of the right age, the parents are conditioned to their own young. They will then neglect or even kill any other young forced upon them (Tinbergen, 1936). Approximately the same results have been obtained in various species of terns (Watson and Lashley, 1915). This learning to 'know' the chicks individually is very remarkable, for the human observer rarely succeeds in distinguishing the young and never reaches the same degree of accuracy as the birds.

The ability of a herring gull to learn its own eggs is, by contrast, amazingly poor. The eggs of different gulls vary a good deal in colour and speckling, in fact they vary much more than the chicks do. Yet even gulls that have eggs of a very distinctive type such as bluish, poorly pigmented eggs, or eggs with exceptionally large or small spots, never show any preference for their own eggs (Fig. 1). The

From *The Study of Instinct* (Oxford: Clarendon Press, 1951).

FIG. 1 Herring gull in choice test, hesitating between its own and another gull's eggs.

innate releasing mechanism of the brooding reactions does not undergo any change by conditioning, so far as the egg itself is concerned. There is, in this respect, a sharp contrast between the reactions to young and those to eggs (Tinbergen, 1936).

The sexual pattern, again, is readily conditioned. Herring gulls, like a great many other birds, are strictly monogamous, and each bird confines its sexual activities to its own mate once the formation of pairs has taken place. Here again the gull's ability to recognize its mate is far superior to our powers of recognizing the gulls. There is proof of the amazing fact that a herring gull instantly recognizes its mate (that is, reacts selectively to it amongst a group of other gulls) from a distance of 30 yards. Nor is the herring gull alone in this respect; similar facts are known about jackdaws, geese, terns, and other birds. Recognition is based partially on visual stimuli, partly on voice.

The fact that many species, man included, seem to distinguish individuals of their own species much more readily than individuals of other species is another aspect of the innate basis of learning.

Other instances of localized learning dispositions have been found in the digger wasp, *Philanthus triangulum*. Females of this species have innate releasing mechanisms directing the chain of prey-hunting activities to the hive bee alone, among hundreds of other insect species. There is no indication of a conditioning of the hunting pattern, apart, perhaps, from the development of a certain preference for favourable hunting territories. Each wasp, however, learns, with astonishing rapidity and precision, the locality of each new nest it builds. It has been proved experimentally that the so-called locality studies (Fig. 2), which have also been observed in numerous other Hymenoptera, are the means of learning the position of the nest in relation to certain landmarks. The best achievement has been observed in the following case (Tinbergen and Kruyt, 1938). A ring of twenty pine-cones was put around a nesting-hole while the wasp

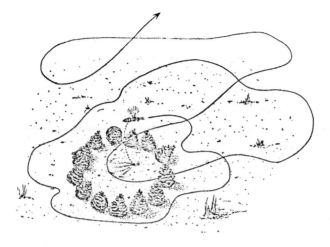

FIG. 2 Locality study of a digger wasp, *Philanthus triangulum.*

was inside. Upon leaving, she made a locality study lasting 6 seconds, and then left. The pine-cones were thereupon taken away and deposited a foot away in the same arrangement. When the wasp returned after about 90 minutes with a captured bee, her choice between the real nest and the displaced beacons was watched thirteen times, the beacon being displaced each time (Fig. 3). She chose the beacons in all the tests and only found the nest after the original situation had been restored. Thus, in a great number of varied experiments, it has been found that the homing ability of *Philanthus* and of other digger wasps depends on an amazing learning capacity (Tinbergen, 1932; Tinbergen and Kruyt, 1938;

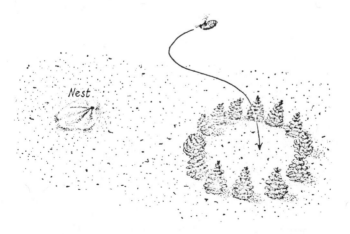

FIG. 3 Orientation experiment. Explanation in the text.

Baerands, 1941; Van Beusekom, 1948). In strong contrast to this, neither the hunting behaviour nor the food-seeking pattern shows any trace of conditioning. This is especially striking when we compare *Philanthus* with the hive bee. Both species suck nectar, but while the honey bee gets readily conditioned to special species of plants and special localities, nothing of the kind could be observed in *Philanthus*. While the homing capacities in the two species are very similar and involve about equal learning capacities, they make a very different use of their learning abilities in the food-seeking instinct.

Another type of this complex interweaving of innate and learned capacities has been reported in jackdaws. In a jackdaw community, as in so many other bird colonies, many relationships between members are based on individually acquired attachments and antagonisms. One such relationship based on learning is the so-called social order. Each individual learns to avoid some of its colony-mates which are stronger or more aggressive, and learns to know which of them can be treated in an unfriendly manner without risk. Now Lorenz (1931) found that when a female that occupies a relatively low position in the social order gets mated with a high-ranking male, her position is at once rated just as high as that of her mate by all the members of the colony. These amazing learning processes are found in the very jackdaws that show such poor learning ability in relation to either eggs or young.

Ravens starting to build nests for the first time in their lives are highly unselective in choosing sticks to build them with. However, they soon learn to select those twigs that can easily be worked into the nest. The selection of a nest site, however, and the building activities themselves, are not changed by conditioning. Improvements in nest-building in older birds have often been interpreted as being caused by experience, but it seems to be settled beyond doubt that it is the consequence of maturation, first-year birds often building clumsy nests because of low (hormonal) motivation (Lorenz, 1937b).

This random selection of pertinent facts shows that in many species there are differences between various parts of the behaviour pattern, with regard to susceptibility to change by learning processes. As part of the innate equipment, such species have inherited certain strictly specific 'dispositions to learn'.

PREFERENTIAL LEARNING

The limitations of learning by innate endowment are not restricted to this phenomenon of localization, as the following instance will show. When the herring gulls' reactions to chicks and to eggs are compared more fully, it is found that, although youngsters about 5 days old are recognized individually wherever they are encountered within or even outside the territory, the reactions to the eggs are, as we have seen, not conditioned to the eggs themselves. They are, however, very rigidly conditioned to the locality of the nest. When a broody herring gull has to choose between the empty nest and the eggs in an artificial nest about a foot away, it will sit in the empty nest because it is on the accustomed site (Fig. 4). The bird will retrieve the eggs, or even occasionally sit on them in the artificial nest, but the attachment to the original site, acquired during the building of the nest, is extremely strong. When the eggs are removed a

FIG. 4 Herring gull incubating on empty nest in full view of eggs.

little farther from the nest, the gull will not respond to them by brooding but will eat them.

This shows that conditioning intervenes in reactions to the eggs as well as to the young, but that the bird selects very different qualities in the two cases: locality in the case of the eggs, neglecting the very conspicuous individual differences of the eggs; subtle individual characters in the case of the young. Here we discover another principle: it seems to be a property of the innate disposition that it directs the conditioning to special parts of the receptual field.

Similar examples have been studied and analysed in the case of orientation to landmarks of hive bees and digger wasps. These insects by no means condition themselves to every available landmark in the environment: they exercise a definite choice. The principles on which this choice is based are not identical in the various species, and are very different from the principles on which man would make a choice (Hertz, 1929, 1930, 1931; Tinbergen and Kruyt, 1938).

CRITICAL PERIODS OF LEARNING

There is not only localization of learning in relation to the reaction concerned, but there is also a certain localization in time, giving rise to the phenomenon of critical periods.

The Eskimo dogs of east Greenland live in packs of 5–10 individuals. The members of the pack defend their group territory against all other dogs. All dogs of an Eskimo settlement have an exact and detailed knowledge of the topography of the territories of other packs; they know where attacks from other packs must be feared. Immature dogs do not defend the territory. Moreover, they often roam through the whole settlement, very often trespassing into other territories, where they are promptly chased. In spite of these frequent attacks, during which they may be severely treated, they do not learn the territories' topography and for the observer their stupidity in this respect is amazing. While the young dogs are growing sexually mature, however, they begin to learn the other territories and within a week their trespassing adventures are over. In two male dogs the first copulation, the first defence of territory, and the first avoidance of strange territory all occurred within one week (Tinbergen, 1942).

Other, more or less similar phenomena are described by Lorenz (1935). Young geese (*Anser anser*) follow their parents soon after hatching. If the parents are removed, however, before the young have seen them or if the young are hatched in an incubator, the young attach themselves to another bird or even to a human being, should this be the first creature they meet. Once the young have adopted the wrong animals as their parents, it is impossible to make them accept members of their own species, even their own parents. This conditioning process takes no longer than a minute or even less. It has been called 'Imprinting' (*Prägung*) by Lorenz, who claims that it is irreversible. Although some authors doubt whether this process of imprinting is fundmentally different from other types of conditioning and believe that there are only differences of degree between them, it is clear that we have to do with an extreme restriction of learning ability to a critical period.

References

Baerends, G. P., 1941: Fortpflanzungsverhalten und Orientierung der Grabwespe *Ammophila campestris* Jur. *Tijdschr. Entomol. 84*, 68—275.

Beusekom, G. Van, 1948: Some experiments on the optical orientation in *Philanthus triangulum* Fabr. *Behaviour*, *1*, 195—225.

Hertz, M., 1929: Die Organisation des optischen Feldes bei der Biene. I. *Zs. vergl. Physiol. 8*, 693—748.

Hertz, M., 1930: Die Organisation des optischen Feldes bei der Biene. II. *Zs. vergl. Physiol. 11*, 107—45.

Hertz, M., 1931: Die Organisation des optischen Feldes bei der Biene. III. *Zs. vergl. Physiol. 14*, 629—74.

Lorenz, K. 1931: Beiträge zur Ethologie sozialer Corviden. *J. Ornithol. 79*, 67—120.

Lorenz, K., 1935: Der Kumpan in der Umwelt des Vogels. *J. Ornithol. 83*, 137—213.

Lorenz, K., 1937b: Über die Bildung des Instinktbegriffs. *Die Naturwissenschaften, 25*, 289—300, 307—18, 324—31.

Tinbergen, N., 1932: Über die Orientierung des Bienenwolfes (*Philanthus triangulum* Fabr.). *Zs. vergl. Physiol. 16*, 305—35.

Tinbergen, N., 1936a: The function of sexual fighting in birds; and the problem of the origin of 'territory'. *Bird Banding, 7*, 1—8.

Tinbergen, N., 1936b: Zur Soziologie der Silbermöwe (*Larus a. argentatus* Pontopp). *Beitr. Fortpflanzungsbiol. Vögel, 12*, 89—96.

Tinbergen, N., 1936c: Eenvoudige proeven over de zintuigfuncties van larve en imago van de geelgerande watertor. *De Levende Natuur, 41*, 225—36.

Tinbergen, N., 1942: An objectivistic study of the innate behaviour of animals. *Biblioth. biotheor. 1*, 39—98.

Tinbergen, N., and W. Kruyt, 1938: Über die Orientierung des Bienenwolfes (*Philanthus triangulum* Fabr.) III. Die Bevorzugung bestimmter Wegmarken. *Zs. vergl. Physiol. 25*, 292—334.

Watson, J. B., and K. S. Lashley, 1915: Homing and related activities of birds. *Carn. Inst. Wash. Publ.* 211.

The next reading is a sterling example of the new comparative psychology which is concerned with finding general laws of learning, while respecting species specificity. Hardy Wilcoxon, William Dragoin, and Paul Kral find that quail are more prepared to associate color than taste with illness, and remarkably that the color-illness association is made with a 30 minute or longer delay of reinforcement. When rats are put through the same procedure, however, they learn about taste but not about color. We would expect this from the natural history of these organisms: birds are largely visual feeders (Brower and Brower, 1969), while rats, as a nocturnal, burrowing species, rely heavily on taste and kinesthetic senses.

24

ILLNESS-INDUCED AVERSIONS IN RAT AND QUAIL: RELATIVE SALIENCE OF VISUAL AND GUSTATORY CUES

Hardy C. Wilcoxon, William B. Dragoin, and Paul A. Kral

Bobwhite quail, like the rat, learn in one trial to avoid flavored water when illness is induced by a drug ½ hour after drinking. In contrast to the rat, quail also learn to avoid water that is merely darkened by vegetable dye. The visual cue is even more salient than the taste cue in quail.

Earlier work on illness-induced aversions to eating and drinking shows rather clearly that the rat, at least, must have either a gustatory or an olfactory cue in order to learn to avoid ingesting a substance if the illness that follows ingestion is delayed by ½ hour or more. Visual, auditory, and tactual cues, even though conspicuously present at the time of ingestion, do not become danger signals for the rat in such circumstances (1, 2). On the other hand, blue jays (*Cyanocitta cristata bromia* Oberholser, Corvidae) easily learn to reject toxic monarch butterflies (*Danaus plexippus* L., subfamily Danainae) on sight, although the model suggested for this learning gives emetic reinstatement of taste during illness a prominent, mediating role (3).

From *Science*, 171 (1971), 826–828.

This research is part of the program of the John F. Kennedy Center for Research on Education and Human Development, George Peabody College for Teachers, Nashville, Tennessee, under a Biomedical Sciences Support grant from the National Institutes of Health. We thank Dr. G. McDaniel of Auburn University for supplying the quail and Dr. P. Tavormina of Mead Johnson Research Center for experimental samples of cyclophosphamide.

252

Impetus for our experiments came from the general view that the behavior of an organism, including what it can and cannot readily learn, is largely a product of its evolutionary history. In view of the rat's highly developed chemical senses, nocturnal feeding habits, and relatively poor vision, its ability to learn to avoid toxic substances on the basis of their taste or smell, rather than their appearance, is not surprising. But how general is this phenomenon across species? Might we not expect a diurnal bird, with its superior visual equipment and greater reliance upon vision in foraging for food and drink, to show a different pattern? Perhaps such birds, even in situations involving long delay between the time of ingestion of some food and the onset of illness, can learn to avoid ingesting substances that are distinctive in appearance only.

We report here two experiments which show that bobwhite quail (*Colinus virginianus*) can associate a purely visual cue with a long-delayed, illness consequence. In the first experiment we investigated the relative salience of a visual cue and a gustatory cue in both rats and quail. In the second experiment, in which we used quail only, we controlled for two variables which, unless accounted for, would not have allowed clear-cut interpretation of the first experiment.

Forty 90-day-old male Sprague-Dawley rats and 40 adult male bobwhite quail were subjects (4) in the first experiment. All were caged individually and had free access to food throughout the experiment. At the start, both species were trained over a period of several days to drink all of their daily water from 30-ml glass Richter tubes. Water was presented at the same time each day, and the time allowed for drinking was gradually reduced to a 10-minute period. Baseline drinking was then measured for 1 week, after which experimental treatments were imposed.

On treatment day, subgroups of each species received an initial 10-minute exposure to water that was either dark blue ($N = 8$), sour ($N = 8$), or both blue and sour ($N = 24$). Water was made blue by the addition of three drops of vegetable food coloring to 100 ml of water. Sour water consisted of a weak hydrochloric acid solution (0.5 ml per liter). One-half hour after removal of the distinctive fluid all subjects were injected intraperitoneally with the illness-inducing drug, cyclophosphamide. The dosage for the rats was 66 mg/kg, a dosage known to be effective for establishing one-trial aversions to distinctive tastes in the rat. We used a larger dose (132 mg/kg) for the quail, however, because exploratory use of the drug with the birds showed that the larger dose was necessary in order to produce the primary symptom of illness that rats exhibit, namely, extensive diarrhea.

For 2 days after treatment all subjects drank plain water at the regular 10-minute daily drinking period. This allowed them time to recover from the illness, as evidenced by remission of diarrhea and a return to baseline amounts of water consumption. Extinction tests were then begun to determine whether aversive conditioning had been established to the cues present in the water on treatment day. Five 10-minute tests were conducted, one every third day, with 2 days intervening between tests during which subjects were allowed to drink plain water to reestablish the baseline.

Animals that drank sour water on treatment day were tested with sour water (S : S); those that drank blue water on treatment day received blue water in the extinction tests (B : B). However, the 24 animals of each species that had drunk blue-sour water on treatment day were divided into three subgroups for testing. One group of each species was tested on blue-sour water (BS : BS), another on sour water (BS : S), and the third on the blue water (BS : B).

Figure 1 shows a comparison of the amount of water drunk by rats and quail over five extinction trials for each of the five treatment: test conditions. Differences between mean drinking scores on treatment day and the first extinction trial (E_1) were assessed for statistical significance by the t-test. Results in the S : S condition show that the sour taste by itself was an effective cue for avoidance in both rat ($P < .02$) and quail ($P < .05$). Only the quail, however, showed reduced drinking ($P < .01$) of water that was colored blue on treatment and test days (B : B). In the BS : BS condition, both species again showed significantly reduced drinking in the tests ($P < .001$).

Perhaps the most striking results were shown by the last two subgroups for which the compound cue (BS) of the treatment day conditioning trial was split for separate testing of each component. In the latter two conditions (BS : S and BS : B) rats and quail showed a remarkable difference with respect to the salience of gustatory and visual cues. When the sour element of the compound conditioning stimulus was the test cue (BS : S), rats avoided it ($P < .001$) but quail did not. On the other hand, when the blue color was the element tested (BS : B), quail avoided it ($P < .01$) but rats did not. The behavior of the quail in these split-cue tests is especially informative. Although the quail learned the aversion to taste alone (S : S condition), removal of the visual element from the compound conditioning stimulus (BS : S condition) apparently constituted such a radical change in stimulus for them that it rendered the remaining taste element ineffective. The results demonstrate, therefore, not only that quail can associate a visual cue with long-delayed illness, but also that a visual cue can be so salient as to overshadow taste when the two cues are compounded.

The most important result of this experiment is that quail were somehow able to associate blue water with a subsequent illness which we induced arbitrarily ½ hour after removal of the drinking tube. Failure of the rats used in our experiments to do so does not, of course, constitute a powerful argument that this species cannot associate a visual cue over a long delay. It is conceivable, although we think it unlikely, that rats see no difference between plain and dark blue water. In any event, Garcia and his co-workers (1) have reported much more convincing evidence than ours that rats do not utilize a visual cue in delayed-illness avoidance learning. Thus, our main concern after the first experiment was whether the results for quail were unequivocal, rather than whether rats could actually see our visual cue.

In the second experiment we attempted to answer two questions: (i) Could the quail have been relying on some subtle taste of the dyed water rather than solely upon its appearance?; and (ii) Was the effective consequence that produced aversion to blue water really the drug-induced illness, or was it the considerable trauma of being caught, handled, and injected?

Birds from each of the five earlier subgroups were assigned to one of two groups, assignment being random except for the restriction that the groups be balanced with respect to prior treatment and test conditions. Procedural details

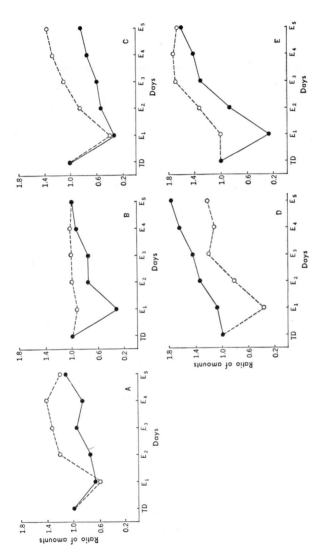

FIG. 1 Comparison of the amount of water consumed by quail (solid lines) and rats (dashed lines) expressed as a ratio of the amount consumed on a given day to the amount consumed on treatment day (TD); E_1 through E_5 are the five extinction trials given at 3-day intervals after the single conditioning trial on TD. (A) Group S : S; (B) group B : B; (C) group BS : BS; (D) group BS : S; (E) group BS : B.

were the same as in the first experiment. On treatment day, however, both groups drank from tinted blue tubes filled with the same plain water to which they were accustomed. One group ($N = 20$) was then injected with cyclophosphamide ½ hour after drinking, whereas the other group ($N = 20$) was injected with normal saline.

Figure 2 shows the result. Birds that received the illness-inducing drug drank less from the tinted tube when they next encountered it ($P < .001$), whereas those injected with saline did not.

Although Figs. 1 and 2 give a clear picture of the relative changes in drinking occasioned by treatment-day and test conditions, they give no information on the absolute amounts ingested or the degree of variability. Accordingly, means and standard deviations are shown in Table 1 for all groups each day from the last baseline day through the first extinction test. Comparison of baseline scores with those of treatment day shows that sour water, whether blue or not, was somewhat aversive to both species at first encounter, that is, before induction of illness; blue water alone was not. The amount of plain water drunk on the two recovery days after treatment shows a return to baseline levels. Effects of the delayed-illness conditioning trial are seen best by comparing scores of treatment day with those of the first extinction test.

Despite the controls introduced in the second experiment, it could be argued that the results represent not true associative learning but only the birds' increased wariness of strange-looking fluids as a result of recent illness. However, studies now completed in our laboratory (4) show that, although such sensitization or heightened neophobia contributes to the effect, there is a

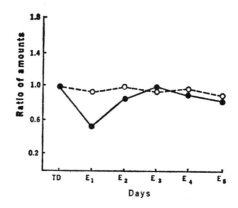

FIG. 2 A comparison of the amount of plain water drunk from tinted tubes by drug-treated quail (solid line) and saline-treated quail (dashed line). The amount drunk is expressed as a ratio of the amount ingested on a given day to the amount consumed on treatment day (TD).

TABLE 1 Means and Standard Deviations (S.D.) of Drinking Scores in All Groups of Both Experiments from the Last Baseline Day through the First Extinction Test (E_1)

Group	N	Last baseline day Mean (ml)	S.D.	TD Mean (ml)	S.D.	First recovery day Mean (ml)	S.D.	Second recovery day Mean (ml)	S.D.	E_1 Mean (ml)	S.D.	P
						Experiment 1						
S : S quail	8	12.9	3.16	9.1	3.24	9.8	4.49	12.6	3.75	6.0	3.77	<.05
S : S rat	8	17.8	4.60	10.6	2.31	17.6	2.04	19.0	3.16	6.2	3.99	<.02
B : B quail	8	12.4	2.52	14.1	2.83	9.5	4.50	11.4	1.90	5.1	3.66	<.01
B : B rat	8	17.4	2.71	19.6	3.70	13.1	2.60	17.6	2.27	18.1	3.71	
BS : BS quail	8	13.0	1.80	6.8	2.49	12.2	3.03	13.0	2.35	2.2	2.68	<.001
BS : BS rat	8	20.4	2.30	13.1	2.29	15.9	3.38	19.4	3.09	5.0	2.92	<.001
BS : S quail	8	13.2	3.07	6.6	3.03	13.2	4.81	12.2	2.59	7.1	3.61	
BS : S rat	8	17.9	2.90	12.0	2.24	17.6	2.53	17.8	2.17	4.5	2.96	<.001
BS : B quail	8	11.5	2.55	8.8	3.19	11.8	3.70	11.9	2.06	2.2	3.19	<.001
BS : B rat	8	18.5	3.08	12.2	3.73	15.9	1.93	17.5	2.96	12.2	4.35	
						Experiment 2, quail only (tinted tube)						
Drug-treated	20	14.1	2.61	13.2	3.58	9.5	3.24	11.4	3.44	7.0	3.63	<.001
Saline-treated	20	13.3	2.86	13.5	3.98	13.0	3.87	13.5	3.30	12.5	3.10	

Probabilities (P) of differences between means of the Treatment Day (TD) and E_1 were calculated by the t-test for repeated measures.

significant associative learning component as well. We are confident, therefore, that at least one avian species can associate a purely visual cue with a delayed illness without mediation by means of peripheral mechanisms such as reinstated taste.

It seems reasonable to expect that this capacity will be widespread among animals whose visual systems are highly developed and whose niches demand great reliance upon vision in foraging. If so, the implications for ecology, behavior theory, and evolutionary theory are of considerable importance.

References

1. J. Garcia and R. A. Koelling. *Psychonom. Sci. 4*, 123 (1966); J. Garcia, B. K. McGowan, F. R. Ervin, R. A. Koelling, *Science 160*, 794 (1968).
2. P. Rozin, *J. Comp. Physiol. Psychol. 67*, 421 (1969).
3. L. P. Brower, W. N. Ryerson, L. L. Coppinger, S. C. Glazier, *Science 161*, 1349 (1968): L. P. Brower, *Sci. Ameri. 220*, 22 (Feb. 1969).
4. H. C. Wilcoxon, W. B. Dragoin, P. A. Kral, in preparation.

When behavioral biologists do turn their attention to broad generalizations concerning the development of behavior, as they may in textbooks (e.g., Hinde, 1966), their presentations are quite inclusive of material from both ethology and psychology, and betray little parochialism. This is a result of a thorough digestion of criticisms by comparative psychologists, especially Lehrman (1953), and of the contributions of learning psychologists. Ethologists have been quicker than psychologists to allow the barriers of academic disciplines to break down, though we hope that the other sections of this book testify to the fact that psychologists are catching up. Typical of the catholic interest of ethologists is the following chapter by Aubrey Manning from his lucid text, An Introdution to Animal Behavior. It includes explicit reference to the relative preparedness of animals to learn some things and their relative unpreparedness to learn others.

25

THE DEVELOPMENT OF BEHAVIOUR

A. Manning

Nearly all the behaviour we observe in animals is adaptive. They respond to appropriate stimuli in an effective manner and thereby feed themselves, find shelter, mate and rear families. Animals are certainly not infallible, but when they do make mistakes it is often because they have been transported into an unnatural environment. We are not surprised if birds make futile attempts to escape when first put into a cage.

INSTINCT AND LEARNING

How does an animal's behaviour become so well fitted to its normal environment? There are two basic ways. Firstly, it may be born with the right responses 'built in' to the nervous system as part of its inherited structure. Honey-bees inherit the ability to form wings and wing muscles for flight; they also inherit the tendency to fly towards flowers and seek nectar and pollen. Such responses are popularly called 'instinctive'—a term which has often been abused but remains useful. Instinctive behaviour evolves gradually, as do structural features, and natural selection modifies it to fit the environment in the best way. It forms a kind of 'species memory' passed on from each generation to its offspring.

Alternatively an animal may be born with few inherited responses but, instead with an ability to modify its behaviour in the light of its experience as it grows up. It learns which responses give the best results and changes its behaviour accordingly.

Instinct and learning both ensure adaptive behaviour, the former by selection operating during the history of a species, the latter during the history of an individual. Stated in this way there is a clear dichotomy, which is rather unrealistic when actual examples are examined. But before we do this it is worth considering the importance of instinct and learning in a general way through the animal kingdom.

From *An Introduction to Animal Behavior* (Reading, Mass.: Addison-Wesley Publishing Company, 1967).

Instinct and Learning in Their Biological Setting

Instinct can equip an animal with a series of adaptive responses which appear ready-made at their first performance. This is clearly advantageous for animals with short lifespans and little or no parental care. The arthropods, for example, show a remarkable development of instinct for no other course is open to them. A female digger-wasp emerges from her underground pupa in spring. Her parents died the previous summer. She has to mate with a male wasp and then perform a whole series of complex patterns connected with digging out a nest hole, constructing cells within it, hunting and killing prey such as caterpillars, provisioning the cells with the prey, laying eggs and finally sealing up the cells. All this must be completed within a few weeks, after which the wasp dies. It is quite inconceivable that she could achieve this tight schedule if she had to learn everything from scratch and by trial and error.

Contrast the digger-wasp's situation with that of a lion cub. Born quite helpless, it is sheltered and fed by its mother until it can move around. It is gradually introduced to solid food and gains agility in playing with its litter mates. It has constant opportunities to watch and copy its parents and other members of the group as they stalk and capture prey. It may catch its first small live prey when 6 months old, but it is 2 years or more before it is fully grown. Its behaviour, and particularly the methods and stratagems it uses in hunting, may change according to circumstances throughout its life.

The digger-wasp which must rely on pre-set instinctive behaviour and the lion who can learn in relative leisure represent two extremes on the behavioural scale. In fact the preceding descriptions have greatly oversimplified their actual behavioural development. The digger-wasp can and must learn many things during its brief life—the exact locality of each of its nests, for example, so that it can return to them after its hunting trips. The young lion possesses some predatory tendencies which are certainly instinctive, even though it has to learn how to direct them.

All animals above the annelid worm level show both kinds of behaviour and each has its own special advantages. This is clearly illustrated from studies on bird calls. Birds often show a strong development of both instinct and learning ability. As we shall discuss later, the song of a male bird often requires the experience both of singing and listening to other males before it takes on its final form. By contrast, in every bird species studied both the production of and response to the alarm calls of the species appear perfect at the first showing. Natural selection has favoured an inherited response where the delay of learning may prove fatal.

The chief advantage of learning over instinct is its greater potential for changing behaviour to meet changing circumstances. Such a consideration is obviously more important to a long-lived animal than to an insect which lives only a few weeks. A further relevant factor may be body size, because highly-developed learning ability requires a relatively large amount of brain tissue, insupportable in a very small animal. Usually body size and life span are positively correlated to some extent and large animals live longer than small ones. Apart from these physical considerations it is clear that natural selection can produce different degrees of learning ability to match a species' life history. The two most advanced orders of the insects, the Hymenoptera (ants, bees and wasps) and the Diptera (two-winged flies), are comparable in size and life span. The Hymenoptera, in addition to a rich instinctive behaviour repertoire, show an extraordinary facility for learning, albeit of a simple type, and this plays an important rôle in their lives. During her brief 3 weeks of foraging a worker honey-bee will learn the precise location of her hive and the locations of the series of flower crops on which she feeds. She may move from one to another of these during the course of a day's foraging because she also learns at what time of day each is secreting the most nectar.

On the other hand, in spite of many attempts, there has been no satisfactory demonstration of learning from the Diptera, although they do show certain types of habituation. Their short lives are governed, with complete success, by inherited responses to food, shelter and a mate.

The Characteristics of Instinct and Learning

We must now examine more closely the characteristics of instinct and learning. There are two conspicuous features of instinctive behaviour which may seem, at first sight, to be unique. First, that it consists of rigid, stereotyped patterns of movement which are very similar in all individuals of a species; all digger-wasps of the same species build their nests in the same way, domestic cockerels all use the same series of movements when courting hens, and so on. Secondly, instinctive patterns can often be evoked most readily be very simple stimuli. When presented with a complex situation the animal responds to one part of it and virtually ignores the rest. A robin displays more aggression to a tuft of red feathers from the breast of a rival male than to a complete bird which lacks only these feathers.

However striking, such characteristics are quite inadequate to distinguish instinctive from learnt behaviour. The latter is often described rather vaguely as being 'more flexible', but in fact the patterns of movement involved may be just as stereotyped as those of instinct. Rats placed in a box where they must learn to press on a projecting lever in order to obtain a pellet of food (Fig. 1) will develop a particular manner of doing so. Some use always their left paw, others press with their chins, and individual rats are very conservative in the method they use. In his delightful book, *King Solomon's Ring*, Lorenz (1952) describes how water shrews learn the geography of their environment in amazing detail. If at one point on a trail they have to jump over a small log, this movement is learnt with such fixity that they continue to make the jump in precisely the same fashion long after the obstacle is removed. There are plenty of other examples where animals have comparable difficulty in 'unlearning' something. The movements appear to become almost 'automatic' and may persist even if they are no longer effective. Learnt patterns nearly always involve responding to particular cues in the environment and, just as with instinctive behaviour, other features may be ignored. It is relatively easy to train animals to discriminate one key stimulus within a complex changing situation.

If we are to make any critical distinction between instinctive and learnt behaviour, it must be based not upon their overt characteristics but upon their

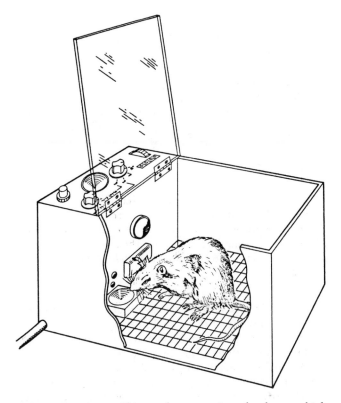

FIG. 1 Rat in a Skinner box pressing the lever which delivers a small pellet of food into the cup.

development within the individual. Rats learn to press a food lever and each does so in a stereotyped way, but this way is unique to the rat and varies between rats. All sexually receptive female rats show the same stereotyped acceptance posture when mounted by a male (Fig. 2). Furthermore if we put a hungry rat into a box with a food lever, it may be hours before, by chance, it pushes against the lever. But if a virgin female rat is brought into receptive condition by a hormone injection, it assumes the acceptance posture on the first occasion it is put with a male.

Here we have the basis for developmental criteria of instinctive behaviour and the commonest way of testing them has been the so-called 'isolation experiment'. Animals are kept individually out of contact with others from as early an age as possible. When mature, their responses to a variety of stimuli are tested and compared with those of animals reared normally. Rather few animals have been tested under really rigorous conditions but some fish and birds have been shown to perform various feeding, sexual and alarm patterns of behaviour quite normally after being reared in isolation. The life histories of many insects are natural isolation experiments which demonstrate vividly that no practice or learning are involved in the behavioural development of the adults.

FIG. 2 Copulation in rats. The female's posture with raised pelvis and deflected tail is very stereotyped in form. The pressure of the male's fore-limbs on her flanks is one of the stimuli necessary for the female to respond. (From Barnett, 1963, *A Study in Behaviour*. Methuen, London.)

There can be no doubt that such behaviour is under genetic control and results from an inherited potentiality of the animal's nervous sytem. But if we leave our consideration of the development of instinct at this point we are losing a great deal of important information. Genes may control behaviour, but they must interact with developing animal's environment. It is obvious that an animal carrying genes for high body weight will not develop its potential if it is half-starved from birth. We may discover factors in the behavioural environment of an animal which influence the development of instinct.

The Effects of Early Experience

Many reflexes—which are as good examples of inherited patterns as can be found—do not develop normally in restricted environments. Riesen (1947) reared chimpanzees from birth in darkness for 40 months. When first tested in the light they showed no eye-blink relfex and this took some 5 days to develop. Clearly the presence of light is necessary for the development of this inherited potentiality. Reyniers (1953) reports another interesting case which was discovered by accident. Infant rats can be removed from a pregnant female by Caesarean section and transferred to a completely sterile environment for studies of germ-free life. When this was first attempted all the babies died after a day although they began to feed well. Post-mortem examination showed that their bladders had ruptured. It turned out that some initial tactile stimuli to the genital region is necessary to start the reflex emptying of the bladder—normally provided by the mother rat. Once set going by this 'trigger' from the environment, the reflex subsequently operates on its own when the bladder is full.

There are now an increasing number of studies on the role of early experience in the development of behaviour, particularly in birds and mammals. In general they show that young animals are sensitive to a wide variety of environmental stimuli. Some experiences have very specific effects on behaviour. Thus stimuli which a young animal perceives during the process of sexual imprinting affect its choice of a sexual partner when it matures. Other types of experience have a more general effect and appear to 'arouse' and accelerate normal behavioural development. Current research is demonstrating that experiences which might be considered quite insignificant can, in fact, produce marked effects on subsequent behaviour. Levine (1962) summarizes some experiments which show that the mere act of lifting young rats or mice out of their nest and then quickly returning them affects their subsequent behaviour. Rats which have been handled mature more quickly in a variety of ways and appear less emotional in frightening situations than do those which are left untouched.

However responsive behaviour is to changes of this rather non-specific type, we cannot deny that the form of much instinctive behaviour, like that of other inherited features which are vital for survival, is very resistant to environmental change. Cockerels raised under hens or in incubators, isolated in battery cages or kept in flocks, may differ in the age at which they first show sexual behaviour and perhaps the frequency of its performance, but they all show the same stereotyped movements, or 'fixed action patterns,' when they court a hen. In contrast, what an animal learns to do will depend to a very great extent on its upbringing. Nevertheless we must avoid any simple dichotomy which ascribes instinct to the genes and learning to the environment. As the examples which follow will show, both genes and environment must be involved in the development of all behaviour. This point might not seem to need such emphasis, but in fact misunderstandings here have been, until quite recently, the basis for a considerable dispute among animal behaviour workers.

Ethologists and Psychologists

After World War II there were two main schools of animal behaviour in the West. The first consisted largely of American experimental psychologists who could claim descent from J. B. Watson (1924), whose book *Behaviourism*, published in 1924, was a landmark in the modern experimental approach to behaviour. The second school—largely European—was founded in the late 1930's by Konrad Lorenz, an Austrian working in Germany. He was joined by Niko Tinbergen from the Netherlands, who collaborated with him in some early work. When the War ended both men rapidly built up groups of research workers and others, usually zoologists, became associated with their approach. This group call themselves 'ethologists', and ethology has been defined simply as 'the scientific study of behaviour.'

Ethologists and American psychologists approached their subject from quite opposite ends. Ethologists studied a wide range of animals under near natural conditions, often in the field with the use of hides. They were impressed by, and concentrated on, the rich variety of adaptive behaviour patterns shown by insects, fish and birds. Reproductive behaviour which is often conspicuous and easy to observe formed a large part of their studies, and ethologists often have great success in keeping animals and getting then to breed in captivity.

The original ethological approach is set out by Tinbergen (1951) in his book, *The Study of Instinct*. It is, in essence, the experimental elucidation of the stimuli which evoke and the motivation which controls the performance of instinctive behaviour, together with a study of its survival value and its evolution. This last aspect is studied in some detail by comparing the behaviour of closely related species and deducing the evolution of particular behaviour patterns, just as a comparative anatomist does for structural features. Ethologists were not much interested in problems related to learning and, though they recognized that their animals could learn, they generally ignored or eliminated this fact from their theories and experiments.

Experimental psychologists, on the other hand, were almost exclusively interested in learning. They largely ignored an animal's behaviour in its natural environment and deliberately confined their subjects to experimental conditions. A maze; a 'shuttle-box' in which it learns to move from one side to another to avoid electric shock; a 'Skinner box' in which it learns to press a lever or peck at a key to receive a reward of food or drink; these were the situations that interested the psychologists. Their aim was to construct 'laws of behaviour' which would describe how an animal's behaviour changes after given levels of practice, reward or punishment and to make predictions, for example, about the efficacy of one or another experimental situation for producing learning.

It is not surprising that the experimental psychologists used a narrower range of animals than the ethologists. Mammals are the best animals for their type of learning study, and were used almost exclusively, with domesticated albino rats providing the great majority of the subjects.

At first the two schools took little note of each other's findings, but after some years cross-fire began and each tended to adopt rather extreme positions. See, for example, Lehrman (1953) for an extreme statement of the case against the ethological concepts then current. The psychologists accused the ethologists, among other things, of grossly underestimating the rôle of the environment in the development of behaviour, of regarding the label 'instinctive' as an adequate explanation in itself and of applying this label far too readily and without sufficient evidence. Conversely, ethologists complained that most experimental psychologists were ignorant of the behaviour of any animal other than the white rat. They suggested that the reality of instinct would become obvious to anybody who could drag himself away from a Skinner box to watch a colony of honey-bees or a nesting male stickleback.

Both sides scored good points and both have subsequently benefited from a dispute which for once did generate more light than heat. Ethologists are now much more cautious in their use of terms and increasingly turn their attention to the development of behaviour. Experimental psychologists are employing a wider range of animals and studying them in a wider range of situations. In particular the studies of physiological psychologists, who mostly remained outside the dispute, now form an excellent link between the two approaches.

THE DEVELOPMENT OF BEHAVIOUR
WITHIN THE INDIVIDUAL

The majority of workers would now agree that any rigid classification of behaviour into 'instinctive' or 'learnt' is inadequate, but that all behaviour presents us with problems of development. What processes are involved in the emergence of fully-formed adult behaviour? This is a very wide topic and here we can only take a few examples to illustrate some of the complex range of influences that must be considered. They will serve to emphasize how meaningless it is to try to press behaviour into categories.

Development Involving Growth or Maturation

The development of an animal's behaviour must obviously be linked to its normal growth processes. For example, the development of sexual behaviour in most vertebrates is linked with the growth of the gonads. Sometimes improvement in the performance of a behaviour pattern can be associated with the development of the animal's nervous sytem and such improvement is usually called 'maturation.'

The behaviour of embryos is determined by their stage of development and their increasing complexity of structure as they develop is paralleled by an increasing repertoire of behaviour, both spontaneous and in response to external stimuli. One of the classic examples is Carmichael's (1926, 1927) study on developing frog tadpoles. Whilst still in the jelly they begin flexing their tails back and forth as in swimming and these movements get more vigorous and complete with time. Is this improvement due to practice or simply to growth? Carmichael kept some developing tadpoles under continuous light anaesthesia which did not slow their growth but prevented all movement. When brought round and released at the age of emerging from the jelly they swam just as proficiently as unanaesthetized tadpoles, which implies that maturation and not practice is the cause of the changes seen in the behaviour of normal tadpoles.

Similar experiments have been made with birds which often appear to 'practice' flying by beating their wings whilst still in the nest. In 1873 Spalding (1873) showed that young swallows reared in cages so small that they could not stretch their wings flew just as well as normally reared birds when released. The ability to fly can be said to 'mature' without practice in these cases, but young fledglings cannot fly as well as adult birds and all the finer points of flying skill are added by practice.

In other cases practice is required from the outset if behaviour is to develop properly. In Chapter 1 Wells' (1958, 1962) experiments with young cuttle-fish were mentioned. It will be recalled that their response to a tiny shrimp presented in a glass tube can be divided into four stages (see Fig. 3):

1. A latency before there is any observable response (Fig. 3a).
2. The nearest eye of the cuttle-fish fixates the shrimp.
3. The cuttle-fish turns towards the shrimp and both eyes fixate (Fig. 3b).
4. It attacks and seizes the shrimp (Fig. 3c).

Stages 2, 3 and 4 usually occupy about 10 seconds and this time varies very little with age or experience. The duration of stage 1 shows a rapid decline with successive tests as shown in Fig. 2.4. After five trials at a rate of one per day, the latency is reduced from about 120 seconds to 10 seconds or less. This change is the same whether the attacks are successful or unsuccessful, whether made with a 1-day-old cuttle-fish or one starved for 5 days before its first test. The only common factor appears to be practice in attacking shrimps. Learning is ruled out because in some other tests Wells finds it impossible to show any sign of learning

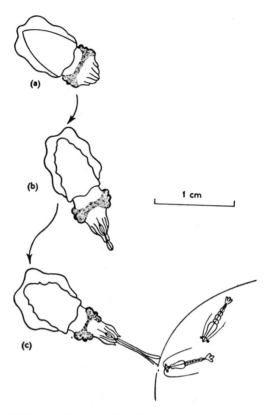

FIG. 3 The attack of *Sepia* on *Mysis*: (a)
Newly-hatched *Sepia* at rest; (b) swimming
towards the prey, the eyes turned forward and
fixating it; (c) stabbing with the long pair of
tentacles at the *Mysis* behind glass. (From
Wells, 1958, *Behaviour*, 13, 96.)

ability until the cuttle-fish are a month old. Baby cuttle-fish go on battering
away at a glass plate behind which they can see a shrimp, until they are
physically exhausted. Nor are they deterred from such attacks by electric
shocks. With similar treatment an adult will stop attacking after a couple of
trials. The vertical lobe of the cuttle-fish brain, which is known to be concerned
with learning in adults, does not develop until relatively late after hatching.

   The development of pecking in newly-hatched chicks provides another
example of the interaction between maturation and practice. Young chicks have
an inherited tendency to peck at objects which contrast with the background,
but their aim is at first rather poor, and various workers have studied how it
improves. One of the most complete studies was made by Cruze (1935). He
hand-fed chicks in the dark on powdered food for periods of up to 5 days before

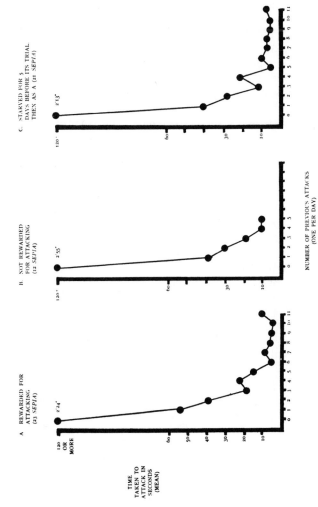

FIG. 4 The rapid decline of latency to attack *Mysis* in newly-hatched *Sepia*. The latency depends on the number of attacks that have already been made and is not affected by reward (a & b) food deprivation or age (c). (From Wells, 1958, *Behaviour*, 13, 96.)

A. REWARDED FOR ATTACKING (23 SEPIA)

B. NOT REWARDED FOR ATTACKING (12 SEPIA)

C. STARVED FOR 5 DAYS BEFORE ITS TRIAL. THEN AS A (21 SEPIA)

TIME TAKEN TO ATTACK IN SECONDS (MEAN)

NUMBER OF PREVIOUS ATTACKS (ONE PER DAY)

testing the accuracy of their pecking. Whilst in the dark they are inactive and have no chance to practise the movement. Cruze measured accuracy by putting the chicks individually into a small arena with a black floor, on to which he scattered two or three grains of millet. Each chick was allowed 25 pecks scored for miss or hit and grains were replaced if the chick swallowed them. After accuracy tests the chicks were allowed to feed naturally in the light and the effects of practice on their accuracy measured again after 12 hours.

Table 1 shows the results of one experiment. There is a steady improvement with age (heavy type), but at any age 12 hours of practice greatly improves accuracy (light type).

More recently an ingenious experiment by Hess (1956) has confirmed Cruze's results whilst avoiding the necessity for keeping chicks in the dark for long periods, which probably affects their visual development. Hess covered the heads of newly-hatched chicks with rubber hoods fitted with prismatic lenses over the eyes which deflected vision by 7° to right or left. Control chicks had plain transparent plastic eyepieces. When 1 day old they were presented with a bright silver nail embedded in Plasticine. As they pecked at this, their bills left marks in the Plasticine scattered around the target nail. The marks of control birds showed a scatter centered on the nail itself; those of birds with deflected vision showed a similar degree of scatter but centreed around a point to the left or right, according to which side the prisms deflected (Figs, 5a and b). For the next 3 days all the chicks fed themselves from bowls of mash or scattered grain. Their pecking patterns at 4 days old are shown in Fig. 5c and d. Both groups show a similar improvement in accuracy, but the prism group had not learnt to correct for the displacement, indeed many of them had lost weight because they couldn't feed themselves well. Their improvment could not have been due to practice, because they never hit the grain at which they were aiming but, if any, another near by. Maturation thus seems the only explanation, although we must bear in mind that mechanisms other than those specifically controlling pecking will influence accuracy. The chicks' legs grow stronger and perhaps their stability improves which would help their aim.

TABLE 1   The Pecking Accuracy of Chicks at Different Ages Before and After 12 Hours of Practice.

Age (hr.)	Practice (hr.)	Av. misses (25 pecks)
24	0	6.04
48	12	1.96
48	0	4.32
72	12	1.76
72	0	3.00
96	12	0.76
96	0	1.88
120	12	0.16
120	0	1.00

Each figure represents an average from 25 chicks. (Modified from Cruze, 1935).

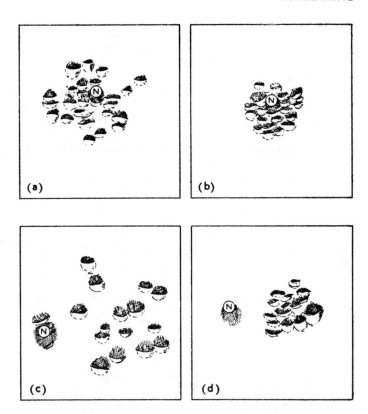

FIG. 5 The accuracy of pecking in chicks as revealed by the marks of their bills in Plasticine around a 'target' brass nail head (N). Each picture is the record of a single chick. (a & b) are from a normal chick at 1 and 4 days old respectively; its accuracy improves greatly. The chick in (c) and (d) wore a hood which deflected its vision 7° to the right. Although it never hits the target its accuracy improves with age in just the same way as in normal chicks. (After photographs from Hess, 1956, *Scientific American*, 195 (1), 71.)

Development Which Involves the Interaction of Inherited Behavior with Learning

In the examples given above, conventional learning has been eliminated as contributing to the development of inherited behaviour. However, it is very common to find that adult behaviour patterns contain elements of both. Lorenz (1966), who continues to emphasize the differences between inherited and learnt behaviour, suggests that where learning modifies the former it does so only in a limited fashion. He points out that 'fixed action patterns' themselves do not change with learning. These are those units of behaviour which are recognized by a stereotyped sequence of muscle contractions—such as the sexual acceptance posture of the female rat or the courtship displays of many birds.

Certainly an animal's ability to learn novel patterns of movement—new motor skills as we might call them—is circumscribed by its inherited behaviour. Many ground-nesting birds retrieve an egg which has slipped out of the nest in the same way. They extend the neck and hook the lower mandible over the egg which is then rolled back by drawing in the head (see Fig. 6). This fixed action pattern can be elicited on the first occasion that an incubating bird is presented with an egg outside the rim of the nest. For a goose to use the bill in this way is reasonably efficient because it has a broad one, but birds with narrower bills such as gulls and waders often have considerable trouble because the egg tends to slip out to one side. It would seem much easier for these birds to use their wing or foot as a scoop, but they show no variation from the fixed pattern.

Perhaps the most vivid example of how resistant inherited fixed action patterns are to change, comes from the work of Dilger (1962) with love-birds. These are members of the parrot family which breed readily in captivity. Within the genus *Agapornis* two types of nest-building behaviour are represented. All species tear strips of material from leaves to build with (in the laboratory newspaper forms an excellent substitute) but whilst some tuck the strips into their rump feathers and fly back to the nest carrying several pieces at once, other

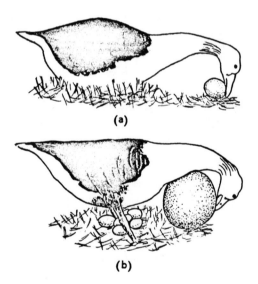

(a)

(b)

FIG. 6 Grey lag goose retrieving an egg which is outside the nest. This movement is very stereotyped in form and used by many ground-nesting birds. The goose attempts to retrieve a giant egg in precisely the same fashion. (From Lorenz and Tinbergen, 1938, *Z. Tierpsychol*, 2, 1.)

species carry the strips singly in their bill. Dilger crossed two species which differed in this respect and watched the nest-building behaviour of the hybrids. For some time such birds were incapable of building a nest at all because they attempted to perform some kind of compromise between the two collecting methods. They might start to tuck a strip between the rump feathers, but either failed to let go of it or failed to tuck it properly. The end result was usually that the strip fell to the ground and the whole process began again. The only success the hybrids had was when they managed to retain a strip in their bill after the attempted tucking procedure. Dilger found that even after months of practice the birds managed successful carrying in only 41% of the trials. Two years later they were successful in nearly all trials, but before carrying a strip in their bill they still made the turning movement of the head which is the preliminary to tucking. Parrots are intelligent birds which are known to learn quickly in other situations, but here the inherited predisposition to perform the tucking sequence outweighed learning for a long time.

However, we often find that inherited components of behaviour become integrated with learnt components during development. For example, Eibl-Eibesfeldt (1961) describes the development of prey-catching in the polecat. He reared a number of them in isolation and never gave them any opportunity to catch live prey. Such polecats when first presented with a live rat showed varying degrees of interest but no hint of attack unless the rat ran away from them. If it did so, they instantly pursued and seized it in their mouth, usually shaking it rapidly in a characteristic way. Their bites were at first badly orientated, but after a few trials they were seizing prey by the nape of the neck and killing with a single bite. Clearly there are inherited components to the killing pattern which are completed by learning. Eibl-Eibesfeldt found that normally polecats picked up the necessary practice during play sessions with their litter mates.

One of the most beautiful examples of the dovetailing of inherited and learnt components during development is that of bird song. Until recently song was difficult to study because there was no way of expressing it graphically. The development of the sound spectrograph has turned this situation inside out and made detailed analysis easier for song than for most behaviour. Bird song is just like any other behaviour pattern—a controlled sequence of muscle contractions which in this case we perceive as sound. It can be recorded on tape and played into the spectrograph which produces a chart showing how much energy was emitted at the various sound frequencies at any time.

Marler and Tamura (1964) have worked on the song development of the American white-crowned sparrow. This small finch has a wide range on the Pacific coast, and birds from different regions have recognizably different song 'dialects'. If young males are taken immediately after hatching and reared alone in sound-proof chambers then, no matter which region they come from, they all eventually sing very similar and simplified versions of the normal song. Obviously they must pick up the local dialect by listening to adult birds and modifying their own simple song pattern accordingly. Marler and Tamura found that this learning process usually takes place during the first 3 months of life and thus before the bird has ever sung itself. Males captured in their first autumn and reared alone begin to sing for the first time with a recognizable version of the local dialect. Up to 3 months of age, isolated males can be 'trained' to sing their own or other dialects by playing to them tape-recorded songs, though the results of such training do not show until the birds begin to sing themselves some months later. Beyond 4 months of age the birds are unreceptive to any further training and their songs when they begin singing are not affected. Here then we have a simple, inherited song pattern which is sensitive to modification by learning but only during early life. The young birds 'carry' the memory of the songs they hear and reproduce them when they first sing.

The analysis has been taken further by the experiments of Konishi (1965). He completely deafened birds at various ages by removing the cochlea of the inner ear. If this is done to a young fledgling just out of the nest, it will subsequently sing, but it produces only a series of disconnected notes. These are quite unlike the song of isolated birds which, though simple in form, would still be recognizable as 'white-crowned sparrow' to an ornithologist. The bird has to be able to hear itself in order to produce this inherited song pattern. Again, if Konishi deafened young birds *after* they had been 'trained' with normal song but *before* they had themselves sung, their subsequent song resembled that of birds deafened as fledglings. They need to hear themselves in order to match up the song they produce with that which they have stored in their memories. Once they have sung properly deafening has no effect on their subsequent singing.

The results of all these experiments are summarized in Fig. 2.7. We have gone over them in some detail because they are an object lesson in the study of behavioural development. They show how subtle and complex are the interactions between inherited tendencies and the environment which finally produce behaviour as we observe it.

Fig. 2.7 also indicates the result of one more experiment with the sparrows which introduces the last aspect of behavioural development to be considered.

The Inheritance of a Predisposition to Learn Particular Things

White-crowned sparrows only learn to sing the white-crowned sparrow song. If the songs of other species are played to males during their 'sensitive period' for learning they have no effect and the birds' subsequent songs sound like those of isolated males. The chaffinch behaves very similarly, and Thorpe (1961) points out that this can scarcely be a result of limitations in its sound-producing organ or syrinx. The related bullfinch and greenfinch have syrinxes of almost identical structure. They have only a poorly developed natural song but are good mimics and will learn to reproduce the songs of many other birds.

Some clue to the chaffinch's limitation is provided by the song of the one species it will learn to imitate reasonably well. This is the tree-pipit, whose song to the human ear also has a chaffinch-like tone, though it is very different in pattern. The chaffinch must have an inherited tendency to single out this tone from all others and to reproduce it.

There are several other cases on record where animals show a singular facility for particular types of learning. Tinbergen's (1953) work with the herring-gull has shown that whereas these birds do not learn to recognize their own eggs, after a few days they do recognize their own chicks and react aggressively

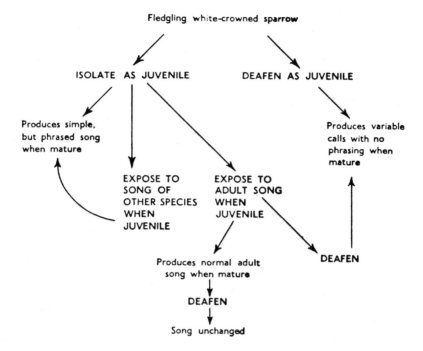

FIG. 7 A summary of the results obtained by Marler, Tamura and Konishi on song development in the white-crowned sparrow.

towards strange ones. From an adaptive viewpoint this makes sense; eggs cannot wander from the nest site, chicks can. Nevertheless it can rarely be possible for a pair of herring-gulls personally to test the wisdom of this, they probably have an inherited tendency to learn details of the plumage of their own chicks. In this connection it is noteworthy that Tschanz (1959) has shown that guillemots, which build no nest but lay their single egg on open cliff ledges, do learn to recognize their own egg. The eggs can roll around and it is clearly adaptive to know which one to retrieve. This may be the reason why guillemot eggs are so variable in ground colour and pattern.

Again, Hinde and Tinbergen (1958) describe how young titmice learn to use their feet to hold down large pieces of food in order to break pieces with their bills. Young chaffinches do not learn to do this even when they are reared by titmice foster-parents and this difference is probably inherited. In Chapter 8 we discuss the phenomenon of imprinting which is based upon an inherited tendency in young animals to approach conspicuous objects and learn their characteristics, so that subsequently they are followed and treated as a 'mother figure.'

It seems certain that further investigation will reveal similar inherited predispositions to learn. The extraordinary facility with which bees and wasps learn landmarks around their nests, or polecats learn to seize their prey by the back of the neck are suggestive examples.

Such examples and all that have been described earlier in this chapter give little encouragement for attempts to classify behaviour into that which is inherited and that which is learnt. It may be possible to do this in some cases but it does not seem a very helpful exercise unless it yields information on how the behaviour develops. In the constant struggle to be well adapted, natural selection usually operates on the end result; it matters little how this is achieved. We have already considered some of the factors that may predispose certain groups to rely mainly on inherited behaviour, others on learning. However, even among close relatives there may be wide variation; Thorpe (1961) has found that the songs of closely related birds may develop in quite different ways.

The study of behavioural development is one of fundamental value. The most important property of the nervous system is its ability to store information. Some of this is fed in by genes during the development of the nervous system, other information is added later by learning. There seems no good reason to regard these two processes as distinct; they may have almost everything in common. Galambos (1961) concludes a paper on mechanisms of learning: 'It could be argued, in brief, that no important gap separates the explanations for how the nervous system comes to be organized during embryological development in the first place; for how it operates to produce the innate responses characteristic of each species in the second place; and for how it becomes reorganized, finally as a result of experiences during life. If this idea should be correct, the solution of any one of these problems would mean that the answer for the others would drop like a ripe plum, so to speak, into our outstretched hands.'

References

Carmichael, L. (1926). The development of behavior in vertebrates experimentally removed from the influence of external stimulation. *Psychol. Rev., 33*, 51–58.

Carmichael, L. (1927). A further study of the development of behavior in vertebrates experimentally removed from the influence of external stimulation. *Psychol. Rev., 34*, 34–47.

Cruze, W. W. (1935). Maturation and learning in chicks. *J. Comp. Psychol., 19*, 371–409.

Dilger, W. C. (1962). The behavior of lovebirds. *Scient. Am., 206*, 88–98.

Eibl-Eibesfeldt, I. Von (1961). The interactions of unlearned behaviour patterns and learning in mammals. In *Brain Mechanisms and Learning*, ed. Delafresnaye, J. F., pp. 53–73. Blackwell Scientific, Oxford.

Galambos, R. (1961). Changing concepts of the learning mechanism. In *Brain Mechanisms and Learning*, ed. Delafresnaye, J. F., pp. 231–41. Blackwell Scientific, Oxford.

Hess, E. H. (1956). Space perception in the chick. *Scient. Am., 195*, 71–80.

Hinde, R. A. and Tinbergen, N. (1958). The comparative study of species-specific behavior. In *Behavior and Evolution*, ed. Roe, A. and Simpson, G. G., pp. 251–68. Yale University Press, New Haven.

Konishi, M. (1965). The rôle of auditory feedback in the control of vocalization in the white-crowned sparrow. *Z. Tierpsychol., 22*, 770–83.

Lehrman, D. S. (1953). A critique of Konrad Lorenz's theory of instinctive behavior. *Q. Rev. Biol., 28*, 337–63.

Levine, S. (1962). Psychophysiological effects of infantile stimulation. In *Roots of Behavior*, ed. Bliss, E. L., pp. 246–53. Harper, New York.

Lorenz, K. Z. (1952). *King Solomon's Ring*. Methuen, London. (Reprinted 1959 by Pan, London.)

Lorenz, K. Z. (1966). *Evolution and Modification of Behavior*. Methuen, London.

Marler, P. and Tamura, M. (1964). Culturally transmitted patterns of vocal behavior in sparrows. *Science*, N. Y., *146*, 1483—86.

Reyniers, J. A. (1953). Germ-free life. *Lancet*, 933—34.

Riesen, A. H. (1947). The development of visual perception in man and chimpanzee. *Science*, N. Y., *106*, 107—8.

Spalding, D. (1873). Instinct: with original observations on young animals. *Macmillan's Mag.*, *27*, 283—93. (Reprinted in *Br. J. Anim. Behav.*, *2*, 1—11, 1954.)

Thorpe, W. H. (1961). *Bird Song*. Cambridge University Press, Cambridge.

Tinbergen, N. (1951). *The Study of Instinct*. Oxford University Press, London.

Tinbergen, N. (1953). *The Herring Gull's World*. Collins, London.

Tschanz, B. (1959). Zur Brutbiologie der Trottelume (*Uria aalge aalge* Pont.) *Behaviour*, *14*, 1—100.

Watson, J. B. (1924). *Behaviorism*. University of Chicago Press, Chicago.

Wells, M. J. (1958). Factors affecting reactions to *Mysis* by newly hatched *Sepia*. *Behaviour*, *13*, 96—111.

Wells, M. J. (1962). Early learning in Sepia. *Symp. zool. Soc. Lond.*, *8*, 149—69.

The importance of Konrad Lorenz's investigations of imprinting for the psychology of learning is difficult to overestimate. Unlike most ethological findings, they came rapidly to the attention of learning theorists, pointed up how intimately "instinct" and "learning" could be interwoven, and violated several acknowledged laws of learning: This kind of prepared response is acquired almost instantaneously during a critical period of development and is extraordinarily resistant to extinction.

Imprinting continues to stimulate considerable experimentation. Gilbert Gottlieb shows here that Peking ducks imprint preferentially, more quickly, more reliably, and more resistantly to the call of their own species than to calls of other species. Equipotentiality is clearly violated by the fact that they are prepared to imprint on the call of their own species.

26

IMPRINTING IN RELATION TO
PARENTAL AND SPECIES
IDENTIFICATION
BY AVIAN NEONATES

Gilbert Gottlieb

Parentally naive ducklings and chicks exhibit a marked preference for the parental call of their own species which is highly resistant to change by learning or by prior experience with parental calls of other species. Existence of an auditory perceptual mechanism for supraindividual identification of species in parentally naive ducklings and chicks would seem to greatly reduce likelihood of birds' becoming imprinted to species other than their own in the normal course of events in nature, though visual learning of species characteristics can certainly take place in the context of this preference. Thus, imprinting would seem to play an important though supporting role in directing avian neonate's social activities toward members of its own species under natural circumstances.

The experiments reported here were designed to examine the imprinting concept as it pertains to the process whereby young birds identify their parent and species. The crux of this aspect of imprinting is contained in the following quotation:

From *Journal of Comparative and Physiological Psychology,* 59 (1965), 345—356.
The execution of the experiments and the analysis of the data were faciliated by the help of Anne W. Smith, William Lynn, Carter Doran, and Marvin Simner. Henry Garren and Clifford Barber of the Poultry Science Department, North Carolina State College, kindly arranged the availability of chick eggs. Financial support came from the North Carolina Department of Mental Health and United States Public Health Service Grants M-6039 and MH-06039-02 from the National Institute of Mental Health (now HD-00878-02 from the National Institute of Child Health and Human Development).

It is a fact most surprising to the layman as well as to the zoologist that most birds do not recognize their own species "instinctively," but that far the greater part of their reactions, whose normal object is represented by a fellow-member of the species, must be conditioned to this object during the individual life of every bird [Lorenz, 1937, pp. 262–263].

Thus, imprinting is pictured as a sort of perceptual learning process through which the young bird learns to identify the general characteristics of its parent and other members of its species, thereby filling the gap left vacant by the absence of instinctive recognition of its own species.

As "imprinting" is a uniquely ethological contribution to the study of animal behavior, it is surprising to many that the evidence for the imprinting formulation did not stem from naturalistic observation (Heinroth, 1910; Lorenz, 1937). Rather, Lorenz's formulation of imprinting relied on observations of young birds (primarily ducklings and goslings) deprived of contact with their biological parents. Thus, the role of imprinting in the establishment of biologically appropriate species identification has been indirectly inferred from isolation and fostering experiments rather than being directly validated by observations and experiments involving species-typical auditory and visual stimulation.

Laboratory research dealing with the approach and following response of young birds has lent credence to the notion that social or perceptual object preferences are or can be induced on the basis of early experience. Such naive perceptual preferences as do exist are of a very general nature and would not seem capable of directing the young animal's attention exclusively to its own species without the benefit of postnatal experience. For example, in the visual modality Hess (1959) has found a graded series of form preferences with the full-fledged adult model being the most *ineffective* for the induction of the following response. Color preferences also seem to be of a rather general nature in naive hatchlings (Gray, 1961; Schaefer & Hess, 1958). In the auditory modality, rather generalized repetitive, low-frequency sounds seem to be the most "innately" effective ones, judging from research with sham sounds (Collias & Collias, 1956; Collias & Joos, 1952).

The apparent relative absence of specificity in the visual and auditory modalities seems to coordinate well with the original suggestion of Lorenz that, in many avian forms, parental and species recognition is a function of postnatal contact with the mother or parent surrogate. Under natural conditions both hole-nesting and ground-nesting hatchlings are exposed to the call of their mother for a relatively long period prior to leaving the nest (Gottlieb, 1963b, 1963c), and this observation would seem to suggest that in nature maternal and possibly species recognition is a function of auditory imprinting which occurs even before the mother leads the young from the nest.

The present experiments are the first ones in a series designed to test the idea that learning or imprinting is requisite to biologically correct parental and species identification in avian neonates. The present method involved exposing parentally naive ducklings and parentally naive chicks to the parental exodus call (i.e., the vocalization of the hen as she leads her young from the nest in nature) of their own and other species, and determining the influence of these calls on the instigation of the following response.

EXPERIMENT 1

Method
In the laboratory, 224 Peking (*Anas platyrhynchos*) duck eggs were incubated and hatched. Prior to incubation the eggs were exposed to a refrigeration technique so that the developmental age of the ducklings could be accurately calculated (Gottlieb, 1963d). During incubation and hatching, a background noise level of 74 db. was maintained inside the incubator; a room air conditioner and an incubator fan supplied the noise. After hatching, Ss were visually isolated (individually) in a brooder (85–90° F.), where the background noise level was maintained at 69–70 db. by a room air conditioner. These and all other sound pressure levels were determined on Scale B of a General Radio sound level meter, Type 1551-A, with a standard sound pressure reference level of 0.0002 microbar at 1,000 cycles.

The ducklings were divided into four separate groups. Three of the groups were exposed to a stuffed replica of a Peking duck hen as it moved about the apparatus (Figure 1) emitting one of three recorded exodus calls through a speaker concealed in its underside. For experimental purposes, each call was rerecorded so that it repeated itself every 3 sec. All of the calls used were free of background sounds such as the cheeping of ducklings or chicks.

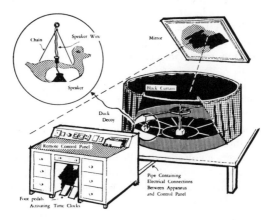

FIG. 1 Experimental apparatus: circular table enclosed by curtains, with observation mirror above. (Foot pedals, when depressed, actuate time clocks. Decoy is equipped with speaker for experiments involving auditory stimulation.)

One group ($N = 60$) was exposed to the exodus call of the Mallard hen (*Anas platyrhynchos*) recorded in the field (Gottlieb, 1963b). For the purpose of the experiment, it is important to note that Peking (domestic) and Mallard (wild) ducks are of the same species. A second group ($N = 59$) was exposed to the exodus call of the Wood duck hen (*Aix sponsa*), also recorded in the field (Gottlieb, 1963c). It will be noted that Peking and Wood ducks are of different genera. A third group ($N = 57$) was exposed to the exodus call of the domestic Chicken hen (*Gallus gallus*). This call was obtained by Collias (1960). A fourth group ($N = 48$) was exposed to the moving model without any auditory stimulation.

Each bird was exposed to one of the above conditions for a 20-min. period at 10–21 hr. after hatching. The developmental ages of the ducklings (calculated from onset of embryonic development) were between 27 days 0 hr. and 28 days and 11 hr. Approximately one-third of the birds were exposed to the model within each of the following three 12-hr. developmental age ranges: 27 days, 0–11 hr.; 27 days, 12–23 hr.; and 28 days, 0-11 hr. A sample of the entire posthatch age spectrum was included within each of the developmental age ranges. For example, the youngest developmental age range (27 days, 0-11 hr.) contained ducks whose posthatch age ranged from 10–21 hr. as did the oldest developmental age range (28 days, 0–11 hr.). In line with the evidence that developmental age is both more sensitive and more reliable than posthatch age for the early phase of postnatal behavior, the experiment was designed around developmental age rather than posthatch age (Fabricius, 1963; Gottlieb, 1961; Gottlieb & Klopfer, 1962; Klopfer & Gottlieb, 1962).

During the experiment background noise (air conditioner) was at 61–62 db. at the point where S was placed in the apparatus. The intensity of all three calls was equated at 65–71 db. at S's starting position 6 in. to the rear of the speaker-rigged model. A temperature of 75° F. was maintained in the testing apparatus. The model moved around a circular (14 ft. circumference) path at the rate of one revolution every 58 sec. This included a 5-sec. pause after every 20 sec. of movement.

Duration of following in seconds and latency of the following response in seconds were recorded for each duck according to previously published criteria (Gottlieb & Klopfer, 1962).

Neither food nor water was available during the experiment. Each duck was housed and trained individually.

All statistical analyses involved two-tailed tests of probability as there were no grounds for predicting the *direction* of differences. The x^2 test was used in comparing incidence of response; the Mann-Whitney U test was used for analyses involving strength and latency of following.

Results

The proportion of ducklings (*Anas platyrhynchos*) which followed the model in each vocal condition is shown in Table 1, along with the latency and duration of following of those birds which followed the model. The exodus call of the Mallard hen (*Anas platyrhynchos*) was more effective in inducing the ducklings to follow than any of the other calls ($p < .01$). Moreover, the exodus call of the

TABLE 1 Incidence, Latency, and Duration of Following Response of Naive Birds Exposed to a Model Emitting the Parental Call of Their Own and Other Species

Experimental condition	N	% following	Latency (in sec.) M	Latency (in sec.) SD	Duration (in sec.) M	Duration (in sec.) SD
Ducklings from Experiment 1						
Mallard	60	85	290.9	253.1	589.6	370.5
Wood duck	59	63	421.7	250.5	468.6	322.9
Chicken	57	40	468.2	307.7	367.9	336.7
Silence	48	4	607.0	151.3	300.5	181.7
Chicks from Experiment 2						
Chicken	79	72	297.4	204.6	371.0	293.8
Mallard	71	37	401.6	220.9	238.6	215.4
Wood duck	75	26	517.7	267.0	117.3	160.1
Silence	63	25	595.9	272.5	89.4	163.2

Wood duck (*Aix sponsa*) was more effective than that of the Chicken (*Gallus gallus*) (*p* = .02), and the Chicken call was more effective than no call at all (*p* < .01).

With respect to strength (persistence) of following of those Ss which responded during the 20-min. period, the Mallard call was possibly more effective (*p* = .10) than the Wood duck call and definitely more effective (*p* < .02) than the Chicken call or no call at all. The Wood duck call was probably no more effective than the exodus call of the chicken (*p* = .20) and the difference between the Chicken call and the silent condition was not statistically reliable. Large standard deviations (Table 1) indicate great individual variability in strength of following.

With regard to latency of response, the Mallard call instigated a significantly swifter approach than either of the other two calls or silence (*p* < .006). There were no significant differences in latency of response among the other three conditions.

"Critical-period" information is shown in Figure 2, where the incidence of following in each condition is broken down into the three developmental age ranges. As can be seen, each call was associated with a somewhat different curve, indicating that the idea of a unitary critical period for the following response is incorrect. The Mallard call differed from *all* the other conditions only during 27 days 0–11 hr., which had been previously identified as a phase of development during which Peking ducklings reared under the present conditions are particularly sensitive to auditory stimulation (Gottlieb, 1963a; Gottlieb & Klopfer, 1962). Compared to the other calls, more Ss exposed to the Mallard call followed (*p* < .01) during this period and they followed more strongly (*p* < .001). There were no statistically significant differences at this period between the Wood duck and Chicken calls, though both of those were superior

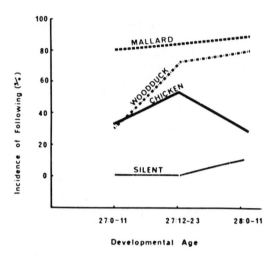

FIG. 2 The proportion of naive ducklings which followed the model in each vocal condition as a function of developmental age.

to no call. Within the Wood duck condition, older Ss (27:12—28:11) were more likely to follow (p = .001) and followed more strongly (p = .001) than the young Ss (27:0—11). There were no significant differences within any of the other conditions.

Discussion

The main finding of Experiment 1 is that in naive ducklings the parental call of their own species was more effective in inducing and maintaining the following response than were the parental calls of other species. This finding indicates that *A. platyrhynchos* ducklings can identify their own species on the basis of auditory stimulation emanating from the parent and that this general identification occurs without the benefit of known forms of learning. Owing to the importance of this conclusion, the experiment was repeated with domestic chicks (*Gallus gallus*).

EXPERIMENT 2

Method

In the laboratory under the conditions outlined in Experiment 1, 288 White Rock (*Gallus gallus*) chick eggs were incubated, hatched, and reared.

The chicks were divided into four groups, each of which was exposed to a stuffed replica of a domestic Chicken hen as it moved about the apparatus, described in Experiment 1. One group (N = 79) was exposed to the call of the domestic Chicken hen (*Gallus gallus*), one (N = 71) to the exodus call of the Mallard hen (*Anas platyrhynchos*), one (N = 75) to the exodus call of the Wood duck hen (*Aix sponsa*), and the fourth group (*N* = 63) to the moving model without any auditory stimulation.

Each *S* was exposed to one of the above conditions for a 20-min. period at 8–50 hr. after hatching. (75% of the *S*s were 8–27 hr. old.) As in Experiment 1, Experiment 2 was designed around developmental age rather than posthatch age. The developmental ages of the chicks differ from those of the ducks because of their shorter incubation period (19–20 days for chicks vs. 26–27 days for ducks). Approximately one-quarter of the *S*s were exposed to the model within each of four developmental age ranges: 20 days, 12–23 hr.; 21 days, 0–11 hr.; 21 days, 12–23 hr.; and 22 days, 0–11 hr. A special effort was made to include a representative sample of the entire posthatch age spectrum within each of the developmental age ranges. For example, the youngest developmental age range contained *S*s whose posthatch age ranged from 8–41 hr. and the oldest developmental age range contained *S*s whose posthatch age ranged from 12–50 hr.

The experimental apparatus, the background noise, and the temperature in the testing area were the same as those outlined in Experiment 1. The intensities of the calls were equated at 70–72 db. at *S*'s starting position. As in Experiment 1, strength of following (in seconds) and latency of the following response (in seconds) were recorded for each *S*.

Results

The proportion of chicks which followed the model in each vocal condition is shown in Table 1, along with the latency and duration (persistence) of following of those *S*s which followed the model. The exodus call of the Chicken hen was much more effective in inducing the chicks to follow than any of the other calls ($p < .001$)—the Mallard and Wood duck exodus calls being no more effective than no call at all.

With respect to strength (persistence) of following of those *S*s which responded during the 20-min. period, the Chicken exodus call was much more effective ($p < .02$) than any of the other conditions. The Mallard exodus call was probably more potent than the Wood duck exodus call ($p = .10$) or no call ($p = .02$), and the Wood duck exodus call was probably more effective than silence ($p = .08$). Large standard deviations (Table 1) indicate great individual variability in duration of following, which ranged as high as 957 sec. in the Chicken Vocal group, 603 sec. in the Mallard Vocal group, 543 sec. in the Wood Duck Vocal group, and 548 sec. in the Silent Model group.

With regard to latency of response, the Chicken exodus call instigated a significantly shorter latency than both the Mallard exodus call ($p = .01$) and the Wood duck exodus call ($p = .001$). The Mallard exodus call promoted a shorter latency than no call ($p = .02$). There was no difference in latency of response between chicks in the Mallard call and Wood duck call groups, and the Wood duck exodus call did not promote a shorter latency than did no call.

Critical-period information is presented in Figure 3, where the incidence of following in each vocal condition is broken down into the four developmental age brackets. There are three main points of interest concerning this information. First, the shape of the so-called critical-period curve is somewhat different

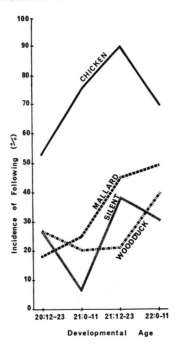

FIG. 3 The proportion of naive chicks which followed the model in each vocal condition as a function of developmental age.

for each condition of stimulation. Second, with 21 days 11 hr. taken as an arbitrary dividing point, older Ss followed more strongly ($p < .05$) than younger Ss within each condition except exposure to the Wood duck exodus call. Third, at each age chicks exposed to the Chicken exodus call followed more strongly ($p < .05$) and in proportionately greater number ($p < .05$) than chicks in the other vocal conditions.

Subsequent Testing for Evidence of Auditory Imprinting. To gain preliminary information on the impact (if any) of the first exposure on the birds' subsequent perceptual behavior, some of the chicks were retested for 10 min. in the same situation 4–8 hr. later using exodus calls which were unfamiliar to them. If auditory imprinting took place during the first exposure, a decrement in strength of following should occur during testing in comparison to control subgroups reexposed to the familiar exodus call. (To make this sort of test valid, the initial response strength of the subgroups was equated as closely as possible.)

The 57 chicks which had following in the Chicken Vocal condition were divided into two groups and reexposed to the model while it emitted the Chicken exodus call or the Wood duck exodus call. In the test, the control group ($N = 29$) followed for an average of 343.58 sec. ($SD = 186.01$), while Ss exposed to the unfamiliar Wood duck call averaged only 86.82 sec. ($SD = 126.34$), a difference reliable at $p < .00006$. Thus, the decrement observed upon retesting chicks which had been previously exposed to the Chicken exodus call indicated that auditory imprinting had taken place. Moreover, the decrement shown by Ss whose original exposure took place at 21 days 12–23 hr. was greater ($p < .05$) than that of any of the other three age groups. This particular developmental age period would seem to be one of unusual sensitivity vis-à-vis the Chicken call in chicks with posthatch ages of 10–31 hr.

The 20 chicks which had followed in the Wood Duck Vocal condition were divided into two groups of 10 and retested with the Wood duck call or the Chicken call. In the test, the control group followed for an average of 269.9 sec. ($SD = 170.25$), while Ss exposed to the unfamiliar Chicken call averaged 313.3 sec. ($SD = 153.09$), a statistically insignificant *increase* in strength of following. Thus, judging from the absence of a decrement in the test, chicks initially exposed to the Wood duck call had not been aurally imprinted.

Finally, the 26 chicks which had followed in the Mallard Vocal condition were divided into two groups and retested with the Mallard call and Chicken call, respectively. In the test, the control group ($N = 12$) averaged 221.2 sec. ($SD = 191.81$) and Ss exposed to the unfamiliar Chicken call ($N = 14$) followed for an average of 419.0 sec. ($SD = 109.64$). This increase was statistically significant ($p < .05$). Thus, based upon the absence of a decrement in the test, the chicks' prior exposure to the Mallard exodus call did not result in auditory imprinting.

Discussion

The Chicken exodus call is a very potent auditory stimulus for naive chicks, both in the sense of initiating the following response and in the sense of reducing responsiveness to other calls when the chick has initially followed the parental call of its own species. When chicks have initially followed the parental call of another species, their subsequent responsiveness is not reduced when they are later given an opportunity to follow a model emitting the exodus call of their own species. Thus, the results of Experiment 2 support the conclusion of Experiment 1: birds can identify their own species on the basis of species-typical auditory stimulation emanating from the parent and this general identification occurs without the benefit of known forms of learning.

EXPERIMENT 3

The next experiments were designed with two purposes in mind: (a) to determine whether parentally naive ducklings would choose the parental call of their own species in a simultaneous discrimination situation, thereby further substantiating the above conclusion, and (b) to delineate the conditions required to shift the duckling's naive preference for the parental call of its own species to that of another species, thereby indicating that a process like auditory learning or auditory imprinting can operate in the establishment of preferential filial contact with species *other* than their own.

Experiment 3 concerns the choice behavior of naive ducklings in a situation in which they could approach or follow a model emitting the parental call of their own species or a model emitting the parental call of the Chicken. The second part of the experiment involved testing the choice behavior of ducklings which had been exposed before testing to the parental call of the Chicken hen while they were in the brooder after hatching; the procedure roughly simulated the natural situation in which ducklings are first exposed to auditory stimulation from the parent, with the important exception that in the field the ducklings would be exposed to the call of the parent of their *own* species prior to leaving the nest (Gottlieb, 1963b).

Method

Forty-nine Peking ducklings (*Anas platyrhynchos*) were hatched and reared under the circumstances specified in Experiment 1 except where otherwise noted.

Within 16–35 hr. after hatching, when their developmental age was 27 days 12 hr. to 28 days 23 hr., the ducklings were placed in the apparatus equidistant from two stuffed replicas of Peking hens. One hen was $90°$ to the left and the other hen $90°$ to the right of the duckling. The speaker in the underside of one model emitted the parental call of the Chicken hen, while the speaker in the underside of the other model emitted the parental call of the Mallard hen (*Anas platyrhynchos*). To rule out possible biasing effects, intensity levels of the two calls at the duckling's starting position were equated at 63–66 db., the speakers in the underside of the models were exactly the same distance from the duckling's starting position, and the calls were systematically rotated between the models (in a counterbalanced design) at the start of testing each duckling.

The simultaneous choice or discrimination test lasted 20 min. and contained three subtests. For the first 4 min. the models were stationary and calling (4-min. approach test), while for the next 10 min. the models were moving and calling (10-min. following test). At 14 min. both models fell silent for 10 sec. while the calls were interchanged (by remote control) between the models. Then, as each model emitted the call previously emitted by the other, the models continued to move for the final 6 min. (6-min. following test) of the 20-min. period.

An approach response was recorded in the 4-min. approach test when the duckling came within 4 in. of the model (gauged by an ellipse painted on the floor below both models). The "strength" of the approach response was measured by the amount of time the duckling stayed within 4 in. of the model. In order for a duckling to be credited with a *choice* or *preference* during any of the subtests, the duckling had to stay with or follow one model more than *twice* the time it accumulated with the other model during that subtest. (Following time was scored according to the same criteria employed previously.)

Previous auditory experience. One group ($N = 24$) was exposed to the choice situation without any prior auditory experience other than that gained by possibly hearing themselves in individual visual isolation (darkness) in the brooder. The other group ($N = 25$), while in the same situation in the brooder, was also exposed to the Chicken call at approximately 72-db. intensity measured in the immediate vicinity of the duckling in its individual carton in the brooder for 4–12 hr. prior to the test, with a minimum of 2 hr. immediately preceding the start of the test. The background noise level for both groups was the same as that reported in Experiment 1.

Results

Tables 2 and 3 show the preference behavior of the two groups of Peking ducklings in the simultaneous choice test. It is clear that in all three stages of the test (a) the parentally naive ducklings strongly favored the parental call of their own species and (b) that prior experience with the parental call of the Chicken hen did not diminish this preference. Further, as can be seen in Table 2, previous exposure to the Chicken call did not affect the latency or strength of the ducklings' response to that call in any way. Rather, in the 10-min. following test, the ducklings given previous experience with the Chicken call began following the model emitting the parental call of their *own* species more quickly and followed that model even more strongly than did the parentally naive ducklings.

EXPERIMENT 4

In Experiment 1, the Wood duck (*Aix sponsa*) call was significantly more effective than the Chicken call in instigating the following response of naive Peking ducklings. Hence, prior experience with the Wood duck call might more readily diminish or alter the Peking duckling's preference for the parental call of its species than did previous experience with the Chicken call. Thus, Experiment 4 is a replication of Experiment 3 using the Wood duck call instead of the Chicken call in competition with the parent call of the species.

Method

The Ss were 30 Peking ducklings, 15 of which were parentally naive and 15 of which were previously exposed to the parental call of the Wood duck. Other experimental details were identical with those of Experiment 3.

Results

In Table 2 it can be seen that without exception the parentally naive Peking ducklings favored the parental call of their own species over that of the Wood duck and that previous experience with the Wood duck call failed to alter that preference.

The data in Table 2 indicate that previous exposure to the Wood duck call did not reduce the latency or enhance the strength with which the ducklings followed that call and that the parental call of the species (Mallard) was vastly superior to the Wood duck call on all measures in both the 4-min. approach test and 10-min. following test.

Discussion

The results of Experiment 3 and 4 indicate (a) that parentally naive ducklings can discriminate the parental call of their own species from the parental calls of other species in a simultaneous discrimination situation, (b that they prefer the parental call of their own species over those of other species, and (c) that sheer passive exposure to the parental call of another species is insufficient to shift the ducklings' preference away from the call of their own species.

TABLE 2 Preference, Latency, and Duration of Responses of Ducklings in Simultaneous Choice Tests between Exodus Calls of Mallard Duck and Other Species

Previous auditory experience	N	% responding	% preference Mallard	% preference Other	Latency Mallard M	Latency Mallard SD	Latency Other M	Latency Other SD	Latency p	Duration Mallard M	Duration Mallard SD	Duration Other M	Duration Other SD	Duration p
					Mallard call vs. Chicken call: 4-min. approach test									
None	24	63	73	20	107.5	73.2	209.7	57.0	.008	89.4	62.8	18.1	32.2	<.001
Chicken call	25	76	79	16	112.0	73.7	184.9	84.7	.005	104.2	75.6	18.0	40.4	<.001
					Mallard call vs. Chicken call: 10-min. following test									
None	24	71	76	24	264.9	253.5	510.4	184.3	.005	225.6	205.2	27.9	74.9	<.001
Chicken call	25	72	89	11	119.2	182.0	546.6	158.8	.001	401.7	188.3	32.8	112.1	<.001
					Mallard call vs. Wood duck call: 4-min. approach test									
None	15	73	100	0	78.3	64.2	223.5	54.6	<.001	120.2	56.8	2.4	7.8	<.001
Wood duck call	15	73	91	9	81.8	71.5	224.2	52.5	<.001	104.3	68.9	14.9	49.5	<.001
					Mallard call vs. Wood duck call: 10-min. following test									
None	15	73	100	0	65.5	70.5	600.0	0.0	<.001	380.9	145.6	.0	.0	<.001
Wood duck call	15	93	100	0	81.9	111.4	572.0	104.8	<.001	295.2	230.0	3.8	14.2	<.001

[a] All comparisons of latencies between groups differing in previous auditory experience only were not significant except the 10-min. following test for those trained on None vs. Chicken call which preferred Mallard call ($p = .05$).

[b] All comparisons of durations between groups differing in previous auditory experience only were not significant except the 10-min. following test for those trained on None vs. Chicken calls which preferred Mallard call ($p < .01$).

[c] In certain instances the preference percentages total less than 100 because all responding animals did not show a preference between the two calls.

TABLE 3   Auditory Preference Changes of Ducklings on 6-Min. Following
Test in Simultaneous Choice Situation

Previous auditory experience	N	% responding	N	Mallard followers		N	Chicken followers	
				Switching to Mallard			Switching to chicken	
				N	%		N	%
Chicken call vs. Mallard call								
None	24	71	13	13	100	4	3	75
Chicken call	25	72	16	13	81	2	0	0
Wood duck call vs. Mallard call								
None	15	73	11	11	100	0	0	0
Wood duck call	15	93	14	12	86	0	0	0

EXPERIMENT 5

In Experiments 3 and 4, passive exposure of Peking ducklings to the exodus call of the Chicken and Wood duck, though it roughly simulated the naturalistic experience which hatchlings have with their *own* species call (Gottlieb, 1963b, 1963c), did not induce a preference for these calls (i.e., did not result in imprinting) when the ducklings were subsequently tested in the presence of the parental call of their own species. It is of interest to determine whether more active commerce with an extraspecific call (e.g., the parental call of the Wood duck hen) might have a greater influence than passive exposure to that call. Thus, in the present experiment naive Peking ducklings were exposed to a single Peking hen model as it emitted the exodus call of the Wood duck hen. Those ducklings which followed the model were subsequently placed in one of two simultaneous discrimination situations: One, in which the choice was between the Wood duck and Mallard calls, and the other in which the choice was between the Wood duck and Chicken calls. The latter situation was employed to show that imprinting, defined as above, occurs quite readily when the parental call of the species (Mallard) is absent from the test.

Method

Peking ducklings were hatched and reared in the laboratory under the same circumstances previously specified.

Within 12–23 hr. after hatching, when their developmental ages were 27 days—28 days 11 hr., the ducklings were placed in the apparatus where they were individually exposed to a moving stuffed Peking hen as it emitted the Wood duck parental exodus call for a 20-min. period. Those (20) ducklings which actively followed the model (following time was scored the same as in previous studies) were returned to the apparatus 2–10 hr. later for one of two choice tests.

The conditions of the simultaneous choice test were the same as those described in Experiment 4. For one group of ducklings ($N = 10$) the speaker in the underside of one model emitted the parental call of the Wood duck hen while the speaker in the underside of the other model emitted the parental call of the Mallard hen. To ascertain the effects of prior experience on subsequent choice behavior when the parental call of the species was not present, the other 10 ducklings were exposed to the two models as one emitted the Wood duck parental call and the other emitted the Chicken parental call. As in previously described simultaneous choice tests, the overall intensity levels of the calls were equated at 63–66 db. The criteria for recording a preference in the choice test were the same as in the previous experiments—a preference was recorded only when the duckling stayed with (approach test) or followed (following test) one model for more than twice the time it accumulated with the other model in any one test.

Results

As indicated in Table 4, one brief active experience with the Wood duck call resulted in imprinting when the ducklings were tested with the Wood duck vs. Chicken calls, i.e., the ducklings preferred the Wood duck over the Chicken call. However, one brief active experience with the Wood duck call was insufficient to establish imprinting when the ducklings were tested with the Wood duck vs. Mallard calls. In the latter test, the large majority of the ducklings chose the parental call of their species (Mallard) even though they had never heard it before. (In the unlikely event that the ducklings chose the Mallard call on the basis of "novelty," the ducklings which received the Wood duck vs. Chicken call test would have chosen the Chicken call, but they did not.)

Discussion

The findings of Experiment 5 demonstrated that one brief active experience with an extraspecific parental call resulted in imprinting only when the duckling was subsequently tested with models emitting calls other than the parental call of their species. One active experience was insufficient to establish imprinting (selective discrimination based on previous experience or learning) when the duckling was subsequently tested with the familiar extraspecific call vs. the parental call of their own species.

EXPERIMENT 6

The final experiment in this series demonstrates that, by increasing the amount of active commerce with the Wood duck call, it is possible to diminish the Peking ducklings' strong naive preference for the Mallard call in a simultaneous choice test.

Method

Twenty Peking ducklings, 10 of which had actively followed the parental Wood duck call during two 20-min. periods and 10 of which had actively followed the Wood duck call during four 20-min. periods, were exposed to a

TABLE 4 Auditory Preferences of Ducklings in Simultaneous Choice Test as a Function of Previous 20-Min. Exposures to Exodus Call of Wood Duck

Experimental condition			4-min. approach test	% preference		10-min. following test	% preference[a]		6-min. following test Wood duck followers	% switching to Wood duck	Followers of other species	% switching to other species
Number of exposures	Test: Wood duck vs.	N	% responding	Wood Duck	Other Species	% responding	Wood Duck	Other Species	N		N	
1	Chicken	10	70	71	29	90	100	0	9	78	0	0
1	Mallard	10	70	29	71	100	10	70	3	0	7	57
2	Mallard	10	70	43	57	100	50	50	5	100	5	60
4	Mallard	10	70	71	29	90	56	33	5	80	3	0

[a]In certain instances the preference percentages total less than 100 because all of the responding animals did not show a preference between the two calls.

simultaneous choice test in which one model emitted the Mallard parental call and the other emitted the parental call of the Wood duck. The 20-min. exposures and the subsequent choice test occurred at intervals of 2–10 hr. The other experimental details were the same as those of Experiment 5, permitting comparisons with the one exposure group from Experiment 5.

Results

In Table 4 it can be seen that increasing the amount of active experience with the Wood duck call to four 20-min. exposures prior to testing eventually resulted in the majority of ducklings choosing that call over the Mallard call in a simultaneous discrimination test. It is of interest that the individual ducklings which preferred the Wood duck call over the Mallard call in the approach and following tests actually did not spend significantly more time actively following the model during the previous training exposures than did the ducklings which chose the Mallard call upon testing.

In Table 5, with respect to the 10-min. following test, it can be seen that as a function of only one 20-min. active exposure to the Wood duck call, the ducklings still followed the Mallard call more strongly and began to follow it more quickly (latency) than they did the Wood duck call. Increasing the amount of previous active exposure to the Wood duck call led to an increase in the latency of response and a decrease in strength of response to the Mallard call, while decreasing the latency and enhancing the strength of response to the Wood duck call. However, it is important to note that increasing the amount of active experience with the Wood duck call did not result in the ducklings following the Wood duck call more strongly or with a shorter latency than the Mallard call in the 10-min. following test.

Discussion

The results of Experiment 6 showed that, by increasing the number of prior active experiences with an extraspecific parental call, it was possible to diminish the ducklings' response to the parental call of their own species while enhancing their response to the familiar extraspecific call during a simultaneous discrimination test. In essence, however, the Peking duckling's naive preference for the parental call of its own species is strongly resistant to modification by experience, though this strong preference does not hamper or preclude the duckling from showing the conventional effects of imprinting when it does not have the subsequent opportunity to respond to the parental call of its own species (i.e., when it is totally deprived of access to the parental call of its species).

DISCUSSION

The present set of experiments demonstrates the existence of an auditory perceptual mechanism for supraindividual identification of species in parentally naive ducklings and chicks. This mechanism arises during ontogeny without the participation of known forms of learning and obviously requires a conceptualization different from learning or imprinting. The presence of such an auditory

TABLE 5 Latency and Duration of Response to Mallard and Wood Duck Calls in Simultaneous Choice Test as a Function of Amount of Previous Active Experience with Wood Duck Call

Number of exposures	N	Latency (in sec.)				Duration (in sec.)			
		Mallard		Wood duck		Mallard		Wood duck	
		M	SD	M	SD	M	SD	M	SD
				4-min. approach test					
1	10	111.9	92.1	150.0	113.1	116.6	88.4	52.0	85.8
2	10	134.1	111.9	173.6	84.6	99.3	105.1	65.6	83.9
4	10	107.4	124.1	120.1	96.1	75.3	110.0	115.4	94.7
				10-min. following test[a]					
1	10	19.7	15.1	398.0	262.9[b]	404.9	177.7	81.7	140.4*
2	10	204.1	276.1	235.8	246.4	164.6	201.2	194.0	220.9
4	10	299.7	290.3	300.2	291.1	194.1	254.1	205.7	220.8

[a]Comparison of 1 and 4 exposure groups yielded significant p values for all 4 comparisons in the 10-min. following test; for Mallard latencies, p = .01; for Wood duck latencies, p = .02; for Mallard durations, p < .05; for Wood duck durations, p = .05.

[b]p < .001.

perceptual mechanism in ducklings and chicks would seem to greatly reduce the likelihood of the birds' becoming imprinted to species other than their own in the normal course of events in nature. Though the naive preference of ducklings and chicks for the parental call of their own species restricts the range of visual stimuli to which they can be imprinted under natural conditions, it is obvious that visual learning of species characteristics can take place in the context of this preference. Thus, imprinting would seem to play an important though secondary (supporting) role in directing the avian neonate's social activities toward members of its own species under natural circumstances.

That newly hatched *A. platyrhynchos* ducklings have the capability of identifying a female adult of their own species on the basis of species-typical auditory stimulation is in accord with impressions of this species presented by Lorenz himself (1937, p. 268). That the same capability is present in domestic chicks confirms the implications for this species found in Spalding's study (1873) as well as in Ramsay's (1951) seminaturalistic work.

Two important questions emerge from the present results. First, what are the ontogenetic (possibly prenatal) events in the history of the individual which give rise to the strong attraction of the parental call of the species in ducklings and chicks? With knowledge of the behavioral and stimulative sequence in the chick embryo (Kuo, 1932) as well as the duck embryo (Gottlieb & Kuo, 1965), it seems worthwhile to try to find an empirical answer to this question rather than positing an unanalyzed factor of instinctive parental or species identification.

The second question concerns the function of imprinting or other forms of learning in further shaping the avian neonate's auditory perceptual preferences and discriminations. With regard to parental recognition and species identification, auditory learning is germane to the problem of individual recognition. For example, auditory learning or auditory imprinting is requisite to the neonate's ability to discriminate the call of its own parent from the call of another parent of the same species. There are small individual peculiarities in the calls of parents of the same species and, in nature, hole-nesting ducklings have been observed to distinguish the call of their own parent from the call of another parent of the same species directly upon leaving the nest (Gottlieb, 1963c, p. 90). Both hole- and ground-nesting species of ducklings are exposed to the call of their parent before leaving the nest (Gottlieb, 1963b), and the phenomenon of individual recognition on the basis of apparently slight auditory differences is worthy of examination under the controlled conditions of the laboratory. In light of present results it would not be surprising to find that avian neonates can learn finer discriminations between calls of their own species than between calls of other species.

The final point to be made concerning auditory learning or auditory imprinting is that such a process can operate in establishing preferential filial contact with species other than the neonate's own (i.e., extraspecific filial attachment). This extraspecific preference can be established readily when the parental call of the duckling's own species is not available to the bird (Experiment 5), but an extraspecific attachment is not easily established when the parental call of its own species *is* available to the bird (Experiment 6). Thus, imprinting can play a role in fostering extraspecific social attachments in those instances when the bird is deprived of auditory contact with its own species.

Finally, with regard to the question of critical periods in behavioral and perceptual development, the present results indicate that the idea of a unitary critical period for the following response is incorrect. Within each species in the present experiments, the shape of "the" critical period differed as the sensory and perceptual attributes of the model were altered. Though this is not new information, the present critical period results offer support for the idea that the shape of any particular critical period curve is a function not only of critical organismic factors, but also of the contemporaneous sensory and perceptual aspects of the parent-surrogate and the stimulation available to the bird prior to exposure to the surrogate (Gottlieb & Klopfer, 1962; Moltz, 1963). In other words, organismic or maturational indices are always partly a function of the stimulative history of the organism from which they cannot be extricated or independently specified.

References

Collias, N. E. An ecological and functional classification of animal sounds. In W. E. Lanyon & W. N. Tavolga (Eds.), *Animal sounds and communication*. Washington, D. C.: Intelligencer, 1960. Pp. 368–391.

Collias, N. E., & Collias, E. C. Some mechanisms of family integration in ducks. *Auk*, 1956, *73*, 378–400.

Collias, N. E., & Joos, M. The spectrographic analysis of sound signals of the domestic fowl. *Behaviour, Leiden*, 1952, *5*, 175–188.

Fabricius, E. Crucial periods in the development of the following response in young nidifugous birds. Paper read at XVII International Congress of Psychology, Washington, D. C., August 1963.

Gottlieb, G. Developmental age as a baseline for determination of the critical period in imprinting. *J. comp. physiol. Psychol.*, 1961, *54*, 422–427.

Gottlieb, G. Following-response initiation in ducklings: Age and sensory stimulation. *Science*, 1963, *140*, 399–400. (a)

Gottlieb, G. "Imprinting" in nature. *Science*, 1963, *139*, 497–498. (b)

Gottlieb, G. A naturalistic study of imprinting in Wood ducklings (*Aix sponsa*). *J. comp. physiol. Psychol.*, 1963, *56*, 86–91. (c)

Gottlieb, G. Refrigerating eggs prior to the incubation as a way of reducing error in calculating developmental age in imprinting experiments. *Anim. Behav.*, 1963, *11*, 290–292. (d)

Gottlieb, G., & Klopfer, P. H. The relation of developmental age to auditory and visual imprinting. *J. comp. physiol. Psychol.*, 1962, *55*, 821–826.

Gottlieb, G., & Kuo, Z.-Y. Development of behavior in the duck embryo. *J. comp. physiol. Psychol.*, 1965, *59*, 183–188.

Gray, P. The releasers of imprinting: Differential reactions to color as a function of maturation. *J. comp. physiol. Psychol.*, 1961, *54*, 597–601.

Heinroth, O. Beiträge zur Biologie, namentlich Ethologie und Physiologie der Anatiden. *Verh. Int. Ornithol. Kongr.*, 1910, *5*, 589–702.

Hess, E. H. Imprinting. *Science*, 1959, *130*, 133–141.

Klopfer, P. H., & Gottlieb, G. Imprinting and behavioral polymorphism: Auditory and visual imprinting in domestic ducks (*Anas platyrhynchos*) and the involvement of the critical period. *J. comp. physiol. Psychol.*, 1962, *55*, 126–130.

Kuo, Z.-Y. Ontogeny of embryonic behavior in aves: IV. The influence of embryonic movements upon the behavior after hatching. *J. comp. Psychol.*, 1932, *14*, 109–121.

Lorenz, K. The companion in the bird's world. *Auk*, 1937, *54*, 245–273.

Moltz, H. Imprinting: An epigenetic approach. *Psychol. Rev.*, 1963, *70*, 123–138.

Ramsay, A. O. Familial recognition in domestic birds. *Auk*, 1951, *68*, 1–16.

Schaefer, H. H., & Hess, E. H. Color preferences in imprinting objects. *Z. Tierpsychol.*, 1958, *16*, 161–172.

Spalding, D. A. Instinct: With original observations on young animals. *MacMillan's Mag.*, 1873, *27*, 282–293. (Reprinted: *Brit. J. anim. Behav.*, 1954, *2*, 2–11).

Animal migration has long been suspected of involving an interaction of instinct and learning as complex as that in imprinting. The elegant work of Arthur Hasler on salmon migration (Hasler, 1966) showed that salmon are prepared to learn about and remember for years the unique odor of their natal stream and use this memory to return there and spawn. Similarly, Steven Emlen shows in the next reading that indigo buntings are prepared to learn about the circumpolar constellations and use these cues in migration. Some biologists had believed that a fixed template for the night sky was genetically given, but by exposing hatchlings to Orion as the polar constellation, Emlen shows that buntings learn selectively about those stars that rotate most slowly in their night "sky," even if they are not the natural circumpolar stars. Such plasticity is evolutionarily important. In 13,000 years, Polaris in the Little Dipper will no longer be the North Star; rather Vega, in Lyra, 47 degrees away from Polaris, will be. It would be a woefully maladaptive indigo bunting that had a genetic template and insisted on migrating toward or away from Polaris 13,000 years from now. Since this is a short time on the evolutionary scale, it seems obvious that prepared plasticity of a kind that Emlen has discovered is highly adaptive.

27

CELESTIAL ROTATION: ITS IMPORTANCE IN THE DEVELOPMENT OF MIGRATORY ORIENTATION

Stephen T. Emlen

Three groups of indigo buntings were hand-raised in various conditions of visual isolation from celestial cues. Birds prevented from viewing the night sky prior to the autumn migration season were unable to select the normal migration direction when tested under planetarium skies. By contrast, individuals allowed exposure to a normal, rotating, planetarium sky as juveniles, displayed typical southerly directional preferences. The third group was exposed to an incorrect planetarium sky in which the stars rotated about a fictitious axis. When tested during the autumn, these birds took up the "correct" migration direction relative to the new axis of rotation.

These results argue against the hypothesis of a "genetic star map." Rather they suggest a maturation process in which stellar cues come to be associated with a directional reference system provided by the axis of celestial rotation.

The ontogenetic development of animal orientation abilities has received very little study. Early workers were impressed by the fact that the young of many species of birds migrate alone, setting out on a course they have never traveled before without the benefit of experienced companions. This suggested that directional tendencies must develop without any prior migratory experience and therefore must be entirely genetically predetermined (1).

From *Science*, 170 (1970), 1198–1201.

This work was supported, in part, by the National Science Foundation *GB 13046 X*. I thank Margaret Platt and Carol Conley for assistance in rearing and testing the birds. I also thank members of Cornell's orientation seminar group for their comments and criticisms. The final manuscript benefited from a critical reading by Howard C. Howland.

Field studies, however, point to a dichotomy of navigation capabilities between young and adult birds. When birds of several species were captured and displaced from their normal autumnal migration routes, the adults corrected for this displacement and returned to the normal winter quarters while immatures (birds on their first autumnal migration) did not (2). Prior migratory experience improved orientation performance.

I arrived at a somewhat similar conclusion from studies of the migratory orientation of caged indigo buntings; the consistency and accuracy of the orientation exhibited by adults was greater than that of young, hand-raised birds (3). Furthermore, young birds prevented from viewing celestial cues during their pre-migratory development showed weaker orientation tendencies than those allowed exposure to the natural surroundings, including the day-night sky. I speculated that the maturation process was a complex one involving the coupling of stellar information with some secondary set of reference cues.

The following experiments were designed to test more precisely the ability of hand-reared birds to use celestial cues, and to determine the possible importance of celestial rotation in providing an axis of reference for direction determination.

Twenty-six nestling indigo buntings between the ages of 4 and 10 days were removed from their nests and hand-raised in the laboratory, where their visual experience with celestial cues was carefully controlled. I housed the birds in 2 x 2 x 2 foot (65 x 65 x 65 cm) cages in an 8 x 8 foot (2.4 x 2.4 m) room equipped with a hung ceiling made of translucent plastic. This prevented the birds from ever viewing a point source of light during their development. Both flourescent and incandescent lights were present above the artificial ceiling and the day length was controlled by an astronomical time clock to simulate that present outdoors.

The birds were hand-fed at frequent intervals until approximately 25 days of age (15 days postfledging), when they became self-sufficient. I then placed them in one of three experimental groups. The first, Group A, never left the 8 x 8 foot living quarters until I tested their orientational tendencies during the autumn migration season. These birds never were allowed to view either the sun or the night sky.

The birds of Group B also were prevented from viewing the sun. However, these individuals were taken into the Cornell research planetarium and exposed to the normal night sky during the months of August and September (4). The artificial sky was set to duplicate that present outdoors and was changed appropriately to simulate the seasonal changes of hour angle positions that occur between August and the migration season. The Spitz star projector was modified to rotate at a speed of one revolution per 24 hours, thus duplicating the normal pattern of celestial rotation. The young buntings continued to live in the room described above, but three times a week they would be removed to the planetarium at 9:00 P. M. and returned to their normal cages between 4:30 and 5:00 A. M. (Eastern Daylight Time).

The birds of Group C also were subjected to planetarium exposure. They were taken on three different nights each week and exposed for a similar length of time to an artificial sky. However, this artificial sky was abnormal in several respects.

Once again I had modified the star projector, this time by constructing a special attachment arm that allowed the celestial sphere to be rotated about any axis of my choosing. For Group C, I selected the bright star Betelgeuse as the new "pole star" and the constellation Orion became the dominant pattern in the new "circumpolar" area of the sky.

This new sky setting was selected for several reasons. First, a bright star is located at the pole of the new axis. Second, a very bright constellation is located in the "circumpolar" area. This area has been determined to be of special importance in the celestial orientation process of this species (5). Third, the "hour angle" position was selected carefully so that the actual northern circumpolar stars (in particular the constellations Ursa Major and Cassiopea and the star Polaris) were present in this artificial sky. They are located just to the south of the new "celestial equator" and move progressively across the sky from east to west as the night progresses.

The logic behind the experiment is this. If celestial rotation provides a reference axis for migratory orientation, then the birds of Group C might adopt this incorrect axis and orient their migratory activity in an inappropriate direction. On the other hand, if young birds possess a genetically predetermined star map as has been proposed by some authors (6), then the birds should orient "south" with reference to the normal circumpolar area of the sky. These two "south" directions should be easily distinguishable since they range from 110 to 180 degrees apart in the planetarium settings of Group C.

During their exposure to these planetarium skies, the buntings were placed in small, funnel-shaped orientation cages (7). In this way they became accustomed to the experimental apparatus that would be used later. The birds from Group A were given comparable experience in the orientation cages but always in the isolation room. I did not record behavior during these sessions, so the degree of nocturnal activity or attentiveness to the artificial skies prior to the migration season is unknown.

Each individual bird from Groups B and C received 22 nights of exposure to the appropriate planetarium sky.

The birds completed the postjuvenal molt and acquired visible subcutaneous fat deposits in late September. This was taken as a criterion for migratory readiness and experiments were conducted throughout the month of October and into early November. The birds were placed under the same planetarium sky that they had been exposed to previously with the exception that the sky was now held stationary. By preventing direct access to rotational information, I tested whether the birds had integrated information from celestial configurations with the potential reference framework provided by the axis of rotation. The experimental design called for testing the same birds under a rotating sky if no directional preferences appeared under these conditions.

I tested up to seven buntings simultaneously, placing their funnel cages as close to the centrally located star projector as possible in order to minimize any distortion of the artificial sky. The only change from the "exposure" situation was that the cages now had a freshly inked floor that permitted the accumulation of directional information by the footprint technique (7). Each experiment lasted 2 hours and the hour-angle position of the planetarium sky was set to correspond with the midpoint of that 2-hour period.

For each data distribution, I tested the null hypothesis of randomness by the "v" modification of the Rayleigh test (8), with the expected orientation being southward. Mean direction was calculated by vector analysis (9).

The results are shown in Figs. 1 through 3 and in Table 1. Of the ten individual buntings of Group A, *none* demonstrated a clear-cut directional tendency. This was true whether one analyzed the total activity of each bird or the mean directions taken during replicate tests (Fig. 1). These results argue against the existence of a hereditary star map that the buntings can refer to for

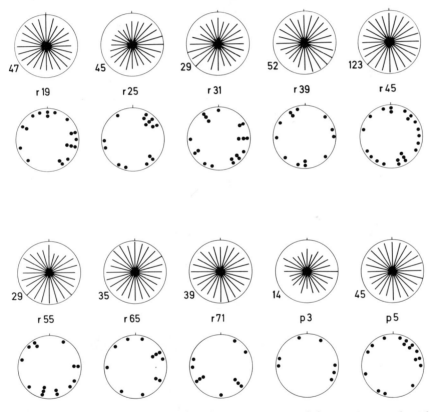

FIG. 1   Orientation of young indigo buntings prevented from viewing celestial cues during their early development. The birds were tested under a stationary, autumnal planetarium sky set for 42°N latitude. Top: Vector-diagram summaries plotted such that the radius equals the greatest number of units of activity in any one 15-degree sector. The number that this represents is written at the lower left of each diagram. Bottom: Distributions of mean directions for all experiments.

navigational information. Rather, they suggest that visual-celestial experience during early ontogeny is important for the normal maturation of stellar orientation abilities.

The results from the buntings of Group B support this interpretation. Of the eight birds, seven exhibited a southerly preference in their nocturnal restlessness, the appropriate direction for their first autumnal migration flight. (Fig. 2). The data from the eighth bird, r47, do not deviate from random. Although the degree of scatter in the data is large (particularly for r41 and r67), the improvement over the performance of isolate birds (Group A) is readily apparent.

Figure 3 shows the findings from Group C when directions are *plotted relative to the new axis of rotation*, that is, with the position of Betelgeuse defining north. All seven birds displayed a "southerly" orientation indicating a realignment of directional behavior to correspond with the new axis of rotation (10).

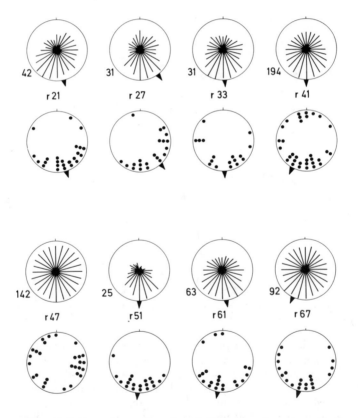

FIG. 2 Orientation of young indigo buntings permitted regular viewings of a normal, rotating, planetarium sky during their early development.

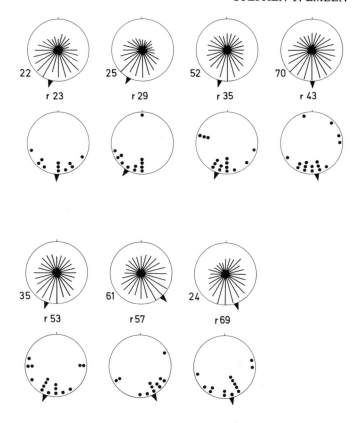

FIG. 3 Orientation of young indigo buntings exposed to a planetarium sky that rotated about an incorrect axis during their early development. The data are plotted with the new "pole star" (Betelgeuse, of the constellation Orion) designating "north" or 0 degrees.

There was no tendency to move toward true stellar south. Once again, these results are inconsistent with the hypothesis of a predetermined template of star positions.

Taken together, these findings provide strong evidence that early visual experience plays an important role in the development of celestial orientation abilities of indigo buntings. I hypothesize that fledgling buntings respond to the apparent rotational motion of the night sky. The fact that stars located near the celestial axis move through much smaller arcs (have a slower linear velocity) than those near the celestial equator allows the birds to locate a north-south directional axis. Stars and patterns of stars are of no value for direction finding until their positions are learned with reference to this rotational framework. Once this coupling of stellar and rotational information has occurred, a bird can locate the rotational axis (and, hence, geographic direction) from star patterns alone. This implies that celestial motion per se should become a secondary or

TABLE 1 Orientation of Young Indigo Buntings Hand-Raised under Various Conditions of Visual Isolation from Celestial Cues

Bird	No. of experiments	Units of activity (total N)	P ("V" test)	Mean direction
Group A				
r19		963	0.649	—
	19		0.836	—
r25		846	0.392	—
	15		0.616	—
r31		573	0.388	—
	19		0.261	—
r39		1,086	0.563	—
	13		0.422	—
r45		2,706	0.147	—
	22		0.356	—
r55		604	0.131	—
	15		0.102	—
r65		762	0.701	—
	12		0.751	—
r71		722	0.270	—
	11		0.069	$(195°)$
p3		238	0.500	—
	7		0.907	—
p5		964	0.695	—
	16		0.943	—
Group B				
r21		684	0.000	$169°$
	24		0.000	$165°$
r27		455	0.006	$145°$
	21		0.003	$138°$
r33		487	0.000	$178°$
	17		0.001	$182°$
r41		3,293	0.000	$182°$
	32		0.024	$208°$
r47		2,932	0.205	—
	28		0.452	—
r51		251	0.000	$181°$
	19		0.000	$186°$
r61		1,024	0.000	$174°$
	21		0.001	$191°$
r67		1,777	0.025	$207°$
	21		0.001	$195°$

Group A: birds prevented from viewing the night sky. Group B: birds permitted view of a normal planetarium sky.

TABLE 1 (continued)

Bird	No. of experiments	Units of activity (total N)	P ("V" test)	Mean direction
Group C				
r23		354	0.003	195°
	11		0.000	186°
r29		343	0.000	207°
	12		0.001	211°
r35		813	0.002	194°
	15		0.000	198°
r43		1,249	0.000	180°
	16		0.001	172°
r53		592	0.014	200°
	16		0.001	201°
r57		1,056	0.005	138°
	12		0.002	156°
r69		379	0.003	161°
	14		0.000	169°

Group C: birds exposed to a planetarium sky that rotated about an incorrect axis. See text for explanation.

redundant orientational cue for adult birds. The accurate orientation of caged migrants under stationary planetarium skies supports this view (11, 12).

This study demonstrates the complexity involved in the maturation of one orientational system available to indigo buntings. Undoubtedly, the picture will become more complex as we learn more about additional components of avian guidance systems.

References and Notes

1. D. R. Griffin, *Bird Migration* (Doubleday & Company, New York, 1964); K. Schmidt-Koenig, in *Advances in the Study of Behavior*, R. Hinde, D. Lehrman, and E. Shaw, Eds. (Academic Press, New York, 1965); G. V. T. Matthews, *Bird Navigation* (2nd edition, Cambridge University Press, New York, 1968).
2. W. Rüppel, *J. Ornith.* 92, 106 (1944). A. C. Perdeck, *Ardea* 46, 1 (1958); 55, 194 (1967); F. Bellrose, *Wilson Bulletin* 70, 20 (1958).
3. S. T. Emlen, *Living Bird* 8, 113 (1969).
4. The Cornell research planetarium is a 30-foot (9-m)-diameter, air-supported dome equipped with a Spitz A-3-P star projector.
5. S. T. Emlen, *Auk* 84, 463 (1967).
6. F. G. Sauer, *Zeit. Tierpsychol.* 14, 29 (1957); *Sci. Amer.* Aug. 44 (1958).
7. S. T. Emlen and J. T. Emlen, Jr., *Auk* 83, 361 (1966). The bottoms of the cages were not inked during the "exposures" to planetarium skies in August and September.
8. D. Durand and J. A. Greenwood, *J. Geol.*, 66, 229 (1958).
9. E. Batschelet, *Amer. Inst. Biol. Sci. Monogr.* 1 (1965). Sample sizes for the Rayleigh test were determined by dividing the total number of units of activity, N, by a

correction factor. This divisor was determined empirically and represents the interval at which activity measures become independent of one another. (See Appendix 5 in reference 3.)

10. The eighth bird in this group, r49, developed the habit of "somersaulting" in the orientation cage. Since the resulting ink smudges represented an aberrant behavior pattern, they were not quantified. F. G. Sauer, *Zeit. Tierpsychol.* 14, 29 (1957). S. T. Emlen, *Auk* 84, 463 (1967); this study.

12. The hypothesis need not imply that buntings directly perceive the slow rate of celestial motion. One easily can locate the axis of rotation by making observations over longer periods of time and comparing the degree of movement of stars located at different points in the celestial sphere.

Comparative psychology has had in its ranks many who resisted general-process learning theory (e.g., Beach, 1950), and opted for an approach to learning which looked carefully at species differences. Schneirla (1959), Lehrman (1953), and others became acquainted with European ethology in the 1940s. Their theories resisted an easy instinct—learning dichotomy, as does ours. Their supporting experiments and criticisms—especially the criticism that behaviors invariant within a species need not be innate but could result from environmental invariance—have been recognized by ethologists as valuable contributions (Klopfer and Hailman, 1965; Eibl-Eibesfeldt, 1970). Some students of behavior express concern that truly comparative psychology has fallen off in recent years, but the following article by one of the foremost comparative psychologists, M. E. Bitterman, should be encouraging. He presents evidence which a general-process learning theorist using an "arbitrary" animal such as the white rat would not have gathered; this evidence indicates that different species may be capable of qualitatively different sorts of learning. Of course, division of learning across species is independent of preparedness, which is a within-species dimension, but recognition of any of the possible variations of the laws of learning in response to evolutionary pressure is central to a comprehensive psychology of learning.

28

PHYLETIC DIFFERENCES
IN LEARNING

M. E. Bitterman

One way to study the role of the brain in learning is to compare the learning of animals with different brains. Differences in brain structure may be produced by surgical means, or they may be found in nature—as when the learning of different species is compared. Of these two approaches the first (the neuro-surgical approach) has been rather popular, but the potentialities of the second still are largely unexplored. Students of learning in animals have been content for the most part to concentrate their attention on a few closely related mammalian forms, chosen largely for reasons of custom and convenience, which they have treated as representative of animals in general. Their work has been dominated almost from its inception by the hypothesis that the laws of learning are the same for all animals—that the wide differences in brain structure which occur in the animal series have a purely quantitative significance.

The hypothesis comes to us from Thorndike (1911), who more than any other man may be credited with having brought the study of animal intelligence into the laboratory. On the basis of his early comparative experiments, Thorndike decided that however much animals might differ in "what" they learned (which could be traced, he thought, to differences in their sensory, motor, and motivational properties), or in the "degree" of their learning ability (some seemed able to learn more than others, and more quickly), the principles which governed their learning were the same. Thorndike wrote:

> If my analysis is true, the evolution of behavior is a rather simple matter. Formally the crab, fish, turtle, dog, cat, monkey and baby have very similar intellects and characters. All are systems of connections subject to change by the laws of exercise and effect [p. 280].

From *American Psychologist,* 20 (1965), 396—410.

This paper was presented in March 1964, under the auspices of the National Science Foundation and of the National Institute of Mental Health, at the Institut de Psychologie in Paris, the Institute of Experimental Psychology in Oxford, the Institut für Hirnforschung in Zurich, and the Nencki Institute of Experimental Biology in Warsaw. The research described was supported by Grant MH-02857 from the National Institute of Mental Health and by Contract Nonr 2829(01) with the Office of Naval Research.

Although Thorndike's hypothesis was greeted with considerable skepticism, experiments with a variety of animals began to turn up functional similarities far more impressive than differences, and before long there was substantial disagreement only as to the *nature* of the laws which were assumed to hold for all animals. As acceptance of the hypothesis grew, the range of animals studied in experiments on learning declined—which, of course, was perfectly reasonable. If the laws of learning were the same everywhere in the animal series, there was nothing to be gained from the study of many different animals; indeed, standardization offered many advantages which it would be foolish to ignore. As the range of animals declined, however, so also did the likelihood of discovering any differences which might in fact exist.

It is difficult for the nonspecialist to appreciate quite how restricted has been the range of animals studied in experiments on animal learning because the restriction is so marked; the novelty of work with lower animals is such that two or three inexpressibly crude experiments with a flatworm may be better publicized than a hundred competent experiments with the rat. Some quantitative evidence on the degree of restriction was provided about 20 years ago by Schneirla, whose conclusion then was that "we do not have a comparative ˜psychology [Harriman, 1946, p. 314]." Schneirla's analysis was carried further by Beach (1950), who plotted the curves which are reproduced in Figure 1. Based on a count of all papers appearing between 1911 and 1948 in the *Journal of Animal Behavior* and its successors, the *Journal of Comparative Psychology*, and the *Journal of Comparative and Physiological Psychology*, the curves show how interest in the rat mounted while interest in submammalian

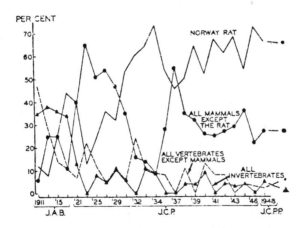

FIG. 1 Percentage of papers dealing with animals in each of four categories which appeared between 1911 and 1948 in the *Journal of Animal Behavior*, the *Journal of Comparative Psychology*, and the *Journal of Comparative and Physiological Psychology* (Beach, 1950). (The points at right, for the decade after 1948, were added by me.)

forms declined. By the '30s, a stable pattern had emerged: about 60% of papers on the rat, 30% on other mammals (mostly primates), and 10% on lower forms. The set of points at the extreme right, which I have added for the decade after 1948, shows no change in the pattern. You will note that these curves are based on papers published only in a single line of journals, and on all papers in those journals—not only the ones which deal with learning; but most of the papers *do* deal with learning, and I know of no other journal which is a richer source of information about learning in submammalians or which, if included in the tabulation, would alter the conclusion that what we know about learning in animals we know primarily from the intensive study of a small number of mammalian forms.

How widespread is the acceptance of Thorndike's hypothesis by contemporary theorists and systematists may be judged from a set of writings recently assembled by Koch (1959). Skinner is quite explicit in his assumption that which animal is studied "doesn't matter." When due allowance has been made for differences in sensory and motor characteristics, he explains, "what remains of . . . behavior shows astonishingly similar properties [Koch, 1959, p. 375]." Tolman, Miller, Guthrie, Estes, and Logan (representing Hull and Spence) rest their perfectly general conclusions about the nature of learning on the data of experiments with a few selected mammals—mostly rat, monkey, and man— skipping lightly back and forth from one to another as if indeed structure did not matter, although Miller "does not deny the possibility that men may have additional capacities which are much less well developed or absent in the lower mammals [Koch, 1959, p. 204]." Harlow alone makes a case for species differences in learning, pointing to the unequal rates of improvement shown by various mammals (mostly primates) trained in long series of discriminative problems, but he gives us no reason to believe that the differences are more than quantitative. While he implies clearly that the capacity for interproblem transfer may be absent entirely in certain lower animals—in the rat, he says, it exists only in a "most rudimentary form [Koch, 1959, p. 505] "—submammalian evidence is lacking.

Although I have been considering thus far only the work of the West, I do not think that things have been very different on the other side of the Curtain. The conditioning has been "classical" rather than "instrumental" in the main, and the favored animal has been the dog rather than the rat, but the range of animals studied in any detail has been small, at least until quite recently, and the principles discovered have been generalized widely. In the words of Voronin (1962), the guiding Pavlovian propositions have been that

> The conditioned reflex is a universal mechanism of activity acquired in the course of the organism's individual life. . . . [and that] In the course of evolution of the animal world there took place only a quantitative growth or complication of higher nervous activity [pp. 161–162].

These propositions are supported, Voronin believes, by the results of some recent Russian comparisons of mammalian and submammalian vertebrates. On the basis of these results, he defines three stages in the evolution of intelligence which are distinguished in terms of the increasing role of learning in the life of the individual organism, and in terms of the precision and delicacy of the learning process. He hastens to assure us, however, that there is nothing really new even at the highest stage, which differs from the others only quantitatively.

The results of the experiments which I shall now describe support quite another view. I began these experiments without very much in the way of conviction as to their outcome, although the formal attractions of the bold Thorndikian hypothesis were rather obvious, and I should have been pleased on purely esthetic grounds to be able to accept it. I was convinced only that the hypothesis had not yet received the critical scrutiny it seemed to warrant, and that it was much too important to be taken any longer on faith. With the familiar rat as a standard, I selected for comparative study another animal—a fish—which I thought similar enough to the rat that it could be studied in analogous experiments, yet different enough to afford a marked neuro-anatomical contrast. I did not propose to compare the two animals in terms of numerical scores, as, for example, the number of trials required for (or the number of errors made in) the mastery of some problem, because such differences would not necessarily imply the operation of different learning processes. I proposed instead to compare them in terms of *functional relations*—to find out whether their performance would be affected in the same way by the same variables (Bitterman, 1960). Why I chose to begin with certain variables rather than others probably is not worth considering—the choice was largely intuitive; whatever the reasons, the experiments soon turned up some substantial differences in the learning of fish and rat. I shall describe here two of those differences, and then present the results of some further experiments which were designed to tell us what they mean.

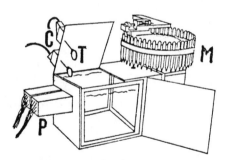

FIG. 2 A situation for the study of discrimination in the fish. (T, targets which are lowered into the water as the cover of the enclosure is brought down; C, phonograph cartridges which hold the targets and register contacts with them; P, projectors for projecting various stimuli on the targets; M, live-worm dispenser.)

One of the situations developed for the study of learning in the fish is illustrated in Figure 2. The animal is brought in its individual living tank to a black Plexiglas enclosure. The manipulanda are two Plexiglas disks (targets) at which the animal is trained to strike. The targets are mounted on rods set into the needle holders of phonograph cartridges in such a way that when the animal makes contact with one of the targets a voltage is generated across its cartridge. This voltage is used to operate a set of relays which record the response and control its consequences. The targets are illuminated with colored lights or patterns projected upon them from behind; on any given trial, for example, the left target ·may be ͵green and the right one red, or the left target may show a triangle and the right one a circle. The reward for correct choice is a *Tubifex* worm discharged into the water through a small opening at the top of the enclosure—the worm is discharged from an eyedropper whose bulb is compressed by a pair of solenoid-operated jaws. When a worm is dropped, a magazine light at the rear of the enclosure is turned on for a few seconds, which signals that a worm has been dropped and provides some diffuse illumination which enables the animal to find it. All of the events of training are programmed automatically and recorded on tape.[1]

I shall talk about two kinds of experiment which have been done in this situation. The first is concerned with *habit reversal*. Suppose an animal is trained to choose one of two stimuli, either for a fixed number of trials or to some criterion level of correct choice, and then the positive and negative stimuli are reversed; that is, the previously unrewarded stimulus now is rewarded, and the previously rewarded stimulus is unrewarded. After the same number of trials as were given in the original problem, or when the original criterion has been reached in the first reversal, the positive and negative stimuli are reversed again—and so forth. In such an experiment, the rat typically shows a dramatic improvement in performance. It may make many errors in the early reversals, but as training proceeds it reverses more and more readily.

---

[1] The response-detection system and a dry-pellet feeder are described in Longo and Bitterman (1959). The liveworm dispenser—which makes it possible to extend the work to species (like the goldfish) that do not take an abundance of dry food—is described in Longo and Bitterman (1963). Programing procedures are described in my chapter on "Animal Learning" in Sidowski (1965). The fully automated technique was developed only after some years of work with less elegant ones which did not permit the complete removal of the experimenter from the experimental situation. The advantages of such removal, from the standpoint of efficiency and of objectivity, should be obvious; yet I have encountered, especially in Europe, a good deal of hostility toward automation. In almost every audience, someone can be counted on to say, rather self-righteously, "*I* like to *watch* my animals." I explain that the automated techniques were developed after a good deal of watching to determine what was worth watching, and that they simply transfer a good part of the watching function to devices more sensitive and reliable than the experimenter, but that they do not rule out the possibility of further watching. In fact, freed of the necessity of programing trials and of recording data, the experimenter now can watch more intently than ever before. The United States has seen great advances in mammalian technique during recent years, while submammalian technique (except for the Skinnerian work with pigeons) has remained terribly primitive. A systematic comparative psychology will require some parallel advances in submammalian technique.

In Figure 3, the performance of a group of African mouthbreeders is compared with that of a group of rats in a series of spatial reversals. (In a spatial problem, the animal chooses between a pair of stimuli which differ only with respect to their position in space, and reinforcement is correlated with position, e.g., the stimulus on the left is reinforced.) The apparatus used for the rat was analogous to the apparatus for the fish which you have already seen. On each trial, the animal was offered a choice between two identically illuminated panels set into the wall of the experimental chamber. It responded by pressing one of the panels, and correct choice operated a feeder which discharged a pellet of food into a lighted food cup. The fish were trained in an early version of the apparatus which you have already seen. For both species, there were 20 trials per day to the criterion of 17 out of 20 correct choices, positive and negative positions being reversed for each animal whenever it met that criterion. Now consider the results. The upper curve of the pair you see here is quite representative of the performance of rats in such a problem—rising at first, and then falling in negatively accelerated fashion to a low level; with a little more training than is shown here, the animals reverse after but a single error. The lower curve is quite representative of the performance of fish in such a problem—there is no progressive improvement, but instead some tendency toward progressive deterioration as training continues.

How is this difference to be interpreted? We may ask first whether the results indicate anything beyond a quantitative difference in the learning of the two animals. It might be contended that reversal learning simply goes on more slowly

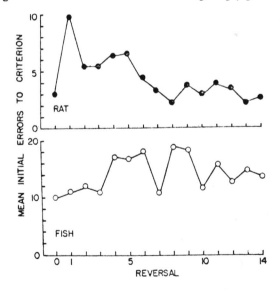

FIG. 3 Spatial habit reversal in fish and rat. (The fish data are taken from Bitterman, Wodinsky, & Candland, 1958; the rat data are from Gonzalez, Roberts, & Bitterman, 1964.)

in the fish than in the rat—that in 10 or 15 more reversals the fish, too, would have shown progressive improvement. In fact, however, the training of fish has been carried much further in later experiments, some animals completing more than 150 reversals without any sign of improvement. I invite anyone who remains skeptical on this point to persist even longer in the search for improvement.

Another possibility to be considered is that the difference between fish and rat which is reflected in these curves is not a difference in learning at all, but a difference in some confounded variable—sensory, motor, or motivational. Who can say, for example, whether the sensory and the motor demands made upon the two animals in these experiments were exactly the same? Who can say whether the fish were just as hungry as the rats, or whether the bits of food given the fish were equal in reward value to those given the rats? It would, I must admit, be a rare coincidence indeed if the conditions employed for the two animals were exactly equal in all of these potentially important respects. How, then, is it possible to find out whether the results obtained are to be attributed to a difference in learning, or to a difference in sensory, or in motor, or in motivational factors? A frank critic might say that it was rather foolish to have made the comparison in the first place, when a moment's thought would have shown that it could not possibly have any meaningful outcome. It is interesting to note that neither Harlow nor Voronin shows any appreciation of this problem. We may doubt, then, whether they have evidence even for quantitative differences in the *learning* of their various animals.

I do not, of course, know how to arrange a set of conditions for the fish which will make sensory and motor demands exactly equal to those which are made upon the rat in some given experimental situation. Nor do I know how to equate drive level or reward value in the two animals. Fortunately, however, meaningful comparisons still are possible, because for *control by equation* we may substitute what I call *control by systematic variation*. Consider, for example, the hypothesis that the difference between the curves which you see here is due to a difference, not in learning, but in degree of hunger. The hypothesis implies that there is a level of hunger at which the fish *will* show progressive improvement, and, put in this way, the hypothesis becomes easy to test. We have only to vary level of hunger widely in different groups of fish, which we know well how to do. If, despite the widest possible variation in hunger, progressive improvement fails to appear in the fish, we may reject the hunger hypothesis. Hypotheses about other variables also may be tested by systematic variation. With regard to the question of reversal learning, I shall simply say here that progressive improvement has appeared in the rat under a wide variety of experimental conditions—it is difficult, in fact, to find a set of conditions under which the rat does not show improvement. In the fish, by contrast, reliable evidence of improvement has failed to appear under a variety of conditions.

I cannot, of course, prove that the fish is incapable of progressive improvement. I only can give you evidence of failure to find it in the course of earnest efforts; and the point is important enough, perhaps, that you may be willing to look at some more negative results. The curves of Figure 4 summarize the outcome of an experiment in which the type of problem was varied. Three

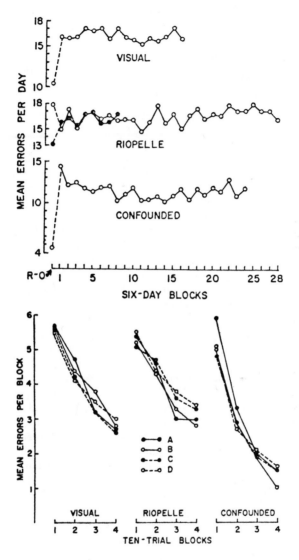

FIG. 4 Visual habit reversal in the fish. (The upper curves show between-sessions performance in each of three problems; the lower curves show within-sessions performance at various stages of training—A, early, D, late—in each problem. These data are taken from some as yet unpublished experiments by Behrend, Domesick, and Bitterman.)

groups of mouthbreeders were given 40 trials per day and reversed daily, irrespective of their performance. In the visual problem, reinforcement was correlated with color and independent of position, which varied randomly from trial to trial; e.g., red positive on odd days and green positive on even days. In the confounded problem, reinforcement was correlated both with color and position; e.g., red always on the left, green always on the right, with red-left positive on odd days and green-right positive on even days. The Riopelle problem was like the visual problem, except that each day's colors were chosen from a group of four, with the restriction that there be no more than partial reversal from one day to the next; i.e., yesterday's negative now positive with a "new" color negative, or yesterday's positive now negative with a "new" color now positive. The upper curves show that there was no improvement over days in any of the three problems (the suggestion of an initial decline in the confounded curve is not statistically reliable). The lower curves show that there was a considerable amount of learning over the 40 trials of each day in each problem and at every stage of training, but that the pattern of improvement over trials did not change as training continued. Negative results of this sort now have been obtained under a variety of conditions wide enough, I think, that the burden of proof now rests with the skeptic. Until someone produces positive results, I shall assume that the fish is incapable of progressive improvement, and that we have come here upon a difference in the learning of fish and rat.

Experiments on *probability learning* also have given different results for rat and fish. Suppose that we train an animal in a choice situation with a ratio of reinforcement other than 100:0; that is, instead of rewarding one alternative on 100% of trials and the other never, we reward one alternative on, say, a random 70% of trials and the other on the remaining 30% of trials, thus constituting what may be called a *70:30 problem*. Under some conditions, rat and fish both "maximize" in such a problem, which is to say that they tend always to choose the more frequently reinforced alternative. Under other conditions—specifically, under conditions in which the distribution of reinforcement is exactly controlled—the rat continues to maximize, but the fish "matches," which is to say that its distribution of choices approximates the distribution of reinforcements: In a 70:30 problem, it chooses the 70% alternative on about 70% of trials and the 30% alternative on the remaining trials.

Figure 5 shows some sample data for a visual problem in which the discriminanda were horizontal and vertical stripes. In the first stage of the experiment, response to one of the stripes was rewarded on a random 70% of each day's 20 trials, and response to the other stripe was rewarded on the remaining 30% of the trials—a 70:30 problem. In the second stage of the experiment the ratio of reinforcement was changed to 100:0, response to the 70% stripe of the first stage being consistently rewarded. The curves shown are plotted in terms of the percentage of each day's responses which were made to the more frequently rewarded alternative. The fish went rapidly from a near-chance level of preference for the 70% stimulus to about a 70% preference, which was maintained from Day 5 until Day 30. With the beginning of the 100:0 training, the preference shifted rapidly upward to about the 95% level. The preference of the rats for the more frequently reinforced stimulus rose gradually

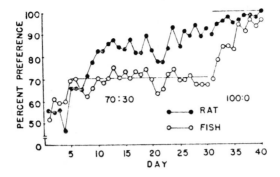

FIG. 5 Visual probability learning in fish and rat (from Bitterman, Wodinsky, & Candland, 1958).

from a near-chance level at the start of the 70:30 training to about the 90% level on Day 30. In the 10 days of 100:0 training, this preference continued to increase gradually, as it might have done irrespective of the shift from inconsistent to consistent reinforcement. Some further evidence of the close correspondence between choice ratio and reward ratio, which is easy to demonstrate in the fish, is presented in Figure 6. The upper portion shows the performance of two groups of mouthbreeders; one trained on a 100:0 and the other on a 70:30 confounded (black-white) problem, and both then shifted to the 0:100 problem (the less frequently rewarded alternative of the first phase now being consistently rewarded). The lower portion shows what happened when one group then was shifted to 40:60 and the other to 20:80, after which both were shifted to 50:50.

Two characteristics of these data should be noted. First, the probability matching which the fish curves demonstrate is an individual, not a group phenomenon—that is, it is not an artifact of averaging. All the animals in the group behave in much the same way. I make this obvious point because some averaged data which have been taken as evidence of matching in the rat are indeed unrepresentative of individual performances.[2] Second, the matching shown by the fish is random rather than systematic. The distribution of choices recorded in the 70:30 problem looks like the distribution of colors which might be obtained by drawing marbles at random from a sack of black and white marbles with a color ratio of 70:30—that is, no sequential dependency is to be found in the data. While the rat typically maximizes, it may on occasion show a correspondence of choice ratio and reward ratio which can be traced to some systematic pattern of choice, like the patterns which are displayed in analogous experiments by human subjects. For example, a correspondence reported by Hickson (1961) has been traced to a tendency in his rats to choose on each trial

---

[2] The averaged data are cited by Estes (1957). The distribution of individual performances is given by Bitterman, Wodinsky, and Candland (1958).

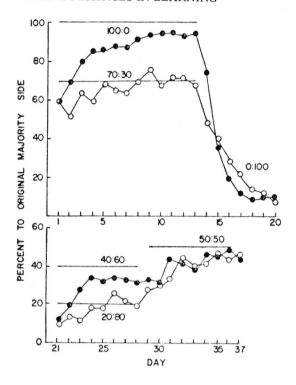

FIG. 6 Probability matching in the fish (from Behrend & Bitterman, 1961).

the alternative which had been rewarded on the immediately preceding trial. Quite the opposite tendency, which also tends to produce a correspondence between choice ratio and reinforcement ratio, has been found in the monkey—a tendency to *avoid* the rewarded alternative of the preceding trial (Wilson, Oscar, & Bitterman, 1964a, 1964b). The matching shown by the fish, which I shall call *random matching*, is a very different sort of thing.

Here then, are two striking differences between rat and fish. In experiments on habit reversal, the rat shows progressive improvement while the fish does not. In experiments on probability learning, the fish shows random matching while the rat does not. These results suggest a number of interesting questions, of which I shall raise here only two: First, there is the question of how the two differences are related. From the point of view of parsimony, the possibility must be considered that they reflect a single underlying difference in the functioning of the two animals—one which has to do with adjustment to inconsistent reinforcement. Inconsistency of reinforcement certainly is involved in both kinds of experiment, between sessions in reversal learning and within sessions in probability learning. It also is possible, however, that the results for reversal learning reflect one functional difference and the results for probability learning quite another. A second question concerns the relation between the observed differences in behavior and differences in brain structure. We may wonder, for example, to what extent the cortex of the rat is responsible for its progressive improvement in habit reversal, or for its failure to show random matching. In an effort to answer such questions we have begun to do some experiments, analogous to those which differentiate fish and normal rat, with a variety of other animals, and with rats surgically deprived in infancy of relevant brain tissues.

I shall describe first some results for extensively decorticated rats (Gonzalez et al., 1964). The animals were operated on at the age of 15 or 16 days in a one-stage procedure which resulted in the destruction of about 70% of the cortex. Two sample lesions, one relatively small and one relatively large, are shown in Figure 7. The experimental work with the operates, like the work with normals, was begun after they had reached maturity—at about 90 days of age. From the methodological viewpoint, work with a brain-injured animal is perfectly equivalent to work with a normal animal of another species, and rats operated in our standard fashion are treated in all respects as such, with systematic variation employed to control for the effects of sensory, motor, and motivational factors. The substantive relation of the work with decorticated rats to the work with normal animals of different species is obvious: We are interested in whether extensive cortical damage will produce in the rat the kinds of behavior which are characteristic of precortical animals, such as the fish, or of animals with only very limited cortical development.

The results for decorticated rats emphasize the importance of the distinction

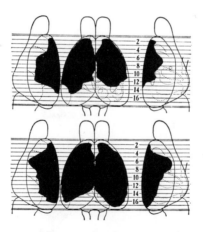

FIG. 7 Extent of cortical destruction in two rats operated at the age of 15 days and sacrificed at the age of 150 days. (The two brains are selected to illustrate the range and general locus of injury produced by the operation. From Gonzalez, Roberts, & Bitterman, 1964.)

between spatial and visual problems. In a pure spatial problem, you will remember, the two alternatives are identical except for position in space, and reinforcement is correlated with position, e.g., the alternative on the left is reinforced. In a pure visual problem, the two alternatives are visually differentiated, each occupying each of the two positions equally often, and reinforcement is correlated with visual appearance—e.g., the green alternative is reinforced independently of its position. The behavior of the decorticated rat is indistinguishable from that of the normal rat in spatial problems, but in visual problems it differs from the normal in the same way as does the fish.

The criterion-reversal performance of a group of decorticated rats trained in a spatial problem is shown in Figure 8 along with that of a group of normal controls. There were 20 trials per day by the correction method, and the criterion of learning was 17 out of 20 correct choices. As you can see, the performance of the two groups was very much the same in the original problem. In the first 10 reversals the operates made more errors than did the normals, but (like the normals) they showed progressive improvement, and in the last 10 reversals, there was no difference between the two groups. The results for two additional groups, decorticated and normal, trained under analogous conditions in a visual problem (a brightness discrimination) are plotted in Figure 9. Again, the performance of normals and operates was much the same in the original problem. In the subsequent reversals, the error scores of the normal animals rose at first and then declined in characteristic fashion, but the error scores of the operates rose much more markedly and showed no subsequent tendency to decline.

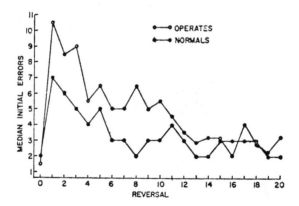

FIG. 8 Spatial habit reversal in normal rats and in rats extensively decorticated in infancy (from Gonzalez, Roberts, & Bitterman, 1964).

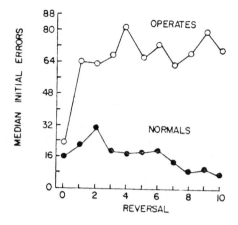

FIG. 9 Visual habit reversal in normal rats and in rats extensively decorticated in infancy (from Gonzalez, Roberts, & Bitterman, 1964).

In spatial probability learning the performance of the operates was indistinguishable from that of normals, but in visual probability learning the operates showed random matching. The asymptotic preferences of operates and normals, first in a 70:30 and then in a 50:50 brightness discrimination, are shown in Table 1. In the 70:30 problem, the operates came to choose the 70% stimulus on about 70% of trials (the mean was 71.7%); in the 50:50 problem they chose the

TABLE 1 Preferences of Decorticated Rats (O) and Normal Controls (N) for the More Frequently Reinforced Alternative in a 70:30 Visual Problem and for the Same Alternative in a Subsequent 50:50 Problem

Subject	70:30 problem	50:50 problem
O-1	68.0	49.5
0-2	69.5	53.0
O-3	71.5	47.0
O-4	73.5	57.0
O-5	76.0	62.0
N-1	64.5	CP
N-2	79.0	CP
N-3	89.5	86.0
N-4	90.0	CP
N-5	90.0	80.0

CP means choice of one position on 90% or more of trials. Data from Gonzalez, Roberts, and Bitterman (1964).

two stimuli about equally often (the mean preference for the former 70% stimulus was 53.7%). No sequential dependencies could be found in their behavior. By contrast, the normal animals tended to maximize in the 70:30 problem. The two whose preferences came closest to 70% adopted rigid position habits (CP) in the 50:50 problem, while one of the others also responded to position, and two continued in the previously established preference. In both spatial experiments, then, the decorticated rats behaved like normal rats, while in both visual experiments they behaved like fish.

These results are compatible with the hypothesis that the cortex of the rat is responsible in some measure for its progressive improvement in habit reversal and for its failure to show random probability matching, at least in visual problems. They are compatible also with the hypothesis that the behavioral differences between fish and rat which appear in the two kinds of experiment are reflections of a single functional difference between the two species. The latter hypothesis is contradicted, however, by some results for the pigeon which I shall now describe. I need not go into any detail about the experimental situation, because it is a fairly familiar one. Suffice it to say that the Skinnerian key-pecking apparatus was adapted for discrete-trials choice experiments directly analogous to those done with fish and rat. The bird, in a darkened enclosure, pecks at one of two lighted keys, correct choice being rewarded by access to grain. Contingencies are programed automatically, and responses are recorded on tape.

In experiments on habit reversal, both visual and spatial, the pigeon behaves like the rat; that is, it gives clear evidence of progressive improvement (Bullock & Bitterman, 1962a). Shown in Figure 10 is the criterion-reversal performance of a group of pigeons trained in a blue-green discrimination. There were 40 trials per day to the criterion of 34 correct choices in the 40 trials, with positive and negative colors reversed for each animal whenever it met that criterion. The results look very much like those obtained in analogous experiments with the rat: There is an initial increase in mean errors to criterion, followed by a progressive, negatively accelerated decline. Now what can we say of the behavior of the pigeon in experiments on probability learning? Figure 11 gives evidence of a correspondence between choice ratio and reward ratio as close in the pigeon as

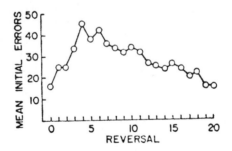

FIG. 10 Visual habit reversal in the pigeon (from Stearns & Bitterman, 1965).

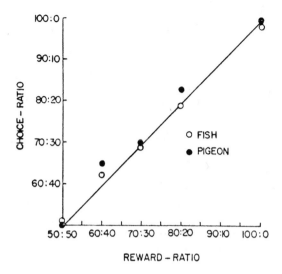

FIG. 11 Probability matching in fish and pigeon. (The points for the fish are based both on spatial and on visual data, while those for the pigeon are based only on visual data.)

in the fish, and statistical analysis shows that the matching is random. The points for the pigeon, like those for the fish, represent the pooled results of a variety of experiments, both published and unpublished, which were carried out in my laboratory. Unlike the points for the fish, however, the points for the pigeon are based only on *visual* data, because the pigeon shows random matching only in visual problems; in spatial problems it tends to maximize (Bullock & Bitterman, 1962b; Graf, Bullock, & Bitterman, 1964).

The results for the pigeon, then, are in a sense intermediate between those for the rat and for the fish. Like the rat, the pigeon shows progressive improvement in habit reversal, but, like the fish, it shows random probability matching—in visual problems if not in spatial ones. One conclusion which may be drawn from these results is that experiments on habit reversal and experiments on probability learning tap somewhat different processes. If the processes were the same, any animal would behave either like the fish, or like the rat, in both kinds of experiment. We have, then, been able to separate the processes underlying the two phenomena which differentiate fish and rat by a method which might be called *phylogenetic filtration*. It is interesting, too, that the visual-spatial dichotomy which appeared in work with the decorticated rat appears again in the probability learning of the pigeon. In experiments on habit reversal, the pigeon behaves like a normal rat; in experiments on probability learning, the pigeon behaves, not like a fish, but like an extensively decorticated rat.

Now let me show you some comparable data for several other species. Being very much interested in the reptilian brain, which is the first to show true cortex, I have devoted a good deal of effort to the development of a satisfactory technique for the study of learning in the painted turtle. After some partial success with a primitive T maze (Kirk & Bitterman, 1963), I came finally to the situation diagramed in Figure 12. As in our latest apparatus for monkey, rat, pigeon, and fish, the turtle is presented with two differentially illuminated targets between which it chooses by pressing against one of them. Correct choice is rewarded with a pellet of hamburger or fish which is rotated into the chamber on a solenoid-driven tray. Some experiments on habit reversal now under way in this situation have yielded the data plotted in Figure 13. One group of turtles was trained on a spatial problem (both targets the same color) and another group on a visual problem (red versus green). There were 20 trials per day, with reversal after every 4 days. As you can see, progressive improvement has appeared in the spatial problem, but not in the visual problem. Some experiments on probability learning also are under way in this situation. In spatial problems, only maximizing and nonrandom matching (reward following) have been found, but in visual problems, random matching has begun to appear. This pattern of results, you will remember, is exactly that which was found in decorticated rats.

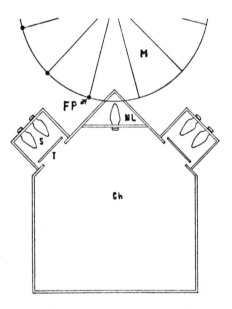

FIG. 12 A situation for the study of discrimination in the turtle. (Ch, animal's chamber; T, target; S, lamps for projecting colored lights on the targets; M, feeder which rotates a pellet of food, FP, into the chamber; ML, magazine lamp which is turned on to signal the presentation of food. From Bitterman, 1964.)

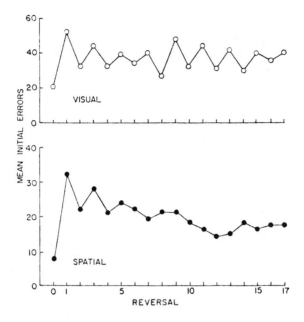

FIG. 13 Visual and spatial habit reversal in the turtle. (The data are taken from some as yet unpublished experiments by Holmes and Bitterman.)

Insofar as performance in these tests is concerned, then, extensive decortication in infancy turns rats into turtles.

I come now to some work with invertebrates. Diagramed in Figure 14 is a Y maze for the cockroach used in the experiments of Longo (1964). The technique is a much cruder one than those used for vertebrates, but it represents, I think, a considerable advance over anything that has yet been done with the cockroach. The motive utilized is shock avoidance: Ten seconds after the animal is introduced into the starting box, shock is turned on, and remains on, until the animal enters the goal box, which is its home cage; if the animal reaches the goal box in less than 10 seconds, it avoids shock entirely. Choices are detected objectively by photocells, but complete automation is not possible, because no satisfactory alternative to handling the animal has been found. The results of an experiment on spatial probability learning in the cockroach, which was patterned after those done with vertebrates, are plotted in Figure 15. Like the fish—but *unlike any higher vertebrate*—the cockroach shows random matching under spatial conditions. The results of an experiment on spatial habit reversal in the cockroach are plotted in Figure 16. Three groups of animals were given 10 trials per day—one group reversed each day, another group reversed every 4 days, and a control group never reversed during the stage of the experiment for which data are plotted. Although the 4-day group showed no significant improvement (its curve hardly declines at all beyond the first point, which is for the original

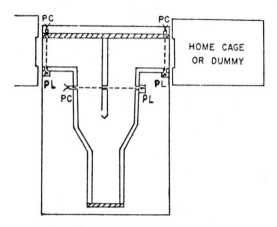

FIG. 14 A Y maze for the cockroach. (PC, photocell; PL, photocell lamp; S, starting compartment. From Longo, 1964.)

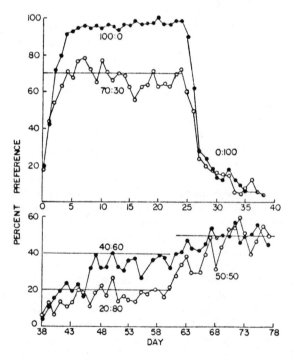

FIG. 15 Spatial probability matching in the cockroach (from Longo, 1964).

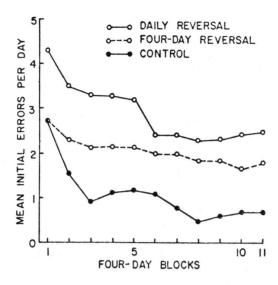

FIG. 16 Spatial habit reversal in the cockroach (from Longo, 1964).

problem), the daily group did show significant improvement (its curve declining in much the same way as that of the control group). What does this result mean? Have we found in the primitive cockroach a capability which does not exist in the fish? A consideration of some results for the earthworm will help to answer this question.

Diagramed in Figure 17 is a T maze developed for the earthworm by Datta (1962). The stem of the maze is bright, warm, and dry, and the animal occasionally is shocked in it. A correct turn at the choice point carries the animal to its dark, moist, cool, shock-free home container, while an incorrect turn is punished with shock from a metal door which converts one arm of the maze into a cul. When the animal is shocked for contact with the door, a sensitive relay in the circuit is energized, thereby providing an objective index of error. This technique, again, is a crude one by vertebrate standards, but it seems to give reliable results. Some sample data on spatial habit reversal are plotted in Figure 18. The worms were given five trials per day and reversed every 4 days. Note that the mean number of errors rose in the first reversal, and thereafter declined progressively, the animals doing better in the fourth and fifth reversals than in the original problem. In a further experiment, however, this improvement was found to be independent of reversal training per se and a function only of general experience in the maze: A control group, trained always to the same side while an experimental group was reversed repeatedly, did not differ from the experimental group when eventually it, too, was reversed. This test for the effects of general experience is feasible in the earthworm, because the turning preferences which it develops do not persist from session to session. The analysis of the progressive improvement shown by the cockroach is, however, a more

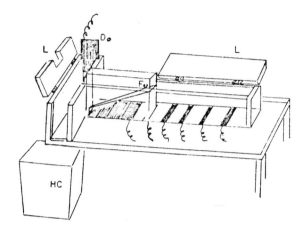

FIG. 17   A T maze for the earthworm. (L, lid; Do, metal door which converts one arm of the maze into a cul and delivers shock for erroneous choice; Fu, funnel to reduce retracing; HC, home container. From Datta, 1962.)

difficult matter, and I must be content here simply to state Longo's opinion that it reflects, as in the earthworm, not an improvement in reversal capability, but an improved adjustment to the maze situation. The course of that general improvement is traced by the curve for the control group, which parallels that of the daily group. Nonspecific improvement probably is not as evident in the vertebrate data because general adjustment to the experimental situation proceeds rapidly and is essentially complete at the end of pretraining.[3]

The results of these experiments on habit reversal and probability learning in a variety of animals are summarized in Table 2. Spatial and visual problems are categorized separately because they give different results. The rows for all the subjects except one are ordered in accordance with the conventional scale of complexity—monkey at the top and earthworm at the bottom. The only subject whose place in the table is not based on preconceived complexity is the decorticated rat, whose placement (with the turtle, between the pigeon and the fish) is dictated by experimental outcomes. The differences between fish and rat which provided points of departure for the subsequent work with other organisms also provide a frame of reference for reading the table: R means that

---

[3] A possibility to be considered is that a portion at least of the cockroach's improvement was due to improvement in the experimenter, of whom the conduct of the experiment required considerable skill. The same may be said of the first in the series of experiments with the fish by Wodinsky and Bitterman (1957) which was the only one to show anything like progressive improvement and whose results have not been replicated in work with automated equipment; the pattern of improvement was, incidentally, quite unlike that found in mammals. A study of another arthropod (the Bermuda land crab) in a simple escape situation, by Datta, Milstein, and Bitterman (1960), gave no evidence of improvement.

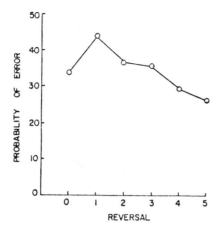

FIG. 18 Spatial habit reversal in the
earthworm (from Datta, 1962).

the results obtained in a given kind of experiment with a given subject are like
those for the rat (that is, progressive improvement in habit reversal and failure of
random matching), while F means that the results obtained are like those for the
fish (that is, random matching and failure of progressive improvement). It should
be understood that these entries are made with varying degrees of confidence.
Where there are no data, there are no entries, but an entry is made even where,
as in the case of the turtle, the data are yet fragmentary and incomplete. All
entries are based on data from my laboratory, except those for reversal learning
in the monkey, which are based on the literature.

TABLE 2 Behavior of a Variety of Animals in Four Classes of Problem which
Differentiate Rat and Fish Expressed in Terms of Similarity to the
Behavior of One or the Other of These Two Reference Animals

	Spatial problems		Visual problems	
Animal	Reversal	Probability	Reversal	Probability
{ Monkey	R	R	R	R
{ *Rat*	R	R	R	R
Pigeon	R	R	R	F
{ Turtle	R	R	F	F
{ Decorticated rat	R	R	F	F
{ *Fish*	F	F	F	F
{ Cockroach	F	F	—	—
{ Earthworm	F	—	—	—

F means behavior like that of the fish (random probability matching and failure of
progressive improvement in habit reversal). R means behavior like that of the rat
(maximizing or nonrandom probability matching and progressive improvement in habit
reversal). Transitional regions are connected by the stepped line. The brackets group animals
which have not yet been differentiated by these problems.

The table is an orderly one. In each column there is a single transition from F to R as the scale of subjects is ascended, although the point of transition varies from column to column, suggesting a certain functional independence: Rat-like behavior in spatial problems of both kinds appears first in decorticated rat and turtle, rat-like behavior is visual reversal learning appears first in pigeon, and rat-like behavior in visual probability learning appears first in rat. The eight subjects fall into four different groupings: monkey and rat in one; pigeon in a second; turtle and decorticated rat in a third; fish, cockroach, and earthworm in a fourth. Monkey and rat fall into the same grouping because they are not differentiated by these experiments when all failures of random probability matching are classified as R. The data for the two mammals do, however, show different kinds of sequential dependency in experiments on probability learning, reward following in the rat giving way in the monkey to the opposite strategy (avoiding the rewarded alternatives of the preceding trial). It is interesting to note that this new strategy of the monkey has been manifested thus far only with respect to the spatial locus of reward, even when the alternatives have been visually distinct. This finding fits the generalization suggested at other points in the table: that as we ascend the phyletic scale new modes of adjustment appear earlier in spatial than in visual contexts.

It is of some interest to ask whether R modes of adjustment are in any sense more effective than F modes, and for habit reversal, at least, the answer is clear. Progressive improvement is on its face a superior adjustment, representing a flexibility that cannot help but be of value in an animal's adjustment to changing life circumstances. The answer for probability learning is less clear, although it can be said that maximizing produces a higher percentage of correct choice than does matching. In a 70:30 problem, for example, the probability of correct choice is .70 for maximizing but only .58—(.70 x .70) + (.30 x .30)—for matching. Nonrandom matching is no more successful than random matching by this criterion, but we know that in human subjects it is the outcome of an effort to find a principle that will permit 100% correct choice; the hypotheses tested reflect the observed reward ratio, and they produce a corresponding choice ratio. To the degree that nonrandom matching in infrahuman subjects is based on an emerging hypothetical or strategic capability, it represents a considerable functional advance over random matching.

The table does, of course, have certain obvious limitations. Clearly, I should like to be able to write *bird* rather than *pigeon*, I should like by *fish* to mean more than *mouthbreeder*, and so forth. It will be interesting to discover how representative of their classes are the particular species studied in these experiments—whose choice was dictated largely by practical considerations—and to extend the comparisons to other classes and phyla. I can say, too, that the behavioral categories used in the table almost certainly will need refining; already the R-F dichotomy is strained by the data on probability learning (with R standing for maximizing, for near maximizing, and for nonrandom matching of several different kinds), while better techniques must be found for isolating the various constituents of progressive improvement in habit reversal. The uncontaminated linear order which now appears in the table, while undeniably esthetic, is rather embarrassing from the standpoint of the far-from-linear evolutionary relationships among the species studied; nonlinearities are perhaps to be expected as the behavioral categories are refined and as the range of tests is broadened.

Whatever its limitations, the table is useful, I think, not only as a summary of results already obtained, but as a guide to further research. Almost certainly, the order in the table will permit us to reduce the amount of parametric variation which must be done before we are satisfied that some phenomenon for which we are looking in a given animal is not to be found. Suppose, for example, that we had begun to work with the turtle before the pigeon, and suppose that we had sought persistently, but in vain, for evidence of random matching in spatial probability learning, being satisfied at last to enter an R for the turtle in the second column of the table. Turning then to the pigeon, we should be prepared after many fewer unsuccessful efforts to enter an R. I do not mean, of course, that systematic parametric variation is no longer important in comparative research; we must continue to do a great deal of it, especially at points of transition in the table, and wherever the entries fail to reflect gross discontinuities in the evolutionary histories of the organisms concerned. I do think, however, that the table will save us some parametric effort *in certain regions*—effort which may be diverted to the task of increasing the range of organisms and the range of tests represented. It does not seem unreasonable to expect that, thus expanded, the table will provide some useful clues to the evolution of intelligence and its relation to the evolution of the brain.

References

Beach, F. A. The snark was a boojum. *American Psychologist*, 1950, *5*, 115–124.

Behrend, E. R., & Bitterman, M. E. Probability-matching in the fish. *American Journal of Psychology,* 1961, *74*, 542–551.

Bitterman, M. E. Toward a comparative psychology of learning. *American Psychologist*, 1960, *15*, 704–712.

Bitterman, M. E. An instrumental technique for the turtle. *Journal of the Experimental Analysis of Behavior*, 1964, *7*, 189–190.

Bitterman, M. E., Wodinsky, J., & Candland, D. K. Some comparative psychology. *American Journal of Psychology*, 1958, *71*, 94–110.

Bullock, D. H., & Bitterman, M. E. Habit reversal in the pigeon. *Journal of Comparative and Physiological Psychology*, 1962, *55*, 958–962. (a)

Bullock, D. H., & Bitterman, M. E. Probability-matching in the pigeon. *American Journal of Psychology*, 1962, *75*, 634–639. (b)

Datta, L. G. Learning in the earthworm, *Lumbricus terrestris*. *American Journal of Psychology*, 1962, *75*, 531–553.

Datta, L. G., Milstein, S., & Bitterman, M. E. Habit reversal in the crab. *Journal of Comparative and Physiological Psychology*, 1960, *53*, 275–278.

Estes, W. K. Of models and men. *American Psychologist*, 1957, *12*, 609–616.

Gonzalez, R. C., Roberts, W. A., & Bitterman, M. E. Learning in adult rats with extensive cortical lesions made in infancy. *American Journal of Psychology*, 1964, 77, 547–562.

Graf, V., Bullock, D. H., & Bitterman, M. E. Further experiments on probability-matching in the pigeon. *Journal of the Experimental Analysis of Behavior*, 1964, 7, 151–157.

Harriman, P. L. (Ed.) *Twentieth century psychology*. New York: Philosophical Library, 1946.

Hickson, R. H. Response probability in a two-choice learning situation with varying probability of reinforcement. *Journal of Experimental Psychology*, 1961, *62*, 138—144.

Kirk, K. L., & Bitterman, M. E. Habit reversal in the turtle. *Quarterly Journal of Experimental Psychology*, 1963, *15*, 52—57.

Koch, S. *Psychology: A study of a science*. Vol. 2. *General systematic formulations, learning, and special processes*. New York: McGraw-Hill, 1959.

Longo, N. Probability-learning and habit-reversal in the cockroach. *American Journal of Psychology*, 1964, *77*, 29—41.

Longo, N., & Bitterman, M. E. Improved apparatus for the study of learning in fish. *American Journal of Psychology*, 1959, *72*, 616—620.

Longo, N., & Bitterman, M. E. An improved live-worm dispenser. *Journal of the Experimental Analysis of Behavior*, 1963, *6*, 279—280.

Sidowski, J. (Ed.) *Experimental methods and instrumentation in psychology*. New York: McGraw-Hill, 1965.

Stearns, E. M., & Bitterman, M. E. A comparison of key-pecking with an ingestive technique for the study of discriminative learning in pigeons. *American Journal of Psychology*, 1965, *78*, in press.

Thorndike, E. L. *Animal intelligence*. New York: Macmillan, 1911.

Voronin, L. G. Some results of comparative-physiological investigations of higher nervous activity. *Psychological Bulletin*, 1962, *59*, 161—195.

Wilson, W. A., Jr., Oscar, M., & Bitterman, M. E. Probability learning in the monkey. *Quarterly Journal of Experimental Psychology*, 1964, *16*, 163—165. (a)

Wilson, W. A., Jr., Oscar, M., & Bitterman, M. E. Visual probability-learning in the monkey. *Psychonomic Science*, 1964, *1*, 71—72. (b)

Wodinsky, J., & Bitterman, M. E. Discrimination-reversal in the fish. *American Journal of Psychology*, 1957, *70*, 569—576.

Peter Marler and his colleagues have gathered what is perhaps the most extensive and systematic evidence for preparedness in the literature of ethology and comparative psychology. For the past decade they have investigated how the white-crowned sparrow learns its song; in the wild, this is normally from listening to adults of the species. If the young do not hear the song between 10 and 50 days of age, however, their adult song is deficient. Learning during this critical period is, moreover, highly selective: They will not learn the song of another species if it is played to them during this time. Marler speculates that a flexible, sensory "template" acts as a crude model if the adult song is not heard during the critical period, or acts as a filter in the presence of stimulation. Finally, Marler points out that both young sparrow and young humans are prepared to focus on the vocalizations of members of their own species, and both seem prepared to develop what could be loosely called "syntactic" structures.

29

A COMPARATIVE APPROACH TO VOCAL LEARNING: SONG DEVELOPMENT IN WHITE-CROWNED SPARROWS[1]

Peter Marler

Unlike nonhuman primates and some other species used in attempts to condition vocal behavior, certain song birds display considerable facility at vocal imitation in the wild state. Species-specific characteristics of the song of the male white-crowned sparrow are normally acquired by learning from adults. Local song dialects result. Males raised in individual or group isolation developed abnormal songs. Exposure to normal song during a critical period of 10–50 days of age resulted in normal song development and in reproduction of the particular training dialect. Exposure to normal song during the 50–100 day age period shifted subsequent song development in a normal direction but details of the training song were not reproduced. Exposure before 10 days and after 100 days of age had no effect. Song

From *Journal of Comparative and Physiological Psychology* 71 (1970), 1–25.

This research was supported by grants from the National Science Foundation and aided by the Zoology Department, University of California, Berkeley, and many individuals, particularly Marcia Kreith, Miwako Tamura, and Inger Bradbury. Help in collecting and raising birds, analyzing data, criticizing and preparing the results for publication was also given by Thomas Bever, Derry Bogert, Kathryn Harpham, Jenny Gerard, Masakazu Konishi, Eric Lenneberg, Marilyn Milligan, James Mulligan, Keith Nelson, Fernando Nottebohm, Anita Pearson, Lewis Petrinovich, Sister Mary Justine Sheil, Thomas Struhsaker, Jerry Verner, and my wife.

learning is selective in that exposure to songs of other species of 10–50 days of age had no effect on song development. Sensory rather than motor constraints seem to be responsible for the selectivity. To explain song development, an auditory template is postulated. At the start of the critical period the template is only a crude specification of normal song, but sufficient to exclude songs of other species. In training the specifications of the template become more precise. Vocalizations are matched to the template subsequently by auditory feedback. No extrinsic reinforcement seems to be necessary. Several analogies are drawn between song learning in white-crowned sparrows and speech development in children.

In broaching the comparative investigation of vocal learning it might seem logical to study the abilities of nonhuman primates in this regard.

This approach has yielded results which, though interesting in themselves, are in some respects disappointing. Although chimpanzees and an orang-utan have been taught to utter two or three words of human speech, the parallel with speech acquisition in children is probably remote. The training required direct manipulation of the animal's tongue, lips, jaw, and nose, and the investigators concur on the extraordinary effort demanded of them and their subjects (Furness, 1916; Hayes, 1951; Hayes, 1950; Hayes & Hayes, 1954; reviewed in Kellogg, 1968). Thus, apes demonstrate no great facility for vocal imitation.

Several other attempts have been made to modify animal vocalization by conditioning. Although the duration and rate of sound production was modifiable, the actual structure or morphology of the vocalizations was changed little or not at all by the conditioning procedures (e.g., Ginsburg, 1960, 1963; Grosslight, Harrison, & Weiser, 1962; Grosslight & Zaynor, 1967; Lane, 1961). Ginsburg (1963) was successful in achieving stimulus control over the production of two words of human speech by a mynah bird, after they were already established in the repertoire. But the training in speech imitation involved not only a conditioning procedure but also repeated presentations of normal and recorded speech without reinforcement, so that the role of conditioning, as such, is uncertain. One attempt to change the morphology of domestic chick calls by conditioning was apparently successful. However, it now seems that interpretations of the results may be equivocal. Comparison of the spectrograms of sounds during continuous reinforcement and extinction (Lane & Shinkman, 1963, Figure 1, top) with records of natural vocalizations of chicks (Collias & Joos, 1953) reveals that all sounds are present in the normal repertoire. Those given during reinforcement are the so-called "pleasure calls." One of those given during extinction, presumed to have novel morphology as a consequence of conditioning, is in fact the normal "distress call" of a chick, given when it is deprived of food. The other is a normal "fear trill" (cf. Collias & Joos, 1953, Figures 1 and 2; Lane & Shinkman, 1963, Figure 1). These two calls must have been used often before the start of the experiment, at 1 mo. of age.

Experiments such as these tend to confirm Skinner's (1957) impression that animal vocalizations are somewhat refractory to effects of operant conditioning as compared with other motor activities. While this a reasonable conclusion to

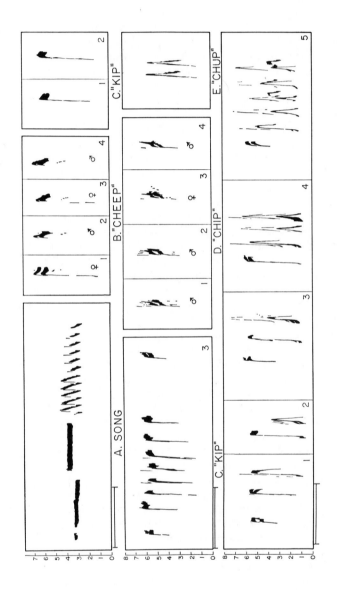

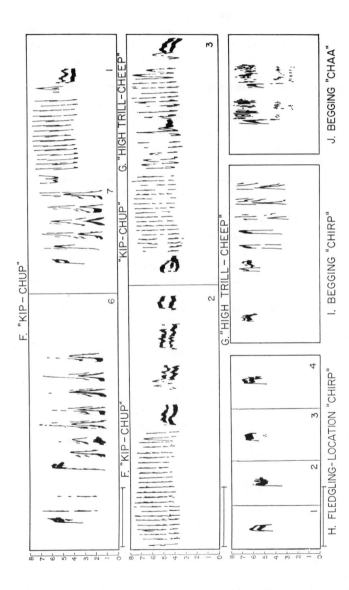

FIG. 1 Sound spectrograms of the major vocalizations of white-crowned sparrows. (A–G: adult calls; H–J: juvenile calls. The song [A] is used only by males. The others are used by both sexes, though the "high trill-cheep" pattern is more common in females than males. B, C, and D are probably connected by a continuous series of intermediates. The time markers indicate ½ sec. The vertical scale is marked in kHz. All sound spectrograms in this paper were made with a wide [300-Hz.] bandpass filter.

draw from psychologists' investigations of vocal learning in animals, there is a body of zoological research that argues otherwise. Some birds display great facility in vocal learning, and in certain species this is a normal means of transmitting vocal morphology from one generation to the next, as in man. There are in fact several analogies between human and avian vocal learning which have not hitherto been acknowledged in the psychological literature. The author will attempt to point some of these out in this study of song learning in a common North American song bird.

The white-crowned sparrow, *Zonotrichia leucophrys nuttalli*, has a repertoire of about seven different sounds (Figure 1). All but one of these vary little from place to place within the species' breeding range, which includes all of North America except the southern and eastern parts (Banks, 1964). The male song is the longest, most elaborate, and most specifically distinctive of the calls. It is restricted to the breeding season, and is characterized by regular repetition over long periods of time. Its geographical variability is widely known and acknowledged as a classic example of dialect variation. Song dialects also occur in the European chaffinch. Auditory experience plays a vital role in song development in the chaffinch (Thorpe, 1958, 1961a), and local dialects may be a clue that the acoustical environment is important in the ontogeny of vocalizations.

This study explores the effects of varying the acoustical environment on the development of singing behavior in one subspecies of the white-crowned sparrow, *Zonotrichia leucophrys nuttali*. An adult male white-crown has a single basic song pattern which is repeated many thousands of times in the course of a breeding season with only minor variations such as repetition or omission of some elements (Figure 2). Songs of males living in the same area have many characters in common, particularly in the detailed syllabic structure of the second part of the song or "trill." There is some individuality, especially in the introductory or "whistle" part of the song. Comparison with birds in other areas reveals consistent differences in some aspects of the song pattern, which are stable from year to year (Marler & Tamura, 1962). The term "dialect" seems appropriate for the song patterns that characterize a given population of this species (Figure 3). As compared with other bird songs that show dialect variation, the white-crown is unusual in the relative homogeneity of song patterns within an area. This is an advantage for developmental study. When a young bird is taken into the laboratory the natural song patterns of the home area provide a firm frame of reference with which to compare vocalizations that develop under experimental conditions.

METHODS OF CAPTURING, RAISING, AND HOUSING THE BIRDS

The subjects were taken as nestlings 2–10 days of age or as fledglings. The latter, already independent from their parents but still in the home area, were taken by driving them into mist nets. Nestlings had to be fed by hand up to an age of about 1 mo. Various foods were used including mashed hard-boiled egg, bird seed which had been soaked in water for 24 hr. and then crushed, a proprietary canary nestling food mixture, mealworms, crickets, wax moth larvae, fly maggots, and a vitamin supplement. The birds were weaned onto a diet of mixed seed previously soaked in water and finally to dry mixed seed. Nestlings were kept in their original nests with a Kleenex lining that was replaced frequently. Food was presented with tweezers or on the tip of a slender wooden spatula. Some weeks after fledgling, birds were sexed by laparotomy. The present paper discusses only the vocalizations of males.

As they were brought in from the field the birds were placed in acoustical isolation. Between 1959 and 1967 a variety of acoustically insulated chambers were used, as designated in the text. Hartshorne boxes consist of three plywood boxes, one inside the other with insulation between them, with windows in the front, and a ventilation fan that circulates air through a system of baffles. Fish boxes are basically similar but with a slightly different construction and a separate ventilation fan connected to the box by a vacuum cleaner hose. The walk-in soundproof box was a commercially made audiometric chamber (Industrial Acoustics Corporation—IAC 112). In all chambers sound attenuation from outside to inside was between at least 40 and 65 db., within the frequency range of the birds' vocalizations (500–7,000 Hz). Acoustical isolation between two birds in separate boxes was complete. No other birds were kept in the room housing the acoustical chambers. To further reduce the chances of one bird hearing another while a box was opened for feeding or cleaning, white noise was broadcast from a loudspeaker in the center of the room at a level of about 60 db. above SPL at 5 ft. from the speaker.

Each box was equipped with a low-impedance microphone and a speaker. Cables to an adjacent room permitted recording of vocalizations and playback of recorded sounds when appropriate. While birds were singing, recordings were made at intervals of 2–3 wk. or less, usually on a two-track Wollensack 1500 tape recorder at a tape speed of 7½ in. per sec. Samples of singing for each date were analyzed on the Kay sound spectrograph using the wide-bandpass filter (300 Hz.) in all cases. After inspection of the sample for a given date a typical example was extracted for the purpose of illustration and traced with ink to facilitate reproduction.

EFFECTS OF ACOUSTICAL ISOLATION

Experiment 1: Two Males in Acoustical Isolation at about 100 Days of Age

In nature a young male leaving the nest about 10 days after hatching (Banks, 1959; Blanchard, 1941) is exposed to abundant singing from its father and neighbors for a period of about 20–100 days, depending on whether it was born early or late in the season. Adult singing declines in frequency during the summer molt. There is sporadic singing in fine weather during the fall and winter and a resumption of full song in early spring. A number of young males were trapped by nets at ages of 30–100 days after hatching, as determined by the state of the plumage. Immediately after capture and sex determination, two of these males with estimated ages of about 35 days were placed in a Hartshorne

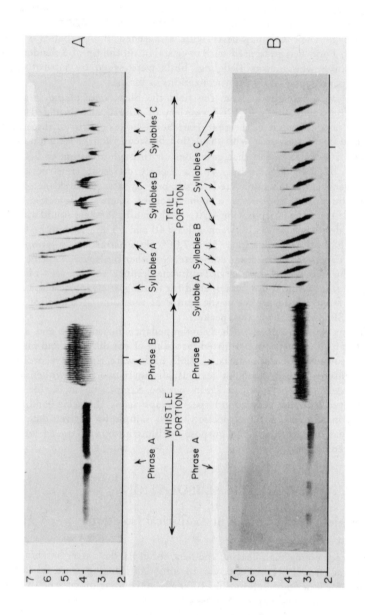

342

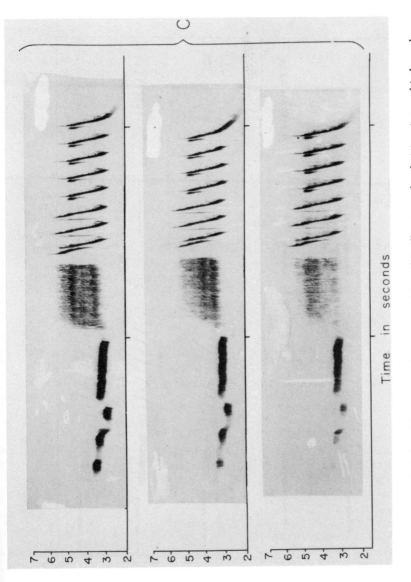

Time in seconds

FIG. 2 Songs of male white-crowned sparrows. (A and B illustrate the division into whistle and trill portions. C illustrates the variation in song renditions of an individual, such as additional repition of a trill syllable or variations in the intensity of whistles.)

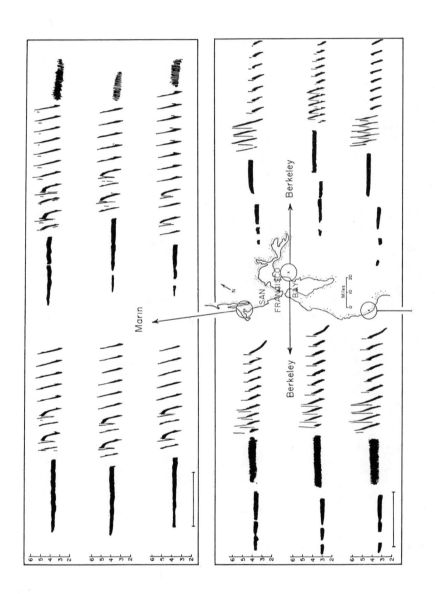

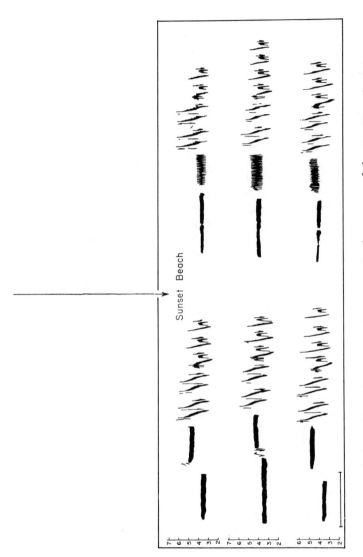

FIG. 3 Song males of 18 white-crowned sparrows in three parts of the San Frnacisco Bay area. (Scales as in Figure 1.)

box with a Masonite partition between them. Cracks around the edges permitted both visual and auditory contact.

In the following spring these two males developed final song patterns which corresponded in many details with the dialect in the part of Marin County from which they were taken (Figure 4, D5 and E5, compare D and EN). The song patterns did not crystallize fully until March and April at an age of about 10 mo., but traces of the syllabic structure of the home dialect can be seen in some of the earliest songs recorded (e.g., Figure 4, E1, age about 3 mo.). General field observation of natural song development in white-crowned sparrows suggests a parallel sequence to that recorded in the laboratory in these two males. Evidently the experimental conditions did not hinder the development of a normal song pattern at the appropriate phase of the life cycle.

Experiment 2: Two Males in Individual Acoustical Isolation from 5 Days after Hatching

If the young are taken from a nest of wild birds 2 or 3 days after hatching, they can readily be raised by artificial feeding in the laboratory, thus reducing the opportunity for them to hear adult male white-crowned sparrow song. We have had no success so far in raising young hatched from eggs in an incubator. Two young males taken at 5 days were placed in separate Fish boxes and raised therein.

They began singing at an age of about 8 mo. and by approximately 12 mo. final song patterns had crystallized. The songs were roughly the same in duration as the home dialect of these birds, but all of the fine detail was lacking (Figure 5, B7, C6, compared with B and CN). The songs were also unlike any that we have recorded in nature. In one bird a syllable "trill" was completely lacking and the song consisted only of broken whistles. In the other (Figure 5, C6) a trill was present, formed by repetitions of another of the calls in the repertoire—a call which develops normally in isolation (cf. Figure 1C).

The course of development differed from that in the previous experiment not only in the failure of the home dialect to appear, but also in the slower rate of development. These birds came into song later and their song patterns were highly variable and slow to crystallize. Even at the age of 1 yr. the successive renderings of the final song were highly variable. The differences might arise because the birds were housed singly, and not in pairs, as in Experiment 1.

Experiment 3: Nine Males in Group Acoustical Isolation after Hatching

A bird raised in individual isolation as was done in the second experiment might suffer from the lack of general social stimulation, to the extent that normal motor development is indirectly impaired. With this possibility in mind, nine males were taken from nests in three different areas at ages 5—8 days after hatching. They were placed in a large walk-in soundproof room, raised there, and left as a group until the next year. Each bird was in a separate cage, free to look at several of its companions, and to hear all of them.

All nine birds developed well-defined final song patterns in the course of the following year. None had any detailed resemblance to the home dialect. Nor could any consistent difference be seen between the song patterns of birds taken from the three areas. In fact, three birds that developed very similar song patterns (Figure 6, A3, B2, C4) came from different areas. As with the previous experiment, these song patterns fall outside the range of variations in wild white-crowned sparrow songs. They consistently lack a syllabic trill. Nevertheless the tonal quality of the whistles that make up these songs would suffice to identify the singer to an ornithologist as a species of the genus *Zonotrichia*, although he could not determine the species, as he easily could with normally reared birds.

Unlike the birds in the previous experiment, several of the nine began singing early, at an age of 2 or 3 mo., and their song patterns also crystallized more rapidly (e.g., Figure 5, A1—6). Nevertheless the songs were as abnormal as in individual isolates. Singing was loud and frequent. Thus the abnormality of the motor patterns does not seem attributable to any deficiency of motivation to sing. The abundant opportunity for social interaction, albeit limited by a wire cage wall, seems to rule out general social deprivation as a cause for song abnormality. The evidence points toward acoustical isolation from adult males as a specific cause of the development of abnormal song.

EFFECTS OF PLAYBACK OF WHITE-CROWNED SPARROW AND OTHER SPECIES SONGS

Experiment 4: One Male Given Brief Playback as a Nestling

In spite of considerable effort, we have been unable to raise white-crowns from the egg as others have done with passerine species. The question arises whether auditory experience during the first few days in the nest, before the birds are brought into the laboratory, affects subsequent vocal development. As an indirect approach, three birds were taken from the nest at 3 days of age and reared in a Fish box. From Day 3 to Day 8, they were given 8 min. of normal song per day through a loudspeaker at a rate of six songs per min. After training they were isolated in separate boxes. One proved to be a male. The training song (Figure 7, AT) was a different song than the home dialect (AN). No trace of either dialect could be discerned in the final song pattern that this bird developed. Like other individually isolated birds, the song patterns were very fluid and slow to crystallize. They were quite abnormal in structure. As in one previous bird (Figure 5, C6) reared in isolation, a syllabic trill was developed by the incorporation of a sequence of calls into the song, a different call in this case (cf. Figure 1F). The experience of normal song in the first week of life seems to have no specific effect on the song patterns subsequently developed.

Experiment 5: One Male Given Playback after Reaching Full Song

The songs from nine males raised as a group in acoustical isolation have been described (Experiment 3). A tenth bird in the group was removed at 11 mo. of

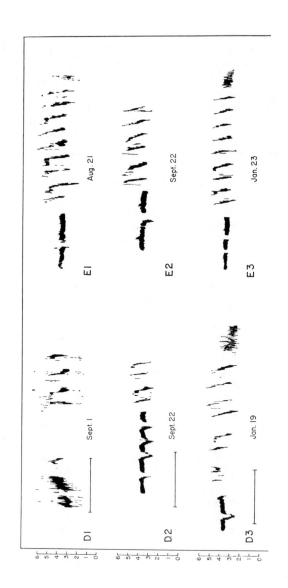

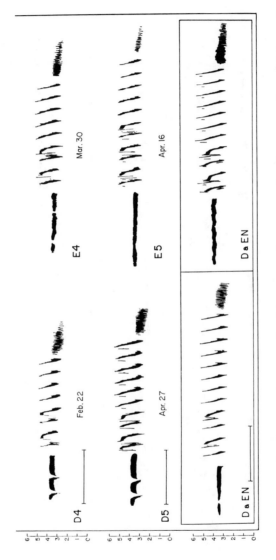

FIG. 4 Song development in two male white-crowned sparrows taken by nets at about 35 days of age and placed in a soundproof box together until they were sexually mature. (D and EN are samples of the local dialect where the birds were caught.)

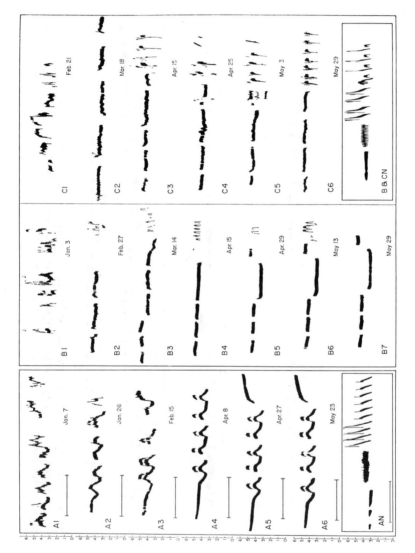

FIG. 5 Song development in the three male white-crowned sparrows raised in isolation from 5 days of age. (B and C were in individual isolation. A was with a group of isolates [cf. Figure 6]. AN is the local dialect for Bird A, B and CN the local dialects for Birds B and C).

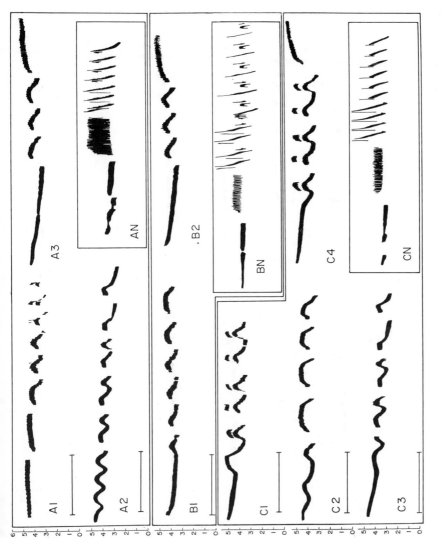

FIG. 6 The full songs of nine males taken as nestlings from three different areas and raised together in a large soundproof room. (Three inserts, AN, BN, and CN, illustrate song dialects in the areas where the birds were born.)

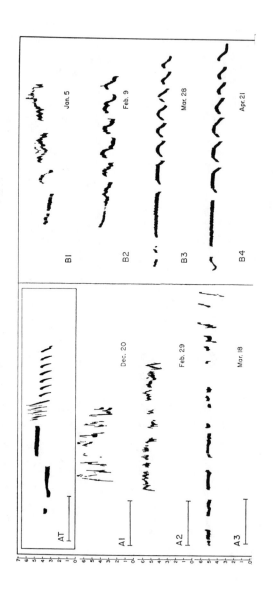

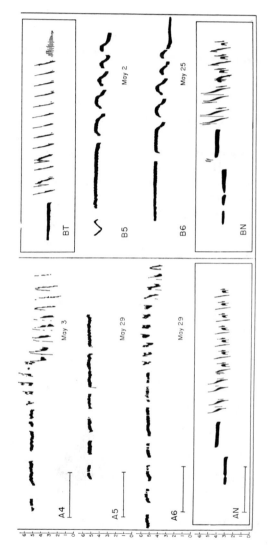

FIG. 7 Song development in two male white-crowned sparrows, one exposed to normal song very early in life and one late. (Bird A was exposed to 8 min. per day of Song AT from the third to the eighth day of age and then left in isolation. AN illustrates its home dialect. Bird B was a member of the group isolated together in experiment 3 until the end of April when it was about 11 mo. of age. It was then removed to another room and exposed to at least 10 min. of daily playback for 10 wk. with Song BT. Its home dialect was BN.)

age, 2 mo. after coming into full song (Figure 7, B1–4). It was then exposed to daily playback with an alien dialect of white-crown song for 10 wk. in an open cage in the laboratory. The treatment had no detectable effect on the song pattern (Figure 7, B5 and 6). This confirms our experience with other birds that varying acoustical conditions have no effect on song patterns after the male has come into full song and its songs have crystallized. This is true even if the song that has crystallized is abnormal. All experimental birds maintained their abnormal song patterns after the first year of life, in spite of being housed within earshot of normal white-crowned sparrow song.

Experiment 6: Five Males Taken at 30–100 Days and Given Playback Song at Various Ages

Eight young males taken by nets in Marin County were placed in pairs in Hartshorne boxes with a Masonite partition between them allowing both visual and auditory contact. Their ages at the time of trapping were estimated at 30–100 days of age. Two were kept in isolation as controls (Experiment 1). The other six were given playback experience of a normal song with a different pattern than their home dialect for a 4-wk. period, 15 min. per day, six songs per min. The three pairs were trained at different times: (a) A pair was trained in August, 1961, at about 100 days of age; (b) a pair was trained in December, 1961, at about 200 days; (c) a pair was trained in February, 1962, at about 300 days of age. One February-trained bird died. The result of training at 200 and 300 days of age (Figure 8, B, C, and D) was unequivocal—it had no effect on song development, which closely paralleled that of the controls (Figure 8, A). The final song patterns are typical of the home area in Marin County where the birds spent their first month or two of life. Only the birds trained in August at approximately 100 days showed any deviation from this pattern (Figure 8, E and F). Their final song patterns did not correspond in detail to the training song. But the losses of terminal buzz and of some detailed syllabic characteristics of the Marin County dialect are evidence of deviation from the normal pattern of development. If auditory experience of adult song is necessary for development of a local dialect, the timing of the experience is obviously important, and the critical period must terminate gradually somewhere around 100 days of age.

The results of these experiments point toward a period between 1 wk. after hatching and about 2 mo. of age as the time when acoustical experience is critical for song development.

Experiment 7: Four Males Given Playback in the Early Fledgling Phase

Concentrating on the effects of training during the first few weeks after leaving the nest, four males were taken as nestlings, three at 5 and one at 9 days of age, and raised in Fish boxes in individual isolation. One was trained from Day 8 to Day 28 (Figure 9B), one from Day 35 to Day 56 (Figure 9A), and two from Day 50 to Day 71 (Figure 10, A and B). The white-crowned sparrow song used in playback was the home dialect for one bird and an alien dialect for the other three.

The song of another species was also presented during the training session in an attempt to get a maximum of information from the experiment. In one case the second species was a Harris' sparrow, *Zonotrichia querula* (Figure 9, AT 2), selected because its song resembles that of the white-crowned sparrow. It does not occur in the area. In the other three cases, a song sparrow, *Melospiza melodia* (Figure 9, BT 2; Figure 10, A BT, right), was used. Its song has a quite different pattern from the white-crown. It is heard abundantly in all of the white-crown nesting areas from which the experimental birds were taken. The training schedules were as follows. The bird whose song is shown in Figure 9A was given 2 min. of white-crowned sparrow song and 2 min. of Harris' sparrow song with a 2 min. pause between, once in the morning and once in the afternoon, for a total of 8 min. of playback per day at a rate of six songs per min. The order of presentation was alternated in morning and afternoon sessions and from day to day, for 21 days. The schedule for the birds in Figures 9B and 10 was similar except that song sparrow song was substituted for the Harris' sparrow song.

Like other individually isolated birds, they came into song rather late. In their earliest utterances the two early-trained birds showed some resemblance to the white-crowned sparrow training song in the detailed structure of syllables (Figure 9). By an age of about 10 mo., both of the early-trained birds produced final song patterns that were good copies of the white-crown model, except that the final vibrato was lacking. No effect of the songs of the two other species could be discerned. The two late-trained birds did not copy either the conspecific or the alien model. One of them (Figure 10A) produced the abnormal song of an isolated bird. The other produced a more normal song, with whistle and trill portions, but the trill syllables did not correspond in detail with any element of a training song (Figure 10B).

It appears then that an otherwise isolated bird given adequate exposure to normal song sometime during the first 50 days after leaving the nest is diverted to a more or less normal course of song development. Exposure to a training song at this age results subsequently in a detailed reproduction of this song pattern. With training between 50 and 100 days of age (cf. also birds in Experiment 6, trained at 100 days) some of the general structural qualities of the training song may be reproduced, so that there is a normal division into whistle and trill portions. The detailed syllabic structure is lacking. Furthermore, the responsiveness of an isolated white-crowned sparrow to playback songs is selective in the sense that songs of two other species presented in the same period, one of them common in the natural environment, had no detectable effects on subsequent development.

Experiment 8: Three Males Given Playback of Another Species' Song in the Early Fledgling Phase

Perhaps white-crowned sparrows might be forced to acquire the song of another species by presenting an alien song alone during the period that a

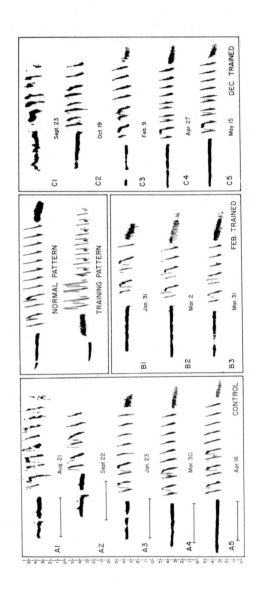

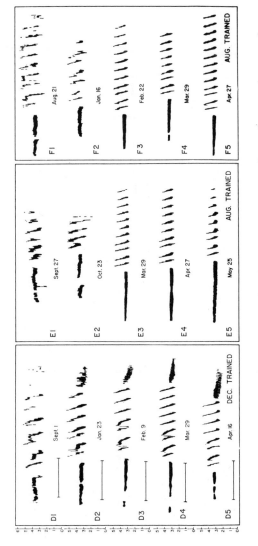

FIG. 8 Song development in five males taken by nets at 30–100 days of age and exposed to a normal training pattern (see insert) for 15 min. per day for 4 wk. (One control bird captured at the same time and kept without training is also illustrated [cf. Figure 4E]. One was trained in February at about 300 days of age, two in December at about 200 days of age, two in August at about 100 days of age.)

357

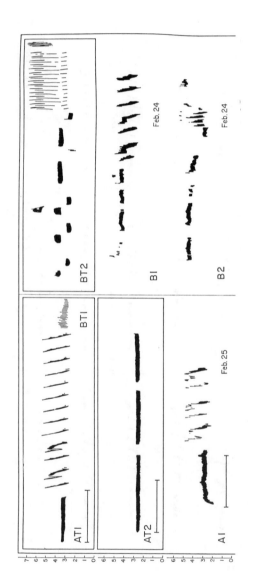

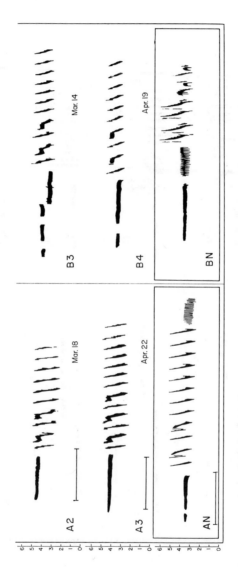

FIG. 9 The emergence of song in two male white-crowned sparrows taken as nestlings at 5 days of age and trained with normal song before 60 days of age. (A heard 2 min. of white-crowned sparrow song [AT1] and 2 min. of Harris' sparrow song [AT2] in the morning and afternoon from Day 35 to Day 56 of age. B was similarly treated but with song sparrow song [BT2] as the alien pattern from the eighth to the twenty-eighth day of age.)

359

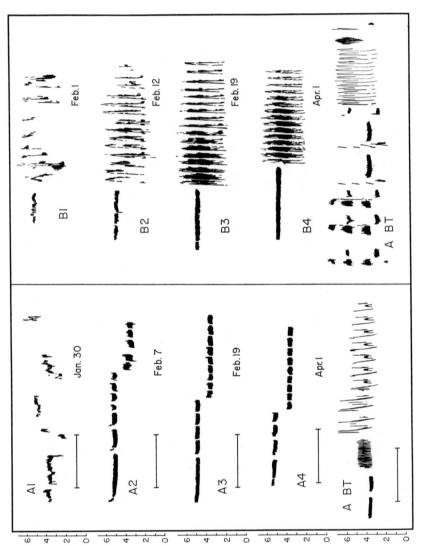

FIG. 10 Song development in two males taken as 5-day nestlings and exposed to 2 min. of normal white-crowned sparrow song (A and BT left) and 2 min. of song sparrow song (A and BT right) each morning and afternoon from Day 50 to Day 71 of age.

conspecific song is learned. Three birds were taken from the nest at 5–6 days of age and raised in individual isolation in Fish boxes. From Day 7 to Day 28 they were given playback of recorded song sparrow songs twice a day. In each training period two song sparrow songs were presented, 2 min. of each at a normal rate of six songs per min. with a 2-min. pause between them. The order was alternated morning and afternoon and on consecutive days.

These birds began singing somewhat earlier than other individual isolates, but they were customarily slow in crystallizing song themes. Their song patterns showed no detectable correspondence to either of the song sparrow training songs (Figure 11). As white-crowned songs they were quite abnormal. This contrasts with the accurate imitation of birds given a conspecific training song in about the same period (Figure 9), and shows that normal development cannot be achieved by playback of songs of other species during the same period.

DISCUSSION

It is perhaps unfortunate that birds such as parrots and mynahs are favorite subjects for investigators with a comparative approach to verbal and vocal development, who study their ability to imitate human speech (Ginsburg, 1963; Grosslight et al., 1962; Grosslight & Zaynor, 1967; Mowrer, 1950, 1958). Although some birds are known to mimic other species in the wild state (Armstrong, 1963), mynahs and parrots only do this in captivity, as far as is known (Thorpe, 1959). If mimicry of other forms plays no part in their natural biology, they are unlikely to bring special phylogenetic predispositions to the task of learning to reproduce sounds of another species, namely man. Does one study processes of speech development by training children to imitate sounds of other species? Only by presenting the child with sounds that have at least some of the structural properties of speech can the special predispositions that the child brings to the problem of language acquisition be understood.

Exploration of the role of such predispositions in vocal learning is urgently needed (Lenneberg, 1967). The prospects of success may be greater if the subjects learn vocalizations in nature, and if the learning process is studied in relation to sounds confronting the species in its natural state. The white-crowned sparrow falls into this category, and it is by no means unique. The European chaffinch is another well-studied example. Males taken as nestlings and raised in acoustical isolation develop most of the repertoire of 14 basic sounds quite normally. A social call and perhaps one alarm call may show some abnormalities (Marler, 1956) but the abnormalities are most striking in the male song (Poulsen, 1951; Thorpe, 1958, 1961a). Similarly, in a variety of other birds the more or less elaborate song of the male is most likely to show abnormalities when birds are raised in isolation (Lanyon, 1960; Marler, 1964).

The song of an isolated male chaffinch is normal in duration and number of notes but much simplified in structure. Normal development requires exposure to the song of older males during the first year or so of life. There is thus a critical period for song learning with two intensive phases, the first at about 3 mo., and the second at about 9 mo. as the young male begins coming into full song. As with the white-crowned sparrow, song development in an isolated male

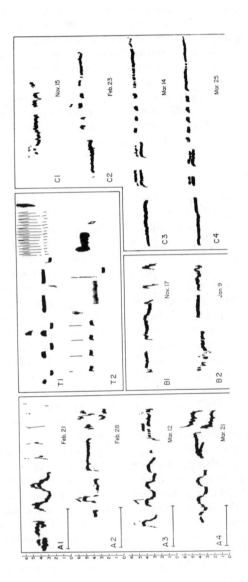

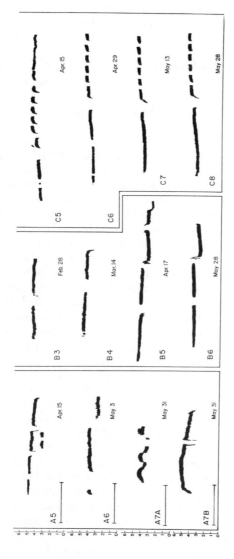

FIG. 11 Song development in three male white-crowned sparrows taken as 5-day nestlings. (They were placed in individual isolation and trained from the seventh to the twenty-eighth day of age with 8 min. per day of recordings of song sparrow song. They were given 2 min. each of T1 and T2 in the morning and the same in the afternoon. The order of T1 and T2 was alternated both morning and afternoon and from one day to the next.)

chaffinch can be restored to normality by playing recordings of a natural song during this period. We have shown that a white-crown learns selectively. The same is true of chaffinches, which learned a jumbled conspecific song, or the rather similar song of a tree pipit, but failed to learn sounds with a very different pattern or tonal quality (Thorpe, 1958).

Song development in the chaffinch differs from that in the white-crowned sparrow in several respects. The period in which learning can occur is much longer—up to a year of age—as compared with 10—50 days in the white-crown. Both come into full song at the same age—about 9 mo. Thus, the learning period of the chaffinch overlaps with the onset of singing, although Thorpe has shown that acoustical experience of normal song restricted to the first 3 mo. or so of life does correct most of the abnormalities of the song of a male chaffinch subsequently left in isolation.

Another contrast between these two species is seen if several nestlings are isolated acoustically as a group and raised together. Male chaffinches raised under these conditions develop more complex songs than individual isolates, apparently as a result of mutual stimulation. Although the songs are still abnormal, there is a significant step towards normal development. As we have seen, this does not occur in white-crowned sparrows which develop similarly abnormal songs in both group and individual isolation.

Learning plays a role in the development not only of the species-specific characteristics of some bird songs but also of population-specific vocal patterns. In addition to the species-specific traits that all white-crowned sparrow songs share, they also exhibit well-marked local dialects such that even populations only a mile or two apart can be reliably distinguished (Marler & Tamura, 1962). The same is true of the chaffinch (Marler, 1952) and of the cardinal (Lemon, 1965; Lemon & Scott, 1966). In all three species the dialect characteristics develop as a result of learning. Some of the other species exhibiting song dialects may be worthy of developmental study.

If vocal learning occurs in some birds and not others one might ask whether it has any taxonomic correlates. Aside from the restriction to passerine and psittacine birds, such correlates are hard to discern. Even close relatives may differ strikingly in the pattern of song development. For example, the white-crowned sparrow has close affinities with the song sparrow and the Arizona and Oregon juncos. The natural songs of these four species are strikingly divergent in many properties. Song develops quite differently when individuals of the four species are raised in isolation (Marler, 1967). An isolated male song sparrow can develop normal song, notwithstanding the fact that its natural song is the most complex of the four species (Mulligan, 1963, 1966). The juncos fall somewhere between, with abnormalities in the songs of isolated males which are less major than those of isolated white-crowns (Marler, Kreith, & Tamura, 1962). Unlike white-crowned sparrows, Arizona juncos raised in groups rather than in individual isolation develop quite normal songs (Marler, 1967). All four species are in fact capable of vocal imitation, but they differ in the way in which this capability is expressed. There must be some differences in their evolutionary history that are responsible for this divergence in their patterns of development but the nature of these differences is still obscure. To put it in another way, they differ in the predispositions they bring to the task of learning new vocalizations. The nature of these predispositions is a major subject for further research.

Selectivity of the Song Learning Process

When Learning Occurs. As with a child developing speech (Chomsky, 1967; Lenneberg, 1967; McNeill, 1966), species of birds in which the normal song is transmitted as a learned tradition seems to bring well-defined predispositions to the task of vocal learning. There are at least two major sets of constraints: (*a*) on the age or stage of the life cycle at which learning most readily occurs, and (*b*) on the particular subset of acoustical experiences selected for vocal acquisition. Consider first the temporal restrictions. In the experiments reported here young male white-crowned sparrows learned to reproduce a species-specific song only if it was heard between about 1–7 wk. of age. Within this critical period there must be another set of temporal constraints relating to the number and time of exposures to the song necessary for effective learning to occur, which have yet to be explored.

Temporal constraints are known to occur in the song learning of other bird species. If normal song development is to occur in a male chaffinch it must be exposed to the song of adults between roughly 2 wk. and a year of age. Within this interval there seem to be two particularly sensitive phases, one early, the other at the end of the period (Thorpe, 1958, 1961a). Once the sensitive period is terminated further exposure has no effect, whether the male has developed an abnormal or a normal song. In meadowlarks and linnets the critical period for song learning extends from the fifth week of age to about 8 mo. of age. As in the chaffinch, it terminates at about the time of onset of full song (Lanyon, 1957, 1960; Poulsen, 1954). For zebra finches the critical period extends to about the eightieth day of life, the time of onset still being uncertain (Immelmann, 1965, 1966, 1969).

Only in one case do we have any hints as to the physiological determinants of the critical period. Nottebohm (1969a) castrated a male chaffinch in youth, before it had come into full song. At 2 yr. of age this bird learned from a recording of natural song while coming into song for the first time under the influence of injections of testosterone a year later than normal. Thus, the termination of the critical period for song learning in this species seems to be a consequence of the high androgen levels experienced in a male's first breeding season. Whether termination results from direct hormonal effects on the brain, or is a consequence of the performance of the motor activity of singing, or some other mechanism, remains to be determined (Konishi & Nottebohm, 1969; Nottebohm, 1966, 1968, 1969a). A different mechanism must be responsible for terminating the critical period in white-crown song learning, for this occurs at a time when androgen levels are insufficient to induce full song, which develops several months later. The capacity for song learning shares with many other types of learning a correlation with age of the organism (Thorpe, 1961b, 1965). In song learning the temporal constraints are imposed with a rare clarity, offering an unusual opportunity to explore the role and nature of critical periods for animal learning.

What Is Learned? White-crowned sparrows presented in the critical period with conspecific songs and songs of another species will selectively learn the song of their own kind. Thorpe (1958) has described essentially the same process in the chaffinch. Birds which do not mimic other species must possess some means of focusing attention upon sounds of their own species while learning song. There are several ways in which this might be brought about.

Preexisting social bonds with members of the species might suffice. Mowrer (1950, 1958) proposed in his autism theory of language learning that speech sounds acquire secondary reinforcing properties as a result of association with primary reinforcement of other kinds from the parents. Nicolai (1959) has evidence that young bullfinches selectively learn both the song and one of the other calls from their father. He discovered this when a male raised by canaries learned some canary phrases and in turn transmitted them to its children. Similarly, the male offspring of a male that was raised by hand and taught to whistle a tune learned the same abnormal song from it, even though normal songs could be heard nearby. Young zebra finches learn the song of a father—or of a foster father (Immelmann, 1965, 1966, 1969). The precise mechanism involved here, whether young birds receive food or specific social stimulation from the father that in turn reinforces song learning, remains to be determined.

No doubt song learning is similarly channeled in other bird species which have enduring social bonds such as exist between parent and young bullfinches through most of the first year of life. Such durable bonds are lacking in many small birds however, notably in the chaffinch and the white-crowned sparrow, whose family breaks up as the young are weaned. Nevertheless, they show selectivity in song learning, and this is manifest when birds receive the sounds through a loudspeaker, with no other concomitant stimulation. Here the mechanism of reinforcement proposed by Mowrer (1958) seems inapplicable (Marler & Tamura, 1964). One gathers that some investigators are also skeptical of the adequacy of Mowrer's autism theory as a complete explanation of speech learning in children. Even with talking birds, where Mowrer felt this hypothesis to be especially relevant, Foss (1964) found that mynah birds learned a whistle sound played through a loudspeaker just as well without concomitant food reinforcement as with it, there being no social stimulation in either case.

The conclusion seems unavoidable that chaffinches and white-crowns are responding selectively to some intrinsic acoustical property of the song rather than to some extrinsic source of reinforcement that occurs in association with song. One can think of at least two kinds of neuromuscular mechanisms that might impose specific constraints on the learning process, one motor, the other sensory. The structure of sound-producing equipment—the syrinx and its associated membranes, muscles, and resonating cavities—must impose constraints on what sounds can be uttered. Could these be specific enough to provide a basis for the selection of conspecific song and rejection of the song of a close relative? There are various reasons for doubting this. No difference can be seen between the syringes of closely related birds such as a white-crowned sparrow and a song sparrow. In fact the structure of the avian syrinx is very conservative and is widely used as a taxonomic trait at the higher levels of phylogenetic classification of birds. Species with similar syringeal structure may produce very different vocalizations. A chaffinch and a bullfinch have very similar syringes, but a bullfinch raised by hand and imprinted on man will imitate a great variety of unnatural sounds, including those of musical instruments (Thorpe, 1955), while, as we have seen, a chaffinch is very restricted in what it will learn. Further evidence is presented in the next section.

In these species the evidence seems to point to a mechanism on the sensory rather than the motor side as being responsible for the selectivity of song learning. The effects of deafening on song seem to be consistent with the idea of a sensory "template" somewhere in the auditory pathway, which focuses attention on sound patterns of a certain type.

Evidence for A Sensory Template from Effects of Deafening on Birdsong

The ability to hear environmental sounds is clearly important for song development in many bird species. What of the bird's ability to hear its own voice? Konishi (1963, 1965) deafened several species of birds at various ages by bilateral removal of the cochlea and studied the effects on their vocal development. In some, a complete repertoire of normal vocalizations developed in birds deafened in early youth, as in domestic chickens (Konishi, 1963). We know the same to be true of ring doves.[1] In all passerine birds deafened in youth, including white-crowned sparrows, there were song abnormalities.

Recall that full song usually develops in young male white-crowned sparrows some 2–6 mo. after the pattern is learned. If a male is deafened either before or after training, but before full song develops, it subsequently sings on schedule, but with a pattern still more elementary than that of an intact isolated bird. The song consists of a rapid trill of repeated notes with a wide frequency range, often with a click or insect-like quality. The only normal trait persisting is the duration of the song (Konishi, 1965). There are many things of interest about this result.

The identity of the outcome with deafening before and after training demonstrates that the bird must hear its own voice if the learned sound pattern is to be translated into motor activity. This immediately hints at a role for audition in song development in addition to the perception of species-specific song during training. Secondly, there is a striking contrast between songs of deaf and intact birds raised in isolation. Although the song of the latter is abnormal in several respects, there are some normal traits, particularly the distinctive sustained whistles with which song usually begins. An experienced field ornithologist listening to recordings of songs of an isolated intact male will hesitantly identify the bird as a member of an unknown species of the genus *Zonotrichia*. He will be completely nonplussed by the song of an early-deafened bird. To realize the potentiality for producing the few normal traits that an isolated bird can generate, it must be able to hear its own voice.

A reasonable hypothesis to explain these results is as follows. At the start of the critical period for song learning a young male white-crown possesses a crude

[1] F. Nottebohm, Vocalizations and breeding behavior of surgically deafened ring doves, 1969.

auditory specification for species-specific song. The author will use the term "template" for this specification, even though this word has a connotation of rigid inflexibility that is inappropriate here. The essential notion is that of active filtering of incoming sensory information, not unrelated to what is implied by von Uexkull's "innate schema" and Lorenz's "innate release mechanism." If the bird is raised in isolation this template is the main sensory guide to development. The manner of guidance is not highly specified, for there is considerable variation in the song patterns that isolated birds produce. If on the other hand the bird is allowed to hear sounds present in its natural environment, this same template will now serve as a kind of filter for focusing attention on sounds that match its crude specification, namely songs of conspecific adult males. As the young male is stimulated selectively by conspecific songs during the critical period the specification of the template will be modified and made more precise. If the training is fully effective the template will now embody not only a complete set of species-specific traits, but also those characteristics of the particular local dialect heard. When full song begins, some months later, vocalizations will be matched to this template and normal song development will occur. But audition is necessary to realize this potentiality, hence the elimination from the song of all traces of training by the deafening operation.

The song of a white-crowned sparrow deafened before singing might be taken as a more basic reflection of the properties of the sound producing equipment than that of a bird which can also use hearing to guide the process of sound production. We have already cast doubt on the proposition that differences in the syrinx of close relatives can be responsible for selectivity of the song learning process. Effects of deafening in youth on the three close relatives of the white-crown that we have studied, the song sparrow and two species of junco, lend further support to this position, for the songs were extraordinarily similar (e.g., Konishi, 1964a, Figure 3, 1965, Figure 2; Mulligan, 1966, Figure 20). All consisted of a rapid sequence of variable notes with a coarse scratchy tone. Recordings of all four might easily be confused. The great divergence in the natural songs of these species (Borror, 1965; Konishi, 1964b; Marler & Isaac, 1961; Marler & Tamura, 1962; Mulligan, 1963) is surely attributable not to differences in syringeal structure, but to different auditory specifications for vocal development.

If deafening is postponed until full song has developed, a quite different result occurs (Konishi, 1965). The established song patterns persist virtually unchanged. Evidently some other mechanism than auditory feedback can support the motor pattern once it is fully established.

The Individual Repertoire

The male white-crowned sparrow is unusual among song birds in the restriction of each individual to a single theme (review in Marler & Hamilton, 1966). A chaffinch typically has a repertoire of two to three song types and a western meadowlark has six to nine (Lanyon, 1957; Marler, 1952). There is some evidence that males raised in isolation have a predisposition to develop a song repertoire of the normal size, whether they are trained or not. For example, several white-crowned sparrows in the present study passed through a phase of development in which two somewhat variable song types were used. As full song was attained and the patterns crystallized one of these dropped out, leaving a single theme as the individual repertoire. Chaffinches reared in isolation often produce more than one song type. Perhaps the most instructive example of conformity of isolated birds to the normal repertoire size comes from the meadowlarks. Wild Eastern meadowlarks have twice the song repertoire of Western meadowlarks and the same difference appeared in captive birds raised under a variety of conditions (Lanyon, 1957; Thorpe, 1958).

The mechanism underlying development of a particular repertoire size remains unknown. We know that the repertoire may develop in birds which cannot hear their own singing. Chaffinches deafened in youth may develop a normal repertoire of two or three song types, even though all are highly abnormal (Nottebohm, 1967). Deaf white-crowns develop only one song type (Konishi, 1965). Perhaps we are dealing here with a motor aspect rather than a sensory property of the underlying neurophysiological mechanisms. A clue that this may be the case is derived from study of the temporal pattern of delivery of song types in the individual. A male chaffinch with a repertoire of three song types will deliver these in bouts, perhaps 10 or 20 renditions of one, followed by a bout of a second type and so on. A chaffinch deafened in youth with three abnormal song types will nevertheless deliver them in bouts as an intact bird does.[2]

Development in the Individual

The song of a male white-crowned sparrow, whether first year or older, does not suddenly appear in complete form. It develops over a period of weeks, passing through an early stage which is reminiscent of the "babbling" phase of speech development in children. The first stage, known to ornithologists as subsong (Lanyon, 1960; Thorpe & Pilcher, 1958), differs from full song in several respects. It is lower in intensity. The components are often given in long, irregular, and unbroken sequences, with other calls from the repertoire occasionally included. The frequency of its component notes tends to fluctuate erratically, giving subsong a wider range of sound frequencies than full song. It is hard to discern any units which are repeated with precision. These characteristics of subsong are shared with many other species. As the male white-crown becomes older the song becomes louder and more clearly segmented (the rehearsed song of Lanyon, 1960). Finally the patterns crystallize into a stereotyped theme, completing the development of full or primary song.

What is the significance of subsong? Is it a by-product of increasing androgen levels, or is the bird in some sense acquiring skills as a necessary stage in the accomplishment of full song? There are reasons for thinking that the second may be true. Thus males coming into song in their second or third years of age pass through the stages from subsong to full song much more quickly than young males, which might be expected once the song pattern has been fully established. In this regard it is illuminating to compare development in white-crowns that have been successfully trained with normal song (e.g., Figures 4 and 9) and birds

[2] F. Nottebohm, personal communication, 1966.

raised in isolation or unsuccessfully trained (Figures 5, 7, 11). Young male white-crowns destined to produce a normal song usually pass through the subsong stage rather quickly. Full song is generally almost fully crystallized within a few weeks after the onset of subsong. Isolated or unsuccessfully trained birds often remain much longer in this transitional stage, and it may be months before the full song is completely crystallized. Thus a bird which will produce abnormal song may persist with variable patterns for a major part of the singing season, behaving almost as though the lack of effective training has left it undecided as to how development should proceed.

Careful examination of the structure of the syllables of subsong reveals another difference between birds that have and have not heard normal song. Compare, for example, Figure 5 C1, an isolated bird, and Figure 9 B1, a trained bird. Birds exposed to normal song during the critical period reveal signs of the training in their subsong. Although their subsong shares many formal properties with that of untrained birds, it is clear from the syllables of early subsong that the training has left its mark. Again one is reminded of speech development in children. Although the late babbling of a Chinese baby makes no more sense than that of an English baby, there is some evidence to suggest that their babbling differs in intonation, already revealing signs of early language training (Weir, 1966).

Are these results consistent with the "auditory template" hypothesis for song development? A bird trained with normal song during the critical period will already possess a highly specified template when singing begins. Nevertheless the accomplishment of a perfect match between vocal output and this template will take time, since novel operations of the sound-producing equipment are required. The sequence of development in a trained bird is what one might expect as it acquires more proficiency in matching vocal output to the specified pattern of auditory feedback.

What of a bird that has been prevented from hearing normal song during the critical period? We have postulated a template which imposes only a crude specification for song development. This will allow considerable latitude, and it might be anticipated that in development guided by such a rough template, crystallization of song patterns would take longer than in a trained bird. Untrained birds show every sign of vacillation, occasionally changing major patterns several times in the course of development. As already mentioned, some males had two song themes at an intermediate stage of development, subsequently rejecting one of them. All were untrained birds.

Carrying this line of argument still further, one might predict that birds deafened in youth, thus deprived of the possibility of reference even to the crude template of a bird that has never heard normal song, would show an even more attenuated and variable sequence of song development. This is precisely what happens. Apart from their abnormal quality and pattern, the most striking characteristic of the songs of male white-crowned sparrows deafened in youth is their instability (Konishi, 1965). Some birds passed through their entire first singing season without a stereotyped theme ever emerging. Many showed some crystallization but they varied much more in successive repetitions than in a normal bird. Even successive repetitions of units within a song varied widely.

The deaf birds seemed to have difficulty in maintaining a steady tone. Many of their traits were reminiscent of an early phase of normal subsong development, a stage which, as a result of deafening, they never get beyond, although their posture and the rhythm of song delivery is more like that of full song.

It seems reasonble then to suppose that the subsong of a young male does indeed have developmental significance and that it is both learning to perform new operations with its sound-producing equipment and also learning by trial and error to match the output with a specified pattern of auditory feedback. Two very similar functions have been postulated for the babbling stage of speech development in children (Fry, 1966). The functions of the brief phase of subsong at the start of each singing season of an older male remains unknown.

There is still another problem to be considered. What is the developmental basis of the template that a previously untrained white-crowned sparrow brings to the task of song learning? Is it a function of previous auditory experience as a nestling or fledgling? We do not know. Training of a nestling 3–8 days of age (Experiment 4) failed to result in normal song. But such early exposure might suffice to establish a crude template, the effects of which would then be manifest in a bird raised in isolation after the nestling stage (Konishi & Nottebohm, 1969; Nottebohm, 1966, 1968).

It should be recalled that all white-crowned sparrows in these experiments were exposed to song for a few days after hatching. Until we hatch and raise birds from the egg in the laboratory, the developmental basis of the so-called song template remains uncertain. It is also possible that experience of the birds' own early vocalizations might make a contribution, as suggested by Nottebohm's (1967, 1968) experiments on the effects of deafening chaffinches at various ages.

The Functional Significance of Song Learning

In language development vocal learning serves to generate a very complex signalling system. The vocal learning of birds clearly has quite different consequences. There is no evidence that the vocal patterns of bird species which learn their songs are any more complex than those of species which do not. What, if any, is the function of avian vocal learning?

We know that white-crowned sparrows can discriminate between the normal song of their own species and that of another, the song sparrow. Milligan (1966) demonstrated this by comparing the frequency with which captive birds sang back in response to recordings of the two species. They replied more frequently to playback of their own species song. This was true even of birds raised in isolation and possessing an abnormal song themselves.

What of the differences between local dialects of white-crown songs; are they discriminable? To answer this question, Milligan and Verner[3] conducted playback experiments in the field. Working in three different areas, they placed loud-speakers in male territories during the breeding season and observed the responses to a standard playback program consisting of 5 min. of silence, 20

[3] M. M. Milligan and J. Verner, Inter-population song dialect discrimination by the white-crowned sparrow, 1969.

songs of one dialect followed by a 5-min. period of silence, 20 songs of a second dialect, another 5-min. period of silence, 20 songs of the first dialect again, and finally 5 min. of silence. Each playback lasted 35 min. and included the subject's own local dialect. The response to hundreds of such playback sessions was recorded. Many males were color banded and the same male was never the subject twice on the same day. During both silent and playback sessions the frequency of the following acts was noted: taking flight, singing (of males), and trills (of females). In addition, the closest approach to the speaker was noted and a weighted score was given for the time taken from start of a session to approach to various distances from the speaker. A composite score assembled from these various measures showed clearly that both males and females are more responsive to playback of the dialect used in the area where they are breeding.

From the learning studies we know that, for males at least, this is also the dialect of the area where they were born. What about females? The females tested by Milligan and Verner (in press) had already started breeding and were exposed to the local dialect of the area. There is no direct evidence that they were born there. However, Konishi (1965) showed that if young female white-crowned sparrows are captured at about 100 days of age and injected with testosterone they come into song and vocalize with the local dialect of the home area where they were taken.

Although the consequence of this learning is not usually manifest as singing behavior, it may guide them in selecting a mate.

Thus it begins to look as though one result of song learning is an increase in the likelihood that male and female white-crowned sparrows will settle in the area where they were born. This might lead to a minor degree of inbreeding in local populations, perhaps permitting the evolution of physiological adaptations to local conditions, as Nottebohm (1969b) has suggested for the South American relative of the white-crowned sparrow, the chingolo, *Zonotrichia capensis*. The use of learned signals to accomplish this end might be a less irrevocable step towards speciation than reproductive isolation by inherited population differences. To put it in another way, the employment of learned behavior patterns to accomplish a limited degree of reproductive isolation of local populations may have the valuable advantage of flexibility, so that populations faced with a change in their habitat, or forced to move to a new one, could still regain access to the main gene pool of the species and shift to another evolutionary tack in the space of a few generations.

BIRD SONG AND SPEECH DEVELOPMENT

The explanation advanced for the important role of learning in the song development of the white-crowned sparrow is clearly speculative. At least it is obvious that the function is entirely different from that in man. In no sense does song learning generate a language. Nevertheless there are many similarities between the processes of song and speech development.

In both, certain kinds of acoustical stimulation play an unexpectedly large role in determining the future structure of the behavior. There are critical periods of life when the ability for the particular kind of learning involved is at its height. Predispositions brought to vocal learning have a prominent role in determining the course that development will take. In both sparrows and man some kind of mechanism exists to focus the young organism's attention on the sounds of members of its own species. Human predispositions to develop certain kinds of syntactic structure have also been postulated.

Audition plays the double role of allowing external sounds to be heard and remembered, and of allowing the organism to hear its own voice and to match the voice to the memory of what has been learned previously (Fry, 1966). In both birds and man the reliance on auditory feedback, that is so critical for normal development, becomes redundant as vocal development is complete. As a man deafened after speech has developed maintains the original basic pattern in spite of slurring of consonants and other speech elements, a monotonous tone, and sudden changes of loudness, so a bird deafened as an adult can maintain normal song. In both birds and man some vocal learning seems to occur independently of extrinsic reinforcement, indicating that the act of matching vocalization with sounds heard may have intrinsic reinforcing properties.

The shaping of vocalizations as a result of prior auditory experience is first manifest in the young bird as subsong and in the child as the transition from "babbling to adult intonation without articulation."[4] In both species these intermediate stages are apparently unavoidable and probably serve an important function in establishing an accurate match between sounds heard and sounds produced. The song of a white-crowned sparrow deafened early in life resembles an early stage of normal subsong, and a child deafened early will babble normally (Lenneberg, 1967), demonstrating in each case that one phase of normal vocal development can proceed without auditory stimulation or feedback.

Are these many parallels mere coincidences? Vocal learning that was not guided by predispositions to develop more readily in some ways than others might easily drift in functionally inappropriate directions. A delay between exposure to a given pattern of sounds and reproduction or rejection of that pattern seems desirable, rather than instantaneous imitation of the pattern, if the predispositions brought to the task are to be given full opportunity to manifest themselves. Perhaps babbling and subsong are significant here as well as in the refinement of skill in using the vocal equipment to match remembered sounds. Rather than reliance upon extrinsic reinforcement of each stage of development, it would seem more efficient if the act of matching auditory feedback to a remembered sound is itself reinforcing, provided that the original sounds have been subjected to some kind of selective filtering. Thus these parallels between song learning of birds and speech development in children perhaps point to a set of conditions to which any system of vocal learning should conform, if it is to function effectively.

References

Armstrong, E. A. *A study of bird song*. London: Oxford University Press, 1963.

Banks, R. C. Development of nestling white-crowned sparrows in central coastal California. *Condor*, 1959, *61*, 96—109.

[4] T. Bever, Personal communication, 1969.

Banks, R. C. Geographic variation in the white-crowned sparrow. *Zonotrichia leucophrys.* *University of California Publications in Zoology*, 1964, *70*, 1–123.

Blanchard, B. D. The white-crowned sparrows (*Zonotricia leucophrys*) of the Pacific seaboard: Environment and annual cycle. *University of California Publications in Zoology*, 1941, *46*, 1–178.

Borror, D. J. Song variation in Maine song sparrows. *Wilson Bulletin*, 1965, *77*, 5–37.

Chomsky, N. The formal nature of language. Appendix A in E. H. Lenneberg (Ed.), *Biological foundations of language*. New York: John Wiley and Sons, 1967.

Collias, N. E., & Joos, M. The spectrographic analysis of sound signals of the domestic fowl. *Behaviour*, 1953, *5*, 175–187.

Foos, B. M. Mimicry in mynas (*Gracula religiosa*): A test of Mowrer's theory. *British Journal of Psychology*, 1964, *55*, 85–88.

Fry, D. B. The development of the phonological system in the normal and the deaf child. In F. Smith & G. A. Miller (Eds.), *The genesis of language*. Cambridge: M.I.T. Press, 1966.

Furness, W. H. Observations of the mentality of chimpanzees and orang-utans. *Proceedings of the American Philosophical Society*, 1916, *55*, 281–290.

Ginsburg, N. Conditioned vocalization in the budgerigar. *Journal of Comparative and Physiological Psychology*, 1960, *53*, 183–186.

Ginsburg, N. Conditioned talking in the mynah bird. *Journal of Comparative and Physiological Psychology*, 1963, *56*, 1061–1063.

Grosslight, J. H., Harrison, P. C., & Weiser, C. M. Reinforcement control of vocal responses in the mynah bird (*Gracula religiosa*). *Psychological Record*, 1962, *12*, 193–201.

Grosslight, J. H., & Zaynor, W. C. Verbal behavior and the mynah bird. In K. Salzinger & S. Salzinger (Eds.), *Research in verbal behavior and some neurophysiological implications*. New York: Academic Press, 1967.

Hayes, C. *The ape in our house*. New York: Harper, 1951.

Hayes, K. J. Vocalization and speech in chimpanzees. *American Psychologist*, 1950, *5*, 275–276.

Hayes, K. J., & Hayes, C. The cultural capacity of chimpanzees. *Human Biology*, 1954, *26*, 288–303.

Immelmann, K. Prägungserscheinungen in der Gesangentwicklung junger Zebrafinken. *Naturwissenschaften*, 1965, *52*, 169–170.

Immelmann, K. Zur ontogenetischen Gesangsentwicklung bei Prachtfinken. *Verhandlungen der Deutschen Zoologischer Gesellschaft (Göttingen)*, 1966, 320–332.

Immelmann, K. Song development in the zebra finch and other estrildid finches. In R. A. Hinde (Ed.), *Bird vocalizations*. Cambridge: Cambridge University Press, 1969.

Kellogg, W. N. Communication and language in the home-raised chimpanzee. *Science*, 1968, *162*, 423–427.

Konishi, M. The role of auditory feedback in the vocal behavior of the domestic fowl. *Zeitschrift für Tierpsychologie*, 1963, *20*, 349–367.

Konishi, M. Effects of deafening on song development in two species of juncos. *Condor*, 1964, *66*, 85–102. (a)

Konishi, M. Song variation in a population of Oregon juncos. *Condor*, 1964, *66*, 423–436. (b)

Konishi, M. The role of auditory feedback in the control of vocalization in the white-crowned sparrow. *Zeitschrift für Tierpsychologie*, 1965, *22*, 770–783.

Konishi, M., & Nottebohm, F. Experimental studies in the ontogeny of avian vocalizations. In R. A. Hinde (Ed.), *Bird vocalizations*. Cambridge: Cambridge University Press, 1969.

Lane, H. Operant control of vocalizing in the chicken. *Journal of the Experimental Analysis of Behavior*, 1961, *4*, 171–177.

Lane, H., & Shinkman, P. G. Methods and findings in an analysis of a vocal operant. *Journal of the Experimental Analysis of Behavior*, 1963, *6*, 179–188.

Lanyon, W. E. The comparative biology of the meadowlarks (*Sturnella*) in Wisconsin. *Publication of the Nuttall Ornithological Club*, 1957, *1*, 1—67.

Lanyon, W. E. The ontogeny of vocalizations in birds. In W. E. Lanyon & W. N. Tavolga (Eds.), *Animal sounds and communication*. Washington, D. C.: American Institute of Biological Sciences, 1960.

Lemon, R. E. The song repertoires of cardinals (*Richmondena cardinalis*) at London, Ontario. *Canadian Journal of Zoology*, 1965, *43*, 559—569.

Lemon, R. E., & Scott, D. M. On the development of song in young cardinals. *Canadian Journal of Zoology*, 1966, *44*, 191—197.

Lenneberg, E. H. *Biological foundations of language*. New York: John Wiley and Sons, 1967.

Marler, P. Variation in the song of the chaffinch, *Fringilla coelebs*. *Ibis*, 1952, *94*, 458—472.

Marler, P. The voice of the chaffinch and its function as language. *Ibis*, 1956, *98*, 231—261.

Marler, P. Inheritance and learning in the development of animal vocalizations. In R. C. Busnel (Ed.), *Acoustic behavior of animals*. Amsterdam: Elsevier, 1964.

Marler, P. Comparative study of song development in sparrows. *Proceedings of the XIV International Ornithological Congress*, 1967, 231—244.

Marler, P., & Hamilton, W. J., III. *Mechanisms of animal behavior*. New York: John Wiley and Sons, 1966.

Marler, P., & Isaac, D. Song variation in a population of Mexican juncos. *Wilson Bulletin*, 1961, *73*, 193—206.

Marler, P., Kreith, M., & Tamura, M. Song development in hand-raised Oregon juncos. *Auk*, 1962, *79*, 12—30.

Marler, P., & Tamura, M. Song dialects in three populations of white-crowned sparrows. *Condor*, 1962, *64*, 368—377.

Marler, P., & Tamura, M. Culturally transmitted patterns of vocal behavior in sparrows. *Science*, 1964, *146*, 1483—1486.

McNeill, D. Developmental psycholinguistics. In F. Smith & G. A. Miller (Eds.), *The genesis of language*. Cambridge: M.I.T. Press, 1966.

Milligan, M. M. Vocal responses of white-crowned sparrows to recorded songs of their own and another species. *Animal Behavior*, 1966, *14*, 356—361.

Mowrer, O. H. On the psychology of "talking birds"—A contribution to language and personality theory. In O. H. Mowrer (Ed.), *Learning theory and personality dynamics*. New York: Ronald Press, 1950.

Mowrer, O. H. Hearing and speaking: An analysis of language learning. *Journal of Speech Hearing Disorders*, 1958, *23*, 143—152.

Mulligan, J. A. A description of song sparrow song based on instrumental analysis. *Proceedings of the XIII International Ornithological Congress*, 1963, 272—284.

Mulligan, J. A. Singing behavior and its development in the song sparrow. *Melospiza melodia*. *University of California Publications in Zoology*, 1966, *81*, 1—76.

Nicolai, J. Familientradition in der Gesangsentwicklung des Gimpels (*Pyrrhula pyrrhula L.*) *Journal für Ornithologie*, 1959, *100*, 39—46.

Nottebohm, F. The role of sensory feedback in the development of avian vocalizations. Unpublished doctoral dissertation, University of California, Berkeley, 1966.

Nottebohm, F. The role of sensory feedback in the development of avian vocalizations. *Proceedings of the XIV International Ornithological Congress*, 1967, 265—280.

Nottebohm, F. Auditory experience and song development in the chaffinch. (*Fringilla coelebs*). *Ibis*, 1968, *110*, 549—568.

Nottebohm, F. The "critical period" for song learning in birds. *Ibis*, 1969, *3*, 386—387. (a)

Nottebohm, F. The song of the chingolo, *Zonotrichia capensis*, in Argentina: Description and evaluation of a system of dialects. *Condor*, 1969, *71*, 299—315. (b)

Poulsen, H. Inheritance and learning in the song of the chaffinch, *Fringilla coelebs L.*

Behaviour, 1951, *3*, 216—228.

Poulsen, H. On the song of the linnet (*Carduelis cannabina L.*) *Dansk Ornithologisk Forenings Tidsskrift*, 1954, *48*, 32—37.

Skinner, B. F. *Verbal behavior*. New York: Appleton-Century-Crofts, 1957.

Thorpe, W. H. Comments on *The bird fancier's delight*, together with notes on imitation in the sub-song of the chaffinch. *Ibis*, 1955, *97*, 247—251.

Thorpe, W. H. The learning of song patterns by birds, with especial reference to the song of the chaffinch *Fringilla coelebs*. *Ibis*, 1958, *100*, 535—570.

Thorpe, W. H. Talking birds and the mode of action of the vocal apparatus of birds. *Proceedings of the Zoological Society of London*, 1959, *132*, 441—455.

Thorpe, W. H. *Bird song: The biology of vocal communication and expression in birds*. Cambridge: Cambridge University Press, 1961. (a)

Thorpe, W. H. Sensitive periods in the learning of animals and men: A study of imprinting with special reference to the induction of cyclic behaviour. In W. H. Thorpe & O. L. Zangwill (Eds.), *Current problems in animal behavior*. Cambridge: Cambridge University Press, 1961. (b)

Thorpe, W. H. The ontogeny of behaviour. In J. A. Moore (Ed.), *Ideas in modern biology. Proceedings of the XVI International Congress of Zoology*, 1965, 485—518.

Thorpe, W. H., & Pilcher, P. M. The nature and characteristics of subsong. *British Birds*, 1958, *51*, 509—514.

Weir, R. H. Some questions on the child's learning of phonology. In F. Smith & G. A. Miller (Eds.), *The genesis of language*. Cambridge: M.I.T. Press, 1966.

V

HUMAN FUNCTIONING:
LANGUAGE,
DEVELOPMENT,
AND PSYCHOPATHOLOGY

And so we turn to Homo sapiens. *There has been a recent trend in psychology to treat man, with his complex cognitive functions, as an animal discontinuous from other animals, and correspondingly the interest of psychologists in findings from nonhumans has been waning. Although the reasons are many, a prominent one is that general-process learning theory has failed to capture and bring into the laboratory phenomena which provide fertile models of complex human learning. This failure may be due in part to the equipotentiality premise. By concentrating on contingencies for which animals are relatively unprepared, the laws and models which general-process learning theories have produced may not be applicable beyond the realm of arbitrary events, arbitrarily connected. This would not be an obstacle if all of human learning was about arbitrary contingencies. But it is not. Man has an evolutionary history and a genetic makeup which has made him relatively prepared to learn some things and contraprepared to learn others. If laws of learning vary with preparedness, it should not be surprising that the laws of unprepared associations are not applicable to all of human learning. This section deals with the biological boundaries of what men can and cannot learn.*

Eric Lenneberg argues that language, and even cognition as we know it, may be forms of species-specific learning not unlike the acquisition of birdsong discussed by Marler in the previous article. The minimal conclusion from Lenneberg's data is that children do not learn language the way rats learn to press a lever for food, contrary to what Skinner (1957) has argued. Lenneberg provides evidence which suggests that language learning does not require careful training or "shaping." We do not need to arrange sets of linguistic contingencies carefully for our children to speak and understand English; in all but the most impoverished linguistic environments, human beings will come to speak and understand. Human acquisition of language, like pigeons' pecking for grain and sparrows' singing, is prepared. From our point of view, it is not surprising that the traditional analysis of instrumental and classical conditioning is inadequate for an analysis of language. This is not because language is a phenomenon sui generis, *but because the laws of instrumental and classical conditioning were developed to explain learning in unprepared situations rather than in prepared situations.*

30

ON EXPLAINING LANGUAGE

Eric H. Lenneberg

Many explanations have been offered for many aspects of language; there is little agreement, however, on how to explain various problems or even on what there is to be explained. Of course, explanations differ with the personal inclinations and interests of the investigator. My interests are in man as a biological species, and I believe that the study of language is relevant to these interests because language has the following six characteristics. (i) It is a form of behavior present in all cultures of the world. (ii) In all cultures its onset is age correlated. (iii) There is only one acquisition strategy—it is the same for all babies everywhere in the world. (iv) It is based intrinsically upon the same formal operating characteristics whatever its outward form (1). (v) Throughout man's recorded history these operating characteristics have been constant. (vi) It is a form of behavior that may be impaired specifically by circumscribed brain lesions which may leave other mental and motor skills relatively unaffected.

Any form of human behavior that has all of these six characteristics may likewise be assumed to have a rather specific biological foundation. This, of course, does not mean that language cannot be studied from different points of view; it can, for example, be investigated for its cultural or social variations, its capacity to reflect individual differences, or its applications. The purpose of this article, however, is to discuss the aspects of language to which biological concepts are applied most appropriately (2). Further, my concern is with the development of language in children—not with its origin in the species.

PREDICTABILITY OF LANGUAGE DEVELOPMENT

A little boy starts washing his hands before dinner no sooner than when his parents decide that training in cleanliness should begin. However, children begin to speak no sooner and no later than when they reach a given stage of physical maturation (Table 1). There are individual variations in development, particularly with respect to age correlation. It is interesting that language development correlates better with motor development than it does with chronological age. If

From *Science*, 164 (1969), 635—643.
I thank H. Levin and M. Seligman for comments and criticisms.

TABLE 1 Correlation of Motor and Language Development

Age (years)	Motor milestones	Language milestones
0.5	Sits using hands for support; unilateral reaching	Cooing sounds change to babbling by introduction of consonantal sounds
1	Stands; walks when held by one hand	Syllabic reduplication; signs of understanding some words; applies some sounds regularly to signify persons or objects, that is, the first words
1.5	Prehension and release fully developed; gait propulsive; creeps downstairs backward	Repertoire of 3 to 50 words not joined in phrases; trains of sounds and intonation patterns resembling discourse; good progress in understanding
2	Runs (with falls); walks stairs with one foot forward only	More than 50 words; two-word phrases most common; more interest in verbal communication; no more babbling
2.5	Jumps with both feet; stands on one foot for 1 second; builds tower of six cubes	Every day new words; utterances of three and more words; seems to understand almost everything said to him; still many grammatical deviations
3	Tiptoes 3 yards (2.7 meters); walks stairs with alternating feet; jumps 0.9 meter	Vocabulary of some 1000 words; about 80 percent intelligibility; grammar of utterances close approximation to colloquial adult; syntacic mistakes fewer in variety, systematic, predictable
4.5	Jumps over rope; hops on one foot; walks on line	Language well established; grammatical anomalies restricted either to unusual constructions or to the more literate aspects of discourse

we take these two variables (motor and language development) and make ordinal scales out of the stages shown in Table 1 and then use them for a correlation matrix, the result is a remarkably small degree of scatter. Since motor development is one of the most important indices of maturation, it is not unreasonable to propose that language development, too, is related to physical growth and development. This impression is further corroborated by examination of retarded children. Here the age correlation is very poor, whereas the correlation between motor and language development continues to be high (3). Nevertheless, there is evidence that the statistical relation between motor and language development is not due to any immediate, causal relation; peripheral motor disabilities can occur that do not delay language acquisition.

Just as it is possible to correlate the variable language development with the variables chronological age or motor development, it is possible to relate it to the physical indications of brain maturation, such as the gross weight of the brain, neurodensity in the cerebral cortex, or the changing weight proportions of given substances in either gray or white matter. On almost all counts, language begins when such maturational indices have attained at least 65 percent of their mature values. (Inversely, language acquisition becomes more difficult when the physical maturation of the brain is complete.) These correlations do not prove causal connections, although they suggest some interesting questions for further research.

EFFECT OF CERTAIN VARIATIONS
IN SOCIAL ENVIRONMENT

In most of the studies on this topic the language development of children in orphanages or socially deprived households has been compared with that of children in so-called normal, middle-class environments. Statistically significant differences are usually reported, which is sometimes taken as a demonstration that language development is contingent on specific language training. That certain aspects of the environment are absolutely essential for language development is undeniable, but it is important to distinguish between what the children actually do, and what they can do.

There is nothing particularly surprising or revealing in the demonstration that language deficits occur in children who hear no language, very little language, or only the discourse of uneducated persons. But what interests us is the underlying capacity for language. This is not a spurious question; for instance, some children have the capacity for language but do not use it, either because of peripheral handicaps such as congenital deafness or because of psychiatric disturbances such as childhood schizophrenia; other children may not speak because they do not have a sufficient capacity for language, on account of certain severely retarding diseases.

There is a simple technique for ascertaining the degree of development of the capacity for speech and language. Instead of assessing it by means of an inventory of the vocabulary, the grammatical complexity of the utterances, the clarity of pronunciation, and the like, and computing a score derived from several subtests of this kind, it is preferable to describe the children's ability in terms of a few broad and general developmental stages, such as those shown in

Table 1. Tests which are essentially inventories of vocabulary and syntactic constructions are likely to reflect simply the deficiencies of the environment; they obscure the child's potentialities and capabilities.

I have used the schema described to compare the speech development of children in many different societies, some of them much more primitive than our own. In none of these studies could I find evidence of variation in developmental rate, despite the enormous differences in social environment.

I have also had an opportunity to study the effect of a dramatically different speech environment upon the development of vocalizations during the first 3 months of life (4). It is very common in our culture for congenitally deaf individuals to marry one another, creating households in which all vocal sounds are decidedly different from those normally heard and in which the sounds of babies cannot be attended to directly. Six deaf mothers and ten hearing mothers were asked, during their last month of pregnancy, to participate in our study. The babies were visited at home when they were no more than 10 days old and were seen biweekly thereafter for at least 3 months. Each visit consisted of 3 hours of observation and 24 hours of mechanical recording of all sounds made and heard by the baby. Data were analyzed quantitatively and qualitatively. Figure 1 shows that although the environment was quantitatively quite different in the experimental and the control groups, the frequency distributions of various baby noises did not differ significantly; as seen in Fig. 2, the developmental histories of cooing noises are also remarkably alike in the two groups. Figure 3 demonstrates that the babies of deaf parents tend to fuss an equal amount, even though the hearing parents are much more likely to come to the child when it fusses. Thus the earliest development of human sounds appears to be relatively independent of the amount, nature, or timing of the sounds made by parents.

I have observed this type of child-rearing through later stages, as well. The hearing children of deaf parents eventually learn two languages and sound systems; those of their deaf parents and those of the rest of the community. In some instances, communication between children and parents is predominantly by gestures. In no case have I found any adverse effects upon the language development of standard English in these children. Although the mothers made sounds different from the children's, and although the children's vocalizations had no significant effect upon attaining what they wanted during early infancy, language in these children invariably began at the usual time and went through the same stages as is normally encountered.

Also of interest may be the following observations on fairly retarded children growing up in state institutions that are badly understaffed. During the day the children play in large, bare rooms, attended by only one person, often an older retardate who herself lacks a perfect command of language. The children's only entertainment is provided by a large television set, playing all day at full strength. Although most of these retarded children have only primitive beginnings of language, there are always some among them who manage, even under these extremely deprived circumstances, to pick up an amazing degree of language skill. Apparently they learn language partly through the television programs, whose level is often quite adequate for them!

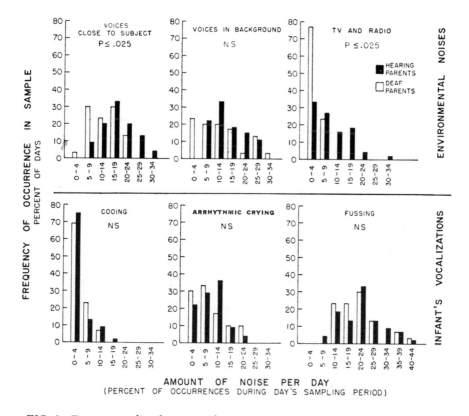

FIG. 1 Frequency distributions of various noises. The basic counting unit is individual recording days.

From these instances we see that language capacity follows its own natural history. The child can avail himself of this capacity if the environment provides a minimum of stimulation and opportunity. His engagement in language activity can be limited by his environmental circumstances, but the underlying capacity is not easily arrested. Impoverished environments are not conducive to good language development, but good language development is not contingent on specific training measures (5); a wide variety of rather haphazard factors seem to be sufficient.

EFFECT OF VARIATIONS IN GENETIC BACKGROUND

Man is an unsatisfactory subject for the study of genetic influences; we cannot do breeding experiments on him and can use only statistical controls. Practically any evidence adduced is susceptible to a variety of interpretations. Nevertheless, there are indications that inheritance is at least partially responsible for deviations in verbal skills, as in the familial occurrence of a deficit termed

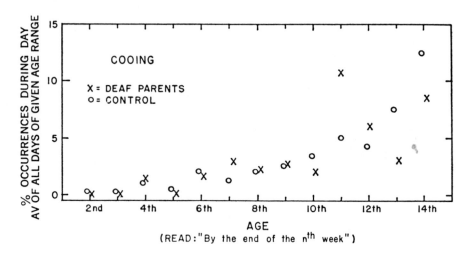

FIG. 2 Each baby's day was divided into 6-minute periods; the presence or absence of cooing was noted for each period; this yielded a percentage for each baby's day; days of all babies were ordered by their ages, and the average was taken for all days of identical age. Nonaveraged data were published in (4).

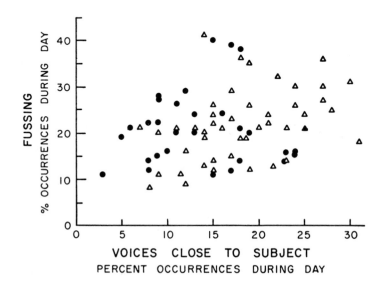

FIG. 3 Relation between the amount of parents' noises heard by the baby and the amount of fussing noises made by the baby. Each symbol is one baby's day; (solid circles) deaf parents; (triangles) hearing parents.

congenital language disability (2, chapter 6). Studies, with complete pedigrees, have been published on the occurrence and distribution of stuttering, of hyperfluencies, of voice qualities, and of many other traits, which constitute supporting though not conclusive evidence that inheritance plays a role in language acquisition. In addition to such family studies, much research has been carried out on twins. Particularly notable are the studies of Luchsinger, who reported on the concordance of developmental histories and of many aspects of speech and language. Zygosity was established in these cases by serology (Fig. 4). Developmental data of this kind are, in my opinion, of greater relevance to our speculations on genetic background than are pedigrees.

The nonbiologist frequently and mistakenly thinks of genes as being directly responsible for one property or another; this leads him to the fallacy, especially when behavior is concerned, of dichotomizing everything as being dependent on either genes or environment. Genes act merely on intracellular biochemical processes, although these processes have indirect effects on events in the individual's developmental history. Many alterations in structure and function indirectly attributable to genes are more immediately the consequence of alterations in the schedule of developmental events. Therefore, the studies on twins are important in that they show that homozygotes reach milestones in language development at the same age, in contrast to heterozygotes, in whom divergences are relatively common. It is also interesting that the nature of the deviations—the symptoms, if you wish—are, in the vast majority, identical in homozygotes but not in heterozygotes.

Such evidence indicates that man's biological heritage endows him with sensitivities and propensities that lead to language development in children, who are spoken to (in contrast to chimpanzee infants, who do not automatically develop language—either receptive or productive—under identical treatment). The endowment has a genetic foundation, but this is not to say that there are "genes for language," or that the environment is of no importance.

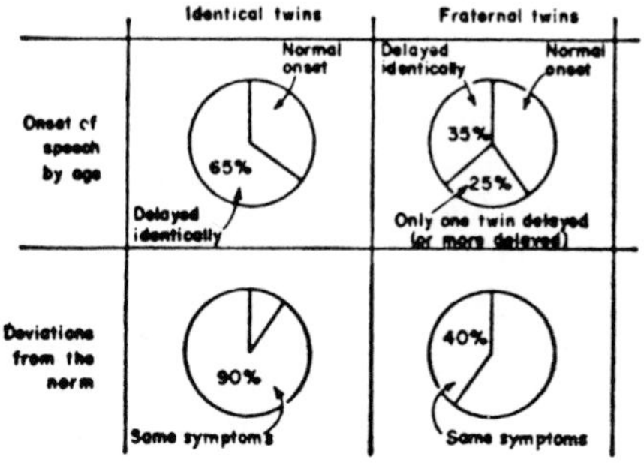

FIG. 4 The onset of speech and its subsequent development tend to be more uniform among identical twins than fraternal twins.

ATTEMPTS TO MODIFY LANGUAGE DEVELOPMENT

Let us now consider children who have the capacity for language acquisition but fail to develop it for lack of exposure. This is the case with the congenitally deaf, who are allowed to grow up without either language or speech until school age, when suddenly language is brought to them in very unnatural ways. Before this time they may have half a dozen words they can utter, read, write, or finger-spell, but I have known of no profoundly deaf child (in New England, where my investigations were conducted) with whom one could communicate by use of the English language before school age.

When deaf children enter an oralist school, lipreading and speech become the major preoccupation of training. However, in most children these activities remain poor for many more years, and in some, throughout life. Their knowledge of language comes through learning to read and write. However, teachers in the oral tradition restrict expression in the graphic medium on the hypothesis that it interferes with lipreading and speech skills. Thus, exposure to language (i) comes much later in these children's lives than is normal, (ii) is dramatically reduced in quantity, (iii) is presented through a different medium and sensory modality, and (iv) is taught to the children rather as a second language is taught, instead of through the simple immersion into a sea of language that most children experience. The deaf children are immediately required to use grammatically correct sentences, and every mistake is discussed and explained to them.

The results of this procedure are interesting but not very encouraging from the educational point of view. During the early years of schooling, the children's spontaneous writings have a very unusual pattern; there is little evidence that the teachers' instruction in "how to compose correct sentences" is of any avail. Yet, careful analysis of their compositions show that some subtleties of English syntax that are usually not part of the grammar taught in the school do make their appearance, sometimes quite early. There can be no question that the children do not simply imitate what they see; some of the teachings fall by the wayside, whereas a number of aspects of language are automatically absorbed from the written material given to the children.

There are other instances in which efforts are made to change a child's language skills by special training, as in the mildly retarded, for example. Many parents believe that their retarded child would function quite normally if somebody could just teach him to speak. At Children's Hospital in Boston I undertook a pilot study in which a speech therapist saw a small number of children with Downe's syndrome (mongolism) for several hours each week, in an effort to speed up language development. Later, two graduate students in linguistics investigated the children's phonetic skills and tried to assess the capacities of each child for clearer enunciation. Throughout these attempts, it was found that if a child had a small repertoire of single words, it was always possible to teach him yet another word, but if he was not joining these words spontaneously into phrases, there was nothing that could be done to induce him to do so. The articulatory skills were somewhat different. It was often possible to make a child who had always had slurred speech say a specific word more clearly. However, the moment the child returned to spontaneous utterances, he would fall back to the style that was usual for him. The most interesting results were obtained when the retarded children were required simply to repeat well-formed sentences. A child who had not developed to a stage in which he used certain grammatical rules spontaneously, who was still missing the syntactic foundations and prerequisites, could not be taught to repeat a sentence that was formed by such higher rules. This was true even in sentences of very few words. Similar observations have since been made on normal children (6), with uniformly similar results; normal children, too, can repeat correctly only that which is formed by rules they have already mastered. This is the best indication that language does not come about by simple imitation, but that the child abstracts regularities or relations from the language he hears, which he then applies to building up language for himself as an apparatus of principles.

WHAT SETS THE PACE OF LANGUAGE DEVELOPMENT

There is a widespread belief that the development of language is dependent on the motor skills of the articulating organs. Some psychologists believe that species other than man fail to develop language only because of anatomical differences in their oral structures. However, we have evidence that this is not so.

It is important that we are clear about the essential nature of language. Since my interests are in language capacities, I am concerned with the development of the child's knowledge of how language works. This is not the same as the acquisition of "the first word." The best test for the presence and development of this knowledge is the manner in which discourse is understood. In most instances, it is true that there is a relation between speech and understanding, but this relation is not a necessary one (7).

By understanding, I mean something quite specific. In the realm of phonology, understanding involves a process that roughly corresponds to the linguists' phonematization (in contrast, for example, to a "pictographic" understanding: phonematization results in seeing similarities between speech sounds, whereas pictographic understanding would treat a word as an indivisible sound pattern). In the realm of semantics, understanding involves seeing the basis on which objects are categorized, thus enabling a child to name an object correctly that he has never seen before. (The child does not start out with a hypothesis that "table" is the proper name of a unique object or that it refers to all things that have four appendages.) In the realm of grammar, understanding involves the extraction of relations between word classes; an example is the understanding of predication. By application of these tests, it can be shown empirically that Aunt Pauline's favorite lapdog does not have a little language knowledge, but in fact, fails the test of understanding on all counts.

A survey of children with a variety of handicaps shows that their grasp of how language works is intimately related to their general cognitive growth, which, in turn, is partly dependent on physical maturation and partly on opportunities to interact with a stimulus-rich environment. In many retarding diseases, for example, language development is predicted best by the rate of advancement in mental age (using tests of nonverbal intelligence). In an investigation of congenitally blind children (8), we are again finding that major milestones for language development are highly correlated with physical development. A naive conception of language development as an accumulation of associations between visual and auditory patterns would be hard put to explain this.

BRAIN CORRELATES

In adults, language functions take place predominantly in the left hemisphere. A number of cortical fields have been related to specific aspects of language. The details are still somewhat controversial and need not concern us here. It is certain, however, that precentral areas of the frontal lobe are principally involved in the production of language, whereas the postcentral parietal and superior temporal fields are involved in sensory functions. These cortical specializations are not present at birth, but become only gradually established during childhood, in a process very similar to that of embryological history; there is evidence of differentiation and regulation of function. In the adult, traumata causing large left-sided central cortical lesions carry a highly pre-dictable prognosis; in 70 percent of all cases, aphasia occurs, and in about half of these, the condition is irreversible (I am basing these figures on our experience with penetrating head injuries incurred in war).

Comparable traumatic lesions in childhood have quite different consequences, the prognosis being directly related to the age at which the insult is incurred. Lesions of the left hemisphere in children under age 2 are no more injurious to future language development than are lesions of the right hemisphere. Children whose brain is traumatized after the onset of language but before the age of 4 usually have transient aphasias; language is quickly reestablished, however, if the right hemisphere remains intact. Often these children regain language by going through stages of language development similar to those of the 2-year-old, but they traverse each stage at greater speed. Lesions incurred before the very early teens also carry an excellent prognosis, permanent residues of symptoms being extremely rare.

The prognosis becomes rapidly worse for lesions that occur after this period; the young men who become casualties of war have symptoms virtually identical with those of stroke patients of advanced age. Experience with the surgical removal of an entire cerebral hemisphere closely parallels this picture. The basis for prognosticating operative success is, again, the age at which the disease has been contracted for which the operation is performed.

If a disturbance in the left hemisphere occurs early enough in life, the right hemisphere remains competent for language throughout life. Apparently this process is comparable to regulation, as we know it from morphogenesis. If the disease occurs after a certain critical period of life, namely, the early teens, this regulative capacity is lost and language is interfered with permanently. Thus the time at which the hemispherectomy is performed is less important than the time of the lesion.

CRITICAL AGE FOR LANGUAGE ACQUISITION

The most reasonable interpretation of this picture of recovery from aphasia in childhood is not that there is vicarious functioning, or taking over, by the right hemisphere because of need, but rather that language functions are not yet confined to the left hemisphere during early life. Apparently both hemispheres are involved at the beginning, and a specialization takes place later (which is the characteristic of differentiation), resulting in a kind of left-right polarization of functions. Therefore, the recovery from aphasia during preteen years may partly be regarded as a reinstatement of activities that had never been lost. There is evidence that children at this age are capable of developing language in the same natural way as do very young children. Not only do symptoms subside, but active language development continues to occur. Similarly, we see that healthy children have a quite different propensity for acquiring foreign languages before the early teens than after the late teens, the period in between being transitional. For the young adult, second-language learning is an academic exercise, and there is a vast variety in degree of proficiency. It rapidly becomes more and more difficult to overcome the accent and interfering influences of the mother tongue.

Neurological material strongly suggests that something happens in the brain during the early teens that changes the propensity for language acquistion. We do not know the factors involved, but it is interesting that the critical period coincides with the time at which the human brain attains its final state of maturity in terms of structure, function, and biochemistry (electroencephalographic patterns slightly lag behind, but become stabilized by about 16 years). Apparently the maturation of the brain marks the end of regulation and locks certain functions into place.

There is further evidence that corroborates the notion of a critical period for primary language acquisition, most importantly, the developmental histories of retarded children. It is dangerous to make sweeping generalizations about all retarded children, because so much depends on the specific disease that causes the retardation. But if we concentrate on diseases in which the pathological condition is essentially stationary, such as microcephaly vera or mongolism, it is possible to make fairly general predictions about language development. If the child's mental developmental age is 2 when he is 4 years old (that is, his I.Q. is 50), one may safely predict that some small progress will be made in language development. He will slowly move through the usual stages of infant language, although the rate of development will gradually slow down. In virtually all of these cases, language development comes to a complete standstill in the early teens, so that these individuals are arrested in primitive stages of language development that are perpetuated for the rest of their lives. Training and motivation are of little help.

Development in the congenitally deaf is also revealing. When they first enter school, their language acquisition is usually quite spectacular, considering the enormous odds against them. However, children who by their early teens have still not mastered all of the principles that underlie the production of sentences appear to encounter almost unsurmountable difficulties in perfecting verbal skills.

There is also evidence of the converse. Children who suddenly lose their hearing (usually a consequence of meningitis) show very different degrees of language skill, depending on whether the disease strikes before the onset of language or after. If it occurs before they are 18 months old, such children encounter difficulties with language development that are very much the same as those encountered by the congenitally deaf. Children who lose their hearing after they have acquired language, however, at age 3 to 4, have a different prospect. Their speech deteriorates rapidly; usually within weeks they stop using language, and so far it has proved impossible to maintain the skill by educational procedures [although new techniques developed in England and described by Fry (9) give promise of great improvement]. Many such children then live without language for a relatively long time, often 2 to 3 years, and when they enter the schools for the deaf, must be trained in the same way that other deaf children are trained. However, training is much more successful, and their language habits stand out dramatically against those of their less fortunate colleagues. There appears to be a direct relation between the length of time during which a child has been exposed to language and the proficiency seen at the time of retraining.

BIOLOGICAL APPROACH:
DEFINING LANGUAGE FURTHER

Some investigators propose that language is an artifact—a tool that man has shaped for himself to serve a purpose. This assumption induces the view that language consists of many individual traits, each independent of the other. However, the panorama of observations presented above suggests a biological predisposition for the development of language that is anchored in the operating characteristics of the human brain (10). Man's cognitive apparatus apparently becomes a language receiver and transmitter, provided the growing organism is exposed to minimum and haphazard environmental events.

However, this assumption leads to a view different from that suggested by the artifact assumption. Instead of thinking of language as a collection of separate and mutually independent traits, one comes to see it as a profoundly integrated activity. Language is to be understood as an operation rather than a static product of the mind. Its modus operandi reflects that of human cognition, because language is an intimate part of cognition. Thus the biological view denies that language is the cause of cognition, or even its effect, since language is not an object (like a tool) that exists apart from a living human brain.

As biologists, we are interested in the operating principles of language because we hope that this will give us some clues about the operating principles of the human brain. We know there is just one species Homo sapiens, and it is therefore reasonable to assume that individuals who speak Turkish, English, or Basque (or who spoke Sanskrit some millennia ago) all have (or had) the same kind of brain, that is, a computer with the same operating principles and the same sensorium. Therefore, in a biological investigation one must try to disregard the differences between the languages of the world and to discover the general principles of operation that are common to all of them. This is not an easy matter; in fact, there are social scientists who doubt the existence of language universals. As students of language we cannot fail to be impressed with the enormous differences among languages. Yet every normal child learns the language to which he is exposed. Perhaps we are simply claiming that common denominators must exist; can we prove their existence? If we discovered a totally isolated tribe with a language unknown to any outsider, how could we find out whether this language is generated by a computer that has the same biological characteristics as do our brains, and how could we prove that it shares the universal features of all languages?

As a start, we could exchange children between our two cultures to discover whether the same language developmental history would occur in those exchanged. Our data would be gross developmental stages, correlated with the emergence of motor milestones. A bioassay of this kind (already performed many times, always with positive results) gives only part of the answer.

In theory, one may also adduce more rigorous proof of similarity among languages. The conception of language universals is difficult to grasp intuitively, because we find it so hard to translate from one language to another and because the grammars appear, on the surface, to be so different. But it is entirely possible that underneath the structural difference that makes it so difficult for the adult speaker to learn a second language (particularly one that is not a cognate of his own) there are significant formal identities.

Virtually every aspect of language is the expression of relations. This is true of phonology (as stressed by Roman Jakobson and his school), semantics, and syntax. For instance, in all languages of the world words label a set of relational principles instead of being labels of specific objects. Knowing a word is never a simple association between an object and an acoustic pattern, but the successful operation of those principles, or application of those rules, that lead to using the word "table" or "house" for objects never before encountered. The language universal in this instance is not the type of object that comes to have a word, nor the particular relations involved; the universal is the generality that words stand for relations instead of being unique names for one object.

Further, no language has ever been described that does not have a second order of relational principles, namely, principles in which relations are being related, that is, syntax in which relations between words are being specified. Once again, the universal is not a particular relation that occurs in all languages (though there are several such relations) but that all languages have relations of relations.

Mathematics may be used as a highly abstract form of description, not of scattered facts but of the dynamic interrelations—the operating principles—found in nature. Chomsky and his students have done this. Their aim has been to develop algorithms for specific languages, primarily English, that make explicit the series of computations that may account for the structure of sentences. The fact that these attempts have only been partially successful is irrelevant to the argument here. (Since every native speaker of English *can* tell a well-formed sentence from an ill-formed one, it is evident that some principles must exist; the question is merely whether the Chomskyites have discovered the correct ones.) The development of algorithms is only one province of mathematics, and in the eyes of many mathematicians a relatively limited one. There is a more exciting prospect; once we know something about the basic relational operating principles underlying a few languages, it should be possible to characterize formally the abstract system *language* as a whole. If our assumption of the existence of basic, structural language universals is correct, one ought to be able to adduce rigorous proof for the existence of homeomorphisms between any natural languages, that is, any of the systems characterized formally. If a category calculus were developed for this sort of thing, there would be one level of generality on which a common denominator could be found; this may be done trivially (for instance by using the product of all systems). However, our present knowledge of the relations, and the relations of relations, found in the languages so far investigated in depth encourages us to expect a significant solution.

ENVIRONMENT AND MATURATION

Everything in life, including behavior and language, is interaction of the individual with its milieu. But the milieu is not constant. The organism itself helps to shape it (this is true of cells and organs as much as of animals and man). Thus, the organism and its environment is a dynamic system and, phylogenetically, developed as such.

The development of language in the child may be elucidated by applying to it the conceptual framework of developmental biology. Maturation may be characterized as a sequence of states. At each state, the growing organism is capable of accepting some specific input; this it breaks down and resynthesizes in such a way that it makes itself develop into a new state. This new state makes the organism sensitive to new and different types of input, whose acceptance transforms it to yet a further state, which opens the way to still different input, and so on. This is called epigenesis. It is the story of embryological development observable in the formation of the body, as well as in certain aspects of behavior.

At various epigenetic states, the organism may be susceptible to more than one sort of input—it may be susceptible to two or more distinct kinds or even to an infinite variety of inputs, as long as they are within determined limits—and the developmental history varies with the nature of the input accepted. In other words, the organism, during development, comes to crossroads; if condition A is present, it goes one way; if condition B is present, it goes another. We speak of states here, but this is, of course, an abstraction. Every stage of maturation is unstable. It is prone to change into specific directions, but requires a trigger from the environment.

When language acquisition in the child is studied from the point of view of developmental biology, one makes an effort to describe developmental stages together with their tendencies for change and the conditions that bring about that change. I believe that the schema of physical maturation is applicable to the study of language development because children appear to be sensitive to successively different aspects of the language environment. The child first reacts only to intonation patterns. With continued exposure to these patterns as they occur in a given language, mechanisms develop that allow him to process the patterns, and in most instances to reproduce them (although the latter is not a necessary condition for further development). This changes him so that he reaches a new state, a new potential for language development. Now he becomes aware of certain articulatory aspects, can process them and possibly also reproduce them, and so on. A similar sequence of acceptance, synthesis, and state of new acceptance can be demonstrated on the level of semantics and syntax.

That the embryological concepts of differentiation, as well as of determination and regulation, are applicable to the brain processes associated with language development is best illustrated by the material discussed above under the headings "brain correlates" and "critical age for language acquisition." Furthermore, the correlation between language development and other maturational indices suggests that there are anatomical and physiological processes whose maturation sets the pace for both cognitive and language development; it is to these maturational processes that the concept differentiation refers. We often transfer the meaning of the word to the verbal behavior itself, which is not unreasonable, although, strictly speaking, it is the physical correlates only that differentiate.

PSEUDO-HOMOLOGIES AND NAIVE "EVOLUTIONIZING"

The relation between species is established on the basis of structural, physiological, biochemical, and often behavioral correspondences, called homologies. The identification of homologies frequently poses heuristic problems. Common sense may be very misleading in this matter. Unless there is cogent evidence that the correspondences noted are due to a common phylogenetic origin, one must entertain the possibility that resemblances are spurious (though perhaps due to convergence). In other words, not all criteria are equally reliable for the discovery of true homologies. The criteria must pass the following two tests if they are to reveal common biological origins. (i) They must be applicable to traits that have a demonstrable (or at least conceivable) genetic basis; and (ii) the traits to which they apply must not have a sporadic and seemingly random distribution over the taxa of the entire animal kingdom. Homologies cannot be established by relying on similarity that rests on superficial inspection (a whale is not a fish); on logical rather than biological aspects (animals that move at 14 miles per hour are not necessarily related to one another); and on anthropocentric imputation of motives (a squirrel's hoarding of nuts may have nothing in common with man's provisions for his future).

Comparisons of language with animal communication that purport to throw light on the problem of its phylogenetic origins infringe on every one of these guidelines. Attempts to write generative grammars for the language of the bees in order to discover in what respect that language is similar to and different from man's language fail to pass test (i). Syntax does not have a genetic basis any more than do arithmetic or algebra; these are calculi used to describe relations. It may be that the activities or circumstances to which the calculi are applied are in some way related to genetically determined capacities. However, merely the fact that the calculus may or may not be applied obviously does not settle that issue.

The common practice of searching the entire animal kingdom for communication behavior that resembles man's in one respect or another fails test (ii). The fact that some bird species and perhaps two or three cetaceans can make noises that sound like words, that some insects use discrete signals when they communicate, or that recombination of signals has been observed to occur in communication systems of a dozen totally unrelated species are not signs of a common phylogeny or genetically based relationship to language. Furthermore, the similarities noted between human language and animal communication all rest on superficial intuition. The resemblances that exist between human language and the language of the bees and the birds are spurious. The comparative criteria are usually logical (12) instead of biological; and the very idea that there must be a common denominator underlying all communication systems of animals and man is based on an anthropocentric imputation.

Everything in biology has a history, and so every communication system is the result of evolution. But traits or skills do not have an evolutionary history of their own, that is, a history that is independent of the history of the species. Contemporary species are discontinuous groups (except for those in the process of branching) with discontinuous communication behavior. Therefore, historical continuity need not lead to continuity between contemporary communication systems, many of which (including man's) constitute unique developments.

Another recent practice is to give speculative accounts of just how, why, and when human language developed. This is a somewhat futile undertaking. The knowledge that we have gained about the mechanisms of evolution does not enable us to give specific accounts of every event of the past. Paleontological evidence points to the nature of its fauna, flora, and climate. The precursors of modern man have left for us their bones, teeth, and primitive tools. None of these bears any necessary or assured relation to any type of communication system. Most speculations on the nature of the most primitive sounds, on the first discovery of their usefulness, on the reasons for the hypertrophy of the brain, or the consequences of a narrow pelvis are in vain. We can no longer reconstruct what the selection pressures were or in what order they came, because we know too little that is securely established by hard evidence about the ecological and social conditions of fossil man. Moreover, we do not even know what the targets of actual selection were. This is particularly troublesome because every genetic alteration brings about several changes at once, some of which must be quite incidental to the selective process.

SPECIES SPECIFICITIES AND COGNITIVE SPECIALIZATION

In the 19th century it was demonstrated that man is not in a category apart from that of animals. Today it seems to be necessary to defend the view (before many psychologists) that man is not identical with all other animals—in fact, that every animal species is unique, and that most of the commonalities that exist are, at best, homologies. It is frequently claimed that the principles of behavioral function are identical—in all vertebrates, for example—and that the differences between species are differences of magnitude, rather than quality. At other times, it is assumed that cognitive functions are alike in two species except that one of the two may have additionally acquired a capacity for a specific activity. I find fault with both views.

Since behavioral capacities (I prefer the term cognition) are the product of brain function, my point can well be illustrated by considering some aspects of brain evolution. Every mammalian species has an anatomically distinct brain. Homologies are common, but innovations can also be demonstrated. When man's brain is compared with the brain of other primates, extensive correspondences can be found, but there are major problems when it comes to the identication of homologies. Dramatic differences exist not only in size but also in details of the developmental histories; together with differences in cerebrocortical histology, topography, and extent, there are differences in subcortical fiber-connections, as pointed out by Geschwind (*13*) most recently and by others before him. The problem is, what do we make of the innovations? Is it possible that each innovation (usually an innovation is not a clear-cut anatomical entity) is like an independent component that is simply added to the components common to all the more old-fashioned brains? And if so, is it likely that the new component is simply adding a routine to the computational facilities already available? Both presumptions are naive. A brain is an integrated organ, and cognition results from the integrated operation of all its tissues and suborgans. Man's brain is not a chimpanzee's brain plus added "association facilities." Its functions have undergone reintegration at the same pace as its evolutionary developments.

The identical argument applies to cognitive functions. Cognition is not made up of isolated processes such as perception, storing, and retrieval. Animals do not all have an identical memory mechanism except that some have a larger storage capacity. As the structure of most proteins, the morphology of most cells, and the gross anatomy of most animals show certain species specificities (as do details of behavioral repertoires), so we may expect that cognition, too, in all of its aspects, has its species specificities. My assumption, therefore, is that man's cognition is not essentially that of every other primate with merely the addition of the capacity for language; instead, I propose that his entire cognitive function, of which his capacity for language is an integral part, is species-specific. I repeat once more that I make this assumption not because I think man is in a category all of his own, but because every animal species must be assumed to have cognitive specificities.

CONCLUSION

The human brain is a biochemical machine; it computes the relations expressed in sentences and their components. It has a print-out consisting of acoustic patterns that are capable of similar relational computation by machines of the same constitution using the same program. Linguists, biologists, and psychologists have all discussed certain aspects of the machine.

Linguists, particularly those developing generative grammar, aim at a formal description of the machine's behavior; they search mathematics for a calculus to describe it adequately. Different calculations are matched against the behavior to test their descriptive adequacy. This is an empirical procedure. The raw data are the way a speaker of a language understands collections of words or the relationships he sees. A totally adequate calculus has not yet been discovered. Once available, it will merely describe, in formal terms, the process of relational interpretation in the realm of verbal behavior. It will describe a set of operations; however, it will not make any claims of isomorphism between the formal operations and the biological operations they describe.

Biologists try to understand the nature, growth, and function of the machine (the human brain) itself. They make little inroads here and there, and generally play catch-as-catch-can; everything about the machine interests them (including the descriptions furnished by linguists).

Traditionally, learning theory has been involved neither in a specific description of this particular machine's behavior nor in its physical constitution. Its concern has been with the use of the machine: What makes it go? Can one make it operate more or less often? What purposes does it serve?

Answers provided by each of these inquiries into language are not intrinsically antagonistic, as has often been claimed. It is only certain overgeneralizations that come into conflict. This is especially so when claims are made that any one of these approaches provides answers to all the questions that matter.

References and Notes

1. E. H. Lenneberg, in *The Structure of Language, Readings in the Philosophy of Language*, J. A. Fodor and J. J. Katz, Eds. (Prentice-Hall, Englewood Cliffs, N. J., 1964).
2. For complete treatment, see E. H. Lenneberg, *Biological Foundations of Language* (Wiley, New York, 1967).
3. E. H. Lenneberg, I. A. Nichols, E. F. Rosenberger, in *Disorders of Communication* D. Rioch, Ed. (Research Publications of Association for Research in Nervous and Mental Disorders, New York, 1964), vol. 42.
4. E. H. Lenneberg, F. G. Rebelsky, I. A. Nichols, *Hum. Develop. 8*, 23 (1965).
5. R. Brown, C. Cazden, U. Bellugi, in *The 1967 Minnesota Symposium on Child Psychology*, J. P. Hill, Ed. (Univ. of Minnesota Press, Minneapolis, in press).
6. D. Slobin, personal communication.
7. E. H. Lenneberg, *J. Abnorm. Soc. Psychol. 65*, 419 (1962).
8. E. H. Lenneberg, S. Fraiberg, N. Stein, research in progress.
9. D. B. Fry, in *The Genesis of Language: A Psycholinguistic Approach*, F. Smith and G. A. Miller, Eds. (MIT Press, Cambridge, 1966).
10. For details, see E. H. Lenneberg, *Perception and Language*, in preparation.
11. N. Chomsky, "The formal nature of language" (in *2*, appendix A).
12. See, for instance, C. F. Hockett, in *Animal Communication*, W. E. Lanyon and W. N. Tavolga, Eds. (American Institute of Biological Sciences, Washington, D. C., 1960); and in *Sci. Amer. 203*, 89 (1960).
13. N. Geschwind, *Brain 88*, 237, 585 (1965).

Allen and Beatrice Gardner's work provides counterpoint to Lenneberg's contention that language is species-specific to man. They discuss their highly successful attempt to teach American Sign Language to their chimpanzee, Washoe. Controversy has swirled about this research from the beginning. At their first major public presentation, at the meeting of the Psychonomic Society in 1967, a highly charged question-and-answer period took place. One member of the audience lambasted the study as unscientific—not an experiment but a demonstration, and therefore insignificant. Keith Hayes, widely known for the Hayes and Hayes (1952) attempt to teach another chimp, Viki, spoken English, then made a dramatic retort. "I want you to know," he began, "that this is the best scientific paper I have ever heard presented at a meeting. As you spoke, I felt stupider and stupider because of all the clever things you thought to do that Catherine and I didn't. But now I know I'm not the stupidest man in the room."

While this work provides a contrast with the view that language is species-specific to man, it begins from a premise strongly allied to Lenneberg's— that ony should pay careful attention to species-specific abilities to learn. For this reason the Gardners chose the language of the deaf rather than spoken language; chimpanzees in nature and in captivity vocalize little but are great manipulators, as anyone who has observed a caged primate will know. Hayes (1968) concluded that the reinforceability of vocalization in chimps may be contraprepared and that Viki failed to learn to speak because of this rather than a lack of cognitive capacity. So by choosing a more prepared response system, the Gardners have been much more successful. Whether what Washoe has is language awaits detailed empirical and analytic comparison with what human children can develop under parallel conditions, but whatever it is, this is one of the most remarkable experiments in the history of psychology.

31

TEACHING SIGN LANGUAGE
TO A CHIMPANZEE

R. Allen Gardner and Beatrice T. Gardner

The extent to which another species might be able to use human language is a classical problem in comparative psychology. One approach to this problem is to consider the nature of language, the processes of learning, the neural mechanisms of learning and of language, and the genetic basis of these mechanisms, and then, while recognizing certain gaps in what is known about these factors, to attempt to arrive at an answer by dint of careful scholarship (1). An alternative approach is to try to teach a form of human language to an animal. We chose the latter alternative, and, in June 1966, began training an infant female chimpanzee, named Washoe, to use the gestural language of the deaf. Within the first 22 months of training it became evident that we had been correct in at least one major aspect of method, the use of a gestural language. Additional aspects of method have evolved in the course of the project. These and some implications of our early results can now be described in a way that may be useful in other studies of communicative behavior. Accordingly, in this article we discuss the considerations which led us to use the chimpanzee as a subject and American Sign Language (the language used by the deaf in North America) as a medium of

From *Science*, 165 (1969), 664–672.

The research described in this article has been supported by National Institute of Mental Health Grants MH-12154 and MH-34953 (Research Scientist Development Award to B. T. Gardner) and by National Science Foundation Grant GB-7432. We acknowledge a great debt to the personnel of the Aeromedical Research Laboratory, Holloman Air Force Base, whose support and expert assistance effectively absorbed all of the many difficulties attendant upon the acquisition of a wild-caught chimpanzee. We are also grateful to Dr. Frances L. Fitz-Gerald of the Yerkes Regional Primate Research Center for detailed advice on the care of an infant chimpanzee. Drs. Emanual Berger of Reno, Nevada, and D. B. Olsen of the University of Nevada have served as medical consultants, and we are grateful to them for giving so generously of their time and medical skills. The faculty of the Sarah Hamilton Fleischmann School of Home Economics, University of Nevada, has generously allowed us to use the facilities of their experimental nursery school on weekends and holidays.

communication; describe the general methods of training as they were initially conceived and as they developed in the course of the project; and summarize those results that could be reported with some degree of confidence by the end of the first phase of the project.

PRELIMINARY CONSIDERATIONS

The Chimpanzee as a Subject

Some discussion of the chimpanzee as an experimental subject is in order because this species is relatively uncommon in the psychological laboratory. Whether or not the chimpanzee is the most intelligent animal after man can be disputed; the gorilla, the orangutan, and even the dolphin have their loyal partisans in this debate. Nevertheless, it is generally conceded that chimpanzees are highly intelligent, and that members of this species might be intelligent enough for our purposes. Of equal or greater importance is their sociability and their capacity for forming strong attachments to human beings. We want to emphasize this trait of sociability; it seems highly likely that it is essential for the development of language in human beings, and it was a primary consideration in our choice of a chimpanzee as a subject.

Affectionate as chimpanzees are, they are still wild animals, and this is a serious disadvantage. Most psychologists are accustomed to working with animals that have been chosen, and sometimes bred, for docility and adaptability to laboratory procedures. The difficulties presented by the wild nature of an experimental animal must not be underestimated. Chimpanzees are also very strong animals; a full-grown specimen is likely to weigh more than 120 pounds (55 kilograms) and is estimated to be from three to five times as strong as man, pound-for-pound. Coupled with the wildness, this great strength presents serious difficulties for a procedure that requires interaction at close quarters with a free-living animal. We have always had to reckon with the likelihood that at some point Washoe's physical maturity will make this procedure prohibitively dangerous.

A more serious disadvantage is that human speech sounds are unsuitable as a medium of communication for the chimpanzee. The vocal apparatus of the chimpanzee is very different from that of man (2). More important, the vocal behavior of the chimpanzee is very different from that of man. Chimpanzees do make many different sounds, but generally vocalization occurs in situations of high excitement and tends to be specific to the exciting situations. Undisturbed, chimpanzees are usually silent. Thus, it is unlikely that a chimpanzee could be trained to make refined use of its vocalizations. Moreover, the intensive work of Hayes and Hayes (3) with the chimpanzee Viki indicates that a vocal language is not appropriate for this species. The Hayeses used modern, sophisticated, psychological methods and seem to have spared no effort to teach Viki to make speech sounds. Yet in 6 years Viki learned only four sounds that approximated English words (4).

Use of the hands, however, is a prominent feature of chimpanzee behavior; manipulatory mechanical problems are their forte. More to the point, even caged, laboratory chimpanzees develop begging and similar gestures spontaneously (5), while individuals that have had extensive contact with human beings have displayed an even wider variety of communicative gestures (6). In our choice of sign language we were influenced more by the behavioral evidence that this medium of communication was appropriate to the species than by anatomical evidence of structural similarity between the hands of chimpanzees and of men. The Hayeses point out that human tools and mechanical devices are constructed to fit the human hand, yet chimpanzees have little difficulty in using these devices with great skill. Nevertheless, they seem unable to adapt their vocalizations to approximate human speech.

Psychologists who work extensively with the instrumental conditioning of animals become sensitive to the need to use responses that are suited to the species they wish to study. Lever-pressing in rats is not an arbitrary response invented by Skinner to confound the mentalists; it is a type of response commonly made by rats when they are first placed in a Skinner box. The exquisite control of instrumental behavior by schedules of reward is achieved only if the original responses are well chosen. We chose a language based on gestures because we reasoned that gestures for the chimpanzee should be analogous to bar-pressing for rats, key-pecking for pigeons, and babbling for humans.

American Sign Language

Two systems of manual communication are used by the deaf. One system is the manual alphabet, or finger spelling, in which configurations of the hand correspond to letters of the alphabet. In this system the words of a spoken language, such as English, can be spelled out manually. The other system, sign language, consists of a set of manual configurations and gestures that correspond to particular words or concepts. Unlike finger spelling, which is the direct encoding of a spoken language, sign languages have their own rules of usage. Word-for-sign translation between a spoken language and a sign language yields results that are similar to those of word-for-word translation between two spoken languages: the translation is often passable, though awkward, but it can also be ambiguous or quite nonsensical. Also, there are national and regional variations in sign languages that are comparable to those of spoken languages.

We chose for this project the American Sign Language (ASL), which, with certain regional variations, is used by the deaf in North America. This particular sign language has recently been the subject of formal analysis (7). The ASL can be compared to pictograph writing in which some symbols are quite arbitrary and some are quite representational or iconic, but all are arbitrary to some degree. For example, in ASL the sign for "always" is made by holding the hand in a fist, index finger extended (the pointing hand), while rotating the arm at the elbow. This is clearly an arbitrary representation of the concept "always." The sign for "flower," however, is highly iconic; it is made by holding the fingers of one hand extended, all five fingertips touching (the tapered hand), and touching the fingertips first to one nostril then to the others, as if sniffing a flower. While this is an iconic sign for "flower," it is only one of a number of conventions by which the concept "flower" could be iconically represented; it is thus arbitrary to some degree. Undoubtedly, many of the signs of ASL that seem quite arbitrary today once had an iconic origin that was lost through years of stylized usage. Thus, the signs of ASL are neither uniformly arbitrary nor uniformly iconic; rather the degree of abstraction varies from sign to sign over a wide range. This would seem to be a useful property of ASL for our research.

The literate deaf typically use a combination of ASL and finger spelling; for purposes of this project we have avoided the use of finger spelling as much as possible. A great range of expression is possible within the limits of ASL. We soon found that a good way to practice signing among ourselves was to render familiar songs and poetry into signs; as far as we can judge, there is no message that cannot be rendered faithfully (apart from the usual problems of translation from one language to another). Technical terms and proper names are a problem when first introduced, but within any community of signers it is easy to agree on a convention for any commonly used term. For example, among ourselves we do not finger-spell the words *psychologist* and *psychology*, but render them as "think doctor" and "think science." Or, among users of ASL, "California" can be finger-spelled but is commonly rendered as "golden playland." (Incidentally, the sign for "gold" is made by plucking at the earlobe with thumb and forefinger, indicating an earring—another example of an iconic sign that is at the same time arbitrary and stylized.)

The fact that ASL is in current use by human beings is an additional advantage. The early linguistic environment of the deaf children of deaf parents is in some respects similar to the linguistic environment that we could provide for an experimental subject. This should permit some comparative evaluation of Washoe's eventual level of competence. For example, in discussing Washoe's early performance with deaf parents we have been told that many of her variants of standard signs are similar to the baby-talk variants commonly observed when human children sign.

Washoe. Having decided on a species and a medium of communication, our next concern was to obtain an experimental subject. It is altogether possible that there is some critical early age for the acquisition of this type of behavior. On the other hand, newborn chimpanzees tend to be quite helpless and vegetative. They are also considerably less hardy than older infants. Nevertheless, we reasoned that the dangers of starting too late were much greater than the dangers of starting too early, and we sought the youngest infant we could get. Newborn laboratory chimpanzees are very scarce, and we found that the youngest laboratory infant we could get would be about 2 years old at the time we planned to start the project. It seemed preferable to obtain a wild-caught infant. Wild-caught infants are usually at least 8 to 10 months old before they are available for research. This is because infants rarely reach the United States before they are 5 months old, and to this age must be added 1 or 2 months before final purchase and 2 or 3 months for quarantine and other medical services.

We named our Chimpanzee Washoe for Washoe County, the home of the University of Nevada. Her exact age will never be known, but from her weight and dentition we estimated her age to be between 8 and 14 months at the end of June 1966, when she first arrived at our laboratory. (Her dentition has continued to agree with this initial estimate, but her weight has increased rather more than would be expected.) This is very young for a chimpanzee. The best available information indicates that infants are completely dependent until the age of 2 years and semi-dependent until the age of 4; the first signs of sexual maturity (for example, menstruation, sexual swelling) begin to appear at about 8 years, and full adult growth is reached between the ages of 12 and 16 (8). As for the complete lifespan, captive specimens have survived for well over 40 years. Washoe was indeed very young when she arrived; she did not have her first canines or molars, her hand-eye coordination was rudimentary, she had only begun to crawl about, and she slept a great deal. Apart from making friends with her and adapting her to the daily routine, we could accomplish little during the first few months.

Laboratory Conditions

At the outset we were quite sure that Washoe could learn to make various signs in order to obtain food, drink, and other things. For the project to be a success, we felt that something more must be developed. We wanted Washoe not only to ask for objects but to answer questions about them and also to ask us questions. We wanted to develop behavior that could be described as conversation. With this in mind, we attempted to provide Washoe with an environment that might be conducive to this sort of behavior. Confinement was to be minimal, about the same as that of human infants. Her human companions were to be friends and playmates as well as providers and protectors, and they were to introduce a great many games and activities that would be likely to result in maximum interaction with Washoe.

In practice, such an environment is readily achieved with a chimpanzee; bonds of warm affection have always been established between Washoe and her several human companions. We have enjoyed the interaction almost as much as Washoe has, within the limits of human endurance. A number of human companions have been enlisted to participate in the project and relieve each other at intervals, so that at least one person would be with Washoe during all her waking hours. At first we feared that such frequent changes would be disturbing, but Washoe seemed to adapt very well to this procedure. Apparently it is possible to provide an infant chimpanzee with affection on a shift basis.

All of Washoe's human companions have been required to master ASL and to use it extensively in her presence, in association with interesting activities and events and also in a general way, as one chatters at a human infant in the course of the day. The ASL has been used almost exclusively, although occasional finger spelling has been permitted. From time to time, of course, there are lapses into spoken English, as when medical personnel must examine Washoe. At one time, we considered an alternative procedure in which we would sign and speak English to Washoe simultaneously, thus giving her an additional source of informative cues. We rejected this procedure, reasoning that, if she should come to understand speech sooner or more easily than ASL, then she might not pay sufficient attention to our gestures. Another alternative, that of speaking English among ourselves and signing to Washoe, was also rejected. We reasoned that this would make it seem that big chimps talk and only little chimps sign, which might give signing an undesirable social status.

The environment we are describing is not a silent one. The human beings can vocalize in many ways, laughing and making sounds of pleasure and displeasure. Whistles and drums are sounded in a variety of imitation games, and hands are clapped for attention. The rule is that all meaningful sounds, whether vocalized or not, must be sounds that a chimpanzee can imitate.

TRAINING METHODS

Imitation

The imitativeness of apes is proverbial, and rightly so. Those who have worked closely with chimpanzees have frequently remarked on their readiness to engage in visually guided imitation. Consider the following typical comment of Yerkes (9): "Chim and Panzee would imitate many of my acts, but never have I heard them imitate a sound and rarely make a sound peculiarly their own in response to mine. As previously stated, their imitative tendency is as remarkable for its specialization and limitations as for its strength. It seems to be controlled chiefly by visual stimuli. Things which are seen tend to be imitated or reproduced. What is heard is not reproduced. Obviously an animal which lacks the tendency to reinstate auditory stimuli—in other words to imitate sounds—cannot reasonably be expected to talk. The human infant exhibits this tendency to a remarkable degree. So also does the parrot. If the imitative tendency of the parrot could be coupled with the quality of intelligence of the chimpanzee, the latter undoubtedly could speak."

In the course of their work with Viki, the Hayeses devised a game in which Viki would imitate various actions on hearing the command "Do this" (10). Once established, this was an effective means of training Viki to perform actions that could be visually guided. The same method should be admirably suited to training a chimpanzee to use sign language; accordingly we have directed much effort toward establishing a version of the "Do this" game with Washoe. Getting Washoe to imitate us was not difficult, for she did so quite spontaneously, but getting her to imitate on command has been another matter altogether. It was not until the 16th month of the project that we achieved any degree of control over Washoe's imitation of gestures. Eventually we got to a point where she would imitate a simple gesture, such as pulling at her ears, or a series of such gestures—first we make a gesture, then she imitates, then we make a second gesture, she imitates the second gesture, and so on -for the reward of being tickled. Up to this writing, however, imitation of this sort has not been an important method for introducing new signs into Washoe's vocabulary.

As a method of prompting, we have been able to use imitation extensively to increase the frequency and refine the form of signs. Washoe sometimes fails to use a new sign in an appropriate situation, or uses another, incorrect sign. At such times we can make the correct sign to Washoe, repeating the performance until she makes the sign herself. (With more stable signs, more indirect forms of prompting can be used—for example, pointing at, or touching, Washoe's hand or a part of her body that should be involved in the sign; making the sign for "sign," which is equivalent to saying "Speak up"; or asking a question in signs, such as "What do you want?" or "What is it?") Again, with new signs, and often with old signs as well, Washoe can lapse into what we refer to as poor "diction." Of course, a great deal of slurring and a wide range of variants are permitted in ASL as in any spoken language. In any event, Washoe's diction has frequently been improved by the simple device of repeating, in exaggeratedly correct form, the sign she has just made, until she repeats it herself in more correct form. On the whole, she has responded quite well to prompting, but there are strict limits to its use with a wild animal—one that is probably quite spoiled, besides. Pressed too hard, Washoe can become completely diverted from her original object; she may ask for something entirely different, run away, go into a tantrum, or even bite her tutor.

Chimpanzees also imitate, after some delay, and this delayed imitation can be quite elaborate (10). The following is a typical example of Washoe's delayed imitation. From the beginning of the project she was bathed regularly and according to a standard routine. Also, from her 2nd month with us, she always had dolls to play with. One day, during the 10th month of the project, she bathed one of her dolls in the way we usually bathed her. She filled her little bathtub with water, dunked the doll in the tub, then took it out and dried it with a towel. She has repeated the entire performance, or parts of it, many times since, sometimes also soaping the doll.

This is a type of imitation that may be very important in the acquisition of language by human children, and many of our procedures with Washoe were devised to capitalize on it. Routine activities—feeding, dressing, bathing, and so on—have been highly ritualized, with appropriate signs figuring prominently in the rituals. Many games have been invented which can be accompanied by appropriate signs. Objects and activities have been named as often as possible, especially when Washoe seemed to be paying particular attention to them. New objects and new examples of familiar objects, including pictures, have been continually brought to her attention, together with the appropriate signs. She likes to ride in automobiles, and a ride in an automobile, including the preparations for a ride, provides a wealth of sights that can be accompanied by signs. A good destination for a ride is a home or the university nursery school, both well stocked with props for language lessons.

The general principle should be clear: Washoe has been exposed to a wide variety of activities and objects, together with their appropriate signs, in the hope that she would come to associate the signs with their referents and later make the signs herself. We have reason to believe that she has come to understand a large vocabulary of signs. This was expected, since a number of chimpanzees have acquired extensive understanding vocabularies of spoken words, and there is evidence that even dogs can acquire a sizable understanding vocabulary of spoken words (11). The understanding vocabulary that Washoe has acquired, however, consists of signs that a chimpanzee can imitate.

Some of Washoe's signs seem to have been originally acquired by delayed imitation. A good example is the sign for "toothbrush." A part of the daily routine has been to brush her teeth after every meal. When this routine was first introduced Washoe generally resisted it. She gradually came to submit with less and less fuss, and after many months she would even help or sometimes brush her teeth herself. Usually, having finished her meal, Washoe would try to leave her highchair; we would restrain her, signing "First, toothbrushing, then you can go." One day, in the 10th month of the project, Washoe was visiting the Gardner home and found her way into the bathroom. She climbed up on the counter, looked at our mug full of toothbrushes, and signed "toothbrush." At the time, we believed that Washoe understood this sign but we had not seen her use it. She had no reason to ask for the toothbrushes, because they were well within her reach, and it is most unlikely that she was asking to have her teeth brushed. This was our first observation, and one of the clearest examples, of behavior in which Washoe seemed to name an object or an event for no obvious motive other than communication.

Following this observation, the toothbrushing routine at mealtime was altered. First, imitative prompting was introduced. Then as the sign became more reliable, her rinsing-mug and toothbrush were displayed prominently until she made the sign. By the 14th month she was making the "toothbrush" sign at the end of meals with little or no prompting; in fact she has called for her toothbrush in a peremptory fashion when its appearance at the end of a meal was delayed. The "toothbrush" sign is not merely a response cued by the end of a meal; Washoe retained her ability to name toothbrushes when they were shown to her at other times.

The sign for "flower" may also have been acquired by delayed imitation. From her first summer with us, Washoe showed a great interest in flowers, and we took advantage of this by providing many flowers and pictures of flowers accompanied by the appropriate sign. Then one day in the 15th month she made the sign, spontaneously, while she and a companion were walking toward a flower garden. As in the case of "toothbrush," we believed that she understood the sign at this time, but we had made no attempt to elicit it from her except by making it ourselves in appropriate situations. Again, after the first observation, we proceeded to elicit this sign as often as possible by a variety of methods, most frequently by showing her a flower and giving it to her if she made the sign for it. Eventually the sign became very reliable and could be elicited by a variety of flowers and pictures of flowers.

It is difficult to decide which signs were acquired by the method of delayed imitation. The first appearance of these signs is likely to be sudden and unexpected; it is possible that some inadvertent movement of Washoe's has been interpreted as meaningful by one of her devoted companions. If the first observer were kept from reporting the observation and from making any direct attempts to elicit the sign again, then it might be possible to obtain independent verification. Quite understandably, we have been more interested in raising the frequency of new signs than in evaluating any particular method of training.

Babbling

Because the Hayeses were attempting to teach Viki to speak English, they were interested in babbling, and during the first year of their project they were encouraged by the number and variety of spontaneous vocalizations that Viki made. But, in time, Viki's spontaneous vocalizations decreased further and further to the point where the Hayeses felt that here was almost no vocal babbling from which to shape spoken language. In planning this project we expected a great deal of manual "babbling," but during the early months we observed very little behavior of this kind. In the course of the project, however, there has been a great increase in manual babbling. We have been particularly encouraged by the increase in movements that involve touching parts of the head and body, since these are important components of many signs. Also, more and more frequently, when Washoe has been unable to get something that she wants, she has burst into a flurry of random flourishes and arm-waving.

We have encouraged Washoe's babbling by our responsiveness; clapping, smiling, and repeating the gesture much as you might repeat "goo goo" to a human infant. If the babbled gesture has resembled a sign in ASL, we have made the correct form of the sign and have attempted to engage in some appropriate activity. The sign for "funny" was probably acquired in this way. It first appeared as a spontaneous babble that lent itself readily to a simple imitation game—first Washoe signed "funny," then we did, then she did, and so on. We would laugh and smile during the interchanges that she initiated, and initiate the game ourselves when something funny happened. Eventually Washoe came to use the "funny" sign spontaneously in roughly appropriate situations.

Closely related to babbling are some gestures that seem to have appeared independently of any deliberate training on our part, and that resemble signs so closely that we could incorporate them into Washoe's repertoire with little or no modification. Almost from the first she had a begging gesture—an extension of her open hand, palm up, toward one of us. She made this gesture in situations in which she wanted aid and in situations in which we were holding some object that she wanted. The ASL signs for "give me" and "come" are very similar to this, except that they involve a prominent beckoning movement. Gradually Washoe came to incorporate a beckoning wrist movement into her use of this sign. In Table 1 we refer to this sign as "come-gimme." As Washoe has come to use it, the sign is not simply a modification of the original begging gesture. For example, very commonly she reaches forward with one hand (palm up) while she gestures with the other hand (palm down) held near her head. (The result resembles a classic fencing posture.)

Another sign of this type is the sign for "hurry," which, so far, Washoe has always made by shaking her open hand vigorously at the wrist. This first appeared as an impatient flourish following some request that she had made in signs; for example, after making the "open" sign before a door. The correct ASL for "hurry" is very close, and we began to use it often, ourselves, in appropriate contexts. We believe that Washoe has come to use the sign in a meaningful way, because she has frequently used it when she, herself, is in a hurry—for example, when rushing to her nursery chair.

Instrumental Conditioning

It seems intuitively unreasonable that the acquisition of language by human beings could be strictly a matter of reiterated instrumental conditioning—that a child acquires language after the fashion of a rat that is conditioned, first, to press a lever for food in the presence of one stimulus, then to turn a wheel in the presence of another stimulus, and so on until a large repertoire of discriminated responses is acquired. Nevertheless, the so-called "trick vocabulary" of early childhood is probably acquired in this way, and this may be a critical stage in the acquisition of language by children. In any case, a minimal objective of this project was to teach Washoe as many signs as possible by whatever procedures we could enlist. Thus, we have not hesitated to use conventional procedures of instrumental conditioning.

Anyone who becomes familiar with young chimpanzees soon learns about their passion for being tickled. There is no doubt that tickling is the most effective reward that we have used with Washoe. In the early months, when we would pause in our tickling, Washoe would indicate that she wanted more tickling by taking our hands and placing them against her ribs or around her neck. The meaning of these gestures was unmistakable, but since we were not studying our human ability to interpret her chimpanzee gestures, we decided to shape an arbitrary response that she could use to ask for more tickling. We noted that, when being tickled, she tended to bring her arms together to cover the place being tickled. The result was a very crude approximation of the ASL sign for "more" (see Table 1). Thus, we would stop tickling and then pull Washoe's arms away from her body. When we released her arms and threatened to resume tickling, she tended to bring her hands together again. If she brought them back together, we would tickle her again. From time to time we would stop tickling and wait for her to put her hands together by herself. At first, any approximation to the "more" sign, however crude, was rewarded. Later, we required closer approximations and introduced imitative prompting. Soon, a very good version of the "more" sign could be obtained, but it was quite specific to the tickling situation.

In the 6th month of the project we were able to get "more" signs for a new game that consisted of pushing Washoe across the floor in a laundry basket. In this case we did not use the shaping procedure but, from the start, used imitative prompting to elicit the "more" sign. Soon after the "more" sign became spontaneous and reliable in the laundry-basket game, it began to appear as a request for more swinging (by the arms)—again, after first being elicited with imitative prompting. From this point on, Washoe transferred the "more" sign to all activities, including feeding. The transfer was usually spontaneous, occurring when there was some pause in a desired activity or when some object was removed. Often we ourselves were not sure that Washoe wanted "more" until she signed to us.

The sign for "open" had a similar history. When Washoe wanted to get through a door, she tended to hold up both hands and pound on the door with her palms or her knuckles. This is the beginning position for the "open" sign (see Table 1). By waiting for her to place her hands on the door and then lift them, and also by imitative prompting, we were able to shape a good approximation of the "open" sign, and would reward this by opening the door. Originally she was trained to make this sign for three particular doors that she used every day. Washoe transferred this sign to all doors; then to containers such as the refrigerator, cupboards, drawers, briefcases, boxes, and jars; and eventually—an invention of Washoe's—she used it to ask us to turn on water faucets.

In the case of "more" and "open" we followed the conventional laboratory procedure of waiting for Washoe to make some response that could be shaped

TABLE 1 Signs Used Reliably by Chimpanzee Washoe within 22 Months of the Beginning of Training

Signs	Description	Context
Come-gimme	Beckoning motion, with wrist or knuckles as pivot.	Sign made to persons or animals, also for objects out of reach. Often combined: "come tickle," "gimme sweet," etc.
More	Fingertips are brought together, usually overhead. (Correct ASL form: tips of the tapered hand touch repeatedly.)	When asking for continuation or repetition of activities such as swinging or tickling, for second helpings of food, etc. Also used to ask for repetition of some performance, such as a somersault.
Up	Arm extends upward, and index finger may also point up.	Wants a lift to reach objects such as grapes on vine, or leaves; or wants to be placed on someone's shoulders; or wants to leave potty-chair.
Sweet	Index or index and second fingers touch tip of wagging tongue. (Correct ASL form: index and second fingers extended side by side.)	For dessert; used spontaneously at end of meal. Also, when asking for candy.
Open	Flat hands are placed side by side, palms down, then drawn apart while rotated to palms up.	At door of house, room, car, refrigerator, or cupboard; on containers such as jars; and on faucets.
Tickle	The index finger of one hand is drawn across the back of the other hand. (Related to ASL "touch.")	For tickling or for chasing games.
Go	Opposite of "come-gimme."	While walking hand-in-hand or riding on someone's shoulders. Washoe usually indicates the direction desired.
Out	Curved hand grasps tapered hand; then tapered hand is withdrawn upward.	When passing through doorways; until recently, used for both "in" and "out." Also, when asking to be taken outdoors.

Sign	Description	Context
Hurry	Open hand is shaken at the wrist. (Correct ASL form: index and second fingers extended side by side.)	Often follows signs such as "come-gimme," "out," "open," and "go," particularly if there is a delay before Washoe is obeyed. Also, used while watching her meal being prepared.
Hear-listen	Index finger touches ear.	For loud or strange sounds: bells, car horns, sonic booms, etc. Also, for asking someone to hold a watch to her ear.
Toothbrush	Index finger is used as brush, to rub front teeth.	When Washoe has finished her meal, or at other times when shown a toothbrush.
Drink	Thumb is extended from fisted hand and touches mouth.	For water, formula, soda pop, etc. For soda pop, often combined with "sweet."
Hurt	Extended index fingers are jabbed toward each other. Can be used to indicate location of pain.	To indicate cuts and bruises on herself or on others. Can be elicited by red stains on a person's skin or by tears in clothing.
Sorry	Fisted hand clasps and unclasps at shoulder. (Correct ASL form: fisted hand is rubbed over heart with circular motion.)	After biting someone, or when someone has been hurt in another way (not necessarily by Washoe). When told to apologize for mischief.
Funny	Tip of index finger presses nose, and Washoe snorts. (Correct ASL form: index and second fingers used; no snort.)	When soliciting interaction play, and during games. Occasionally, when being pursued after mischief.
Please	Open hand is drawn across chest. (Correct ASL form: fingertips used, and circular motion.)	When asking for objects and activities. Frequently combined: "Please go," "Out, please," "Please drink."
Food-eat	Several fingers of one hand are placed in mouth. (Correct ASL form: fingertips of tapered hand touch mouth repeatedly.)	During meals and preparation of meals.

TABLE 1 (continued)

Signs	Description	Content
Flower	Tip of index finger touches one or both nostrils. (Correct ASL form: tips of tapered hand touch first one nostril, then the other.)	For flowers.
Cover-blanket	Draws one hand toward self over the back of the other.	At bedtime or naptime, and, on cold days, when Washoe wants to be taken out.
Dog	Repeated slapping on thigh.	For dogs and for barking.
You	Index finger points at a person's chest.	Indicates successive turns in games. Also used in response to questions such as "Who tickle?" "Who brush?"
Napkin-bib	Fingertips wipe the mouth region.	For bib, for washcloth, and for Kleenex.
In	Opposite of "out."	Wants to go indoors, or wants someone to join her indoors.
Brush	The fisted hand rubs the back of the open hand several times. (Adapted from ASL "polish.")	For hairbrush, and when asking for brushing.
Hat	Palm pats top of head.	For hats and caps.
I-me	Index finger points at, or touches, chest.	Indicates Washoe's turn, when she and a companion share food, drink, etc. Also used in phrases, such as "I drink," and in reply to questions such as "Who tickle?" (Washoe: "you"); "Who I tickle?" (Washoe: "Me.")
Shoes	The fisted hands are held side by side and strike down on shoes or floor. (Correct ASL form: the sides of the fisted hands strike against each other.)	For shoes and boots.

Sign	Description	Context
Smell	Palm is held before nose and moved slightly upward several times.	For scented objects: tobacco, perfume, sage, etc.
Pants	Palms of the flat hands are drawn up against the body toward waist.	For diapers, rubber pants, trousers.
Clothes	Fingertips brush down the chest.	For Washoe's jacket, nightgown, and shirts; also for our clothing.
Cat	Thumb and index finger grasp cheek hair near side of mouth and are drawn outward (representing cat's whiskers).	For cats.
Key	Palm of one hand is repeatedly touched with the index finger of the other. (Correct ASL form: crooked index finger is rotated against palm.)	•Used for keys and locks and to ask us to unlock a door.
Baby	One forearm is placed in the crook of the other, as if cradling a baby.	For dolls, including animal dolls such as a toy horse and duck.
Clean	The open palm of one hand is passed over the open palm of the other.	Used when Washoe is washing, or being washed, or when a companion is washing hands or some other object. Also used for "soap."

The signs are listed in the order of their original appearance in her repertoire (see text for the criterion of reliability and for the method of assigning the date of original appearance).

into the sign we wished her to acquire. We soon found that this was not necessary; Washoe could acquire signs that were first elicited by our holding her hands, forming them into the desired configuration, and then putting them through the desired movement. Since this procedure of guidance is usually much more practical than waiting for a spontaneous approximation to occur at a favorable moment, we have used it much more frequently.

RESULTS

Vocabulary

In the early stages of the project we were able to keep fairly complete records of Washoe's daily signing behavior. But, as the amount of signing behavior and the number of signs to be monitored increased, our initial attempts to obtain exhaustive records became prohibitively cumbersome. During the 16th month we settled on the following procedure. When a new sign was introduced we waited until it had been reported by three different observers as having occurred in an appropriate context and spontaneously (that is, with no prompting other than a question such as "What is it?" or "What do you want?"). The sign was then added to a checklist in which its occurrence, form, context, and the kind of prompting required were recorded. Two such checklists were filled out each day, one for the first half of the day and one for the second half. For a criterion of acquisition we chose a reported frequency of at least one appropriate and spontaneous occurrence each day over a period of 15 consecutive days.

In Table 1 we have listed 30 signs that met this criterion by the end of the 22nd month of the project. In addition, we have listed four signs ("dog," "smell," "me," and "clean") that we judged to be stable, despite the fact that they had not met the stringent criterion before the end of the 22nd month. These additional signs had, nevertheless, been reported to occur appropriately and spontaneously on more than half of the days in a period of 30 consecutive days. An indication of the variety of the signs that Washoe used in the course of a day is given by the following data: during the 22nd month of the study, 28 of the 34 signs listed were reported on at least 20 days, and the smallest number of different signs reported for a single day was 23, with a median of 29 (12).

The order in which these signs first appeared in Washoe's repertoire is also given in Table 1. We considered the first appearance to be the date on which three different observers reported appropriate and spontaneous occurrences. By this criterion, 4 new signs first appeared during the first 7 months, 9 new signs during the next 7 months, and 21 new signs during the next 7 months. We chose the 21st month rather than the 22nd month as the cutoff for this tabulation so that no signs would be included that do not appear in Table 1. Clearly, if Washoe's rate of acquisition continues to accelerate, we will have to assess her vocabulary on the basis of sampling procedures. We are now in the process of developing procedures that could be used to make periodic tests of Washoe's performance on samples of her repertoire. However, now that there is evidence that a chimpanzee can acquire a vocabulary of more than 30 signs, the exact number of signs in her current vocabulary is less significant than the order of magnitude—50, 100, 200 signs, or more—that might eventually be achieved.

Differentiation

In Table 1, column 1, we list English equivalents for each of Washoe's signs. It must be understood that this equivalence is only approximate, because equivalence between English and ASL, as between any two human languages, is only approximate, and because Washoe's usage does differ from that of standard ASL. To some extent her usage is indicated in the column labeled "Context" in Table 1, but the definition of any given sign must always depend upon her total vocabulary, and this has been continually changing. When she had very few signs for specific things, Washoe used the "more" sign for a wide class of requests. Our only restriction was that we discouraged the use of "more" for first requests. As she acquired signs for specific requests, her use of "more" declined until, at the time of this writing, she was using this sign mainly to ask for repetition of some action that she could not name, such as a somersault. Perhaps the best English equivalent would be "do it again." Still, it seemed preferable to list the English equivalent for the ASL sign rather than its current referent for Washoe, since further refinements in her usage may be achieved at a later date.

The differentiation of the signs for "flower" and "smell" provides a further illustration of usage depending upon size of vocabulary. As the "flower" sign became more frequent, we noted that it occurred in several inappropriate contexts that all seemed to include odors; for example, Washoe would make the "flower" sign when opening a tobacco pouch or when entering a kitchen filled with cooking odors. Taking our cue from this, we introduced the "smell" sign by passive shaping and imitative prompting. Gradually Washoe came to make the appropriate distinction between "flower" contexts and "smell" contexts in her signing, although "flower" (in the single-nostril form) (see Table 1) has continued to occur as a common error in "smell" contexts.

Transfer

In general, when introducing new signs we have used a very specific referent for the initial training—a particular door for "open," a particular hat for "hat." Early in the project we were concerned about the possibility that signs might become inseparable from their first referents. So far, however, there has been no problem of this kind: Washoe has always been able to transfer her signs spontaneously to new members of each class of referents. We have already described the transfer of "more" and "open." The sign for "flower" is a particularly good example of transfer, because flowers occur in so many varieties, indoors, outdoors, and in pictures, yet Washoe uses the same sign for all. It is fortunate that she has responded well to pictures of objects. In the case of "dog" and "cat" this has proved to be important because live dogs and cats can be too exciting, and we have had to use pictures to elicit most of the "dog" and "cat" signs. It is noteworthy that Washoe has transferred the "dog" sign to the sound of barking by an unseen dog.

The acquisition and transfer of the sign for "key" illustrates a further point. A great many cupboards and doors in Washoe's quarters have been kept secure by small padlocks that can all be opened by the same simple key. Because she was immature and awkward, Washoe had great difficulty in learning to use these keys and locks. Because we wanted her to improve her manual dexterity, we let her practice with these keys until she could open the locks quite easily (then we had to hide the keys). Washoe soon transferred this skill to all manner of locks and keys, including ignition keys. At about the same time, we taught her the sign for "key," using the original padlock keys as a referent. Washoe came to use this sign both to name keys that were presented to her and to ask for the keys to various locks when no key was in sight. She readily transferred the sign to all varieties of keys and locks.

Now, if an animal can transfer a skill learned with a certain key and lock to new types of key and lock, it should not be surprising that the same animal can learn to use an arbitrary response to name and ask for a certain key and then transfer that sign to new types of keys. Certainly, the relationship between the use of a key and the opening of locks is as arbitrary as the relationship between the sign for "key" and its many referents. Viewed in this way, the general phenomenon of transfer of training and the specifically linguistic phenomenon of labeling become very similar, and the problems that these phenomena pose for modern learning theory should require similar solutions. We do not mean to imply that the problem of labeling is less complex than has generally been supposed; rather, we are suggesting that the problem of transfer of training requires an equally sophisticated treatment.

Combinations

During the phase of the project covered by this article we made no deliberate attempts to elicit combinations or phrases, although we may have responded more readily to strings of two or more signs than to single signs. As far as we can judge, Washoe's early use of signs in strings was spontaneous. Almost as soon as she had eight or ten signs in her repertoire, she began to use them two and three at a time. As her repertoire increased, her tendency to produce strings of two or more signs also increased, to the point where this has become a common mode of signing for her. We, of course, usually signed to her in combinations, but if Washoe's use of combinations has been imitative, then it must be a generalized sort of imitation, since she has invented a number of combinations, such as "gimme tickle" (before we had ever asked her to tickle us), and "open food drink" (for the refrigerator—we have always called it the "cold box").

Four signs—"please," "come-gimme," "hurry," and "more"—used with one or more other signs, account for the largest share of Washoe's early combinations. In general, these four signs have functioned as emphasizers, as in "please open hurry" and "gimme drink please."

Until recently, five additional signs—"go," "out," "in," "open," and "hear-listen"—accounted for most of the remaining combinations. Typical examples of combinations using these four are, "go in" or "go out" (when at some distance from a door), "go sweet" (for being carried to a raspberry bush), "open flower" (to be let through the gate to a flower garden), "open key" (for a locked door), "listen eat" (at the sound of an alarm clock signaling mealtime), and "listen dog" (at the sound of barking by an unseen dog). All but the first and last of these six examples were inventions of Washoe's. Combinations of this type tend to amplify the meaning of the single signs used. Sometimes, however, the function of these five signs has been about the same as that of the emphasizers, as in "open out" (when standing in front of a door).

Toward the end of the period covered in this article we were able to introduce the pronouns "I-me" and "you," so that combinations that resemble short sentences have begun to appear.

CONCLUDING OBSERVATIONS

From time to time we have been asked questions such as, "Do you think that Washoe has language?" or "At what point will you be able to say that Washoe has language?" We find it very difficult to respond to these questions because they are altogether foreign to the spirit of our research. They imply a distinction between one class of communicative behavior that can be called language and another class that cannot. This in turn implies a well-established theory that could provide the distinction. If our objectives had required such a theory, we would certainly not have been able to begin this project as early as we did.

In the first phase of the project we were able to verify the hypothesis that sign language is an appropriate medium of two-way communication for the chimpanzee. Washoe's intellectual immaturity, the continuing acceleration of her progress, the fact that her signs do not remain specific to their original referents but are transferred spontaneously to new referents, and the emergence of rudimentary combinations all suggest that significantly more can be accomplished by Washoe during the subsequent phases of this project. As we proceed, the problems of these subsequent phases will be chiefly concerned with the technical business of measurement. We are now developing a procedure for testing Washoe's ability to name objects. In this procedure, an object or a picture of an object is placed in a box with a window. An observer, who does not know what is in the box, asks Washoe what she sees through the window. At present, this method is limited to items that fit in the box; a more ingenious method will have to be devised for other items. In particular, the ability to combine and recombine signs must be tested. Here, a great deal depends upon reaching a stage at which Washoe produces an extended series of signs in answer to questions. Our hope is that Washoe can be brought to the point where she describes events and situations to an observer who has no other source of information.

At an earlier time we would have been more cautious about suggesting that a chimpanzee might be able to produce extended utterances to communicate information. We believe now that it is the writers—who would predict just what it is that no chimpanzee will ever do—who must proceed with caution. Washoe's accomplishments will probably be exceeded by another chimpanzee, because it is unlikely that the conditions of training have been optimal in this first attempt. Theories of language that depend upon the identification of aspects of language that are exclusively human must remain tentative until a considerably larger body of intensive research with other species becomes available.

416   TEACHING SIGN LANGUAGE TO A CHIMPANZEE

SUMMARY

We set ourselves the task of teaching an animal to use a form of human language. Highly intelligent and highly social, the chimpanzee is an obvious choice for such a study, yet it has not been possible to teach a member of this species more than a few spoken words. We reasoned that a spoken language, such as English, might be an inappropriate medium of communication for a chimpanzee. This led us to choose American Sign Language, the gestural system of communication used by the deaf in North America, for the project.

The youngest infant that we could obtain was a wild-born female, whom we named Washoe, and who was estimated to be between 8 and 14 months old when we began our program of training. The laboratory conditions, while not patterned after those of a human family (as in the studies of Kellogg and Kellogg and of Hayes and Hayes), involved a minimum of confinement and a maximum of social interaction with human companions. For all practical purposes, the only verbal communication was in ASL, and the chimpanzee was maximally exposed to the use of this language by human beings.

It was necessary to develop a rough-and-ready mixture of training methods. There was evidence that some of Washoe's early signs were acquired by delayed imitation of the signing behavior of her human companions, but very few if any, of her early signs were introduced by immediate imitation. Manual babbling was directly fostered and did increase in the course of the project. A number of signs were introduced by shaping and instrumental conditioning. A particularly effective and convenient method of shaping consisted of holding Washoe's hands, forming them into a configuration, and putting them through the movements of a sign.

We have listed more than 30 signs that Washoe acquired and could use spontaneously and appropriately by the end of the 22nd month of the project. The signs acquired earliest were simple demands. Most of the later signs have been names for objects, which Washoe has used both as demands and as answers to questions. Washoe readily used noun signs to name pictures of objects as well as actual objects and has frequently called the attention of her companions to pictures and objects by naming them. Once acquired, the signs have not remained specific to the original referents but have been transferred spontaneously to a wide class of appropriate referents. At this writing, Washoe's rate of acquistion of new signs is still accelerating.

From the time she had eight or ten signs in her repertoire, Washoe began to use them in strings of two or more. During the period covered by this article we made no deliberate effort to elicit combinations other than by our own habitual use of strings of signs. Some of the combined forms that Washoe has used may have been imitative, but many have been inventions of her own. Only a small proportion of the possible combinations have, in fact, been observed. This is because most of Washoe's combinations include one of a limited group of signs that act as combiners. Among the signs that Washoe has recently acquired are the pronouns "I-me" and "you." When these occur in combinations the result resembles a short sentence. In terms of the eventual level of communication that a chimpanzee might be able to attain, the most promising results have been spontaneous naming, spontaneous transfer to new referents, and spontaneous combinations and recombinations of signs.

References and Notes

1. See, for example, E. H. Lenneberg, *Biological Foundations of Language* (Wiley, New York, 1967).
2. A. L. Bryan, *Curr. Anthropol. 4*, 297 (1963).
3. K. J. Hayes and C. Hayes, *Proc. Amer. Phil. Soc. 95*, 105 (1951).
4. K. J. Hayes, personal communication. Dr. Hayes also informed us that Viki used a few additional sounds which, while not resembling English words, were used for specific requests.
5. R. M. Yerkes, *Chimpanzees* (Yale Univ. Press, New Haven, 1943).
6. K. J. Hayes and C. Hayes, in *The Non-Human Primates and Human Evolution*, J. A. Gavan, Ed. (Wayne Univ. Press, Detroit, 1955), p. 110; W. N. Kellogg and L.A. Kellogg, *The Ape and the Child* (Hafner, New York, 1967; originally published by McGraw-Hill, New York, 1933); W. N. Kellogg, *Science 162*, 423 (1968).
7. W. C. Stokoe, D. Casterline, C. G. Croneberg, *A Dictionary of American Sign Language* (Gallaudet College Press, Washington, D. C., 1965); E. A. McCall, thesis, University of Iowa (1965).
8. J. Goodall, in *Primate Behavior*, I. DeVore, Ed. (Holt, Rineheart & Winston, New York, 1965), p. 425; A. J. Riopelle and C. M. Rogers in *Behavior of Nonhuman Primates*, A. M. Schrier, H. F. Harlow, F. Stollnitz, Eds. (Academic Press, New York, 1965), p. 449.
9. R. M. Yerkes and B. W. Learned, *Chimpanzee Intelligence and Its Vocal Expression* (William & Wilkins, Baltimore, 1925), p. 53.
10. K. J. Hayes and C. Hayes, *J. Comp. Physiol. Psychol. 45*, 450 (1952).
11. C. J. Warden and L. H. Warner, *Quart. Rev. Biol. 3*, 1 (1928).
12. The development of Washoe's vocabulary of signs is being recorded on motion-picture film. At the time of this writing, 30 of the 34 signs listed in Table 1 are on film.

Preparedness varies not only from contingency to contingency within a species but also developmentally for a given contingency within a species. A young animal may be differentially prepared to learn about two contingencies, both of which he can master equally well later in life. The human infant, as Arnold Sameroff points out, is a clear example of this. There has been a long and checkered history of trying to teach newborn humans various things. Investigators failed to classically condition foot withdrawal with such arbitrary stimuli as tones paired with foot shock, but succeeded in shaping sucking for food reinforcement. Sameroff accounts for this by pointing out that in the unsuccessful conditioning studies, investigators tried to get the infant to learn a relationship between two previously unrelated stimuli from different modalities; he postulates that a newborn infant cannot coordinate two separate "schema." When classical conditioning is done with a tactile CS and a tactile US, conditioning occurs. So man, even at birth, can learn but only about relationships for which he is prepared at that stage of development.

32

CAN CONDITIONED RESPONSES BE
ESTABLISHED IN THE
NEWBORN INFANT: 1971?

Arnold J. Sameroff

The learning capabilities of the human newborn are evaluated. Classical conditioning is difficult to demonstrate in the newborn, while operant conditioning is possible. Two hypotheses are evaluated as explanations for difficulties in conditioning the newborn: (a) The newborn is unable to respond to stimulus change. (b) The newborn is able to respond to a general change but cannot respond to specific differences in stimulation. It is proposed that classical conditioning may involve the integration of two sensory modalities: that of the CS and that of the US. The newborn infant must first develop cognitive systems, through his experience with various stimuli, to differentiate each modality separately before he can integrate any two modalities in classical conditioning. The roles of the orienting reaction and defensive reaction are discussed.

The title of this article is taken from Dorothy Marquis who asked the same question in 1931. She answered that question in the affirmative, but recent data suggest that her conclusion may have been premature. For the purpose of

From *Developmental Psychology*, 5 (1971), 411–442.

An earlier version of this article was presented at the Eastern Regional Meeting of the Society for Research in Child Development, Worcester, Massachusetts, 1968. This study was supported by United States Public Health Service, National Institute of Child Health and Human Development Grant No. HD-03454. The author wishes to thank Michael Davidson and James Ison for their criticisms which were helpful in sharpening some of the ideas in this article.

exploring the issue of newborn learning in detail, the present author has divided the literature into two parts. The section on studies of infant activity focuses on the infant's ability to alter his behavior in experimental situations. The section on studies of infant reactivity deals with the newborn's ability to respond to stimulus change in his environment. In a later section the relation between the infant's ability to react to stimuli and his ability to form new associations to these stimuli is explored. The operational definition of the newborn period used in this article is the length of time that the infant remains in the hospital after birth, currently from 3 to 10 days.

STUDIES OF ACTIVITY

In Kessen's (1963) description of infants as active as well as reactive, he suggested that the child is engaged in the process of integrating his experience and thereby constructing his world, and is not atomistically accepting the contingencies of which he finds himself a part. An empirical question that would help in the definition of a theoretical position is, What are the kinds of contingencies to which the newborn can respond; that is, which experimental paradigms will be effective in showing learning, and which paradigms will not show alteration in the performance of the infant? The major two paradigms of consequence for learning studies are the classical or respondent and the instrumental or operant.

There have been many investigations in which attempts were made to show classical conditioning in newborn infants. These studies were uniformly unsuccessful or inconclusive. A prototype of this kind of study is one done by Wickens and Wickens in 1940, who elicited foot withdrawal by using an electrotactual shock as an unconditioned stimulus. In their experimental group, they paired a buzzer with the shock for 36 trials over 3 days. On the third day, they tested for conditioning by presenting the buzzer alone and got, as they had hoped, the foot withdrawal response. However, in a control group which also had 36 trials of electrotactual shock, but without a buzzer, they were also able to get a foot withdrawal response when the infants were stimulated with the buzzer. It appeared that pairing the buzzer with the shock was irrelevant to the results they obtained. They concluded from this study that if they had conditioned anything it was to a sudden change in stimulation.

Encouraged by advances in technology over the intervening decades, Crowell (in Bijou & Baer, 1965), Gullickson (in Bijou & Baer, 1965), and Marum (in Lipsitt, 1963) each did experiments in which they tried to condition foot withdrawal elicited by electrotactual shock to an auditory stimulus. These investigators were equally unsuccessful. Lipsitt and Kaye (in Lipsitt, 1963) worked with a different aversive response. They paired a tone with the presentation of acetic acid vapor to the infant's nose. The unconditioned response was withdrawal from the vapor or heightened activity. They were also unsuccessful in obtaining this response.

There is a second group of studies[1] in which conditioning effects were purportedly found, but a number of imporant questions were left unanswered about control groups or peculiarities in results. These studies have been criticized by a number of authors including Lipsitt (1963) and Bijou and Baer (1965). Among these are Spelt's (1948) report of fetal conditioning, Marquis's (1931) report of conditioning sucking movements to a buzzer, Marquis's (1941) later report of conditioning infants to their feeding schedules, and Lipsitt and Kaye's (1964) recent attempt to condition sucking movements to a tone.

During the last few years a change in paradigm took place and investigators using operant techniques have been able to find positive evidence of learning abilities in the newborn. Lipsitt, Kaye, and Bosack (1966) were able to increase the infant's sucking rate to a rubber tube by reinforcing the sucking with dextrose solution. They demonstrated both extinction and retraining effects.

Sameroff (1968) was able to differentially alter two components of the sucking response. Infants had been noted to get milk out of a nipple either by expression, that is, squeezing the nipple between tongue and palate, or by suction, that is, enlarging the oral cavity and creating a vacuum which pulls the milk out of the nipple. When the expression component was reinforced, that is, squeezing the nipple, the suction component was diminished and in many cases disappeared during the training period. When the newborns had to express above certain pressure thresholds to obtain milk, they changed their performance to match the thresholds.

Siqueland (1968) was able to influence the head turning response in newborns by operant training. He succeeded in increasing the rate of head turning in two groups (one of which was put on a 2:1 fixed-ratio schedule), and to decrease head turning in a third group which was reinforced for holding the head still.

Using a modified classical conditioning paradigm, Siqueland and Lipsitt (1966) performed three experiments using Papousek's (1961) head turning method. They stroked the cheeks of newborn infants which under normal conditions elicited ipsilateral head turns about 25% of the time. In their first experiment they paired a buzzer with the stroking and, if the infant turned his head, he received an immediate dextrose solution reinforcement. In their experimental group, the rate of head turning to the tactual stimulus increased to 80%, while in a control group in which the reinforcement was given only 8–10 seconds after the tone-touch stimulation, the rate remained at 25%. However, there was no evidence that the auditory stimulus had any influence on the results, since the head turn did not occur until the stroke was performed.

In the second experiment, Siqueland and Lipsitt investigated differentiation of two auditory stimuli, a buzzer and a tone. The positive stimulus was paired with a tactual stimulus eliciting head turning to one side, while on alternate trials the

[1] The author has classed all studies in which sucking on a nipple was the UR and anticipatory sucking without a nipple was the CR in the questionable group because of the prepotency of the sucking response in the hungry infant. Jensen (1933) has reported onset of sucking to squeezing the infant's toe or pulling his hair. More recent evidence has indicated an unconditioned sucking response to onset of auditory stimulation (Keen, 1964; Semb & Lipsitt, 1968). The potentiation of this response and the inability of the investigator to truly decide what elicted the response (Was it the infant touching his tongue to his lips or merely touching the two lips together?) when it occurs makes sucking a complex response to control in studies of classical conditioning. It is an example of what Seligman (1970) has called a prepared response.

negative stimulus was paired with tactual stimulation eliciting head turning to the other side. After training by reinforcing the response to the positive stimulus with dextrose solution, they were able to show an increase of head turning to the stroke on the positive side as opposed to no increase of head turning to the stroke on the negative side. Again, however, there was no evidence that the auditory stimuli played any role in the learning since the infants responded only to the differential stroking of the cheek to one side or the other.

In the third experiment, the same authors showed some evidence for differentiation of the auditory stimuli. They used the same buzzer and tone as positive and negative stimuli, presented alternately as in the previous experiment; but, this time both were paired with a tactual perioral stimulus eliciting head turning on only one side. When the positive stimulus sounded, the tactual stimulus was applied and if a head turn occurred the infant was reinforced with dextrose solution. When the negative stimulus sounded, the infant was stroked on the same side, but a head turn did not result in reinforcement. In this situation, the infant increased his responding to the tactual stimulus following the positive auditory stimulus while the stroke associated with the negative stimulus did not increase in effectiveness in eliciting head turns. These results are interesting, both from the point of view of having a differentiation of response associated with the two auditory stimuli, and the failure to demonstrate the infant's ability to be classically conditioned. The auditory signal still did not elicit the head turning response anticipatorily; it was only after the tactual stimulus was presented that the head turn was elicited.

What differentiates those studies in which investigators were able to show learning effects in newborns from those where there was less success? Is there any generalization that can be made which will help to understand the behavior of these newborns better? One clear difference is between the classical and operant conditioning paradigms. The unsuccessful studies have typically been attempts at classical conditioning, attempts to relate a previously neutral stimulus to an unconditioned stimulus and response.

On the other hand, the successful experiments either have not been in the classical conditioning paradigm or have not yielded classical results. In all cases, a previous relationship has already existed between the stimulus and response in question. No previously neutral stimuli have been associated. The results of the various training procedures have been to strengthen or alter what Kessen (1967) has described as *organized patterns of behavior* in the newborn. In the Lipsitt, Kaye, and Bosack (1966) study, an already existing low sucking rate to an oral stimulus was enhanced. In the Sameroff (1968) study, already existing expression and suction components of the sucking response were modified. In Siqueland's (1968) operant conditioning of head turning, an already existing organized component of the rooting-sucking-feeding complex was modified; and in Siqueland and Lipsitt's (1966) three experiments, an already existing relation between tactual perioral stimulation and head turning was enhanced.

If classical conditiong has not been demonstrated in the newborn, when can it be said to have been reliably shown? Polikanina (1961) paired a tone CS with ammonia vapor as an US eliciting motoric avoidance as a response. She found a conditioned response to the tone in 50% of the trials after 3–5 weeks. Papousek

(1967) worked with the head turning response. He paired a bell CS with stroking the infant's cheek and found stable conditioned responses after an average of 3 weeks (i.e., the bell alone regularly elicited the head turn). Thus, it seems that some time during the first few weeks of life something changes so that the same classical conditioning which was not demonstrated in the first week of life in the work of Lipsitt and Kaye (in Lipsitt, 1963) and Siqueland and Lipsitt (1966) became possible during the third week of life, as seen in the work of Polikanina (1961) and Papousek (1967).

A *caveat* must be included here about considering the Polikanina (1961) or Papousek (1967) studies as evidence for successful classical conditioning. The Polikanina study included no controls for pseudoconditioning. As a result, her findings may be identical in origin to those of Wickens and Wickens (1940). The Papousek head turning paradigm that was also used in the Siqueland and Lipsitt (1966) studies is not true classical conditioning. The milk reinforcement as a consequence of the head turning made the procedure a mixed model during training, and an operant after criterion was reached. Morgan and Morgan (1944), also without controls, claimed no eyeblink conditioning was possible before 45 days of life. Janos (1965) presented the best case for conditional eyeblink, but he got it only after 86 days. He was also able to show differentiation of response to two auditory cues.

The failure to classically condition newborns requires that an attempt be made at some theoretical explanation of the data. A starting point for such an explanation will be an analysis of the task. Since the problem seems to be related to the establishment of an association to a previously neutral stimulus, a first requirement for the subject in the classical conditioning paradigm is that he be able to perceive this neutral stimulus. A starting hypothesis can be that the newborn is unable to detect changes in his environment. To test this hypothesis, a series of studies related to the infant's abilities to respond to stimulus change is reviewed in the next section.

STUDIES OF REACTIVITY

The focus of studies in this class is on the infant's response to stimulation and the changes in this response as the stimulation is either varied or repeated. For example, studies of perception using habituation or eye orientation fall into this class. The main concern, however, is with a group of responses which the Russians, especially Sokolov (1963), have called the orienting reaction.

The function of the orienting reaction is to prepare the organism to deal with novel stimulation (Lynn, 1966). Lynn (1966), following Sokolov (1963), lists five classes of responses in the orienting reaction. They include (a) increases in the sensitivity of the sense organs, (b) motor orientation of the sense organs toward the source of stimulation, (c) changes in general skeletal musculature, (d) desynchronization of the EEG with accompanying lowered amplitude and increased frequency, and (e) a number of autonomic responses consisting of GSR, vasoconstriction in the limbs and vasodilation in the head, decrease in respiratory frequency with increase in amplitude, and heart-rate deceleration. In the last decade, several studies have produced evidence for the existence of various components of the orienting reaction in the newborn. They are listed below following Lynn's (1966) categorization.

Increase in the Sensitivity of the Sense Organs

Stechler, Bradford, and Levy (1966) stimulated newborn infants with an air puff to the abdomen in two conditions while measuring the GSR. In the first condition, the infants were awake with eyes open and fixated on a patterned visual stimulus. In the second condition the infants were awake with eyes open but not fixated on any apparent stimulus. The electrodermal response was much stronger in the fixated condition as compared with the unfixated condition. The existence of the orienting reaction can be inferred from the lower sensory thresholds for GSR elicitation in the fixating group.

Motor Orientation of Sense Organs

Motor orientation of head and/or eyes to visual stimuli have been found by Fantz (1963), Hershenson (1964), Wolff (1966), and Salapatek and Kessen (1966). Eye orientation to auditory stimulation has been reported by Wolff (1966) and Turkewitz, Moreau, and Birch (1966). The rooting reflex is an orientation of the head to perioral tactual stimulation.

Changes in General Skeletal Musculature

Motor quieting and cessation of ongoing activity to novel stimuli have been found by Papousek (1967) and Bronshtein and Petrowa (1952).

Desynchronization of the EEG

Generalized EEG responses have been reported by Dreyfuss-Brissac and Blanc (1956) and Ellingson (1967) to indicate that the newborn can react to novel stimuli with a change to the low amplitude, fast activity which has been described as part of the orienting reaction.

Autonomic Responses

Sokolov (1963) used the vasomotor responses as one of his prime indicators for the orienting reaction. However, as yet, vasomotor responses have not been investigated in the newborn, so little can be said about them. More work has been done with other autonomic responses. Until recently there was some question as to whether the GSR could be found in newborns. However, Crowell, Davis, Chun, and Spellacy (1965) and Stechler, Bradford, and Levy (1966) in a study cited above, both found the GSR by careful experimental preparation. Respiration has not received much attention as an orienting reaction component. Sameroff (1970) has found respiratory slowing to auditory stimulation in some conditions. Steinschneider (1968) reported that white noise stimuli between 55 and 100 decibels increased respiratory rate. However, if only the first respiratory cycle following stimulus change was considered, the low intensity stimuli, 55 and 70 decibels, resulted in respiratory deceleration. The different direction of response to the low intensity stimuli might be interpreted as an orienting reaction component.

The one response that seems to be quite different from what was expected in an orienting reaction is the heart-rate response. Authors working with newborns have consistently shown heart-rate acceleration to novel stimuli. The heart-rate-decelerative response to stimulation does exist in the 4-month-old infant (Kagan & Lewis, 1965). Lipton, Steinschneider, and Richmond (1966) found some heart-rate deceleration before acceleration in infants 2½ months of age, and Lewis, Bartels, and Goldberg (1966) also found initial deceleration before acceleration in a third of their awake subjects between the ages of 2 and 8 weeks. Schulman (1968), in a recent study, was able to find consistent deceleration in awake 1-week-olds, further lowering the age boundary. In newborns, Schachter, Williams, Khachaturian, Tobin, and Druger (1968) found a triphasic response to auditory clicks, the first phase being a short deceleration.

From this survey of the newborn orienting reaction literature, it can be seen that the field has moved in the last 10 years from little or no knowledge to an almost complete outline of newborn reactivity. Apparently, the one component of the orienting reaction about which there is some serious question is the heart-rate response. Is the heart-rate-decelerative component of the orienting reaction undeveloped, or can some other explanation be put forth as to why acceleration seems to be the predominate heart-rate response in the newborn? One hypothesis is related to the significance of the heart-rate-accelerative response. Graham and Clifton (1966) have shown that the heart-rate-accelerative response is a part of the adult's reaction to many stimulus situations. It has a role in a reaction to stimulation different from the orienting reaction, the defensive reaction.

According to Sokolov (1963) the defensive reaction differs from the orienting reaction in that rather than increase in the sensitivity of the sensory systems, there is a decrease and a reaction away from the source of stimulation. The defensive reaction avoids the stimulus source, whereas the orienting reaction approaches the source of stimulation. Perhaps the heart-rate acceleration to stimulation found in newborn infants is part of the defensive reaction rather than a sign of an immature orienting reaction.

A question which immediately arises is, What kind of stimulation gives rise to one reaction over another? Sokolov (1963) defined the defensive reaction as occurring when stimulation increases above a certain limit and threatens the integrity of the body, that is, becomes painful. However, in the case of the newborn there are stimuli which are not painful, but which elicit defensive reactions (Kessen & Mandler, 1961). Loud noises or loss of support evoke obvious defensive reactions in the form of startles or Moro reflexes. Less obvious defensive reactions, expressed only autonomically, can occur to any intense stimulus.

It may be that there are two kinds of defensive reactions, a quantitative one and a qualitative one. The quantitative defensive reaction would be the response to the high intensity stimuli which Sokolov (1963) discussed. The qualitative defensive reaction would be to stimuli for which there is no cognitive or neuronal model. Given the limited experience of the newborn, it would be expected that there would not be a model for most of the stimuli he encounters.

Therefore, it can be expected that the newborn's initial reaction to most novel stimulation is defensive and that for an orienting reaction to occur there must first be a habituation of this defensive reaction. Bartoshuk (1962), Bridger (1961), and Graham, Clifton, and Hatton (1968) have shown habituation of the accelerative heart-rate response and startle response to auditory stimulation. Sameroff (1970) found a change in direction of respiratory response to auditory stimuli from acceleration in 1-day-old infants to deceleration in 4-day-olds.

Studies of orientation to visual stimulation in which defensive reactions have not been found might be thought to contradict this position. However, no study has been performed on the just born newborn, so that it can be hypothesized that the defensive reaction to general low intensity visual stimuli has already been habituated by the time the first experiments were performed, possibly *in utero*. Studies using low-intensity stimuli are different from studies where loud sounds or bright lights, which would seem to be novel for the newborn, lead to clear defensive reactions. The point could be confirmed if heart-rate response to the kinds of low-level visual stimuli that elicit orientation behavior in the newborn were to be studied. A finding of heart-rate deceleration would further support the existence of the full orienting reaction in the newborn.

Another hypothesis explaining the change from accelerative heart-rate responses in the newborn to decelerative responses in the 3-month-old has been proposed by Graham and Jackson (1970). They suggested the difference in findings might be a function of the state of the infant during the experimental sessions, that newborns are typically examined while they are asleep or drowsy, and 3-month-olds are examined while they are awake. The ability of Schulman (1968) and Lewis, Bartels, and Goldberg (1966) to find the decelerative response only in waking infants support the Graham and Jackson (1970) hypothesis.

The significance of the preceding discussion as to whether or not the orienting reaction exists in the newborn is in the light it throws on the infant's ability to respond to changes in his environment, especially novel ones. Sokolov (1963) maintained that preceding conditioning, there must be an initial orienting reaction to the conditional stimulus. Therefore, if the orienting reaction is incomplete in the newborn, there can be no conditioning until it matures.

For learning to occur, the infant must react to new contingencies in his environment. If he is unable to respond to new situations, it is unlikely that he can show changes in his behavior related to these new situations. That the orienting reaction seems to be present in the newborn, boosts the infant one rung up the ladder.

The second rung on the ladder is related to the distinction between a "neutral" stimulus and a "new" stimulus. Classical conditioning is defined as the association of a previously neutral CS with the nonneutral US. An additional problem in newborn conditioning is that a neutral stimulus is also a new stimulus. How many newborns have had previous experience with electric shock or acetic acid vapors or even bells and buzzers? Since, from the studies described in this section, it seems that the newborn can respond to general changes in stimulation, the first hypothesis related to his inability to be classically conditioned seems disconfirmed. The next hypothesis to explain his inability could be that the newborn is unable to respond differentially to the specific stimuli that have been used in studies of early classical conditioning. To elaborate this hypothesis, one must move away from the empirical base of the preceding two sections and explore some theoretical positions in the next section.

COGNITIVE SCHEMAS

Until now stimuli and responses have been discussed only as observables. The attempt to explain all of behavior on the basis of observables has been a goal of radical behaviorists for a number of decades. A high point in this attempt was Skinner's (1957) explanation of language behavior. However, Skinner's work was judged by Chomsky (1959) to be inadequate for linguistic analysis. Learning theorists of a less fundamentalist bent have dealt with the issue of nonobservables in the explanation of complex human behavior (Kendler, 1963) by inferring covert analogies of overt S-R processes. The use of covert mediation to reinforce the reductionism in the S-R approach to behavior has not resolved the inability of a nonhierarchical model to explain complex thought processes (Scheerer, 1954). Piaget (1960) also believed that the associationist position was inadequate to explain the complexities of logical behavior and language. Instead, Piaget formulated a theory in which the same cognitive *functions* were used to explain both the complex symbolic behavior of the adult and the simple sensory-motor behavior of the infant, while at the same time the cognitive structural elements associated with the two age periods were quite different. The addition that Piaget makes to behaviorism is to fill in the black box with a cognitive organization composed of structural elements called *schemas*. The schema is a cognitive structure which is adapted through the organism's interaction with the environment. The general function of adaptation is composed of two subfunctions: assimilation, the incorporation of a stimulus into a previously organized schema; and accommodation, the process by which a schema alters itself in order to incorporate new inputs. Focusing on the active internal organization that accompanies the adaptation process, Piaget (1960) is able to trace the development from innate sensory-motor schemas to the formal logical operations of the adult human. What for many may seem to be an unnecessary complication in theory for understanding simple behaviors is for Piaget an excellent application of Occam's razor. Piaget has extended accepted principles of biology which function in the development of chemical and physical systems to the sphere of psychology. Intelligent behavior from a Piagetian viewpoint can be regarded as a more complexly organized *adaptive* system of the human animal in keeping with his parallel more complexly organized biological system. However, the functions of assimilation, accommodation, and their organization need not be different for the two systems.

Initially the infant comes into the world with a set of built-in reflex schemas. These schemas may have been previously tuned or adapted *in utero* to an optimal input, but almost immediately begin adapting to new inputs. For example, the sucking schema seems optimally fitted to the tactual input of the nipple, but is readily adapted to sucking on a finger, tube, tongue, blanket, or anything else that stimulates the lips. Experiments such as Lipsitt and Kaye (1964), Lipsitt, Kaye, and Bosack (1966), and Sameroff (1968) have shown that the sucking schema is sensitive to many input contingencies and can be readily altered by manipulating variables directly related to food getting. It is through the adaptation of these already existing reflex schemas that any demonstration of learning has been possible in the newborn.

It is when one departs from these built-in schemas that difficulties arise. In the typical classical conditioning problem, there is an attempt to relate two previously unrelated stimuli in different sensory modalities. For adults, both the CS and the US already are part of various schematic hierarchies. In the typical newborn study, only the US is part of the schema, for example, tactual stimulation leading to head turning. The "newness" of the CS for the infant also means that it is unrelated to any of his activity schemas other than through the possibility of generalizing assimilation. As a consequence, there is no place for the CS in the infant's cognitive structure.

The failure of classical conditioning attempts can occur for two possible reasons. The first is that the infant cannot coordinate two separate schemas in the newborn period; the second is that an independent schema for the CS must first exist before a coordination can be made between the US-UR and CS schemas. Both reasons are probably true in the context of the development of the entire schematic structure. Werner (1957) made the point in his orthogenetic principle that development proceeds through both differentiation *and* hierarchic integration. There is a simultaneous process of differentiation in the sensory systems as various stimuli are related to different activities of the organism, and at the same time these various activities are integrated at higher levels.

The relations to be established in experimental classical conditioning situations might be placed midway in the developmental sequence between (a) the differentiation of innate schemas and (b) the subsequent integration of these schema systems. In an experiment, an attempt is made to coordinate schemas artifically that are not coordinated in the organism's real world. For control purposes, the experimental association is made between elements different from those which arise in the organism's normal environment. As a result of this controlled reliable relationship, the organism might be able to make coordinations which would only appear at a later stage in the more erratic real world.

To return to the initial problem, how would it be possible to obtain classical conditioning in the infant? The answer cannot be found by generalizing from a procedure used with adult dogs. There is no compelling reason to differentiate between the adult dog or rat and the older prelinguistic child. Both can have perceptually differentiated the world, and can have established differentiated modalities of perception.

In contrast, the newborn rat, dog, or infant has not yet achieved this differentiation. It is not even clear that the infant initially differentiates inputs from the auditory, visual, or tactual systems other than at the level of the perceiving organ, the reflex schema. The sensory system in the mouth seems to be highly developed (Jensen, 1932; Sameroff, 1968). The same cannot be said for the visual system, as recent studies by Salapatek (1968) and Salapatek and

Kessen (1966) have indicated; nor for the auditory system (Stubbs, 1934). Before a specific auditory input can be related to other response schemas, the auditory schema must itself become differentiated. An interactionist position is called for, since it does not seem appropriate to call a perceptual system immature if its maturity depends on an interaction with the environment. If conditioning is to occur in the classical sense that a specific previously neutral stimulus will now elicit a response, the organism must first be able to differentiate that stimulus from the other stimuli in its environment. For Piaget (1952), the only possibility of recognizing an input is through the subject's response to it, through what has been called motor recognition or recognitory assimilation. Until the response to one specific stimulus is adequately differentiated from responses to other specific stimuli in the auditory schematic hierarchy, there can be no connection of these to other schemas.

For example, it may be that in the typical conditioning study the modality of the CS and the modality of the US are distant on some dimension, thus making their schematic coordination difficult. Using a CS and US in modalities that are less different might lead to more successful results. Ignoring the differentiation problem for the present, the earliest and most stable conditioning should occur if the sensory modalities of the CS and US are identical. There is evidence that this is, indeed, the case. Kasatkin (1948), on the basis of Russian research, ranks the sensory modalities of CSs on the basis of the age at which they can first be used in successful conditioning. Earliest on the list are changes of body position which involve proprioceptive as well as vestibular stimulation. Neurologically, the interrelations between proprioceptive receptors and motor centers are very close, from the gamma efferent fibers through the cerebellum and into cortical areas.

Brackbill, Lintz, and Fitzgerald (1968; Abrahamson, Brackbill, Carpenter, & Fitzgerald, in press) made a more general point in differentiating the conditioning of autonomic versus somatic responses. Rather than accepting a developmental progression from one to the other in conditionability, they have demonstrated in the first months of life that they could obtain an autonomic CR to an autonomic CS (temporal conditioning of the pupillary response) and somatic CR to a sensory CS (tactual stimulus associated with eyeblink), but could not cross-condition between the somatic and autonomic systems, that is, obtain an eyeblink to temporal conditioning or a pupillary response to a tactual stimulus.

SCHEMA DIFFERENTIATION

There is no reason to believe that the response systems associated with perception are any more differentiated at birth than the response systems associated with motor activity. Researchers from Gesell and Amatruda (1945) to White, Castle, and Held (1964) have spelled out the development from global responses to specific, directed motor functioning in coordination with other response systems. Recent research indicates the same can be said for the perceptual systems.

The case is clearer for the differentiation of stimuli leading to sucking behavior, but a parallel case can be made for audition. Initially, there is an innate global response to suck on anything sensed by the mouth that does not elicit a defensive reaction, such as a hot nipple. Differentiation occurs through accommodation of the response to the specific object sucked upon, and is evidenced by the increase in coordination and stability of sucking in the first days of life found by Halverson (1944), Kron, Stein, and Goddard (1963), and Sameroff (1967). However, the infant does not act differently on the basis of this differentiation of response. He will suck on a dry nipple for 20 minutes even though he is hungry (Sameroff, 1967).

This situation changes after a few weeks. The 3-week-old infant will begin to reject a nonnutritive nipple when hungry (Piaget, 1952). The differentiation between sucking alone and the complex of sucking, warm feeling in the mouth, and swallowing, now makes a difference in the infant's behavior. There is an integration of new elements into the set of schemas which permits differentiations to be made in the infant's response to his environment.

An analogous case can be made for auditory stimuli. The initial differentiation of auditory inputs found in Siqueland and Lipsitt's (1966) third experiment could not be integrated at that stage with other response schemas. It was only after a period of differentiation and stabilization of the auditory schema that it could be coordinated with other behaviors, as was evidenced by Papousek's (1967) success in obtaining head turning to the tone alone without mediating oral stimulation after 3 weeks of age.

Papousek's (1967) research is a case study of the infant's changing ability to respond to auditory stimuli. When number of trials to a conditioning criterion was compared for groups of newborns, 3-month-old infants, and 5-month-old infants, the data showed an inverse correlation with age: 177, 42, and 28 trials, respectively. The longer experience that the older infants had in responding to differential auditory stimuli in their natural environment was reflected in their faster conditioning in the experimental situation. An alternate hypothesis is that the infants' had somehow matured neurologically, thus making faster conditioning possible. However, a maturation hypothesis is weakened by Papousek's extinction data. The three age groups extinguished their responses in almost identical numbers of trials: 27, 25, and 27, respectively. The extinction data indicate that the neurological mechanisms are not radically different in the three age groups, so that the differential ability to be conditioned must lie in the differential development of the cognitive organization.

More recently, Papousek (1969) has found further related effects in attempts to condition infants to differentiate head turning responses. A bell signal indicated that a head turn to one side would be reinforced; a buzzer indicated that a head turn in the opposite direction would be reinforced. In Papousek's (1967) original work, differentiation training began when the newborn group was an average of 44 days old, because it followed three other procedures—conditioning, extinction, and reconditioning. In the later study, Papousek (1969) investigated the ability of younger infants to learn the differentiation. In one group, he began training at an average age of 31 days when the infants had completed only one previous procedure—conditioning of a head turn to the left.

In another group, he began differentiation training with newborns, completely eliminating any previous procedures. The results were surprising in that, while the group that began differentiation at 44 days took 224 trials, reaching criterion at an average age of 72 days, the group that began at 31 days took 278 trials and reached criterion at an average of 71 days of age. Thus, the younger subjects were unable to capitalize on their earlier start.

To support a maturation hypothesis, the newborn group should also have reached criterion at around 72 days of age. However, they provided surprising results. They required an average of 814 trials, and were 128 days old when the differentiation criterion was reached, almost double the age of the other two groups. It thus seems that not only must the auditory schemas become differentiated before conditioning can take place, but also that the infant's experience must be paced or an input overload of the schema can occur with consequent retardation in its development.

SUMMARY

Rather than hypothesize stages of development in the newborn period, the proposed theory has a progression in cognitive structure based on differentiation and hierarchic integration of schemas. On the activity side, the newborn initially can respond with prenatally organized cognitive schemas, which can assimilate, that is, are adapted either genetically or *in utero* to include specific stimuli. Development is through the increasing differentiation and enlargement of the activity schemas by accommodation to a growing number of stimuli. The initial limited range of stimuli to which the reflex was sensitive is expanded as a function of feedback from the infant's experience with differential effects of his responding.

On the reactivity side, suprathreshold novel stimuli, that is, those which are not assimilated by the innate reflex schemas, elicit a defensive reaction. Repeated exposure to novel stimuli builds up the infant's schema repertoire. As the repertoire grows, the likelihood of encountering a stimulus for which there is no differentiated schema declines, reducing the chances for eliciting the qualitative defensive reaction. Subsequently, the response to the novel stimulus will be an orienting reaction. The activity-reactivity dichotomy is more than a division between those stimuli that can be assimilated to existing schemas and those that cannot, because it also includes the dynamic experiential aspect of the qualitative defensive reaction and orienting reaction in the adaptation process. Eventually, sufficient plasticity is achieved within the cognitive framework. Separate schema systems can then be coordinated making possible the association necessary for classical conditioning in the experimental situation.

To conclude, the evidence strongly indicates that before classical conditioning can occur there must be a differentiation of the schema systems related to both the US and CS. For distance receptors, this development seems to take about 3 weeks, after which the infant begins to be able to coordinate his differentiated perceptual response systems with other sensory-motor schemas such as sucking or head turning.

References

Abrahamson, D., Brackbill, Y., Carpenter, R., & Fitzgerald, H. E. Interaction of stimulus and response in infant conditioning. In H. E. Fitzgerald & Y. Brackbill (Eds.), *Design and method in infant research*. Chicago: University of Chicago Press, in press.

Bartoshuk, A. K. Response decrement with repeated elicitation of human neonatal cardiac acceleration to sound. *Journal of Comparative and Physiological Psychology*, 1962, *55*, 9—13.

Brackbill, Y., Lintz, L. M., & Fitzgerald, H. E. Differences in the autonomic and somatic conditioning of infants. *Psychosomatic Medicine*, 1968, *30*, 193—201.

Bijou, S. W., & Baer, D. M. *Child development. II: University stage of infancy*. New York: Appleton-Century-Crofts, 1965.

Bridger, W. H. Sensory habituation and discrimination in the human neonate. *American Journal of Psychiatry*, 1961, *117*, 991—996.

Bronschtein, A. I., & Petrowa, J. P. Die Erforschung des akustischen Analysators bei Neugeborenen und Kinder im frühen Säuglingsalter. *Pawlow-Zeitschrift für höhere Nerventätigkeit*, 1952, *2*, 441—455.

Chomsky, N. Review of B. F. Skinner's *Verbal behavior. Language*, 1959, *35*, 26—58.

Crowell, D. H., David, C. M., Chun, B. J., & Spellacy, F. J. Galvanic skin reflex in newborn humans. *Science*, 1965, *148*, 1108—1111.

Dreyfus-Brisac, C., & Blanc, C. Electro-encephalogramme et maturation cerebrale. *Encephale*, 1956, *3*, 205—245.

Ellingson, R. J. The study of brain electrical activity in infants. In L. P. Lipsitt & C. C. Spiker (Eds.), *Advances in child development and behavior*. Vol. 3. New York: Academic Press, 1967.

Fantz, R. L. Pattern vision in newborn infants. *Science*, 1963, *140*, 296—297.

Gesell, A. L. & Amatruda, C. S. *The embryology of behavior: The beginnings of the human mind*. New York: Harper, 1945.

Graham, F. K. & Clifton, R. K. Heartrate change as a component of the orienting response. *Psychological Bulletin*, 1966, *65*, 305—320.

Graham, F. K., Cliton, R. K. & Hatton, H. M. Habituation of the heartrate response to repeated auditory stimulation during the first five days of life. *Child Development*, 1968, *39*, 35—52.

Graham, F. K., & Jackson, J. C. Arousal systems and infant heart rate responses. In H. W. Reese & L. P. Lipsitt (Eds.), *Advances in child development and behavior*. Vol. 5. New York: Academic Press, 1970.

Halverson, H. M. Mechanisms of early infant feeding. *Journal of Genetic Psychology*, 1944, *64*, 185—223.

Hershenson, M. Visual discrimination in the human newborn. *Journal of Comparative and Physiological Psychology*, 1964, *58*, 270—276.

Janos, O. *Vekove a individualni rozdily ve vyssi nervove cinnosti kojenco*. [Age and individual differences in the higher nervous activity of the infant] Prague: Statni Zdravotnicke Nakladatelstvi, 1965.

Jensen, K. Differential reactions to taste and temperature stimuli in newborn infants. *Genetic Psychology Monographs*, 1932, *12*, 361—479.

Kagan, J., & Lewis, A. Studies of attention in the human infant. *Merrill-Palmer Quarterly*, 1965, *11*, 95—128.

Kasatkin, N. I. *Rannie uslovnye reflexsy v ontogeneze cheloveka*. [Early conditioned reflexes in human ontogenesis] Moscow: Izdatelstvo Akademiye Medistvo Nauk SSR, 1948.

Keen, R. Effects of auditory stimulation on sucking behavior in the human neonate. *Journal of Experimental Child Psychology*, 1964, *1*, 348—354.

Kendler, T. S. Development of mediating responses in children. *Monographs of the Society for Research in Child Development*, 1963, *28* (28, Serial No. 86).

Kessen, W. Research in the psychological development of infants: An overview. *Merrill-Palmer Quarterly of Behavior and Development*, 1963, *9*, 83—94.

Kessen, W. Sucking and looking: Two organized congenital patterns of behavior in the human newborn. In H. W. Stevenson, E. H. Hess, & H. L. Rheingold (Eds.), *Early behavior*. New York: Wiley, 1967.

Kessen, W., & Mandler, G. Anxiety, pain, and the inhibition of distress. *Psychological Review*, 1961, *68*, 396—404.

Kron, R. E., Stein, M., & Goddard, K. E. A method of measuring sucking behavior of newborn infants. *Psychosomatic Medicine*, 1963, *25*, 181—191.

Lewis, M., Bartels, B., & Goldberg, S. State as a determinant of infants' heartrate reponse to stimulation. *Science*, 1966, *155*, 486—488.

Lipsitt, L. P. Learning in the first year of life. In L. P. Lipsitt & C. C. Spiker (Eds.), *Advances in child development and behavior*. Vol. 1. New York: Academic Press, 1963.

Lipsitt, L. P., & Kaye, H. Conditioned sucking in the human newborn. *Psychonomic Science*, 1964, *1*, 29—30.

Lipsitt, L. P., Kaye, H., & Bosack, T. N. Enhancement of neonatal sucking through reinforcement. *Journal of Experimental Child Psychology*, 1966, *4*, 163—168.

Lipton, E. L., Steinschneider, A., & Richmond, J. B. Autonomic function in the neonate: VII. Maturational changes in cardiac control. *Child Development*, 1966, *37*, 1—16.

Lynn, R. *Attention, arousal and the orientation reaction*. Oxford: Pergamon, 1966.

Marquis, D. P. Can conditioned reflexes be established in the new born infant? *Journal of Genetic Psychology*, 1931, *39*, 479—492.

Marquis, D. P. Learning in the neonate: The modification of behavior under three feeding schedules. *Journal of Experimental Psychology*, 1941, *29*, 263—282.

Morgan, J. J. B., & Morgan, S. S. Infant learning as a developmental index. *Journal of Genetic Psychology*, 1944, *65*, 281—289.

Papousek, H. Conditioned head rotation reflexes in infants in the first months of life. *Acta Paediatrica*, 1961, *50*, 565—576.

Papousek, H. Experimental studies of appetitional behavior in human newborns and infants. In H. W. Stevenson, E. H. Hess, & H. L. Rheingold (Eds.), *Early behavior*. New York: Wiley, 1967.

Papousek, H. Elaborations of conditioned headturning. Paper presented at the meeting of the XIX International Congress of Psychology, London, 1969.

Piaget, J. *The origins of intelligence in children*. New York: International Universities Press, 1952.

Piaget, J. *Psychology of intelligence*. New York: Littlefield, Adams, 1960.

Polikanina, R. I. The relation between autonomic and somatic components in the development of the conditioned reflex in premature infants. *Pavlov Journal of Higher Nervous Activity*, 1961, *11*, 51—58.

Salapatek, P. Visual scanning of geometric figures by the human newborn. *Journal of Comparative and Physiological Psychology*, 1968, *66*, 247—248.

Salapatek, P., & Kessen, W. Visual scanning of triangles in the human newborn. *Journal of Experimental Child Psychology*, 1966, *3*, 155—167.

Sameroff, A. J. Nonnutritive sucking in newborns under visual and auditory stimulation. *Child Development*, 1967, *38*, 443—452.

Sameroff, A. J. The components of sucking in the human newborn. *Journal of Experimental Child Psychology*, 1968, *6*, 607—623.

Sameroff, A. J. Respiration and sucking as components of the orienting reaction in newborns. *Psychophysiology*, 1970, *7*, 213—222.

Schacter, J., Williams, T. A. Khachaturian, Z., Tobin, M., & Druger, R. The multiphasic heart rate response to auditory clicks in neonates. Paper presented at the meeting of the Society for Psychophysiological Research, Washington, D. C., 1968.

Scheerer, M. Cognitive theory. In G. Lindzey (Ed.), *Handbook of social psychology*. Vol. 1. Cambridge, Mass.: Addison-Wesley, 1954.

Schulman, C. A. Effects of auditory stimulus on heartrate in high-risk and low-risk premature infants as a function of state. Paper presented at the meeting of the Eastern Psychological Association, Washington, D. C., April, 1968.

Seligman, M. E. P. On the generality of the laws of learning. *Psychological Review*, 1970, 77, 406–418.

Semb, G., & Lipsitt, L. P. The effects of acoustic stimulation on cessation and initiation of nonnutritive sucking in neonates. *Journal of Experimental Child Psychology*, 1968, 6, 585–597.

Siqueland, E. R. Reinforcement patterns and extinction in human newborns. *Journal of Experimental Child Psychology*, 1968, 6, 431–442.

Siqueland, E. R., & Lipsitt, L. P. Conditioned head-turning behavior in newborns. *Journal of Experimental Child Psychology*, 1966, 3, 356–376.

Skinner, B. F. *Verbal behavior*. New York: Appleton, 1957.

Sokolov, Ye. N. *Perception and the conditioned reflex*. New York: Macmillan, 1963.

Spelt, D. K. The conditioning of the human fetus in utero. *Journal of Experimental Psychology*, 1948, 38, 338–346.

Stechler, G., Bradford, S., & Levy, H. Attention in the newborn: Effect on motility and skin potential. *Science*, 1966, 151, 1246-1248.

Steinschneider, A. Sound intensity and respiratory responses in the neonate. *Psychosomatic Medicine*, 1968, 30, 534–541.

Stubbs, E. M. The effect of the factor of duration, intensity, and pitch of sound stimuli on the responses of newborn infants. *University of Iowa Studies in Child Welfare*, 1934, 9(4), 75–135.

Turkewitz, G., Moreau, T., & Birch, H. G. Head position and receptor organization in the human neonate. *Journal of Experimental Child Psychology*, 1966, 4, 169–177.

Werner, H. The concept of development from a comparative and organismic view. In D. B. Harris (Ed.), *The concept of development*. Minneapolis: University Minnesota Press, 1957.

White, B. L., Castle, P., & Held, R. Observations on the development of visually-directed reaching. *Child Development*, 1964, 35, 349–364.

Wickens, D. D., & Wickens, C. A study of conditioning in the neonate. *Journal of Experimental Psychology*, 1940, 25, 94–102.

Wolff, P. H. The causes, controls, and organization of behavior in the neonate. *Psychological Issues*, 1966, 5(1, Whole No. 17).

What is the relationship of cognition to preparedness? Lenneberg (this volume, p. 379) argues that cognition itself, as well as the language which expresses it, is species-specific. The next selection is taken from Hans Furth's exegesis of the work of the world's foremost developmental psychologist, Jean Piaget. It is argued that human intelligence, "like other organs," has evolved to regulate interaction with the environment. Cognition is a biological phenomenon, but not in the sense of being innately programmed to run off in a fixed way; rather only the "sources of organization" are fixed. Human cognitive organization frees the species from hereditary preprogramming, permitting constructive self-regulation. In our terms, cognition is the mechanism which underlies unprepared learning and allows men to deal so well with arbitrary contingencies.

33

BIOLOGY AND KNOWLEDGE

Jean Piaget

This is the final section of a comprehensive book in which Piaget explicitly gives a broad biological basis for his entire theory of knowledge. In the preceding section Piaget outlines the place of knowledge within a theoretical evolutionary perspective. He considers that a biological organization as an "open system" is subject to the vicissitudes of the surrounding environment. While it has an inherent tendency to extend itself into the environment, at the same time it must tend to close the system in order to conserve its own organization. External behavior in general is seen as fulfilling this double function with, however, only incomplete success. Knowing is a further step in this evolutionary direction. With its tendency towards reversible regulations and towards a stable equilibrium, knowledge can eventually attain what external behavior could not do. Knowledge can extend itself to an indefinite variety of situations, to the entire universe and all potential, thinkable situations and yet conserve the stability of its structure through complete compensation. The reason for this lies in the dissociation between the general forms of knowledge and the particular content to which the forms are applied. This dissociation, slowly prepared for in evolutionary history, implies for men the possibility as well as the necessity of social interaction. The human subject who is the carrier of knowledge is therefore not an isolated individual. The biological intelligence which Piaget explores in the "epistemic" subject is as much a social as an individual intelligence.

Continuing in this perspective Piaget asks in subsection I the old philosophical question: Where should we look for truth? His answer, as a scientist, is to look into the biological organization, which includes within its own nature the tendency to go beyond itself.

ORGANIC REGULATIONS AND COGNITIVE REGULATIONS

This collective surpassing of forms already constructed, beginning with the biological organization, puts in a proper perspective the conclusions which we

From H. G. Furth, *Piaget and Knowledge: Theoretical Foundation* (Englewood Cliffs, N. J.: Prentice-Hall, Inc., 1969). Originally published in French in Jean Piaget, *Biologie et connaissance* (Paris: Gallimard, 1967), pp. 413–423. Translated by Hans G. Furth, by permission of the publishers.

must now draw from the whole series of our analyses. It remains to justify the hypothesis that cognitive functions are a specialized organ for regulating exchanges with the external environment and that they yet derive their instruments from general forms of biological organization.

Life and Truth

One could say that the necessity of a differentiated organ is obvious since it is characteristic of knowledge to attain truth, while the characteristic of life is only the search for continued life. But while one does not know exactly what life consists of one knows even less what is understood by cognitive "truth." In general, one agrees to see in truth something other than a simple copy conforming to the real for the good reason that such a copy is impossible. In fact, only the copy would furnish the knowledge of the model to be copied and yet that knowledge would in turn be necessary for the copy! Nonetheless the attempt to follow the copy theory has resulted in a simple phenomenalism in which the subjectivity of the self constantly interferes with perceptual data. Such a situation by itself demonstrates an inextricable mesh between subject and object.

If truth is not a copy, it is then an organization of the real. But an organization on the part of what kind of subject? If it is only the human subject, this case, with only minimal gain, would risk the enlargement of egocentrism into anthropocentrism which at the same time would be sociocentrism. Consequently all philosophers seriously concerned with the absolute have recourse to a transcendent subject that goes beyond man and particularly beyond "nature." They place truth beyond spatio-temporal and physical contingencies and make "nature" intelligible in a timeless or eternal perspective. But the question arises whether it is possible to jump over one's own shadow to attain the "subject" in itself without it remaining in spite of all "human, all too human" as Nietzsche said. Unfortunately, from Plato to Husserl, the transcendent subject has constantly changed its appearance, without any other progress except that due to the sciences themselves, hence to the real model and not the transcendent model.

Our intention is therefore not to flee from nature which no one can escape but to understand it more deeply step by step with the efforts of science. In spite of what philosophers may say, nature is still far from having disclosed its secrets. It may be worthwhile, before placing the absolute in the clouds, to look into the interior of things. Moreover, if truth is an organization of the real, the preliminary question concerns the understanding of how an organization is organized. This is a biological question. In other words, since the epistemological problem is to know how science is possible, one should exhaust the resources of the immanent organization before taking recourse to a transcendent organization.

However, if truth is not egocentric and should not be anthropocentric either, must one reduce it to a biocentric organization? From the fact that truth goes beyond man, must one look for it in protozoa, termites, or chimpanzees? It would be an impoverished result to define truth as only that which all living beings, including man, have in common in their vision of the world. But if it is characteristic of life constantly to evolve further and if one looks for the secret of the rational organization in the biological organization *including its evolving*, the method then consists in trying to understand knowledge by its own construction. This is reasonable since knowledge is *essentially a construction*.

> In subsection II, Piaget describes the triple deficiencies of the organism with regard to (1) its extension into the environment, (2) its maintenance or conservation, (3) its regulation. The reason for these deficiencies is linked with (1) the hereditary mechanisms tied to genetic recombinations and (2) the phenotypic, i.e., individual, interactions with the environment that follow a rigidly built-in reaction norm. Behavior can be viewed as partly compensating for these deficiencies by a "functional" extension of organic forms. The regulations of the assimilative and accommodative activities of behavior emerge as cognitive functions.

The Deficiencies of the Organism

This evolving appears to us from a cognitive viewpoint inherent in the biological organization and is therefore essential as a primary datum. An organization involves a system of exchanges with the environment; it tends therefore to extend itself to the totality of the environment yet with only limited success; hence we can see the role of knowledge which is capable of functionally assimilating the entire universe without staying limited to physiological, material assimilations. Biological organization also creates forms and tends to conserve them with complete stability, again with only limited success; hence we can see the role of knowledge which extends material forms into forms of actions or operations; as these forms are dissociated from contents they are capable of conservation in their diverse applications. Finally, this biological organization is a source of homeostasis at all levels, and possesses regulations that ensure equilibrium by quasi-reversible mechanisms. This equilibrium remains fragile, however, and only resists the surrounding irreversibility by momentary stabilizations. Thus evolution appears like a series of disequilibria and re-equilibrations that tends toward an unattainable goal of integrated construction and reversible mobility. Only the cognitive mechanisms are able to realize this goal by integrating the regulation in their construction in the form of "operations."

In short, the need for differentiated organs that regulate exchanges with the external environment results from the deficiencies of the biological organization to realize its own program written in the laws of its organization. The program involves two points. (1) The organization has genetic mechanisms which construct and not merely transmit. But the modes of construction as far as is known, namely recombinations of genes, comprise only a limited sector of construction. This limitation is due to the requirements of a hereditary programming which is restricted for two reasons. First, it does not harmonize construction and conservation in one coherent dynamism (this is done by knowledge) and secondly, it does not possess sufficiently flexible information about the environment. (2) The phenotypes actualize in a particular manner the interaction with the environment and are distributed along reaction norms which are themselves limited. Moreover, each individual actualization remains limited and without influence on the total system, since there are no social or exterior interactions such as are possible only to man in his cognitive exchanges. The only influence on the total system is the genetic recombinations with the above-mentioned limitations.

This double deficiency of organisms in their material exchanges with the environment is in part compensated by the construction of behavior. Behavior emerges from the biological organization as an extension of its internal program. In effect, behavior is nothing else but the organization of life, applied and generalized to an enlarged sector of exchanges with the environment. The exchanges become functional as distinct from the material and energy exchanges which the physiological organization already takes care of; "functional" implies that one deals with actions and forms (or schemes of action) which extend organic forms. These new exchanges, as all others, consist in accomodations to the environment, taking account of its events and its temporal succession and above all in assimilations that utilize the environment. These assimilations frequently impose forms on the environment by the construction and arrangement of objects to suit the needs of the organism.

This behavior, like all organization, involves regulations. Their function is to control accommodations and constructive assimilations on the basis of results of actions or anticipations through which the organism can foresee favorable events or obstacles and ensure the required compensations. These regulations, differentiated from internal regulations of the organism (since it is now a question of behavior), are the cognitive functions. The problem is to understand how regulations can go beyond the organic regulations to the point of accomplishing the internal program of the biological organization without being limited by the mentioned deficiencies.

> In subsection III, Piaget·first provides a quick glance at the evolution of cognitive functions from early levels in which they are hardly differentiated from organic functions to the final stage of scientific, objective knowledge in its twin forms of experiential knowledge and logical knowledge that involves logical necessity.
>
> Piaget proceeds to clarify the nature of instinctual knowledge, the type of knowledge that is tied to organic hereditary programming but yet carries in it the seed of its final transformation. Possibilities for change are foreshadowed in certain behavioral adaptations of instinct that point toward further evolutionary progress in cognitive regulations.

Instinct, Learning and Logico-Mathematical Structures

The fundamental facts in this regard are as follows. Cognitive regulations begin by using only the instruments which served organic adaptation in general, i.e., heredity with its limited variations and phenotypic accommodations: such regulations are the hereditary forms of knowledge and in particular the instincts. But then the same deficiencies which were observed in the initial organization and which the new stage of behavior corrects to only a limited degree are found at this level of innate knowledge: hence in the superior stages of evolution a final breakup leads to a dissociation of instinct according to its two components of internal organization and phenotypic accommodation. As a result, and by complementary reconstructions in two opposed directions—and not, as one has seen, from the dissociation itself—there emerge both logico-mathematical structures and experiential knowledge, as yet undifferentiated in the practical intelligence of the anthropoids (who are geometricians as well as technicians) and in the technical intelligence at the beginning of humanity.

The three fundamental types of knowledge are: innate know-how, the prototype of which is instinct; knowledge of the physical world which extends learning as a function of environmental data; and logico-mathematical knowledge. The relation between the first and latter two types of knowledge appears essential for comprehending how the superior forms of knowledge are, in fact, an organ for regulating exchanges. Therefore we elaborate this point as a fitting conclusion.

Instinct undoubtedly involves certain cognitive regulations: as evidence, for example, there is the system of feedbacks constituted by the "stigmergies" of Grassé. [Stigmergies are a type of hereditary and behavioral regulation in termite colonies.] But these regulations stay limited and rigid, precisely because they take place in a frame of hereditary programming and because a programmed regulation is not able to make new discoveries. It does happen that an animal succeeds in dealing with some unforeseen situations by means of readjustments that foreshadow intelligence. We have seen previously that the coordinations of schemes produced in those situations can be compared to the innate coordinations of the instinctual cycle that concerns the species and not the individual. Here is an interesting indication of the possible parentage of functioning between instinct and intelligence in spite of characteristic differences on epigenetic and phenotypic levels. Yet these phenotypic extensions of the instinct remain quite restricted and do not correct the systematic deficiency. Evidently a form of knowledge that remains tied only to the instruments of organic adaptation, even with some faint indications of cognitive regulations, scarcely advances in the direction of the achievements which intelligence must bring to life.

Although the area of learning proper, going beyond the innate, may well begin at the level of protozoa, it enlarges only very slowly up to the cerebralization of the higher vertebrates. This area, apart from some significant exceptions noted already at the level of insects, shows no systematic new start before the primates.

> As Piaget points out in subsection IV, a new type of knowing appears only quite late in evolutionary history. The mechanisms of instinctual behavior finally burst and give way to new constructions; the two essential components of instinct are taken over by the new type of knowing while the central part of hereditary programming that dominated all instinct disappears. The two components are (1) the general organized functioning that regulates instinct from within and (2) the extension of the organization in external encounters. Analo-

gously, the new knowing turns (1) inward towards its own sources and (2) towards acquisition and learning from its interaction with the external environment. Corresponding new regulations appear that become part of the constructs of knowledge so that regulations are no longer differentiated from the constructs. In mature intelligence all constructs are formed within the framework of general regulations: in other words, all empirical abstractions are carried out under the control of reflective, formal abstraction. Indeed for Piaget, the relation of intelligence to instinct illustrates an essential characteristic of a reflective formal abstraction as a "convergent reconstruction with further evolving."

The new cognitive regulations are flexible in the sense that they are not tied to specific, innately given information. Knowledge is free to apply itself to any or all particular instances. Moreover, since flexible regulation cannot be programmed within the genotype, a period of active acquisition is required. The higher an organization develops by its own activity the more incomplete are the innate regulations. The utter helplessness of the human newborn is the reverse side of the intellectual mastery which his development achieves.

The Breakup of Instinct
The basic fact of the breakup of instinct, in other words, of the nearly total disappearance in anthropoids and in man of a cognitive organization that was predominate during the entire evolution of animal behavior is itself highly significant. This is not, as one says quite commonly, because a new mode of knowledge, namely, intelligence considered as a whole, replaces the now extinguished mode. Much more profoundly, significance lies in the fact that a form of knowledge until now nearly organic extends into new forms of regulations. While this new mode of knowledge takes the place of the former, it does not properly speaking replace instinct. Rather, the change involves the dissociation and utilization of its components in two complementary directions.

What disappears with the breakup of instinct is the hereditary programming in favor of two kinds of new cognitive self-regulations, which are flexible and constructive. One might say, this is a replacement, indeed a total change. But one forgets two essential factors. Instincts do not consist exclusively of hereditary programming. As Viaud expresses it so well, such a concept views instinct at its extreme limit. On the one hand, instinct derives its programming and particularly its "logic" from an organized functioning which is implicit in the most general forms of biological organization. On the other hand, instinct extends this programming in individual or phenotypic actions that involve a considerable margin of accommodation and even of assimilation that is partly learned and in certain cases quasi-intelligent.

With the dissolution of instinctual behavior, what disappears is only the central or middle part, i.e., the programmed regulations, while the other two realities remain: the sources of organization and the results of individual or phenotypic adjustment. Intelligence inherits therefore what belongs to instinct while rejecting the method of programmed regulation in favor of constructive self-regulation. That which intelligence retains makes it possible to branch out in the two complementary directions, interiorization towards the inner sources and exteriorization towards learned or even experimentally controlled adjustments.

A preliminary condition for this double progress is of course the construction of a new mode of regulations. These regulations, from now on flexible and no longer programmed, start by the usual interplay of corrections based on the results of actions and of anticipations. Tied to the construction of schemes of assimilation and the coordination of schemes, the regulations tend by a combination of proactive and retroactive effects in the direction of the operations themselves. In this manner they become precorrective rather than corrective regulations. Moreover, inverse operations ensure a complete and not merely approximate reversibility.

These novel regulations are a differentiated organ for deductive verification as well as for construction. Thanks to them, intelligence manifests itself simultaneously in the two above-mentioned directions of reflective interiorization and experimental exteriorization. One can understand that this double direction does not simply divide up the remaining functions of the instinct, namely, its function as a source of organization and its outgoing explorations and individual experimentations. As the work of intelligence consists in going deeper into the sources and in extending the explorations, it makes new constructions of two types. One type is the operational schemes that derive from reflecting abstraction and focus on the necessary conditions of general coordinations of action; the other type assimiliates experiential data to these operational schemes. In this way these two processes extend the former components of instinctual tendencies.

After the breakup of instinct, a new cognitive evolution begins. In fact it is a beginning again from zero, since the innate programming of the instinct has disappeared. Although the cerebral nervous sytem as well as intelligence insofar as it is a capacity to learn and to discover is hereditary, the activity that has to be accomplished is henceforth phenotypic. Just because this intellectual development begins from zero, one does not readily relate it to biological organization and especially to the constructions of the instinct in spite of their importance. Intelligence provides an apt example of what we have called "convergent reconstructions with further evolving." In the case of human knowledge this reconstruction appears complete to such a degree that hardly one theoretician of logico-mathematical knowledge has thought to search for an explanation in the indispensable framework of biological organization. It is only quite recently that mechano-physiology has shown the interrelation of logic, cybernetic models, and the functioning of the brain and that McCulloch has spoken of a "logic of neurons."

In subsection V Piaget links the presence of an interindividual system of exchanges to operational objective knowledge. This provides a partial answer to a criticism often heard that Piaget neglects the role of society. His answer is indicated in this section when he asserts that biological intelligence in the case of man includes man in his social aspect.

Knowledge and Society

Such a complete reconstruction is possible only because intelligence gives up the instinctual cycle that transcends the individual in order to rely on interindividual and social interactions. There does not seem to be any discontinuity in this regard since even chimpanzees work only in social groups. This direction towards social interaction takes place at the same time as intelligence loses the support furnished by hereditary programming and proceeds in the direction of constructed and phenotypic regulations.

From a cognitive viewpoint, as already mentioned, the social group plays here the same role as does "population" from a genetic and consequently an instinctual viewpoint. In this sense society is the supreme unity and the individual succeeds with his discoveries and intellectual constructions only insofar as he himself is the place of collective interactions. The level and the value of these interactions depend naturally on the society as a whole. The great man who seems to launch new movements is but a point of intersection or of synthesis, of ideas that were elaborated by continuous cooperation. Even if he is opposed to current opinions he responds to underlying needs which he himself has not created. This is why the social milieu effectively fulfills for intelligence that function which in evolution is carried out by the genetic recombinations of the total population, or in instincts by the species-specific cycle.

In a sense the modes of transmission and interaction in a society are external and educative as opposed to the hereditary transmissions or combinations. Nonetheless society is still a product of life. The "collective representations," to quote Durkheim, presuppose the existence of a nervous system in the members of the group. Therefore the important question is not to weigh the relative merits of the individual and the group (a problem that is analogous to the chicken and the egg); it is rather to distinguish the logic found in individual reflection and in cooperative efforts from the errors or insanities that occur in collective opinion or in the individual conscience. In spite of Tarde there are not two kinds of logic, one belonging to the group, the other to the individual: there is only one way in which to coordinate the actions A and B according to relations of class ordering and serial ordering. It makes no difference whether these are actions or distinct individuals, some of A, others of B, or whether they are of the same individual who certainly did not discover them by himself since he is part of the whole society. In this sense cognitive regulations or operations are identical in a single brain and in a system of cooperations (is not this the meaning of the word "cooperation"?).

The final subsection VI, besides some personal remarks that may be typical for a French-speaking author but that seem inappropriate to an English-speaking audience—many adjectives and insinuations have been softened here by the translator—ends with a strong plea for the continuance of scientific epistemology. This is not a sentimental wish on Piaget's part. It is the serious concern of a scientist who has not been inclined to or not been able to build a school as Freud did, who has not a large number of pupils and who is not generally recognized for what he is. Piaget's work and his Center of Genetic Epistemology have yet to make their full revolutionary impact in the world of philosophy, epistemology, biology, mathematics, the theory of science, and last, but not least, psychology.

Conclusions

In general we believe that we have verified the two hypotheses that formed the main theme directing this work: the hypothesis that cognitive functions extend organic regulations and that they are a differentiated organ regulating exchanges with the external environment. This organ is only partially differentiated at the level of innate knowledge, but it becomes more and more so with the logico-mathematical structures as well as the exchanges inherent in all experience (including social experience).

These are perhaps rather obvious hypotheses. But it seems necessary to stress and deepen them, all the more because, curiously enough, some specialists in epistemology and especially in mathematics forget too readily the biological perspective, and biologists as a rule fail to see the relevance of such questions as why mathematics is so well adapted to physical reality.

The entire book may have all sorts of deficiencies. There is perhaps a lack of strict proofs, and propositions are advanced which are based on facts but go beyond them. Nevertheless we have thought it useful to write this essay because the kind of collaboration between biologists, psychologists, and epistemologists needed for the above proofs hardly exists and is highly desirable. Only through an interdisciplinary effort is scientific epistemology possible and this cooperation is still much too infrequent for the problems at hand. We have attempted to set forth the ideas contained in this volume in the hope of encouraging this cooperation.

Preparedness plays a role in normal human functioning and development and it may also illuminate problems in the most tangled field in psychology—abnormal functioning. The final two articles speculate on the role of biological constraints in the treatment and etiology of psychopathology. In recent years, general-process learning theory, in the guise of behavior therapy, has had considerable impact on psychopathology. Using principles which learning theorists derived from animal experiments, behavior therapists have successfully treated phobias and other specific behavioral disorders, and have been influential in propounding a learning view of the causes of psychopathology. So, for example, fear of snakes can be broken up by pairing unconditioned relaxation with the CS of fear-evoking snakes and talking can be reinstated in catatonic mutes by progressive shaping of verbalization (Ullmann and Krasner, 1965). Behavior therapists have argued that if conditioning and training can break up psychopathology, the behaviors may have been established in the same way.

Since behavior therapists have based their work on general learning principles and since we have seen that the equipotentiality premise is untenable, preparedness has direct implications. G. Terence Wilson and Gerald Davison suggest that Garcia's findings be applied to aversion therapy, a technique in which some undesirable behavior such as alcoholism is punished by a noxious stimulus. The therapy could be improved, they argue, if a prepared US such as nausea is chosen to punish drinking, rather than more arbitrary US's such as shock.

34

AVERSION TECHNIQUES IN BEHAVIOR THERAPY: SOME THEORETICAL AND METATHEORETICAL CONSIDERATIONS

G. Terence Wilson and Gerald C. Davison

Recent psychophysiological research indicates that certain cues may be singularly appropriate as functional conditioned stimuli for certain response systems. Such findings raise into question the trend in the aversion conditioning literature away from chemically produced aversion and toward fear produced by painful electric shock. Although this shift from the chemical to the electrical is being made on sound functional grounds, the physiological research on appropriateness of cues suggests that contrary to prevalent assumptions in behavior therapy, one must consider most carefully the topographical nature of stimuli and responses. At the metatheoretical level, this research makes still more persuasive the argument that behavior modification as a field be concerned with areas of psychology outside of learning and conditioning.

An important issue in the use of aversion techniques concerns the nature of the noxious stimulus. Earlier versions of aversion treatment favored the use of chemically produced aversion in the form of a nausea-producing drug. (cf. Lemere & Voegtlin, 1950). Current trends, however, almost exclusively emphasize electrical aversive stimulation. Rachman (1965) and Rachman and Teasdale (1969) detail the reasons which have dictated this shift to electrical noxious stimuli. At a practical level, the use of nausea-producing drugs results in an unpleasant and unsavory experience for client and clinical staff alike. At a more theoretical level, Eysenck and Rachman (1965) have suggested that these

From *Journal of Consulting and Clinical Psychology*, 33 (1968), 327–329.

drugs act as central nervous system neural depressants, and thereby are likely to impede the conditionability of the client in accord with Eysenck's personality theory. Yet these factors are really secondary to the most cogent of Rachman and Teasdale's points, namely, the difficulty in adhering to the *traditional conditioning paradigm* (in both classical and anticipatory avoidance conditioning) when using chemical aversion. The crucial parameters here are temporal, that is, getting optimal interstimulus intervals; sequential, that is, having the CS precede the UCS; the frequency of repetition of CS-UCS pairings; and finally, precision in specifying the intensity and duration of the stimuli. Variable and fluctuating individual differences in reactions to emetic drugs virtually proscribe the precision required by the conditioning paradigm for successful application.

Given their premise of the traditional conditioning paradigm, Rachman and Teasdale's points are both well taken and compelling. However, some recent findings from the physiological psychology literature raise questions for current practices in aversion therapy, and suggest also some metatheoretical considerations for behavior therapy.

Garcia and his associates have recently demonstrated that the procedure of pairing a perceptible cue with an effective reinforcer does not lead automatically to effective associative learning. Rather, it seems that the cue must be "appropriate" for the consequences that ensue. Thus, Garcia and Koelling (1966) have shown that avoidance learning with gastrointestinal disturbances produced by ionizing radiation as the UCS readily transferred to a gustatory stimulus, but not to audiovisual and tactile stimuli. On the other hand, avoidance learning with electric shock as the UCS transferred to the audiovisual and tactile stimuli, but not to the gustatory stimulus. Garcia and Koelling (1967) reported the same differential effect following the injection of a drug. Garcia, McGowan, Ervin, and Koelling (1968) paired either flavor or size of food pellets as conditioned stimuli with either malaise induced by X ray or electric shock as the UCS in four groups of rats. The combination of flavor and illness resulted in a significant conditioned decrease in food consumption, but that of size and illness did not. Conversely, the combination of size and pain produced an inhibition of eating while flavor and pain did not. The authors argue that since flavor is closely related to the chemical composition of food, natural selection would favor associative mechanisms relating flavor and olfaction to the aftereffects of ingestion; and they suggest how effective associative learning depends on central neural convergence of the paired afferent input.

These data appear to discredit the commonly made procedural prescription that, in the treatment of an alcoholic, for instance, shock be used to condition aversion to the sight, smell, and taste of alcohol, to exogenous as well as to endogenous stimuli. It seems that fear responses from a shock UCS may be conditioned only to nongustatory attributes of alcohol in our example, and not to the taste and/or smell of alcohol. Any radical change in these conditioned stimuli, such as could be produced by a different environmental complex, could be expected to lead to the "spontaneous recovery" of the consumption of alcohol (Estes, 1955). The best strategy would seem to be to create a chemically based aversion to the taste and/or smell of alcohol and not to the complex of visual, personal, and other stimuli defining the treatment situation.

Garcia, Ervin, Yorke, and Koelling (1967) and Revusky (1968) have extended this notion of the peculiar "appropriateness" of cues to reinforcers, finding that reinforcement can be delayed well beyond the time interval posited as mandatory for effective reinforcement by the traditional S-R model of associative learning. It will be recalled that one of the major arguments in favor of electrical aversion relates to the temporal control it allows.

Interestingly enough, Lazarus (1968) has independently and from a purely clinical standpoint expressed similar views. He reports the case of an alcoholic whose alcohol consumption remained recalcitrant to faradic shock but disappeared rapidly when a singularly foul-smelling admixture of smelling salts was substituted as the noxious UCS. He goes on to observe that whereas faradic shock seems "appropriate" when the concern is with visual and/or tactile stimuli, as would be the case in a handwashing compulsion, it may be inappropriate in handling overeating and alcoholic consumption. Of course these and similar clinical observations (e.g., Cautela, 1967; Davison, 1968) are in line with Garcia's psychophysiological findings.

The foregoing raises also some interesting issues on the metatheoretical level. The learning-oriented behavior modification literature, especially the operant, emphasizes the overriding importance of *functional* definitions of problems in distinct contrast to *topographical* (e.g., Ferster, 1965; Staats & Staats, 1963). In the attempt to extrapolate from research with infrahumans to research with humans, learning theory oriented behavior modifiers seem, on reflection, to have had little choice but to stress the functional to the virtual exclusion of the topographical, nay, physiological nature of stimuli and responses. Thus, one terms a response as topographically complex as "walking to the door" an "operant" if it can be shown to relate functionally to antecedent and consequent stimuli in the same fashion as more carefully delineated operants in the Skinner box. The same holds true for behavior therapy approaches which stress the classical conditioning paradigm: Pavlov (1928) himself proposed that "every imaginable phenomenon of the outer world affecting a specific receptive surface of the body may be converted into a CS [p. 88]."

The Garcia research obviously raises the serious question of this preoccupation with functional identities to the exclusion of the specific nature of the particular stimuli and responses within one's presumed conditioning paradigm. This work also illustrates most clearly the possible dangers inherent within a limited conception of "behavior modification" as deriving from "modern learning theory" or, more properly, learning principles. Familiarity with such psychophysiological work as Garcia's (inter alia) makes clear the desirability of expanding the field of behavior modification to include general experimental psychology as a whole (cf. Davison, 1969).

References

Cautela, J. Covert sensitization. *Psychological Reports*, 1967, *20*, 459—468.

Davison, G. C. Elimination of a sadistic fantasy by a client-controlled counterconditioning technique: A case study. *Journal of Abnormal Psychology*, 1968, *73*, 84—90.

Davison, G. C. Appraisal of behavior modification techniques with adults in institutional settings. In C. M. Franks (Ed.), *Assessment and status of the behavioral therapies and associated developments.* New York: McGraw-Hill, 1969.

disregarding his explicit rejections of the interpretation. Wolpe and Rachman's exposé of the looseness of psychoanalytic argument and evidence is perhaps as clearheaded a critique of analytic inference as exists in the literature. They also outlined a learning theory view of little Hans's phobia. What little Hans was afraid of, in their view, was not his father, but horses. To quote their interpretation:

In brief, phobias are regarded as conditioned anxiety (fear) reactions. Any "neutral" stimulus, simple or complex, that happens to make an impact on an individual at about the time that a fear reaction is evoked, acquires the ability to evoke fear subsequently. If the fear at the original conditioning situation is of high intensity or if the conditioning is many times repeated, the conditioned fear will show the persistence that is characteristic of *neurotic* fear; and there will be generalization of fear reactions to stimuli resembling the conditioned stimulus.

Hans, we are told, was a sensitive child who "was never unmoved if someone wept in his presence" and long before the phobia developed became "uneasy on seeing horses in the merry-go-round being beaten" (p. 254). It is our contention that the incident to which Freud refers as merely the exciting cause of Hans' phobia was in fact the cause of the entire disorder. Hans actually says, "No. I only got it (the phobia) then. When the horse in the bus fell down, it gave me such a fright, really! That was when I got the nonsense" (p. 192). The father says, "All of this was confirmed by my wife, as well as the fact that the anxiety broke out immediately afterwards" (p. 193).

Horses became phobic via Hans via classical conditioning because he saw rses at the same time as being frightened. Such a view has much *prima facie* usibility. The conditioning of fear has been demonstrated repeatedly in the oratory both in humans and animals. Watson and Rayner (1920) paired a rtling noise with a white rat to "Little Albert," and Albert became afraid of , rabbits, and other furry objects. The classical conditioning of fear was sequently brought into the animal laboratory by Estes and Skinner (1941), the literature on it is now truly voluminous (e.g., Campbell & Church, 1969; sh, 1971).

urther impetus for a learning interpretation of the cause of phobias comes n the dramatic success which behavior therapists have had in breaking up bias using learning techniques (e.g., Wolpe & Lazarus, 1969). Phobias can be inguished" by counterconditioning relaxation to representations of a phobic ulus. If phobias can be extinguished by techniques developed in the learning ratory, this suggests, but by no means proves, that they were originally ired by such learning.

here are some salient problems with the learning interpretation of phobias h seem related to inadequacies of theories of learning themselves. These culties also crop up in learning accounts of other forms of human hopathology, but we shall discuss only phobias here.

e first problem is that phobias do not extinguish under conventional edures which reliably extinguish classically conditioned fear in the labora- When an individual with a cat phobia imagines a cat or comes across a cat,

---

Estes, W. K. Statistical theory of spontaneous recovery and regression. *Psychological Review*, 1955, *62*, 145–154.

Eysenck, H. J., & Rachman, S. *The causes and cures of neurosis*. London: Routledge & Kegan Paul, 1965.

Ferster, C. B. Classification of behavioral pathology. In L. Krasner & L. P. Ullmann (Eds.), *Research in behavior modification*. New York: Holt, 1965.

Garcia, J., Ervin, F. R., Yorke, C. H., & Koelling, R. A. Conditioning with delayed vitamin injections. *Science*, 1967, *155*, 716.

Garcia, J., & Koelling, R. A. Relation of cue to consequence in avoidance learning. *Psychonomic Science*, 1966, *4*, 123–124.

Garcia, J., & Koelling, R. A. A comparison of aversions induced by X-rays, toxins, and drugs in the rat. *Radiation Research*, 1967, 7, 439.

Garcia, J., McGowan, B. K., Ervin, F. R., & Koelling, R. A. Cues: Their relative effectiveness as a function of the reinforcer. *Science*, 1968, *160*, 794–795.

Lazarus, A. A. Aversion therapy and sensory modalities: Clinical impressions. *Perceptual and Motor Skills*, 1968, *27*, 178.

Lemere, G., & Voegtlin, W. An evaluation of the aversion treatment of alcoholism. *Quarterly Journal for the Study of Alcoholism*, 1950, *11*, 199–204.

Pavlov, I. P. *Lectures on conditioned reflexes*. New York: International, 1928.

Rachman, S. Aversion therapy: Chemical or electrical? *Behaviour Research and Therapy*, 1965, *2*, 289–300.

Rachman, S., & Teasdale, J. D. Aversion therapy. In C. M. Franks (Eds.), *Assessment and status of the behavioral therapies and associated developments*. New York: McGraw-Hill, 1969.

Revusky, S. H. Aversion to sucrose produced by contingent X-irradiation: Temporal and dosage parameters. *Journal of Comparative and Physiological Psychology*, 1968, *65*, 17–22.

Staats, A. W., & Staats, C. K. *Complex human behavior*. New York: Holt, 1963.

So prepared contingencies may be more effective than arbitrary ones in psychotherapy, and similar considerations may hold for the way psychopatho-logical symptoms are learned. The extraordinary persistence of phobias and other disorders in the face of extinction and punishment is difficult for general-process learning theory to handle. In our final selection, Martin Seligman argues that humans are prepared to fear a nonarbitrary range of events, and that preparedness answers the question of why horse phobias, fly phobias, and rat phobias are common, and electric-outlet phobias, grass phobias, and knife phobias are rare. Further, since prepared associations are resistant to extinction, the nonarbitrary nature of phobias may account for their persistence, and may even permit a reconstruction of Freudian symbolism.

PHOBIAS AND PREPAⅠ

Martin E.⁣

Some inadequacies of the classical conditioning ana are discussed: phobias are highly resistant to extir laboratory fear conditioning, unlike avoidance cond guishes rapidly; phobias comprise a nonarbitrary and objects, whereas fear conditioning is thought to occur range of conditioned stimuli. Furthermore, phobias, u fear conditioning, are often acquired in one trial resistant to change by "cognitive" means. An analysis a more contemporary model of fear conditioning is ɪ view, phobias are seen as instances of highly "pɪ (Seligman, 1970). Such prepared learning is selective, ɪ extinction, probably noncognitive and can be acquir reconstruction of the notion of symbolism is suggested

Behavior therapists have proposed a plausible learnin psychoanalytic view of phobias. This paper examines some learning model and suggests a way of accounting for phobia biological and learning points of view. Ironically, wha resembles the psychoanalytic view, and it may help to rec symbolism.

Wolpe and Rachman (1960) have clearly stated the case interpretation of phobias. They examined Freud's class (1909), and proposed an alternative approach. To refresh Little Hans was a 5-year-old boy who developed a interpreted the fear of horses as an outcome of the (desired his mother sexually, wished his father out of the father's retribution (castration), displaced the fear on Rachman effectively criticized Freud's use of evidence, focusing only on material from Hans which confirmed tl

From *Behavior Therapy*, 2 (1971), 307–320.
Supported by PHS grant MH19604 to the author.

he is exposed to an extinction *procedure.* By the learning account, the cat (CS) was once paired with some fear evoking trauma, unconditioned stimulus (UCS), and as a consequence the cat became an elicitor of fear. *When the cat is presented without the original UCS, the association should diminish.* But it is commonplace that exposure to the phobic stimulus or brooding about the phobic object does not diminish fear and may even enhance it. It will not do to say that the cat itself became a UCS, because this is merely a restatement of the problem. Why should cats become UCS's when paired with trauma, and not tones which are paired with shock in the laboratory?

There is a common misconception among clinicians about the extinction of conditioned fear in the laboratory, and it is worthwhile examining the evidence at some length. The misconception arises from a careless interpretation of the avoidance learning literature, a leap from the fact that avoidance responding does not extinguish to the mistaken inference that conditioned fear does not extinguish.

In a typical laboratory avoidance procedure, an animal is exposed to the following contingencies: (1) some CS such as a tone is paried with strong electric shock (UCS). Such pairing causes the classical conditioning of fear to the tone. (2) If the animal responds, e.g., by running to the other side of the shuttle box after the shock comes on, both the shock and the tone terminate. This instrumental escape response is reinforced by the termination of the painful shock, possibly by the termination of the fear-evoking CS and also by the nonoccurrence of shock. Which of these reinforcements is more effective is in dispute (e.g., Rescorla & Solomon, 1967; Herrnstein, 1969; Bolles, this volume, p. 189), but is irrelevant for the present discussion. It is well documented that, once an animal begins avoiding reliably, if the shock is now disconnected (a so-called extinction procedure) the animal will continue to respond, not infrequently outlasting the experimenter's patience (e.g., Solomon, Kamin, & Wynne, 1953; Seligman & Campbell, 1965). What many have inferred from this, however, is that fear once learned does not extinguish. But it does not follow from failure of avoidance to extinguish that classical conditioning of fear does not extinguish. Notice that, as the contingencies are arranged, if the animal avoids on every trial (i.e., responds to the tone and terminates it before the shock would have appeared) it is not exposed to the fact that the tone no longer predicts shock. That is to say: an extinction of avoidance procedure does not necessarily entail an extinction of classically conditioned fear procedure. It turns out that, if the avoidance response is prevented, thus forcibly exposing the animal to the fact that tone is no longer followed by shock, avoidance readily extinguishes (for an extensive review, see Baum, 1970). Avoidance extinguishes after blocking because fear is extinguished, since the subject is exposed to the CS, no longer predicting the UCS. Avoidance fails to extinguish before blocking because the response is continually reinforced by shock prevention and by CS termination. The animal has no way of "finding out" that shock would not have occurred if he had not responded. If the animal continues to respond every time, disconnecting the shock is the experimenter's secret. Moreover, if an instrumental avoidance paradigm is not used, so that fear is conditioned without an instrumental contingency, the fear extinguishes to the CS. This is true of both behavioral indexes of fear (e.g., Wagner, Siegel, & Fein, 1967) as well as physiological (e.g., Black, Carlson, & Solomon, 1962). In fact, this is such common knowledge among people working in these fields that not much systematic study of it has been published, rather it is assumed in their procedures. For example, after fear has been classically conditioned, the effects of the CS are commonly tested only for the first few trials of extinction. After that, the CS soon becomes impotent (e.g., Rescorla & LoLordo, 1965; Kamin, 1965).

Although the weight of evidence indicates extinction of conditioned fear, sophisticated readers may be aware of the paradoxical "Napalkov" (1963) effect (see also Eysenck, 1968). It is observed that, occasionally fear is actually enhanced during presentation of the CS unreinforced by shock (Rohrbaugh & Riccio, 1970). There seems to be no ready explanation for the conditions under which this relatively rare phenomenon occurs; but it will hardly do as a refuge for those who want to hold that it explains the failure of phobias to extinguish. First, because the most common observation is monotonically decreasing fear in extinction, and second, because extinction probably sets in after a few trials of paradoxical enhancement (Rohrbaugh & Riccio, 1970).

There is one way out and that is to claim that phobias involve avoidance and so do not extinguish because they are analogous to laboratory avoidance (Eysenck & Rachman, 1965). So, e.g., when Freud's notorious Little Hans thinks of horses, he also performs some avoidance response which he believes prevents the real UCS, and he never finds out that horses are no longer paired with the unconditionally frightening event. By avoiding, he never exposes himself to the fact that the CS is no longer paired with the UCS and the CR remains. This way out is unpalatable because it postulates on unobservable avoidance response in the absence of independent evidence for such a process. Incidentally, this avoidance formulation should not be confused with a very real avoidance component in phobias: that people go to great length to avoid the phobic object—but this is an example of avoiding the CS, not of being exposed to the CS and avoiding the UCS. For example, a woman afraid of heights will actively avoid getting herself into a situation in which she is very far off the ground. In such a case, fear of heights should remain, since she cannot be exposed to heights no longer paired with the original UCS. Our concern is not with cases in which the person successfully avoids any exposure to the CS and, therefore, avoids exposure to the extinction contingency, but rather with those individuals who are exposed to the CS when it is no longer paired with UCS. The problem we are tackling is that phobics actually exposed to the CS do not extinguish, and avoidance of the CS is irrelevant to this problem. For example, a spider phobic individual will think about spiders, see pictures of spiders, and even actually see spiders. All of these situations constitute exposure to the CS (more or less) no longer paired with the original UCS. Yet it is commonplace that such inadvertent exposures rarely weaken, and may even strengthen, the phobia.

Before leaving the difference in extinguishability of phobias and laboratory conditioned fear, we should mention another difference. Implicit in the general process learning view of phobias is the assumption that they can be learned in one trial: It must be enough for one traumatic experience paired with a CS to produce a phobia. One-trial conditioning of fear is the exception, not the rule, in laboratory fear conditioning. The conditioning of fear commonly takes between three and six trials (e.g., Kamin, 1969; Seligman, 1968). If extremely traumatic UCSs are used, such as fear of imminent death (Campbell, Sanderson, & Laverty, 1964), one-trial conditioning can be obtained. But let us keep in mind that fear conditioning in the laboratory is only rarely full-blown in one trial, but for phobias it should be commonplace.

In summary, one difficulty for the behavior therapy view of phobias is that they are hard to extinguish, while the alleged laboratory model of classically conditioned fear extinguishes readily. A homier way of making the same point is to say that phobias are irrational. Telling a phobic, however persuasively, that cats (CS) won't do him any harm, or showing him that the UCS doesn't occur when cats are around is rarely effective. Showing an animal that the CS no longer predicts the UCS usually results in extinction (Black, 1958). The "laws" of fear conditioning (Rescorla & Solomon, 1967) look very much like expectations: CSs that are paired with shock become fearful and stop being fearful when they predict no shock. Conditioned and differential inhibitors, CSs that predict the absence of shock, become active inhibitors of fear (Rescorla, 1969). Very long CSs which end in shock inhibit fear at their outset and evoke fear at their termination (Rescorla, 1967; Seligman & Meyer, 1970). We shall later try to account for the noncognitive nature of phobias, their inextinguishability, and their one-trial acquisition.

Before doing so, let us look at another neglected property of phobias which is difficult to model by ordinary classical conditioning of fear. According to Pavlov's view of conditioning, the choice of CS is a matter of indifference. "Any natural phenomenon chosen at will may be converted into a conditioned stimulus . . . any visual stimulus, any desired sound, any odor and the stimulation of any part of the skin" (Pavlov, 1928, p. 86). This is the heart of the general process view of learning and, by this widely held view, any CS which happens to be associated with trauma should become phobic. But a neglected fact about phobias is that, by and large, they comprise a relatively nonarbitrary and limited set of objects: agoraphobia, fear of specific animals, insect phobias, fear of heights, and fear of the dark, etc. All these are relatively common phobias. And only rarely, if ever, do we have pajama phobias, grass phobias, electric-outlet phobias, hammer phobias, even though these things are likely to be associated with trauma in our world. The set of potentially phobic events may be nonarbitrary: events related to the survival of the human species through the long course of evolution (see Marks, 1970, pp. 63–68, for a clearheaded discussion of the nonarbitrariness of phobic stimuli).

What is it about phobias that makes them (1) selective, (2) so resistant to extinction, (3) irrational, and (4) capable of being learned in one trial? *Phobias are highly prepared to be learned by humans, and, like other highly prepared relationships, they are selective and resistant to extinction, learned even with degraded input, and probably are noncognitive.* Phobias may be instances of classically conditioned fear, but not unprepared conditioned fear such as a tone paired with shock. Rather, they are instances of prepared conditioning of fear.

So phobias can indeed be modelled by a "simple learning process," but one needs to modify general process learning theory to do it. The modification argued at length throughout this volume, may be summarized as follows:

Since the time of Pavlov and Thorndike, the laws of learning have been formulated using arbitrary sets of events, such as a click paired with meat powder for dogs, and the pressing of levers for flour pellets in rats. At the base of such endeavors is the premise that the laws found would be general from one set of events to another. Arbitrarily chosen relationships were at a premium, since the laws that emerged should be uncontaminated by the idiosyncratic past experience that the animal brings to the situation or by the biological characteristics of his particular species. However, one danger in such a strategy is that the laws so found would be peculiar to arbitrary events arbitrarily concatenated. This danger is particularly acute when one realizes that animals and humans do a great deal of learning about contingencies which their species has faced for eons. Not only do birds learn to turn wheels for grain, which their ancestors never did, but they also *learn* to migrate away from the North Star in the fall (Emlen, this volume, p.300), a contingency their ancestors faced before them. Not only do humans learn to fear crossing busy streets, but also to fear the dark. All this learning may not be the same.

A dimension of preparedness has been operationally defined:

"confront an organism with a CS paired with UCS or with a response which produces an outcome. Depending on the specifics, the organism can be either prepared, unprepared, or contraprepared for learning about the events. The relative preparedness of an organism for learning about a situation is defined by the amount of input (e.g., numbers of trials, pairings, bits of information, etc.) which must occur before that output (responses, acts, repertoire, etc.), which is construed as evidence of acquisition, reliably occurs. It does not matter how input or output are specified, as long as that specification can be used consistently for all points on the continuum. Thus, using the preparedness dimension is independent of whether one happens to be an S-R theorist, a cognitive theorist, an information processing theorist, an ethologist, or what have you. Let us illustrate how one can place an experimental situation at various points on the continuum for classical conditioning. If the organism makes the indicated response consistently from the very first presentation of the CS on, such "learning" represents a clear case of instinctive responding, the extreme of the prepared end of the dimension. If the organism makes the response consistently after only a few pairings, it is somewhat prepared. If the response emerges only after many pairings, the organism is unprepared. If acquisition occurs only after very many pairings or does not occur at all, the organism is said to be contraprepared. The number of pairings is the measure that makes the dimension a continuum, and implicit in this dimension is the notion that "learning" and "instinct" are continuous. Typically ethologists have studied situations from the prepared side of the dimension, while general process learning theorists have largely restricted themselves to the unprepared region. The contraprepared part of the dimension has been largely uninvestigated, or at least unpublished" (Seligman, p. 408, 1970).

By now, it has been well documented that some contingencies are learned about much more readily than others. In virtually every major paradigm, that learning theorists have used, some contingencies are learned with highly degraded input (one trial, long delay of reinforcement) while others are learned only painstakingly. A few examples follow.

Many readers have probably acquired some taste aversion after being sick to their stomachs. Garcia and associates (for review, see Garcia, McGowan, & Green, this volume, p. 21) have found that this is a prepared form of classical conditioning. Rats learn to associate tastes, rather than external cues like lights, with nausea, and they can learn this in one trial even with a several hour delay between the taste and the illness. Pairing a light with foot shock, on the other hand, takes several trials to acquire and can bridge a delay of only a few seconds. Note that this prepared learning reflects a real contingency which rodents have faced through the course of evolution: tastes are paired with poisoning, and the effects of poisons do not usually begin immediately. Such prepared learning gives a selective advantage.

In the realm of instrumental learning, Brown and Jenkins (this volume, p. 146) showed that pigeons learn to peck a lighted key which is paired with grain, even though pecking the key has no effect on grain. Yet rats learn only by trial and error to press a bar for food and only if bar pressing produces food. In avoidance learning, birds have a great deal of trouble learning to peck a key to prevent shock, but can learn to hop up (Emlen, 1970) or fly away (Bedford & Anger, 1967) to avoid shock. Rats have trouble learning to bar press to avoid, but learn to jump up to avoid in one trial (Baum, 1966). In discrimination learning, dogs learn readily to go to the left rather than to the right, if the cues which tell them which way to go are in different places, but can't learn if the cues differ in quality, rather than place. Conversely they can learn to put their paw up or keep it down if the cues differ in quality, but not if they differ in location (Dobrzecka, Szwejkowska, & Konorski, this volume p. 131). Seligman (1970 and this volume) discuss many other examples of prepared, unprepared, and contraprepared learning. The upshot of these examples is that learning itself may be quite different depending on how prepared the organism is for the particular contingency he confronts.

We can now return to phobias: The difficulty that learning theory has in modelling phobias by the classical conditioning of fear does not result from phobias' being phenomena *sui generis*, but, rather, results because the conditioning used as a model was unprepared rather than prepared conditioning. Prepared learning provides a better fit with phobias than unprepared learning because we have reason to believe that it (1) can be acquired in one trial, (2) is selective, (3) is resistant to extinction, and (4) may be noncognitive. Let us now look at the evidence that leads in this direction.

In the first place, prepared classical conditioning by definition occurs in one or a very few trials. It is defined as conditioning that occurs with minimal or even degraded input. Like phobias, the contingencies around which prepared learning revolves are not arbitrary, but rather those that may have been intimately involved in the survival of the species. Prepared learning is highly selective: When a rat becomes ill, taste aversion develops but not aversions to the sounds and sights that were also contiguous with illness. When grain is presented, pigeons peck at lighted keys, but do not step on treadles or turn wheels. When chaffinches develop, they learn the song of their species, and ignore the similar songs of other species (Marler, this volume, p. 336). Reevaluate Watson's classical experiment with Little Albert. Furry things, like rats and rabbits, became aversive to Little Albert, but Watson and Rayner themselves probably did not. Maybe this experiment really is a more adequate model of human phobias than fear conditioning in the rat. Conditioning occurred in two trials, making it operationally prepared and it was also selective. Bregman (1934), probably aware of the difficulty of making children afraid of scissors and electric outlets, repeated the Little Albert experiment using common household CSs like curtains and blocks instead of furry things. She got no fear conditioning at all. Furthermore, English (1929) did not get fear conditioning to a wooden duck, even after many pairings with a startling noise.

Aside from being selective, Watson and Rayner's prepared fear conditioning does not extinguish readily. Special procedures, such as counterconditioning (Jones, 1924) are necessary to produce remission of fear. It seems likely that prepared learning like phobic learning is highly resistant to extinction. Garcia's taste aversions are somewhat persistent, even though the animal must drink the fluid to survive. Rozin's (this volume, p. 51) taste aversions persisted even after his rats were restored to health. Wild rats, who become poisoned on a new taste, will often starve to death before eating other new flavors (Rzoska, 1953). Human taste aversions are also resistant to change—they may dissipate in time, rather than with trials of unreinforced exposure. Other forms of prepared learning, unlike unprepared learning, are highly resistant to extinction. Williams and Williams (this volume, p. 158) made the "auto-shaped" key pecking of pigeons counterproductive—pecking the lighted key was no longer independent of grain presentation, it actually *prevented* grain. The pigeons pecked anyway. Stimbert (this volume, p. 175) trained rats to make the correct choice in a maze either using another rat as the cue or with masking tape, over the course the cue rat had traversed as the cue. The "rat" cue was learned readily (prepared), whereas the masking tape cue was learned painstakingly (unprepared). The cue rat did not lose his cuing ability even after 150 trials in which food was no longer presented, but the masking tape cue extinguished in 20 trials. Seligman, Ives, Ames, and Mineka (1970) conditioned drinking in rats by pairing a compound CS with thirst-inducing NaCl-procaine. When mild thirst was part of the CS, conditioning did not extinguish; but if mild thirst were not part of the CS, conditioning occurred and extinguished rapidly.

Thus, if phobias are seen as prepared classical conditioning, their one-trial acquisition, their selectivity and their persistence may follow. The "irrationality" of phobias is also compatible with what data exists on prepared classical conditioning. Seligman (1970) suggested that unprepared contingencies are learned and extinguish cognitively, i.e., by such mechanisms as expectations, intentions, beliefs, or attention, while   prepared   associations are learned more primitively or noncognitively. Prepared associations may be the blind associations that Pavlov and Thorndike had thought they were studying, whereas they wound up working on the laws of unprepared learning or expectancies.

The noncognitive nature of prepared associations is illustrated by at least one observation: Knowing that the stomach flu and not the sauce Bearnaise caused the vomiting does not inhibit the aversion to the sauce. In addition, there are several experiments which suggest that, unlike unprepared conditioning, prepared conditioning is not readily modified by information. When unprepared CSs such as tones are paired with shock, information plays a large role in learning. Kamin (1969) has demonstrated that, when tone is paired with shock and then both tone and light are paired with shock, no fear conditioning occurs to the light. Prior conditioning with tone "blocks" the rat's learning that the redundant light also predicts shock. Kalat and Rozin (this volume, p. 115) repeated the blocking study with the more prepared contingency of taste and illness. The redundant CS was *not* blocked in their studies, indicating that taste-nausea conditioning may be primitive and noncognitive. Garcia, Kovner, and Green (this volume, p. 238) reported a related finding. Rats learned to avoid shock with taste as the discriminative stimulus in a shuttle box. When tested in the home cage, no aversion to taste was found. When the rats had the taste as a stimulus for illness, however, aversion was total even in the home cage. In the taste-shock contingency, taste merely becomes a *cue* for shock in the shuttlebox. But when taste predicts illness, the taste aversion is full-blown even though the rat is in a different place. The taste may actually take on some qualities of the illness. Finally, Roll and Smith (this volume, p. 98) demonstrated that taste aversion could occur even when the rat was anesthetized, and Nachman (this volume, p. 104) reported that electroconvulsive shock, which eliminates fear conditioning, did not eliminate the memory of taste aversion.

Human phobias are similar. Showing or telling a phobic that cats are not going to hurt him is rarely effective. *Phobic* fear is by definition not readily inhibited by rational means. Rather, one needs to resort to special procedures, such as the counterconditioning employed in systematic desensitization. We do not yet know much about how to get rid of prepared associations like taste-illness, imprinting, and auto-shaping, although we know that mere extinction is not very effective. Might counterconditioning be an effective procedure in these cases? At any rate, we may now be in the position to develop a fruitful animal model of phobias, and discover how best to produce extinction; for we can do fear conditioning not with a tone or light, as is usual, but with more natural CSs such as the picture and sound of snakes or hawks paired with shock for a rat. It would not be surprising to find one trial fear conditioning and great resistance to extinction. Such experiments would allow us to explore the ways of getting rid of fear, and might suggest new therapeutic techniques with phobias.

There is one subtlety to the form of the argument which should be underlined. It is not argued that no phobia about objects of modern technology exists, or that all phobias are noncognitive. People sometimes talk themselves into phobias. There are airplane phobias and fears of electric shock. The preparedness view is not disconfirmed by isolated examples: it points to the fact that the great majority of phobias are about objects of natural importance to the survival of the species. It does not deny that other phobias are possible, it only claims that they should be less frequent, since they are less prepared.

In some ways, we have come full circle. We began by concurring in the rejection of the psychoanalytic interpretation of phobias, e.g., that horses were fearful to Little Hans because they symbolized his father's retribution. We modified the learning reconstruction of phobias by suggesting a modification of general process learning theory. Phobias, in our view, are not instances of unprepared fear conditioning, but of prepared fear conditioning. Nonarbitrary stimuli seem particularly ready to become phobic objects for human beings and this may also be true of "soteria," the opposite number from phobias (e.g., Linus' blanket). Particular CSs are readily conditioned to particular UCSs. Perhaps this is a way of reconstructing symbolism. Is it possible that there really is something to horses and wolves, etc., that makes them highly associable with certain kinds of traumas, perhaps even sexual ones? Does anyone have a lamb phobia? This is testable. When Little Hans acquired his phobia, there were not only horses around, but other things, such as his nurse or a bus and yet these did not become phobic objects. Why only horses? If children were given horses and blackboards, both paired with anxiety-arousal, would they learn readily to be afraid of horses but not of blackboards?

So, for a biologically oriented learning theorist, to what can the notion of symbolism amount? A is symbolic of B, if and only if human beings are prepared, in the sense defined, to learn that A is associated with B. If humans can acquire with A the properties of B after only minimal input, then it is meaningful to say that A is symbolic of B.

Even more speculatively, does preparedness range beyond simple symbolic associations? Are there ways of thinking in which humans are particularly prepared to engage, as Lenneberg (1967) has argued for language and cognition? If association, causal inference, and forms of cognition are prepared, are there stories that man is prepared to formulate and accept? If so, a meaningful version of the racial unconscious lurks close behind.

References

Baum, M. Rapid extinction of an avoidance response following a period of response prevention. *Psychological Reports*, 1966, *18*, 59—64.

Baum, M. Extinction of avoidance responding through response prevention (flooding). *Psychological Bulletin*, 1970, *74*, 276—284.

Bedford, J., & Anger, D. Flight as an avoidance response in pigeons. Paper presented at the meeting of the Psychonomic Society, St. Louis, Mo., October, 1967.

Black, A. H. The extinction of avoidance responding under curare. *Journal of Comparative and Physiological Psychology*, 1958, *51*, 519—524.

Black, A. H., Carlson, N. J., & Solomon, R. L. Exploratory studies of the conditioning of autonomic responses in curarized dogs. *Psychological Monographs*, 1962, 1—31, Whole number 548.

Bolles, R. Species-specific defense reactions and avoidance learning. This volume, pp. 189—211.

Bregman, E. An attempt to modify the emotional attitude of infants by the conditioned response technique. *Journal of Genetic Psychology*, 1934, *45*, 169—198.

Brown, P., & Jenkins, H. Autoshaping of the pigeon's key peck. This volume, pp. 146—156.

Brush, R. R. (ed.) *Aversive conditioning and learning.* New York: Academic Press, 1971.

Campbell, B. A., & Church, R. M. *Punishment and aversive behavior.* New York: Appleton-Century-Crofts, 1969.

Campbell, D., Sanderson, R. E., & Laverty, S. G. Characteristics of a conditioned response in human subjects during extinction trials following a simple traumatic conditioning trial. *Journal of Abnormal and Social Psychology,* 1964, *68,* 627–639.

Dobrzecka, C., Szwejkowska, G., & Konorski, J. Qualitative versus directional cues in two forms of differentiation. This volume, pp. 131–134.

Emlen, S. The influence of magnetic information on the orientation of the indigo bunting (*Passerina Cyanea*). *Animal Behavior,* 1970, *18,* 215–224.

Emlen, S. Celestial rotation: its importance in the development of migratory orientation. This volume, pp. 300–308.

English, H. B. Three cases of the "conditioned fear response." *Journal of Abnormal and Social Psychology,* 1929, *34,* 221–225.

Estes, W. K., & Skinner, B. F. Some quantitative properties of anxiety. *Journal of Experimental Psychology,* 1941, *29,* 390–400.

Eysenck, H. J. A theory of the incubation of anxiety/fear response. *Behavior Research and Therapy,* 1968, *6,* 309–321.

Eysenck, H. J., & Rachman, S. *The causes and cures of neurosis.* London: Routledge and Kegan Paul, 1965.

Freud, S. The analysis of a phobia in a five-year old boy. (1909). In *Collected Papers,* Vol. 3. London: Hogarth, 1950.

Garcia, J., Kovner, R., & Green, K. Cue properties of flavors in avoidance. This volume, pp. 238–242.

Garcia, J., McGowan, B., & Green, K. Sensory quality and integration: constraints on conditioning? This volume, pp. 21–43.

Herrnstein, R. J. Method and theory in the study of avoidance. *Psychological Review,* 1969, *76,* 49–69.

Jones, M. C. The elimination of children's fears. *Journal of Experimental Psychology,* 1924, *7,* 383–390.

Kalat, J., & Rozin, P. You can lead a rat to poison but you can't make him think. This volume, pp. 115–122.

Kamin, L. J. Temporal and intensity characteristics of the conditioned stimulus. In W. Prokasy (Ed.), *Classical conditioning.* New York: Appleton-Century-Crofts, 1965. Pp. 279–290.

Kamin, L. J. Predictability, surprise, attention, and conditioning. In B. A. Campbell and R. M. Church (Eds.), *Punishment and aversive behavior.* New York: Appleton-Century-Crofts, 1969, Pp. 317–332.

Lenneberg, E. *The biological foundations of language.* New York: Wiley, 1967.

Marks, I. *Fears and phobias.* New York: Academic Press, 1970.

Marler, P. A comparative approach to vocal learning. This volume, pp. 336–376.

Nachman, M. Limited effects of electroconvulsive shock on memory of taste stimulation. This volume, pp. 104–113.

Napalkov, A. V. Information process of the brain. In N. Wener and J. G. Sefade Eds.), *Progress of brain research, nerve, brain, and memory models.* 1963, Vol. 2, 59–69. New York: American Elsevier.

Pavlov, I. P. *Lectures on conditioned reflexes.* New York: International Publishers, 1928.

Rescorla, R. A. Inhibition of delay in Pavlovian fear conditioning. *Journal of Comparative and Physiological Psychology,* 1967, *64,* 114–120.

Rescorla, R. A. Pavlovian conditioned inhibition. *Psychological Bulletin,* 1969, *72,* 77–94.

Rescorla, R. A., & LoLordo, V. M. Inhibition of avoidance behavior. *Journal of Comparative and Physiological Psychology,* 1965, *59,* 406–412.

Rescorla, R. A., & Solomon, R. L.Two process learning theory: relations between Pavlovian conditioning and instrumental learning. *Psychological Review*, 1967, *74*, 151–182.

Roll, D., & Smith, J. Conditioned taste aversion in anesthetized rats. This volume, pp. 98–103.

Rohrbaugh, M., & Riccio, D. Paradoxical enhancement of learned fear. *Journal of Abnormal Psychology*, 1970, *75*, 210–216.

Rozin, P. Specific aversions as components of specific hungers. This volume, pp. 51–58.

Rzoska, J. Bait shyness, a study in rat behaviour. *British Journal of Animal Behaviour*, 1953, *1*, 128–135.

Seligman, M. E. P. Chronic fear produced by unpredictable electric shock. *Journal of Comparative and Physiological Psychology*, 1968, *66*, 402–411.

Seligman, M. E. P. On the generality of the laws of learning. *Psychological Review*, 1970, 77, 406–418.

Seligman, M. E. P., & Campbell, B. A. Effect of intensity and duration of punishment on extinction of an avoidance response. *Journal of Comparative and Physiological Psychology*, 1965, *59*, 295–297.

Seligman, M. E. P., Ives, C. I., Ames, H., & Mineka, S. Conditioned drinking and its failure to extinguish: Avoidance, preparedness or functional autonomy? *Journal of Comparative and Physiological Psychology*, 1970, *71*, 411–419.

Seligman, M. E. P., & Meyer, B. Chronic fear and ulcers in rats as a function of the unpredictability of safety. *Journal of Comparative and Physiological Psychology*, 1970, *73*, 202–208.

Solomon, R. L., Kamin, L. J., & Wynne, L. C. Traumatic avoidance learning; the outcomes of several extinction procedures with dogs. *Journal of Abnormal and Social Psychology*, 1953, *48*, 291.

Stimbert, V. A comparison of learning based on social or nonsocial discriminative stimuli. This volume, pp. 175–183

Wagner, A. R., Siegel, L. S., & Fein, G. G. Extinction of conditioned fear as a function of percentage of reinforcement. *Journal of Comparative and Physiological Psychology*, 1967, *63*, 160–164.

Watson, J. B., & Rayner, R. Conditioned emotional reactions. *Journal of Experimental Psychology*, 1920, *3*, 1–14.

Williams, D. R., & Williams, H. Auto-maintenance in the pigeon: sustained pecking despite contingent nonreinforcement. This volume, pp. 158–173.

Wolpe, J., & Lazarus, A. *The practice of behavior therapy*. London: Pergamon, 1969.

Wolpe, J., & Rachman, S. Psychoanalytic evidence: A critique of Freud's case of Little Hans. *Journal of Nervous and Mental Diseases*, 1960, *130*, 198–220.

SUMMARY AND AFTERWORD

Animals, man included, learn some things easily, others only painstakingly, and still others not at all. Some species learn particular things better than other things and better than other species. Within a species, some individuals can learn particular things better than other things. Further, an individual will learn some things better at one stage of development than at another stage. Some of these differences are environmental, others evolutionary. It is hard to deny these differences but easy to ignore them. As a matter of scientific strategy, general-process learning theorists elected to ignore them.

They chose instead the equipotentiality premise: It is a matter of relative indifference what an animal is required to learn about. A set of laws can be abstracted from the thorough investigation of contingencies between any response and reinforcer, and these laws will hold for contingencies between any other CS and US or response and reinforcer. The general-process view puts a premium on the investigation of unnatural contingencies, between arbitrary events, such as tones and meat powder, or lever pressing and sugar pellets. The danger of this approach is that regularities discovered may apply only to equally unnatural contingencies. For in the real world animals learn not only about random contingencies but also about contingencies their species has faced for eons. And this learning may be different in kind.

Preparedness recognizes that learning apparatus may be just as specialized as perceptual and motor apparatus, and therefore attends to natural and unnatural contingencies, as well as arbitrary contingencies. How prepared an animal is for a given contingency is specified by how degraded input can be before learning occurs. If the behavior which indicates learning occurs at the first exposure to the contingency, the animal is at the prepared end of the continuum with respect to this contingency. This end is commonly called "instinct" or "reflex." If the behavior occurs after limited exposure, the animal is highly prepared. If the animal learns only after considerable exposure, he is unprepared. And if he fails to learn even then, he may be contraprepared. Preparedness thus stands in direct contradiction to equipotentiality, and supporting data are now voluminous in the annals of experimental psychology, comparative psychology, and ethology.

Classical conditioning experiments have revealed highly evolved forms of learning. Rats instantly learn to associate tastes with gastrointestinal illness despite very long taste-illness intervals; they are contraprepared to associate lights and tones contiguous with the illness. Unlike the nocturnal rat, birds are visual feeders and they are prepared to associate colors with illness over long delays, while ignoring contiguous tastes. Taste-illness preparedness allows us to understand the puzzling phenomenon of specific hungers; animals ill with vitamin deficiencies stop eating the old diet because they associate its taste with illness. Therefore, they seek out new foods and come to prefer the one that is vitamin enriched because they associate its taste with recovery.

Instrumental learning paradigms have revealed that cats are contraprepared to lick or scratch themselves to escape. In contrast, pigeons are so highly prepared to peck lighted keys for grain that they acquire this response even when pecking and grain are independent. Dogs are contraprepared to learn which paw to move when the discriminative stimuli are different tones coming from the same place, but are prepared to learn this when tones differ only in location. Conversely, they are prepared to learn to move a paw or keep it still to different tones but not to different locations.

Animals learn readily to avoid electric shock, when the avoidance response is part of their natural defensive repertoire. Rats readily learn to jump and run away to avoid, but have difficulty learning to bar press or run back and forth. Birds learn to hop, fly, or run to avoid, but not to key peck.

Ethology and comparative psychology provide a wealth of evidence for preparedness. Herring gulls learn readily to recognize their own hatchlings but never their own eggs. Peking ducks imprint more readily on the call of their own species than on that of any other species. Indigo buntings are prepared to learn about circumpolar constellations for navigation, and contraprepared to learn about those lower in the sky.

Preparedness is more than just a name for the dimension of ease of learning. As we have seen, the preparedness of organisms probably reflects the selective pressure that their species has faced. There is, moreover, some evidence to suggest that the laws of learning vary with preparedness. Extinction, for example, proceeds very slowly for prepared learning: Imprinting, as its name implies, resists modification and the autoshaped key peck persists even when it costs the pigeon grain. In contrast, unprepared associations extinguish gradually and contraprepared associations may extinguish precipitously. Different physiological mechanisms may underlie prepared as opposed to unprepared learning: Relatively implastic physiological structures are implied by the fact that prepared taste-illness associations can be made under anesthesia and are not readily eliminated by electroconvulsive shock; unprepared mechanisms appear more flexible and are less likely to be reflected in anatomical proximity. Finally, unprepared learning may be cognitive while prepared is more primitive: Tone-shock associations are not made if the CS is redundant, while even redundant tastes become CS's for illness.

So the equipotentiality premise is false, and learning proceeds differently depending on the evolutionary history of the species. What implications does this fact have for the general-process view of learning? We believe that some form of general-process learning theory is salvageable, for there are surely levels of generality at which laws of learning are possible. At a lower level, of course, are laws which describe only unprepared behavior. But a higher level of generality may be possible—laws which describe systematic differences in learning along the dimension of preparedness. Whether adequate laws can be formulated at this level is a largely uninvestigated matter. If, for example, we find that the families of extinction functions vary systematically along the dimension, we could formulate a more general law of extinction. Thus, if prepared responses extinguish very slowly, unprepared responses gradually, and contraprepared responses precipitously, as we suspect, such a systematic differences in *laws* would be a truly general law of extinction. But before such general laws can be formulated, we must investigate the laws of prepared and contraprepared learning. We cannot say in advance that such an investigation will yield general laws, for it may turn out that laws of such high generality are as much a will-o'-the-wisp as those originally sought by general-process learning theorists. Evolutionary pressure may have operated to produce highly peculiar forms of learning, and future theorists may have to content themselves with laws which are restricted to particular species in their particular evolutionary niches. But our intuitions lead us to be more hopeful than this, for scientists are prepared to create order out of chaos.

Preparedness is a thesis about human learning as well as animal learning. While investigations of the biological boundaries of human learning are in their infancy, initial evidence suggests that language, child development, and psychopathological behavior are subject to evolutionary constraints. Language is universal within the human species and men come to speak and understand in all but the most degraded linguistic environments. Human neonates can learn, but only about highly prepared contingencies, and the cognitive capacities of the human adult can be seen as an organ evolved to deal effectively with the wide range of unprepared contingencies which our species has faced. Even in man's most bizarre behaviors, psychopathology, we see the hand of evolution. Human phobias are largely restricted to objects that have threatened survival, potential predators, unfamiliar places, and the dark. We can also ask if man's aggressiveness and sexuality are not highly prepared.

We reject the *tabula rasa* view of learning: Animals are not blank slates upon which experience can write anything it wishes with equal facility. But there are *tabula rasa* views of other psychological phenomena, and such an approach to any behavior of evolved organisms now appears as naive as ignoring the evolutionary constraints upon their anatomy. So we might question the generality of psychophysical functions based solely on the study of men listening for barely audible blips in acoustic chambers in expectation of monetary rewards. Might these functions be different for scared subjects listening for predators? So too we have doubts about the generality of laws of memory based on the study of adults memorizing pairs of nonsense syllables. Rejecting the *tabula rasa* view might help educational psychology to understand the waxing and waning of curiosity, the relative merits of learning by discovery, by example or by rote, the critical periods for second-language learning and other subjects, and the naturalness of learning to read by syllabization as opposed to phonemization.

To what extent are we prepared to understand, perceive, believe, and remember, and to what extent will we be forever unprepared? Dimensions of experience and categories of thought are open to us: causation, violence, space and time, love, rational inquiry. But consider that we cannot visualize four-dimensional space, that we do not have access to other minds, and that we cannot know the future as we do the past. These dimensions of experience and modes of thought are not open to us—not yet, perhaps never. It is our task to find the boundaries that limit us simply because we are *homo sapiens*, an animal that has a long evolution behind it and that is evolving yet.

References

Baum, M. Dissociation of respondent and operant processes in avoidance learning. *Journal of Comparative and Physiological Psychology*, Vol. 67 (1969), pp. 83—88.

Beach, F. A. The Snark was a boojum. *American Psychologist*, Vol. 5 (1950), pp. 115—124.

Bedford, J., and Anger, D. Flight as an avoidance response in pigeons. Paper read at meeting of Psychonomic Society (St. Louis, 1968).

Best, P., and Zuckerman, K. Subcortical mediation of learned taste aversion. *Physiology and Behavior*, Vol. 7 (1971), 317—320.

Bregman, E. An attempt to modify the emotional attitude of infants by the conditioned response technique. *Journal of Genetic Psychology*, Vol. 45 (1934), pp. 169—198.

Breland, K., and Breland, M. *Animal behavior* (New York: Macmillan, 1966).

Brower, L., and Brower, J. Ethological chemistry. *Scientific American*, Vol. 220 (1969), pp. 22—24.

D'Amato, M., and Fazzaro, J. Discriminated lever-press avoidance learning as a function of type and intensity of shock. *Journal of Comparative and Physiological Psychology*, Vol. 61 (1966), pp. 313—315.

D'Amato, M., and Schiff, J. Long term discriminated avoidance performance in the rat. *Journal of Comparative and Physiological Psychology*, Vol. 57 (1964), pp. 123—126.

Egger, M. D., and Miller, N. E. Secondary reinforcements in rats as a function of information value and reliability of the stimulus. *Journal of Experimental Psychology*, Vol. 64 (1962), pp. 97—104.

Eibl-Eibesfeldt, I. *Ethology: The biology of behavior* (New York: Holt, Rinehart and Winston, 1970).

Emlen, S. T. The influence of magnetic information on the orientation of the Indigo Bunting, *Passerina cyanea. Animal Behavior*, Vol. 18 (1970), pp. 215—224.

Estes, W. K. The statistical approach to learning theory. In S. Koch (ed.), *Psychology: A study of a science*, Vol. 2 (New York: McGraw-Hill, 1959).

Fantino, E., Sharp, D., and Cole, M. Factors facilitating lever press avoidance. *Journal of Comparative and Physiological Psychology*, Vol. 63 (1966), pp. 214—217.

Harris, L. J., Clay, J., Hargreaves, F., and Ward, A. Appetite and choice of diet: The ability of the vitamin B deficient rat to discriminate between diets containing and lacking the vitamin. *Proceedings of the Royal Society*, London, Series B, Vol. 113 (1933), pp. 161—190.

Hasler, G. D. *Underwater guideposts: Homing of salmon.* (Madison, Wisc.: University of Wisconsin Press, 1966).

Hayes, K. J. Spoken and gestural language learning in chimpanzees. Paper presented at the meeting of the Psychonomic Society, St. Louis, October, 1968.

Hayes, K. J., and Hayes, C. Imitation in a home-raised chimpanzee. *Journal of Comparative and Physiological Psychology*, Vol. 45 (1952), pp. 450—459.

Hemmes, N. S. DRL efficiency depends upon the operant. Paper presented at Psychonomic Society (San Antonio, Texas, November, 1970).

Hinde, R. A. *Animal behavior* (New York: McGraw-Hill, 1966).

Hovland, C. The generalization of conditioned responses. I. The sensory generalization of conditioned responses with varying frequencies of tone. *Journal of Genetic Psychology*, Vol. 17 (1937), pp. 279—291.

Huxley, Julian. *Essays of a humanist* (New York: Harper & Row, 1964).

Kamin, L. J. Predictability, surprise, attention and conditioning. In B. A. Campbell and R. M. Church (Eds.), *Punishment and aversive behavior* (New York: Appleton-Century-Crofts, 1969).

Klopfer, P. H., and Hailman, J. P. Habitat selection in birds. *Advances in the Study of Behavior*, Vol. 1 (1965), pp. 279—303.

Konorski, J. *Integretive activity of the brain* (Chicago: University of Chicago Press, 1967).

Kuhn, T. S. *The structure of scientific revolution*. (Chicago: University of Chicago Press, 1962).

Lehrman, D. S. A critique of Konrad Lorenz's theory of instructive behavior. *Quarterly Review of Biology*, Vol. 28 (1953), pp. 337—363.

MacPhail, E. M. Avoidance response in pigeons. *Journal of the Experimental Analysis of Behavior*, Vol. 11 (1968), pp. 625—632.

Miller, N. E. Learnable drives and rewards. In S. S. Stevens (Ed.), *Handbook of experimental psychology* (New York: Wiley, 1951).

Pavlov, I. P. *Conditioned reflexes* (New York: Dover, 1927).

Pavlov, I. P. *Lectures on conditioned reflexes* (New York: International Publishers, 1928).

Rescorla, R. A., and Wagner, A. R. A theory of Pavlovian conditioning; Variation in the effectiveness of reinforcement and nonreinforcement. In A. H. Black and W. F. Prokasy (Eds.), *Classical conditioning II: Current Research and Theory* (New York: Appleton-Century-Crofts, 1972).

Schneirla, T. C. An evolutionary and developmental theory of biphasic processes underlying approach and withdrawal. In *Nebraska Symposium on Motivation* (Lincoln: University of Nebraska Press, 1959), pp. 1—41.

Schwartz, B. Two kinds of key-peck in the pigeon: Some properties of responses maintained by a negative response-reinforcer contingency. Paper presented at EPA, New York, April, 1971.

Schwartz, B., and Williams, D. Discrete-trials DRL in the pigeon: The dependence of efficient performance on the availability of a stimulus for collateral pecking. *Journal of the Experimental Analysis of Behavior* (1971), Vol. 16 (1971), pp. 155—160.

Skinner, B. F. *The behavior of organisms* (New York: Appleton-Century-Crofts, 1938).

Skinner, B. F. *Verbal behavior* (New York: Appleton-Century-Crofts, 1957).

Thorndike, E. L. *Animal intelligence: An experimental study of the associative processes in animals* (New York: Columbia University Press, 1898).

Thorndike, E. L. *The psychology of wants, interests and attitudes* (New York: Appleton-Century-Crofts, 1935).

Ullman, L. P., and Krasner, L. *Case studies in behavior modification* (New York: Holt, Rinehart and Winston, 1965).

Watson, J. B., and Rayner, R. Conditioned emotional reactions. *Journal of Experimental Psychology*, Vol. 3 (1920), pp. 1—14.

NAME INDEX

Abrahamson, D., 432
Adelman, H. M., 144
Allison, J., 222–226
Amatruda, C. S., 429, 432
American Psychologist, 181, 310
Ames, H., 458, 462
Anger, D., 206, 208, 212, 460, 466
Appel, J. B., 220
Armstrong, E. A., 373
Azrin, N. H., 173, 213–214, 220, 221

Bach-y-Rita, G., 41
Baer, D. M., 421, 432
Baerends, G. P., 250
Banks, J. H., 179
Banks, R. C., 374
Banuazizi, A., 112
Barelare, B., Jr., 95
Barnes, G. W., 136, 139, 144
Barnett, S. A., 10, 13, 19, 41, 48, 58, 93
Bartels, B., 425, 426, 433
Bartoshuk, A. K., 426, 432
Batschelet, E., 307
Baum, M., 212, 460, 466
Beach, F. A., 22, 41, 181, 186, 309, 311–312, 333, 466
Bedarf, E. W., 32, 43, 44–48, 83, 95
Bedford, J., 212, 460, 466
Behavior Therapy, 419, 451
Behrend, E. R., 333
Bellrose, F., 307
Bellugi, U., 396
Berger, B., 121
Best, P., 103, 121, 466
Bever, T., 96
Bijou, S. W., 421, 432
Birch, H. G., 424, 434
Bitterman, M. E., 28, 41, 88–89, 93, 94, 155, 156, 309–333, 334
Bivens, L. W., 113
Black A. H., 21, 460, 467
Black, M., 113
Blanc, C., 424, 432
Blanchard, B. D., 374
Bliss, E. L., 276
Borror, D. J., 374

Bolles, R. C., 6n, 58, 135–143, 188–208, 209, 211, 212, 460
Borer, K. T., 32, 41
Bosack, T. N., 421, 428, 433
Bower, C. H., 95
Bower G., 156, 201, 209
Brackbill, Y., 429, 432
Bradford, S., 424, 434
Braveman, N., 93
Bregman, E., 124, 458, 460, 466
Breland, K., 6n, 22, 23, 41, 114n, 172, 173, 180–186, 466
Breland, M., 6n, 22, 23, 41, 114n, 172, 173, 180–186, 466
Bremner, F. J., 209
Bridger, W. H., 426, 432
Brogden, W. J., 194, 209
Bronschtein, A. I., 424, 432
Brookshire, K. H., 96
Brower, L., 36–37, 41, 86, 93, 242, 251, 258, 466
Brown, P. L., 145–156, 158–159, 173, 180, 212, 215, 220, 457, 461
Brown, R., 396
Brush, E. S., 210
Brush, F. R., 209
Brush, R. R., 461
Bryan, A. L., 417
Buchwald, N. A., 41
Bullock, D. H., 333
Bykov, K. M., 40, 41

Campbell, B. A., 122, 144, 461, 462, 467
Campbell, C., 93
Campbell, D., 461
Candland, D. K., 93, 333
Capretta, P. J., 41, 93
Carlson, N. J., 460
Carmichael, L., 267, 276
Carpenter, R., 432
Carrol, H. W., 42, 101
Casterline, D., 417
Castle, P., 429, 434
Catania, A. C., 173
Cautela, J., 448
Cazden, C., 396
Chitty, D., 93
Cho, C., 210

Parenthetical citations have not been indexed.

SUBJECT INDEX